W9-BKM-649

The Oxford Book of American Poetry

The Oxford Book of American Poetry

Chosen and Edited by

DAVID LEHMAN

Associate Editor

JOHN BREHM

2006

OXFORD
UNIVERSITY PRESS

Oxford University Press, Inc., publishes works that further
Oxford University's objective of excellence
in research, scholarship, and education.

Oxford New York
Auckland Cape Town Dar es Salaam Hong Kong Karachi
Kuala Lumpur Madrid Melbourne Mexico City Nairobi
New Delhi Shanghai Taipei Toronto

With offices in
Argentina Austria Brazil Chile Czech Republic France Greece
Guatemala Hungary Italy Japan Poland Portugal Singapore
South Korea Switzerland Thailand Turkey Ukraine Vietnam

Published by Oxford University Press, Inc.
198 Madison Avenue, New York, New York, 10016
http://www.oup.com/us

Library of Congress Cataloging-in-Publication Data
The Oxford book of American poetry / [edited by] David Lehman.
p. cm.
Rev. ed of: Oxford book of American verse. 1950.
Includes bibliographical references and index.
ISBN-13: 978-0-19-516251-6 (hardcover : acid-free paper)

1. American poetry. I. Lehman, David, 1948- II. Oxford book of American verse.
PS583.O82 2006
811.008--dc22
2005036590

Printing number: 19 18 17 16 15 14 13 12 11 10

Printed in the United States of America
on acid-free paper

The Oxford Book of American Poetry

Introduction

The past—that foreign country where they do things differently—is neither a fixed entity nor a finished narrative but a changing landscape of the mind where travelers come and go, talking of Michelangelo, *Hamlet*, T. S. Eliot, and much else less lofty. It may be that what we call the present defines itself in the disagreements we have about the past and the complicated negotiations we undertake to resolve our differences. This means at bottom that virtually all events, periods, tendencies, and climates of opinion are subject to continual reassessment and revision. New facts come to light, old testimony comes into question; our belief system changes and we need to adjust our understanding of history to bring it in line with our governing assumptions. And so, for example, a story once held to be "true" in the sense that it "actually happened" is modified into a legend or a fiction that may still be "true" but only in some attenuated and entirely different sense.

The principle of continual change applies not only to, say, the causes of World War I but even to some "monuments of unageing intellect," as William Butler Yeats called them in "Sailing to Byzantium": to works of art and literature that long ago took their final form. In his seminal essay "Tradition and the Individual Talent," T. S. Eliot wrote that "what happens when a new work of art is created is something that happens simultaneously to all the works of art which preceded it." What Eliot called "the new (the really new) work of art" revises the tradition it joins. The successful new poem makes us see its antecedents in a clarifying light. So pervasive is this view that even a critic as generally hostile to Eliot as Harold Bloom has taken it to heart in elaborating his idea that a successful poet must overcome the anxiety-inducing influence of an earlier poet, a father figure of fearsome power, to the point that the newcomer can claim priority. It stretches Bloom's theory somewhat, but only somewhat, to cite it in support of the notion that Wallace Stevens retroactively influenced John Keats, who died more than half a century before Stevens was born.

Eliot's own poetry illustrates the point a little less hyperbolically. As a result of Eliot's persuasive argumentation, his perceived authority, and his uncanny ability to pluck superb lines from their original context and use them as epigraphs to poems or as quotations embedded within poems, the stock of such seventeenth-century poets as John Donne and Andrew Marvell went sky-high in the early twentieth century while the stock of the Romantic stalwart Percy Bysshe Shelley plummeted and has never fully recovered. The tradition of English lyric poetry from the Renaissance to 1900 looked different in 1940 from the way it looked in 1910, as a comparison of anthologies dated in those years would attest. The paradox is that our sense of timelessness—of literary immortality—itself exists in time. The text of an important poem, or any poem that has lasted, may not change (although poets who incessantly revise their work do create quandaries). What is certain to change is the value we attach to the work; the value moves up and down and probably could be graphed in the manner of the Dow Jones industrial index.

The canon of English lyric poetry that Eliot changed has changed again in the forty years since his death. The changes reflect shifts and even revolutions in taste and sensibility, and sometimes reflect the emergence of figures long forgotten or previously little known. There has been a widening of focus, an enlargement of what it is acceptable to do in verse or prose. Disliking academic jargon, I resist referring, as some do, to American "poetries," but the point of the term is plain enough. Where once there was a mainstream that absorbed all our sight, today we see a complex pattern of intersecting tributaries and brooks feeding more rivers than one. The posthumous discovery of an unknown or underappreciated poet keeps happening because new art occurs in advance of an audience and because some poets put their energy into their writing and let publication take care of itself—or not. "Publication," wrote the unpublished Emily Dickinson defiantly, "is the Auction / Of the mind of man"; it is a "foul thing," she added, that reduces "Human Spirit / To Disgrace of Price." Once only did Dickinson submit her poems to the perusal of a magazine editor, Thomas Wentworth Higginson of the *Atlantic Monthly*. It was in 1862, a year in which she wrote a poem every day. She was thirty-one. She sent Higginson four of her works, including the famous one beginning "Safe in their alabaster chambers." Higginson, who meant well, advised her not to publish. So much for the wisdom of experts. Though Dickinson's poems are now universally acknowledged to be among the prime glories of American literature, they were all but unknown at the time of her death in 1886, and for more than half of the twentieth century they remained too unconventional in appearance to get past the copyeditors who thought they were doing her a favor by substituting commas for her characteristic dashes. The secretive poet had fashioned a brilliant system of punctuation, and it took a while for the rest of the world to catch on and catch up.

"We had the experience but missed the meaning," Eliot wrote in *Four Quartets*, summarizing a common condition; he had found a new way of saying that the unexamined life was not worth living. But flip the terms and you come upon an equally valid truth. Many readers, including brilliant ones, have the meaning but miss the experience of poems. They are so busy hunting down clues, unpacking deep psychic structures, industriously applying a methodology or imposing a theoretical construct that they fail to confront the poem as it is, in all its mysterious otherness. The enjoyment of a great poem begins with the recognition of its fundamental strangeness. Can you yield yourself to it the way Keats recommends yielding yourself to uncertainties and doubts without any irritable reaching after fact? If you can, the experience is yours to have. And the experience of greatness demands attention before analysis. In a celebrated poem, Dickinson likens herself to a "Loaded Gun," whose owner has the "power to die," which is as much greater than the gun's "power to kill" as the categorical "must" is greater than the contingent "may." It may be irresistible to try to solve this poem's riddles. Who is the owner? In what sense is Dickinson herself a "Loaded Gun"? But it would be a mistake to adopt an allegorical interpretation that solves these questions too neatly, or not neatly enough, at the cost of the poem's deep and uncanny mysteriousness. The aesthetic and moral experience of "My Life had stood—a Loaded Gun—" is greater than the sense one makes of the poem, though it is also true that the effort of making sense of its opening metaphor and its closing paradoxes may clear a path toward that incomparable experience.

Posterity, which is intolerant of fakes and indifferent to reputations, will find the marvelous eccentric talent whose writings had known no public. And distance allows for clarity if the reader is prepared to meet the poets as they are, 'more truly and more strange' (in Wallace Stevens's phrase) than we could have expected. Reading a poem by Dickinson or by Walt Whitman in the year 2006 is an experience no one has had before: we read more aware than ever of the differences between ourselves and the selves we behold on the page. And because the poems have power, because they have genius, they can speak to us with uncanny prescience, as Whitman's "Crossing Brooklyn Ferry" does:

It avails not, time nor place—distance avails not,
I am with you, you men and women of a generation, or ever so many generations
hence,
Just as you feel when you look on the river and sky, so I felt,
Just as any of you is one of a living crowd, I was one of a crowd,
Just as you are refresh'd by the gladness of the river and the bright flow, I was
refresh'd,
Just as you stand and lean on the rail, yet hurry with the stiff current, I stood yet was
hurried,
Just as you look on the numberless masts of ships and the thick-stemm'd pipes of
steamboats, I look'd.

The language changes; styles go in and out of favor. The poets of a new generation resurrect the deceased visionary who toiled in the dark. For these reasons and others, the need to replace the retrospective anthologies of the past is as constant as the need to render classic works in new translations with up-to-date idioms. But what may sound like an obligation quickly becomes an enormous promise, an opportunity to renew the perhaps unexpected pleasures of Henry Wadsworth Longfellow or Edwin Arlington Robinson; to revisit and reassess the conservative Allen Tate and the liberal Archibald MacLeish, two eminences who argued out their positions in civil verse; to read Emma Lazarus's sonnets and realize just how good they are—and what a masterpiece is "The New Colossus," which gave the Statue of Liberty its universal meaning; to consider Hart Crane's "The Broken Tower" in relation to his friend Leonie Adams's "Bell Tower," or to be struck once again by how much Crane's "Emblems of Conduct" owes to the poem entitled "Conduct" by the poor, consumptive, self-taught Samuel Greenberg, who died young but lives on in Crane's work as well as in his own.

An anthology like this one is, to borrow Crane's central metaphor, a bridge connecting us to the past, the past that loves us, the great past. It is also perforce a critical statement performed by editorial means. There are readers who will say that I overrate Gertrude Stein, the mother of all radical experimentation, who retains her power to shake the complacent and give any reader a jolt, or that I underrate Fiddler Jones or Madame La Fleurie or So-and-So reclining on her couch.[1] That is part of the deal. The editor must make difficult choices—must even omit some poems he greatly admires—simply because the amount of space is limited and the competition fierce. The task is difficult almost beyond presumption if you hold the view, as I do, that it is possible to value and derive pleasure from poets who saw themselves as being irreconcilably opposed to and incompatible with each other. William Carlos Williams clashed with T. S. Eliot, and the split widened to the point that in the 1960s, the decade when the two men died, the whole of American poetry seemed divided between them in an oversimplification that felt compelling at the time. Eliot was understood to be the captain of the mainstream squad—the standard-bearer of the traditional, the formally exacting, the intellectual (as opposed to the instinctive), the poetry of complexity endorsed by the New Criticism, the poetry that the academy had assimilated. Williams was at the forefront of the opposition, call it what you will: the nontraditional, the "alternative," the colloquial, the adversarial; Williams was what the Beats and the San Francisco Renaissance and the Black Mountain movement had in common. Williams felt that Eliot's "The Waste Land" was an unmitigated disaster for American poetry, but the reader today who falls in love with Williams's "Danse Russe" or "To a Poor Old Woman" or "Great Mullen" need not renounce the aesthetic of fragmentation and echo and the collage method that made "The Waste Land" the most revolutionary modern poem. American poetry is larger than any faction or sect. You can love the poetry of Richard Wilbur and have your Robert Creeley, too.

* * *

The paramount purpose of virtually any literary anthology is to distill, convey, and preserve the best writing in the field. "The typical anthologist is a sort of Gallup Poll with connections—often astonishing ones; it is hard to know whether he is printing a poem because he likes it, because his acquaintances tell him he ought to, or because he went to high school with the poet," Randall Jarrell wrote. What you need and do not often get, he emphasized, is "taste." There is more than a little truth to this. Some decisions made by anthologists defy reason or seem to be the result of pressure, whim, sentiment, committee deliberations, or intrigue. At the same time, editors would be foolish not to exploit their circles of acquaintance. Even the most receptive reader will have blind spots. The editor is lucky who has friends with areas of expertise that do not narrowly replicate his or her own. It is, after all, often through a friend's or a

[1]"Fiddler Jones," "Madame Fleurie," and "So-and-So Reclining on her Couch" are the titles of specific poems by Edgar Lee Masters ("Fiddler Jones") and Wallace Stevens (the other two) but can stand for the names of poets who advanced far in the editorial process yet did not make the final cut.

writer's recommendation that one had picked up a certain poet or poem in the first place. To learn from a Richard Wilbur essay that "Fairy-Land" was Elizabeth Bishop's favorite poem by Edgar Allan Poe, for example, is not inconsequential if the information prompts one to look up the poem and see just how good it is. Nevertheless Jarrell's larger point remains valid. There is no substitute for taste, where that word means something more developed than a grab bag of opinions.

"To ask the hard question is simple," W. H. Auden wrote in an early poem. "But the answer / Is hard and hard to remember." What makes a poem good? What makes a good poem great? The questions are simple enough to express, but the "hard to remember" part is that no listing of criteria will satisfactorily dispose of them. I prize, as do many readers, eloquence, passion, intelligence, conviction, wit, originality, pride of craft, an eye for the genuine, an ear for speech, an instinct for the truth. I ask of a poem that it have a beguiling surface, but I also want it to imply something more—enough to compel a second reading and make it a surprise. It would be hard to argue with Marianne Moore, who felt that the reader "interested in poetry" has a right to demand "the raw material of poetry in / all its rawness and / that which is on the other hand / genuine." Perhaps Matthew Arnold had the smartest idea when he proposed and illustrated the concept of *touchstones*—lines of such quality that they can be held up as models of excellence by which to judge other works. And perhaps on a wide scale that is what this anthology means to do: to assemble the touchstones of American poetry. Discussing the merits of a poet ultimately not included, I told the book's associate editor, John Brehm, that I "couldn't find anything that was truly great, exceptionally interesting, or not done better by someone else." As John pointed out in reply, that sentence implies a trio of bottom-line criteria. Yet we know these can be dismissed as merely rhetorical and thoroughly subjective. That is why I have long felt that Frank O'Hara's advice in his mock-manifesto "Personism" might make a suitable motto for any anthologist: "You just go on your nerve. If someone's chasing you down the street with a knife you just run, you don't turn around and shout, 'Give it up! I was a track star for Mineola Prep.'"

* * *

This new edition of *The Oxford Book of American Poetry* is the first since Richard Ellmann edited *The New Oxford Book of American Verse* in 1976. Twenty-six years earlier F. O. Matthiessen had chosen and edited the book Ellmann revised, *The Oxford Book of American Verse*. It is an honor to join the company of two such accomplished scholars and skillful anthologists. Matthiessen (1902–1950), a renowned Harvard professor, wrote an early book expounding T. S. Eliot's achievement. He also wrote *American Renaissance* (1941), a classic study of five nineteenth-century writers. Ellmann, who died in 1987 at the age of sixty-nine, held a titled professorship at Oxford and later at Emory University. He was justly acclaimed for his biographies of James Joyce and Oscar Wilde. Less well-known are Ellmann's excellent translations of Henri Michaux, which introduced American poets to this hero of the French prose poem. Though my task in creating this book necessarily involves overhauling Matthiessen's and Ellmann's, I mean to build on both. It is my good fortune to inherit their work, which has served my own as scaffolding or source.

The Oxford Book of American Poetry is a comprehensive, one-volume anthology of American poetry from its seventeenth-century origins to the present. The words *canon* and *canonical* acquired layers of unfortunate connotation during the culture wars of the past quarter century, but we should not shy away from such terms when they fit the case, as they do here. The goal of this volume is to establish a canon wider and more inclusive than those that formerly prevailed, but to do so on grounds that are fundamentally literary and artistic in nature. Not one selection was dictated by a political imperative. Matthiessen in 1950 picked fifty-one poets. Ellmann's anthology contained seventy-eight. There are two hundred and ten in this volume.

The discrepancy in the number of poets included is not attributable to the difference in cutoff years alone. Naturally, I needed and wanted to include poets born since 1934, the birth year of Ellmann's youngest poet, but I was determined also to rescue many who had been eligible but were overlooked in previous editions. To make room for the new you need to subject the old to stringent reevaluation, and so I needed not only to reconsider Ellmann's selections but to ask whether such major figures as Emerson, Whitman, Dickinson, Frost, Stevens, Williams, Moore, and Bishop can be better represented than they were formerly. It is especially vital to reassess the selection of poets who were barely hitting mid-career when Ellmann made his selections—poets of the magnitude of A. R. Ammons, John Ashbery, and James Merrill.

In Matthiessen the youngest poet was born in 1917; in Ellmann, 1934. Needing to advance the cutoff date, I settled on 1950, which virtually replicates the previous interval and has the additional advantage of being both the exact midpoint of the twentieth century and the year Matthiessen's selection was published. Making an anthology involves making a lot of lists—beginning with a list of the poets too young to be considered by Ellmann in 1976. Thirty years have gone by since then, and I can hear America clamoring. Scores of fine poets born since 1950 are rapping on the doors, pressing their case for admission. It would be tricky enough to accommodate the impatient newcomers under any circumstances. But what makes things infinitely more complicated is that the list of outstanding poets who were eligible in 1976 but were not included may be even longer. Missing from Ellmann is W. H. Auden. (Matthiessen had included him in 1950, but Ellmann—in the single parenthetical sentence he devotes to the question—explains that he considered Auden "English to the bone.") The omission of Gertrude Stein goes unexplained, but then it would doubtlessly astonish both Matthiessen and Ellmann to learn that this relentlessly abstract writer should have the continuing and growing influence on American poetry that she has. In Ellmann you will not find any evidence of the Objectivist movement (Louis Zukofsky, George Oppen, Charles Reznikoff, Lorine Niedecker). Absent, too, are New York School pillars Kenneth Koch and James Schuyler and eminent San Franciscans Kenneth Rexroth and Jack Spicer. Not in Ellmann are James Weldon Johnson, Paul Laurence Dunbar, Angelina Weld Grimke, Jean Toomer, Claude McKay, Melvin Tolson, Sterling Brown, Robert Hayden, and other African American poets who have become better known in recent years. Nor in Ellmann are such smart-set poets of wit and satire as Dorothy Parker and Ogden Nash, who lacked gravitas at a time when that quality was deemed essential, as though real poetry (as opposed to light verse) had to be as deadly as a press conference with a presidential hopeful.

Some of the poets overlooked in 1976 were once celebrated, later deprecated (Amy Lowell); some died young and obscure (Samuel Greenberg, Joan Murray); some were once in fashion but fell into disregard (H. Phelps Putnam, Leonie Adams); some may have struck a donnish reader as Caliban crashing the muse's party (Charles Bukowski). Others may have seemed too eccentric (John Wheelwright, William Bronk) or were underrated until somebody else made it his or her business to champion them (Weldon Kees) or were better known for their work in a different field (as were Lincoln Kirstein, the director of the New York City Ballet, and Edwin Denby, the foremost dance critic of his time). Some were overshadowed by a great contemporary, as Josephine Miles (born 1911) and May Swenson (born 1913) were overshadowed by Elizabeth Bishop (born 1911). Some may have been resented and therefore overlooked because of their perceived editorial power (Howard Moss, poetry editor of *The New Yorker*); some were just plain overlooked (Donald Justice, John Hollander). Yet others never got the attention they deserved (Ruth Herschberger, Joseph Ceravolo) or were acknowledged or dismissed for reasons having little to do with their actual writing (Laura Riding, who was Robert Graves's companion and collaborator and who later renounced poetry and became a first-class crank). What many of these poets have in common is that they stood outside the prevailing tradition, the mainline of American poetry as the academic literary establishment conceived it in 1976. It was not very difficult to leave them out.

Donald Hall, in a critique of Ellmann's anthology, wrote that *The New Oxford Book of American Verse* "gives us poetry by the Star System." There is a friendlier way of putting this. Matthiessen in his introduction to the 1950 edition said pithily that his first rule was "fewer poets, with more space for each." Matthiessen—and Ellmann as well—aimed for amplitude; they wanted to present the best poets in full measure, at the expense of "several delicately accomplished lyric poets whose continuing life is in a few anthology pieces" (Matthiessen). In Ellmann, the major figures get star treatment—thirty-nine pages for John Greenleaf Whittier, including all of "Snow-Bound," twenty-nine pages for William Carlos Williams, twenty-eight for Robert Frost, twenty-three for Marianne Moore—while minor figures such as Stephen Crane and Trumbull Stickney are lucky to get two pages apiece.

To the extent that hierarchy is an inescapable ordering principle, some of this is inevitable. Walt Whitman is and should be the gold standard in number of pages allotted, Emily Dickinson in number of poems included. They are our poetic grandparents, these two, and yet no two poets could seem less alike: on the one hand, a robust and expansive bard who wrote in long lines and proposed his poems as a visionary embodiment of American democracy, and on the other hand a reclusive shut-in who wrote in short-breath utterances broken by dashes and made her interior life a cosmos. People who habitually divide everything in two may contend that all poets make themselves in the image of one or the other of these two great predecessors. And it is likely that the leading poets of our time have all read certain poets—Eliot, Pound, Moore, Stevens, Williams, Frost, Bishop, Ashbery—whom we must therefore take pains to represent at length. Nevertheless there are alternatives to the star system. "We used to make anthologies not of poets but of poems," Donald Hall said, and it is possible to balance the claims of major figures with the case for great poems by poets sometimes considered peripheral. That is the path I have elected to follow. As comprehensiveness tends to vary inversely with focus, the gain in variety and ecumenicism may not come cost-free, but then the making of an anthology is neither an exact science nor a pure art but instead is a vision projected and sustained to fulfillment.

There are other rules governing this anthology besides the requirement that the poet be born in 1950 or earlier. The poetry has to be written in English. (This is a rule that would not have required articulation in the past.) I am inclined toward a construction of "American" that is broad enough to include poets who were born in other countries but came to the United States to live and contributed tangibly to American poetry. The example of the Canadian poet Anne Carson, who has taught in the United States and has a wide following among younger poets, reminds me that the word "North" is invisible but no less present in the phrase "American poetry." W. H. Auden, who became a U.S. citizen, belongs here not only because of the poems that he wrote in and sometimes about places like New York City ("I sit in one of the dives / On Fifty Second Street") but because of his importance to a whole generation of American poets.[2] My claiming both Auden and Eliot for this book would not prevent me from claiming both of them for *The Oxford Book of English Verse* (1999), as that book's editor, Christopher Ricks, has done. The way the two poets traded places in parallel career paths—Eliot from Harvard to London, Auden from Oxford to New York—marked a high point in Anglo-American literary relations: the last time the two cultures seemed to have a common poetry.

I hold Matthiessen's *Oxford Book of American Verse* in high esteem. It is, I think, one of the finest anthologies of American poetry ever made. I have gone back to it for poems by Oliver Wendell Holmes ("Contentment"), Edgar Allan Poe ("To One in Paradise"), Walt Whitman ("Reconciliation"), Robert Frost ("Meeting and Passing," "The Road Not Taken," "Birches," "Out, Out—"), Wallace Stevens ("Domination of Black," "Disillusionment of Ten O'Clock," "The Poems of Our Climate," "Of Modern Poetry"), Marianne Moore ("To a Steam Roller," "No Swan So Fine"), William Carlos Williams ("Nantucket," "Fine Work with Pitch and Copper"), E. E. Cummings ("next to of course god america i"). I have restored seven poets who were in the Matthiessen canon in 1950 but fell out in 1976: Phelps Putnam, Edna St. Vincent Millay, Elinor Wylie, Stephen Vincent Benet, Karl Shapiro, Amy Lowell, and Auden.[3]

Matthiessen's introduction begins with a summary statement of his criteria. The irony is that I generally agree with his reasoning and yet in practice find myself frequently obliged to do the opposite. I mentioned that his first rule is "fewer poets, with

[2] Richard Ellmann, who felt that Auden was too English for *The New Oxford Book of American Verse*, chose T. S. Eliot's "Little Gidding" for the volume. I concur with this choice and have duplicated it here. Of the four long poems constituting Eliot's *Four Quartets*, it is the one that seems to set a crown upon his lifetime's effort. I would, however, point out that this magnificent work, written long after Eliot adopted British citizenship, is as "English" a poem as Eliot ever wrote. The poet's declaration that "in a secluded chapel, / History is now and England," is in its way as proud an Englishman's boast as the hero's rejection of "all temptations / To belong to other nations" in Gilbert and Sullivan's *H.M.S. Pinafore*. Nevertheless Eliot's birth in St. Louis, his American upbringing, and his enduring influence are all the justification one needs to include "Little Gidding," and by the same permissive logic it is hard to exclude certain poems that Auden wrote before setting foot on American soil, such as "As I Walked Out One Evening" (1937).

[3] Of Ellmann's chosen seventy-eight, I have dropped only seven poets—eight entities, if "folk songs" is counted.

more space for each." In this book there are more poets, with less space for most. Matthiessen's second rule is "to include nothing on merely historical grounds, and the third [rule] is similar, to include nothing that the anthologist does not really like." Here I am enthusiastically with him, but even so the exceptions stand up. Do I, do you, "like" Julia Ward Howe's "The Battle Hymn of the Republic," or is "like" not quite the right word for how we feel about this stirring anthem? Oliver Wendell Holmes's "Old Ironsides" is credited with saving a battleship. Is this a dimension of the poem that the editor ought to ignore? Poetry is an art with a history, and shouldn't a poem that changes the consciousness of an era, as Edwin Markham's "The Man with the Hoe" did, have a place in such a book as this? Matthiessen's fourth rule is "not too many sonnets." This rule implies a great deal about the popularity of the sonnet form in American poetry before 1950, but it is not a major concern in 2006. Matthiessen's fifth rule is to represent each poet with "poems of some length"—a rule impossible to observe if you are quadrupling the number of poets in the volume. Matthiessen's sixth and final rule is "no excerpts." I agree with this sentiment entirely; I deplore the practice of excerpting long works, and I observe respectfully that just as Matthiessen breaks this rule by printing a part of a Pound Canto and parts of a long poem by James Russell Lowell, I have done the same in both of these cases and in others. Wherever possible I have used only excerpts that are self-contained and have an integrity separate from the larger work of which they are a part, as do the sections here of Hart Crane's *The Bridge* and Allen Ginsberg's *Kaddish*.

Philip Larkin, who edited *The Oxford Book of Twentieth-Century English Verse* in 1973, spoke of wanting that book to have a "wide rather than deep representation." Asked by an interviewer to elaborate on this distinction, Larkin dodged the question but gave an excellent account of the available options and their limitations:

> You could produce a purely historical anthology: this is what poetry in this century was like—it may not be the best poetry, it may not be the most enjoyable poetry, but this is what it was like. Well, that's one way of doing it. The other way, or *an* other way, is the critical approach: this is the best poetry of the century. And there would be about thirty names on it, and it would be full of poems that everybody already possesses, and it would be critically irreproachable. But it wouldn't be historically true, and it might not always be as enjoyable as it might have been if you'd let in a few little strays. The third way is to pick just the poems you personally find enjoyable, but that would have been too personal: it would have left out things that were critically accepted, it would have left out people who, like Everest, were there. In the end, you have to compromise. Sometimes you are acting historically, sometimes you are acting critically, sometimes you're acting just as a reader who reaches out to his bedside table and picks up a book and wants to have a quick change of mood and enjoy himself. I tried to cater for all these people.

I, too, have a weakness for "strays," an inclination to pick and choose among models and methods of assemblage, a willingness to compromise, and a realization that there is no court of final appeal beyond your own taste, eclectic or focused, wide or narrow, as the case may be.

The spirit of our age is friendly to peripheral figures and able to entertain mutually exclusive positions. It is as though the culture has enshrined F. Scott Fitzgerald's statement that the "test of a first-rate intelligence is the ability to hold two opposed ideas in the mind at the same time, and still retain the ability to function." We have become more pluralist since 1950 or 1976, more willing to acknowledge the validity of styles, movements, or idioms other than our own. We have broadened our sense of poetic diction and have loosened our sense of propriety, and so we can now hear Charles Bukowski's rough-edged poetry. No longer do we need to punish Edna St. Vincent Millay for enjoying her sexuality or for having committed the even worse crime of being tremendously popular early in her life. In the same volume we can have a terse, biting J. V. Cunningham epigram and a satirical rant by Kenneth Fearing. Each is pretty much the best of its kind, and enjoyment of one implies no disloyalty to the other. At the same time, we can no longer safely omit anything—"A Visit from St. Nicholas," "Paul Revere's Ride," "Casey at the Bat"—on the presumption that everyone knows it. The fact is that nothing can be taken for granted. I envy readers who have not yet encountered "Out of the Cradle Endlessly Rocking" or "Eros Turannos" or "Sunday Morning" and can look forward to reading these great poems for the first time. Rereading is a major pleasure, but nothing quite measures up to the thrill of discovery.

* * *

Undoubtedly the greatest long poem by an American is Walt Whitman's "Song of Myself." Both Matthiessen and Ellmann include it, and I do, too. But here is the rub: Whitman constantly revised his poetry. He did not write multiple books, in the modern fashion. Instead he augmented and replenished the one book, *Leaves of Grass*. Both Matthiessen and Ellmann print the so-called "deathbed edition" of "Song of Myself," which Whitman prepared in 1891 and 1892. (He died in 1892.) So this may seem a safe choice. But I am among those who strongly prefer the 1855 edition of "Song of Myself," the original version of the poem, when it was still untitled. *Leaves of Grass* was privately printed by Whitman, who also distributed it, publicized it, and wrote the only favorable reviews that it got in 1855. It was this, the edition published on July 4, 1855, that spurred Emerson to write to Whitman what is probably the greatest letter a young American poet has ever received: "I greet you at the beginning of a great career, which yet must have had a long foreground somewhere, for such a start. I rubbed my eyes a little to see if this sunbeam were no illusion; but the solid sense of the book is a sober certainty. It has the best merits, namely, of fortifying & encouraging."

Here is how the 1855 version of "Song of Myself" begins:

> I celebrate myself,
> And what I assume, you shall assume,
> For every atom belonging to me as good belongs to you.
>
> I loafe and invite my soul,
> I lean and loafe at my ease . . . observing a spear of summer grass.

Now here is part one of "Song of Myself" as Whitman revised it:

> I celebrate myself, and sing myself,
> And what I assume, you shall assume,
> For every atom belonging to me as good belongs to you.
>
> I loafe and invite my soul,
> I lean and loafe at my ease observing a spear of summer grass.
>
> My tongue, every atom of my blood, form'd from this soil, this air,
> Born here of parents born here from parents the same, and their parents the same;
> I, now thirty-seven years old and in perfect health begin,
> Hoping to cease not till death.
>
> Creeds and schools in abeyance,
> Retiring back a while sufficed at what they are, but never forgotten,
> I harbor for good or bad, I permit to speak at every hazard,
> Nature without check with original energy.

I submit that in this representative instance, Whitman weakened the poem by revising it. Line one as originally written is incomparably stronger because it relies on one verb instead of dividing its action between two. The eight additional lines in the later version seem not only unnecessary but work to dilute the egalitarian message by stressing the writer's American roots. The gain in specificity—the poet telling us he is thirty-seven years old, the son of people who were born in this country—masks a loss in universality. Does the poet of *Democratic Vistas* really wish to deny equal grace to the immigrant and the naturalized citizen?

Here is another telling revision. In 1855, when the poet names himself in his poem, he is "Walt Whitman, an American, one of the roughs, a kosmos." In 1892, the line reads as follows: "Walt Whitman, a kosmos, of Manhattan the son." Again it seems to me that the original is superior. The claim made for the poet is that his identity consists of three parts; he is, in order, an American, a "rough," and a whole cosmos. In the later version, the primitive energy that Whitman delights in is omitted, and instead of being "an American," he is "of Manhattan the son"—an unnecessary localism and a poetical inversion of the sort that Whitman at his best eschews. The later version is more refined, less rough, and therefore less accurate, *and* it has lost the musical charm of "Walt Whitman, an American, one of the roughs, a kosmos." I could cite other revisions, but I think these will suffice to explain why I have elected to deviate from Ellmann and Matthiessen in using the 1855 version of "Song of Myself." I can think of only one major anthology that represents Whitman with the 1855 "Song of Myself," a fact that astounds me and reinforces my resolve to break with the pack.

The whole issue of revisions and how to deal with them is unavoidable. Of Marianne Moore's "Poetry," arguably her most famous poem, there are multiple versions. She revised it one final time in her *Complete Poems*, a volume that she prefaced with the declaration that "Omissions are not accidents." The reader, turning to the page on which "Poetry" appears, might be astonished to find that most of the poem has been omitted. It is a breathtaking and audacious revision: a page-long poem reduced to less than its first three lines.[4] But I am not convinced by it—the original is better, and not only because it is the version I grew up with. I believe if all we had of that poem were the second version, we would not remember it nearly so well or with as much affection. The revised version exhibits the virtues of brevity and unadorned pith. But it lacks the great "imaginary gardens with real toads in them." It gets rid of the unusual zoological imagery, the critic "twitching his skin like a horse that feels / a flea." The revision is a summary statement; the original is a full argument with Moore's signature quotations in place of logical propositions. On the other hand, there are Moore's own intentions to take into account. What to do? How to proceed when your aesthetic instincts clash with the author's stated wishes? Moore's own baroque solution was to publish the original version of her poem as a footnote in her *Complete Poems*. I decided to include both versions, leaving it to readers and students to debate the merits of each.

It may not be a universal maxim that a poem changed after it has appeared in print is a poem worsened by the change. But the maxim applies to W. H. Auden, another compulsive self-revisionist. I went with the original versions of "In Memory of W. B. Yeats," "September 1, 1939," and "In Praise of Limestone." I was assisted in this judgment by my students at the New School in New York City, who were asked in various classes to imagine themselves the editors of a new anthology based on Ellmann's *New Oxford Book of American Verse*. We found that the stanzas that troubled Auden the most—the penultimate stanza of "September 1, 1939" and stanzas two to four of part III of "In Memory of W. B. Yeats," all of which Auden dropped at one time or another—are particularly worthy of study. The reason Auden renounced some of the poems and prose poems he wrote prior to 1940 had more to do with morals than with aesthetics; he felt that the sentiments he expressed in such poems were highly objectionable. The idea that time would pardon a writer for airing odious views in melodious verse—that barbarous content is excused by grace of form—seemed to him, in retrospect, a wicked doctrine. Auden therefore removed the three stanzas that aired this doctrine in his Yeats elegy, and it is undeniable that the poem thus altered is politically more in tune with his later, more mature views. As for "September 1, 1939," the line "We must love one another or die" so offended its author that at various times he (a) disowned the poem altogether, (b) printed the poem without the stanza that concludes with the line, and (c) changed the line to "We must love one another *and* die" (italics added). It seems to me that Auden's objections to the line as written—that it is mere rhetoric or that it sentimentalizes the power of love—are not adequately met by any of the changes he proffered, all of which would fatally compromise a poem that reaches its climax precisely with the controversial line. I cross Auden's wishes knowing that Edward Mendelson, Auden's faithful literary executor, has done the same in

[4] Readers of the fifth edition of the *Norton Anthology of Poetry* (2005) learn in a footnote that Moore reduced the poem to "the first three lines." This is not quite accurate. Originally the first line read, "I, too, dislike it: there are things that are important beyond all this fiddle." In the revision the opening line is reduced to its first four words.

the *Selected Poems* (1979), though for somewhat different reasons. Mendelson says he wanted to produce a "historical edition" that reflects "the author's work as it first appeared in public rather than his final version of it." Mendelson takes pains to defend Auden's revisions and would disagree with the maxim that begins this paragraph. But readers can make up their own minds: that is one of the prerogatives of readership. You are entitled to overrule an author's decision, reminding yourself complacently that had Max Brod heeded Franz Kafka's wishes, we would have no Kafka today. Moreover, you reserve the right to accept or reject anything—and to reverse your position at some future date. As James Schuyler wrote of James Joyce's *Ulysses*, "The book I suppose is a masterpiece. Freedom of choice is better."[5]

* * *

A note on songs. A problem any anthologist of American verse must face is the status of popular song lyrics. I love and admire the lyrics of Lorenz Hart, Johnny Mercer, Ira Gershwin, Cole Porter, Oscar Hammerstein, Irving Berlin, Dorothy Fields, Sammy Cahn, Yip Harburg, Frank Loesser, Carolyn Leigh, and numerous other songwriters. Yet I feel that what they wrote forms a different genre—that in an important sense, Ira Gershwin's lyrics for "Can't Get Started" need the music of Vernon Duke just as Lorenz Hart's words for "The Lady is a Tramp" need Richard Rodgers's tune. The lyrics do not quite exist independently of the notes and chords. Mind you, I feel there are few modern love poems as affecting as "All the Things You Are" (lyrics by Oscar Hammerstein, music by Jerome Kern) or "That Old Black Magic" (lyrics by Johnny Mercer, music by Harold Arlen). But the great American songbook is a category all its own, and so you will not find Lorenz Hart's "Mountain Greenery" or Dorothy Fields's "A Fine Romance" or Cole Porter's "I've Got You Under My Skin" in these pages though each is a great American invention and all have a permanent place in my heart. A few anthems of central cultural importance ("A Defense of Fort McHenry," "America the Beautiful") are included. Otherwise I made only three exceptions to the rule against song lyrics: I included a Bessie Smith blues and a Robert Johnson blues in part because of the argument, based on the work of Langston Hughes and others, that the blues is a literary form. I also included Bob Dylan's "Desolation Row," of which it can be said, as it cannot be said of "Some Enchanted Evening," "I Get a Kick Out of You," "Come Rain or Come Shine," "Cheek to Cheek," or "Someone to Watch over Me," that the lyrics have an existence apart from the music. The placement of "Desolation Row" in this anthology in the specific company of Dylan's contemporaries—among them Charles Simic, Frank Bidart, Robert Hass, Lyn Hejinian, Louise Glück, and James Tate—may help advance consideration of the claims put forth aggressively by Christopher Ricks and others regarding Dylan's achievement as a poet.

---

[5] Auden bowdlerized only one line of "In Praise of Limestone." In the sanitized version, the line reads as follows: "For her son, the flirtatious male who lounges / Against a rock in the sunlight." Readers are encouraged to compare this to the version of the line printed here, its fig leaf removed.

To the instructor who adopts this book for classroom use. As a teacher, I have found it useful to pair poems by different authors on the same theme or in the same form. Here are some linkages that may stimulate classroom discussion. Both Mark Strand ("Orpheus Alone") and Jorie Graham ("Orpheus and Eurydice") treat the myth of Orpheus. Sylvia Plath's "Mirror" might be paired with "The Mirror" of Louise Glück, Ruth Stone's "Train Ride" with the poem of the same title by John Wheelwright. Rae Armantrout's "Traveling through the Yard" responds pungently to William Stafford's "Traveling through the Dark." Both Wallace Stevens ("The Snow Man") and Richard Wilbur ("Boy at the Window") have poems about snowmen. Both Henry Wadsworth Longfellow and Hart Crane wrote poems entitled "The Bridge." Both Kay Ryan and Katha Pollitt have poems entitled "Failure," and there are poems about the nature of "Inspiration" by Henry David Thoreau, James Tate, and William Matthews. The "things to do" genre seems to have been invented concurrently by two poets working independently, James Schuyler and Gary Snyder, whose initiating efforts are included here. About World War II, there is testimony from Randall Jarrell, Kenneth Koch, Lincoln Kirstein, Karl Shapiro, Josephine Miles, Gwendolyn Brooks, and Charles Simic. There is an entire genre of two-line poems that merits exploration. Examples here in diverse styles come from Charles Reznikoff, J. V. Cunningham, A. R. Ammons, Charles Simic, and Robert Pinsky. There are self-portraits by Charles Wright ("Self-Portrait"), Donald Justice ("Self-Portrait as Still Life"), John Ashbery ("Self-Portrait in a Convex Mirror"), and James Merrill ("Self-Portrait in Tyvek™ Windbreaker"). Paintings by Brueghel are treated in poems by Auden and William Carlos Williams ("Landscape with the Fall of Icarus") and by John Berryman and Williams ("The Hunters in the Snow"). There are villanelles by Edwin Arlington Robinson, W. H. Auden, Theodore Roethke, Elizabeth Bishop, Donald Justice, Mark Strand, and John Koethe; sestinas by Elizabeth Bishop (two), Anthony Hecht, Harry Mathews, and James Cummins; ballads by Whittier, Longfellow, Auden, Elinor Wylie, James Merrill, and Dana Gioia; sonnets by Jones Very, Frederick Goddard Tuckerman, Emma Lazarus, Edwin Arlington Robinson, Claude McKay, Edna St. Vincent Millay, Elinor Wylie, Donald Hall, Edwin Denby, Ted Berrigan, and Bernadette Mayer, among others; and prose poems by such poets as Delmore Schwartz, Stanley Kunitz, Karl Shapiro, Allen Ginsberg, W. S. Merwin, Russell Edson, Robert Hass, Lyn Hejinian, Carolyn Forche, and James Tate.

I should add that Anthony Hecht's "The Dover Bitch" and Tom Clark's "Dover Beach" demand to be read as reactions to Matthew Arnold's "Dover Beach"; that Pound's "The Lake Isle" is a complex response to Yeats's "The Lake Isle of Innisfree" and presupposes a knowledge of that poem, though it can be enjoyed without it; that the student of Emma Lazarus's "the New Colossus" may profit from reading it in the light of Shelley's "Ozymandias"; That Billy Collins's "Lines Composed Over Three Thousand Miles from Tintern Abbey "can serve as a charming gloss on Wordsworth's great ode; and that Elizabeth Bishop's "Crusoe in England" makes a reference to Wordsworth's "I Wandered Lonely as a Cloud," which ideally should be read concurrently with or just before one reads Bishop's "Crusoe."

A note on dates. No real consistency is possible in assigning dates to the poems. Generally we opted for the year of first publication in a book by the author, which in most cases is easier to find than the year of composition, even though this practice leads to such absurdities as giving the year 1939 to a poem by the seventeenth-century Edward Taylor for the reason that Taylor's works, unearthed by a scholar, came into print that year. It is often difficult to establish when a given poem was written, or completed, or abandoned, but when strong evidence suggests a certain year, we have gone with that to avoid anachronisms.

A last note. I have opted to provide succinct headnotes for each of the poets in the pages that follow. I hope that these notes stimulate further reading of the poets and their critics, biographers, and historians. And I would echo F. O. Matthiessen's closing declaration from 1950, which applies with even greater force today: "We have produced by now a body of poetry of absorbing quality. If this poetry reveals violent contrasts and unresolved conflicts, it corresponds thereby to American life."

Ithaca, New York
December 2005

Acknowledgments

I owe a special debt to John Brehm, associate editor of this book, who assisted me ably in every aspect of the enterprise. Mark Bibbins, Steven Dube, Betsy Johnson-Miller, Kelly Nichols, Danielle Pafunda, Karl Parker, and Carly Sachs contributed valuable research. They have my heartfelt thanks, as does Natalie Gerber who made thoughtful recommendations concerning early American poetry. Fred Muratori, a poet as well as a reference librarian at Cornell University, managed heroic feats of scholarship—tracking down a poem, nailing down a date—with impressive speed.

I am grateful to my students at the New School University, who were asked in various classes to imagine themselves the editors of a new anthology based on Richard Ellmann's *New Oxford Book of American Verse*, and to students of "Great Poems" at NYU on whom I tried out some selections. I also benefited from conversations with the following, who made suggestions I took to heart, shared enthusiasms, or provided factual or other information that helped my work on the headnotes: Nin Andrews, Molly Arden, John Ashbery, Angela Ball, Frank Bidart, Tamar Brazis, J. D. Bullard, Sofiya Cabalquinto, Michael Cirelli, Marc Cohen, Theresa Collins, Shanna Compton, Douglas Crase, Laura Cronk, Wende Crow, Heather Currier, Mary Donnelly, Peter Drake, Steven Dube, Denise Duhamel, Will Edmiston, Julia Farkis, Erica Miriam Fabri, John Findura, Peter Fortunato, Claire Fuqua, Amy Gerstler, Roger Gilbert, Katy Gilliam, Dana Gioia, Peter Gizzi, Louise Glück, Laurence Goldstein, Lainie Goldwert, Anna Ojascastro Guzon, Judith Hall, Jack Hanley, William Harmon, Michael Harris, Glen Hartley, Stacey Harwood, Ron Horning, Jennifer Huh, Salwa Jabado, Megin Jiminez, Peter Johnson, Betsy Johnson-Miller, Lawrence Joseph, Mookie Katigbak, Yusef Komunyakaa, Anastasios Kozaitis, Deborah Landau, David Levi, Gianmarc Manzione, Edward Mendelson, Susan Mitchell, Michael Montlack, Honor Moore, Robert Mueller, Geoffrey O'Brien, Danielle Pafunda, Karl Parker, Robert Pinsky, Robert Polito, Aaron Raymond, Liam Rector, Eugene Richie, Hester Rock, Allyson Salazar, Paul Schwartzberg, Laurie Sheck, Charles Simic, Monica Stahl, Shelley Stenhouse, Nicole Steinberg, Mark Strand, James Tate, Gabriella Torres, Ben Turner, Lee Upton, David Wagoner, Susan Wheeler, Elizabeth Willis, Antonia Wright, and Matthew Yeager.

Some of the poems in this book were chosen for *The Best American Poetry* of the year following the year they appeared in periodicals. To the eighteen guest editors of *The Best American Poetry* since 1988 I renew my thanks: John Ashbery, Donald Hall,

Jorie Graham, Mark Strand, Charles Simic, Louise Glück, A. R. Ammons, Richard Howard, Adrienne Rich, James Tate, John Hollander, Robert Bly, Rita Dove, Robert Hass, Robert Creeley, Yusef Komunyakaa, Lyn Hejinian, and Paul Muldoon.

For expert editorial advice and support, it gives me pleasure to acknowledge Casper Grathwohl and Benjamin Keene of Oxford University Press and, as always, my agents, Glen Hartley and Lynn Chu of Writers' Representatives, Inc.

Contents

The Oxford Book of American Poetry

Anne Bradstreet (c. 1612–1672)

Born Anne Dudley in Northampton, England, the first American poet had rheumatic fever as a child and contracted smallpox just before marrying Cambridge graduate Simon Bradstreet. With John Winthrop's fleet in 1630, the couple sailed to America, where both Bradstreet's husband and her father would serve as governors of Massachusetts. Anne Bradstreet became the mother of eight children and the author of a manuscript that her brother-in-law brought back to London and published without her knowledge in 1650 under the title *The Tenth Muse Lately Sprung Up in America*. Six years after her death a second and enlarged edition of her poems appeared in Boston. John Berryman found it expedient to adopt her voice in his long poem *Homage to Mistress Bradstreet* (1953). "I didn't like her work, but I loved her—I sort of fell in love with her," he explained.

The Prologue

I

To sing of Wars, of Captaines, and of Kings,
Of Cities founded, Common-wealths begun,
For my mean Pen, are too superiour things,
And how they all, or each, their dates have run:
Let Poets, and Historians set these forth,
My obscure Verse, shal not so dim their worth.

II

But when my wondring eyes, and envious heart,
Great *Bartas* sugar'd lines doe but read o're;
Foole, *I* doe grudge, the Muses did not part
'Twixt him and me, that over-fluent store;
A *Bartas* can, doe what a *Bartas* wil,
But simple I, according to my skill.

III

From School-boyes tongue, no Rhethorick we expect,
Nor yet a sweet Confort, from broken strings,
Nor perfect beauty, where's a maine defect,
My foolish, broken, blemish'd Muse so sings;
And this to mend, alas, no Art is able,
'Cause Nature made it so irreparable.

IV

Nor can I, like that fluent sweet tongu'd *Greek*
Who lisp'd at first, speake afterwards more plaine.
By Art, he gladly found what he did seeke,
A full requitall of his striving paine:
Art can doe much, but this maxime's most sure,
A weake or wounded braine admits no cure.

V

I am obnoxious to each carping tongue,
Who sayes, my hand a needle better fits,
A Poets Pen, all scorne, I should thus wrong;
For such despight they cast on female wits:
If what I doe prove well, it wo'nt advance,
They'l say its stolne, or else, it was by chance.

VI

But sure the antick *Greeks* were far more milde,
Else of our Sex, why feigned they those nine,
And poesy made, *Calliope's* owne childe,
So 'mongst the rest, they plac'd the Arts divine:
But this weake knot they will full soone untye,
The *Greeks* did nought, but play the foole and lye.

VII

Let *Greeks* be *Greeks*, and Women what they are,
Men have precedency, and still excell,
It is but vaine, unjustly to wage war,
Men can doe best, and Women know it well;
Preheminence in each, and all is yours,
Yet grant some small acknowledgement of ours.

VIII

And oh, ye high flown quils, that soare the skies,
And ever with your prey, still catch your praise,
If e're you daigne these lowly lines, your eyes
Give wholsome Parsley wreath, I aske no Bayes:
This meane and unrefined stuffe of mine,
Will make your glistering gold but more to shine.

1650

from *Contemplations*

When I behold the heavens as in their prime,
    And then the earth, though old, still clad in green,
The stones and trees insensible of time,
    Nor age nor wrinkle on their front are seen;
If winter come, and greenness then doth fade,
A spring returns, and they're more youthful made.
But man grows old, lies down, remains where once he's laid.

By birth more noble than those creatures all,
    Yet seems by nature and by custom cursed —
No sooner born but grief and care make fall
    That state obliterate he had at first;

Nor youth, nor strength, nor wisdom spring again,
Nor habitations long their names retain,
But in oblivion to the final day remain.

Shall I then praise the heavens, the trees, the earth,
    Because their beauty and their strength last longer?
Shall I wish there or never to had birth,
    Because they're bigger and their bodies stronger?
Nay, they shall darken, perish, fade, and die,
And when unmade so ever shall they lie;
But man was made for endless immortality.

1650

The Author to Her Book

Thou ill-formed offspring of my feeble brain,
Who after birth didst by my side remain,
Till snatched from thence by friends, less wise than true,
Who thee abroad, expos'd to publick view,
Made thee in raggs, halting to th' press to trudg,
Where errors were not lessened (all may judge).
At thy return my blushing was not small,
My rambling brat (in print) should mother call,
I cast thee by as one unfit for light,
Thy Visage was so irksome in my sight;
Yet being mine own, at length affection would
Thy blemishes amend, if so I could:
I wash'd thy face, but more defects I saw,
And rubbing off a spot still made a flaw.
I stretched thy joynts to make thee even feet,
Yet still thou run'st more hobling than is meet;
In better dress to trim thee was my mind,
But nought save homespun Cloth i' th' house I find[.]
In this array 'mongst Vulgars may'st thou roam[.]
In Criticks hands, beware thou dost not come;
And take thy way where yet thou art not known;
If for thy Father asked, say thou hadst none;
And for thy Mother, she alas is poor,
Which caus'd her thus to send thee out of door.

1678

Before the Birth of One of Her Children

All things within this fading world hath end,
Adversity doth still our joys attend;
No ties so strong, no friends so dear and sweet,

But with death's parting blow is sure to meet.
The sentence past is most irrevocable,
A common thing, yet oh inevitable.
How soon, my Dear, death may my steps attend,
How soon't may be thy Lot to lose thy friend,
We are both ignorant, yet love bids me
These farewell lines to recommend to thee,
That when that knot's untied that made us one,
I may seem thine, who in effect am none.
And if I see not half my dayes that's due,
What nature would, God grant to yours and you;
The many faults that well you know I have
Let be interr'd in my oblivious grave;
If any worth or virtue were in me,
Let that live freshly in thy memory
And when thou feel'st no grief, as I no harms,
Yet love thy dead, who long lay in thine arms.
And when thy loss shall be repaid with gains
Look to my little babes[,] my dear remains.
And if thou love thyself, or loved'st me[,]
These o protect from step Dames injury.
And if chance to thine eyes shall bring this verse,
With some sad sighs honour my absent Herse;
And kiss this paper for thy loves dear sake,
Who with salt tears this last Farewel did take.

1678

To My Dear and Loving Husband

If ever two were one, then surely we.
If ever man were lov'd by wife, then thee;
If ever wife was happy in a man,
Compare with me ye women if you can.
I prize thy love more than whole Mines of gold,
Or all the riches that the East doth hold.
My love is such that Rivers cannot quench,
Nor ought but love from thee, give recompense.
Thy love is such I can no way repay,
The heavens reward thee manifold, I pray.
Then while we live, in love lets so persever,
That when we live no more, we may live ever.

1678

Edward Taylor (1642–1729)

Edward Taylor was born in Leicestershire, England. He emigrated to New England in 1668, graduated from Harvard University, became a minister in the frontier village of Westfield, Massachusetts, and applied his powers of oratory to his pastoral duties. His poems remained unknown until the scholar Thomas H. Johnson discovered them in a bound manuscript book at the Yale University Library and published a selection in 1937. Taylor "was a Puritan minister in the 1680s on the remotest American frontier writing an often ecstatic poetry in a style strongly reminiscent of George Herbert but verging on a continental, Roman Catholic baroque, a minister who also, it should be added, was the author of a number of virulently anti-Papist works" (Robert Hass). When Taylor died, the only book of English verse in his library was by Anne Bradstreet.

Meditation III (Canticles I:3: Thy Good Ointment)

How Sweet a Lord is mine? If any should
  Guarded, Engarden'd, nay, Imbosomd bee
In reechs of Odours, Gales of Spices, Folds
  Of Aromaticks, Oh! how Sweet was hee?
  He would be Sweet, and yet his sweetest Wave
  Compar'de to thee my Lord, no Sweet would have.

A Box of Ointments, broke; Sweetness most sweet
  A surge of Spices: Odours Common Wealth,
A Pillar of Perfume: a Steaming Reech
  Of Aromatick Clouds: All Saving Health
  Sweetness itselfe thou art: And I presume
  In Calling of thee Sweet, who art Perfume.

But Woe is mee! who have so quick a Sent
  To Catch perfumes pufft out from Pincks, and Roses
And other Muscadalls, as they get Vent,
  Out of their Mothers Wombs to bob our noses.
  And yet thy sweet perfume doth seldom latch
  My Lord, within my Mammulary Catch.

Am I denos'de? or doth the Worlds ill Sents
  Engarison my nosthrills narrow bore?
Or is my Smell lost in these Damps it Vents?
  And shall I never finde it any more?
  Or is it like the Hawks, or Hownds whose breed
  Take Stincking Carrion for Perfume indeed?

This is my Case. All things smell sweet to mee:
  Except thy sweetness, Lord. Expell these damps.
Break up this Garison: and let me see
  Thy Aromaticks pitching in these Camps.

Oh! let the Clouds of thy sweet Vapours rise,
And both my Mammularies Circumcise.

Shall spirits thus my Mammularies Suck?
(As Witches Elves their teats,) and draw from thee
My Dear, Dear Spirit after fumes of muck?
Be Dunghill Damps more sweet than Graces bee?
Lord, clear these Caves; these Passes take, and keep.
And in these Quarters lodge thy Odours sweet.

Lord, breake thy Box of Ointment on my Head;
Let thy sweet Powder powder all my hair:
My Spirits let with thy perfumes be fed.
And make thy Odours, Lord, my nosthrills fare.
My Soule shall in thy Sweets then Soar to thee:
I'le be thy Love, thou my Sweet Lord shalt bee.

c. 1682

Meditation VI (Canticles II:1: I am . . . the lily of the valleys.)

Am I thy gold? Or Purse, Lord, for thy Wealth;
Whether in mine or mint refinde for thee?
Ime counted so, but count me o're thyselfe,
Lest gold washt face, and brass in Heart I bee.
I Feare my Touchstone touches when I try
Mee, and my Counted Gold too overly.

Am I new minted by thy Stamp indeed?
Mine Eyes are dim; I cannot clearly see.
Be thou my Spectacles that I may read
Thine Image and Inscription stampt on mee.
If thy bright Image do upon me stand,
I am a Golden Angell in thy hand.

Lord, make my Soule thy Plate: thine Image bright
Within the Circle of the same enfoile.
And on its brims in golden Letters write
Thy Superscription in an Holy style.
Then I shall be thy Money, thou my Hord:
Let me thy Angell bee, bee thou my Lord.

c. 1682

The Preface [to God's Determinations*]*

Infinity, when all things it beheld
In Nothing, and of Nothing all did build,

Upon what Base was fixt the Lath, wherein
He turn'd this Globe, and riggalld it so trim?
Who blew the Bellows of his Furnace Vast?
Or held the Mould wherein the world was Cast?
Who laid its Corner Stone? Or whose Command?
Where stand the Pillars upon which it stands?
Who Lac'de and Fillitted the earth so fine,
With Rivers like green Ribbons Smaragdine?
Who made the Sea's its Selvedge, and it locks
Like a Quilt Ball within a Silver Box?
Who spread its Canopy? Or Curtains Spun?
Who in this Bowling Alley bowld the Sun?
Who made it always when it rises set
To go at once both down, and up to get?
Who th'Curtain rods made for this Tapistry?
Who hung the twinckling Lanthorns in the Sky?
Who? who did this? or who is he? Why, know
Its Onely Might Almighty this did doe.
His hand hath made this noble worke which Stands
His Glorious Handywork not made by hands.
Who spake all things from nothing; and with ease
Can speake all things to nothing, if he please.
Whose Little finger at his pleasure Can
Out mete ten thousand worlds with halfe a Span:
Whose Might Almighty can by half a looks
Root up the rocks and rock the hills by th'roots.
Can take this mighty World up in his hande,
And shake it like a Squitchen or a Wand.
Whose single Frown will make the Heavens shake
Like as an aspen leafe the Winde makes quake.
Oh! what a might is this Whose single frown
Doth shake the world as it would shake it down?
Which All from Nothing fet, from Nothing, All:
Hath All on Nothing set, lets Nothing fall.
Gave All to nothing Man indeed, whereby
Through nothing man all might him Glorify.
In Nothing then imbosst the brightest Gem
More pretious than all pretiousness in them.
But Nothing man did throw down all by Sin:
And darkened that lightsom Gem in him.
  That now his Brightest Diamond is grown
  Darker by far than any Coalpit Stone.

c. 1685

Upon a Spider Catching a Fly

Thou sorrow, venom Elfe.
  Is this thy play,

To spin a web out of thyselfe
  To Catch a Fly?
    For Why?

I saw a pettish wasp
  Fall foule therein.
Whom yet thy Whorle pins did not clasp
  Lest he should fling
    His sting.

But as affraid, remote
  Didst stand hereat
And with thy little fingers stroke
  And gently tap
    His back.

Thus gently him didst treate
  Lest he should pet,
And in a froppish, waspish heate
  Should greatly fret
    Thy net.

Whereas the silly Fly,
  Caught by its leg
Thou by the throate tookst hastily
  And 'hinde the head
    Bite Dead.

This goes to pot, that not
  Nature doth call.
Strive not above what strength hath got
  Lest in the brawle
    Thou fall.

This Frey seems thus to us.
  Hells Spider gets
His intrails spun to whip Cords thus
  And wove to nets
    And sets.

To tangle Adams race
  In's stratigems
To their Destructions, spoil'd, made base
  By venom things
    Damn'd Sins.

But mighty, Gracious Lord
  Communicate

Thy Grace to breake the Cord, afford
　Us Glorys Gate
　　And State.

We'l Nightingaile sing like
　When pearcht on high
In Glories Cage, thy glory, bright,
　And thankfully,
　　For joy.

published 1939

Huswifery

Make me, O Lord, thy Spining Wheele compleate.
　Thy Holy Worde my Distaff make for mee.
Make mine Affections thy Swift Flyers neate
　And make my Soule thy holy Spoole to bee.
　My Conversation make to be thy Reele
　And reele the yarn thereon spun of thy Wheele.

Make me thy Loome then, knit therein this Twine:
　And make thy Holy Spirit, Lord, winde quills:
Then weave the Web thyselfe. Thy yarn is fine.
　Thine Ordinances make my Fulling Mills.
　Then dy the same in Heavenly Colours Choice,
　All pinkt with Varnisht Flowers of Paradise.

Then cloath therewith mine Understanding, Will,
　Affections, Judgement, Conscience, Memory
My Words, and Actions, that their shine may fill
　My wayes with glory and thee glorify.
　Then mine apparell shall display before yee
　That I am Cloathd in Holy robes for glory.

published 1939

PHILIP FRENEAU (1752–1832)

Philip Freneau, the "Poet of the American Revolution," was also (in F. O. Matthiessen's words) "the first American to think of himself as a professional poet." Freneau hobnobbed with presidents. He roomed with James Madison at Princeton University and would later bring his silver tongue to bear on the side of Madison and Thomas Jefferson in their ideological disputes with Alexander Hamilton. The poet fought in the Revolutionary War, and in 1780 he was captured by the British, held for six weeks, and treated brutally on the prison ship *Scorpion*. Freneau wrote much satirical journalism (under the pseudonym Robert Slender), edited an anti-Federalist newspaper that rankled President Washington, and served more than once as a ship's captain. His *Poems Written and Published during the American Revolutionary War* appeared in two volumes in 1809. On his way home on foot from a tavern, he lost his way in a snowstorm and died on 18 December 1832.

On the Emigration to America and Peopling the Western Country

To western woods, and lonely plains,
Palemon from the crowd departs,
Where Nature's wildest genius reigns,
To tame the soil, and plant the arts —
What wonders there shall freedom show,
What mighty states successive grow!

From Europe's proud, despotic shores
Hither the stranger takes his way,
And in our new found world explores
A happier soil, a milder sway,
Where no proud despot holds him down,
No slaves insult him with a crown.

What charming scenes attract the eye,
On wild Ohio's savage stream!
There Nature reigns, whose works outvie
The boldest pattern art can frame;
There ages past have rolled away,
And forests bloomed but to decay.

From these fair plains, these rural seats,
So long concealed, so lately known,
The unsocial Indian far retreats,
To make some other clime his own,
When other streams, less pleasing flow,
And darker forests round him grow.

Great sire of floods! whose varied wave
Through climes and countries takes its way,
To whom creating Nature gave
Ten thousand streams to swell thy sway!
No longer shall they useless prove,
Nor idly through the forests rove;

Nor longer shall your princely flood
From distant lakes be swelled in vain,
Nor longer through a darksome wood
Advance, unnoticed, to the main,

Far other ends, the heavens decree —
And commerce plans new freights for thee.

While virtue warms the generous breast,
There heaven-born freedom shall reside,
Nor shall the voice of war molest,
Nor Europe's all-aspiring pride —
There Reason shall new laws devise,
And order from confusion rise.

Forsaking kings and regal state,
With all their pomp and fancied bliss,
The traveler owns, convinced though late,
No realm so free, so blessed as this —
The east is half to slaves consigned,
Where kings and priests enchain the mind.

O come the time, and haste the day,
When man shall man no longer crush,
When Reason shall enforce her sway,
Nor these fair regions raise our blush,
Where still the African complains,
And mourns his yet unbroken chains.

Far brighter scenes a future age,
The muse predicts, these states will hail,
Whose genius may the world engage,
Whose deeds may over death prevail,
And happier systems bring to view,
Than all the eastern sages knew.

1785

The Wild Honey Suckle

Fair flower, that dost so comely grow,
Hid in this silent, dull retreat,
Untouched thy honied blossoms blow,
Unseen thy little branches greet:
  No roving foot shall crush thee here,
  No busy hand provoke a tear.

By Nature's self in white arrayed
She bade thee shun the vulgar eye,
And planted here the guardian shade,
And sent soft waters murmuring by;
  Thus quietly thy summer goes,
  Thy days declining to repose.

Smit with those charms, that must decay,
I grieve to see your future doom;
They died — nor were those flowers more gay,
The flowers that did in Eden bloom;
  Unpitying frosts, and Autumn's power
  Shall leave no vestige of this flower.

From morning suns and evening dews
At first thy little being came:
If nothing once, you nothing lose,
For when you die you are the same;
  The space between, is but an hour,
  The frail duration of a flower.

1786

The Indian Burying Ground

In spite of all the learned have said,
I still my old opinion keep;
The *posture*, that *we* give the dead,
Points out the soul's eternal sleep.

Not so the ancients of these lands —
The Indian, when from life released,
Again is seated with his friends,
And shares again the joyous feast.

His imaged birds, and painted bowl,
And venison, for a journey dressed.
Bespeak the nature of the soul,
ACTIVITY, that knows no rest.

His bow, for action ready bent,
And arrows, with a head of stone,
Can only mean that life is spent,
And not the old ideas gone.

Thou, stranger, that shalt come this way,
No fraud upon the dead commit —
Observe the swelling turf, and say
They do not *lie*, but here they *sit*,

Here still a lofty rock remains,
On which the curious eye may trace
(Now wasted, half, by wearing rains)
The fancies of a ruder race.

Here still an aged elm aspires,
Beneath whose far-projecting shade
(And which the shepherd still admires)
The children of the forest played!

There oft a restless Indian queen
(Pale *Shebah*, with her braided hair)
And many a barbarous form is seen
To chide the man that lingers there.

By midnight moons, o'er moistening dews,
In habit for the chase arrayed,
The hunter still the deer pursues,
The hunter and the deer, a shade!

And long shall timorous fancy see
The painted chief, and pointed spear,
And Reason's self shall bow the knee
To shadows and delusions here.

1788

PHILLIS WHEATLEY (c. 1753–1784)

A slave ship brought Phillis Wheatley from West Africa to Boston in 1761. John Wheatley, a wealthy tailor, and his wife, Susannah, purchased her and gave her an American name. Her first poem appeared in print in a Newport, Rhode Island, newspaper in 1767. In 1773, thirty-nine of her poems were published in London as *Poems on Various Subjects, Religious and Moral.* This, her only collection of poems, was the first published book by an African-American. She was freed in 1778 and married a freedman, John Peters, but the marriage turned out badly. Abandoned by Peters, she lived in penury in Boston. She had already lost two children, and a third lay mortally ill, when she died and was buried in an unmarked grave.

On Being Brought from Africa to America

'Twas mercy brought me from my *Pagan* land,
Taught my benighted soul to understand
That there's a God, that there's a *Saviour* too:
Once I redemption neither sought nor knew.
Some view our sable race with scornful eye,
"Their colour is a diabolic die."
Remember, *Christians*, *Negroes*, black as *Cain*,
May be refin'd, and join th' angelic train.

1773

To The Right Honorable William, Earl of Dartmouth

Hail, happy day, when, smiling like the morn,
Fair Freedom rose New England to adorn:
The northern clime beneath her genial ray,
Dartmouth, congratulates thy blissful sway:
Elate with hope her race no longer mourns,
Each soul expands, each grateful bosom burns,
While in thine hand with pleasure we behold
The silken reins, and Freedom's charms unfold.
Long lost to realms beneath the northern skies
She shines supreme, while hated faction dies:
Soon as appear'd the Goddess long desir'd,
Sick as the view, she languish'd and expir'd;
Thus from the splendors of the morning light
The owl in sadness seeks the caves of night.
No more America in mournful strain
Of wrongs, and grievance unredress'd complain,
No longer shalt thou dread the iron chain,
Which wanton Tyranny with lawless hand
Had made, and which it meant t' enslave the land.

Should you, my lord, while you peruse my song,
Wonder from whence my love of Freedom sprung,
Whence flow these wishes for the common good,
By feeling hearts alone best understood,
I, young in life, by seeming cruel fate
Was snatch'd from Afric's fancy'd happy seat:
What pangs excruciating must molest,
What sorrows labour in my parent's breast!
Steel'd was the soul and by no misery mov'd
That from a father seiz'd his babe belov'd.
Such, such my case. And can I then but pray
Others may never feel tyrannic sway?
For favours past, great Sir, our thanks are due,
And thee we ask thy favours to renew,
Since in thy pow'r, as in thy will before,
To sooth the griefs, which thou did'st once deplore.
May heav'nly grace the sacred sanction give
To all thy works, and thou for ever live
Not only on the wings of fleeting Fame,
Though praise immortal crowns the patriot's name,
But to conduct to heav'n's refulgent fane,
May fiery courses sweep th' ethereal plain,
And bear thee upwards to that blest abode,
Where, like prophet, thou shalt find thy God.

1773

JOEL BARLOW (1754–1812)

The son of a wealthy Connecticut farmer, Joel Barlow volunteered for the American army while a Yale undergraduate. He joined a circle of "Hartford wits" in the 1780s before leaving with his wife for Europe, where he lived for seventeen years. Like Freneau, he counted Thomas Jefferson and James Madison among his friends. "Hasty pudding," which has been called "colonial America's fast food," provoked Barlow to write his mirthful poem in 1793. Appointed U.S. ambassador to France in 1811, Barlow traveled from Paris to Vilna to negotiate a trade agreement with Napoleon. He was caught in the retreat of the French army from Russia and died near Kraków in Poland on the day before Christmas, 1812.

The Hasty-Pudding

Canto I

Ye Alps audacious, thro' the Heavens that rise,
To cramp the day and hide me from the skies;
Ye Gallic flags, that o'er their heights unfurl'd,
Bear death to kings, and freedom to the world,
I sing not you. A softer theme I chuse,
A virgin theme, unconscious of the Muse,
But fruitful, rich, well suited to inspire
The purest frenzy of poetic fire.
   Despise it not, ye Bards to terror steel'd,
Who hurl'd your thunders round the epic field;
Nor ye who strain your midnight throats to sing
Joys that the vineyard and the still-house bring;
Or on some distant fair your notes employ,
And speak of raptures that you ne'er enjoy.
I sing the sweets I know, the charms I feel,
My morning incense, and my evening meal,
The sweets of Hasty-Pudding. Come, dear bowl,
Glide o'er my palate, and inspire my soul.
The milk beside thee, smoking from the kine,
Its substance mingled, married in with thine,
Shall cool and temper thy superior heat,
And save the pains of blowing while I eat.
   Oh! could the smooth, the emblematic song
Flow like thy genial juices o'er my tongue,
Could those mild morsels in my numbers chime,
And, as they roll in substance, roll in rhyme,
No more thy aukward unpoetic name
Should shun the Muse, or prejudice thy fame;
But rising grateful to the accustom'd ear,
All Bards should catch it, and all realms revere!
   Assist me first with pious toil to trace
Thro' wrecks of time thy lineage and thy race;
Declare what lovely squaw, in days of yore,

(Ere great Columbus sought thy native shore)
First gave thee to the world; her works of fame
Have liv'd indeed, but liv'd without a name.
Some tawny Ceres, goddess of her days,
First learn'd with stones to crack the well-dry'd maize,
Thro' the rough sieve to shake the golden show'r,
In boiling water stir the yellow flour.
The yellow flour, bestrew'd and stir'd with haste,
Swells in the flood and thickens to a paste,
Then puffs and wallops, rises to the brim,
Drinks the dry knobs that on the surface swim:
The knobs at last the busy ladle breaks,
And the whole mass its true consistence takes.
　Could but her sacred name, unknown so long,
Rise like her labors, to the sons of song,
To her, to them, I'd consecrate my lays,
And blow her pudding with the breath of praise.
If 'twas Oella, whom I sang before,
I here ascribe her one great virtue more.
Not thro' the rich Peruvian realms alone
The fame of Sol's sweet daughter should be known,
But o'er the world's wide climes should live secure,
Far as his rays extend, as long as they endure.
　Dear Hasty-Pudding, what unpromis'd joy
Expands my heart, to meet thee in Savoy!
Doom'd o'er the world thro' devious paths to roam,
Each clime my country, and each house my home,
My soul is sooth'd, my cares have found an end,
I greet my long-lost, unforgotten friend.
　For thee thro' Paris, that corrupted town,
How long in vain I wandered up and down,
Where shameless Bacchus, with his drenching hoard
Cold from his cave usurps the morning board.
London is lost in smoke and steep'd in tea;
No Yankey there can lisp the name of thee:
The uncouth word, a libel on the town,
Would call a proclamation from the crown.
For climes oblique, that fear the sun's full rays,
Chill'd in their fogs, exclude the generous maize;
A grain whose rich luxuriant growth requires
Short gentle showers, and bright etherial fires.
　But here tho' distant from our native shore,
With mutual glee we meet and laugh once more,
The same! I know thee by that yellow face,
That strong complexion of true Indian race,
Which time can never change, nor soil impair,
Nor Alpine snows, nor Turkey's morbid air;
For endless years, thro' every mild domain,
Where grows the maize, there thou art sure to reign.

But man, more fickle, the bold licence claims,
In different realms to give thee different names.
Thee the soft nations round the warm Levant
Palanta call, the French of course *Polante*;
E'en in thy native regions, how I blush
To hear the Pennsylvanians call thee *Mush*!
On Hudson's banks, while men of Belgic spawn
Insult and eat thee by the name *suppawn*.
All spurious appellations, void of truth:
I've better known thee from my earliest youth,
Thy name is *Hasty-Pudding*! thus our sires
Were wont to greet thee fuming from their fires;
And while they argu'd in thy just defence
With logic clear, they thus explained the sense: —
"In *haste* the boiling cauldron o'er the blaze,
Receives and cooks the ready-powder'd maize;
In *haste* 'tis serv'd, and then in equal *haste*,
With cooling milk, we make the sweet repast.
No carving to be done, no knife to grate
The tender ear, and wound the stony plate;
But the smooth spoon, just fitted to the lip,
And taught with art the yielding mass to dip,
By frequent journies to the bowl well stor'd,
Performs the hasty honors of the board."
Such is thy name, significant and clear,
A name, a sound to every Yankey dear,
But most to me, whose heart and palate chaste
Preserve my pure hereditary taste.
There are who strive to stamp with disrepute
The luscious food, because it feeds the brute;
In tropes of high-strain'd wit, while gaudy prigs
Compare thy nursling man to pamper'd pigs;
With sovereign scorn I treat the vulgar jest,
Nor fear to share thy bounties with the beast.
What though the generous cow gives me to quaff
The milk nutritious; am I then a calf?
Or can the genius of the noisy swine,
Tho' nurs'd on pudding, thence lay claim to mine?
Sure the sweet song, I fashion to thy praise,
Runs more melodious than the notes they raise.
My song resounding in its grateful glee,
No merit claims; I praise myself in thee.
My father lov'd thee through his length of days:
For thee his fields were shaded o'er with maize;
From thee what health, what vigour he possest,
Ten sturdy freemen sprung from him attest;
Thy constellation rul'd my natal morn,
And all my bones were made of Indian corn.
Delicious grain! whatever form it take,

To roast or boil, to smother or to bake,
In every dish 'tis welcome still to me,
But most, my Hasty-Pudding, most in thee.
  Let the green Succatash with thee contend,
Let beans and corn their sweetest juices blend,
Let butter drench them in its yellow tide,
And a long slice of bacon grace their side;
Not all the plate, how fam'd soe'er it be,
Can please my palate like a bowl of thee.
  Some talk of Hoe-cake, fair Virginia's pride,
Rich Johnny-cake this mouth has often tri'd;
Both please me well, their virtues much the same;
Alike their fabric, as allied their fame,
Except in dear New-England, where the last
Receives a dash of pumpkin in the paste,
To give it sweetness and improve the taste.
But place them all before me, smoaking hot,
The big round dumplin rolling from the pot;
The pudding of the bag, whose quivering breast,
With suet lin'd leads on the Yankey feast;
The Charlotte brown, within whose crusty sides
A belly soft the pulpy apple hides;
The yellow bread, whose face like amber glows,
And all of Indian that the bake-pan knows —
You tempt me not — my fav'rite greets my eyes,
To that lov'd bowl my spoon by instinct flies.

1793

Francis Scott Key (1779–1843)

On 14 September 1814, when the United States was at war with Britain, Francis Scott Key witnessed the British bombardment of Baltimore, which lasted twenty-five hours. At dawn, observing the American flag still waving over Fort McHenry, Key wrote the words of "The Star-Spangled Banner" (as it came to be known) to the tune of an eighteenth-century drinking song (John Stafford Smith's "To Anacreon in Heaven"). It was published as "Defence of Fort McHenry" in the *Baltimore American* on 21 September 1814. Shortly after, Thomas Carr's Baltimore music store published Key's words and Smith's music under the title "The Star-Spangled Banner." It became enormously popular and was made the national anthem by an act of Congress in 1931.

Defence of Fort McHenry

O! say can you see, by the dawn's early light,
What so proudly we hail'd at the twilight's last gleaming,

Whose broad stripes and bright stars through the perilous fight,
O'er the ramparts we watch'd, were so gallantly streaming?
And the rockets' red glare, the bombs bursting in air,
Gave proof through the night that our flag was still there —
O, say, does that star-spangled banner yet wave
O'er the land of the free, and the home of the brave?

On the shore, dimly seen through the mists of the deep,
Where the foe's haughty host in dread silence reposes,
What is that which the breeze o'er the towering steep,
As it fitfully blows, half conceals, half discloses?
Now it catches the gleam of the morning's first beam,
In full glory reflected now shines on the stream —
'Tis the star-spangled banner, O! long may it wave
O'er the land of the free, and the home of the brave.

And where is that band who so vauntingly swore
That the havoc of war and the battle's confusion
A home and a country should leave us no more?
Their blood has wash'd out their foul foot-steps' pollution.
No refuge could save the hireling and slave,
From the terror of flight or the gloom of the grave;
And the star-spangled banner in triumph doth wave
O'er the land of the free, and the home of the brave.

O! thus be it ever, when freemen shall stand
Between their lov'd home, and the war's desolation,
Blest with vict'ry and peace, may the heav'n-rescued land
Praise the power that hath made and preserv'd us a nation!
Then conquer we must, when our cause it is just,
And this be our motto — "In God is our trust!"
And the star-spangled banner in triumph shall wave
O'er the land of the free, and the home of the brave.

1814

CLEMENT MOORE (1779–1863)

Clement Moore was the only son of Benjamin Moore, president of Columbia College and bishop of the Protestant Episcopal Church in New York City. A graduate of Columbia College, he married Catherine Elizabeth Taylor in 1813, and they settled in Chelsea, in what was then a country estate beyond the city limits. He wrote "A Visit from Saint Nicholas" in 1822 as a Christmas gift for his children.

A Visit from St. Nicholas

'Twas the night before Christmas, when all through the house
Not a creature was stirring, not even a mouse;
The stockings were hung by the chimney with care,
In hopes that ST. NICHOLAS soon would be there;
The children were nestled all snug in their beds,
While visions of sugar-plums danced in their heads;
And Mamma in her 'kerchief, and I in my cap,
Had just settled down for a long winter's nap;
When out on the lawn there arose such a clatter,
I sprang from the bed to see what was the matter.
Away to the window I flew like a flash,
Tore open the shutters and threw up the sash.
The moon on the breast of the new-fallen snow,
Gave the lustre of mid-day to objects below,
When, what to my wondering eyes should appear,
But a miniature sleigh, and eight tiny rein-deer,
With a little old driver, so lively and quick,
I knew in a moment it must be St. Nick.
More rapid than eagles his coursers they came,
And he whistled, and shouted, and called them by name;
"Now, *Dasher*! now, *Dancer*! now, *Prancer* and *Vixen*!
On, *Comet*! on *Cupid*! on, *Donder* and *Blitzen*!
To the top of the porch! to the top of the wall!
Now dash away! dash away! dash away all!"
As dry leaves that before the wild hurricane fly,
When they meet with an obstacle, mount to the sky;
So up to the house-top the coursers they flew,
With the sleigh full of Toys, and St. Nicholas too.
And then, in a twinkling, I heard on the roof,
The prancing and pawing of each little hoof —
As I drew in my head, and was turning around,
Down the chimney St. Nicholas came with a bound.
He was dressed all in fur, from his head to his foot,
And his clothes were all tarnished with ashes and soot;
A bundle of Toys he had flung on his back,
And he look'd like a pedlar just opening his pack.
His eyes — how they twinkled! his dimples how merry!
His cheeks were like roses, his nose like a cherry!
His droll little mouth was drawn up like a bow,
And the beard of his chin was as white as the snow;
The stump of a pipe he held tight in his teeth,
And the smoke it encircled his head like a wreath;
He had a broad face and a little round belly,
That shook when he laughed, like a bowlfull of jelly.
He was chubby and plump, a right jolly old elf,
And I laughed when I saw him, in spite of myself,

A wink of his eye and a twist of his head,
Soon gave me to know I had nothing to dread;
He spoke not a word, but went straight to his work,
And fill'd all the stockings; then turned with a jerk,
And laying his finger aside of his nose,
And giving a nod, up the chimney he rose;
He sprang to his sleigh, to his team gave a whistle,
And away they all flew like the down of a thistle.
But I heard him exclaim, ere he drove out of sight,
"Happy Christmas to all, and to all a good-night!"

1822

FITZ-GREENE HALLECK (1790–1867)

Fitz-Greene Halleck was born in Guilford, Connecticut. He worked at a bank in New York City, mastered what he called "this bank-note world," and went on to become John Jacob Astor's personal secretary. In the anthology *From Confucius to Cummings*, Ezra Pound included selections from Halleck's narrative poem *Fanny*, claiming that the American poet compared favorably with Lord Byron. While it is difficult to credit this claim, Halleck's overlooked narrative demonstrates the vitality of an American comic tradition. A statue of Fitz-Greene Halleck is in Central Park at East 66th Street in New York City.

from *Fanny*

I

Fanny was younger once than she is now,
  And prettier of course: I do not mean
To say that there are wrinkles on her brow;
  Yet, to be candid, she is past eighteen —
Perhaps past twenty — but the girl is shy
About her age, and Heaven forbid that I

II

Should get myself in trouble by revealing
  A secret of this sort; I have too long
Loved pretty women with a poet's feeling,
  And when a boy, in day dream and in song,
Have knelt me down and worshipp'd them: alas!
They never thank'd me for't — but let that pass.

V

Her father kept, some fifteen years ago,
  A retail dry-good shop in Chatham-street,

And nursed his little earnings, sure though slow,
   Till, having muster'd wherewithal to meet
The gaze of the great world, he breathed the air
Of Pearl-street — and "set up" in Hanover-square.

VI

Money is power, 'tis said — I never tried;
   I'm but a poet — and bank-notes to me
Are curiosities, as closely eyed,
   Whene'er I get them, as a stone would be,
Toss'd from the moon on Doctor Mitchill's table,
Or classic brickbat from the tower of Babel.

VII

But he I sing of well has known and felt
   That money hath a power and a dominion;
For when in Chatham-street the good man dwelt,
   No one would give a *sous* for his opinion.
And though his neighbours were extremely civil,
Yet, on the whole, they thought him — a poor devil,

VIII

A decent kind of person; one whose head
   Was not of brains particularly full;
It was not known that he had ever said
   Any thing worth repeating — 'twas a dull,
Good, honest man — what Paulding's muse would call
A "cabbage head" — but he excelled them all

IX

In that most noble of the sciences,
   The art of making money; and he found
The zeal for quizzing him grew less and less,
   As he grew richer; till upon the ground
Of Pearl-street, treading proudly in the might
And majesty of wealth, a sudden light

X

Flash'd like the midnight lightning on the eyes
   Of all who knew him; brilliant traits of mind,
And genius, clear and countless as the dies
   Upon the peacock's plumage; taste refined,
Wisdom and wit, were his — perhaps much more.
'Twas strange they had not found it out before.

XXV

Dear to the exile is his native land,
   In memory's twilight beauty seen afar:

Dear to the broker is a note of hand,
   Collaterally secured — the polar star
Is dear at midnight to the sailor's eyes,
And dear are Bristed's volumes at "half price;"

XXVI

But dearer far to me each fairy minute
   Spent in that fond forgetfulness of grief;
There is an airy web of magic in it,
   As in Othello's pocket-handkerchief,
Veiling the wrinkles on the brow of sorrow,
The gathering gloom to-day, the thunder cloud to-morrow.

XLI

Since that wise pedant, Johnson, was in fashion,
   Manners have changed as well as moons; and he
Would fret himself once more into a passion,
   Should he return (which heaven forbid!), and see,
How strangely from his standard dictionary,
The meaning of some words is made to vary.

XLII

For instance, an *undress* at present means
   The wearing a pelisse, a shawl, or so;
Or any thing you please, in short, that screens
   The face, and hides the form from top to toe;
Of power to brave a quizzing-glass, or storm —
'Tis worn in summer, when the weather's warm.

XLIII

But a full dress is for a winter's night.
   The most genteel is made of "woven air;"
That kind of classic cobweb, soft and light,
   Which Lady Morgan's Ida used to wear.
And ladies, this aërial manner dress'd in,
Look Eve-like, angel-like, and interesting.

1821

WILLIAM CULLEN BRYANT (1794–1878)

Born in a log cabin in Cummington, Massachusetts, William Cullen Bryant wrote "Thanatopsis" when he was seventeen years old. The author Richard Henry Dana thought it was a hoax: "No one, on this side of the Atlantic, is capable of writing such verses." In Richard Wilbur's view, Bryant's "To a Waterfowl" may be "America's first flawless poem." (Matthew

Arnold had previously called it "the most perfect brief poem in the language.") Bryant gave up a law practice to pursue a literary career. In 1829 he became editor of the *New York Evening Post*, a position he held for nearly fifty years. In his seventies, Bryant translated the *Iliad* and the *Odyssey*. After dedicating a statue of the Italian patriot Giuseppe Mazzini in Central Park on 29 May 1878, he collapsed in the heat and died two weeks later.

Thanatopsis

To him who in the love of Nature holds
Communion with her visible forms, she speaks
A various language; for his gayer hours
She has a voice of gladness, and a smile
And eloquence of beauty, and she glides
Into his darker musings, with a mild
And healing sympathy, that steals away
Their sharpness, ere he is aware. When thoughts
Of the last bitter hour come like a blight
Over thy spirit, and sad images
Of the stern agony, and shroud, and pall,
And breathless darkness, and the narrow house,
Make thee to shudder, and grow sick at heart; —
Go forth, under the open sky, and list
To Nature's teachings, while from all around —
Earth and her waters, and the depths of air —
Comes a still voice — Yet a few days, and thee
The all-beholding sun shall see no more
In all his course; nor yet in the cold ground,
Where thy pale form was laid, with many tears,
Nor in the embrace of ocean, shall exist
Thy image. Earth, that nourished thee, shall claim
Thy growth, to be resolved to earth again,
And, lost each human trace, surrendering up
Thine individual being, shalt thou go
To mix for ever with the elements,
To be a brother to the insensible rock
And to the sluggish clod, which the rude swain
Turns with his share, and treads upon. The oak
Shall send his roots abroad, and pierce thy mould.

Yet not to thine eternal resting-place
Shalt thou retire alone, nor couldst thou wish
Couch more magnificent. Thou shalt lie down
With patriarchs of the infant world — with kings,
The powerful of the earth — the wise, the good,
Fair forms, and hoary seers of ages past,
All in one mighty sepulchre. The hills
Rock-ribbed and ancient as the sun, — the vales

Stretching in pensive quietness between;
The venerable woods — rivers that move
In majesty, and the complaining brooks
That make the meadows green; and, poured round all,
Old Ocean's gray and melancholy waste, —
Are but the solemn decorations all
Of the great tomb of man. The golden sun,
The planets, all the infinite host of heaven,
Are shining on the sad abodes of death,
Through the still lapse of ages. All that tread
The globe are but a handful to the tribes
That slumber in its bosom. — Take the wings
Of morning, pierce the Barcan wilderness,
Or lose thyself in the continuous woods
Where rolls the Oregon, and hears no sound,
Save his own dashings — yet the dead are there:
And millions in those solitudes, since first
The flight of years began, have laid them down
In their last sleep — the dead reign there alone.
So shalt thou rest, and what if thou withdraw
In silence from the living, and no friend
Take note of thy departure? All that breathe
Will share thy destiny. The gay will laugh
When thou art gone, the solemn brood of care
Plod on, and each one as before will chase
His favorite phantom; yet all these shall leave
Their mirth and their employments, and shall come
And make their bed with thee. As the long train
Of ages glide away, the sons of men,
The youth in life's green spring, and he who goes
In the full strength of years, matron and maid,
The speechless babe, and the gray-headed man —
Shall one by one be gathered to thy side,
By those, who in their turn shall follow them.

So live, that when thy summons comes to join
The innumerable caravan, which moves
To that mysterious realm, where each shall take
His chamber in the silent halls of death,
Thou go not, like the quarry-slave at night,
Scourged to his dungeon, but, sustained and soothed
By an unfaltering trust, approach thy grave,
Like one who wraps the drapery of his couch
About him, and lies down to pleasant dreams.

1811

To a Waterfowl

Whither, midst falling dew,
While glow the heavens with the last steps of day,
Far, through their rosy depths, dost thou pursue
Thy solitary way?

Vainly the fowler's eye
Might mark thy distant flight to do thee wrong,
As, darkly seen against the crimson sky,
Thy figure floats along.

Seek'st thou the plashy brink
Of weedy lake, or marge of river wide,
Or where the rocking billows rise and sink
On the chafed ocean-side?

There is a Power whose care
Teaches thy way along that pathless coast —
The desert and illimitable air —
Lone wandering, but not lost.

All day thy wings have fanned,
At that far height, the cold, thin atmosphere,
Yet stoop not, weary, to the welcome land,
Though the dark night is near.

And soon that toil shall end;
Soon shalt thou find a summer home, and rest,
And scream among thy fellows; reeds shall bend,
Soon, o'er thy sheltered nest.

Thou'rt gone, the abyss of heaven
Hath swallowed up thy form; yet, on my heart
Deeply has sunk the lesson thou hast given,
And shall not soon depart.

He who, from zone to zone,
Guides through the boundless sky thy certain flight,
In the long way that I must tread alone,
Will lead my steps aright.

1817

Sonnet — To an American Painter Departing for Europe

Thine eyes shall see the light of distant skies:
Yet, Cole! thy heart shall bear to Europe's strand
A living image of thy native land,

Such as on thy own glorious canvass lies.
Lone lakes — savannahs where the bison roves —
    Rocks rich with summer garlands — solemn streams —
    Skies, where the desert eagle wheels and screams —
Spring bloom and autumn blaze of boundless groves.
Fair scenes shall greet thee where thou goest — fair,
    But different — every where the trace of men,
    Paths, homes, graves, ruins, from the lowest glen
To where life shrinks from the fierce Alpine air.
    Gaze on them, till the tears shall dim thy sight,
    But keep that earlier, wilder image bright.

1829

RALPH WALDO EMERSON (1803–1882)

Ralph Waldo Emerson was born in Boston, went to Harvard, completed his studies for the ministry and became, in 1830, the sole pastor of the Second Unitarian Church in Boston. A crisis of faith caused him to resign his position in 1833 and to strike out on his own. The great American essayist and orator thought himself a poet first but wrote his truest poetry in his prose. In retrospect, such indispensable essays as "Self-Reliance," "Nature," "Compensation," and "The Poet" seem to contain a series of predictions and prophecies that have come to pass. Emerson seems sometimes to have invented, or at least envisioned, American literature as an entity unto itself rather than as a tributary of a mainstream English or British tradition. Read Walt Whitman in the light of Emerson's essays and you see a pattern. Emerson will make a robust declaration in aphoristic prose ("A foolish consistency is the hobgoblin of little minds, adored by little statesmen and philosophers and divines") and Whitman will take the same sentiment and turn it into a lyric cry ("Do I contradict myself?/Very well then. . . . I contradict myself./I am large. . . . I contain multitudes"). Whitman acknowledged the debt: "I was simmering, simmering, simmering; Emerson brought me to a boil." It is irresistible to quote Emerson, the "sage of Concord." The American "bard," he wrote, must "mount to paradise/By the stairway of surprise." On the autonomy of the self: "There is a time in every man's education when he arrives at the conviction that envy is ignorance; that imitation is suicide." On love: "From the necessity of loving none are exempt, and he that loves must utter his desires." On death: "I think we may be sure that, whatever may come after death, no one will be disappointed."

A Letter

Dear brother, would you know the life,
Please God, that I would lead?
On the first wheels that quit this weary town
Over yon western bridges I would ride
And with a cheerful benison forsake
Each street and spire and roof incontinent.
Then would I seek where God might guide my steps,

Deep in a woodland tract, a sunny farm,
Amid the mountain counties, Hant, Franklin, Berks,
Where down the rock ravine a river roars,
Even from a brook, and where old woods
Not tamed and cleared cumber the ground
With their centennial wrecks.
Find me a slope where I can feel the sun
And mark the rising of the early stars.
There will I bring my books, — my household gods,
The reliquaries of my dead saint, and dwell
In the sweet odor of her memory.
Then in the uncouth solitude unlock
My stock of art, plant dials in the grass,
Hang in the air a bright thermometer
And aim a telescope at the inviolate sun.

1831

Concord Hymn

Sung at the completion of the Battle Monument, July 4, 1837

By the rude bridge that arched the flood,
   Their flag to April's breeze unfurled,
Here once the embattled farmers stood
   And fired the shot heard round the world.

The foe long since in silence slept;
   Alike the conqueror silent sleeps;
And Time the ruined bridge has swept
   Down the dark stream which seaward creeps.

On this green bank, by this soft stream,
   We set to-day a votive stone;
That memory may their deed redeem,
   When, like our sires, our sons are gone.

Spirit, that made those heroes dare
   To die, and leave their children free,
Bid Time and Nature gently spare
      The shaft we raise to them and thee.

1837

Each and All

Little thinks, in the field, yon red-cloaked clown
Of thee from the hill-top looking down;
The heifer that lows in the upland farm,

Far-heard, lows not thine ear to charm;
The sexton, tolling his bell at noon,
Deems not that great Napoleon
Stops his horse, and lists with delight,
Whilst his files sweep round yon Alpine height;
Nor knowest thou what argument
Thy life to thy neighbor's creed has lent.
All are needed by each one;
Nothing is fair or good alone.
I thought the sparrow's note from heaven,
Singing at dawn on the alder bough;
I brought him home, in his nest, at even;
He sings the song, but it cheers not now,
For I did not bring home the river and sky; —
He sang to my ear, — they sang to my eye.
The delicate shells lay on the shore;
The bubbles of the latest wave
Fresh pearls to their enamel gave,
And the bellowing of the savage sea
Greeted their safe escape to me.
I wiped away the weeds and foam,
I fetched my sea-born treasures home;
But the poor, unsightly, noisome things
Had left their beauty on the shore
With the sun and the sand and the wild uproar.
The lover watched his graceful maid,
As 'mid the virgin train she strayed,
Nor knew her beauty's best attire
Was woven still by the snow-white choir,
At last she came to his hermitage,
Like the bird from the woodlands to the cage; —
The gay enchantment was undone,
A gentle wife, but fairy none.
Then I said, "I covet truth;
Beauty is unripe childhood's cheat;
I leave it behind with the games of youth:" —
As I spoke, beneath my feet
The ground-pine curled its pretty wreath,
Running over the club-moss burrs;
I inhaled the violet's breath;
Around me stood the oaks and firs;
Pine-cones and acorns lay on the ground;
Over me soared the eternal sky,
Full of light and of deity;
Again I saw, again I heard,
The rolling river, the morning bird; —
Beauty through my senses stole;
I yielded myself to the perfect whole.

1839

Water

The water understands
Civilization well;
It wets my foot, but prettily,
It chills my life, but wittily,
It is not disconcerted,
It is not broken-hearted:
Well used, it decketh joy,
Adorneth, doubleth joy:
Ill used, it will destroy,
In perfect time and measure
With a face of golden pleasure
Elegantly destroy.

1841

Blight

Give me truths;
For I am weary of the surfaces,
And die of inanition. If I knew
Only the herbs and simples of the wood,
Rue, cinquefoil, gill, vervain and agrimony,
Blue-vetch and trillium, hawkweed, sassafras,
Milkweeds and murky brakes, quaint pipes and sundew,
And rare and virtuous roots, which in these woods
Draw untold juices from the common earth,
Untold, unknown, and I could surely spell
Their fragrance, and their chemistry apply
By sweet affinities to human flesh,
Driving the foe and stablishing the friend, —
O, that were much, and I could be a part
Of the round day, related to the sun
And planted world, and full executor
Of their imperfect functions.
But these young scholars, who invade our hills,
Bold as the engineer who fells the wood,
And travelling often in the cut he makes,
Love not the flower they pluck, and know it not,
And all their botany is Latin names.
The old men studied magic in the flowers,
And human fortunes in astronomy,
And an omnipotence in chemistry,
Preferring things to names, for these were men,
Were unitarians of the united world,
And, wheresoever their clear eye-beams fell,

They caught the footsteps of the SAME. Our eyes
Are armed, but we are strangers to the stars,
And strangers to the mystic beast and bird,
And strangers to the plant and to the mine.
The injured elements say, "Not in us;"
And night and day, ocean and continent,
Fire, plant and mineral say, "Not in us;"
And haughtily return us stare for stare.
For we invade them impiously for gain;
We devastate them unreligiously,
And coldly ask their pottage, not their love.
Therefore they shove us from them, yield to us
Only what to our griping toil is due;
But the sweet affluence of love and song,
The rich results of the divine consents
Of man and earth, of world beloved and lover,
The nectar and ambrosia, are withheld;
And in the midst of spoils and slaves, we thieves
And pirates of the universe, shut out
Daily to a more thin and outward rind,
Turn pale and starve. Therefore, to our sick eyes,
The stunted trees look sick, the summer short,
Clouds shade the sun, which will not tan our hay,
And nothing thrives to reach its natural term;
And life, shorn of its venerable length,
Even at its greatest space is a defeat,
And dies in anger that it was a dupe;
And, in its highest noon and wantonness,
Is early frugal, like a beggar's child;
Even in the hot pursuit of the best aims
And prizes of ambition, checks its hand,
Like Alpine cataracts frozen as they leaped,
Chilled with a miserly comparison
Of the toy's purchase with the length of life.

1843

The Rhodora

On being asked, whence is the flower?

In May, when sea-winds pierced our solitudes,
I found the fresh Rhodora in the woods,
Spreading its leafless blooms in a damp nook,
To please the desert and the sluggish brook.
The purple petals, fallen in the pool,
Made the black water with their beauty gay;

Here might the red-bird come his plumes to cool,
And court the flower that cheapens his array.
Rhodora! if the sages ask thee why
This charm is wasted on the earth and sky,
Tell them, dear, that if eyes were made for seeing,
Then Beauty is its own excuse for being:
Why thou wert there, O rival of the rose!
I never thought to ask, I never knew:
But, in my simple ignorance, suppose
The self-same Power that brought me there brought you.

1846

The Snow-Storm

Announced by all the trumpets of the sky,
Arrives the snow, and, driving o'er the fields,
Seems nowhere to alight: the whited air
Hides hills and woods, the river, and the heaven,
And veils the farm-house at the garden's end.
The sled and traveller stopped, the courier's feet
Delayed, all friends shut out, the housemates sit
Around the radiant fireplace, enclosed
In a tumultuous privacy of storm.

Come see the north wind's masonry.
Out of an unseen quarry evermore
Furnished with tile, the fierce artificer
Curves his white bastions with projected roof
Round every windward stake, or tree, or door.
Speeding, the myriad-handed, his wild work
So fanciful, so savage, nought cares he
For number or proportion. Mockingly,
On coop or kennel he hangs Parian wreaths;
A swan-like form invests the hidden thorn;
Fills up the farmer's lane from wall to wall,
Maugre the farmer's sighs; and at the gate
A tapering turret overtops the work.
And when his hours are numbered, and the world
Is all his own, retiring, as he were not,
Leaves, when the sun appears, astonished Art
To mimic in slow structures, stone by stone,
Built in an age, the mad wind's night-work,
The frolic architecture of the snow.

1846

Hamatreya

Bulkeley, Hunt, Willard, Hosmer, Meriam, Flint,
Possessed the land which rendered to their toil
Hay, corn, roots, hemp, flax, apples, wool and wood.
Each of these landlords walked amidst his farm,
Saying, "'T is mine, my children's and my name's.
How sweet the west wind sounds in my own trees!
How graceful climb those shadows on my hill!
I fancy these pure waters and the flags
Know me, as does my dog: we sympathize;
And, I affirm, my actions smack of the soil."

Where are these men? Asleep beneath their grounds:
And strangers, fond as they, their furrows plough.
Earth laughs in flowers, to see her boastful boys
Earth-proud, proud of the earth which is not theirs;
Who steer the plough, but cannot steer their feet
Clear of the grave.
They added ridge to valley, brook to pond,
And sighed for all that bounded their domain;
"This suits me for a pasture; that's my park;
We must have clay, lime, gravel, granite-ledge,
And misty lowland, where to go for peat.
The land is well, — lies fairly to the south.
'T is good, when you have crossed the sea and back,
To find the sitfast acres where you left them."
Ah! the hot owner sees not Death, who adds
Him to his land, a lump of mould the more.
Hear what the Earth says: —

Earth-Song

"Mine and yours;
 Mine, not yours.
Earth endures;
Stars abide —
Shine down in the old sea;
Old are the shores;
But where are old men?
I who have seen much,
Such have I never seen.

"The lawyer's deed
 Ran sure,
In tail,
To them, and to their heirs
Who shall succeed,
Without fail,
Forevermore.

"Here is the land,
 Shaggy with wood,
With its old valley,
Mound and flood.
But the heritors? —
Fled like the flood's foam.
The lawyer, and the laws,
And the kingdom,
Clean swept hereform.

"They called me theirs,
 Who controlled me;
Yet every one
Wished to stay, and is gone,
How am I theirs,
If they cannot hold me,
But I hold them?"

When I heard the Earth-song
I was no longer brave;
My avarice cooled
Like lust in the chill of the grave.

1845

Fable

The mountain and the squirrel
Had a quarrel;
And the former called the latter "Little Prig."
Bun replied,
"You are doubtless very big;
But all sorts of things and weather
Must be taken in together,
To make up a year
And a sphere.
And I think it no disgrace
To occupy my place.
If I'm not so large as you,
You are not so small as I,
And not half so spry.
I'll not deny you make
A very pretty squirrel track;
Talents differ; all is well and wisely put;
If I cannot carry forests on my back,
Neither can you crack a nut."

1845

Ode

Inscribed to W. H. Channing

Though loath to grieve
The evil time's sole patriot,
I cannot leave
My honied thought
For the priest's cant,
Or statesman's rant.

If I refuse
My study for their politique,
Which at the best is trick,
The angry Muse
Puts confusion in my brain.

But who is he that prates
Of the culture of mankind,
Of better arts and life?
Go, blindworm, go,
Behold the famous States
Harrying Mexico
With rifle and with knife!

Or who, with accent bolder,
Dare praise the freedom-loving mountaineer?
I found by thee, O rushing Contoocook!
And in thy valleys, Agiochook!
The jackals of the negro-holder.

The God who made New Hampshire
Taunted the lofty land
With little men; —
Small bat and wren
House in the oak: —
If earth-fire cleave
The upheaved land, and bury the folk,
The southern crocodile would grieve.
Virtue palters; Right is hence;
Freedom praised, but hid;
Funeral eloquence
Rattles the coffin-lid.

What boots thy zeal,
O glowing friend,
That would indignant rend
The northland from the south?
Wherefore? to what good end?

Boston Bay and Bunker Hill
Would serve things still; —
Things are of the snake.

The horseman serves the horse,
The neatherd serves the neat,
The merchant serves the purse,
The eater serves his meat;
'T is the day of the chattel,
Web to weave, and corn to grind;
Things are in the saddle,
And ride mankind.

There are two laws discrete,
Not reconciled, —
Law for man, and law for thing;
The last builds town and fleet,
But it runs wild,
And doth the man unking.

'T is fit the forest fall,
The steep be graded,
The mountain tunnelled,
The sand shaded,
The orchard planted,
The glebe tilled,
The prairie granted,
The steamer built.

Let man serve law for man;
Live for friendship, live for love,
For truth's and harmony's behoof;
The state may follow how it can,
As Olympus follows Jove.

Yet do not I implore
The wrinkled shopman to my sounding woods,
Nor bid the unwilling senator
Ask votes of thrushes in the solitudes.
Every one to his chosen work; —
Foolish hands may mix and mar;
Wise and sure the issues are.
Round they roll till dark is light,
Sex to sex, and even to odd; —
The over-god
Who marries Right to Might,
Who peoples, unpeoples, —
He who exterminates
Races by stronger races,

Black by white faces, —
Knows to bring honey
Out of the lion;
Grafts gentlest scion
On pirate and Turk.

The Cossack eats Poland,
Like stolen fruit;
Her last noble is ruined,
Her last poet mute:
Straight, into double band
The victors divide;
Half for freedom strike and stand; —
The astonished Muse finds thousands at her side.

1846

Give All to Love

Give all to love;
Obey thy heart;
Friends, kindred, days,
Estate, good-frame,
Plans, credit and the Muse, —
Nothing refuse.

'T is a brave master;
Let it have scope:
Follow it utterly,
Hope beyond hope;
High and more high
It dives into noon,
With wing unspent,
Untold intent:
But it is a god,
Known its own path
And the outlets of the sky.

It was never for the mean;
It requireth courage stout.
Souls above doubt,
Valor unbending,
It will reward, —
They shall return
More than they were,
And ever ascending.

Leave all for love;
Yet, hear me, yet,
One word more thy heart behoved,
One pulse more of firm endeavour, —
Keep thee to-day,
To-morrow, forever,
Free as an Arab
Of thy beloved.

Cling with life to the maid;
But when the surprise,
First vague shadow of surmise
Flits across her bosom young,
Of a joy apart from thee,
Free be she, fancy-free;
Nor thou detain her vesture's hem,
Nor the palest rose she flung
From her summer diadem.

Though thou loved her as thyself,
As a self of purer clay,
Though her parting dims the day,
Stealing grace from all alive;
Heartily know,
When half-gods go,
The gods arrive.

1847

Bacchus

Bring me wine, but wine which never grew
In the belly of the grape
Or grew on vine whose tap-roots, reaching through
Under the Andes to the Cape,
Suffer no savor of the earth to scape.

Let its grapes the morn salute
From a nocturnal root,
Which feels the acrid juice
Of Styx and Erebus;
And turns the woe of Night,
By its own craft, to a more rich delight.

We buy ashes for bread;
We buy diluted wine;
Give me of the true, —
Whose ample leaves and tendrils curled

Among the silver hills of heaven
Draw everlasting dew;
Wine of wine,
Blood of the world,
Form of forms, and mould of statures,
That I intoxicated,
And by the draught assimilated,
May float at pleasure through all natures;
The bird-language rightly spell,
And that which roses say so well.

Wine that is shed
Like the torrents of the sun
Up the horizon walls,
Or like the Atlantic streams, which run
When the South Sea calls.

Water and bread,
Food which needs no transmuting,
Rainbow-flowering, wisdom-fruiting,
Wine which is already man,
Food which teach and reason can.

Wine which Music is, —
Music and wine are one, —
That I, drinking this,
Shall hear far Chaos talk with me;
Kings unborn shall walk with me;
And the poor grass shall plot and plan
What it will do when it is man.
Quickened so, will I unlock
Every crypt of every rock.

I thank the joyful juice
For all I know; —
Winds of remembering
Of the ancient being blow,
And seeming-solid walls of use
Open and flow.

Pour, Bacchus! the remembering wine;
Retrieve the loss of me and mine!
Vine for vine be antidote,
And the grape requite the lote!
Haste to cure the old despair, —
Reason in Nature's lotus drenched,
The memory of ages quenched;
Give them again to shine;
Let wine repair what this undid;
And where the infection slid,

A dazzling memory revive;
Refresh the faded tints,
Recut the aged prints,
And write my old adventures with the pen
Which on the first day drew,
Upon the tablets blue,
The dancing Pleiads and eternal men.

1847

Brahma

If the red slayer think he slays,
   Or if the slain think he is slain,
They know not well the subtle ways
   I keep, and pass, and turn again.

Far or forgot to me is near;
   Shadow and sunlight are the same;
The vanished gods to me appear;
   And one to me are shame and fame.

They reckon ill who leave me out;
   When me they fly, I am the wings;
I am the doubter and the doubt,
   And I the hymn the Brahmin sings.

The strong gods pine for my abode,
   And pine in vain the sacred Seven;
But thou, meek lover of the good!
   Find me, and turn thy back on heaven.

1856

Days

Daughters of Time, the hypocritic Days,
Muffled and dumb like barefoot dervishes,
And marching single in an endless file,
Bring diadems and fagots in their hands.
To each they offer gifts after his will,
Bread, kingdoms, stars, and sky that holds them all.
I, in my pleached garden, watched the pomp,
Forgot my morning wishes, hastily
Took a few herbs and apples, and the Day
Turned and departed silent. I, too late,
Under her solemn fillet saw the scorn.

1857

Henry Wadsworth Longfellow (1807–1882)

The best-loved poet of his time, Henry Wadsworth Longfellow achieved great popularity with his narrative poems, such as "Evangeline" and "The Song of Hiawatha." Read aloud, his "Paul Revere's Ride" can still prove spellbinding. But Longfellow fell out of favor; Robert Lowell characterized him perhaps too neatly as "Tennyson without gin," and he is now underrated. James Merrill, who began his epic vision of the afterlife with a volume entitled *Divine Comedies*, regarded Longfellow's translation of Dante's *Divine Comedy* as the best in English. Robert Frost took the title of his first book of poems, *A Boy's Will*, from Longfellow's "My Lost Youth."

The Bridge

I stood on the bridge at midnight,
As the clocks were striking the hour,
And the moon rose o'er the city,
Behind the dark church-tower.

I saw her bright reflection
In the waters under me,
Like a golden goblet falling
And sinking into the sea.

And far in the hazy distance
Of that lovely night in June,
The blaze of the flaming furnace
Gleamed redder than the moon.

Among the long, black rafters
The wavering shadows lay,
And the current that came from the ocean
Seemed to lift and bear them away;

As, sweeping and eddying through them,
Rose the belated tide,
And, streaming into the moonlight,
The seaweed floated wide.

And like those waters rushing
Among the wooden piers,
A flood of thoughts came o'er me
That filled my eyes with tears.

How often, O, how often,
In the days that had gone by,
I had stood on that bridge at midnight
And gazed on that wave and sky!

How often, O, how often,
  I had wished that the ebbing tide
Would bear me away on its bosom
  O'er the ocean wild and wide!

For my heart was hot and restless,
  And my life was full of care,
And the burden laid upon me
  Seemed greater than I could bear.

But now it has fallen from me,
  It is buried in the sea;
And only the sorrow of others
  Throws its shadow over me.

Yet whenever I cross the river
  On its bridge with wooden piers,
Like the odor of brine from the ocean
  Comes the thought of other years.

And I think how many thousands
  Of care-encumbered men,
Each bearing his burden of sorrow,
  Have crossed the bridge since then.

I see the long procession
  Still passing to and fro,
The young heart hot and restless,
  And the old subdued and slow!

And forever and forever,
  As long as the river flows,
As long as the heart has passions,
  As long as life has woes;

The moon and its broken reflection
  And its shadows shall appear,
As the symbol of love in heaven,
  And its wavering image here.

1845

The Fire of Drift-wood

We sat within the farm-house old,
  Whose windows, looking o'er the bay,
Gave to the sea-breeze damp and cold,
  An easy entrance, night and day.

Not far away we saw the port,
The strange, old-fashioned, silent town,
The lighthouse, the dismantled fort,
The wooden houses, quaint and brown.

We sat and talked until the night,
Descending, filled the little room;
Our faces faded from the sight,
Our voices only broke the gloom.

We spake of many a vanished scene,
Of what we once had thought and said,
Of what had been, and might have been,
And who was changed, and who was dead;

And all that fills the hearts of friends,
When first they feel, with secret pain,
Their lives thenceforth have separate ends,
And never can be one again;

The first slight swerving of the heart,
That words are powerless to express,
And leave it still unsaid in part,
Or say it in too great excess.

The very tones in which we spake
Had something strange, I could but mark;
The leaves of memory seemed to make
A mournful rustling in the dark.

Oft died the words upon our lips,
As suddenly, from out the fire
Built of the wreck of stranded ships,
The flames would leap and then expire.

And, as their splendor flashed and failed,
We thought of wrecks upon the main,
Of ships dismasted, that were hailed
And sent no answer back again.

The windows, rattling in their frames,
The oceans, roaring up the beach,
The gusty blast, the bickering flames,
All mingled vaguely in our speech;

Until they made themselves a part
Of fancies floating through the brain,
The long-lost ventures of the heart,
That send no answers back again.

O flames that glowed! O hearts that yearned!
  They were indeed too much akin,
The drift-wood fire without that burned,
  The thoughts that burned and glowed within.

1849

The Jewish Cemetery at Newport

How strange it seems! These Hebrews in their graves,
  Close by the street of this fair seaport town,
Silent beside the never-silent waves,
  At rest in all this moving up and down!

The trees are white with dust, that o'er their sleep
  Wave their broad curtains in the south-wind's breath,
While underneath these leafy tents they keep
  The long, mysterious Exodus of Death.

And these sepulchral stones, so old and brown,
  That pave with level flags their burial-place,
Seem like the tablets of the Law, thrown down
  And broken by Moses at the mountain's base.

The very names recorded here are strange,
  Of foreign accent, and of different climes;
Alvares and Rivera interchange
  With Abraham and Jacob of old times.

"Blessed be God! for he created Death!"
  The mourners said, "and Death is rest and peace;"
Then added, in the certainty of faith,
  "And giveth Life that nevermore shall cease."

Closed are the portals of their Synagogue,
  No Psalms of David now the silence break,
No Rabbi reads the ancient Decalogue
  In the grand dialect the Prophets spake.

Gone are the living, but the dead remain,
  And not neglected; for a hand unseen,
Scattering its bounty, like a summer rain,
  Still keeps their graves and their remembrance green.

How came they here? What burst of Christian hate,
  What persecution, merciless and blind,
Drove o'er the sea — that desert desolate —
  These Ishmaels and Hagars of mankind?

They lived in narrow streets and lanes obscure,
  Ghetto and Judenstrass, in mirk and mire;
Taught in the school of patience to endure
  The life of anguish and the death of fire.

All their lives long, with the unleavened bread
  And bitter herbs of exile and its fears,
The wasting famine of the heart they fed,
  And slaked its thirst with marah of their tears.

Anathema maranatha! was the cry
  That rang from town to town, from street to street;
At every gate the accursed Mordecai
  Was mocked and jeered, and spurned by Christian feet.

Pride and humiliation hand in hand
  Walked with them through the world where'er they went;
Trampled and beaten were they as the sand,
  And yet unshaken as the continent.

For in the background figures vague and vast
  Of patriarchs and of prophets rose sublime,
And all the great traditions of the Past
  They saw reflected in the coming time.

And thus for ever with reverted look
  The mystic volume of the world they read,
Spelling it backward, like a Hebrew book,
  Till life became a Legend of the Dead.

But ah! what once has been shall be no more!
  The groaning earth in travail and in pain
Brings forth its races, but does not restore,
  And the dead nations never rise again.

1858

My Lost Youth

Often I think of the beautiful town
  That is seated by the sea;
Often in thought go up and down
The pleasant streets of that dear old town,
  And my youth comes back to me.
    And a verse of a Lapland song
    Is haunting my memory still:
  "A boy's will is the wind's will,
And the thoughts of youth are long, long thoughts."

I can see the shadowy lines of its trees,
   And catch, in sudden gleams,
The sheen of the far-surrounding seas,
And islands that were the Hesperides
   Of all my boyish dreams.
      And the burden of that old song,
      It murmurs and whispers still:
   "A boy's will is the wind's will,
And the thoughts of youth are long, long thoughts."

I remember the black wharves and the slips,
   And the sea-tides tossing free;
And Spanish sailors with bearded lips,
And the beauty and mystery of the ships,
   And the magic of the sea.
      And the voice of that wayward song
      Is singing and saying still:
   "A boy will is the wind's will,
And the thoughts of youth are long, long thoughts."

I remember the bulwarks by the shore,
   And the fort upon the hill;
The sunrise gun, with its hollow roar,
The drum-beat repeated o'er and o'er,
   And the bugle wild and shrill.
      And the music of that old song
      Throbs in my memory still:
   "A boy's will is the wind's will,
And the thoughts of youth are long, long thoughts."

I remember the sea-fight far away,
   How it thundered o'er the tide!
And the dead captains, as they lay
In their graves, o'erlooking the tranquil bay,
   Where they in battle died.
      And the sound of that mournful song
      Goes through me with a thrill:
   "A boy's will is the wind's will,
And the thoughts of youth are long, long thoughts."

I can see the breezy dome of groves,
   The shadow of Deering's Woods;
And the friendships old and the early loves
Come back with a Sabbath sound, as of doves
   In quiet neighborhoods.
      And the verse of that sweet old song,
      It flutters and murmurs still:
   "A boy's will is the wind's will,
And the thoughts of youth are long, long thoughts."

I remember the gleams and glooms that dart
Across the school-boy's brain;
The song and the silence in the heart,
That in part are prophecies, and in part
Are longings wild and vain.
And the voice of that fitful song
Sings on, and is never still:
"A boy's will is the wind's will,
And the thoughts of youth are long, long thoughts."

There are things of which I may not speak;
There are dreams that cannot die;
There are thoughts that make the strong heart weak,
And bring a pallor into the cheek,
And a mist before the eye.
And the words of that fatal song
Come over me like a chill:
"A boy's will is the wind's will,
And the thoughts of youth are long, long thoughts."

Strange to me now are the forms I meet
When I visit the dear old town;
But the native air is pure and sweet,
And the trees that o'ershadow each well-known street,
As they balance up and down,
Are singing the beautiful song,
Are singing and whispering still:
"A boy's will is the wind's will,
And the thoughts of youth are long, long thoughts."

And Deering's Woods are fresh and fair,
And with joy that is almost pain
My heart goes back to wander there,
And among the dreams of the days that were,
I find my lost youth again.
And the strange and beautiful song,
The groves are repeating it still:
"A boy's will is the wind's will,
And the thoughts of youth are long, long thoughts."

1858

Paul Revere's Ride

Listen, my children, and you shall hear
Of the midnight ride of Paul Revere,
On the eighteenth of April, in Seventy-five;
Hardly a man is now alive
Who remembers that famous day and year.

He said to his friend, "If the British march
By land or sea from the town to-night,
Hang a lantern aloft in the belfry arch
Of the North Church tower as a signal light, —
One, if by land, and two, if by sea;
And I on the opposite shore will be,
Ready to ride and spread the alarm
Through every Middlesex village and farm,
For the country-folk to be up and to arm."

Then he said "Good night!" and with muffled oar
Silently rowed to the Charlestown shore,
Just as the moon rose over the bay,
Where swinging wide at her moorings lay
The Somerset, British man-of-war;
A phantom ship, with each mast and spar
Across the moon like a prison bar,
And a huge black hulk, that was magnified
By its own reflection in the tide.

Meanwhile, his friend, through alley and street,
Wanders and watches with eager ears,
Till in the silence around him he hears
The muster of men at the barrack door,
The sound of arms, and the tramp of feet,
And the measured tread of the grenadiers,
Marching down to their boats on the shore.

Then he climbed the tower of the Old North Church,
By the wooden stairs, with stealthy tread,
To the belfry-chamber overhead,
And startled the pigeons from their perch
On the sombre rafters, that round him made
Masses and moving shapes of shade, —
By the trembling ladder, steep and tall,
To the highest window in the wall,
Where he paused to listen and look down
A moment on the roofs of the town,
And the moonlight flowing over all.

Beneath, in the churchyard, lay the dead,
In their night-encampment on the hill,
Wrapped in silence so deep and still
That he could hear, like a sentinel's tread,
The watchful night-wind, as it went
Creeping along from tent to tent,
And seeming to whisper, "All is well!"
A moment only he feels the spell
Of the place and the hour, and the secret dread

Of the lonely belfry and the dead;
For suddenly all his thoughts are bent
On a shadowy something far away,
Where the river widens to meet the bay, —
A line of black that bends and floats
On the rising tide, like a bridge of boats.

Meanwhile, impatient to mount and ride,
Booted and spurred, with a heavy stride
On the opposite shore walked Paul Revere.
Now he patted his horse's side,
Now gazed at the landscape far and near,
Then, impetuous, stamped the earth,
And turned and tightened his saddle-girth;
But mostly he watched with eager search
The belfry-tower of the Old North Church,
As it rose above the graves on the hill,
Lonely and spectral and sombre and still.
And lo! as he looks, on the belfry's height
A glimmer, and then a gleam of light!
He springs to the saddle, the bridle he turns,
But lingers and gazes, till full on his sight
A second lamp in the belfry burns!

A hurry of hoofs in a village street,
A shape in the moonlight, a bulk in the dark,
And beneath, from the pebbles, in passing, a spark
Struck out by a steed flying fearless and fleet:
That was all! And yet, through the gloom and the light,
The fate of a nation was riding that night;
And the spark struck out by that steed, in his flight,
Kindled the land into flame with its heat.

He has left the village and mounted the steep,
And beneath him, tranquil and broad and deep,
Is the Mystic, meeting the ocean tides;
And under the alders, that skirt its edge,
Now soft on the sand, now loud on the ledge,
Is heard the tramp of his steed as he rides.

It was twelve by the village clock
When he crossed the bridge into Medford town.
He heard the crowing of the cock,
And the barking of the farmer's dog,
And felt the damp of the river fog,
That rises after the sun goes down.

It was one by the village clock,
When he galloped into Lexington.

He saw the gilded weathercock
Swim in the moonlight as he passed,
And the meeting-house windows, black and bare,
Gaze at him with a spectral glare,
As if they already stood aghast
At the bloody work they would look upon.

It was two by the village clock,
When he came to the bridge in Concord town.
He heard the bleating of the flock,
And the twitter of birds among the trees,
And felt the breath of the morning breeze
Blowing over the meadow, brown.
And one was safe and asleep in his bed
Who at the bridge would be first to fall,
Who that day would be lying dead,
Pierced by a British musket-ball.

You know the rest. In the books you have read,
How the British Regulars fired and fled, —
How the farmers gave them ball for ball,
From behind each fence and farm-yard wall,
Chasing the red-coats down the lane,
Then crossing the fields to emerge again
Under the trees at the turn of the road,
And only pausing to fire and load.

So through the night rode Paul Revere;
And so through the night went his cry of alarm
To every Middlesex village and farm, —
A cry of defiance and not of fear,
A voice in the darkness, a knock at the door,
And a word that shall echo forevermore!
For, borne on the night-wind of the Past,
Through all our history, to the last,
In the hour of darkness and peril and need,
The people will waken and listen to hear
The hurrying hoof-beats of that steed,
And the midnight message of Paul Revere.

1860

The Tide Rises, the Tide Falls

The tide rises, the tide falls,
The twilight darkens, the curlew calls;
Along the sea-sands damp and brown
The traveller hastens toward the town,
   And the tide rises, the tide falls.

Darkness settles on roofs and walls,
But the sea, the sea in the darkness calls;
The little waves, with their soft, white hands,
Efface the footprints in the sands,
   And the tide rises, the tide falls.

The morning breaks; the steeds in their stalls
Stamp and neigh, as the hostler calls;
The day returns, but nevermore
Returns the traveller to the shore,
   And the tide rises, the tide falls.

1880

JOHN GREENLEAF WHITTIER (1807–1892)

Born in a poor but devout Quaker household, the self-taught John Greenleaf Whittier, a fierce abolitionist, attended the Philadelphia convention that founded the American Anti-Slavery Society in December 1833. "I set a higher value on my name as appended to the Anti-Slavery Declaration of 1833 than on the title-page of any book," he said. When he edited *The Pennsylvania Freeman*, an antislavery newspaper, a rioting mob torched its offices, shouting, "Hang Whittier!" He narrowly escaped. His long poem "Snow-Bound" (1866) won him literary fame and earned him a comfortable living. Of "Telling the Bees" (1858), Whittier wrote, "A remarkable custom, brought from the Old Country, formerly prevailed in the rural districts of New England. On the death of a member of the family, the bees were at once informed of the event, and their hives dressed in mourning. This ceremonial was supposed to be necessary to prevent the swarm from leaving their hives and seeking a new home."

For Righteousness' Sake

Inscribed to Friends Under Arrest for
Treason Against the Slave Power

The age is dull and mean. Men creep,
   Not walk; with blood too pale and tame
   To pay the debt they owe to shame;
Buy cheap, sell dear; eat, drink, and sleep
   Down-pillowed, deaf to moaning want;
Pay tithes for soul-insurance; keep
   Six days to Mammon, one to Cant.

In such a time, give thanks to God,
   That somewhat of the holy rage
   With which the prophets in their age
On all its decent seemings trod,
   Has set your feet upon the lie,

That man and ox and soul and clod
   Are market stock to sell and buy!

The hot words from your lips, my own,
   To caution trained, might not repeat;
   But if some tares among the wheat
Of generous thought and deed were sown,
   No common wrong provoked your zeal;
The silken gauntlet that is thrown
   In such a quarrel rings like steel.

The brave old strife the fathers saw
   For Freedom calls for men again
   Like those who battled not in vain
For England's Charter, Alfred's law;
   And right of speech and trial just
Wage in your name their ancient war
   With venal courts and perjured trust.

God's ways seem dark, but, soon or late,
   They touch the shining hills of day;
   The evil cannot brook delay,
The good can well afford to wait.
   Give ermined knaves their hour of crime;
Ye have the future grand and great,
   The safe appeal of Truth to Time!

1855

Telling the Bees

Here is the place; right over the hill
   Runs the path I took;
You can see the gap in the old wall still,
   And the stepping-stones in the shallow brook.

There is the house, with the gate red-barred,
   And the poplars tall;
And the barn's brown length, and the cattle-yard,
   And the white horns tossing above the wall.

There are the beehives ranged in the sun;
   And down by the brink
Of the brook are her poor flowers, weed-o'errun,
   Pansy and daffodil, rose and pink.

A year has gone, as the tortoise goes,
   Heavy and slow;

And the same rose blows, and the same sun glows,
　And the same brook sings of a year ago.

There's the same sweet clover-smell in the breeze;
　And the June sun warm
Tangles his wings of fire in the trees,
　Setting, as then, over Fernside farm.

I mind me how with a lover's care
　From my Sunday coat
I brushed off the burrs, and smoothed my hair,
　And cooled at the brookside my brow and throat.

Since we parted, a month had passed, —
　To love, a year;
Down through the beeches I looked at last
　On the little red gate and the well-sweep near.

I can see it all now, — the slantwise rain
　Of light through the leaves,
The sundown's blaze on her window-pane,
　The bloom of her roses under the eaves.

Just the same as a month before, —
　The house and the trees,
The barn's brown gable, the vine by the door, —
　Nothing changed but the hives of bees.

Before them, under the garden wall,
　Forward and back,
Went drearily singing the chore-girl small,
　Draping each hive with a shred of black.

Trembling, I listened: the summer sun
　Had the chill of snow;
For I knew she was telling the bees of one
　Gone on the journey we all must go!

Then I said to myself, "My Mary weeps
　For the dead to-day:
Haply her blind old grandsire sleeps
　The fret and the pain of his age away."

But her dog whined low; on the doorway sill,
　With his cane to his chin,
The old man sat; and the chore-girl still
　Sang to the bees stealing out and in.

And the song she was singing ever since
  In my ear sounds on: —
"Stay at home, pretty bees, fly not hence!
  Mistress Mary is dead and gone!"

1858

Barbara Frietchie

Up from the meadows rich with corn,
Clear in the cool September morn,

The clustered spires of Frederick stand
Green-walled by the hills of Maryland.

Round about them orchards sweep,
Apple and peach trees fruited deep,

Fair as the garden of the Lord
To the eyes of the famished rebel horde,

On that pleasant morn of the early fall
When Lee marched over the mountain-wall;

Over the mountains winding down,
Horse and foot, into Frederick town.

Forty flags with their silver stars,
Forty flags with their crimson bars,

Flapped in the morning wind: the sun
Of noon looked down, and saw not one.

Up rose old Barbara Frietchie then,
Bowed with her fourscore years and ten;

Bravest of all in Frederick town,
She took up the flag the men hauled down;

In her attic window the staff she set,
To show that one heart was loyal yet.

Up the street came the rebel tread,
Stonewall Jackson riding ahead.

Under his slouched hat left and right
He glanced; the old flag met his sight.

"Halt!" — the dust-brown ranks stood fast.
"Fire!" — out blazed the rifle-blast.

It shivered the window, pane and sash;
It rent the banner with seam and gash.

Quick, as it fell, from the broken staff
Dame Barbara snatched the silken scarf.

She leaned far out on the window-sill,
And shook it forth with a royal will.

"Shoot, if you must, this old gray head,
But spare your country's flag," she said.

A shade of sadness, a blush of shame,
Over the face of the leader came;

The nobler nature within him stirred
To life at that woman's deed and word;

"Who touches a hair of yon gray head
Dies like a dog! March on!" he said.

All day long through Frederick street
Sounded the tread of marching feet:

All day long that free flag tost
Over the heads of the rebel host.

Ever its torn folds rose and fell
On the loyal winds that loved it well;

And through the hill-gaps sunset light
Shone over it with a warm good-night.

Barbara Frietchie's work is o'er,
And the Rebel rides on his raids no more.

Honor to her! and let a tear
Fall, for her sake, on Stonewall's bier.

Over Barbara Freitchie's grave,
Flag of Freedom and Union, wave!

Peace and order and beauty draw
Round thy symbol of light and law;

And ever the stars above look down
On thy stars below in Frederick town!

1863

What the Birds Said

The birds against the April wind
  Flew northward, singing as they flew;
They sang, "The land we leave behind
  Has swords for corn-blades, blood for dew."

"O wild-birds, flying from the South,
  What saw and heard ye, gazing down?"
"We saw the mortar's upturned mouth,
  The sickened camp, the blazing town!

"Beneath the bivouac's starry lamps,
  We saw your march-worn children die;
In shrouds of moss, in cypress swamps,
  We saw your dead uncoffined lie.

"We heard the starving prisoner's sighs,
  And saw, from line and trench, your sons
Follow our flight with home-sick eyes
  Beyond the battery's smoking guns."

"And heard and saw ye only wrong
  And pain," I cried, "O wing-worn flocks?"
"We heard," they sang, "the freedman's song,
  The crash of Slavery's broken locks!

"We saw from new, uprising States
  The treason-nursing mischief spurned,
As, crowding Freedom's ample gates,
  The long-estranged and lost returned.

"O'er dusky faces, seamed and old,
  And hands horn-hard with unpaid toil,
With hope in every rustling fold,
  We saw your star-dropt flag uncoil.

"And struggling up through sounds accursed,
  A grateful murmur clomb the air;
A whisper scarcely heard at first,
  It filled the listening heavens with prayer.

"And sweet and far, as from a star,
   Replied a voice which shall not cease,
Till, drowning all the noise of war,
   It sings the blessed song of peace!"

So to me, in a doubtful day
   Of chill and slowly greening spring,
Low stooping from the cloudy gray,
   The wild-birds sang or seemed to sing.

They vanished in the misty air,
   The song went with them in their flight;
But lo! they left the sunset fair,
   And in the evening there was light.

1864

OLIVER WENDELL HOLMES (1809–1894)

Born in Cambridge, Massachusetts, Oliver Wendell Holmes studied law at Harvard and medicine in Paris. In 1830 he wrote "Old Ironsides," the poem that was credited with saving the frigate *Constitution*, which had defeated the British *Guerriere* in the War of 1812, from being dismantled. He began a medical practice in 1836 and served as professor of anatomy for many years at Harvard. Essays he contributed to periodicals under the heading *The Autocrat of the Breakfast-Table* were gathered into a volume with the same title in 1858. When the editors of an ambitious new magazine wondered what to name it, Holmes suggested *The Atlantic Monthly* (1857). The eldest of his three children became a justice of the U.S. Supreme Court. In his introduction to the 1950 *Oxford Book of American Verse*, F. O. Matthiessen wrote "To those who have been elaborately bored by the forensic periods of 'The Chambered Nautilus,' it may come as a delight to find, in 'Contentment,' Holmes the ripely sophisticated wit, with his mocking acceptance of his desire to build 'more stately mansions' on the water side of Beacon Street." Richard Ellmann in the 1976 *Oxford* restored "The Chambered Nautilus" and deleted "Contentment." The poems appear here together.

Old Ironsides

September 14, 1830

Ay, tear her tattered ensign down!
      Long has it waved on high,
And many an eye has danced to see
      That banner in the sky;
Beneath it rung the battle shout,
      And burst the cannon's roar; —

The meteor of the ocean air
Shall sweep the clouds no more.

Her deck, once red with heroes' blood,
Where knelt the vanquished foe,
When winds were hurrying o'er the flood,
And waves were white below,
No more shall feel the victor's tread,
Or know the conquered knee; —
The harpies of the shore shall pluck
The eagle of the sea!

O better that her shattered hulk
Should sink beneath the wave;
Her thunders shook the mighty deep,
And there should be her grave;
Nail to the mast her holy flag,
Set every thread-bare sail,
And give her to the god of storms, —
The lightning and the gale!

1830

The Chambered Nautilus

This is the ship of pearl, which, poets feign,
Sails the unshadowed main, —
The venturous bark that flings
On the sweet summer wind its purpled wings
In gulfs enchanted, where the Siren sings,
And coral reefs lie bare,
Where the cold sea-maids rise to sun their streaming hair.

Its webs of living gauze no more unfurl;
Wrecked is the ship of pearl!
And every chambered cell,
Where its dim dreaming life was wont to dwell,
As the frail tenant shaped his growing shell,
Before thee lies revealed, —
Its irised ceiling rent, its sunless crypt unsealed!

Year after year beheld the silent toil
That spread his lustrous coil;
Still, as the spiral grew,
He left the past year's dwelling for the new,
Stole with soft step its shining archway through,
Built up its idle door,
Stretched in his last-found home, and knew the old no more.

Thanks for the heavenly message brought by thee,
   Child of the wandering sea,
   Cast from her lap, forlorn!
From thy dead lips a clearer note is born
Than ever Triton blew from wreathèd horn!
   While on mine ear it rings,
Through the deep caves of thought I hear a voice that sings: —

Build thee more stately mansions, O my soul,
   As the swift seasons roll!
   Leave thy low-vaulted past!
Let each new temple, nobler than the last,
Shut thee from heaven with a dome more vast,
   Till thou at length art free,
Leaving thine outgrown shell by life's unresting sea!

1858

Contentment

"Man wants but little here below"

Little I ask; my wants are few;
   I only wish a hut of stone,
(A *very plain* brown stone will do,)
   That I may call my own; —
And close at hand is such a one,
In yonder street that fronts the sun.

Plain food is quite enough for me;
   Three courses are as good as ten; —
If Nature can subsist on three,
   Thank Heaven for three. Amen!
I always thought cold victual nice; —
My *choice* would be vanilla-ice.

I care not much for gold or land; —
   Give me a mortgage here and there, —
Some good bank-stock, some note of hand,
   Or trifling railroad share, —
I only ask that Fortune send
A *little* more than I shall spend.

Honors are silly toys, I know,
   And titles are but empty names;
I would, *perhaps*, be Plenipo, —
   But only near St. James;
I'm very sure I should not care
   To fill our Gubernator's chair.

Jewels are baubles; 't is a sin
To care for such unfruitful things; —
One good-sized diamond in a pin, —
Some, *not so large*, in rings, —
A ruby, and a pearl, or so,
Will do for me; — I laugh at show.

My dame should dress in cheap attire;
(Good, heavy silks are never dear;) —
I own perhaps *I might* desire
Some shawls of true Cashmere, —
Some marrowy crapes of China silk,
Like wrinkled skins on scalded milk.

I would not have the horse I drive
So fast that folks must stop and stare;
An easy gait — two, forty-five —
Suits me; I do not care; —
Perhaps, for just a *single spurt*,
Some seconds less would do no hurt.

Of pictures, I should like to own
Titians and Raphaels three or four, —
I love so much their style and tone,
One Turner, and no more,
(A landscape, — foreground golden dirt, —
The sunshine painted with a squirt.)

Of books but few, — some fifty score
For daily use, and bound for wear;
The rest upon an upper floor; —
Some *little* luxury *there*
Of red morocco's gilded gleam
And vellum rich as country cream.

Busts, cameos, gems, — such things as these,
Which others often show for pride,
I value for their power to please,
And selfish churls deride; —
One Stradivarius, I confess,
Two Meerschaums, I would fain possess.

Wealth's wasteful tricks I will not learn,
Nor ape the glittering upstart fool; —
Shall not carved tables serve my turn,
But *all* must be of buhl?
Give grasping pomp its double share, —
I ask but *one* recumbent chair.

Thus humble let me live and die,
   Nor long for Midas' golden touch;
If Heaven more generous gifts deny,
   I shall not miss them *much*, —
Too grateful for the blessing lent
Of simple tastes and mind content!

1858

Edgar Allan Poe (1809–1849)

Born in Boston, Edgar Allan Poe was the inventor of the detective story, a celebrated poet, a professional writer and editor, and the author of unforgettable tales of horror, the uncanny, and the supernatural. A kind of uncle of French symbolism, he was venerated by Charles Baudelaire (who translated him) and Stéphane Mallarmé (who wrote in an elegy that Poe had "given a purer sense to the dialect of the tribe"). Poe lived a luridly sensational life. "Poe was going to get the ecstasy and the heightening, cost what it might," wrote D. H. Lawrence in *Studies in Classic American Literature*. "Poe tried alcohol, and any drug he could lay his hand on. He also tried any human being he could lay his hands on." Poe liked making lofty pronouncements; he declared that a long poem "is simply a flat contradiction in terms," which did not prevent him from writing and publishing a lengthy prose treatise entitled *Eureka* and subtitled "A Prose Poem." Numerous writers have condescended to Poe. Emerson called Poe the "jingle man." T. S. Eliot likened Poe's mind to that of "a highly gifted young person before puberty." Richard Wilbur maintains nevertheless that "of American writers, it is Poe who most challenges the reader not only to read him but to solve him."

Dreams

Oh! that my young life were a lasting dream!
My spirit not awak'ning till the beam
Of an Eternity should bring the morrow.
Yes! tho' that long dream were of hopeless sorrow,
'T were better than the cold reality
Of waking life, to him whose heart must be,
And hath been still, upon the lovely earth,
A chaos of deep passion, from his birth.
But should it be — that dream eternally
Continuing — as dreams have been to me
In my young boyhood — should it thus be giv'n,
'T were folly still to hope for higher Heav'n.
For I have revell'd, when the sun was bright
I' the summer sky, in dreams of living light
And loveliness, — have left my very heart
In climes of mine imagining, apart
From mine own home, with beings that have been
Of mine own thought — what more could I have seen?

'T was once — and only once — and the wild hour
From my remembrance shall not pass — some pow'r
Or spell had bound me — 't was the chilly wind
Came o'er me in the night, and left behind
Its image on my spirit — or the moon
Shone on my slumbers in her lofty noon
Too coldly — or the stars — howe'er it was,
That dream was as that night-wind — let it pass.
I *have been* happy, tho' but in a dream.
I have been happy — and I love the theme:
Dreams! In their vivid coloring of life,
As in that fleeting, shadowy, misty strife
Of semblance with reality which brings
To the delirious eye, more lovely things
Of Paradise and Love — and all our own!
Than young Hope in his sunniest hour hath known.

1828

Fairy-Land

Dim vales — and shadowy floods —
And cloudy-looking woods,
Whose forms we can't discover
For the tears that drip all over
Huge moons there wax and wane —
Again — again — again —
Every moment of the night —
Forever changing places —
And they put out the star-light
With the breath from their pale faces.
About twelve by the moon-dial
One more filmy than the rest
(A kind which, upon trial,
They have found to be the best)
Comes down — still down — and down
With its centre on the crown
Of a mountain's eminence,
While its wide circumference
In easy drapery falls
Over hamlets, over halls,
Wherever they may be —
O'er the strange woods — o'er the sea —
Over spirits on the wing —
Over every drowsy thing —
And buries them up quite
In a labyrinth of light —
And then, how deep! — O, deep!

Is the passion of their sleep.
In the morning they arise,
And their moony covering
Is soaring in the skies,
With the tempests as they toss,
Like — almost any thing —
Or a yellow Albatross.
They use that moon no more
For the same end as before —
Videlicet a tent —
Which I think extravagant:
Its atomies, however,
Into a shower dissever,
Of which those butterflies,
Of Earth, who seek the skies,
And so come down again
(Never-contented things!)
Have brought a specimen
Upon their quivering wings.

1829

To Helen

Helen, thy beauty is to me
   Like those Nicéan barks of yore,
That gently, o'er a perfumed sea,
   The weary, way-worn wanderer bore
   To his own native shore.

On desperate seas long wont to roam,
   Thy hyacinth hair, thy classic face,
Thy Naiad airs have brought me home
   To the glory that was Greece,
And the grandeur that was Rome.

Lo! in yon brilliant window-niche
   How statue-like I see thee stand,
   The agate lamp within thy hand!
Ah, Psyche, from the regions which
   Are Holy-Land!

1831

The City in the Sea

Lo! Death has reared himself a throne
In a strange city lying alone

Far down within the dim West,
Where the good and the bad and the worst and the best
Have gone to their eternal rest.
There shrines and palaces and towers
(Time-eaten towers that tremble not!)
Resemble nothing that is ours.
Around, by lifting winds forgot,
Resignedly beneath the sky
The melancholy waters lie.

No rays from the holy heaven come down
On the long night-time of that town;
But light from out the lurid sea
Streams up the turrets silently —
Gleams up the pinnacles far and free
Up domes — up spires — up kingly halls —
Up fanes — up Babylon-like walls —
Up shadowy long-forgotten bowers
Of sculptured ivy and stone flowers —
Up many and many a marvellous shrine
Whose wreathèd friezes intertwine
The viol, the violet, and the vine.

Resignedly beneath the sky
The melancholy waters lie.
So blend the turrets and shadows there
That all seem pendulous in air,
While from a proud tower in the town
Death looks gigantically down.

There open fanes and gaping graves
Yawn level with the luminous waves;
But not the riches there that lie
In each idol's diamond eye —
Not the gaily-jewelled dead
Tempt the waters from their bed;
For no ripples curl, alas!
Along that wilderness of glass —
No swellings tell that winds may be
Upon some far-off happier sea —
No heavings hint that winds have been
On seas less hideously serene.

But lo, a stir is in the air!
The wave — there is a movement there!
As if the towers had thrust aside,
In slightly sinking, the dull tide —
As if their tops had feebly given
A void within the filmy Heaven.

The waves have now a redder glow —
The hours are breathing faint and low —
And when, amid no earthly moans,
Down, down that town shall settle hence,
Hell, rising from a thousand thrones,
Shall do it reverence.

1831

To One in Paradise

Thou wast that all to me, love,
  For which my soul did pine —
A green isle in the sea, love,
  A fountain and a shrine,
All wreathed with fairy fruits and flowers,
  And all the flowers were mine.

Ah, dream too bright to last!
  Ah, starry Hope! that didst arise
But to be overcast!
  A voice from out the Future cries,
"On! on!" — but o'er the Past
  (Dim gulf!) my spirit hovering lies
Mute, motionless, aghast!

For, alas! alas! with me
  The light of Life is o'er!
  No more — no more — no more —
(Such language holds the solemn sea
  To the sands upon the shore)
Shall bloom the thunder-blasted tree,
  Or the stricken eagle soar!

And all my days are trances,
  And all my nightly dreams
Are where thy grey eye glances,
  And where thy footstep gleams —
In what ethereal dances,
  By what eternal streams.

1834

The Haunted Palace

In the greenest of our valleys
  By good angels tenanted,

Once a fair and stately palace —
   Radiant palace — reared its head.
In the monarch Thought's dominion —
   It stood there!
Never seraph spread a pinion
   Over fabric half so fair!

Banners yellow, glorious, golden,
   On its roof did float and flow
(This — all this — was in the olden
   Time long ago),
And every gentle air that dallied,
   In that sweet day,
Along the ramparts plumed and pallid,
   A wingèd odor went away.

Wanderers in that happy valley,
   Through two luminous windows, saw
Spirits moving musically,
   To a lute's well-tunèd law,
Round about a throne where, sitting,
   Porphyrogene,
In state his glory well befitting
   The ruler of the realm was seen.

And all with pearl and ruby glowing
   Was the fair palace door,
Through which came flowing, flowing flowing,
   And sparkling evermore,
A troop of Echoes, whose sweet duty
   Was but to sing,
In voices of surpassing beauty,
   The wit and wisdom of their king.

But evil things, in robes of sorrow,
   Assailed the monarch's high estate.
(Ah, let us mourn! — for never morrow
   Shall dawn upon him, desolate!)
And round about his home the glory
   That blushed and bloomed,
Is but a dim-remembered story
   Of the old-time entombed.

And travellers, now, within that valley,
   Through the encrimsoned windows see
Vast forms that move fantastically
   To a discordant melody,
While, like a ghastly rapid river,
   Through the pale door

A hideous throng rush out forever
  And laugh — but smile no more.

1838

The Raven

Once upon a midnight dreary, while I pondered, weak and weary,
Over many a quaint and curious volume of forgotten lore —
While I nodded, nearly napping, suddenly there came a tapping,
As of some one gently rapping, rapping at my chamber door —
" 'Tis some visitor," I muttered, "tapping at my chamber door —
    Only this and nothing more."

Ah, distinctly I remember it was in the bleak December;
And each separate dying ember wrought its ghost upon the floor.
Eagerly I wished the morrow; — vainly I had sought to borrow
From my books surcease of sorrow — sorrow for the lost Lenore —
For the rare and radiant maiden whom the angels name Lenore —
    Nameless *here* for evermore.

And the silken, sad, uncertain rustling of each purple curtain
Thrilled me — filled me with fantastic terrors never felt before;
So that now, to still the beating of my heart, I stood repeating,
" 'Tis some visiter entreating entrance at my chamber door —
Some late visiter entreating entrance at my chamber door; —
    This it is and nothing more."

Presently my soul grew stronger; hesitating then no longer,
"Sir," said I, "or Madam, truly your forgiveness I implore;
But the fact is I was napping, and so gently you came rapping,
And so faintly you came tapping, tapping at my chamber door,
That I scarce was sure I heard you" — here I opened wide the door; —
    Darkness there and nothing more.

Deep into that darkness peering, long I stood there wondering, fearing,
Doubting, dreaming dreams no mortal ever dared to dream before;
But the silence was unbroken, and the stillness gave no token,
And the only word there spoken was the whispered word, "Lenore?"
This I whispered, and an echo murmured back the word "Lenore!"
    Merely this and nothing more.

Back into the chamber turning, all my soul within me burning,
Soon again I heard a tapping somewhat louder than before.
"Surely," said I, "surely that is something at my window lattice;
Let me see, then, what thereat is, and this mystery explore —
Let my heart be still a moment and this mystery explore; —
    'Tis the wind and nothing more!"

Open here I flung the shutter, when, with many a flirt and flutter,
In there stepped a stately Raven of the saintly days of yore:
Not the least obeisance made he; not a minute stopped or stayed he;
But, with mien of lord or lady, perched above my chamber door —
Perched upon a bust of Pallas just above my chamber door —
Perched, and sat, and nothing more.

Then this ebony bird beguiling my sad fancy into smiling,
By the grave and stern decorum of the countenance it wore:
"Though thy crest be shorn and shaven, thou," I said, " art sure no craven,
Ghastly grim and ancient Raven wandering from the Nightly shore —
Tell me what thy lordly name is on the Night's Plutonian shore!"
Quoth the Raven "Nevermore."

Much I marvelled this ungainly fowl to hear discourse so plainly,
Though its answer little meaning — little relevancy bore:
For we cannot help agreeing that no living human being
Ever yet was blessed with seeing bird above his chamber door —
Bird or beast upon the sculptured bust above his chamber door,
With such name as "Nevermore."

But the Raven, sitting lonely on the placid bust, spoke only
That one word, as if his soul in that one word he did outpour.
Nothing farther then he uttered — not a feather then he fluttered —
Till I scarcely more than muttered "Other friends have flown before —
On the morrow *he* will leave me, as my Hopes have flown before."
Then the bird said "Nevermore."

Startled at the stillness broken by reply so aptly spoken,
"Doubtles," said I, "What it utters is its only stock and store
Caught from some unhappy master whom unmerciful Disaster
Followed fast and followed faster till his songs one burden bore —
Till the dirges of his Hope that melancholy burden bore
Of 'Never — nevermore.' "

But the Raven still beguiling my sad fancy into smiling,
Straight I wheeled a cushioned seat in front of bird, and bust and door;
Then, upon the velvet sinking, I betook myself to linking
Fancy unto fancy, thinking what this ominous bird of yore —
What this grim, ungainly, ghastly, gaunt, and ominous bird of yore
Meant in croaking "Nevermore."

This I sat engaged in guessing, but no syllable expressing
To the fowl whose fiery eyes now burned into my bosom's core;
This and more I sat divining, with my head at ease reclining
On the cushion's velvet lining that the lamp-light gloated o'er,
But whose velvet-violet lining with the lamp-light gloating o'er,
She shall press, ah, nevermore!

Then, methought, the air grew denser, perfumed from an unseen censer
Swung by seraphim whose foot-falls tinkled on the tufted floor.
"Wretch," I cried, "thy God hath lent thee — by these angels he hath
  sent thee
Respite — respite and nepenthe from thy memories of Lenore;
Quaff, oh quaff this kind nepenthe and forget this lost Lenore!"
  Quoth the Raven "Nevermore."

"Prophet!" said I, "thing of evil! — prophet still, if bird or devil! —
Whether Tempter sent, or whether tempest tossed thee here ashore,
Desolate yet all undaunted, on this desert land enchanted —
On this home by Horror haunted — tell me truly, I implore —
Is there — *is* there balm in Gilead? — tell me — tell me, I implore!"
  Quoth the Raven "Nevermore."

"Prophet!" said I, "thing of evil! — prophet still, if bird or devil! —
By that Heaven that bends above us — by that God we both adore —
Tell this soul with sorrow laden if, within the distant Aidenn,
It shall clasp a sainted maiden whom the angels name Lenore —
Clasp a rare and radiant maiden whom the angels name Lenore."
  Quoth the Raven "Nevermore."

"Be that word our sign of parting, bird or fiend!" I shrieked, upstarting —
"Get thee back into the tempest and the Night's Plutonian shore!
Leave no black plume as a token of that lie thy soul hath spoken!
Leave my loneliness unbroken! — quit the bust above my door!
Take thy beak from out my heart, and take thy form from off my door!"
  Quoth the Raven "Nevermore."

And the Raven, never flitting, still is sitting, *still* is sitting
On the pallid bust of Pallas just above my chamber door;
And his eyes have all the seeming of a demon's that is dreaming,
And the lamp-light o'er him streaming throws his shadow on the floor;
And my soul from out that shadow that lies floating on the floor
  Shall be lifted — nevermore!

1845

Ulalume — A Ballad

The skies they were ashen and sober;
  The leaves they were crispéd and sere —
  The leaves they were withering and sere:
It was night, in the lonesome October
  Of my most immemorial year:
It was hard by the dim lake of Auber,
  In the misty mid region of Weir: —

It was down by the dank tarn of Auber,
  In the ghoul-haunted woodland of Weir.

Here once, through an alley Titanic,
  Of cypress, I roamed with my Soul —
  Of cypress, with Psyche, my Soul.
These were days when my heart was volcanic
  As the scoriac rivers that roll —
  As the lavas that restlessly roll
Their sulphurous currents down Yaanek,
  In the ultimate climes of the Pole —
That groan as they roll down Mount Yaanek,
  In the realms of the Boreal Pole.

Our talk had been serious and sober,
  But our thoughts they were palsied and sere —
  Our memories were treacherous and sere;
For we knew not the month was October,
  And we marked not the night of the year —
  (Ah, night of all nights in the year!)
We noted not the dim lake of Auber,
  (Though once we had journeyed down here)
We remembered not the dank tarn of Auber,
  Nor the ghoul-haunted woodland of Weir.

And now, as the night was senescent,
  And star-dials pointed to morn —
  As the star-dials hinted of morn —
At the end of our path a liquescent
  And nebulous lustre was born,
Out of which a miraculous crescent
  Arose with a duplicate horn —
Astarte's bediamonded crescent,
  Distinct with its duplicate horn.

And I said — "She is warmer than Dian;
  She rolls through an ether of sighs —
  She revels in a region of sighs.
She has seen that the tears are not dry on
  These cheeks where the worm never dies,
And has come past the stars of the Lion,
  To point us the path to the skies —
  To the Lethean peace of the skies —
Come up, in despite of the Lion,
  To shine on us with her bright eyes —
Come up, through the lair of the Lion,
  With love in her luminous eyes."

But Psyche, uplifting her finger,
  Said — "Sadly this star I mistrust —
  Her pallor I strangely mistrust —
Ah, hasten! — ah, let us not linger!
  Ah, fly! —let us fly! —for we must."
In terror she spoke; letting sink her
  Wings till they trailed in the dust —
In agony sobbed; letting sink her
  Plumes till they trailed in the dust —
  Till they sorrowfully trailed in the dust.

I replied — "This is nothing but dreaming.
  Let us on, by this tremulous light!
  Let us bathe in this crystalline light!
Its Sibyllic splendor is beaming
  With Hope and in Beauty to-night —
  See! — it flickers up the sky through the night!
Ah, we safely may trust to its gleaming
  And be sure it will lead us aright —
We surely may trust to a gleaming
  That cannot but guide us aright
Since it flickers up to Heaven through the night."

Thus I pacified Psyche and kissed her,
  And tempted her out of her gloom —
  And conquered her scruples and gloom;
And we passed to the end of the vista —
  But were stopped by the door of a tomb, —
  By the door of a legended tomb: —
And I said — "What is written, sweet sister,
  On the door of this legended tomb?"
  She replied — "Ulalume — Ulalume! —
  'T is the vault of thy lost Ulalume!"

Then my heart it grew ashen and sober
  As the leaves that were crispéd and sere —
  As the leaves that were withering and sere —
And I cried — "It was surely October,
  On *this* very night of last year,
  That I journeyed — I journeyed down here! —
  That I brought a dread burden down here —
  On this night, of all nights in the year,
  Ah, what demon hath tempted me here?
Well I know, now, this dim lake of Auber —
  This misty mid region of Weir: —
Well I know, now, this dank tarn of Auber —
  This ghoul-haunted woodland of Weir."

1847

A Dream Within a Dream

Take this kiss upon the brow!
And, in parting from you now,
Thus much let me avow —
You are not wrong, who deem
That my days have been a dream;
Yet if hope has flown away
In a night, or in a day,
In a vision, or in none,
Is it therefore the less *gone?*
All that we see or seem
Is but a dream within a dream.

I stand amid the roar
Of a surf-tormented shore,
And I hold within my hand
Grains of the golden sand —
How few! yet how they creep
Through my fingers to the deep,
While I weep — while I weep!
O God! Can I not grasp
Them with a tighter clasp?
O God! can I not save
One from the pitiless wave?
Is *all* that we see or seem
But a dream within a dream?

1849

Annabel Lee

It was many and many a year ago,
   In a kingdom by the sea,
That a maiden there lived whom you may know
   By the name of Annabel Lee; —
And this maiden she lived with no other thought
   Than to love and be loved by me.

She was a child and *I* was a child,
   In this kingdom by the sea,
But we loved with a love that was more than love —
   I and my Annabel Lee —
With a love that the wingéd seraphs of Heaven
   Coveted her and me.

And this was the reason that, long ago,
   In this kingdom by the sea,

A wind blew out of a cloud by night
  Chilling my Annabel Lee;
So that her highborn kinsmen came
  And bore her away from me,
To shut her up in a sepulchre
  In this kingdom by the sea.

The angels, not half so happy in Heaven,
  Went envying her and me: —
Yes! that was the reason (as all men know,
  In this kingdom by the sea)
That the wind came out of the cloud, chilling
  And killing my Annabel Lee.

But our love it was stronger by far than the love
  Of those who were older than we —
  Of many far wiser than we —
And neither the angels in Heaven above
  Nor the demons down under the sea
Can ever disserver my soul from the soul
  Of the beautiful Annabel Lee: —

For the moon never beams without bringing me dreams
  Of the beautiful Annabel Lee;
And the stars never rise but I see the bright eyes
  Of the beautiful Annabel Lee;
And so, all the night-tide, I lie down by the side
Of my darling, my darling, my life and my bride
  In her sepulchre there by the sea —
  In her tomb by the side of the sea.

1849

JONES VERY (1813–1880)

Born in 1813 to first cousins who never married, Jones Very, the "laureate of Salem," was educated at Harvard, where he went on to teach Greek. As a result of a mystical experience, he was locked up in McLean Asylum for a month in the autumn of 1838. It was then that he wrote the visionary sonnets on which his poetic reputation is based. "And he is gone into the multitude as solitary as Jesus," Emerson wrote in his journals after a visit from Very. "In dismissing him I seem to have discharged an arrow into the heart of society. Wherever that young enthusiast goes he will astonish and disconcert men by dividing for them the cloud that covers the profound gulf that is in man." Very lived with his sister Frances, who had an enormous shaggy gray cat named Walt Whitman.

The New Birth

'Tis a new life; — thoughts move not as they did
With slow uncertain steps across my mind,
In thronging haste fast pressing on they bid
The portals open to the viewless wind
That comes not save when in the dust is laid
The crown of pride that gilds each mortal brow,
And from before man's vision melting fade
The heavens and earth; — their walls are falling now. —
Fast crowding on, each thought asks utterance strong;
Storm-lifted waves swift rushing to the shore,
On from the sea they send their shouts along,
Back through the cave-worn rocks their thunders roar;
And I a child of God by Christ made free
Start from death's slumbers to Eternity.

1839

The Dead

I see them, — crowd on crowd they walk the earth
Dry leafless trees to autumn wind laid bare;
And in their nakedness find cause for mirth,
And all unclad would winter's rudeness dare;
No sap doth through their clattering branches flow,
Whence springing leaves and blossoms bright appear;
Their hearts the living God have ceased to know
Who gives the spring time to th' expectant year;
They mimic life, as if from him to steal
His glow of health to paint the livid cheek;
They borrow words for thoughts they cannot feel,
That with a seeming heart their tongue may speak;
And in their show of life more dead they live
Than those that to the earth with many tears they give.

1839

The Garden

I saw the spot where our first parents dwelt;
And yet it wore to me no face of change,
For while amid its fields and groves, I felt
As if I had not sinned, nor thought it strange;
My eye seemed but a part of every sight,
My ear heard music in each sound that rose;
Each sense forever found a new delight,

Such as the spirit's vision only knows;
Each act some new and ever-varying joy
Did by my Father's love for me prepare;
To dress the spot my ever fresh employ,
And in the glorious whole with Him to share;
No more without the flaming gate to stray,
No more for sin's dark stain the debt of death to pay.

1839

The New World

The night that has no star lit up by God,
The day that round men shines who still are blind,
The earth their grave-turned feet for ages trod,
And sea swept over by His mighty wind;
All these have passed away; the melting dream
That flitted o'er the sleeper's half-shut eye,
When touched by morning's golden-darting beam;
And he beholds around the earth and sky
That ever real stands; the rolling spheres
And heaving billows of the boundless main,
That show though time is past no trace of years,
And earth restored he sees as his again;
The earth that fades not, and the heavens that stand;
Their strong foundations laid by God's right hand!

1839

Yourself

'T is to yourself I speak; you cannot know
Him whom I call in speaking such an one,
For thou beneath the earth liest buried low,
Which he alone as living walks upon;
Thou mayst at times have heard him speak to you,
And often wished perchance that you were he;
And I must ever wish that it were true,
For then thou couldst hold fellowship with me;
But now thou hear'st us talk as strangers, met
Above the room wherein thou liest abed;
A word perhaps loud spoken thou mayst get,
Or hear our feet when heavily they tread;
But he who speaks, or him who's spoken to,
Must both remain as strangers still to you.

1839

HENRY DAVID THOREAU (1817–1862)

Henry David Thoreau wrote several of our classics in prose, notably "Walden" — his journal of living in the woods at Walden Pond (1854) — and his essay on "Civil Disobedience" (1849). Emerson wrote of Thoreau in his journals: "It was a pleasure to know him and a privilege to walk with him. He knew the country like a fox or a bird, and passed through it as freely by paths of his own. He knew every track in the snow or on the ground, and what creature had taken this path before him." Thoreau lived in an intimate relation with the birds and the flowers. When Thoreau and Emerson walked together one day (the latter wrote), "He thought that, if waked up from a trance, in this swamp, he could tell by the plants what time of the year it was within two days." When Thoreau heard the "night-warbler," having searched for it in vain for twelve years, he told Emerson, "What you seek in vain for, half your life, one day you come full upon, all the family at dinner. You seek it like a dream, and as soon as you find it you become its prey."

I Am a Parcel of Vain Strivings Tied

I am a parcel of vain strivings tied
By a chance bond together,
Dangling this way and that, their links
Were made so loose and wide,
Methinks,
For milder weather.

A bunch of violets without their roots,
And sorrel intermixed,
Encircled by a wisp of straw
Once coiled about their shoots,
The law
By which I'm fixed.

A nosegay which Time clutched from out
Those fair Elysian fields,
With weeds and broken stems, in haste,
Doth make the rabble rout
That waste
The day he yields.

And here I bloom for a short hour unseen,
Drinking my juices up,
With no root in the land
To keep my branches green,
But stand
In a bare cup.

Some tender buds were left upon my stem
In mimicry of life,

But ah! the children will not know,
Till time has withered them,
The woe
With which they're rife.

But now I see I was not plucked for naught,
And after in life's vase
Of glass set while I might survive,
But by a kind hand brought
Alive
To a strange place.

That stock thus thinned will soon redeem its hours,
And by another year,
Such as God knows, with freer air,
More fruits and fairer flowers
Will bear,
While I droop here.

1841

Inspiration

Whate'er we leave to God, God does,
And blesses us;
The work we choose should be our own,
God lets alone.

If with light head erect I sing,
Though all the muses lend their force,
From my poor love of anything,
The verse is weak and shallow as its source.

But if with bended neck I grope,
Listening behind me for my wit,
With faith superior to hope,
More anxious to keep back than forward it,

Making my soul accomplice there
Unto the flame my heart hath lit,
Then will the verse forever wear, —
Time cannot bend the line which God hath writ.

Always the general show of things
Floats in review before my mind,
And such true love and reverence brings,
That sometimes I forget that I am blind.

But now there comes unsought, unseen,
  Some clear, divine electuary,
And I who had but sensual been,
  Grow sensible, and as God is, am wary.

I hearing get who had but ears,
  And sight, who had but eyes before,
I moments live who lived but years,
  And truth discern who knew but learning's lore.

I hear beyond the range of sound,
  I see beyond the range of sight,
New earths and skies and seas around,
  And in my day the sun doth pale his light.

A clear and ancient harmony
  Pierces my soul through all its din,
As through its utmost melody, —
  Farther behind than they — farther within.

More swift its bolt than lightning is,
  Its voice than thunder is more loud,
It doth expand my privacies
  To all, and leave me single in the crowd.

It speaks with such authority,
  With so serene and lofty tone,
That idle Time runs gadding by,
  And leaves me with Eternity alone.

Then chiefly is my natal hour,
  And only then my prime of life,
Of manhood's strength it is the flower,
  'Tis peace's end and war's beginning strife.

'T 'hath come in summer's broadest noon,
  By a grey wall or some chance place,
Unseasoned time, insulted June,
  And vexed the day with its presuming face.

Such fragrance round my couch it makes,
  More rich than are Arabian drugs,
That my soul scents its life and wakes
  The body up beneath its perfumed rugs.

Such is the Muse — the heavenly maid,
  The star that guides our mortal course,
Which shows where life's true kernel's laid,
  Its wheat's fine flower, and its undying force.

She with one breath attunes the spheres,
  And also my poor human heart,
With one impulse propels the years
  Around, and gives my throbbing pulse its start.

I will not doubt forever more,
  Nor falter from a steadfast faith,
For though the system be turned o'er,
  God takes not back the word which once he saith.

I will then trust the love untold
  Which not my worth nor want has bought,
Which wooed me young and woos me old,
  And to this evening hath me brought.

My memory I'll educate
  To know the one historic truth,
Remembering to the latest date
  The only true and sole immortal youth.

Be but thy inspiration given,
  No matter through what danger sought,
I'll fathom hell or climb to heaven,
  And yet esteem that cheap which love has bought.

Fame cannot tempt the bard
  Who's famous with his God,
Nor laurel him reward
  Who hath his Maker's nod.

c. 1841

JULIA WARD HOWE (1819–1910)

The staunch abolitionist who wrote the song that became the Union Army's unofficial anthem in the Civil War was born into a wealthy New York family. Julia Ward Howe and her husband published the abolitionist newspaper *The Commonwealth*. "The Battle Hymn of the Republic" appeared in the *Atlantic Monthly* in February 1862. After the war, Howe campaigned for the causes of women's suffrage and prison reform.

The Battle Hymn of the Republic

Mine eyes have seen the glory of the coming of the Lord:
He is trampling out the vintage where the grapes of wrath are stored;
He hath loosed the fateful lightning of His terrible swift sword:
His truth is marching on.

I have seen Him in the watch-fires of a hundred circling camps,
They have builded Him an altar in the evening dews and damps;
I can read His righteous sentence by the dim and flaring lamps:
His day is marching on.

I have read a fiery gospel writ in burnished rows of steel:
"As ye deal with my contemners, so with you my grace shall deal;
Let the Hero, born of woman, crush the serpent with his heel,
Since God is marching on."

He has sounded forth the trumpet that shall never call retreat;
He is sifting out the hearts of men before His judgement seat:
Oh, be swift, my soul, to answer Him! Be jubilant, my feet!
Our God is marching on.

In the beauty of the lilies Christ was born across the sea,
With a glory in his bosom that transfigures you and me:
As he died to make men holy, let us die to make men free,
While God is marching on.

1862

JAMES RUSSELL LOWELL (1819–1891)

James Russell Lowell was born in Cambridge, Massachusetts, and educated at Harvard. He had a talent for satirical verse, which he used to advance political causes: opposition to the Mexican War, support of the Union in the Civil War. "A Fable for Critics" (1848), his best work, satirizes his contemporaries. In 1855, Lowell became professor of modern languages at Harvard, a position he held until 1876. In addition to teaching, he served as first editor (1857–1861) of the *Atlantic Monthly*. In 1877 he was appointed ambassador to England, where he remained until 1885. Robert Lowell, his great-grandnephew, unsentimentally called him "a poet pedestaled for oblivion."

from *A Fable for Critics*

Emerson

"There comes Emerson first, whose rich words, every one,
Are like gold nails in temples to hang trophies on,

Whose prose is grand verse, while his verse, the Lord knows,
Is some of it pr— No, 't is not even prose;
I'm speaking of metres; some poems have welled
From those rare depths of soul that have ne'er been excelled;
They're not epics, but that doesn't matter a pin,
In creating, the only hard thing's to begin;
A grass-blade's no easier to make than an oak;
If you've once found the way, you've achieved the grand stroke;
In the worst of his poems are mines of rich matter,
But thrown in a heap with a crash and a clatter;
Now it is not one thing nor another alone
Makes a poem, but rather the general tone,
The something pervading, uniting the whole,
The before unconceived, unconceivable soul,
So that just in removing this trifle or that, you
Take away, as it were, a chief limb of the statue;
Roots, wood, bark, and leaves singly perfect may be,
But, clapt hodge-podge together, they don't make a tree.

"But, to come back to Emerson (whom by the way,
I believe we left waiting), — his is, we may say,
A Greek head on right Yankee shoulders, whose range
Has Olympus for one pole, for t'other the Exchange;
He seems, to my thinking (although I'm afraid
The comparison must, long ere this, have been made),
A Plotinus-Montaigne, where the Egyptian's gold mist
And the Gascon's shrewd wit cheek-by-jowl coexist;
All admire, and yet scarcely six converts he's got
To I don't (nor they either) exactly know what;
For though he builds glorious temples, 't is odd
He leaves never a doorway to get in a god.
'T is refreshing to old-fashioned people like me
To meet such a primitive Pagan as he,
In whose mind all creation is duly respected
As parts of himself — just a little projected;
And who's willing to worship the stars and the sun,
A convert to — nothing but Emerson.
So perfect a balance there is in his head,
That he talks of things sometimes as if they were dead;
Life, nature, love, God, and affairs of that sort,
He looks at as merely ideas; in short,
As if they were fossils stuck round in a cabinet,
Of such vast extent that our earth's a mere dab in it;
Composed just as he is inclined to conjecture her,
Namely, one part pure earth, ninety-nine parts pure lecturer;
You are filled with delight at his clear demonstration,
Each figure, word, gesture, just fits the occasion,
With the quiet precision of science he'll sort 'em,
But you can't help suspecting the whole a *post mortem.*

"There are persons, mole-blind to the soul's make and style,
Who insist on a likeness 'twixt him and Carlyle;
To compare him with Plato would be vastly fairer,
Carlyle's the more burly, but E. is the rarer;
He sees fewer objects, but clearlier, truelier,
If C.'s as original, E.'s more peculiar;
That he's more of a man you might say of the one,
Of the other he's more of an Emerson;
C.'s the Titan, as shaggy of mind as of limb, —
E. the clear-eyed Olympian, rapid and slim;
The one's two thirds Norseman, the other half Greek,
Where the one's most abounding, the other's to seek;
C.'s generals require to be seen in the mass, —
E.'s specialties gain if enlarged by the glass;
C. gives nature and God his fits of the blues,
And rims common-sense things with mystical hues, —
E. sits in a mystery calm and intense,
And looks coolly around him with sharp common-sense;
C. shows you how every-day matters unite
With the dim transdiurnal recesses of night, —
While E., in a plain, preternatural way,
Makes mysteries matters of mere every day;
C. draws all his characters quite *à la* Fuseli, —
No sketching their bundles of muscles and thews illy,
He paints with a brush so untamed and profuse,
They seem nothing but bundles of muscles and thews;
E. is rather like Flaxman, lines strait and severe,
And a colorless outline, but full, round, and clear; —
To the men he thinks worthy he frankly accords
The design of a white marble statue in words.
C. labors to get at the centre, and then
Take a reckoning from there of his actions and men;
E. calmly assumes the said centre as granted,
And, given himself, has whatever is wanted.

"He has imitators in scores, who omit
No part of the man but his wisdom and wit, —
Who go carefully o'er the sky-blue of his brain,
And when he has skimmed it once, skim it again;
If at all they resemble him, you may be sure it is
Because their shoals mirror his mists and obscurities,
As a mud-puddle seems deep as heaven for a minute,
While a cloud that floats o'er is reflected within it.

"There comes ——, for instance; to see him 's rare sport,
Tread in Emerson's tracks with legs painfully short;
How he jumps, how he strains, and gets red in the face,
To keep step with the mystagogue's natural pace!
He follows as close as a stick to a rocket,
His fingers exploring the prophet's each pocket.

Fie, for shame, brother bard; with good fruit of your own,
Can't you let Neighbor Emerson's orchards alone?
Besides, 't is no use, you'll not find e'en a core, —
—— has picked up all the windfalls before.
They might strip every tree, and E. never would catch 'em,
His Hesperides have no rude dragon to watch 'em;
When they send him a dishful, and ask him to try 'em,
He never suspects how the sly rogues came by 'em;
He wonders why 't is there are none such his trees on,
And thinks 'em the best he has tasted this season.

Poe and Longfellow

"There comes Poe, with his raven, like Barnaby Rudge,
Three fifths of him genius and two fifths sheer fudge,
Who talks like a book of iambs and pentameters,
In a way to make people of common sense damn metres,
Who has written some things quite the best of their kind,
But the heart somehow seems all squeezed out by the mind,
Who — But hey-day! What's this? Messieurs Mathews and Poe,
You must n't fling mud-balls at Longfellow so,
Does it make a man worse that his character's such
As to make his friends love him (as you think) too much?
Why, there is not a bard at this moment alive
More willing than he that his fellows should thrive;
While you are abusing him thus, even now
He would help either one of you out of a slough;
You may say that he's smooth and all that till you're hoarse,
But remember that elegance also is force;
After polishing granite as much as you will,
The heart keeps its tough old persistency still;
Deduct all you can, *that* still keeps you at bay;
Why, he'll live till men weary of Collins and Gray.
I 'm not over-fond of Greek metres in English,
To me rhyme's a gain, so it be not too jinglish,
And your modern hexameter verses are no more
Like Greek ones than sleek Mr, Pope is like Homer;
As the roar of the sea to the coo of a pigeon is,
So, compared to your moderns, sounds old Melesigenes;
I may be too partial, the reason, perhaps, o't is
That I 've heard the old blind man recite his own rhapsodies,
And my ear with that music impregnate may be,
Like the poor exiled shell with the soul of the sea,
Or as one can't bear Strauss when his nature is cloven
To its deeps within deeps by the stroke of Beethoven;
But, set that aside, and 't is truth that I speak,
Had Theocritus written in English, not Greek,
I believe that his exquisite sense would scarce change a line
In that rare, tender, virgin-like pastoral Evangeline.
That 's not ancient nor modern, its place is apart

Where time has no sway, in the realm of pure Art,
'T is a shrine of retreat from Earth's hubbub and strife
As quiet and chaste as the author's own life.

1848

WALT WHITMAN (1819–1892)

Walt Whitman was born on Long Island (which he called by its Indian name, Paumanok) and lived in Brooklyn, where he worked as a newspaperman and printer. The self-published *Leaves of Grass* appeared in 1855. "An American bard at last!" Thus opens one of the first reviews the book received. The reviewer continues: "One of the roughs, large, proud, affectionate, eating, drinking, and breeding, his costume manly and free, his face sunburnt and bearded, his posture strong and erect, his voice bringing hope and prophecy to the generous races of young and old." Whitman himself wrote this review in 1855. Not every critic concurred. During the Civil War, Whitman served for three years as a wound dresser and solace giver to injured soldiers in and around Washington. In 1865, when his Civil War poems and his elegy for President Lincoln ("When Lilacs Last in the Dooryard Bloom'd") were published in *Drum-Taps*, Henry James addressed the author directly: "What would be bald nonsense and dreary platitudes in any one else becomes sublimity in you. But all this is a mistake. To become adopted as a national poet, it is not enough to discard everything in particular and to accept everything in general, to amass crudity upon crudity, to discharge the undigested contents of your blotting-book into the lap of the public." Later writers addressed him, too: Ezra Pound proposed a surly "pact" with Whitman, Hart Crane clasped him by the hand, and Allen Ginsberg spied him in the aisles of a supermarket in California. In the prose preface to *Leaves of Grass*, Whitman declares that "the United States themselves are essentially the greatest poem," a statement that bears contemplating. He is generous with his advice.

> This is what you shall do: Love the earth and sun and the animals, despise riches, give alms to every one that asks, stand up for the stupid and crazy, devote your income and labor to others, hate tyrants, argue not concerning God, have patience and indulgence toward the people, take off your hat to nothing known or unknown or to any man or number of men, go freely with powerful uneducated persons and with the young and with the mothers of families, read these leaves in the open air every season of every year of your life, re-examine all you have been told at school or church or in any book, dismiss whatever insults your own soul, and your very flesh shall be a great poet and have the richest fluency not only in its words but in the silent lines of its lips and face and between the lashes of your eyes and in every motion and joint of your body.

Song of Myself (1855 edition)

I

I celebrate myself,
And what I assume you shall assume,
For every atom belonging to me as good belongs to you.

I loafe and invite my soul,
I lean and loafe at my ease . . . . observing a spear of summer grass.

II

Houses and rooms are full of perfumes . . . . the shelves are crowded with perfumes,
I breathe the fragrance myself, and know it and like it,
The distillation would intoxicate me also, but I shall not let it.

The atmosphere is not a perfume . . . . it has no taste of the distillation . . . . it is odorless,
It is for my mouth forever . . . . I am in love with it,
I will go to the bank by the wood and become undisguised and naked,
I am mad for it to be in contact with me.

The smoke of my own breath,
Echoes, ripples, and buzzed whispers . . . . loveroot, silkthread, crotch and vine,
My respiration and inspiration . . . . the beating of my heart . . . . the passing of blood and air through my lungs,
The sniff of green leaves and dry leaves, and of the shore and darkcolored sea-rocks, and of hay in the barn,
The sound of the belched words of my voice . . . . words loosed to the eddies of the wind,
A few light kisses . . . . a few embraces . . . . a reaching around of arms,
The play of shine and shade on the trees as the supple boughs wag,
The delight alone or in the rush of the streets, or along the fields and hillsides,
The feeling of health . . . . the full-noon trill . . . . the song of me rising from bed and meeting the sun.

Have you reckoned a thousand acres much? Have you reckoned the earth much?
Have you practiced so long to learn to read?
Have you felt so proud to get at the meaning of poems?

Stop this day and night with me and you shall possess the origin of all poems,
You shall possess the good of the earth and sun . . . . there are millions of suns left,
You shall no longer take things at second or third hand . . . . nor look through the eyes of the dead . . . . nor feed on the spectres in books,
You shall not look through my eyes either, nor take things from me,
You shall listen to all sides and filter them from yourself.

III

I have heard what the talkers were talking . . . . the talk of the beginning and the end,
But I do not talk of the beginning or the end.

There was never any more inception than there is now,
Nor any more youth or age than there is now;
And will never be any more perfection than there is now,
Nor any more heaven or hell than there is now.

Urge and urge and urge,
Always the procreant urge of the world.

Out of the dimness opposite equals advance . . . . Always substance and increase,
Always a knit of identity . . . . always distinction . . . . always a breed of life.

To elaborate is no avail . . . . Learned and unlearned feel that it is so.

Sure as the most certain sure . . . . plumb in the uprights, well entretied, braced in the beams,
Stout as a horse, affectionate, haughty, electrical,
I and this mystery here we stand.

Clear and sweet is my soul . . . . and clear and sweet is all that is not my soul.

Lack one lacks both . . . . and the unseen is proved by the seen,
Till that becomes unseen and receives proof in its turn.

Showing the best and dividing it from the worst, age vexes age,
Knowing the perfect fitness and equanimity of things, while they discuss I am silent, and go bathe and admire myself.

Welcome is every organ and attribute of me, and of any man hearty and clean,
Not an inch nor a particle of an inch is vile, and none shall be less familiar than the rest.

I am satisfied . . . . I see, dance, laugh, sing;
As God comes a loving bedfellow and sleeps at my side all night and close on the peep of the day,
And leaves for me baskets covered with white towels bulging the house with their plenty,
Shall I postpone my acceptation and realization and scream at my eyes,
That they turn from gazing after and down the road,
And forthwith cipher and show me to a cent,
Exactly the contents of one, and exactly the contents of two, and which is ahead?

IV

Trippers and askers surround me,
People I meet . . . . the effect upon me of my early life . . . . of the ward and city I live in . . . . of the nation,
The latest news . . . . discoveries, inventions, societies . . . . authors old and new,
My dinner, dress, associates, looks, business, compliments, dues,
The real or fancied indifferences of some man or woman I love,
The sickness of one of my folks — or of myself . . . . or ill-doing . . . . or loss or lack of money . . . . or depressions or exaltations,
They come to me days and nights and go from me again,
But they are not the Me myself.

Apart from the pulling and hauling stands what I am,
Stands amused, complacent, compassionating, idle, unitary,
Looks down, is erect, bends an arm on an impalpable certain rest,
Looks with its sidecurved head curious what will come next,
Both in and out of the game, and watching and wondering at it.

Backward I see in my own days where I sweated through fog with linguists and contenders,
I have no mockings or arguments . . . . I witness and wait.

V

I believe in you my soul . . . . the other I am must not abase itself to you,
And you must not be abased to the other.

Loafe with me on the grass . . . . loose the stop from your throat,
Not words, not music or rhyme I want . . . . not custom or lecture, not even the best,
Only the lull I like, the hum of your valved voice.

I mind how we lay in June, such a transparent summer morning;
You settled your head athwart my hips and gently turned over upon me,
And parted the shirt from my bosom-bone, and plunged your tongue to my barestript heart,
And reached till you felt my beard, and reached till you held my feet.

Swiftly arose and spread around me the peace and joy and knowledge that pass all the art and argument of the earth;
And I know that the hand of God is the elderhand of my own,
And I know that the spirit of God is the eldest brother of my own,
And that all the men ever born are also my brothers . . . . and the women my sisters and lovers,
And that a kelson of the creation is love;
And limitless are leaves stiff or drooping in the fields,

And brown ants in the little wells beneath them,
And mossy scabs of the wormfence, and heaped stones, and elder and mullen and pokeweed.

VI

A child said, What is the grass? fetching it to me with full hands;
How could I answer the child? . . . . I do not know what it is any more than he.

I guess it must be the flag of my disposition, out of hopeful green stuff woven.

Or I guess it is the handkerchief of the Lord,
A scented gift and remembrancer designedly dropped,
Bearing the owner's name someway in the corners, that we may see and remark, and say Whose?

Or I guess the grass is itself a child . . . . the produced babe of the vegetation.

Or I guess it is a uniform hieroglyphic,
And it means, Sprouting alike in broad zones and narrow zones,
Growing among black folks as among white,
Kanuck, Tuckahoe, Congressman, Cuff, I give them the same, I receive them the same.

And now it seems to me the beautiful uncut hair of graves.

Tenderly will I use you curling grass,
It may be you transpire from the breasts of young men,
It may be if I had known them I would have loved them;
It may be you are from old people and from women, and from offspring taken soon out of their mothers' laps,
And here you are the mothers' laps.

This grass is very dark to be from the white heads of old mothers,
Darker than the colorless beards of old men,
Dark to come from under the faint red roofs of mouths.

O I perceive after all so many uttering tongues!
And I perceive they do not come from the roofs of mouths for nothing.

I wish I could translate the hints about the dead young men and women,
And the hints about old men and mothers, and the offspring taken soon out of their laps.

What do you think has become of the young and old men?
And what do you think has become of the women and children?

They are alive and well somewhere;
The smallest sprout shows there is really no death,
And if ever there was it led forward life, and does not wait at the
 end to arrest it,
And ceased the moment life appeared.

All goes onward and outward . . . . and nothing collapses,
And to die is different from what any one supposed, and luckier.

VII

Has any one supposed it lucky to be born?
I hasten to inform him or her it is just as lucky to die, and I know it.

I pass death with the dying, and birth with the new-washed babe . . . .
 and am not contained between my hat and boots,
And peruse manifold objects, no two alike, and every one good,
The earth good, and the stars good, and their adjuncts all good.

I am not an earth nor an adjunct of an earth,
I am the mate and companion of people, all just as immortal and
 fathomless as myself;
They do not know how immortal, but I know.

Every kind for itself and its own . . . . for me mine male and female,
For me all that have been boys and that love women,
For me the man that is proud and feels how it stings to be slighted,
For me the sweetheart and the old maid . . . . for me mothers and
 the mothers of mothers,
For me lips that have smiled, eyes that have shed tears,
For me children and the begetters of children.

Who need be afraid of the merge?
Undrape . . . . you are not guilty to me, nor stale nor discarded,
I see through the broadcloth and gingham whether or no,
And am around, tenacious, acquisitive, tireless . . . . and can never
 be shaken away.

VIII

The little one sleeps in its cradle,
I lift the gauze and look a long time, and silently brush away flies
 with my hand.

The youngster and the redfaced girl turn aside up the bushy hill,
I peeringly view them from the top.

The suicide sprawls on the bloody floor of the bedroom,
It is so . . . . I witnessed the corpse . . . . there the pistol had fallen.

The blab of the pave . . . . the tires of carts and sluff of bootsoles
and talk of the promenaders,
The heavy omnibus, the driver with his interrogating thumb, the
clank of the shod horses on the granite floor,
The carnival of sleighs, the clinking and shouted jokes and pelts of
snowballs;
The hurrahs for popular favorites . . . . the fury of roused mobs,
The flap of the curtained litter — the sick man inside, borne to the
hospital,
The meeting of enemies, the sudden oath, the blows and fall,
The excited crowd — the policeman with his star quickly working his
passage to the centre of the crowd;
The impassive stones that receive and return so many echoes,
The souls moving along . . . . are they invisible while the least atom
of the stones is visible?
What groans of overfed or half-starved who fall on the flags
sunstruck or in fits,
What exclamations of women taken suddenly, who hurry home and
give birth to babes,
What living and buried speech is always vibrating here . . . . what
howls restrained by decorum,
Arrests of criminals, slights, adulterous offers made, acceptances,
rejections with convex lips,
I mind them or the resonance of them . . . . I come again and again.

IX

The big doors of the country-barn stand open and ready,
The dried grass of the harvest-time loads the slow-drawn wagon,
The clear light plays on the brown gray and green intertinged,
The armfuls are packed to the sagging mow:
I am there . . . . I help . . . . I came stretched atop of the load,
I felt its soft jolts . . . . one leg reclined on the other,
I jump from the crossbeams, and seize the clover and timothy,
And roll head over heels, and tangle my hair full of wisps.

X

Alone far in the wilds and mountains I hunt,
Wandering amazed at my own lightness and glee,
In the late afternoon choosing a safe spot to pass the night,
Kindling a fire and broiling the freshkilled game,
Soundly falling asleep on the gathered leaves, my dog and gun by
my side.
The Yankee clipper is under her three skysails . . . . she cuts the
sparkle and scud,
My eyes settle the land . . . . I bend at her prow or shout joyously
from the deck.

The boatmen and clamdiggers arose early and stopped for me,
I tucked my trowser-ends in my boots and went and had a good time,
You should have been with us that day round the chowder-kettle.

I saw the marriage of the trapper in the open air in the far-west . . . . the bride was a red girl,
Her father and his friends sat near by crosslegged and dumbly smoking . . . . they had moccasins to their feet and large thick blankets hanging from their shoulders;
On a bank lounged the trapper . . . . he was dressed mostly in skins . . . . his luxuriant beard and curls protected his neck,
One hand rested on his rifle . . . . the other hand held firmly the wrist of the red girl,
She had long eyelashes . . . . her head was bare . . . . her coarse straight locks descended upon her voluptous limbs and reached to her feet.

The runaway slave came to my house and stopped outside,
I heard his motions crackling the twigs of the woodpile,
Through the swung half-door of the kitchen I saw him limpsey and weak,
And went where he sat on a log, and led him in and assured him,
And brought water and filled a tub for his sweated body and bruised feet,
And gave him a room that entered from my own, and gave him some coarse clean clothes,
And remember perfectly well his revolving eyes and his awkwardness,
And remember putting plasters on the galls of his neck and ankles;
He staid with me a week before he was recuperated and passed north,
I had him sit next me at table . . . . my firelock leaned in the corner.

XI

Twenty-eight young men bathe by the shore,
Twenty-eight young men, and all so friendly,
Twenty-eight years of womanly life, and all so lonesome.

She owns the fine house by the rise of the bank,
She hides handsome and richly drest aft the blinds of the window.

Which of the young men does she like the best?
Ah the homeliest of them is beautiful to her.

Where are you off to, lady? for I see you,
You splash in the water there, yet stay stock still in your room.

Dancing and laughing along the beach came the twenty-ninth bather,
The rest did not see her, but she saw them and loved them.

The beards of the young men glistened with wet; it ran from their
long hair,
Little streams passed all over their bodies.

An unseen hand also passed over their bodies,
It descended tremblingly from their temples and ribs.

The young men float on their backs, their white bellies swell to the
sun . . . . they do not ask who seizes fast to them,
They do not know who puffs and declines with pendant and
bending arch,
They do not think whom they souse with spray.

XII

The butcher-boy puts off his killing-clothes, or sharpens his knife
at the stall in the market,
I loiter enjoying his repartee and his shuffle and breakdown.

Blacksmiths with grimed and hairy chests environ the anvil,
Each has his main-sledge . . . . they are all out . . . . there is a great
heat in the fire.

From the cinder-strewed threshold I follow their movements,
The lithe sheer of their waists plays even with their massive arms,
Overhand the hammers roll — overhand so slow — overhand so sure,
They do not hasten, each man hits in his place.

XIII

The negro holds firmly the reins of his four horses . . . . the block
swags underneath on its tied-over chain,
The negro that drives the huge dray of the stoneyard . . . . steady
and tall he stands poised on one leg on the stringpiece,
His blue shirt exposes his ample neck and breast and loosens over
his hipband,
His glance is calm and commanding . . . . he tosses the slouch of his
hat away from his forehead,
The sun falls on his crispy hair and moustache . . . . falls on the
black of his polish'd and perfect limbs.

I behold the picturesque giant and love him . . . . and I do not stop
there,
I go with the team also.

In me the caresser of life wherever moving . . . . backward as well
as forward slueing,
To niches aside and junior bending.

Oxen that rattle the yoke or halt in the shade, what is that you
express in your eyes?
It seems to me more than all the print I have read in my life.

My tread scares the wood-drake and wood-duck on my distant and
daylong ramble,
They rise together, they slowly circle around.
. . . . I believe in those winged purposes,
And acknowledge the red yellow and white playing within me,
And consider the green and violet and the tufted crown intentional;
And do not call the tortoise unworthy because she is not something
else,
And the mocking bird in the swamp never studied the gamut, yet
trills pretty well to me,
And the look of the bay mare shames silliness out of me.

XIV

The wild gander leads his flock through the cool night,
Ya-honk! he says, and sounds it down to me like an invitation;
The pert may suppose it meaningless, but I listen closer,
I find its purpose and place up there toward the November sky.

The sharphoofed moose of the north, the cat on the housesill, the
chickadee, the prairie-dog,
The litter of the grunting sow as they tug at her teats,
The brood of the turkeyhen, and she with her halfspread wings,
I see in them and myself the same old law.

The press of my foot to the earth springs a hundred affections,
They scorn the best I can do to relate them.

I am enamoured of growing outdoors,
Of men that live among cattle or taste of the ocean or woods,
Of the builders and steerers of ships, of the wielders of axes and
mauls, of the drivers of horses,
I can eat and sleep with them week in and week out.

What is commonest and cheapest and nearest and easiest is Me,
Me going in for my chances, spending for vast returns,
Adorning myself to bestow myself on the first that will take me,
Not asking the sky to come down to my goodwill,
Scattering it freely forever.

XV

The pure contralto sings in the organloft,
The carpenter dresses his plank . . . . the tongue of his foreplane
whistles its wild ascending lisp,
The married and unmarried children ride home to their
thanksgiving dinner,

The pilot seizes the king-pin, he heaves down with a strong arm,
The mate stands braced in the whaleboat, lance and harpoon are ready,
The duck-shooter walks by silent and cautious stretches,
The deacons are ordained with crossed hands at the altar,
The spinning-girl retreats and advances to the hum of the big wheel,
The farmer stops by the bars of a Sunday and looks at the oats and rye,
The lunatic is carried at last to the asylum a confirmed case,
He will never sleep any more as he did in the cot in his mother's bedroom;
The jour printer with gray head and gaunt jaws works at his case,
He turns his quid of tobacco, his eyes get blurred with the manuscript;
The malformed limbs are tied to the anatomist's table,
What is removed drops horribly in a pail;
The quadroon girl is sold at the stand . . . . the drunkard nods by the barroom stove,
The machinist rolls up his sleeves . . . . the policeman travels his beat . . . . the gatekeeper marks who pass,
The young fellow drives the express-wagon . . . . I love him though I do not know him;
The half-breed straps on his light boots to compete in the race,
The western turkey-shooting draws old and young . . . . some lean on their rifles, some sit on logs,
Out from the crowd steps the marksman and takes his position and levels his piece;
The groups of newly-come immigrants cover the wharf or levee,
The woollypates hoe in the sugarfield, the overseer views them from his saddle;
The bugle calls in the ballroom, the gentlemen run for their partners, the dancers bow to each other;
The youth lies awake in the cedar-roofed garret and harks to the musical rain,
The Wolverine sets traps on the creek that helps fill the Huron,
The reformer ascends the platform, he spouts with his mouth and nose,
The company returns from its excursion, the darkey brings up the rear and bears the well-riddled target,
The squaw wrapt in her yellow-hemmed cloth is offering moccasins and beadbags for sale,
The connoisseur peers along the exhibition-gallery with halfshut eyes bent sideways,
The deckhands make fast the steamboat, the plank is thrown for the shoregoing passengers,
The young sister holds out the skein, the elder sister winds it off in a ball and stops now and then for the knots,
The one-year wife is recovering and happy, a week ago she bore her first child,

The cleanhaired Yankee girl works with her sewing-machine or in the factory or mill,
The nine months' gone is in the parturition chamber, her faintness and pains are advancing;
The pavingman leans on his twohanded rammer — the reporter's lead flies swiftly over the notebook — the signpainter is lettering with red and gold,
The canal-boy trots on the towpath — the bookkeeper counts at his desk — the shoemaker waxes his thread,
The conductor beats time for the band and all the performers follow him,
The child is baptised — the convert is making the first professions,
The regatta is spread on the bay . . . . how the white sails sparkle!
The drover watches his drove, he sings out to them that would stray,
The pedlar sweats with his pack on his back — purchaser higgles about the odd cent,
The camera and plate are prepared, the lady must sit for her daguerreotype,
The bride unrumples her white dress, the minutehand of the clock moves slowly,
The opium eater reclines with rigid head and just-opened lips,
The prostitute draggles her shawl, her bonnet bobs on her tipsy and pimpled neck,
The crowd laugh at her blackguard oaths, the men jeer and wink to each other,
(Miserable! I do not laugh at your oaths nor jeer you,)
The President holds a cabinet council, he is surrounded by the great secretaries,
On the piazza walk five friendly matrons with twined arms;
The crew of the fish-smack pack repeated layers of halibut in the hold,
The Missourian crosses the plains toting his wares and his cattle,
The fare-collector goes through the train — he gives notice by the jingling of loose change,
The floormen are laying the floor — the tinners are tinning the roof — the masons are calling for mortar,
In single file each shouldering his hod pass onward the laborers;
Seasons pursuing each other the indescribable crowd is gathered . . . . it is the Fourth of July . . . . what salutes of cannon and small arms!
Seasons pursuing each other the plougher ploughs and the mower mows and the wintergrain falls in the ground;
Off on the lakes the pikefisher watches and waits by the hole in the frozen surface,
The stumps stand thick round the clearing, the squatter strikes deep with his axe,
The flatboatmen make fast toward dusk near the cottonwood or pekantrees,

The coon-seekers go now through the regions of the Red river,
or through those drained by the Tennessee, or through those of
the Arkansas,
The torches shine in the dark that hangs on the Chattahoochee or
Altamahaw;
Patriarchs sit at supper with sons and grandsons and great grandsons
around them,
In walls of adobie, in canvas tents, rest hunters and trappers after
their day's sport.
The city sleeps and the country sleeps,
The living sleep for their time . . . . the dead sleep for their time,
The old husband sleeps by his wife and the young husband sleeps
by his wife;
And these one and all tend inward to me, and I tend outward to
them,
And such as it is to be of these more or less I am.

XVI

I am of old and young, of the foolish as much as the wise,
Regardless of others, ever regardful of others,
Maternal as well as paternal, a child as well as a man,
Stuffed with the stuff that is coarse, and stuffed with the stuff that
is fine,
One of the great nations, the nation of many nations — the smallest
the same and the largest the same,
A southerner soon as a northerner, a planter nonchalant and
hospitable,
A Yankee bound my own way . . . . ready for trade . . . . my joints
the limberest joints on earth and the sternest joints on earth,
A Kentuckian walking the vale of the Elkhorn in my deerskin
leggings,
A boatman over the lakes or bays or along coasts . . . . a Hoosier, a
Badger, a Buckeye,
A Louisianian or Georgian, a poke-easy from sandhills and pines,
At home on Canadian snowshoes or up in the bush, or with
fishermen off Newfoundland,
At home in the fleet of iceboats, sailing with the rest and tacking,
At home on the hills of Vermont or in the woods of Maine or the
Texan ranch,
Comrade of Californians . . . . comrade of free northwesterners,
loving their big proportions,
Comrade of raftsmen and coalmen — comrade of all who shake hands
and welcome to drink and meat;
A learner with the simplest, a teacher of the thoughtfulest,
A novice beginning experient of myriads of seasons,
Of every hue and trade and rank, of every caste and religion,
Not merely of the New World but of Africa Europe or Asia . . . . a
wandering savage,

A farmer, mechanic, or artist . . . . a gentleman, sailor, lover or quaker,
A prisoner, fancy-man, rowdy, lawyer, physician or priest.

I resist anything better than my own diversity,
And breathe the air and leave plenty after me,
And am not stuck up, and am in my place.

The moth and the fisheggs are in their place,
The suns I see and the suns I cannot see are in their place,
The palpable is in its place and the impalpable is in its place.

XVII

These are the thoughts of all men in all ages and lands, they are not original with me,
If they are not yours as much as mine they are nothing or next to nothing,
If they do not enclose everything they are next to nothing,
If they are not the riddle and the untying of the riddle they are nothing,
If they are not just as close as they are distant they are nothing.

This is the grass that grows wherever the land is and the water is,
This is the common air that bathes the globe.

This is the breath of laws and songs and behaviour,
This is the tasteless water of souls . . . . this is the true sustenance,
It is for the illiterate . . . . it is for the judges of the supreme court . . . . it is for the federal capitol and the state capitols,
It is for the admirable communes of literary men and composers and singers and lecturers and engineers and savans,
It is for the endless races of working people and farmers and seamen.

XVIII

This is the trill of a thousand clear cornets and scream of the octave flute and strike of triangles.
I play not a march for victors only . . . . I play great marches for conquered and slain persons.

Have you heard that it was good to gain the day?
I also say it is good to fall . . . . battles are lost in the same spirit in which they are won.

I sound triumphal drums for the dead . . . . I fling through my embouchures the loudest and gayest music to them,
Vivas to those who have failed, and to those whose war-vessels sank in the sea, and those themselves who sank in the sea,
And to all generals that lost engagements, and all overcome heroes, and the numberless unknown heroes equal to the greatest heroes known.

XIX

This is the meal pleasantly set . . . . this is the meat and drink for natural hunger,
It is for the wicked just the same as the righteous . . . . I make appointments with all,
I will not have a single person slighted or left away,
The keptwoman and sponger and thief are hereby invited . . . . the heavy-lipped slave is invited . . . . the venerealee is invited,
There shall be no difference between them and the rest.

This is the press of a bashful hand . . . . this is the float and odor of hair,
This is the touch of my lips to yours . . . . this is the murmur of yearning,
This is the far-off depth and height reflecting my own face,
This is the thoughtful merge of myself and the outlet again.

Do you guess I have some intricate purpose?
Well I have . . . . for the April rain has, and the mica on the side of a rock has.

Do you take it I would astonish?
Does the daylight astonish? or the early redstart twittering through the woods?
Do I astonish more than they?

This hour I tell things in confidence,
I might not tell everybody but I will tell you.

XX

Who goes there! hankering, gross, mystical, nude?
How is it I extract strength from the beef I eat?

What is a man anyhow? What am I? and what are you?
All I mark as my own you shall offset it with your own,
Else it were time lost listening to me.

I do not snivel that snivel the world over,
That months are vacuums and the ground but wallow and filth,
That life is a suck and a sell, and nothing remains at the end but threadbare crape and tears.

Whimpering and truckling fold with powders for invalids . . . . conformity goes to the fourth-removed,
I cock my hat as I please indoors or out.

Shall I pray? Shall I venerate and be ceremonious?
I have pried through the strata and analyzed to a hair,
And counselled with doctors and calculated close and found no sweeter fat than sticks to my own bones.

In all people I see myself, none more and not one a barleycorn less,
And the good or bad I say of myself I say of them.

And I know I am solid and sound,
To me the converging objects of the universe perpetually flow,
All are written to me, and I must get what the writing means.

And I know I am deathless,
I know this orbit of mine cannot be swept by a carpenter's compass,
I know I shall not pass like a child's carlacue cut with a burnt stick
at night.

I know I am august,
I do not trouble my spirit to vindicate itself or be understood,
I see that the elementary laws never apologize,
I reckon I behave no producer than the level I plant my house by
after all.

I exist as I am, that is enough,
If no other in the world be aware I sit content,
And if each and all be aware I sit content.

One world is aware, and by far the largest to me, and that is myself,
And whether I come to my own today or in ten thousand or ten
million years,
I can cheerfully take it now, or with equal cheerfulness I can wait.

My foothold is tenoned and mortised in granite,
I laugh at what you call dissolution,
And I know the amplitude of time.

XXI

I am the poet of the body,
And I am the poet of the soul.

The pleasures of heaven are with me, and the pains of hell are with
me,
The first I graft and increase upon myself . . . . the latter I translate
into a new tongue.

I am the poet of the woman the same as the man,
And I say it is as great to be a woman as to be a man,
And I say there is nothing greater than the mother of men.

I chant a new chant of dilation or pride,
We have had ducking and deprecating about enough,
I show that size is only development.

Have you outstript the rest? Are you the President?
It is a trifle . . . . they will more than arrive there every one, and
still pass on.

I am he that walks with the tender and growing night;
I call to the earth and sea half-held by the night.

Press close barebosomed night! Press close magnetic nourishing night!
Night of south winds! Night of the large few stars!
Still nodding night! Mad naked summer night!

Smile O voluptuous coolbreathed earth!
Earth of the slumbering and the liquid trees!
Earth of the departed sunset! Earth of the mountains misty-topt!
Earth of the vitreous pour of the full moon just tinged with blue!
Earth of shine and dark mottling the tide of the river!
Earth of the limpid gray of clouds brighter and clearer for my sake!
Far-swooping elbowed earth! Rich apple-blossomed earth!
Smile, for your lover comes!

Prodigal! you have given me love! . . . . therefore I to you give love!
O unspeakable passionate love!

Thruster holding me tight and that I hold tight!
We hurt each other as the bridegroom and the bride hurt each other.

XXII

You sea! I resign myself to you also . . . . I guess what you mean,
I behold from the beach your crooked inviting fingers,
I believe you refuse to go back without feeling of me;
We must have a turn together . . . . I undress . . . . hurry me out of
sight of the land,
Cushion me soft . . . . rock me in billowy drowse,
Dash me with amorous wet . . . . I can repay you.

Sea of stretched ground-swells!
Sea breathing broad and convulsive breaths!
Sea of the brine of life! Sea of unshovelled and always-ready graves!
Howler and scooper of storms! Capricious and dainty sea!
I am integral with you . . . . I too am of one phase and of all phases.

Partaker of influx and efflux . . . . extoller of hate and conciliation,
Extoller of amies and those that sleep in each others' arms.

I am he attesting sympathy;
Shall I make my list of things in the house and skip the house that
supports them?

I am the poet of commonsense and of the demonstrable and of
immortality;
And am not the poet of goodness only . . . . I do not decline to be
the poet of wickedness also.

Washes and razors for foofoos . . . . for me freckles and a bristling
beard.

What blurt is it about virtue and about vice?
Evil propels me, and reform of evil propels me . . . . I stand indifferent,
My gait is no faultfinder's or rejecter's gait,
I moisten the roots of all that has grown.

Did you fear some scrofula out of the unflagging pregnancy?
Did you guess the celestial laws are yet to be worked over and
rectified?

I step up to say that what we do is right and what we affirm is
right . . . . and some is only the ore of right,
Witnesses of us . . . . one side a balance and the antipodal side a
balance,
Soft doctrine as steady help as stable doctrine,
Thoughts and deeds of the present our rouse and early start.

This minute that comes to me over the past decillions,
There is no better than it and now.

What behaved well in the past or behaves well today is not such a
wonder,
The wonder is always and always how there can be a mean man or
an infidel.

XXIII

Endless unfolding of words of ages!
And mine a word of the modern . . . . a word en masse.

A word of the faith that never balks,
One time as good as another time . . . . here or henceforward it is
all the same to me.

A word of reality . . . . materialism first and last imbuing.

Hurrah for positive science! Long live exact demonstration!
Fetch stonecrop and mix it with cedar and branches of lilac;
This is the lexicographer or chemist . . . . this made a grammar of
the old cartouches,
These mariners put the ship through dangerous unknown seas,
This is the geologist, and this works with the scalpel, and this is a
mathematician.

Gentlemen I receive you, and attach and clasp hands with you,
The facts are usefull and real . . . . they are not my dwelling . . . . I enter by them to an area of the dwelling.

I am less the reminder of property or qualities, and more the reminder of life,
And go on the square for my own sake and for other's sake,
And make short account of neuters and geldings, and favor men and women fully equipped,
And beat the gong of revolt, and stop with fugitives and them that plot and conspire.

XXIV

Walt Whitman, an American, one of the roughs, a kosmos,
Disorderly fleshy and sensual . . . . eating drinking and breeding,
No sentimentalist . . . . no stander above men and women or apart from them . . . . no more modest than immodest.

Unscrew the locks from the doors!
Unscrew the doors themselves from their jambs!

Whoever degrades another degrades me . . . . and whatever is done or said returns at last to me,
And whatever I do or say I also return.

Through me the afflatus surging and surging . . . . through me the current and index.

I speak the password primeval . . . . I give the sign of democracy;
By God! I will accept nothing which all cannot have their counterpart on the same terms.

Through me many long dumb voices,
Voices of the interminable generations of slaves,
Voices of prostitutes and of deformed persons,
Voices of the diseased and despairing, and of thieves and dwarfs,
Voices of cycles of preparation and accretion,
And of the threads that connect the stars — and of wombs, and of the fatherstuff,
And of the rights of them the others are down upon,
Of the trivial and flat and foolish and despised,
Of fog in the air and beetles rolling balls of dung.

Through me forbidden voices,
Voices of sexes and lusts . . . . voices veiled, and I remove the veil,
Voices indecent by me clarified and transfigured.

I do not press my finger across my mouth,
I keep as delicate around the bowels as around the head and heart,
Copulation is no more rank to me than death is.

I believe in the flesh and the appetites,
Seeing hearing and feeling are miracles, and each part and tag of
 me is a miracle.

Divine am I inside and out, and I make holy whatever I touch or
 am touched from;
The scent of these arm-pits is aroma finer than prayer,
This head is more than churches or bibles or creeds.

If I worship any particular thing it shall be some of the spread of my
 body;
Translucent mould of me it shall be you,
Shaded ledges and rests, firm masculine coulter, it shall be you,
Whatever goes to the tilth of me it shall be you,
You my rich blood, your milky stream pale strippings of my life;
Breast that presses against other breasts it shall be you,
My brain it shall be your occult convolutions,
Root of washed sweet-flag, timorous pond-snipe, nest of guarded
 duplicate eggs, it shall be you,
Mixed tussled hay of head and beard and brawn it shall be you,
Trickling sap of maple, fibre of manly wheat, it shall be you;
Sun so generous it shall be you,
Vapors lighting and shading my face it shall be you,
You sweaty brooks and dews it shall be you,
Winds whose soft-tickling genitals rub against me it shall be you,
Broad muscular fields, branches of liveoak, loving lounger in my
 winding paths, it shall be you,
Hands I have taken, face I have kissed, mortal I have ever touched,
 it shall be you.

I dote on myself . . . . there is that lot of me, and all so luscious,
Each moment and whatever happens thrills me with joy.

I cannot tell how my ankles bend . . . . nor whence the cause of my
 faintest wish,
Nor the cause of the friendship I emit . . . . nor the cause of the
 friendship I take again.

To walk up my stoop is unaccountable . . . . I pause to consider if it
 really be,
That I eat and drink is spectacle enough for the great authors and
 schools,
A morning-glory at my window satisfies me more than the
 metaphysics of books.

To behold the daybreak!
The little light fades the immense and diaphanous shadows,
The air tastes good to my palate.

Hefts of the moving world at innocent gambols, silently rising,
    freshly exuding,
Scooting obliquely high and low.

Something I cannot see puts upward libidinous prongs,
Seas of bright juice suffuse heaven.

The earth by the sky staid with .... the daily close of their junction,
The heaved challenge from the east that moment over my head,
The mocking taunt, See then whether you shall be master!

XXV

Dazzling and tremendous how quick the sunrise would kill me,
If I could not now and always send sunrise out of me.

We also ascend dazzling and tremendous as the sun,
We found our own my soul in the calm and cool of the daybreak.

My voice goes after what my eyes cannot reach,
With the twirl of my tongue I encompass worlds and volumes of
    worlds.

Speech is the twin of my vision .... it is unequal to measure itself.
It provokes me forever,
It says sarcastically, Walt, you understand enough .... why don't
    you let it out then?

Come now I will not be tantalized .... you conceive too much of
    articulation.

Do you not know how the buds beneath are folded?
Waiting in gloom protected by frost,
The dirt receding before my prophetical screams,
I underlying causes to balance them at last,
My knowledge my live parts .... it keeping tally with the meaning
    of things,
Happiness .... which whoever hears me let him or her set out in
    search of this day.

My final merit I refuse you .... I refuse putting from me the best
    I am.

Encompass worlds but never try to encompass me,
I crowd your noisiest talk by looking toward you.

Writing and talk do not prove me,
I carry the plenum of proof and every thing else in my face,
With the hush of my lips I confound the topmost skeptic.

XXVI

I think I will do nothing for a long time but listen,
And accrue what I hear into myself . . . . and let sounds contribute
toward me.

I hear the bravuras of birds . . . . the bustle of growing wheat . . . .
gossip of flames . . . . clack of sticks cooking my meals.

I hear the sound of the human voice . . . . a sound I love,
I hear all sounds as they are tuned to their uses . . . . sounds of the
city and sounds out of the city . . . . sounds of the day and night;
Talkative young ones to those that like them . . . . the recitative of
fish-pedlars and fruit-pedlars . . . . the loud laugh of workpeople
at their meals,
The angry base of disjointed friendship . . . . the faint tones of
the sick,
The judge with hands tight to the desk, his shaky lips pronouncing
a death-sentence,
The heave'e'yo of stevedores unlading ships by the wharves . . . . the
refrain of the anchor-lifters;
The ring of alarm-bells . . . . the cry of fire . . . . the whirr of swift-
streaking engines and hose-carts with premonitory tinkles
and colored lights,
The steam-whistle . . . . the solid roll of the train of approaching cars;
The slow-march played at night at the head of the association,
They go to guard some corpse . . . . the flag-tops are draped with
black muslin.

I hear the violincello or man's heart complaint,
And hear the keyed cornet or else the echo of sunset.

I hear the chorus . . . . it is a grand-opera . . . . this indeed is music!

A tenor large and fresh as the creation fills me,
The orbic flex of his mouth is pouring and filling me full.

I hear the trained soprano . . . . she convulses me like the climax of
my love-grip;
The orchestra whirls me wider than Uranus flies;
It wrenches unnamable ardors from my breast,
It throbs me to gulps of the farthest down horror,
It sails me . . . . I dab with bare feet . . . . they are licked by the
indolent waves,
I am exposed . . . . cut by bitter and poisoned hail,
Steeped amid honeyed morphine . . . . my windpipe squeezed in the
fakes of death,
Let up again to feel the puzzle of puzzles,
And that we call Being.

XXVII

To be in any form, what is that?
If nothing lay more developed the quahaug and its callous shell were enough.

Mine is no callous shell,
I have instant conductors all over me whether I pass or stop,
They seize every object and lead it harmlessly through me.

I merely stir, press, feel with my fingers, and am happy,
To touch my person to some one else's is about as much as I can stand.

XXVIII

Is this then a touch? . . . . quivering me to a new identity,
Flames and ether making a rush for my veins,
Treacherous tip of me reaching and crowding to help them,
My flesh and blood playing out lightning, to strike what is hardly different from myself,
On all sides prurient provokers stiffening my limbs,
Straining the udder of my heart for its withheld drip,
Behaving licentious toward me, taking no denial,
Depriving me of my best as for a purpose,
Unbuttoning my clothes and holding me by the bare waist,
Deluding my confusion with the calm of the sunlight and pasture fields,
Immodestly sliding the fellow-senses away,
They bribed to swap off with touch, and go and graze at the edges of me,
No consideration, no regard for my draining strength or my anger,
Fetching the rest of the herd around to enjoy them awhile,
Then all uniting to stand on a headland and worry me.

The sentries desert every other part of me,
They have left me helpless to a red marauder,
They all come to the headland to witness and assist against me.

I am given up by traitors;
I talk wildly . . . . I have lost my wits . . . . I and nobody else am the greatest traitor,
I went myself first to the headland . . . . my own hands carried me there.

You villain touch! what are you doing? . . . . my breath is tight in its throat;
Unclench your floodgates! you are too much for me.

XXIX

Blind loving wrestling touch! Sheathed hooded sharptoothed touch!
Did it make you ache so leaving me?

Parting tracked by arriving . . . . perpetual payment of the perpetual
loan,
Rich showering rain, and recompense richer afterward.

Sprouts take and accumulate . . . . stand by the curb prolific and vital,
Landscapes projected masculine full-sized and golden.

XXX

All truths wait in all things,
They neither hasten their own delivery nor resist it,
They do not need the obstetric forceps of the surgeon,
The insignificant is as big to me as any,
What is less or more than a touch?

Logic and sermons never convince,
The damp of the night drives deeper into my soul.

Only what proves itself to every man and woman is so,
Only what nobody denies is so.

A minute and a drop of me settle my brain;
I believe the soggy clods shall become lovers and lamps,
And a compend of compends is the meat of a man or woman,
And a summit and flower there is the feeling they have for each other,
And they are to branch boundlessly out of that lesson until it
becomes omnific,
And until every one shall delight us, and we them.

XXXI

I believe a leaf of grass is no less than the journeywork of the stars,
And the pismire is equally perfect, and a grain of sand, and the egg
of the wren,
And the tree-toad is a chef-d'œuvre for the highest,
And the running blackberry would adorn the parlors of heaven,
And the narrowest hinge in my hand puts to scorn all machinery,
And the cow crunching with depressed head surpasses any statue,
And a mouse is miracle enough to stagger sextillions of infidels,
And I could come every afternoon of my life to look at the farmer's
girl boiling her iron tea-kettle and baking shortcake.

I find I incorporate gneiss and coal and long-threaded moss and
fruits and grains and esculent roots,
And am stucco'd with quadrupeds and birds all over,
And have distanced what is behind me for good reasons,
And call any thing close again when I desire it.

In vain the speeding or shyness,
In vain the plutonic rocks send their old heat against my approach,
In vain the mastodon retreats beneath its own powdered bones,

In vain objects stand leagues off and assume manifold shapes,
In vain the ocean settling in hollows and the great monsters lying low,
In vain the buzzard houses herself with the sky,
In vain the snake slides through the creepers and logs,
In vain the elk takes to the inner passes of the woods,
In vain the razorbilled auk sails far north to Labrador,
I follow quickly . . . . I ascend to the nest in the fissure of the cliff.

XXXII

I think I could turn and live awhile with the animals . . . . they are
so placid and self-contained,
I stand and look at them sometimes half the day long.

They do not sweat and whine about their condition,
They do not lie awake in the dark and weep for their sins,
They do not make me sick discussing their duty to God,
Not one is dissatisfied . . . . not one is demented with the mania of
owning things,
Not one kneels to another nor to his kind that lived thousands of
years ago,
Not one is respectable or industrious over the whole earth.

So they show their relations to me and I accept them;
They bring me tokens of myself . . . . they evince them plainly in
their possession.

I do not know where they got those tokens,
I must have passed that way untold times ago and negligently dropt
them,
Myself moving forward then and now and forever,
Gathering and showing more always and with velocity,
Infinite and omnigenous and the like of these among them;
Not too exclusive toward the reachers of my remembrancers,
Picking out here one that shall be my amie,
Choosing to go with him on brotherly terms.

A gigantic beauty of a stallion, fresh and responsive to my caresses,
Head high in the forehead and wide between the ears,
Limbs glossy and supple, tail dusting the ground,
Eyes well apart and full of sparkling wickedness . . . . ears finely cut
and flexibly moving.

His nostrils dilate . . . . my heels embrace him . . . . his well built limbs
tremble with pleasure . . . . we speed around and return.

I but use you a moment and then I resign you stallion . . . . and do
not need your paces, and outgallop them,
And myself as I stand or sit pass faster than you.

XXXIII

Swift wind! Space! My Soul! Now I know it is true what I guessed at;
What I guessed when I loafed on the grass,
What I guessed when I lay alone in my bed . . . . and again as I walked the beach under the paling stars of the morning.

My ties and ballasts leave me . . . . I travel . . . . I sail . . . . my elbows rest in the sea-gaps,
I skirt the sierras . . . . my palms cover continents,
I am afoot with my vision.

By the city's quadrangular houses . . . . in log-huts, or camping with lumbermen,
Along the ruts of the turnpike . . . . along the dry gulch and rivulet bed,
Hoeing my onion-patch, and rows of carrots and parsnips . . . . crossing savannas . . . . trailing in forests,
Prospecting . . . . gold-digging . . . . girdling the trees of a new purchase,
Scorched ankle-deep by the hot sand . . . . hauling my boat down the shallow river;
Where the panther walks to and fro on a limb overhead . . . . where the buck turns furiously at the hunter,
Where the rattlesnake suns his flabby length on a rock . . . . where the otter is feeding on fish,
Where the alligator in his tough pimples sleeps by the bayou,
Where the black bear is searching for roots or honey . . . . where the beaver pats the mud with his paddle-tail;
Over the growing sugar . . . . over the cottonplant . . . . over the rice in its low moist field;
Over the sharp-peaked farmhouse with its scalloped scum and slender shoots from the gutters;
Over the western persimmon . . . . over the longleaved corn and the delicate blue-flowered flax;
Over the white and brown buckwheat, a hummer and a buzzer there with the rest,
Over the dusky green of the rye as it ripples and shades in the breeze;
Scaling mountains . . . . pulling myself cautiously up . . . . holding on by low scragged limbs,
Walking the path worn in the grass and beat through the leaves of the brush;
Where the quail is whistling betwixt the woods and the wheatlot,
Where the bat flies in the July eve . . . . where the great goldbug drops through the dark;
Where the flails keep time on the barn floor,
Where the brook puts out of the roots of the old tree and flows to the meadow,
Where cattle stand and shake away flies with the tremulous shuddering of their hides,

Where the cheese-cloth hangs in the kitchen, and andironus straddle
the hearth-slab, and cobwebs fall in festoons from the rafters;
Where triphammers crash . . . . where the press is whirling its
cylinders;
Wherever the human heart beats with terrible throes out of its ribs;
Where the pear-shaped balloon is floating aloft . . . . floating in it
myself and looking composedly down;
Where the life-car is drawn on the slipnoose . . . . where the heat
hatches pale-green eggs in the dented sand,
Where the she-whale swims with her calves and never forsakes them,
Where the steamship trails hindways its long pennant of smoke,
Where the ground-shark's fin cuts like a black chip out of the water,
Where the half-burned brig is riding on unknown currents,
Where shells grow to her slimy deck, and the dead are corrupting
below;
Where the striped and starred flag is borne at the head of the
regiments;
Approaching Manhattan, up by the long-stretching island,
Under Niagara, the cataract falling like a veil over my countenance;
Upon a door-step . . . . upon the horse-block of hard wood outside,
Upon the race-course, or enjoying pic-nics or jigs or a good game
of base-ball,
At he-festivals with blackguard jibes and ironical license and bull-
dances and drinking and laughter,
At the cider-mill, tasting the sweet of the brown squash . . . . sucking
the juice through a straw,
At apple-peelings, wanting kisses for all the red fruit I find,
At musters and beach-parties and friendly bees and huskings and
house-raisings;
Where the mockingbird sounds his delicious gurgles, and cackles and
screams and weeps,
Where the hay-rick stands in the barnyard, and the dry-stalks are
scattered, and the brood cow waits in the hovel,
Where the bull advances to do his masculine work, and the stud to
the mare, and the cock is treading the hen,
Where the heifers browse, and the geese nip their food with short jerks;
Where the sundown shadows lengthen over the limitless and lone-
some prairie,
Where the herds of buffalo make a crawling spread of the square
miles far and near;
Where the hummingbird shimmers . . . . where the neck of the
longlived swan is curving and winding;
Where the laughing-gull scoots by the slappy shore and laughs her
near-human laugh;
Where beehives range on a gray bench in the garden half-hid by
the high weeds;
Where the band-necked partridges roost in a ring on the ground
with their heads out;

Where burial coaches enter the arched gates of a cemetery;
Where winter wolves bark amid wastes of snow and icicled trees;
Where the yellow-crowned heron comes to the edge of the marsh at
night and feeds upon small crabs;
Where the splash of swimmers and divers cools the warm noon;
Where the katydid works her chromatic reed on the walnut-tree
over the well;
Through patches of citrons and cucumbers with silver-wired leaves,
Through the salt-lick or orange glade . . . . or under conical firs;
Through the gymnasium . . . . through the curtained saloon . . . .
through the office or public hall;
Pleased with the native and pleased with the foreign . . . . pleased
with the new and old,
Pleased with women, the homely as well as the handsome,
Pleased with the quakeress as she puts off her bonnet and talks
melodiously,
Pleased with the primitive tunes of the choir of the whitewashed
church,
Pleased with the earnest words of the sweating Methodist preacher,
or any preacher . . . . looking seriously at the camp-meeting;
Looking in at the shop-windows in Broadway the whole forenoon
. . . . pressing the flesh of my nose to the thick plate-glass,
Wandering the same afternoon with my face turned up to the clouds;
My right and left arms round the sides of two friends and I in the
middle;
Coming home with the bearded and dark-cheeked bush-boy . . . .
riding behind him at the drape of the day;
Far from the settlements studying the print of animals' feet, or the
moccasin print;
By the cot in the hospital reaching lemonade to a feverish patient,
By the coffined corpse when all is still, examining with a candle;
Voyaging to every port to dicker and adventure;
Hurrying with the modern crowd, as eager and fickle as any,
Hot toward one I hate, ready in my madness to knife him;
Solitary at midnight in my back yard, my thoughts gone from me a
long while,
Walking the old hills of Judea with the beautiful gentle god by my
side;
Speeding through space . . . . speeding through heaven and the stars,
Speeding amid the seven satellites and the broad ring and the
diameter of eighty thousand miles,
Speeding with tailed meteors . . . . throwing fire-balls like the rest,
Carrying the crescent child that carries its own full mother in its
belly:
Storming enjoying planning loving cautioning,
Backing and filling, appearing and disappearing,
I tread day and night such roads.

I visit the orchards of God and look at the spheric product,
And look at quintillions ripened, and look at quintillions green.

I fly the flight of the fluid and swallowing soul,
My course runs below the soundings of plummets.

I help myself to material and immaterial,
No guard can shut me off, no law can prevent me.

I anchor my ship for a little while only,
My messengers continually cruise away or bring their returns
to me.

I go hunting polar furs and the seal . . . . leaping chasms with a
pike-pointed staff . . . . clinging to topples of brittle and blue.

I ascend to the foretruck . . . . I take my place late at night in the
crow's nest . . . . we sail through the arctic sea . . . . it is plenty
light enough,
Through the clear atmosphere I stretch around on the wonderful
beauty,
The enormous masses of ice pass me and I pass them . . . . the
scenery is plain in all directions,
The white-topped mountains point up in the distance . . . . I fling
out my fancies toward them;
We are about approaching some great battlefield in which we are
soon to be engaged,
We pass the colossal outposts of the encampment . . . . we pass with
still feet and caution;
Or we are entering by the suburbs some vast and ruined city . . . .
the blocks and fallen architecture more than all the living cities
of the globe.

I am a free companion . . . . I bivouac by invading watchfires.

I turn the bridegroom out of bed and stay with the bride myself,
And tighten her all night to my thighs and lips.

My voice is the wife's voice, the screech by the rail of the stairs,
They fetch my man's body up dripping and drowned.

I understand the large hearts of heroes,
The courage of present times and all times;
How the skipper saw the crowded and rudderless wreck of the
steamship, and death chasing it up and down the storm,
How he knuckled tight and gave not back one inch, and was
faithful of days and faithful of nights,
And chalked in large letters on a board, Be of good cheer, We will
not desert you;

How he saved the drifting company at last,
How the lank loose-gowned women looked when boated from the
 side of their prepared graves,
How the silent old-faced infants, and the lifted sick, and the sharp-
 lipped unshaved men;
All this I swallow and it tastes good . . . . I like it well, and it
 becomes mine,
I am the man . . . . I suffered . . . . I was there.

The disdain and calmness of martyrs,
The mother condemned for a witch and burnt with dry wood, and
 her children gazing on;
The hounded slave that flags in the race and leans by the fence,
 blowing and covered with sweat,
The twinges that sting like needles his legs and neck,
The murderous buckshot and the bullets,
All these I feel or am.

I am the hounded slave . . . . I wince at the bite of the dogs,
Hell and despair are upon me . . . . crack and again crack the
 marksmen,
I clutch the rails of the fence . . . . my gore dribs thinned with the
 ooze of my skin,
I fall on the weeds and stones,
The riders spur their unwilling horses and haul close,
They taunt my dizzy ears . . . . they beat me violently over the head
with their whip-stocks.

Agonies are one of my changes of garments;
I do not ask the wounded person how he feels . . . . I myself
 become the wounded person,
My hurt turns livid upon me as I lean on a cane and observe.

I am the mashed fireman with breastbone broken . . . . tumbling
 walls buried me in their debris,
Heat and smoke I inspired . . . . I heard the yelling shouts of my
 comrades,
I heard the distant click of their picks and shovels;
They have cleared the beams away . . . . they tenderly lift me forth.

I lie in the night air in my red shirt . . . . the pervading hush is for
 my sake,
Painless after all I lie, exhausted but not so unhappy,
White and beautiful are the faces around me . . . . the heads are
 bared of their fire-caps,
The kneeling crowd fades with the light of the torches.

Distant and dead resuscitate,
They show as the dial or move as the hands of me . . . . and I am the clock myself.

I am an old artillerist, and tell of some fort's bombardment . . . . and am there again.

Again the reveille of drummers . . . . again the attacking cannon and mortars and howitzers,
Again the attacked send their cannon responsive.

I take part . . . . I see and hear the whole,
The cries and curses and roar . . . . the plaudits for well aimed shots,
The ambulanza slowly passing and trailing its red drip,
Workmen searching after damages and to make indispensable repairs,
The fall of grenades through the rent roof . . . . the fan-shaped explosion,
The whizz of limbs heads stone wood and iron high in the air.

Again gurgles the mouth of my dying general . . . . he furiously waves with his hand,
He gasps through the clot . . . . Mind not me . . . . mind . . . . the entrenchments.

XXXIV

I tell not the fall of Alamo . . . . not one escaped to tell the fall of Alamo,
The hundred and fifty are dumb yet at Alamo.

Hear now the tale of a jetblack sunrise,
Hear of the murder in cold blood of four hundred and twelve young men.

Retreating they had formed in a hollow square with their baggage for breastworks,
Nine hundred lives out of the surrounding enemy's nine times their number was the price they took in advance,
Their colonel was wounded and their ammunition gone,
They treated for an honorable capitulation, received writing and seal, gave up their arms, and marched back prisoners of war.

They were the glory of the race of rangers,
Matchless with a horse, a rifle, a song, a supper or a courtship,
Large, turbulent, brave, handsome, generous, proud and affectionate,
Bearded, sunburnt, dressed in the free costume of hunters,
Not a single one over thirty years of age.

The second Sunday morning they were brought out in squads and massacred . . . . it was beautiful early summer,
The work commenced about five o'clock and was over by eight.

None obeyed the command to kneel,
Some made a mad and helpless rush . . . . some stood stark and straight,
A few fell at once, shot in the temple or heart . . . . the living and dead lay together,
The maimed and mangled dug in the dirt . . . . the new-comers saw them there;
Some half-killed attempted to crawl away,
There were dispatched with bayonets or battered with the blunts of muskets;
A youth not seventeen years old seized his assassin till two more came to release him,
The three were all torn, and covered with the boy's blood.

At eleven o'clock began the burning of the bodies;
And that is the tale of the murder of the four hundred and twelve young men,
And that was a jetblack sunrise.

XXXV

Did you read in the seabooks of the oldfashioned frigate-fight?
Did you learn who won by the light of the moon and stars?

Our foe was no skulk in his ship, I tell you,
His was the English pluck, and there is no tougher or truer, and never was, and never will be;
Along the lowered eve he came, horribly raking us.

We closed with him . . . . the yards entangled . . . . the cannon touched,
My captain lashed fast with his own hands.

We had received some eighteen-pound shots under the water,
On our lower-gun-deck two large pieces had burst at the first fire, killing all around and blowing up overhead.

Ten o'clok at night, and the full moon shining and the leaks on the gain, and five feet of water reported,
The master-at-arms loosing the prisoners confined in the after-hold to give them chance for themselves.

The transit to and from magazine was now stopped by the sentinels,
They saw so many strange faces they did not know whom to trust.

Our frigate was afire . . . . the other asked if we demanded quarters?
    if our colors were struck and the fighting done?

I laughed content when I heard the voice of my little captain,
We have not struck, he composedly cried, We have just begun our
    part of the fighting.

Only three guns were in use,
One was directed by the captain himself against the enemy's
    mainmast,
Two well-served with grape and canister silenced his musketry and
    cleared his decks.

The tops alone seconded the fire of this little battery, especially the
    maintop,
They all held out bravely during whole of the action.

Not a moment's cease,
The leaks gained fast on the pumps . . . . the fire eat toward the
    powder-magazine,
One of the pumps was shot away . . . . it was generally thought we
    were sinking.

Serene stood the little captain,
He was not hurried . . . . his voice was neither high nor low,
His eyes gave more light to us than our battle-lanterns.

Toward twelve at night, there in the beams of the moon they
surrendered to us.

XXXVI

Stretched and still lay the midnight,
Two great hulls motionless on the breast of the darkness,
Our vessel riddled and slowly sinking . . . . preparations to pass to the
    one we had conquered,
The captain on the quarter deck coldly giving his orders through a
    countenance white as a sheet,
Near by the corpse of the child that served in the cabin,
The dead face of an old salt with long white hair and carefully
    curled whiskers,
The flames spite of all that could be done flickering aloft and
    below,
The husky voices of the two or three officers yet fit for duty,
Formless stacks of bodies and bodies by themselves . . . . dabs of flesh
    upon the masts and spars,
The cut of cordage and dangle of rigging . . . . the slight shock of the
    soothe of waves,

Black and impassive guns, and litter of powder-parcels, and the strong scent,
Delicate sniffs of the seabreeze . . . . smells of sedgy grass and fields by the shore . . . . death-messages given in charge to survivors,
The hiss of the surgeon's knife and the gnawing teeth of his saw,
The wheeze, the cluck, the swash of falling blood . . . . the short wild scream, the long dull tapering groan,
These so . . . . these irretrievable.

XXXVII

O Christ! My fit is mastering me!
What the rebel said gaily adjusting his throat to the rope-noose,
What the savage at the stump, his eye-sockets empty, his mouth spirting whoops and defiance,
What stills the traveler come to the vault at Mount Vernon,
What sobers the Brooklyn boy as he looks down the shores of the Wallabout and remembers the prison ships,
What burnt the gums of the redcoat at Saratoga when he surrendered his brigades,
These become mine and me every one, and they are but little,
I become as much more as I like.

I become any presence or truth of humanity here,
And see myself in prison shaped like another man,
And feel the dull unintermitted pain.

For me the keepers of convicts shoulder their carbines and keep watch,
It is I let out in the morning and barred at night.

Not a mutineer walks handcuffed to the jail, but I am handcuffed to him and walk by his side,
I am less the jolly one there, and more the silent one with sweat on my twitching lips.

Not a youngster is taken for larceny, but I go too and am tried and sentenced.

Not a cholera patient lies at the last gasp, but I also lie at the last gasp,
My face is ash-colored, my sinews gnarl . . . . away from me people retreat.

Askers embody themselves in me, and I am embodied in them,
I project my hat and sit shamefaced and beg.

I rise extatic through all, and sweep with the true gravitation,
The whirling and whirling is elemental within me.

XXXVIII

Somehow I have been stunned. Stand back!
Give me a little time beyond my cuffed head and slumbers and dreams and gaping
I discover myself on a verge of the usual mistake.

That I could forget the mockers and insults!
That I could forget the trickling tears and the blows of the bludgeons and hammers!
That I could look with a separate look on my own crucifixion and bloody crowning!

I remember . . . . I resume the overstaid fraction,
The grave of rock multiplies what has been confided to it . . . . or to any graves,
The corpses rise . . . . the gashes heal . . . . the fastenings roll away.

I troop forth replenished with supreme power, one of an average unending procession,
We walk the roads of Ohio and Massachusetts and Virginia and Wisconsin and New York and New Orleans and Texas and Montreal and San Francisco and Charleston and Savannah and Mexico,
Inland and by the seacoast and boundary lines . . . . and we pass the boundary lines.

Our swift ordinances are on their way over the whole earth,
The blossoms we wear in our hats are the growth of two thousand years.

Eleves I salute you,
I see the approach of your numberless gangs . . . . I see you understand yourselves and me,
And know that they who have eyes are divine, and the blind and lame are equally divine,
And that my steps drag behind yours yet go before them,
And are aware how I am with you no more than I am with everybody.

XXXIX

The friendly and flowing savage . . . . Who is he?
Is he waiting for civilization or past it and mastering it?

Is he some southwesterner raised outdoors? Is he Canadian?
Is he from the Mississippi country? or from Iowa, Oregon or California? or from the mountain? or prairie life or bush-life? or from the sea?

Wherever he goes men and women accept and desire him,
They desire he should like them and touch them and speak to them and stay with them.

Behaviour lawless as snow-flakes .... words simple as grass .... uncombed head and laughter and naivete;
Slowstepping feet and the common features, and the common modes and emanations,
They descend in new forms from the tips of his fingers,
They are wafted with the odor of his body or breath .... they fly out of the glance of his eyes.

XL

Flaunt of the sunshine I need not your bask .... lie over,
You light surfaces only .... I force the surfaces and the depths also.

Earth! you seem to look for something at my hands,
Say old topknot! what do you want?

Man or woman! I might tell how I like you, but cannot,
And might tell what it is in me and what it is in you, but cannot,
And might tell the pinings I have .... the pulse of my nights and days.

Behold I do not give lectures or a little charity,
What I give I give out of myself.

You there, impotent, loose in the knees, open your scarfed chops till I blow grit within you,
Spread your palms and lift the flaps of your pockets,
I am not to be denied .... I compel .... I have stores plenty and to spare,
And any thing I have I bestow.

I do not ask who you are .... that is not important to me,
You can do nothing and be nothing but what I will infold you.

To a drudge of the cottonfields or emptier of privies I lean .... on his right cheek I put the family kiss,
And in my soul I swear I never will deny him.

On women fit for conception I start bigger and nimbler babes,
This day I am jetting the stuff of far more arrogant republics.

To any one dying .... thither I speed and twist the knob of the door,
Turn the bedclothes toward the foot of the bed,
Let the physician and the priest go home.

I seize the descending man . . . . I raise him with resistless will.

O despairer, here is my neck,
By God! you shall not go down! Hang your whole weight upon me.

I dilate you with tremendous breath . . . . I buoy you up;
Every room of the house do I fill with an armed force . . . . lovers of
me, bafflers of graves:
Sleep! I and they keep guard all night;
Not doubt, not decease shall dare to lay finger upon you,
I have embraced you, and henceforth possess you to myself,
And when you rise in the morning you will find what I tell you is so.

XLI

I am he bringing help for the sick as they pant on their backs,
And for strong upright men I bring yet more needed help.

I heard what was said of the universe,
Heard it and heard of several thousand years;
It is middling well as far as it goes . . . . but is that all?

Magnifying and applying come I,
Outbidding at the start the old cautious hucksters,
The most they offer for mankind and eternity less than a spirit of my
own seminal wet,
Taking myself the exact dimensions of Jehovah and laying them away,
Lithographing Kronos and Zeus his son, and Hercules his grandson,
Buying drafts of Osiris and Isis and Belus and Brahma and Adonai,
In my portfolio placing Manito loose, and Allah on a leaf, and the
crucifix engraved,
With Odin, and the hideous-faced Mexitli, and all idols and images,
Honestly taking them all for what they are worth, and not a cent more,
Admitting they were alive and did the work of their day,
Admitting they bore mites as for unfledged birds who have now
to rise and fly and sing for themselves,
Accepting the rough deific sketches to fill out better in myself . . . .
bestowing them freely on each man and woman I see,
Discovering as much or more in a framer framing a house,
Putting higher claims for him there with his rolled-up sleeves, driving
the mallet and chisel;
Not objecting to special revelations . . . . considering a curl of smoke
or a hair on the back of my hand as curious as any revelation;
Those ahold of fire-engines and hook-and-ladder ropes more to me
than the gods of the antique wars,
Minding their voices peal through the crash of destruction,
Their brawny limbs passing safe over charred laths . . . . their white
foreheads whole and unhurt out of the flames;

By the mechanic's wife with her babe at her nipple interceding for
every person born;
Three scythes at harvest whizzing in a row from three lusty angels
with shirts bagged out at their waists;
The snag-toothed hostler with red hair redeeming sins past and to
come,
Selling all he possesses and traveling on foot to fee lawyers for his
brother and sit by him while he is tried for forgery:
What was strewn in the amplest strewing the square rod about me,
and not filling the square rod then;
The bull and the bug never worshipped half enough,
Dung and dirt more admirable than was dreamed,
The supernatural of no account . . . . myself waiting my time to be
one of the supremes,
The day getting ready for me when I shall do as much good as the
best, and be as prodigious,
Guessing when I am it will not tickle me much to receive puffs out of
pulpit or print;
By my life-lumps! becoming already a creator!
Putting myself here and now to the ambushed womb of the shadows!

XLII

. . . . A call in the midst of the crowd,
My own voice, orotund sweeping and final.

Come my children,
Come my boys and girls, and my women and household and intimates,
Now the performer launches his nerve . . . . he has passed his
prelude on the reeds within.

Easily written loosefingered chords! I feel the thrum of their climax
and close.

My head evolves on my neck,
Music rolls, but not from the organ . . . . folks are around me, but
they are no household of mine.

Ever the hard and unsunk ground,
Ever the eaters and drinkers . . . . ever the upward and downward
sun . . . . ever the air and ceaseless tides,
Ever myself and my neighbors, refreshing and wicked and real,
Ever the old inexplicable query . . . . ever that thorned thumb — that
breath of itches and thirsts,
Ever the vexer's hoot! hoot! till we find where the sly one hides and
bring him forth;
Ever love . . . . ever the sobbing liquid of life,
Ever the bandage under the chin . . . . ever the trestles of death.

Here and there with dimes on the eyes walking,
To feed the greed of the belly the brains liberally spooning,
Tickets buying or taking or selling, but in to the feast never once
 going;
Many sweating and ploughing and thrashing, and then the chaff
 for payment receiving,
A few idly owning, and they the wheat continually claiming.

This is the city . . . . and I am one of the citizens;
Whatever interests the rest interests me . . . . politics, churches,
 newspapers, schools,
Benevolent societies, improvements, banks, tariffs, steamships,
 factories, markets,
Stocks and stores and real estate and personal estate.

They who piddle and patter here in collars and tailed coats I
 am aware who they are . . . . and that they are not worms
 or fleas,
I acknowledge the duplicates of myself under all the scrape-lipped
 and pipe-legged concealments.

The weakest and shallowest is deathless with me,
What I do and say the same waits for them,
Every thought that flounders in me the same flounders in them.

I know perfectly well my own egotism,
And know my omnivorous words, and cannot say any less,
And would fetch you whoever you are flush with myself.

My words are words of a questioning, and to indicate reality;
This printed and bound book . . . . but the printer and the printing-
 office boy?
The marriage estate and settlement . . . . but the body and mind of
 the bridegroom? also those of the bride?
The panorama of the sea . . . . but the sea itself?
The well-taken photographs . . . . but your wife or friend close and
 solid in your arms?
The fleet of ships of the line and all the modern improvements . . . .
 but the craft and pluck of the admiral?
The dishes and fare and furniture . . . . but the host and hostess, and
 the look out of their eyes?
The sky up there . . . . yet here or next door or across the way?
The saints and sages in history . . . . but you yourself?
Sermons and creeds and theology . . . . but the human brain, and
 what is called reason, and what is called love, and what is
 called life?

XLIII

I do not despise you priests;
My faith is the greatest of faiths and the least of faiths,

Enclosing all worship ancient and modern, and all between ancient and modern,
Believing I shall come again upon the earth after five thousand years,
Waiting responses from oracles . . . . honoring the gods . . . . saluting the sun,
Making a fetish of the first rock or stump . . . . powowing with sticks in the circle of obis,
Helping the lama or brahmin as he trims the lamps of the idols,
Dancing yet through the streets in a phalic procession . . . . rapt and austere in the woods, a gymnosophist,
Drinking mead from the skull-cup . . . . to shasta and vedas admirant . . . . minding the koran,
Walking the teokallis, spotted with gore from the stone and knife — beating the serpent-skin drum;
Accepting the gospels, accepting him that was crucified, knowing assuredly that he is divine,
To the mass kneeling — to the puritan's prayer rising — sitting patiently in a pew,
Ranting and frothing in my insane crisis — waiting dead-like till my spirit arouses me;
Looking forth on pavement and land, and outside of pavement and land,
Belonging to the winders of the circuit of circuits.

One of that centripetal and centrifugal gang,
I turn and talk like a man leaving charges before a journey.

Down-hearted doubters, dull and excluded,
Frivolous sullen moping angry affected disheartened atheistical,
I know every one of you, and know the unspoken interrogatories,
By experience I know them.

How the flukes splash!
How they contort rapid as lightning, with spasms and spouts of blood!

Be at peace bloody flukes of doubters and sullen mopers,
I take my place among you as much as among any;
The past is the push of you and me and all precisely the same,
And the day and night are for you and me and all,
And what is yet untried and afterward is for you and me and all.

I do not know what is untried and afterward,
But I know it is sure and alive and sufficient.

Each who passes is considered, and each who stops is considered, and not a single one can it fail.

It cannot fail the young man who died and was buried,
Nor the young woman who died and was put by his side,

Nor the little child that peeped in at the door and then drew back
and was never seen again,
Nor the old man who has lived without purpose, and feels it with
bitterness worse than gall,
Nor him in the poorhouse tubercled by rum and the bad disorder,
Nor the numberless slaughtered and wrecked .... nor the brutish
koboo, called the ordure of humanity,
Nor the sacs merely floating with open mouths for food to slip in,
Nor any thing in the earth, or down in the oldest graves of the earth,
Nor any thing in the myriads of spheres, nor one of the myriads of
myriads that inhabit them,
Nor the present, nor the least wisp that is known.

XLIV

It is time to explain myself . . . . let us stand up.

What is known I strip away . . . . I launch all men and women
forward with me into the unknown.

The clock indicates the moment . . . . but what does eternity
indicate?

Eternity lies in bottomless reservoirs . . . . its buckets are rising
forever and ever,
They pour and they pour and they exhale away.

We have thus far exhausted trillions of winters and summers;
There are trillions ahead, and trillions ahead of them.

Births have brought us richness and variety,
And other births will bring us richness and variety.

I do not call one greater and one smaller,
That which fills its period and place is equal to any.

Were mankind murderous or jealous upon you my brother or my
sister?
I am sorry for you . . . . they are not murderous or jealous
upon me;
All has been gentle with me . . . . I keep no account with
lamentation;
What have I to do with lamentation?

I am an acme of things accomplished, and I an encloser of things
to be.

My feet strike an apex of the apices of the stairs,
On every step bunches of ages, and larger bunches between the
steps,
All below duly traveled — and still I mount and mount.

Rise after rise bow the phantoms behind me,
Afar down I seethe huge first Nothing, the vapor from the nostrils of death,
I know I was even there . . . . I waited unseen and always,
And slept while God carried me through the lethargic mist,
And took my time . . . . and took no hurt from the fœtid carbon.

Long I was hugged close . . . . long and long.

Immense have been the preparations for me,
Faithful and friendly the arms that have helped me.

Cycles ferried my cradle, rowing and rowing like cheerful boatmen;
For room to me stars kept aside in their own rings,
They sent influences to look after what was to hold me.

Before I was born out of my mother generations guided me,
My embryo has never been torpid . . . . nothing could overlay it;
For it the nebula cohered to an orb . . . . the long slow strata piled to rest it on . . . . vast vegetables gave it sustenance,
Monstrous sauroids transported it in their mouths and deposited it with care.

All forces have been steadily employed to complete and delight me,
Now I stand on this spot with my soul.

XLV

Span of youth! Ever-pushed elasticity! Manhood balanced and florid and full!

My lovers suffocate me!
Crowding my lips, and thick in the pores of my skin,
Jostling me through streets and public halls . . . . coming naked to me at night,
Crying by day Ahoy from the rocks of the river . . . . swinging and chirping over my head,
Calling my name from flowerbeds or vines or tangled underbrush,
Or while I swim in the bath . . . . or drink from the pump at the corner . . . . or the curtain is down at the Opera . . . . or I glimpse at a woman's face in the railroad car;
Lighting on every moment of my life,
Bussing my body with soft and balsamic busses,
Noiselessly passing handfuls out of their hearts and giving them to be mine.

Old age superbly rising! Ineffable grace of dying days!

Every condition promulges not only itself . . . . it promulges what grows after and out of itself,
And the dark hush promulges as much as any.

I open my scuttle at night and see the far-sprinkled systems,
And all I see, multiplied as high as I can cipher, edge but the rim
of the farther systems.

Wider and wider they spread, expanding and always expanding,
Outward and outward and forever outward.

My sun has his sun, and round him obediently wheels,
He joins with his partners a group of superior circuit,
And greater sets follow, making specks of the greatest inside them.

There is no stoppage, and never can be stoppage;
If I and you and the worlds and all beneath or upon their surfaces,
and all the palpable life, were this moment reduced back to a
pallid float, it would not avail in the long run,
We should surely bring up again where we now stand,
And as surely go as much farther, and then farther and farther.

A few quadrillions of eras, a few octillions of cubic leagues, do not
hazard the span, or make it impatient,
They are but parts . . . . any thing is but a part.

See ever so far . . . . there is limitless space outside of that,
Count ever so much . . . . there is limitless time around that.

Our rendezvous is fitly appointed . . . . God will be there and wait
till we come.

XLVI

I know I have the best of time and space — and that I was never
measured, and never will be measured.

I tramp a perpetual journey,
My signs are a rain-proof coat and good shoes and a staff cut from
the woods;
No friend of mine takes his ease in my chair,
I have no chair, nor church nor philosophy;
I lead no man to a dinner-table or library or exchange,
But each man and each woman of you I lead upon a knoll,
My left hand hooks you round the waist,
My right hand points to landscapes of continents, and a plain
public road.

Not I, not any one else can travel that road for you,
You must travel it for yourself.

It is not far . . . . it is within reach,
Perhaps you have been on it since you were born, and did not
know,
Perhaps it is every where on water and on land.

Shoulder your duds, and I will mine, and let us hasten forth;
Wonderful cities and free nations we shall fetch as we go.

If you tire, give me both burdens, and rest the chuff of your hand
    on my hip,
And in due time you shall repay the same service to me;
For after we start we never lie by again.

This day before dawn I ascended a hill and looked at the
    crowded heaven,
And I said to my spirit, When we become the enfolders of those
    orbs and the pleasure and knowledge of every thing in them,
    shall we be filled and satisfied then?
And my spirit said No, we level that lift to pass and continue beyond.

You are also asking me questions, and I hear you;
I answer that I cannot answer . . . . you must find out for yourself.

Sit awhile wayfarer,
Here are biscuits to eat and here is milk to drink,
But as soon as you sleep and renew yourself in sweet clothes I will
    certainly kiss you with my goodbye kiss and open the gate for
    your egress hence.

Long enough have you dreamed contemptible dreams,
Now I wash the gum from your eyes,
You must habit yourself to the dazzle of the light and of every
    moment of your life.

Long have you timidly waded, holding a plank by the shore,
Now I will you to be a bold swimmer,
To jump off in the midst of the sea, and rise again and nod to me
    and shout, and laughingly dash with your hair.

XLVII

I am the teacher of athletes,
He that by me spreads a wider breast than my own proves the
    width of my own,
He most honors my style who learns under it to destroy the teacher.

The boy I love, the same becomes a man not through derived
    power but in his own right,
Wicked, rather than virtuous out of conformity or fear,
Fond of his sweetheart, relishing well his steak,
Unrequited love or a slight cutting him worse than a wound cuts,
First rate to ride, to fight, to hit the bull's eye, to sail a skiff, to
    sing a song or play on the banjo,
Preferring scars and faces pitted with smallpox over all latherers and
    those that keep out of the sun.

I teach straying from me, yet who can stray from me?
I follow you whoever you are from the present hour;
My words itch at your ears till you understand them.

I do not say these things for a dollar, or to fill up the time while I wait for a boat;
It is you talking just as much as myself . . . . I act as the tongue of you,
It was tied in your mouth . . . . in mine it begins to be loosened.

I swear I will never mention love or death inside a house,
And I swear I never will translate myself at all, only to him or her who privately stays with me in the open air.

If you would understand me go to the heights or water-shore,
The nearest gnat is an explanation and a drop or the motion of waves a key,
The maul the oar and the handsaw second my words.

No shuttered room or school can commune with me,
But roughs and little children better than they.

The young mechanic is closest to me . . . . he knows me pretty well,
The woodman that takes his axe and jug with him shall take me with him all day,
The farmboy ploughing in the field feels good at the sound of my voice,
In vessels that sail my words must sail . . . . I go with fishermen and seamen, and love them,
My face rubs to the hunter's face when he lies down alone in his blanket,
The driver thinking of me does not mind the jolt of his wagon,
The young mother and old mother shall comprehend me,
The girl and the wife rest the needle a moment and forget where they are,
They and all would resume what I have told them.

XLVIII

I have said that the soul is not more than the body,
And I have said that the body is not more than the soul,
And nothing, not God, is greater to one than one's-self is,
And whoever walks a furlong without sympathy walks to his own funeral, dressed in his shroud,
And I or you pocketless of a dime may purchase the pick of the earth,
And to glance with an eye or show a bean in its pod confounds the learning of all times,
And there is no trade or employment but the young man following it may become a hero,

And there is no object so soft but it makes a hub for the wheeled
universe,
And any man or woman shall stand cool and supercilious before a
million universes.

And I call to mankind, Be not curious about God,
For I who am curious about each am not curious about God,
No array of terms can say how much I am at peace about God
and about death.

I hear and behold God in every object, yet I understand God not
in the least,
Nor do I understand who there can be more wonderful than myself.

Why should I wish to see God better than this day?
I see something of God each hour of the twenty-four, and each
moment then,
In the faces of men and women I see God, and in my own face in
the glass;
I find letters from God dropped in the street, and every one is
signed by God's name,
And I leave them where they are, for I know that others will
punctually come forever and ever.

XLIX

And as to you death, and you bitter hug of mortality .... it is idle
to try to alarm me.

To his work without flinching the accoucheur comes,
I see the elderhand pressing receiving supporting,
I recline by the sills of the exquisite flexible doors .... and mark
the outlet, and mark the relief and escape.

And as to you corpse I think you are good manure, but that
does not offend me,
I smell the white roses sweetscented and growing,
I reach to the leafy lips .... I reach to the polished breasts of
melons,

And as to you life, I reckon you are the leavings of many deaths,
No doubt I have died myself ten thousand times before.

I hear you whispering there O stars of heaven,
O suns .... O grass of graves .... O perpetual transfers and
promotions .... if you do not say anything how can I say
anything?

Of the turbid pool that lies in the autumn forest,
Of the moon that descends the steeps of the soughing twilight,

Toss, sparkles of day and dusk . . . . toss on the black stems that decay in the muck,
Toss to the moaning gibberish of the dry limbs.

I ascend from the moon . . . . I ascend from the night,
And I perceive of the ghastly glitter the sunbeams reflected,
And debouch to the steady and central from the offspring great or small.

L

There is that in me . . . . I do not know what it is . . . . but I know it is in me.

Wrenched and sweaty . . . . calm and cool then my body becomes;
I sleep . . . . I sleep long.

I do not know it . . . . it is without name . . . . it is a word unsaid,
It is not in any dictionary or utterance or symbol.

Something it swings on more than the earth I swing on,
To it the creation is the friend whose embracing awakes me.

Perhaps I might tell more . . . . Outlines! I plead for my brothers and sisters.

Do you see O my brothers and sisters?
It is not chaos or death . . . . it is form and union and plan . . . . it is eternal life . . . . it is happiness.

LI

The past and present wilt . . . . I have filled them and emptied them,
And proceed to fill my next fold of the future.

Listener up there! Here you . . . . what have you to confide to me?
Look in my face while I snuff the sidle of evening,
Talk honestly, for no one else hears you, and I stay only a minute longer.

Do I contradict myself?
Very well then . . . . I contradict myself;
I am large . . . . I contain multitudes.

I concentrate toward them that are nigh . . . . I wait on the door-slab.

Who had done his day's work and will soonest be through with his supper?
Who wishes to walk with me?

Will you speak before I am gone? Will you prove already too late?

LII

The spotted hawk swoops by and accuses me . . . . he complains of
my gab and my loitering.

I too am not a bit tamed . . . . I too am untranslatable,
I sound my barbaric yawp over the roofs of the world.

The last scud of day holds back for me,
It flings my likeness after the rest and true as any on the shadowed
wilds,
It coaxes me to the vapor and the dusk.

I depart as air . . . . I shake my white locks at the runaway sun,
I effuse my flesh in eddies and drift it in lacy jags.

I bequeath myself to the dirt to grow from the grass I love,
If you want me again look for me under your bootsoles.

You will hardly know who I am or what I mean,
But I shall be good health to you nevertheless,
And filter and fibre your blood.

Failing to fetch me at first keep encouraged,
Missing me one place search another,
I stop some where waiting for you

1855

Crossing Brooklyn Ferry

I

Flood-tide below me! I see you face to face!
Clouds of the west — sun there half an hour high — I see you also
face to face.

Crowds of men and women attired in the usual costumes, how curious
you are to me!
On the ferry-boats the hundreds and hundreds that cross, returning
home, are more curious to me than you suppose,
And you that shall cross from shore to shore years hence are more to
me, and more in my meditations, than you might suppose.

II

The impalpable sustenance of me from all things at all hours of the day,
The simple, compact, well-join'd scheme, myself disintegrated, every
one disintegrated yet part of the scheme,
The similitudes of the past and those of the future,
The glories strung like beads on my smallest sights and hearings, on the
walk in the street and the passage over the river,

The current rushing so swiftly and swimming with me far away,
The others that are to follow me, the ties between me and them,
The certainty of others, the life, love, sight, hearing of others.

Others will enter the gates of the ferry and cross from shore to shore,
Others will watch the run of the flood-tide,
Others will see the shipping of Manhattan north and west, and the heights of Brooklyn to the south and east,
Others will see the islands large and small;
Fifty years hence, others will see them as they cross, the sun half an hour high,
A hundred years hence, or ever so many hundred years hence, others will see them,
Will enjoy the sunset, the pouring-in of the flood-tide, the falling-back to the sea of the ebb-tide.

III

It avails not, time nor place — distance avails not,
I am with you, you men and women of a generation, or ever so many generations hence,
Just as you feel when you look on the river and sky, so I felt,
Just as any of you is one of a living crowd, I was one of a crowd,
Just as you are refresh'd by the gladness of the river and the bright flow, I was refresh'd,
Just as you stand and lean on the rail, yet hurry with the swift current, I stood yet was hurried,
Just as you look on the numberless masts of ships and the thick-stemm'd pipes of steamboats, I look'd.

I too many and many a time cross'd the river of old,
Watched the Twelfth-month sea-gulls, saw them high in the air floating with motionless wings, oscillating their bodies,
Saw how the glistening yellow lit up parts of their bodies and left the rest in strong shadow,
Saw the slow-wheeling circles and the gradual edging toward the south,
Saw the reflection of the summer sky in the water,
Had my eyes dazzled by the shimmering track of beams,
Look'd at the fine centrifugal spokes of light round the shape of my head in the sunlit water,
Look'd on the haze on the hills southward and south-westward,
Look'd on the vapor as it flew in fleeces tinged with violet,
Look'd toward the lower bay to notice the vessels arriving,
Saw their approach, saw aboard those that were near me,
Saw the white sails of schooners and sloops, saw the ships at anchor,
The sailors at work in the rigging or out astride the spars,
The round masts, the swinging motion of the hulls, the slender serpentine pennants,
The large and small steamers in motion, the pilots in their pilot-houses,

The white wake left by the passage, the quick tremulous whirl of the
wheels,
The flags of all nations, the falling of them at sunset,
The scallop-edged waves in the twilight, the ladled cups, the frolicsome
crests and glistening,
The stretch afar growing dimmer and dimmer, the gray walls of the
granite storehouses by the docks,
On the river the shadowy group, the big steam-tug closely flank'd on
each side by the barges, the hay-boat, the belated lighter,
On the neighboring shore the fires from the foundry chimneys burning
high and glaringly into the night,
Casting their flicker of black contrasted with wild red and yellow light
over the tops of houses, and down into the clefts of streets.

IV

These and all else were to me the same as they are to you,
I loved well those cities, loved well the stately and rapid river,
The men and women I saw were all near to me,
Others the same — others who look back on me because I look'd forward
to them,
(The time will come, though I stop here to-day and to-night.)

V

What is it then between us?
What is the count of the scores or hundreds of years between us?

Whatever it is, it avails not — distance avails not, and place avails not,
I too lived, Brooklyn of ample hills was mine,
I too walk'd the streets of Manhattan island, and bathed in the waters
around it,
I too felt the curious abrupt questionings stir within me,
In the day among crowds of people sometimes they came upon me,
In my walks home late at night or as I lay in my bed they came upon me,
I too had been struck from the float forever held in solution,
I too had receiv'd identity by my body,
That I was I knew was of my body, and what I should be I knew I
should be of my body.

VI

It is not upon you alone the dark patches fall,
The dark threw its patches down upon me also,
The best I had done seem'd to me blank and suspicious,
My great thoughts as I supposed them, were they not in reality meagre?
Nor is it you alone who know what it is to be evil,
I am he who knew what it was to be evil,
I too knitted the old knot of contrariety,
Blabb'd, blush'd, resented, lied, stole, grudg'd,
Had guile, anger, lust, hot wishes I dared not speak,
Was wayward, vain, greedy, shallow, sly, cowardly, malignant,

The wolf, the snake, the hog, not wanting in me,
The cheating look, the frivolous word, the adulterous wish, not wanting,
Refusals, hates, postponements, meanness, laziness, none of these
wanting,
Was one with the rest, the days and haps of the rest,
Was call'd by my nighest name by clear loud voices of young men as
they saw me approaching or passing,
Felt their arms on my neck as I stood, or the negligent leaning of their
flesh against me as I sat,
Saw many I loved in the street or ferry-boat or public assembly, yet
never told them a word,
Lived the same life with the rest, the same old laughing, gnawing,
sleeping,
Play'd the part that still looks back on the actor or actress,
The same old role, the role that is what we make it, as great as we like,
Or as small as we like, or both great and small.

VII

Closer yet I approach you,
What thought you have of me now, I had as much of you — I laid in
my stores in advance,
I consider'd long and seriously of you before you were born.

Who was to know what should come home to me?
Who knows but I am enjoying this?
Who knows, for all the distance, but I am as good as looking at you
now, for all you cannot see me?

VIII

Ah, what can ever be more stately and admirable to me than mast-hemm'd
Manhattan?
River and sunset and scallop-edg'd waves of flood-tide?
The sea-gulls oscillating their bodies, the hay-boat in the twilight, and
the belated lighter?
What gods can exceed these that clasp me by the hand, and with
voices I love call me promptly and loudly by my nighest name
as I approach?
What is more subtle than this which ties me to the woman or man that
looks in my face?
Which fuses me into you now, and pours my meaning into you?

We understand then do we not?
What I promis'd without mentioning it, have you not accepted?
What the study could not teach — what the preaching could not
accomplish is accomplish'd, it is not?

IX

Flow on, river! flow with the flood-tide, and ebb with ebb-tide!
Frolic on, crested and scallop-edg'd waves!

Gorgeous clouds of the sunset! drench with your splendor me, or the
men or women generations after me!
Cross from shore to shore, countless crowds of passengers!
Stand up, tall masts of Mannahatta! stand up, beautiful hills of
Brooklyn!
Throb, baffled and curious brain! throw out questions and answers!
Suspend here and everywhere, eternal float of solution!
Gaze, loving and thirsting eyes, in the house or street or public assembly!
Sound out, voices of young men! loudly and musically call me by my
nighest name!
Live, old life! play the part that looks back on the actor or actress!
Play the old role, the role that is great or small according as one makes it!
Consider, you who peruse me, whether I may not in unknown ways
be looking upon you;
Be firm, rail over the river, to support those who lean idly, yet haste
with the hasting current;
Fly on, sea-birds! fly sideways, or wheel in large circles high in the air;
Receive the summer sky, you water, and faithfully hold it till all downcast
eyes have time to take it from you!
Diverge, fine spokes of light, from the shape of my head, or any one's
head, in the sunlit water!
Come on, ships from the lower bay! pass up or down, white-sail'd
schooners, sloops, lighters!
Flaunt away, flags of all nations! be duly lower'd at sunset!
Burn high your fires, foundry chimneys! cast black shadows at nightfall!
cast red and yellow light over the tops of the houses!
Appearances, now or henceforth, indicate what you are,
You necessary film, continue to envelope the soul,
About my body for me, and your body for you, be hung our divinest
aromas,
Thrive, cities — bring your freight, bring your shows, ample and
sufficient rivers,
Expand, being than which none else is perhaps more spiritual,
Keep your places, objects than which none else is more lasting.

You have waited, you always wait, you dumb, beautiful ministers,
We receive you with free sense at last, and are insatiate henceforward,
Not you any more shall be able to foil us, or withhold yourselves from us,
We use you, and do not cast you aside — we plant you permanently
within us,
We fathom you not — we love you — there is perfection in you also,
You furnish your parts toward eternity,
Great or small, you furnish your parts toward the soul.

1856

Out of the Cradle Endlessly Rocking

Out of the cradle endlessly rocking,
Out of the mocking-bird's throat, the musical shuttle,
Out of the Ninth-month midnight,
Over the sterile sands and the fields beyond, where the child leaving his
bed wander'd alone, bareheaded, barefoot,
Down from the shower'd halo,
Up from the mystic play of shadows twining and twisting as if they
were alive,
Out from the patches of briers and blackberries,
From the memories of the bird that chanted to me,
From your memories sad brother, from the fitful risings and fallings I heard,
From under that yellow half-moon late-risen and swollen as if with tears,
From those beginning notes of yearning and love there in the mist,
From the thousand responses of my heart never to cease,
From the myriad thence-arous'd words,
From the word stronger and more delicious than any,
From such as now they start the scene revisiting,
As a flock, twittering, rising, or overhead passing,
Borne hither, ere all eludes me, hurriedly,
A man, yet by these tears a little boy again,
Throwing myself on the sand, confronting the waves,
I, chanter of pains and joys, uniter of here and hereafter,
Taking all hints to use them, but swiftly leaping beyond them,
A reminiscence sing.

Once Paumanok,
When the lilac-scent was in the air and Fifth-month grass was growing,
Up this seashore in some briers,
Two feather'd guests from Alabama, two together,
And their nest, and four light-green eggs spotted with brown,
And every day the he-bird to and fro near at hand,
And every day the she-bird crouch'd on her nest, silent, with bright eyes,
And every day I, a curious boy, never too close, never disturbing them,
Cautiously peering, absorbing, translating.

Shine! shine! shine!
Pour down your warmth, great sun!
While we bask, we two together!

Two together!
Winds blow south, or winds blow north,
Day come white, or night come black,
Home, or rivers and mountains from home,
Singing all time, minding no time,
While we two keep together.

Till of a sudden,
May-be kill'd, unknown to her mate,
One forenoon the she-bird crouch'd not on the nest,
Nor return'd that afternoon, nor the next,
Nor ever appear'd again.

And thenceforward all summer in the sound of the sea,
And at night under the full of the moon in calmer weather,
Over the hoarse surging of the sea,
Of flitting from brier to brier by day,
I saw, I heard at intervals the remaining one, the he-bird,
The solitary guest from Alabama.

Blow! blow! blow!
Blow up sea-winds along Paumanok's shore;
I wait and I wait till you blow my mate to me.

Yes when the stars glisten'd,
All night long on the prong of a moss-scallop'd stake,
Down almost amid the slapping waves,
Sat the lone singer wonderful causing tears.

He call'd on his mate,
He pour'd forth the meanings which I of all men know.

Yes, my brother I know,
The rest might not, but I have treasur'd every note,
For more than once dimly down to the beach gliding,
Silent, avoiding the moonbeams, blending myself with the shadows,
Recalling now the obscure shapes, the echoes, the sounds and sights
    after their sorts,
The white arms out in the breakers tirelessly tossing,
I, with bare feet, a child, the wind wafting my hair,
Listen'd long and long.

Listen'd to keep, to sing, now translating the notes,
Following you my brother.

Soothe! soothe! soothe!
Close on its wave soothes the wave behind,
And again another behind embracing and lapping, every one close,
But my love soothes not me, not me.

Low hangs the moon, it rose late,
It is lagging — O I think it is heavy with love, with love.

O madly the sea pushes upon the land,
With love, with love.

O night! do I not see my love fluttering out among the breakers?
What is that little black thing I see there in the white?

Loud! loud! loud!
Loud I call to you, my love!

High and clear I shoot my voice over the waves,
Surely you must know who is here, is here,
You must know who I am, my love.

Low-hanging moon!
What is that dusky spot in your brown yellow?
O it is the shape, the shape of my mate!
O moon do not keep her from me any longer.

Land! land! O land!
Whichever way I turn, O I think you could give me my mate back again if you only would,
For I am almost sure I see her dimly whichever way I look.

O rising stars!
Perhaps the one I want so much will rise, will rise with some of you.

O throat! O trembling throat!
Sound clearer through the atmosphere!
Pierce the woods, the earth,
Somewhere listening to catch you must be the one I want.

Shake out carols!
Solitary here, the night's carols!
Carols of lonesome love! death's carols!
Carols under that lagging, yellow, waning moon!
O under that moon where she droops almost down into the sea!
O reckless despairing carols.

But soft! sink low!
Soft! let me just murmur,
And do you wait a moment you husky-nois'd sea,
For somewhere I believe I heard my mate responding to me,
So faint, I must be still, be still to listen,
But not altogether still, for then she might not come immediately to me.

Hither my love!
Here I am! here!
With this just-sustain'd note I announce myself to you,
This gentle call is for you my love, for you.

Do not be decoy'd elsewhere,
That is the whistle of the wind, it is not my voice,

That is the fluttering, the fluttering of the spray,
Those are the shadows of leaves.

O darkness! O in vain!
O I am very sick and sorrowful.

O brown halo in the sky near the moon, drooping upon the sea!
O troubled reflection in the sea!
O throat! O throbbing heart!
And I singing uselessly, uselessly all the night.

O past! O happy life! O songs of joy!
In the air, in the woods, over fields,
Loved! loved! loved! loved! loved!
But my mate no more, no more with me!
We two together no more.

The aria sinking,
All else continuing, the stars shining,
The winds blowing, the notes of the bird continuous echoing,
With angry moans the fierce old mother incessantly moaning,
On the sands of Paumanok's shore gray and rustling,
The yellow half-moon enlarged, sagging down, drooping, the face of the sea almost touching,
The boy ecstatic, with his bare feet the waves, with his hair the atmosphere dallying,
The love in the heart long pent, now loose, now at last tumultuously bursting,
The aria's meaning, the ears, the soul, swiftly depositing,
The strange tears down the cheeks coursing,
The colloquy there, the trio, each uttering,
The undertone, the savage old mother incessantly crying,
To the boy's soul's questions sullenly timing, some drown'd secret hissing,
To the outsetting bard.

Demon or bird (said the boy's soul,)
Is it indeed toward your mate you sing? or is it really to me?
For I, that was a child, my tongue's use sleeping, now I have heard you,
Now in a moment I know what I am for, I awake,
And already a thousand singers, a thousand, songs, clearer, louder and more sorrowful than yours,
A thousand warbling echoes have started to life within me, never to die.

O you singer solitary, singing by yourself, projecting me,
O solitary me listening, never more shall I cease perpetuating you,
Never more shall I escape, never more the reverberations,
Never more the cries of unsatisfied love be absent from me,

Never again leave me to be the peaceful child I was before what there
in the night,
By the sea under the yellow and sagging moon,
The messenger there arous'd, the fire, the sweet hell within,
The unknown want, the destiny of me.

O give me the clew! (it lurks in the night here somewhere,)
O if I am to have so much, let me have more!

A word then, (for I will conquer it,)
The word final, superior to all,
Subtle, sent up — what is it? — I listen;
Are you whispering it, and have been all the time, you sea-waves?
Is that it from your liquid rims and wet sands?

Whereto answering, the sea,
Delaying not, hurrying not,
Whisper'd me through the night, and very plainly before daybreak,
Lisp'd to me the low and delicious word death,
And again death, death, death, death,
Hissing melodious, neither like the bird nor like my arous'd child's heart,
But edging near as privately for me rustling at my feet,
Creeping thence steadily up to my ears and laving me softly all over,
Death, death, death, death, death.

Which I do not forget,
But fuse the song of my dusky demon and brother,
That he sang to me in the moonlight on Paumanok's gray beach,
With the thousand responsive songs at random,
My own songs awaked from that hour,
And with them the key, the word up from the waves,
The word of the sweetest song and all songs,
That strong and delicious word which, creeping to my feet,
(Or like some old crone rocking the cradle, swathed in sweet garments,
bending aside,)
The sea whisper'd me.

1859

As I Ebb'd with the Ocean of Life

I

As I ebb'd with the ocean of life,
As I wended the shores I know,
As I walk'd where the ripples continually wash you Paumanok,
Where they rustle up hoarse and sibilant,
Where the fierce old mother endlessly cries for her castaways,
I musing late in the autumn day, gazing off southward,

Held by this electric self out of the pride of which I utter poems,
Was seiz'd by the spirit that trails in the lines underfoot,
The rim, the sediment that stands for all the water and all the land of
the globe.

Fascinated, my eyes reverting from the south, dropt, to follow those
slender windrows,
Chaff, straw, splinters of wood, weeds, and the sea-gluten,
Scum, scales from shining rocks, leaves of salt-lettuce, left by the tide,
Miles walking, the sound of breaking waves the other side of me,
Paumanok there and then as I thought the old thought of likenesses,
These you presented to me you fish-shaped island,
As I wended the shores I know,
As I walk'd with that electric self seeking types.

II

As I wend to the shores I know not,
As I list to the dirge, the voices of men and women wreck'd,
As I inhale the impalpable breezes that set in upon me,
As the ocean so mysterious rolls toward me closer and closer,
I too but signify at the utmost a little wash'd-up drift,
A few sands and dead leaves to gather,
Gather, and merge myself as part of the sands and drift.

O baffled, balk'd, bent to the very earth,
Oppress'd with myself that I have dared to open my mouth,
Aware now that amid all that blab whose echoes recoil upon me I have
not once had the least idea who or what I am,
But that before all my arrogant poems the real Me stands yet untouch'd,
untold, altogether unreach'd,
Withdrawn far, mocking me with mock-congratulatory signs and bows,
With peals of distant ironical laughter at every word I have written,
Pointing in silence to these songs, and then to the sand beneath.

I perceive I have not really understood any thing, not a single object,
and that no man ever can,
Nature here in sight of the sea taking advantage of me to dart upon me
and sting me,
Because I have dared to open my mouth to sing at all.

III

You oceans both, I close with you,
We murmur alike reproachfully rolling sands and drift, knowing not
why,
These little shreds indeed standing for you and me and all.

You friable shore with trails of debris,
You fish-shaped island, I take what is underfoot,
What is yours is mine my father.

I too Paumanok,
I too have bubbled up, floated the measureless float, and been wash'd
on your shores,
I too am but a trail of drift and debris,
I too leave little wrecks upon you, you fish-shaped island.

I throw myself upon your breast my father,
I cling to you so that you cannot unloose me,
I hold you so firm till you answer me something.
Kiss me my father,
Touch me with your lips as I touch those I love,
Breathe to me while I hold you close the secret of the murmuring I envy.

IV

Ebb, ocean of life, (the flow will return,)
Cease not your moaning you fierce old mother,
Endlessly cry for your castaways, but fear not, deny not me,
Rustle not up so hoarse and angry against my feet as I touch you or
gather from you.

I mean tenderly by you and all,
I gather for myself and for this phantom looking down where we lead,
and following me and mine.

Me and mine, loose windrows, little corpses,
Froth, snowy white, and bubbles,
(See, from my dead lips the ooze exuding at last,
See, the prismatic colors glistening and rolling,)
Tufts of straw, sands, fragments,
Buoy'd hither from many moods, one contradicting another,
From the storm, the long calm, the darkness, the swell,
Musing, pondering, a breath, a briny tear, a dab of liquid or soil,
Up just as much out of fathomless workings fermented and thrown,
A limp blossom or two, torn, just as much over waves floating, drifted
at random,
Just as much for us that sobbing dirge of Nature,
Just as much whence we come that blare of the cloud-trumpets,
We, capricious, brought hither we know not whence, spread out before
you,
You up there walking or sitting,
Whoever you are, we too lie in drifts at your feet.

1860

I Saw in Louisiana a Live-Oak Growing

I saw in Louisiana a live-oak growing,
All alone stood it and the moss hung down from the branches,

Without any companion it grew there uttering joyous leaves of dark
green,
And its look, rude, unbending, lusty, made me think of myself,
But I wonder'd how it could utter joyous leaves standing alone there
without its friend near, for I knew I could not,
And I broke off a twig with a certain number of leaves upon it, and
twined around it a little moss,
And brought it away, and I have placed it in sight in my room,
It is not needed to remind me as of my own dear friends,
(For I believe lately I think of little else than of them,)
Yet it remains to me a curious token, it makes me think of manly love;
For all that, and though the live-oak glistens there in Louisiana solitary
in a wide flat space,
Uttering joyous leaves all its life without a friend a lover near,
I know very well I could not.

1860

Scented Herbage of My Breast

Scented herbage of my breast,
Leaves from you I glean, I write, to be perused best afterwards,
Tomb-leaves, body-leaves growing up above me above death,
Perennial roots, tall leaves, O the winter shall not freeze you
delicate leaves,
Every year shall you bloom again, out from where you retired you
shall emerge again;
O I do not know whether many passing by will discover you or
inhale your faint odor, but I believe a few will;
O slender leaves! O blossoms of my blood! I permit you to tell
in your own way of the heart that is under you,
O I do not know what you mean there underneath yourselves, you
are not happiness,
You are often more bitter than I can bear, you burn and sting me,
Yet you are beautiful to me you faint tinged roots, you make me
think of death,
Death is beautiful from you, (what indeed is finally beautiful except
death and love?)
O I think it is not for life I am chanting here my chant of lovers,
I think it must be for death,
For how calm, how solemn it grows to ascend to the atmosphere
of lovers,
Death or life I am then indifferent, my soul declines to prefer,
(I am not sure but the high soul of lovers welcomes death most,)
Indeed O death, I think now these leaves mean precisely the same
as you mean,
Grow up taller sweet leaves that I may see! grow up out of my breast!

Spring away from the conceal'd heart there!
Do not fold yourself so in your pink-tinged roots timid leaves!
Do not remain down there so ashamed, herbage of my breast!
Come I am determin'd to unbare this broad breast of mine, I
have long enough stifled and choked;
Emblematic and capricious blades I leave you, now you serve me
not,
I will say what I have to say by itself,
I will sound myself and comrades only, I will never again utter a
call only their call,
I will raise with it immortal reverberations through the States,
I will give an example to lovers to take permanent shape and
will through the States,
Through me shall the words be said to make death exhilarating,
Give me your tone therefore O death, that I may accord with it,
Give me yourself, for I see that you belong to me now above all, and are
folded inseparably together, you love and death are,
Nor will I allow you to balk me any more with what I was calling life,
For now it is convey'd to me that you are the purports essential,
That you hide in these shifting forms of life, for reasons, and that
they are mainly for you,
That you beyond them come forth to remain, the real reality,
That behind the mask of materials you patiently wait, no matter
how long,
That you will one day perhaps take control of all,
That you will perhaps dissipate this entire show of appearance,
That may-be you are what it is all for, but it does not last so very long,
But you will last very long.

1860

To a Stranger

Passing stranger! you do not know how longingly I look upon you,
You must be he I was seeking, or she I was seeking, (it comes to me
as of a dream,)
I have somewhere surely lived a life of joy with you,
All is recall'd as we flit by each other, fluid, affectionate, chaste, matured,
You grew up with me, were a boy with me or a girl with me,
I ate with you and slept with you, your body has become not yours only
nor left my body mine only,
You give me the pleasure of your eyes, face, flesh, as we pass, you take
of my beard, breast, hands, in return,
I am not to speak to you, I am to think of you when I sit alone or wake
at night alone,
I am to wait, I do not doubt I am to meet you again,
I am to see to it that I do not lose you.

1860

When I Heard the Learn'd Astronomer

When I heard the learn'd astronomer,
When the proofs, the figures, were ranged in columns
before me,
When I was shown the charts and diagrams, to add, divide,
and measure them,
When I sitting heard the astronomer where he lectured
with much applause in the lecture-room,
How soon unaccountable I became tired and sick,
Till rising and gliding out I wander'd off by myself,
In the mystical moist night-air, and from time to time,
Look'd up in perfect silence at the stars.

1865

Reconciliation

Word over all, beautiful as the sky,
Beautiful that war and all its deeds of carnage must in time be utterly
lost,
That the hands of the sisters Death and Night incessantly softly wash
again, and ever again, this soil'd world;
For my enemy is dead, a man divine as myself is dead,
I look where he lies white-faced and still in the coffin — I draw near,
Bend down and touch lightly with my lips the white face in the coffin.

1865

When Lilacs Last in the Dooryard Bloom'd

I

When lilacs last in the dooryard bloom'd,
And the great star early droop'd in the western sky in the night,
I mourn'd, and yet shall mourn with ever-returning spring.

Ever-returning spring, trinity sure to me you bring,
Lilac blooming perennial and drooping star in the west,
And thought of him I love.

II

O powerful western fallen star!
O shades of night — O moody, tearful night!
O great star disappear'd — O the black murk that hides the star!
O cruel hands that hold me powerless — O helpless soul of me!
O harsh surrounding cloud that will not free my soul.

III

In the dooryard fronting an old farm-house near the white-wash'd palings,
Stands the lilac-bush tall-growing with heart-shaped leaves of rich green,
With many a pointed blossom rising delicate, with the perfume strong I love,
With every leaf a miracle — and from this bush in the dooryard,
With delicate-color'd blossoms and heart-shaped leaves of rich green,
A sprig with its flower I break.

IV

In the swamp in secluded recesses,
A shy and hidden bird is warbling a song.

Solitary the thrush,
The hermit withdrawn to himself, avoiding the settlements,
Sings by himself a song.

Song of the bleeding throat,
Death's outlet song of life, (for well dear brother I know,
If thou wast not granted to sing thou would'st surely die.)

V

Over the breast of the spring, the land, amid cities,
Amid lanes and through old woods, where lately the violets peep'd from the ground, spotting the gray debris,
Amid the grass in the fields each side of the lanes, passing the endless grass,
Passing the yellow-spear'd wheat, every grain from its shroud in the dark-brown fields uprisen,
Passing the apple-tree blows of white and pink in the orchards,
Carrying a corpse to where it shall rest in the grave,
Night and day journeys a coffin.

VI

Coffin that passes through lanes and streets,
Through day and night with the great cloud darkening the land,
With the pomp of the inloop'd flags with the cities draped in black,
With the show of the States themselves as of crape-veil'd women standing,
With processions long and winding and the flambeaus of the night,
With the countless torches lit, with the silent sea of faces and the unbared heads,
With the waiting depot, the arriving coffin, and the sombre faces,
With dirges through the night, with the thousand voices rising strong and solemn,
With all the mournful voices of the dirges pour'd around the coffin,
The dim-lit churches and the shuddering organs — where amid these you journey,
With the tolling tolling bells' perpetual clang,

Here, coffin that slowly passes,
I give you my sprig of lilac.

VII

(Nor for you, for one alone,
Blossoms and branches green to coffins all I bring,
For fresh as the morning, thus would I chant a song for you O sane and sacred death.

All over bouquets of roses,
O death, I cover you over with roses and early lilies,
But mostly and now the lilac that blooms the first,
Copious I break, I break the sprigs from the bushes,
With loaded arms I come, pouring for you,
For you and the coffins all of you O death.)

VIII

O western orb sailing the heaven,
Now I know what you must have meant as a month since I walk'd,
As I walk'd in silence the transparent shadowy night,
As I saw you had something to tell as you bent to me night after night,
As you droop'd from the sky low down as if to my side, (while the other stars all look'd on,)
As we wander'd together the solemn night, (for something I know not what kept me from sleep,)
As the night advanced, and I saw on the rim of the west how full you were of woe,
As I stood on the rising ground in the breeze in the cool transparent night,
As I watch'd where you pass'd and was lost in the netherward black of the night,
As my soul in its trouble dissatisfied sank, as where you sad orb,
Concluded, dropt in the night, and was gone.

IX

Sing on there in the swamp,
O singer bashful and tender, I hear your notes, I hear your call,
I hear, I come presently, I understand you,
But a moment I linger, for the lustrous star has detain'd me,
The star my departing comrade holds and detains me.

X

O how shall I warble myself for the dead one there I loved?
And how shall I deck my song for the large sweet soul that has gone?
And what shall my perfume be for the grave of him I love?
Sea-winds blown from east and west,
Blown from the Eastern sea and blown from the Western sea, till there on the prairies meeting,
These and with these and the breath of my chant,
I'll perfume the grave of him I love.

XI

O what shall I hang on the chamber walls?
And what shall the pictures be that I hang on the walls,
To adorn the burial-house of him I love?

Pictures of growing spring and farms and homes,
With the Fourth-month eve at sundown, and the gray smoke lucid and bright,
With floods of the yellow gold of the gorgeous, indolent, sinking sun, burning, expanding the air,
With the fresh sweet herbage under foot, and the pale green leaves of the trees prolific,
In the distance the flowing glaze, the breast of the river, with a wind-dapple here and there,
With ranging hills on the banks, with many a line against the sky, and shadows,
And the city at hand with dwellings so dense, and stacks of chimneys,
And all the scenes of life and the workshops, and the workmen homeward returning.

XII

Lo, body and soul — this land,
My own Manhattan with spires, and the sparkling and hurrying tides, and the ships,
The varied and ample land, the South and the North in the light, Ohio's shores and flashing Missouri,
And ever the far-spreading prairies cover'd with grass and corn.

Lo, the most excellent sun so calm and haughty,
The violet and purple morn with just-felt breezes,
The gentle soft-born measureless light,
The miracle spreading bathing all, the fulfill'd noon,
The coming eve delicious, the welcome night and the stars,
Over my cities shining all, enveloping man and land.

XIII

Sing on, sing on you gray-brown bird,
Sing from the swamps, the recesses, pour your chant from the bushes,
Limitless out of the dusk, out of the cedars and pines.

Sing on dearest brother, warble your reedy song,
Loud human song, with voice of uttermost woe.

O liquid and free and tender!
O wild and loose to my soul — O wondrous singer!
You only I hear — yet the star holds me, (but will soon depart,)
Yet the lilac with mastering odor holds me.

XIV

Now while I sat in the day and look'd forth,
In the close of the day with its light and the fields of spring, and the farmers preparing their crops,
In the large unconscious scenery of my land with its lakes and forests,
In the heavenly aerial beauty, (after the perturb'd winds and the storms,)
Under the arching heavens of the afternoon swift passing, and the voices of children and women,
The many-moving sea-tides, and I saw the ships how they sail'd,
And the summer approaching with richness, and the fields all busy with labor,
And the infinite separate houses, how they all went on, each with its meals and minutia of daily usages,
And the streets how their throbbings throbb'd, and the cities pent — lo, then and there,
Falling upon them all and among them all, enveloping me with the rest,
Appear'd the cloud, appear'd the long black trail,
And I knew death, its thought, and the sacred knowledge of death.

Then with the knowledge of death as walking one side of me,
And the thought of death close-walking the other side of me,
And I in the middle as with companions, and as holding the hands of companions,
I fled forth to the hiding receiving night that talks not,
Down to the shores of the water, the path by the swamp in the dimness,
To the solemn shadowy cedars and ghostly pines so still.

And the singer so shy to the rest receiv'd me,
The gray-brown bird I know receiv'd us comrades three,
And he sang the carol of death, and a verse for him I love.

From deep secluded recesses,
From the fragrant cedars and the ghostly pines so still,
Came the carol of the bird.

And the charm of the carol rapt me,
As I held as if by their hands my comrades in the night,
And the voice of my spirit tallied the song of the bird.

Come lovely and soothing death,
Undulate round the world, serenely arriving, arriving,
In the day, in the night, to all, to each,
Sooner or later delicate death.

Prais'd be the fathomless universe,
For life and joy, and for objects and knowledge curious,
And for love, sweet love — but praise! praise! praise!
For the sure-enwinding arms of cool-enfolding death.

Dark mother always gliding near with soft feet,
Have none chanted for thee a chant of fullest welcome?
Then I chant it for thee, I glorify thee above all,
I bring thee a song that when thou must indeed come, come unfalteringly.

Approach strong deliveress,
When it is so, when thou hast taken them I joyously sing the dead,
Lost in the loving floating ocean of thee,
Laved in the flood of thy bliss O death.

From me to thee glad serenades,
Dances for thee I propose saluting thee, adornments and feastings for thee,
And the sights of the open landscape and the high-spread sky are fitting,
And life and the fields, and the huge and thoughtful night.

The night in silence under many a star,
The ocean shore and the husky whispering wave whose voice I know,
And the soul turning to thee O vast and well-veil'd death,
And the body gratefully nestling close to thee.

Over the tree-tops I float thee a song,
Over the rising and sinking waves, over the myriad fields and the prairies wide,
Over the dense-pack'd cities all and the teeming wharves and ways,
I float this carol with joy, with joy to thee O death.

XV

To the tally of my soul,
Loud and strong kept up the gray-brown bird,
With pure deliberate notes spreading filling the night.

Loud in the pines and cedars dim,
Clear in the freshness moist and the swamp-perfume,
And I with my comrades there in the night.

While my sight that was bound in my eyes unclosed,
As to long panoramas of visions.

And I saw askant the armies,
I saw as in noiseless dreams hundreds of battle-flags,
Borne through the smoke of the battles and pierc'd with missiles I saw them,
And carried hither and yon through the smoke, and torn and bloody,
And at last but a few shreds left on the staffs, (and all in silence,)
And the staffs all splinter'd and broken.

I saw battle-corpses, myriads of them,
And the white skeletons of young men, I saw them,
I saw the debris and debris of all the slain soldiers of the war,
But I saw they were not as was thought,
They themselves were fully at rest, they suffer'd not,
The living remain'd and suffer'd, the mother suffer'd,
And the wife and the child and the musing comrade suffer'd,
And the armies that remain'd suffer'd.

XVI

Passing the visions, passing the night,
Passing, unloosing the hold of my comrades' hands,
Passing the song of the hermit bird and the tallying song of my soul,
Victorious song, death's outlet song, yet varying ever-altering song,
As low and wailing, yet clear the notes, rising and falling, flooding the
night,
Sadly sinking and fainting, as warning and warning, and yet again burst-
ing with joy,
Covering the earth and filling the spread of the heaven,
As that powerful psalm in the night I heard from recesses,
Passing, I leave thee lilac with heart-shaped leaves,
I leave thee there in the door-yard, blooming, returning with spring.

I cease from my song for thee,
From my gaze on thee in the west, fronting the west, communing with
thee,
O comrade lustrous with silver face in the night.

Yet each to keep and all, retrievements out of the night,
The song, the wondrous chant of the gray-brown bird,
And the tallying chant, the echo arous'd in my soul,
With the lustrous and drooping star with the countenance full of woe,
With the holders holding my hand nearing the call of the bird,
Comrades mine and I in the midst, and their memory ever to keep,
for the dead I loved so well,
For the sweetest, wisest soul of all my days and lands — and this for his
dear sake,
Lilac and star and bird twined with the chant of my soul,
There in the fragrant pines and the cedars dusk and dim.

1865

A Noiseless Patient Spider

A noiseless patient spider,
I mark'd where on a little promontory it stood isolated,
Mark'd how to explore the vacant vast surrounding,
It launch'd forth filament, filament, filament, out of itself,
Ever unreeling them, ever tirelessly speeding them.

And you O my soul where you stand,
Surrounded, detached, in measureless oceans of space,
Ceaselessly musing, venturing, throwing, seeking the spheres to connect
them,
Till the bridge you will need be form'd, till the ductile anchor hold,
Till the gossamer thread you fling catch somewhere, O my soul.

1868

HERMAN MELVILLE (1819–1891)

"Failure is the true test of greatness," Herman Melville wrote, and it was a test fate compelled him to meet. His first novels were successes, but *Moby-Dick* (1851) had an unenthusiastic reception and *Pierre* a year later was savaged by the critics. "Herman has taken to writing poetry," wrote his wife in 1859. He collected his poems about the Civil War in *Battle-Pieces and Aspects of the War* (1866). In July 1863, he wrote "The House-Top" when Irish mobs in New York City, rioting against military conscription, lynched black men and hanged them from lampposts. Whitman (in such poems as "Reconciliation" and "Vigil Strange I Kept on the Field One Night") wrote about soldiers and wounds, close up; Melville wrote about the "great historic tragedy" from a distance. In *Call Me Ishmael* (1947), a personal reverie based on an academic undertaking, Charles Olson wrote: "The man made a mess of things. He got all balled up with Christ. He made a white marriage. He had one son die of tuberculosis, the other shoot himself. He only rode his own space once—*Moby-Dick*. He had to be wild or he was nothing in particular. He had to go fast, like an American, or he was all torpor. Half horse half alligator." (A "white marriage" is an unconsummated one.) "After the Pleasure Party," a late poem, presents Melville's dark vision of the relations between man and woman. In his copy of Emerson's *Essays*, where Emerson had written, "Trust men, and they will be true to you," Melville wrote in the margin, "God help the poor fellow who squares his life according to this."

The Portent

Hanging from the beam,
   Slowly swaying (such the law),
Gaunt the shadow on your green,
   Shenandoah!
The cut is on the crown
(Lo, John Brown),
And the stabs shall heal no more.

Hidden in the cap
   Is the anguish none can draw;
So your future veils its face,
   Shenandoah!
But the streaming beard is shown

(Weird John Brown),
The meteor of the war.

1859

Misgivings

When ocean-clouds over inland hills
  Sweep storming in late autumn brown,
And horror the sodden valley fills,
  And the spire falls crashing in the town,
I muse upon my country's ills —
The tempest bursting from the waste of Time
On the world's fairest hope linked with man's foulest crime.

Nature's dark side is heeded now —
  (Ah! optimist-cheer disheartened flown) —
A child may read the moody brow
  Of yon black mountain lone.
With shouts the torrents down the gorges go,
And storms are formed behind the storm we feel:
The hemlock shakes in the rafter, the oak in the driving keel.

1860

Ball's Bluff

A Reverie
(*October, 1861*)

One noonday, at my window in the town,
  I saw a sight — saddest that eyes can see —
  Young soldiers marching lustily
        Unto the wars,
With fifes, and flags in mottoed pageantry;
  While all the porches, walks, and doors
Were rich with ladies cheering royally.

They moved like Juny morning on the wave,
  Their hearts were fresh as clover in its prime
  (It was the breezy summer time),
        Life throbbed so strong,
How should they dream that Death in a rosy clime
  Would come to thin their shining throng?
Youth feels immortal, like the gods sublime.

Weeks passed; and at my window, leaving bed,
   By night I mused, of easeful sleep bereft,
   On those brave boys (Ah War! thy theft);
         Some marching feet
Found pause at last by cliffs Potomac cleft;
   Wakeful I mused, while in the street
Far footfalls died away till none were left.

1861

Shiloh

A Requiem

Skimming lightly, wheeling still,
   The swallows fly low
Over the field in clouded days,
   The forest-field of Shiloh —
Over the field where April rain
Solaced the parched ones stretched in pain
Through the pause of night
That followed the Sunday fight
   Around the church of Shiloh —
The church so lone, the log-built one,
That echoed to many a parting groan
      And natural prayer
   Of dying foemen mingled there —
Foemen at morn, but friends at eve —
   Fame or country least their care:
(What like a bullet can undeceive!)
   But now they lie low,
While over them the swallows skim,
   And all is hushed at Shiloh.

1862

The House-Top

A Night Piece

No sleep. The sultriness pervades the air
And binds the brain — a dense oppression, such
As tawny tigers feel in matted shades,
Vexing their blood and making apt for ravage.
Beneath the stars the roofy desert spreads

Vacant as Libya. All is hushed near by.
Yet fitfully from far breaks a mixed surf
Of muffled sound, the Atheist roar of riot.
Yonder, where parching Sirius set in drought,
Balefully glares red Arson — there — and there.
The Town is taken by its rats — ship-rats
And rats of the wharves. All civil charms
And priestly spells which late held hearts in awe —
Fear-bound, subjected to a better sway
Than sway of self; these like a dream dissolve,
And man rebounds whole æons back in nature.
Hail to the low dull rumble, dull and dead,
And ponderous drag that shakes the wall.
Wise Draco comes, deep in the midnight roll
Of black artillery; he comes, though late;
In code corroborating Calvin's creed
And cynic tyrannies of honest kings;
He comes, nor parlies; and the Town, redeemed,
Gives thanks devout; nor, being thankful, heeds
The grimy slur on the Republic's faith implied,
Which holds that Man is naturally good,
And — more — is Nature's Roman, never to be scourged.

1863

The Maldive Shark

About the Shark, phlegmatical one,
Pale sot of the Maldive sea,
The sleek little pilot-fish, azure and slim,
How alert in attendance be.
From his saw-pit of mouth, from his charnel of maw
They have nothing of harm to dread,
But liquidly glide on his ghastly flank
Or before his Gorgonian head;
Or lurk in the port of serrated teeth
In white triple tiers of glittering gates,
And there find a haven when peril's aboard,
An asylum in jaws of the Fates!
They are friends; and friendly they guide him to prey,
Yet never partake of the treat —
Eyes and brains to the dotard lethargic and dull,
Pale ravener of horrible meat.

1888

After the Pleasure Party

LINES TRACED
UNDER AN IMAGE OF
AMOR THREATENING

Fear me, virgin whosoever
Taking pride from love exempt,
Fear me, slighted. Never, never
Brave me, nor my fury tempt:
Downy wings, but wroth they beat
Tempest even in reason's seat.

Behind the house the upland falls
With many an odorous tree —
White marbles gleaming through green halls —
Terrace by terrace, down and down,
And meets the star-lit Mediterranean Sea.

'Tis Paradise. In such an hour
Some pangs that rend might take release.
Nor less perturbed who keeps this bower
Of balm, nor finds balsamic peace?
From whom the passionate words in vent
After long revery's discontent?

"Tired of the homeless deep,
Look how their flight yon hurrying billows urge
Hitherward but to reap
Passive repulse from the iron-bound verge!
Insensate, can they never know
'Tis mad to wreck the impulsion so?

"An art of memory is, they tell:
But to forget! forget the glade
Wherein Fate sprung Love's ambuscade,
To flout pale years of cloistral life
And flush me in this sensuous strife.
'Tis Vesta struck with Sappho's smart.
No fable her delirious leap:
With more of cause in desperate heart,
Myself could take it — but to sleep!

"Now first I feel, what all may ween,
That soon or late, if faded e'en,
One's sex asserts itself. Desire,
The dear desire through love to sway,
Is like the Geysers that aspire —
Through cold obstruction win their fervid way.

But baffled here — to take disdain,
To feel rule's instinct, yet not reign;
To dote, to come to this drear shame —
Hence the winged blaze that sweeps my soul
Like prairie-fires that spurn control,
Where withering weeds incense the flame.

"And kept I long heaven's watch for this,
Contemning love, for this, even this?
O terrace chill in Northern air,
O reaching ranging tube I placed
Against yon skies, and fable chased
Till, fool, I hailed for sister there
Starred Cassiopea in Golden Chair.
In dream I throned me, nor I saw
In cell the idiot crowned with straw.

"And yet, ah yet, scarce ill I reigned,
Through self-illusion self-sustained,
When now — enlightened, undeceived —
What gain I, barrenly bereaved!
Than this can be yet lower decline —
Envy and spleen, can these be mine?

"The peasant-girl demure that trod
Beside our wheels that climbed the way,
And bore along a blossoming rod
That looked the sceptre of May-Day —
On her — to fire this petty hell,
His softened glance how moistly fell!
The cheat! on briers her buds were strung;
And wiles peeped forth from mien how meek.
The innocent bare-foot! young, so young!
To girls, strong man's a novice weak.
To tell such beads! And more remain,
Sad rosary of belittling pain.

"When after lunch and sallies gay
Like the Decameron folk we lay
In sylvan groups; and I — let be!
O, dreams he, can he dream that one
Because not roseate feels no sun?
The plain lone bramble thrills with Spring
As much as vines that grapes shall bring.

"Me now fair studies charm no more.
Shall great thoughts writ, or high themes sung
Damask wan cheeks — unlock his arm
About some radiant ninny flung?

How glad, with all my starry lore,
I'd buy the veriest wanton's rose
Would but my bee therein repose.

"Could I remake me! or set free
This sexless bound in sex, then plunge
Deeper than Sappho, in a lunge
Piercing Pan's paramount mystery!
For, Nature, in no shallow surge
Against thee either sex may urge,
Why hast thou made us but in halves —
Co-relatives? This makes us slaves.
If these co-relatives never meet
Self-hood itself seems incomplete.
And such the dicing of blind fate
Few matching halves here meet and mate.
What Cosmic jest or Anarch blunder
The human integral clove asunder
And shied the fractions through life's gate?

"Ye stars that long your votary knew
Rapt in her vigil, see me here!
Whither is gone the spell ye threw
When rose before me Cassiopea?
Usurped on by love's stronger reign —
But, lo, your very selves do wane:
Light breaks — truth breaks! Silvered no more,
But chilled by dawn that brings the gale
Shivers yon bramble above the vale,
And disillusion opens all the shore."

One knows not if Urania yet
The pleasure-party may forget;
Or whether she lived down the strain
Of turbulent heart and rebel brain;
For Amor so resents a slight,
And hers had been such haught disdain,
He long may wreak his boyish spite,
And boy-like, little reck the pain.

One knows not, no. But late in Rome
(For queens discrowned a congruous home)
Entering Albani's porch she stood
Fixed by an antique pagan stone
Colossal carved. No anchorite seer,
Not Thomas à Kempis, monk austere,
Religious more are in their tone;
Yet far, how far from Christian heart

That form august of heathen Art.
Swayed by its influence, long she stood,
Till surged emotion seething down,
She rallied and this mood she won:

"Languid in frame for me,
To-day by Mary's convent-shrine,
Touched by her picture's moving plea
In that poor nerveless hour of mine,
I mused — A wanderer still must grieve.
Half I resolved to kneel and believe,
Believe and submit, the veil take on.
But thee, arm'd Virgin! less benign,
Thee now I invoke, thou mightier one.
Helmeted woman — if such term
Befit thee, far from strife
Of that which makes the sexual feud
And clogs the aspirant life —
O self-reliant, strong and free,
Thou in whom power and peace unite,
Transcender! raise me up to thee,
Raise me and arm me!"

Fond appeal.
For never passion peace shall bring,
Nor Art inanimate for long
Inspire. Nothing may help or heal
While Amor incensed remembers wrong.
Vindictive, not himself he'll spare;
For scope to give his vengeance play
Himself he'll blaspheme and betray.

Then for Urania, virgins everywhere,
O pray! Example take too, and have care.

1891

FREDERICK GODDARD TUCKERMAN (1821–1873)

Frederick Goddard Tuckerman was born in Boston, a merchant's son. He gave up a law practice to pursue studies in astronomy, botany, and literature, with the result that he published astronomical observations, gained recognition as an authority on local flora, and had his *Poems* printed privately in 1860. Tuckerman was forgotten after his death until the poet Witter Bynner took up his banner in 1931. Yvor Winters declared that only Wordsworth among the Romantics surpassed Tuckerman "in the description of natural detail."

Dank fens of cedar, hemlock branches gray

Dank fens of cedar, hemlock branches gray
With trees and trail of mosses, wringing-wet;
Beds of the black pitchpine in dead leaves set
Whose wasted red has wasted to white away;
Remnants of rain and droppings of decay, —
Why hold ye so my heart, nor dimly let
Through your deep leaves the light of yesterday,
The faded glimmer of a sunshine set?
Is it that in your darkness, shut from strife,
The bread of tears becomes the bread of life?
Far from the roar of day, beneath your boughs
Fresh griefs beat tranquilly, and loves and vows
Grow green in your gray shadows, dearer far
Even than all lovely lights and roses are?

1860

An upper chamber in a darkened house

An upper chamber in a darkened house,
Where, ere his footsteps reached ripe manhood's brink,
Terror and anguish were his lot to drink, —
I cannot rid the thought nor hold it close;
But dimly dream upon that man alone; —
Now though the autumn clouds most softly pass;
The cricket chides beneath the doorstep stone,
And greener than the season grows the grass.
Nor can I drop my lids nor shade my brows,
But there he stands beside the lifted sash;
And — with a swooning of the heart, I think
Where the black shingles slope to meet the boughs,
And — shattered on the roof like smallest snows —
The tiny petals of the mountain-ash.

1860

How oft in schoolboy-days

How oft in schoolboy-days, from the school's sway
Have I run forth to Nature as to a friend, —
With some pretext of o'erwrought sight, to spend
My school-time in green meadows far away!
Careless of summoning bell, or clocks that strike,
I marked with flowers the minutes of my day:
For still the eye that shrank from hated hours,
Dazzled with decimal and dividend,
Knew each bleached alder-root that plashed across

The bubbling brook, and every mass of moss;
Could tell the month, too, by the vervain-spike, —
How far the ring of purple tiny flowers
Had climbed; just starting, may-be, with the May,
Half-high, or tapering off at Summer's end.

1860

Sometimes I walk where the deep water dips

Sometimes I walk where the deep water dips
Against the land. Or on where fancy drives
I walk and muse aloud, like one who strives
To tell his half-shaped thought with stumbling lips,
And view the ocean sea, the ocean ships,
With joyless heart: still but myself I find
And restless phantoms of my restless mind:
Only the moaning of my wandering words,
Only the wailing of the wheeling plover,
And this high rock beneath whose base the sea
Has wormed long caverns, like my tears in me:
And hard like this I stand, and beaten and blind,
This desolate rock with lichens rusted over,
Hoar with salt-sleet and chalkings of the birds.

1860

HENRY TIMROD (1828–1867)

Henry Timrod was born in Charleston, South Carolina. He enlisted in the confederate army but was discharged because of ill health; he suffered from and eventually died of tuberculosis. As a war correspondent for the *Charleston Mercury*, he witnessed the retreat from Shiloh. In 1950, F. O. Matthiessen wrote that Timrod's "few war poems, which state the Southern cause with deep conviction, endure with a classic hardness. I am encouraged in the belief that Timrod is the best Southern poet of his time by knowing that it is also held by the leading Southern poets of our time, [John Crowe] Ransom and [Allen] Tate."

Charleston

Calm as that second summer which precedes
   The first fall of the snow,
In the broad sunlight of heroic deeds,
   The City bides the foe.

As yet, behind their ramparts stern and proud,
   Her bolted thunders sleep —

Dark Sumter, like a battlemented cloud,
   Looms o'er the solemn deep.

No Calpe frowns from lofty cliff or scar
   To guard the holy strand;
But Moultrie holds in leash her dogs of war
   Above the level sand.

And down the dunes a thousand guns lie couched,
   Unseen, beside the flood —
Like tigers in some Orient jungle crouched
   That wait and watch for blood.

Meanwhile, through streets still echoing with trade,
   Walk grave and thoughtful men,
Whose hands may one day wield the patriot's blade
   As lightly as the pen.

And maidens, with such eyes as would grow dim
   Over a bleeding hound,
Seem each one to have caught the strength of him
   Whose sword she sadly bound.

Thus girt without and garrisoned at home,
   Day patient following day,
Old Charleston looks from roof, and spire, and dome,
   Across her tranquil bay.

Ships, through a hundred foes, from Saxon lands
   And spicy Indian ports,
Bring Saxon steel and iron to her hands,
   And Summer to her courts.

But still, along yon dim Atlantic line,
   The only hostile smoke
Creeps like a harmless mist above the brine,
   From some frail, floating oak.

Shall the Spring dawn, and she still clad in smiles,
   And with an unscathed brow,
Rest in the strong arms of her palm-crowned isles,
   As fair and free as now?

We know not; in the temple of the Fates
   God has inscribed her doom;
And, all untroubled in her faith, she waits
   The triumph or the tomb.

published 1873

EMILY DICKINSON (1830–1886)

Emily Dickinson was born in Amherst, Massachusetts, and spent nearly all her life within its confines. The death-obsessed recluse who seldom left her house had this criterion for judging a poem: "If I read a book [and] it makes my whole body so cold no fire can ever warm me I know *that* is poetry. If I feel physically as if the top of my head were taken off, I know *that* is poetry. These are the only way [*sic*] I know it. Is there any other way." Only seven of her 1,775 poems were published in her lifetime, none with her full consent. Not until 1890, four years after her death, did a selection of her poems appear in print. During the years 1862 and 1863, as the Civil War raged, she wrote approximately one poem a day, none of them dealing directly with that terrible conflict. She wrote in a letter: "Life is a spell so exquisite that everything conspires to break it." Some of her poems are soluble riddles, but her insoluble ones are even more compelling, as she explained herself: "The Riddle we can guess/We speedily despise — / Not anything is stale so long/As Yesterday's surprise —" (#1,222). She and Walt Whitman are our two poetic grandparents, yet he had never heard of her, and she, when asked for her opinion of *Leaves of Grass*, said of Whitman, "I never read his book — but was told that he was disgraceful." Charles Simic has written: "Whitman and Dickinson are the prototypes of what an American poet could be, a bard commensurate in optimism with his people versus a recluse and a secret blasphemer." (See Donald Hall's poem "The Impossible Marriage," about these two unwed poets on their imaginary wedding day, in this volume.) From Dickinson's poems one might derive the illusion that she had died and written them posthumously. "To have been immortal transcends to become so," she wrote, as though having been in both positions.

Success is counted sweetest (67)

Success is counted sweetest
By those who ne'er succeed.
To comprehend a nectar
Requires sorest need.

Not one of all the purple Host
Who took the Flag today
Can tell the definition
So clear of Victory

As he defeated — dying —
On whose forbidden ear
The distant strains of triumph
Burst agonized and clear!

1859

"Faith" is a fine invention (185)

"Faith" is a fine invention
When Gentlemen can *see* —

But *Microscopes* are prudent
In an Emergency.

1860

I taste a liquor never brewed (214)

I taste a liquor never brewed —
From Tankards scooped in Pearl —
Not all the Frankfort Berries
Yield such an Alcohol!

Inebriate of Air — am I —
And Debauchee of Dew —
Reeling — thro endless summer days —
From inns of Molten Blue —

When "Landlords" turn the drunken Bee
Out of the Foxglove's door —
When Butterflies — renounce their "drams" —
I shall but drink the more!

Till Seraphs swing their snowy Hats —
And Saints — to windows run —
To see the little Tippler
From Manzanilla come!

1860

Safe in their Alabaster Chambers (216)

Safe in their Alabaster Chambers —
Untouched by Morning
And untouched by Noon —
Sleep the meek members of the Resurrection —
Rafter of satin,
And Roof of stone.

Light laughs the breeze
In her Castle above them —
Babbles the Bee in a stolid Ear,
Pipe the Sweet Birds in ignorant cadence —
Ah, what sagacity perished here!

1859

Safe in their Alabaster Chambers —
Untouched by Morning —
And untouched by Noon —
Lie the meek members of the Resurrection —
Rafter of Satin — and Roof of Stone!

Grand go the Years — in the Crescent — above them —
Worlds scoop their Arcs —
And Firmaments — row —
Diadems — drop — and Doges — surrender —
Soundless as dots — on a Disc of Snow —

1861

Wild Nights — Wild Nights! (249)

Wild Nights — Wild Nights!
Were I with thee
Wild Nights should be
Our luxury!

Futile — the Winds —
To a Heart in port —
Done with the Compass —
Done with the Chart!

Rowing in Eden —
Ah, the Sea!
Might I but moor — Tonight —
In Thee!

1861

"Hope" is the thing with feathers (254)

"Hope" is the thing with feathers —
That perches in the soul —
And sings the tune without the words —
And never stops — at all —

And sweetest — in the Gale — is heard —
And sore must be the storm —
That could abash the little Bird
That kept so many warm —

I've heard it in the chillest land —
And on the strangest Sea —

Yet, never, in Extremity,
It asked a crumb — of Me.

1861

There's a certain Slant of light (258)

There's a certain Slant of light,
Winter Afternoons —
That oppresses, like the Heft
Of Cathedral Tunes —

Heavenly Hurt, it gives us —
We can find no scar,
But internal difference,
Where the Meanings, are —

None may teach it — Any —
'Tis the Seal Despair —
An imperial affliction
Sent us of the Air —

When it comes, the Landscape listens —
Shadows — hold their breath —
When it goes, 'tis like the Distance
On the look of Death —

1861

I felt a Funeral, in my Brain (280)

I felt a Funeral, in my Brain,
And Mourners to and fro
Kept treading — treading — till it seemed
That Sense was breaking through —

And when they all were seated,
A Service, like a Drum —
Kept beating — beating — till I thought
My Mind was going numb —

And then I heard them lift a Box
And creak across my Soul
With those same Boots of Lead, again,
Then Space — began to toll,

As all the Heavens were a Bell,
And Being, but an Ear,
And I, and Silence, some strange Race
Wrecked, solitary, here —

And then a Plank in Reason, broke,
And I dropped down, and down —
And hit a World, at every plunge,
And Finished knowing — then —

1861

I'm Nobody! Who are you? (288)

I'm Nobody! Who are you?
Are you — Nobody — too?
Then there's a pair of us!
Don't tell! they'd banish us — you know!

How dreary — to be — Somebody!
How public — like a Frog —
To tell your name — the livelong June —
To an admiring Bog!

1861

The Soul selects her own Society (303)

The Soul selects her own Society —
Then — shuts the Door —
To her divine Majority —
Present no more —

Unmoved — she notes the Chariots — pausing —
At her low Gate —
Unmoved — an Emperor be kneeling
Upon her Mat —

I've known her — from an ample nation —
Choose One —
Then — close the Valves of her attention —
Like Stone —

1862

A Bird came down the Walk (328)

A Bird came down the Walk —
He did not know I saw —
He bit an Angleworm in halves
And ate the fellow, raw,

And then he drank a Dew
From a convenient Grass —
And then hopped sidewise to the Wall
To let a Beetle pass —

He glanced with rapid eyes
That hurried all around —
They looked like frightened Beads, I thought —
He stirred his Velvet Head

Like one in danger, Cautious,
I offered him a Crumb
And he unrolled his feathers
And rowed him softer home —

Than Oars divide the Ocean,
Too silver for a seam —
Or Butterflies, off Banks of Noon
Leap, plashless as they swim.

1862

After great pain, a formal feeling comes (341)

After great pain, a formal feeling comes —
The Nerves sit ceremonious, like Tombs —
The stiff Heart questions was it He, that bore,
And Yesterday, or Centuries before?

The Feet, mechanical, go round —
Of Ground, or Air, or Ought —
A Wooden way
Regardless grown,
A Quartz contentment, like a stone —

This is the Hour of Lead —
Remembered, if outlived,
As Freezing persons, recollect the Snow —
First — Chill — then Stupor — then the letting go —

1862

Dare you see a Soul at the White Heat? *(365)*

Dare you see a Soul *at the White Heat?* —
Then crouch within the door —
Red — is the Fire's common tint —
But when the vivid Ore
Has vanquished Flame's conditions,
It quivers from the Forge
Without a color, but the light
Of unanointed Blaze.
Least Village has its Blacksmith
Whose Anvil's even ring
Stands symbol for the finer Forge
That soundless tugs — within —
Refining these impatient Ores
With Hammer, and with Blaze
Until the Designated Light
Repudiate the Forge —

1862

Much Madness is divinest Sense (435)

Much Madness is divinest Sense —
To a discerning Eye —
Much Sense — the starkest Madness —
'Tis the Majority
In this, as All, prevail —
Assent — and you are sane —
Demur — you're straightway dangerous —
And handled with a Chain —

1862

This was a Poet — It is That (448)

This was a Poet — It is That
Distills amazing sense
From ordinary Meanings —
And Attar so immense

From the familiar species
That perished by the Door —
We wonder it was not Ourselves
Arrested it — before —

Of Pictures, the Discloser —
The Poet — it is He —
Entitles Us — by Contrast —
To ceaseless Poverty —

Of Portion — so unconscious —
The Robbing — could not harm —
Himself — to Him — a Fortune —
Exterior — to Time —

1862

I died for Beauty — but was scarce (449)

I died for Beauty — but was scarce
Adjusted in the Tomb
When One who died for Truth, was lain
In an adjoining Room —

He questioned softly "Why I failed"?
"For Beauty", I replied —
"And I — for Truth — Themself are One —
We Bretheren, are", He said —

And so, as Kinsmen, met a Night —
We talked between the Rooms —
Until the Moss had reached our lips —
And covered up — our names —

1862

I heard a Fly buzz — when I died (465)

I heard a Fly buzz — when I died —
The Stillness in the Room
Was like the Stillness in the Air —
Between the Heaves of Storm —

The Eyes around — had wrung them dry —
And Breaths were gathering firm
For that last Onset — when the King
Be witnessed — in the Room —

I willed my Keepsakes — Signed away
What portion of me be
Assignable — and then it was
There interposed a Fly —

With Blue — uncertain stumbling Buzz —
Between the light — and me —
And then the Windows failed — and then
I could not see to see —

1862

I am alive — I guess (470)

I am alive—I guess —
The Branches on my Hand
Are full of Morning Glory —
And at my finger's end —

The Carmine — tingles warm —
And if I hold a Glass
Across my Mouth — it blurs it —
Physician's — proof of Breath —

I am alive — because
I am not in a Room —
The Parlor — Commonly — it is —
So Visitors may come —

And lean — and view it sidewise —
And add "How cold — it grew" —
And "Was it conscious — when it stepped
In Immortality?"

I am alive — because
I do not own a House —
Entitled to myself — precise —
And fitting no one else —

And marked my Girlhood's name —
So Visitors may know
Which Door is mine — and not mistake —
And try another Key —

1862

I would not paint — a picture (505)

I would not paint — a picture —
I'd rather be the One
Its bright impossibility
To dwell — delicious — on —

And wonder how the fingers feel
Whose rare — celestial — stir —
Evokes so sweet a Torment —
Such sumptuous — Despair —

I would not talk, like Cornets —
I'd rather be the One
Raised softly to the Ceilings —
And out, and easy on —
Through Villages of Ether —
Myself endued Balloon
By but a lip of Metal —
The pier to my Pontoon —

Nor would I be a Poet —
It's finer — own the Ear —
Enamored — impotent — content —
The License to revere,
A privilege so awful
What would the Dower be,
Had I the Art to stun myself
With Bolts of Melody!

1862

It was not Death, for I stood up (510)

It was not Death, for I stood up,
And all the Dead, lie down —
It was not Night, for all the Bells
Put out their Tongues, for Noon.

It was not Frost, for on my Flesh
I felt Siroccos — crawl —
Nor Fire — for just my Marble feet
Could keep a Chancel, cool —

And yet, it tasted, like them all,
The Figures I have seen
Set orderly, for Burial,
Reminded me, of mine —

As if my life were shaven,
And fitted to a frame,
And could not breathe without a key,
And 'twas like Midnight, some —

When everything that ticked — has stopped —
And Space stares all around —
Or Grisly frosts — first Autumn morns,
Repeal the Beating Ground —

But, most, like Chaos — Stopless — cool —
Without a Chance, or Spar —
Or even a Report of Land —
To justify — Despair.

1862

The Soul has Bandaged moments (512)

The Soul has Bandaged moments —
When too appalled to stir —
She feels some ghastly Fright come up
And stop to look at her —

Salute her — with long fingers —
Caress her freezing hair —
Sip, Goblin, from the very lips
The Lover — hovered — o'er —
Unworthy, that a thought so mean
Accost a Theme — so — fair —

The Soul has moments of Escape —
When bursting all the doors —
She dances like a Bomb, abroad,
And swings upon the Hours,

As do the Bee — delirious borne —
Long Dungeoned from his Rose —
Touch Liberty — then know no more,
But Noon, and Paradise —

The Soul's retaken moments —
When, Felon led along,
With shackles on the plumed feet,
And staples, in the Song,

The Horror welcomes her, again,
These, are not brayed of Tongue —

1862

The Heart asks Pleasure — first (536)

The Heart asks Pleasure — first —
And then — Excuse from Pain —
And then — those little Anodynes
That deaden suffering —

And then — to go to sleep —
And then — if it should be
The will of its Inquisitor
The privilege to die —

1862

I reckon — when I count at all (569)

I reckon — when I count at all —
First — Poets — Then the Sun —
Then Summer — then the Heaven of God —
And then — the List is done —

But, looking back — the First so seems
To Comprehend the Whole —
The Others look a needless Show —
So I write — Poets — All —

Their Summer — lasts a Solid Year —
They can afford a Sun
The East — would deem extravagant —
And if the Further Heaven —

Be Beautiful as they prepare
For Those who worship Them —
It is too difficult a Grace —
To justify the Dream —

1862

I like to see it lap the Miles (585)

I like to see it lap the Miles —
And lick the Valleys up —
And stop to feed itself at Tanks
And then — prodigious step

Around a Pile of Mountains —
And supercilious peer

In Shanties — by the sides of Roads
And then a Quarry pare

To fit its sides
And crawl between
Complaining all the while
In horrid — hooting stanza —
Then chase itself down Hill —

And neigh like Boanerges —
Then — prompter than a Star
Stop — docile and omnipotent
At its own stable door —

1862

They shut me up in Prose (613)

They shut me up in Prose —
As when a little Girl
They put me in the Closet —
Because they like me "still" —

Still! Could themself have peeped —
And seen my Brain — go round —
They might as wise have lodged a Bird
For Treason — in the Pound —

Himself has but no will
And easy as a Star
Look down upon Captivity —
And laugh — No more have I —

1862

The Brain — is wider than the Sky (632)

The Brain — is wider than the Sky —
  For — put them side by side —
The one the other will contain
  With ease — and You — beside.

The Brain is deeper than the sea —
  For — hold them — Blue to Blue —
The one the other will absorb —
  As Sponges — Buckets — do —

The Brain is just the weight of God —
   For — Heft them — Pound for Pound —
And they will differ, if they do,
   As Syllable from Sound —

1862

I cannot live with You (640)

I cannot live with You —
It would be Life —
And Life is over there —
Behind the Shelf

The Sexton keeps the Key to —
Putting up
Our Life — His Porcelain —
Like a Cup —

Discarded of the Housewife —
Quaint — or Broke —
A newer Sevres pleases —
Old Ones crack —

I could not die — with You —
For One must wait
To shut the Other's Gaze down —
You — could not —

And I — Could I stand by
And see You — freeze —
Without my Right of Frost —
Death's privilege?

Nor could I rise — with You —
Because Your Face
Would put out Jesus' —
That New Grace

Glow plain — and foreign
On my homesick Eye —
Except that You than He
Shone closer by —

They'd judge Us — How —
For You — served Heaven — You know,
Or sought to —
I could not —

Because You saturated Sight —
And I had no more Eyes
For sordid excellence
As Paradise

And were You lost, I would be —
Though My Name
Rang loudest
On the Heavenly fame —

And were You — saved —
And I — condemned to be
Where You were not —
That self — were Hell to Me —

So We must meet apart —
You there — I —here —
With just the Door ajar
That Oceans are — and Prayer —
And that White Sustenance —
Despair —

1862

Pain — has an Element of Blank (650)

Pain — has an Element of Blank —
It cannot recollect
When it begun — or if there were
A time when it was not —

It has no Future — but itself —
Its Infinite contain
Its Past — enlightened to perceive
New Periods — of Pain.

1862

I dwell in Possibility (657)

I dwell in Possibility —
A fairer House than Prose —
More numerous of Windows —
Superior — for Doors —

Of Chambers as the Cedars —
Impregnable of Eye —

And for an Everlasting Roof
The Gambrels of the Sky —

Of Visiters — the fairest —
For Occupation — This —
The spreading wide my narrow Hands
To gather Paradise —

1862

Title divine — is mine! (1072)

Title divine — is mine!
The Wife — without the Sign!
Acute Degree — conferred on me —
Empress of Calvary!
Royal — all but the Crown!
Betrothed — without the swoon
God sends us Women —
When you — hold — Garnet to Garnet —
Gold — to Gold —
Born — Bridalled — Shrouded —
In a Day —
Tri Victory
"My Husband" — women say —
Stroking the Melody —
Is *this* — the way?

1862

Publication — is the Auction (709)

Publication — is the Auction
Of the Mind of Man —
Poverty — be justifying
For so foul a thing

Possibly — but We — would rather
From Our Garret go
White — Unto the White Creator —
Than invest — Our Snow —

Thought belong to Him who gave it —
Then — to Him Who bear
Its Corporeal illustration — Sell
The Royal Air —

In the Parcel — Be the Merchant
Of the Heavenly Grace —
But reduce no Human Spirit
To Disgrace of Price —

1863

Because I could not stop for Death (712)

Because I could not stop for Death —
He kindly stopped for me —
The Carriage held but just Ourselves —
And Immortality.

We slowly drove — He knew no haste
And I had put away
My labor and my leisure too,
For His Civility —

We passed the School, where Children strove
At Recess — in the Ring —
We passed the Fields of Gazing Grain —
We passed the Setting Sun —

Or rather — He passed Us —
The Dews drew quivering and chill —
For only Gossamer, my Gown —
My Tippet — only Tulle —

We paused before a House that seemed
A Swelling of the Ground —
The Roof was scarcely visible —
The Cornice — in the Ground —

Since then — 'tis Centuries — and yet
Feels shorter than the Day
I first surmised the Horses Heads
Were toward Eternity —

1863

My Life had stood — a Loaded Gun (754)

My Life had stood — a Loaded Gun —
In Corners — till a Day
The Owner passed — identified —
And carried Me away —

And now We roam in Soverign Woods —
And now We hunt the Doe —
And every time I speak for Him —
The Mountains straight reply —

And do I smile, such cordial light
Upon the Valley glow —
It is as a Vesuvian face
Had let its pleasure through —

And when at Night — Our good Day done —
I guard My Master's Head —
'Tis better than the Eider-Duck's
Deep Pillow — to have shared —

To foe of His — I'm deadly foe —
None stir the second time —
On whom I lay a Yellow Eye —
Or an emphatic Thumb —

Though I than He — may longer live
He longer must — than I —
For I have but the power to kill,
Without — the power to die —

1863

A narrow Fellow in the Grass (986)

A narrow Fellow in the Grass
Occasionally rides —
You may have met Him — did you not
His notice sudden is —

The Grass divides as with a Comb —
A spotted shaft is seen —
And then it closes at your feet
And opens further on —

He likes a Boggy Acre
A Floor too cool for Corn —
Yet when a Boy, and Barefoot —
I more than once at Noon

Have passed, I thought, a Whip lash
Unbraiding in the Sun
When stooping to secure it
It wrinkled, and was gone —

Several of Nature's People
I know, and they know me —
I feel for them a transport
Of cordiality —

But never met this Fellow
Attended, or alone
Without a tighter breathing
And Zero at the Bone —

1865

Bee! I'm expecting you! (1035)

Bee! I'm expecting you!
Was saying Yesterday
To Somebody you know
That you were due —

The Frogs got Home last Week —
Are settled, and at work —
Birds, mostly back —
The Clover warm and thick —

You'll get my Letter by
The seventeenth; Reply
Or better, be with me —
Yours, Fly.

1865

Further in Summer than the Birds (1068)

Further in Summer than the Birds
Pathetic from the Grass
A minor Nation celebrates
It's unobtrusive Mass.

No Ordinance be seen
So gradual the Grace
A pensive Custom it becomes
Enlarging Loneliness.

Antiquest felt at Noon
When August burning low
Arise this spectral Canticle
Repose to typify

Remit as yet no Grace
No Furrow on the Glow
Yet a Druidic Difference
Enhances Nature now

1866

Tell all the Truth but tell it slant (1129)

Tell all the Truth but tell it slant —
Success in Circuit lies
Too bright for our infirm Delight
The Truth's superb surprise
As Lightning to the Children eased
With explanation kind
The Truth must dazzle gradually
Or every man be blind —

c. 1868

The Riddle we can guess (1222)

The Riddle we can guess
We speedily despise —
Not anything is stale so long
As Yesterday's surprise —

c. 1870

There is no Frigate like a Book (1263)

There is no Frigate like a Book
To take us Lands away
Nor any Coursers like a Page
Of prancing Poetry —
This Traverse may the poorest take
Without oppress of Toll —
How frugal is the Chariot
That bears the Human soul.

c. 1873

Escape is such a thankful Word (1347)

Escape is such a thankful Word
I often in the Night
Consider it unto myself
No spectacle in sight

Escape — it is the Basket
In which the Heart is caught
When down some awful Battlement
The rest of Life is dropt —

'Tis not to sight the savior —
It is to be the saved —
And that is why I lay my Head
Upon this trusty word —

c. 1875

"Go tell it" — What a Message (1554)

"Go tell it" — What a Message —
To whom — is specified —
Not murmur — not endearment —
But simply — we — obeyed —
Obeyed — a Lure — a Longing?
Oh Nature — none of this —
To Law — said sweet Thermopylae
I give my dying Kiss —

c. 1882

My life closed twice before its close (1732)

My life closed twice before its close;
It yet remains to see
If Immortality unveil
A third event to me,

So huge, so hopeless to conceive
As these that twice befel.
Parting is all we know of heaven,
And all we need of hell.

published 1896

Fame is a bee (1763)

Fame is a bee.
   It has a song —
It has a sting —
   Ah, too, it has a wing.

published 1898

EMMA LAZARUS (1849–1887)

Emma Lazarus, the daughter of a wealthy sugar merchant, came from a Sephardic Jewish family that had settled in New York City long before the Colonies declared their independence from Britain. She wrote her most famous poem for an auction to raise the cash needed to build a pedestal for the Statue of Liberty. At the ceremony dedicating the statue on 28 October 1886, no one read Lazarus's sonnet. Not until the 1930s, when Europeans in droves began seeking asylum from Fascist persecution, came the widespread recognition that "The New Colossus" expressed the true intention of the statue. As the title indicates, the Statue of Liberty is a replacement for the Colossus of Rhodes, "the brazen giant of Greek fame." The great bronze monument to the sun god, one of the Seven Wonders of the World, stood in the harbor of Rhodes. (It crumbled in an earthquake in 224 BC.) It is instructive to compare "The New Colossus" with Percy Bysshe Shelley's "Ozymandias," also a sonnet, which describes the ruin of a grandiose monument in Egypt built by an ancient emperor to memorialize his imperial self. The Egyptian monument's legend reads: "My name is Ozymandias, king of kings; / Look on my works, ye Mighty, and despair!" The triumphant epitaph is mocked in the wreckage and in the "lone and level" desert sands stretching out on all sides around it. Where Shelley's sonnet pivots on a boast made hollow by the monument's fate, the "Mother of Exiles" in Lazarus's poem issues not a boast but a vow, with the stress not on the glorification of the self but on the rescue of others.

The New Colossus

Not like the brazen giant of Greek fame,
With conquering limbs astride from land to land;
Here at our sea-washed, sunset gates shall stand
A mighty woman with a torch, whose flame
Is the imprisoned lightning, and her name
Mother of Exiles. From her beacon-hand
Glows world-wide welcome; her mild eyes command
The air-bridged harbor that twin cities frame.
"Keep, ancient lands, your storied pomp!" cries she
With silent lips. "Give me your tired, your poor,
Your huddled masses yearning to breathe free,
The wretched refuse of your teeming shore.
Send these, the homeless, tempest-tost to me,
I lift my lamp beside the golden door!"

1883

Venus of the Louvre

Down the long hall she glistens like a star,
The foam-born mother of Love, transfixed to stone,
Yet none the less immortal, breathing on.
Time's brutal hand hath maimed but could not mar.
When first the enthralled enchantress from afar
Dazzled mine eyes, I saw not her alone,

Serenely poised on her world-worshipped throne,
As when she guided once her dove-drawn car, —
But at her feet a pale, death-stricken Jew,
Her life adorer, sobbed farewell to love.
Here *Heine* wept! Here still he weeps anew,
Nor ever shall his shadow lift or move,
While mourns one ardent heart, one poet-brain,
For vanished Hellas and Hebraic pain.

1888

Long Island Sound

I see it as it looked one afternoon
In August,—by a fresh soft breeze o'erblown.
The swiftness of the tide, the light thereon,
A far-off sail, white as a crescent moon.
The shining waters with pale currents strewn,
The quiet fishing-smacks, the Eastern cove,
The semi-circle of its dark, green grove.
The luminous grasses, and the merry sun
In the grave sky; the sparkle far and wide,
Laughter of unseen children, cheerful chirp
Of crickets, and low lisp of rippling tide,
Light summer clouds fantastical as sleep
Changing unnoted while I gazed thereon.
All these fair sounds and sights I made my own.

1888

1492

Thou two-faced year, Mother of Change and Fate,
Didst weep when Spain cast forth with flaming sword,
The children of the prophets of the Lord,
Prince, priest, and people, spurned by zealot hate.
Hounded from sea to sea, from state to state,
The West refused them, and the East abhorred.
No anchorage the known world could afford,
Close-locked was every port, barred every gate.

Then smiling, thou unveil'dst, O two-faced year,
A virgin world where doors of sunset part,
Saying, "Ho, all who weary, enter here!
There falls each ancient barrier that the art
Of race or creed or rank devised, to rear
Grim bulwarked hatred between heart and heart!"

1888

EDWIN MARKHAM (1852–1940)

Edwin Markham was born in Oregon City, Oregon. Inspired by Millet's painting of a bowed and overburdened worker, Markham universalized the plight of the French peasant in "The Man with the Hoe." This poem of social protest appeared in the *San Francisco Examiner* on 15 January 1899, and quickly became that rare thing, a poem that galvanizes public opinion. The text that follows is the revised version of 1920.

The Man with the Hoe

(Written after seeing Millet's world-famous painting)

Bowed by the weight of centuries he leans
Upon his hoe and gazes on the ground,
The emptiness of ages in his face,
And on his back the burden of the world.
Who made him dead to rapture and despair,
A thing that grieves not and that never hopes,
Stolid and stunned, a brother to the ox?
Who loosened and let down this brutal jaw?
Whose was the hand that slanted back this brow?
Whose breath blew out the light within this brain?

Is this the Thing the Lord God made and gave
To have dominion over sea and land;
To trace the stars and search the heavens for power;
To feel the passion of Eternity?
Is this the dream He dreamed who shaped the suns
And marked their ways upon the ancient deep?
Down all the caverns of Hell to their last gulf
There is no shape more terrible than this —
More tongued with censure of the world's blind greed —
More filled with signs and portents for the soul —
More packt with danger to the universe.

What gulfs between him and the seraphim!
Slave of the wheel of labor, what to him
Are Plato and the swing of Pleiades?
What the long reaches of the peaks of song,
The rift of dawn, the reddening of the rose?
Through this dread shape the suffering ages look;
Time's tragedy is in that aching stoop;
Through this dread shape humanity betrayed,
Plundered, profaned, and disinherited,
Cries protest to the Judges of the World,
A protest that is also prophecy.

O masters, lords and rulers in all lands,
Is this the handiwork you give to God,
This monstrous thing distorted and soul-quenched?
How will you ever straighten up this shape;
Touch it again with immortality;
Give back the upward looking and the light;
Rebuild in it the music and the dream;
Make right the immemorial infamies,
Perfidious wrongs, immedicable woes?

O masters, lords and rulers in all lands,
How will the Future reckon with this man?
How answer his brute question in that hour
When whirlwinds of rebellion shake all shores?
How will it be with kingdoms and with kings —
With those who shaped him to the thing he is —
When this dumb Terror shall rise to judge the world,
After the silence of the centuries?

1899

KATHARINE LEE BATES (1859–1929)

In 1893, Katharine Lee Bates, a professor at Wellesley College, visited the World's Fair in Chicago and the Rocky Mountains in Colorado. When she climbed Pike's Peak she began writing "America the Beautiful" while "looking out over the sea-like expanse of fertile country." She published the hymn in 1895 and revised it in 1904. Sung to the tune of Samuel A. Ward's hymn "Materna," it has become hugely popular and is sometimes advocated as a replacement for "The Star-Spangled Banner" as the national anthem on the grounds that it is both easier to sing and less bellicose.

America the Beautiful

I

O beautiful for spacious skies,
   For amber waves of grain,
For purple mountain majesties
   Above the fruited plain!
   America! America!
   God shed his grace on thee
And crown thy good with brotherhood
From sea to shining sea!

II

O beautiful for pilgrim feet
   Whose stern impassioned stress

A thoroughfare for freedom beat
  Across the wilderness!
  America! America!
  God mend thine every flaw,
Confirm thy soul in self-control,
Thy liberty in law!

III

O beautiful for heroes proved
  In liberating strife,
Who more than self the country loved
  And mercy more than life!
  America! America!
  May God thy gold refine
Till all success be nobleness
And every gain divine!

IV

O beautiful for patriot dream
  That sees beyond the years
Thine alabaster cities gleam
  Undimmed by human tears!
  America! America!
  God shed his grace on thee
And crown thy good with brotherhood
From sea to shining sea!

1911

Ernest Lawrence Thayer (1863–1940)

Ernest Lawrence Thayer, the son of a mill owner, grew up in Worcester, Massachusetts, and graduated from Harvard with William Randolph Hearst. "Casey at the Bat" appeared first in Hearst's *San Francisco Examiner* on 3 June 1888. Thayer, who was not proud of the poem, received $5 for it. Why has "Casey" endured? "Casey must strike out: Casey's failure is the poem's success," Donald Hall explains. The poem's "language is a small consistent comic triumph of irony." A mock-epic, the poem is a critique of hero worship, a point that is intimated by the poem's original subtitle, "A Ballad of the Republic."

Casey at the Bat

A Ballad of the Republic, Sung in the Year 1888

The outlook wasn't brilliant for the Mudville nine that day;
The score stood four to two with but one inning more to
    play.

And then when Cooney died at first, and Barrows did the
same,
A sickly silence fell upon the patrons of the game.

A straggling few got up to go in deep despair. The rest
Clung to that hope which springs eternal in the human
breast;
They thought if only Casey could but get a whack at that —
We'd put up even money now with Casey at the bat.

But Flynn preceded Casey, as did also Jimmy Blake,
And the former was a lulu and the latter was a cake;
So upon that stricken multitude grim melancholy sat,
For there seemed but little chance of Casey's getting to the
bat.

But Flynn let drive a single, to the wonderment of all,
And Blake, the much despis-ed, tore the cover off the ball;
And when the dust had lifted, and the men saw what had
occurred,
There was Jimmy safe at second and Flynn a-hugging third.

Then from 5,000 throats and more there rose a lusty yell;
It rumbled through the valley, it rattled in the dell;
It knocked upon the mountain and recoiled upon the flat,
For Casey, mighty Casey, was advancing to the bat.

There was ease in Casey's manner as he stepped into his
place;
There was pride in Casey's bearing and a smile on Casey's
face.
And when, responding to the cheers, he lightly doffed his
hat,
No stranger in the crowd could doubt 'twas Casey at the
bat.

Ten thousand eyes were on him as he rubbed his hands
with dirt;
Five thousand tongues applauded when he wiped them on
his shirt.
Then while the writhing pitcher ground the ball into his
hip,
Defiance gleamed in Casey's eye, a sneer curled Casey's lip.

And now the leather-covered sphere came hurtling through
the air,
And Casey stood a-watching it in haughty grandeur there.

Close by the sturdy batsman the ball unheeded sped —
"That ain't my style," said Casey. "Strike one," the umpire
said.

From the benches, black with people, there went up a
muffled roar,
Like the beating of the storm-waves on a stern and distant
shore.
"Kill him! Kill the umpire!" shouted some one on the stand;
And it's likely they'd have killed him had not Casey raised
his hand.

With a smile of Christian charity great Casey's visage
shone;
He stilled the rising tumult; he bade the game go on;
He signaled to the pitcher, and once more the spheroid
flew;
But Casey still ignored it, and the umpire said, "Strike
two."

"Fraud!" cried the maddened thousands, and echo answered
fraud;
But one scornful look from Casey and the audience was
awed.
They saw his face grow stern and cold, they saw his
muscles strain,
And they knew that Casey wouldn't let that ball go by
again.

The sneer is gone from Casey's lip, his teeth are clinched in
hate;
He pounds with cruel violence his bat upon the plate.
And now the pitcher holds the ball, and now he lets it go,
And now the air is shattered by the force of Casey's blow.

Oh, somewhere in this favored land the sun is shining
bright;
The band is playing somewhere, and somewhere hearts are
light,
And somewhere men are laughing, and somewhere children
shout;
But there is no joy in Mudville — mighty Casey has struck
out.

1888

EDGAR LEE MASTERS (1868–1950)

Edgar Lee Masters was born in Garnett, Kansas, and grew up in the Illinois towns of Petersburg and Lewistown, near the Spoon River. Randall Jarrell described *Spoon River Anthology*, Masters's collection of verse portraits of small-town characters, as "a 'Main Street' through whose mud the old buggies and the new horseless carriages are still pushing." Louise Bogan detected a "hint of nostalgia" in Masters's presentation of "these thin, baffled, sour lives."

The Hill

Where are Elmer, Herman, Bert, Tom and Charley,
The weak of will, the strong of arm, the clown, the boozer, the fighter?
All, all, are sleeping on the hill.

One passed in a fever,
One was burned in a mine,
One was killed in a brawl,
One died in a jail,
One fell from a bridge toiling for children and wife —
All, all are sleeping, sleeping, sleeping on the hill.

Where are Ella, Kate, Mag, Lizzie and Edith,
The tender heart, the simple soul, the loud, the proud, the happy
    one? —
All, all, are sleeping on the hill.

One died in shameful child-birth,
One of a thwarted love,
One at the hands of a brute in a brothel,
One of a broken pride, in the search for heart's desire,
One after life in far-away London and Paris
Was brought to her little space by Ella and Kate and Mag —
All, all are sleeping, sleeping, sleeping on the hill.

Where are Uncle Isaac and Aunt Emily,
And old Towny Kincaid and Sevigne Houghton,
And Major Walker who had talked
With venerable men of the revolution? —
All, all, are sleeping on the hill.

They brought them dead sons from the war,
And daughters whom life had crushed,
And their children fatherless, crying —
All, all are sleeping, sleeping, sleeping on the hill.

Where is Old Fiddler Jones
Who played with life all his ninety years,
Braving the sleet with bared breast,
Drinking, rioting, thinking neither of wife nor kin,
Nor gold, nor love, nor heaven?
Lo! he babbles of the fish-frys of long ago,
Of the horse-races of long ago at Clary's Grove,
Of what Abe Lincoln said
One time at Springfield.

1915

Editor Whedon

To be able to see every side of every question;
To be on every side, to be everything, to be nothing long;
To pervert truth, to ride it for a purpose,
To use great feelings and passions of the human family
For base designs, for cunning ends;
To wear a mask like the Greek actors —
Your eight-page paper — behind which you huddle,
Bawling through the megaphone of big type;
"This is I, the giant."
Thereby also living the life of a sneak-thief,
Poisoned with the anonymous words
Of your clandestine soul.
To scratch dirt over scandal for money,
And exhume it to the winds for revenge,
Or to sell papers,
Crushing reputations, or bodies, if need be;
To win at any cost, save your own life.
To glory in demoniac power, ditching civilization,
As a paranoiac boy puts a log on the track
And derails the express train.
To be an editor, as I was.
Then to lie here close by the river over the place
Where the sewage flows from the village,
And the empty cans and garbage are dumped,
And abortions are hidden.

1915

Anne Rutledge

Out of me unworthy and unknown
The vibrations of deathless music;

"With malice toward none, with charity for all."
Out of me the forgiveness of millions toward millions,
And the beneficent face of a nation
Shining with justice and truth.
I am Anne Rutledge who sleep beneath these weeds,
Beloved in life of Abraham Lincoln,
Wedded to him, not through union,
But through separation.
Bloom forever, O Republic,
From the dust of my blossom!

1915

Amanda Barker

Henry got me with child,
Knowing that I could not bring forth life
Without losing my own.
In my youth therefore I entered the portals of dust.
Traveler, it is believed in the village where I lived
That Henry loved me with a husband's love,
But I proclaim from the dust
That he slew me to gratify his hatred.

1915

Archibald Higbie

I loathed you, Spoon River. I tried to rise above you,
I was ashamed of you. I despised you
As the place of my nativity.
And there in Rome, among the artists,
Speaking Italian, speaking French,
I seemed to myself at times to be free
Of every trace of my origin.
I seemed to be reaching the heights of art
And to breathe the air that the masters breathed,
And to see the world with their eyes.
But still they'd pass my work and say:
"What are you driving at, my friend?
Sometimes the face looks like Apollo's,
At others it has a trace of Lincoln's."
There was no culture, you know, in Spoon River,
And I burned with shame and held my peace.
And what could I do, all covered over
And weighted down with western soil,
Except aspire, and pray for another

Birth in the world, with all of Spoon River
Rooted out of my soul?

1915

Edwin Arlington Robinson (1869–1935)

Edwin Arlington Robinson grew up in Gardiner, Maine. He moved to New York in 1897 and was barely able to make ends meet. "I starved for twenty years, and in my opinion no one should write poetry unless he is willing to starve for it," he said. *The Children of the Night* (1897) "is one of the hinges upon which American poetry was able to turn from the sentimentality of the nineties toward modern veracity and psychological truth," Louise Bogan wrote. "It is filled with portraits of men who are misfits when they are not actual outcasts; and into each is incorporated something of Robinson's own lonely and eccentric nature." Robinson created memorable characters (the butcher Reuben Bright, the dissatisfied Miniver Cheevy). In "Eros Turannos," his best poem, he paints a haunting picture of marriage as a domestic prison and the god of love as a tyrant. President Theodore Roosevelt took a liking to Robinson's published verse and arranged a job for the poet as a customs inspector at the New York Customs House in 1905. Starting in 1911, Robinson spent summers—and wrote many of his poems—at the MacDowell Colony in New Hampshire.

The House on the Hill

They are all gone away,
   The House is shut and still,
There is nothing more to say.

Through broken walls and gray
   The winds blow bleak and shrill:
They are all gone away.

Nor is there one to-day
   To speak them good or ill:
There is nothing more to say.

Why is it then we stray
   Around that sunken sill?
They are all gone away.

And our poor fancy-play
   For them is wasted skill:
There is nothing more to say.

There is ruin and decay
   In the House on the Hill:

They are all gone away,
There is nothing more to say.

1894

An Old Story

Strange that I did not know him then,
    That friend of mine!
I did not even show him then
    One friendly sign;

But cursed him for the ways he had
    To make me see
My envy of the praise he had
    For praising me.

I would have rid the earth of him
    Once, in my pride! . . .
I never knew the worth of him
    Until he died.

1897

Luke Havergal

Go to the western gate, Luke Havergal,
There where the vines cling crimson on the wall,
And in the twilight wait for what will come.
The leaves will whisper there of her, and some,
Like flying words, will strike you as they fall;
But go, and if you listen she will call.
Go to the western gate, Luke Havergal —
Luke Havergal.

No, there is not a dawn in eastern skies
To rift the fiery night that's in your eyes;
But there, where western glooms are gathering,
The dark will end the dark, if anything:
God slays Himself with every leaf that flies,
And hell is more than half of paradise.
No, there is not a dawn in eastern skies —
In eastern skies.

Out of a grave I come to tell you this,
Out of a grave I come to quench the kiss
That flames upon your forehead with a glow

That blinds you to the way that you must go.
Yes, there is yet one way to where she is,
Bitter, but one that faith may never miss.
Out of a grave I come to tell you this —
To tell you this.

There is the western gate, Luke Havergal,
There are the crimson leaves upon the wall.
Go, for the winds are tearing them away, —
Nor think to riddle the dead words they say,
Nor any more to feel them as they fall;
But go, and if you trust her she will call.
There is the western gate, Luke Havergal —
Luke Havergal.

1897

Richard Cory

Whenever Richard Cory went down town,
We people on the pavement looked at him:
He was a gentleman from sole to crown,
Clean favored, and imperially slim.

And he was always quietly arrayed,
And he was always human when he talked;
But still he fluttered pulses when he said,
"Good-morning," and he glittered when he walked.

And he was rich —yes, richer than a king —
And admirably schooled in every grace:
In fine, we thought that he was everything
To make us wish that we were in his place.

So on we worked, and waited for the light,
And went without the meat, and cursed the bread;
And Richard Cory, one calm summer night,
Went home and put a bullet through his head.

1897

Reuben Bright

Because he was a butcher and thereby
Did earn an honest living (and did right),
I would not have you think that Reuben Bright
Was any more a brute than you or I:
For when they told him that his wife must die,

He started at them, and shook with grief and fright,
And cried like a great baby half that night,
And made the women cry to see him cry.

And after she was dead, and he had paid
The singers and the sexton and the rest,
He packed a lot of things that she had made
Most mournfully away in an old chest
Of hers, and put some chopped-up cedar boughs
In with them, and tore down the slaughter house.

1897

Credo

I cannot find my way: there is no star
In all the shrouded heavens anywhere;
And there is not a whisper in the air
Of any living voice but one so far
That I can hear it only as a bar
Of lost, imperial music, played when fair
And angel fingers wove, and unaware,
Dead leaves to garlands where no roses are.

No, there is not a glimmer, nor a call,
For one that welcomes, welcomes when he fears,
The black and awful chaos of the night;
For through it all — above, beyond it all —
I know the far-sent message of the years,
I feel the coming glory of the Light.

1897

Miniver Cheevy

Miniver Cheevy, child of scorn,
   Grew lean while he assailed the seasons;
He wept that he was ever born,
   And he had reasons.

Miniver loved the days of old
   When swords were bright and steeds were prancing;
The vision of a warrior bold
   Would set him dancing.

Miniver sighed for what was not,
   And dreamed, and rested from his labors;
He dreamed of Thebes and Camelot,
   And Priam's neighbors.

Miniver mourned the ripe renown
   That made so many a name so fragrant;
He mourned Romance, now on the town,
   And Art, a vagrant.

Miniver loved the Medici,
   Albeit he had never seen one;
He would have sinned incessantly
   Could he have been one.

Miniver cursed the commonplace
   And eyed a khaki suit with loathing;
He missed the mediæval grace
   Of iron clothing.

Miniver scorned the gold he sought,
   But sore annoyed was he without it;
Miniver thought, and thought, and thought,
   And thought about it.

Miniver Cheevy, born too late,
   Scratched his head and kept on thinking;
Miniver coughed, and called it fate,
   And kept on drinking.

1910

For a Dead Lady

No more with overflowing light
Shall fill the eyes that now are faded,
Nor shall another's fringe with night
Their woman-hidden world as they did.
No more shall quiver down the days
The flowing wonder of her ways,
Whereof no language may requite
The shifting and the many-shaded.

The grace, divine, definitive,
Clings only as a faint forestalling;
The laugh that love could not forgive
Is hushed, and answers to no calling;
The forehead and the little ears
Have gone where Saturn keeps the years;
The breast where roses could not live
Has done with rising and with falling.

The beauty, shattered by the laws
That have creation in their keeping,
No longer trembles at applause,
Or over children that are sleeping;
And we who delve in beauty's lore
Know all that we have known before
Of what inexorable cause
Makes Time so vicious in his reaping.

1910

Cassandra

I heard one who said: 'Verily,
   What word have I for children here?
Your Dollar is your only Word,
   The wrath of it your only fear.

'You build it altars tall enough
   To make you see, but you are blind;
You cannot leave it long enough
   To look before you or behind.

'When Reason beckons you to pause,
   You laugh and say that you know best;
But what is it you know, you keep
   As dark as ingots in a chest.

'You laugh and answer, "We are young;
   O leave us now, and let us grow." —
Not asking how much more of this
   Will Time endure or Fate bestow.

'Because a few complacent years
   Have made your peril of your pride,
Think you that you are to go on
   Forever pampered and untried?

'What lost eclipse of history,
   What bivouac of the marching stars,
Has given the sign for you to see
   Millenniums and last great wars?

'What unrecorded overthrow
   Of all the world has ever known,
Or ever been, has made itself
   So plain to you, and you alone?

'Your Dollar, Dove and Eagle make
A Trinity that even you
Rate higher than you rate yourselves;
It prays, it flatters, and it's new.

'And though your very flesh and blood
Be what your Eagle eats and drinks,
You'll praise him for the best of birds,
Not knowing what the Eagle thinks.

'The power is yours, but not the sight;
You see not upon what you tread;
You have the ages for your guide,
But not the wisdom to be led.

'Think you to tread forever down
The merciless old verities?
And are you never to have eyes
To see the world for what it is?

'Are you to pay for what you have
With all you are?' — No other word
We caught, but with a laughing crowd
Moved on. None heeded, and few heard.

1916

Eros Turannos

She fears him, and will always ask
What fated her to choose him;
She meets in his engaging mask
All reasons to refuse him;
But what she meets and what she fears
Are less than are the downward years,
Drawn slowly to the foamless weirs
Of age, were she to lose him.

Between a blurred sagacity
That once had power to sound him,
And Love, that will not let him be
The Judas that she found him,
Her pride assuages her almost,
As if it were alone the cost. —
He sees that he will not be lost,
And waits and looks around him.

A sense of ocean and old trees
Envelops and allures him;

Tradition, touching all he sees,
   Beguiles and reassures him;
And all her doubts of what he says
Are dimmed with what she knows of days —
Till even prejudice delays
   And fades, and she secures him.

The falling leaf inaugurates
   The reign of her confusion:
The pounding wave reverberates
   The dirge of her illusion;
And home, where passion lived and died,
Becomes a place where she can hide,
While all the town and harbor side
   Vibrate with her seclusion.

We tell you, tapping on our brows,
   The story as it should be, —
As if the story of a house
   Were told, or ever could be;
We'll have no kindly veil between
Her visions and those we have seen, —
As if we guessed what hers have been,
   Or what they are or would be.

Meanwhile we do no harm; for they
   That with a god have striven,
Not hearing much of what we say,
   Take what the god has given;
Though like waves breaking it may be
Or like a changed familiar tree,
Or like a stairway to the sea
   Where down the blind are driven.

1916

Mr. Flood's Party

Old Eben Flood, climbing alone one night
Over the hill between the town below
And the forsaken upland hermitage
That held as much as he should ever know
On earth again of home, paused warily.
The road was his with not a native near;
And Eben, having leisure, said aloud,
For no man else in Tilbury Town to hear:

"Well, Mr. Flood, we have the harvest moon
Again, and we may not have many more;

The bird is on the wing, the poet says,
And you and I have said it here before.
Drink to the bird." He raised up to the light
The jug that he had gone so far to fill,
And answered huskily: "Well, Mr. Flood,
Since you propose it, I believe I will."

Alone, as if enduring to the end
A valiant armor of scarred hopes outworn,
He stood there in the middle of the road
Like Roland's ghost winding a silent horn.
Below him, in the town among the trees,
Where friends of other days had honored him,
A phantom salutation of the dead
Rang thinly till old Eben's eyes were dim.

Then, as a mother lays her sleeping child
Down tenderly, fearing it may awake,
He set the jug down slowly at his feet
With trembling care, knowing that most things break;
And only when assured that on firm earth
It stood, as the uncertain lives of men
Assuredly did not, he paced away,
And with his hand extended paused again:

"Well, Mr. Flood, we have not met like this
In a long time; and many a change has come
To both of us, I fear, since last it was
We had a drop together. Welcome home!"
Convivially returning with himself,
Again he raised the jug up to the light;
And with an acquiescent quaver said:
"Well, Mr. Flood, if you insist, I might.

"Only a very little, Mr. Flood —
For auld lang syne. No more, sir; that will do."
So, for the time, apparently it did,
And Eben evidently thought so too;
For soon amid the silver loneliness
Of night he lifted up his voice and sang,
Secure, with only two moons listening,
Until the whole harmonious landscape rang —

"For auld lang syne." The weary throat gave out,
The last word wavered, and the song was done.
He raised again the jug regretfully
And shook his head, and was again alone.
There was not much that was ahead of him,
And there was nothing in the town below —

Where strangers would have shut the many doors
That many friends had opened long ago.

1921

The Sheaves

Where long the shadows of the wind had rolled,
Green wheat was yielding to the change assigned;
And as by some vast magic undivined
The world was turning slowly into gold.
Like nothing that was ever bought or sold
It waited there, the body and the mind;
And with a mighty meaning of a kind
That tells the more the more it is not told.

So in a land where all days are not fair,
Fair days went on till on another day
A thousand golden sheaves were lying there,
Shining and still, but not for long to stay —
As if a thousand girls with golden hair
Might rise from where they slept and go away.

1925

STEPHEN CRANE (1871–1900)

Born in Newark, New Jersey, after the Civil War, Stephen Crane is perhaps best known as the author of *The Red Badge of Courage* (1895), his novel set during that bloody conflict. He covered the Greco-Turkish War in 1897 and the Spanish-American War (for Joseph Pulitzer's *New York World*) in 1898. Crane had survived the shipwreck of a gunrunning steamer, an episode he made the basis of a story, "The Open Boat," about human cooperation in the face of nature's indifference. The story begins with the sentence, "None of them knew the color of the sky." Crane's poems—terse, dark, trenchant parables, in plain speech stripped of decorative elements—were anomalous in their time but have shown lasting power. John Berryman saw in Crane's poems the "sincerity of a frightened savage anxious to learn what his dream means."

In the desert

In the desert
I saw a creature, naked, bestial,
Who, squatting upon the ground,
Held his heart in his hands,
And ate of it.

I said: "Is it good, friend?"
"It is bitter — bitter," he answered;
"But I like it
Because it is bitter,
And because it is my heart."

1895

Once there came a man

Once there came a man
Who said:
"Range me all men of the world in rows."
And instantly
There was terrific clamor among the people
Against being ranged in rows.
There was a loud quarrel, world-wide.
It endured for ages;
And blood was shed
By those who would not stand in rows,
And by those who pined to stand in rows.
Eventually, the man went to death, weeping.
And those who stayed in bloody scuffle
Knew not the great simplicity.

1895

I saw a man pursuing the horizon

I saw a man pursuing the horizon;
Round and round they sped.
I was disturbed at this;
I accosted the man.
"It is futile," I said,
"You can never —"

"You lie," he cried,
And ran on.

1895

Behold, the grave of a wicked man

Behold, the grave of a wicked man,
And near it, a stern spirit.

There came a drooping maid with violets,
But the spirit grasped her arm.
"No flowers for him," he said.
The maid wept:
"Ah, I loved him."
But the spirit, grim and frowning:
"No flowers for him."

Now, this is it —
If the spirit was just,
Why did the maid weep?

1895

A man saw a ball of gold in the sky

A man saw a ball of gold in the sky;
He climbed for it,
And eventually he achieved it —
It was clay.

Now this is the strange part:
When the man went to the earth
And looked again,
Lo, there was the ball of gold.
Now this is the strange part:
It was a ball of gold.
Aye, by the heavens, it was a ball of gold.

1895

I walked in a desert

I walked in a desert.
And I cried:
"Ah, God, take me from this place!"
A voice said: "It is no desert."
I cried: "Well, but —
The sand, the heat, the vacant horizon."
A voice said: "It is no desert."

1895

The impact of a dollar upon the heart

The impact of a dollar upon the heart
Smiles warm red light

Sweeping from the hearth rosily upon the white table,
With the hanging cool velvet shadows
Moving softly upon the door.

The impact of a million dollars
Is a crash of flunkeys
And yawning emblems of Persia
Cheeked against oak, France and a sabre,
The outcry of old beauty
Whored by pimping merchants
To submission before wine and chatter.
Silly rich peasants stamp the carpets of men,
Dead men who dreamed fragrance and light
Into their woof, their lives;
The rug of an honest bear
Under the feet of a cryptic slave
Who speaks always of baubles,
Forgetting place, multitude, work and state,
Champing and mouthing of hats
Making ratful squeak of hats,
Hats.

1899

JAMES WELDON JOHNSON (1871–1938)

James Weldon Johnson was born in Jacksonville, Florida, to a middle-class African-American family. He studied law, started a newspaper, and wrote popular songs; *Lift Ev'ry Voice and Sing* became known as the "Negro National Anthem." He moved to New York City in 1901 or 1902. He served as United States consul to Venezuela (1906–1909) and to Nicaragua (1909–1912) and later committed himself to the struggle for civil rights, as field secretary and later general secretary of the National Association for the Advancement of Colored People (NAACP). He edited *The Book of American Negro Poetry* (1922) and two anthologies of spirituals, and wrote an autobiography, *Along This Way* (1933). He died in a car crash in 1938.

O Black and Unknown Bards

O Black and unknown bards of long ago,
How came your lips to touch the sacred fire?
How, in your darkness, did you come to know
The power and beauty of the minstrel's lyre?
Who first from midst his bonds lifted his eyes?
Who first from out the still watch, lone and long,
Feeling the ancient faith of prophets rise
Within his dark-kept soul, burst into song?

Heart of what slave poured out such melody
As "Steal away to Jesus"? On its strains
His spirit must have nightly floated free,
Though still about his hands he felt his chains.
Who heard great "Jordan roll"? Whose starward eye
Saw chariot "swing low"? And who was he
That breathed that comforting, melodic sigh,
"Nobody knows de trouble I see"?

What merely living clod, what captive thing,
Could up toward God through all its darkness grope,
And find within its deadened heart to sing
These songs of sorrow, love, and faith, and hope?
How did it catch that subtle undertone,
That note in music heard not with the ears?
How sound the elusive reed, so seldom blown,
Which stirs the soul or melts the heart to tears?

Not that great German master in his dream
Of harmonies that thundered 'mongst the stars
At the creation, ever heard a theme
Nobler than "Go down, Moses." Mark its bars,
How like a mighty trumpet-call they stir
The blood. Such are the notes that men have sung,
Going to valorous deeds; such tones there were
That helped make history when Time was young.

There is a wide, wide wonder in it all,
That from degraded rest and service toil
The fiery spirit of the seer should call
These simple children of the sun and soil.
O black slave singers, gone, forgot, unfamed,
You — you alone, of all the long, long line
Of those who've sung untaught, unknown, unnamed,
Have stretched out upward, seeking the divine.

You sang not deeds of heroes or of kings;
No chant of bloody war, no exulting pæan
Of arms-won triumphs; but your humble strings
You touched in chord with music empyrean.
You sang far better than you knew; the songs
That for your listeners' hungry hearts sufficed
Still live, — but more than this to you belongs:
You sang a race from wood and stone to Christ.

1908

The Creation

And God stepped out on space,
And he looked around and said:
I'm lonely —
I'll make me a world.

And far as the eye of God could see
Darkness covered everything,
Blacker than a hundred midnights
Down in a cypress swamp.

Then God smiled,
And the light broke,
And the darkness rolled up on one side,
And the light stood shining on the other,
And God said: That's good!

Then God reached out and took the light in his hands,
And God rolled the light around in his hands
Until he made the sun;
And he set that sun a-blazing in the heavens.
And the light that was left from making the sun
God gathered it up in a shining ball
And flung it against the darkness,
Spangling the night with the moon and stars.
Then down between
The darkness and the light
He hurled the world;
And God said: That's good!

Then God himself stepped down —
And the sun was on his right hand,
And the moon was on his left;
The stars were clustered about his head,
And the earth was under his feet.
And God walked, and where he trod
His footsteps hollowed the valleys out
And bulged the mountains up.

Then he stopped and looked and saw
That the earth was hot and barren.
So God stepped over to the edge of the world
And he spat out the seven seas —
He batted his eyes, and the lightnings flashed —
He clapped his hands, and the thunders rolled —
And the waters above the earth came down,
The cooling waters came down.

Then the green grass sprouted,
And the little red flowers blossomed,
The pine tree pointed his finger to the sky,
And the oak spread out his arms,
The lakes cuddled down in the hollows of the ground,
And the rivers ran down to the sea;
And God smiled again,
And the rainbow appeared,
And curled itself around his shoulder.

Then God raised his arm and he waved his hand
Over the sea and over the land,
And he said: Bring forth! Bring forth!
And quicker than God could drop his hand,
Fishes and fowls
And beasts and birds
Swam the rivers and the seas,
Roamed the forests and the woods,
And split the air with their wings.
And God said: That's good!

Then God walked around,
And God looked around
On all that he had made.
He looked at his sun,
And he looked at his moon,
And he looked at his little stars;
He looked on his world
With all its living things,
And God said: I'm lonely still.

Then God sat down —
On the side of a hill where he could think;
By a deep, wide river he sat down;
With his head in his hands,
God thought and thought,
Till he thought: I'll make me a man!

Up from the bed of the river
God scooped the clay;
And by the bank of the river
He kneeled him down;
And there the great God Almighty
Who lit the sun and fixed it in the sky,
Who flung the stars to the most far corner of the night,
Who rounded the earth in the middle of his hand;
This Great God,
Like a mammy bending over her baby,
Kneeled down in the dust

Toiling over a lump of clay
Till he shaped it in his own image;

Then into it he blew the breath of life,
And man became a living soul.
Amen. Amen.

1920

Paul Laurence Dunbar (1872–1906)

Paul Laurence Dunbar was born in Dayton, Ohio, to two former slaves from Kentucky. In school he edited "The Dayton Tatler" with his school friends Orville and Wilbur Wright. William Dean Howells praised Dunbar in an article in *Harper's* in 1895, singling out his dialect poems for special praise. Dunbar was grateful for the endorsement, though he came to regard it as a mixed blessing, and he is represented here with three poems in Standard English, including his best-known poem, "We Wear the Mask," a rondeau. He suffered from tuberculosis and depression, and died in 1906.

Dawn

An angel, robed in spotless white,
Bent down and kissed the sleeping Night.
Night woke to blush; the sprite was gone.
Men saw the blush and called it Dawn.

1895

We Wear the Mask

We wear the mask that grins and lies,
It hides our cheeks and shades our eyes, —
This debt we pay to human guile;
With torn and bleeding hearts we smile,
And mouth with myriad subtleties.

Why should the world be overwise,
In counting all our tears and sighs?
Nay, let them only see us, while
        We wear the mask.

We smile, but, O great Christ, our cries
To thee from tortured souls arise.

We sing, but oh the clay is vile
Beneath our feet, and long the mile;
But let the world dream otherwise,
    We wear the mask!

1895

He Had His Dream

He had his dream, and all through life,
Worked up to it through toil and strife.
Afloat fore'er before his eyes,
It colored for him all his skies:
    The storm-cloud dark
    Above his bark,
The calm and listless vault of blue
Took on its hopeful hue,
It tinctured every passing beam —
    He had his dream.

He labored hard and failed at last,
His sails too weak to bear the blast,
The raging tempests tore away
And sent his beating bark astray.
    But what cared he
    For wind or sea!
He said, "The tempest will be short,
My bark will come to port."
He saw through every cloud a gleam —
    He had his dream.

1895

A Choice

They please me not — these solemn songs
That hint of sermons covered up.
'Tis true the world should heed its wrongs,
  But in a poem let me sup,
Not simples brewed to cure or ease
Humanity's confessed disease,
But the spirit-wine of a singing line,
  Or a dew-drop in a honey cup!

1899

ROBERT FROST (1874–1963)

Robert Frost, though born in San Francisco, was raised in New Hampshire and seemed to embody the genius of New England. In London in 1912, at age 38 and still unknown, he chanced upon a newspaper headline that announced, "ENGLAND IN THE GRIP OF FROST." Converting a weather report into a forecast of personal glory, Frost published his first two books, *A Boy's Will* (1913) and *North of Boston* (1914), in England. He had uncanny skill at balancing the conversational idioms of the American vernacular with the strict demands of rhyme and meter. Free verse he dismissed as the equivalent of playing tennis without a net. A poem "begins in delight and ends in wisdom," Frost wrote; "it begins in delight, it inclines to the impulse, it assumes direction with the first line laid down, it runs a course of lucky events, and ends in a clarification of life — not necessarily a great clarification, such as sects and cults are founded on, but in a momentary stay against confusion." Great fame was his, four Pulitzer Prizes, yet — as Robert Lowell quotes him in a poem — "When I am too full of joy, I think how little good my health did anyone near me." (One daughter went mad, a second died of puerperal fever; one son died at three, a second grew up a failed poet and committed suicide.) Lionel Trilling at Frost's 85th birthday party created a ruckus when he delivered a toast hailing Frost as a "tragic" and even "terrifying" poet who represented "the terrible actualities of life in a new way." Some of Frost's possessive admirers took offense at a characterization that challenged their image of the poet as a benign sage and Yankee folk hero. But Trilling's assessment has prevailed, resulting not in a diminution of Frost's reputation but in its enhancement. At the inauguration of John F. Kennedy on 20 January 1961, Frost, the cold warrior, with his shock of white hair, was blinded by the sunlight. Unable to read his prepared text, he recited from memory "The Gift Outright."

Mending Wall

Something there is that doesn't love a wall,
That sends the frozen-ground-swell under it
And spills upper boulders in the sun,
And makes gaps even two can pass abreast.
The work of hunters is another thing:
I have come after them and made repair
Where they have left not one stone on a stone,
But they would have the rabbit out of hiding,
To please the yelping dogs. The gaps I mean,
No one has seen them made or heard them made,
But at spring mending-time we find them there.
I let my neighbor know beyond the hill;
And on a day we meet to walk the line
And set the wall between us once again.
We keep the wall between us as we go.
To each the boulders that have fallen to each.
And some are loaves and some so nearly balls
We have to use a spell to make them balance:
"Stay where you are until our backs are turned!"
We wear our fingers rough with handling them.
Oh, just another kind of outdoor game,

One on a side. It comes to little more:
There where it is we do not need the wall:
He is all pine and I am apple orchard.
My apple trees will never get across
And eat the cones under his pines, I tell him.
He only says, "Good fences make good neighbors."
Spring is the mischief in me, and I wonder
If I could put a notion in his head:
"*Why* do they make good neighbors? Isn't it
Where there are cows? But here there are no cows.
Before I built a wall I'd ask to know
What I was walling in or walling out,
And to whom I was like to give offense.
Something there is that doesn't love a wall,
That wants it down." I could say "Elves" to him,
But it's not elves exactly, and I'd rather
He said it for himself. I see him there,
Bringing a stone grasped firmly by the top
In each hand, like an old-stone savage armed.
He moves in darkness as it seems to me,
Not of woods only and the shade of trees.
He will not go behind his father's saying,
And he likes having thought of it so well
He says again, "Good fences make good neighbors."

1914

The Death of the Hired Man

Mary sat musing on the lamp-flame at the table
Waiting for Warren. When she heard his step,
She ran on tip-toe down the darkened passage
To meet him in the doorway with the news
And put him on his guard. "Silas is back."
She pushed him outward with her through the door
And shut it after her. "Be kind," she said.
She took the market things from Warren's arms
And set them on the porch, then drew him down
To sit beside her on the wooden steps.

"When was I ever anything but kind to him?
But I'll not have the fellow back," he said.
"I told him so last haying, didn't I?
'If he left then,' I said, 'that ended it.'
What good is he? Who else will harbour him
At his age for the little he can do?
What help he is there's no depending on.
Off he goes always when I need him most.

'He thinks he ought to earn a little pay,
Enough at least to buy tobacco with,
So he won't have to beg and be beholden.'
'All right,' I say, 'I can't afford to pay
Any fixed wages, though I wish I could,'
'Someone else can.' 'Then someone else will have to.'
I shouldn't mind his bettering himself
If that was what it was. You can be certain,
When he begins like that, there's someone at him
Trying to coax him off with pocket-money, —
In haying time, when any help is scarce.
In winter he comes back to us. I'm done."

"Sh! not so loud: he'll hear you," Mary said.

"I want him to: he'll have to soon or late."

"He's worn out. He's asleep beside the stove.
When I came up from Rowe's I found him here,
Huddled against the barn-door fast asleep,
A miserable sight, and frightening, too —
You needn't smile — I didn't recognise him —
I wasn't looking for him — and he's changed.
Wait till you see."

"Where did you say he'd been?"

"He didn't say. I dragged him to the house,
And gave him tea and tried to make him smoke.
I tried to make him talk about his travels.
Nothing would do: he just kept nodding off."

"What did he say? Did he say anything?"

"But little."

"Anything? Mary, confess
He said he'd come to ditch the meadow for me."

"Warren!"

"But did he? I just want to know."

"Of course he did. What would you have him say?
Surely you wouldn't grudge the poor old man
Some humble way to save his self-respect.
He added, if you really care to know,
He meant to clear the upper pasture, too.
That sounds like something you have heard before?

Warren, I wish you could have heard the way
He jumbled everything. I stopped to look
Two or three times — he made me feel so queer —
To see if he was talking in his sleep.
He ran on Harold Wilson — you remember —
The boy you had in haying four years since.
He's finished school, and teaching in his college.
Silas declares you'll have to get him back.
He says they two will make a team for work:
Between them they will lay this farm as smooth!
The way he mixed that in with other things.
He thinks young Wilson a likely lad, though daft
On education — you know how they fought
All through July under the blazing sun,
Silas up on the cart to build the load,
Harold along beside to pitch it on."

"Yes, I took care to keep well out of earshot."

"Well, those days trouble Silas like a dream.
You wouldn't think they would. How some things linger!
Harold's young college boy's assurance piqued him.
After so many years he still keeps finding
Good arguments he sees he might have used.
I sympathise. I know just how it feels
To think of the right thing to say too late.
Harold's associated in his mind with Latin.
He asked me what I thought of Harold's saying
He studied Latin like the violin
Because he liked it — that an argument!
He said he couldn't make the boy believe
He could find water with a hazel prong —
Which showed how much good school had ever done him.
He wanted to go over that. But most of all
He thinks if he could have another chance
To teach him how to build a load of hay —"

"I know, that's Silas' one accomplishment.
He bundles every forkful in its place,
And tags and numbers it for future reference,
So he can find and easily dislodge it
In the unloading. Silas does that well.
He takes it out in bunches like big birds' nests.
You never see him standing on the hay
He's trying to lift, straining to lift himself."

"He thinks if he could teach him that, he'd be
Some good perhaps to someone in the world.
He hates to see a boy the fool of books.

Poor Silas, so concerned for other folk,
And nothing to look backward to with pride,
And nothing to look forward to with hope,
So now and never any different."

Part of a moon was falling down the west,
Dragging the whole sky with it to the hills.
Its light poured softly in her lap. She saw it
And spread her apron to it. She put out her hand
Among the harp-like morning-glory strings,
Taut with the dew from garden bed to eaves,
As if she played unheard some tenderness
That wrought on him beside her in the night.
"Warren," she said, "he has come home to die:
You needn't be afraid he'll leave you this time."

"Home," he mocked gently.

"Yes, what else but home?
It all depends on what you mean by home.
Of course he's nothing to us, any more
Than was the hound that came a stranger to us
Out of the woods, worn out upon the trail."
"Home is the place where, when you have to go there,
They have to take you in."

"I should have called it
Something you somehow haven't to deserve."

Warren learned out and took a step or two,
Picked up a little stick, and brought it back
And broke it in his hand and tossed it by.
"Silas has better claim on us you think
Than on his brother? Thirteen little miles
As the road winds would bring him to his door.
Silas has walked that far no doubt to-day.
Why didn't he go there? His brother's rich,
A somebody — director in the bank."

"He never told us that."

"We know it though."

"I think his brother ought to help, of course.
I'll see to that if there is need. He ought of right
To take him in, and might be willing to —
He may be better than appearances.
But have some pity on Silas. Do you think
If he had any pride in claiming kin

Or anything he looked for from his brother,
He'd keep so still about him all this time?"

"I wonder what's between them."

"I can tell you.
Silas is what he is — we wouldn't mind him —
But just the kind that kinsfolk can't abide.
He never did a thing so very bad.
He don't know why he isn't quite as good
As anybody. Worthless though he is,
He won't be made ashamed to please his brother."

"*I* can't think Si ever hurt anyone."

"No, but he hurt my heart the way he lay
And rolled his old head on that sharp-edged chair-back.
He wouldn't let me put him on the lounge.
You must go in and see what you can do.
I made the bed up for him there to-night.
You'll be surprised at him — how much he's broken.
His working days are done; I'm sure of it."

"I'd not be in a hurry to say that."

"I haven't been. Go, look, see for yourself.
But, Warren, please remember how it is:
He's come to help you ditch the meadow.
He has a plan. You mustn't laugh at him.
He may not speak of it, and then he may.
I'll site and see if that small sailing cloud
Will hit or miss the moon."

It hit the moon.
Then there were three there, making a dim row,
The moon, the little silver cloud, and she.

Warren returned — too soon, it seemed to her,
Slipped to her side, caught up her hand and waited.

"Warren?" she questioned.

"Dead," was all he answered.

1914

After Apple-Picking

My long two-pointed ladder's sticking through a tree
Toward heaven still,
And there's a barrel that I didn't fill
Beside it, and there may be two or three
Apples I didn't pick upon some bough.
But I am done with apple-picking now.
Essence of winter sleep is on the night,
The scent of apples: I am drowsing off.
I cannot rub the strangeness from my sight
I got from looking through a pane of glass
I skimmed this morning from the drinking trough
And held against the world of hoary grass.
It melted, and I let it fall and break.
But I was well
Upon my way to sleep before it fell,
And I could tell
What form my dreaming was about to take.
Magnified apples appear and disappear,
Stem end and blossom end,
And every fleck of russet showing clear.
My instep arch not only keeps the ache,
It keeps the pressure of ladder-round.
I feel the ladder sway as the boughs bend.
And I keep hearing from the cellar bin
The rumbling sound
Of load on load of apples coming in.
For I have had too much
Of apple-picking: I am overtired
Of the great harvest I myself desired.
There were ten thousand thousand fruit to touch,
Cherish in hand, lift down, and not let fall.
For all
That struck the earth,
No matter if not bruised or spiked with stubble,
Went surely to the cider-apple heap
As of no worth.
One can see what will trouble
This sleep of mine, whatever sleep it is.
Were he not gone,
The woodchuck could say whether it's like his
Long sleep, as I described its coming on,
Or just some human sleep.

1914

Home Burial

He saw her from the bottom of the stairs
Before she saw him. She was starting down,
Looking back over her shoulder at some fear.
She took a doubtful step and then undid it
To raise herself and look again. He spoke
Advancing toward her: "What is it you see
From up there always? — for I want to know."
She turned and sank upon her skirts at that,
And her face changed from terrified to dull.
He said to gain time: "What is it you see?"
Mounting until she cowered under him.
"I will find out now — you must tell me, dear."
She, in her place, refused him any help,
With the least stiffening of her neck and silence.
She let him look, sure that he wouldn't see,
Blind creature; and awhile he didn't see.
But at last he murmured, "Oh," and again, "Oh."

"What is it — what?" she said.

"Just that I see."

"You don't," she challenged. "Tell me what it is."

"The wonder is I didn't see at once.
I never noticed it from here before.
I must be wonted to it — that's the reason.
The little graveyard where my people are!
So small the window frames the whole of it.
Not so much larger than a bedroom, is it?
There are three stones of slate and one of marble,
Broad-shouldered little slabs there in the sunlight
On the sidehill. We haven't to mind *those*.
But I understand: it is not the stones,
But the child's mound —— "

"Don't, don't, don't,
don't," she cried.

She withdrew, shrinking from beneath his arm
That rested on the banister, and slid downstairs;
And turned on him, with such a daunting look,
He said twice over before he knew himself:
"Can't a man speak of his own child he's lost?"

"Not you! — Oh, where's my hat? Oh, I don't need it!
I must get out of here. I must get air. —
I don't know rightly whether any man can."

"Amy! Don't go to someone else this time.
Listen to me. I won't come down the stairs."
He sat and fixed his chin between his fists.
"There's something I should like to ask you, dear."

"You don't know how to ask it."
"Help me, then."

Her fingers moved the latch for all reply.

"My words are nearly always an offense.
I don't know how to speak of anything
So as to please you. But I might be taught,
I should suppose. I can't say I see how.
A man must partly give up being a man
With womenfolk. We could have some arrangement
By which I'd bind myself to keep hands off
Anything special you're a-mind to name.
Though I don't like such things 'twixt those that love.
Two that don't love can't live together without them.
But two that do can't live together with them."
She moved the latch a little. "Don't — don't go.
Don't carry it to someone else this time.
Tell me about it if it's something human.
Let me into your grief. I'm not so much
Unlike other folks as your standing there
Apart would make me out. Give me my chance.
I do think, though, you overdo it a little.
What was it brought you up to think it the thing
To take your mother-loss of a first child
So inconsolably — in the face of love.
You'd think his memory might be satisfied —— "

"There you go sneering now!"
"I'm not. I'm not!
You make me angry. I'll come down to you.
God, what a woman! And it's come to this,
A man can't speak of his own child that's dead."

"You can't because you don't know how to speak.
If you had any feeling, you that dug
With your own hand — how could you? — his little grave;
I saw you from that very window there,
Making the gravel leap and leap in air,
Leap up, like that, like that, and land so lightly
And roll back down the mound beside the hole.
I thought, who is that man? I didn't know you.
And I crept down the stairs and up the stairs

To look again, and still your spade kept lifting.
Then you came in. I heard your rumbling voice

Out in the kitchen, and I don't know why,
But I went near to see with my own eyes.
You could sit there with the stains on your shoes
Of the fresh earth from your own baby's grave
And talk about your everyday concerns.
You had stood the spade up against the wall
Outside there in the entry, for I saw it."

"I shall laugh the worst laugh I ever laughed.
I'm cursed. God, if I don't believe I'm cursed."

"I can repeat the very words you were saying:
'Three foggy mornings and one rainy day
Will rot the best birch fence a man can build.'
Think of it, talk like that at such a time!
What had how long it takes a birch to rot
To do with what was in the darkened parlor?
You *couldn't* care! The nearest friends can go
With anyone to death, comes so far short
They might as well not try to go at all.
No, from the time when one is sick to death,
One is alone, and he dies more alone.
Friends make pretense of following to the grave,
But before one is in it, their minds are turned
And making the best of their way back to life
And living people, and things they understand.
But the world's evil. I won't have grief so
If I can change it. Oh, I won't, I won't!"

"There, you have said it all and you feel better.
You won't go now. You're crying. Close the door.
The heart's gone out of it: why keep it up?
Amy! There's someone coming down the road!"

"*You* — oh, you think the talk is all. I must go —
Somewhere out of this house. How can I make you —— "

"If — you — do!" She was opening the door wider.
"Where do you mean to go? First tell me that.
I'll follow and bring you back by force. I *will*! — "

1914

The Wood-Pile

Out walking in the frozen swamp one gray day,
I paused and said, "I will turn back from here.
No, I will go on farther — and we shall see."
The hard snow held me, save where now and then
One foot went through. The view was all in lines
Straight up and down of tall slim trees
Too much alike to mark or name a place by
So as to say for certain I was here
Or somewhere else: I was just far from home.
A small bird flew before me. He was careful
To put a tree between us when he lighted,
And say no word to tell me who he was
Who was so foolish as to think what *he* thought.
He thought that I was after him for a feather —
The white one in his tail; like one who takes
Everything said as personal to himself.
One flight out sideways would have undeceived him.
And then there was pile of wood for which
I forgot him and let his little fear
Carry him off the way I might have gone,
Without so much as wishing him good-night.
He went behind it to make his last stand.
It was a cord of maple, cut and split
And piled — and measured, four by four by eight.
And not another like it could I see.
No runner tracks in this year's snow looped near it.
And it was older sure than this year's cutting,
Or even last year's or the year's before.
The wood was gray and the bark warping off it
And the pile somewhat sunken. Clematis
Had wound strings round and round it like a bundle.
What held it, though, on one side was a tree
Still growing, and on one a stake and prop,
These latter about to fall. I thought that only
Someone who lived in turning to fresh tasks
Could so forget his handiwork on which
He spent himself, the labor of his ax,
And leave it there far from a useful fireplace
To warm the frozen swamp as best it could
With the slow smokeless burning of decay.

1914

The Road Not Taken

Two roads diverged in a yellow wood,
And sorry I could not travel both

And be one traveler, long I stood
And looked down one as far as I could
To where it bent in the undergrowth;

Then took the other, as just as fair,
And having perhaps the better claim,
Because it was grassy and wanted wear;
Though as for that, the passing there
Had worn them really about the same,

And both that morning equally lay
In leaves no step had trodden black.
Oh, I kept the first for another day!
Yet knowing how way leads on to way,
I doubted if I should ever come back.

I shall be telling this with a sigh
Somewhere ages and ages hence:
Two roads diverged in a wood, and I —
I took the one less traveled by,
And that has made all the difference.

1916

Birches

When I see birches bend to left and right
Across the lines of straighter darker trees,
I like to think some boy's been swinging them.
But swinging doesn't bend them down to stay
As ice storms do. Often you must have seen them
Loaded with ice a sunny winter morning
After a rain. They click upon themselves
As the breeze rises, and turn many-colored
As the stir cracks and crazes their enamel.
Soon the sun's warmth makes them shed crystal shells
Shattering and avalanching on the snow crust —
Such heaps of broken glass to sweep away
You'd think the inner dome of heaven had fallen.
They are dragged to the withered bracken by the load,
And they seem not to break; though once they are bowed
So low for long, they never right themselves:
You may see their trunks arching in the woods
Years afterwards, trailing their leaves on the ground
Like girls on hands and knees that throw their hair
Before them over their heads to dry in the sun.
But I was going to say when Truth broke in
With all her matter of fact about the ice storm,
I should prefer to have some boy bend them

As he went out and in to fetch the cows —
Some boy too far from town to learn baseball,
Whose only play was what he found himself,
Summer or winter, and could play alone.
One by one he subdued his father's trees
By riding them down over and over again
Until he took the stiffness out of them,
And not one but hung limp, not one was left
For him to conquer. He learned all there was
To learn about not launching out too soon
And so not carrying the tree away
Clear to the ground. He always kept his poise
To the top branches, climbing carefully
With the same pains you use to fill a cup
Up to the brim, and even above the brim.
Then he flung outward, feet first, with a swish,
Kicking his way down through the air to the ground.
So was I once myself a swinger of birches.
And so I dream of going back to be.
It's when I'm weary of considerations,
And life is too much like a pathless wood
Where your face burns and tickles with the cobwebs
Broken across it, and one eye is weeping
From a twig's having lashed across it open.
I'd like to get away from earth awhile
And then come back to it and begin over.
May no fate willfully misunderstand me
And half grant what I wish and snatch me away
Not to return. Earth's the right place for love:
I don't know where it's likely to go better.
I'd like to go by climbing a birch tree,
And climb black branches up a snow-white trunk
Toward heaven, till the tree could bear no more,
But dipped its top and set me down again.
That would be good both going and coming back.
One could do worse than be a swinger of birches.

1916

Meeting and Passing

As I went down the hill along the wall
There was a gate I had leaned at for the view
And had just turned from when I first saw you
As you came up the hill. We met. But all
We did that day was mingle great and small
Footprints in summer dust as if we drew
The figure of our being less than two

But more than one as yet. Your parasol
Pointed the decimal off with one deep thrust.
And all the time we talked you seemed to see
Something down there to smile at in the dust.
(Oh, it was without prejudice to me!)
Afterward I went past what you had passed
Before we met and you what I had passed.

1916

Putting in the Seed

You come to fetch me from my work tonight
When supper's on the table, and we'll see
If I can leave off burying the white
Soft petals fallen from the apple tree.
(Soft petals, yes, but not so barren quite,
Mingled with these, smooth bean and wrinkled pea)
And go along with you ere you lose sight
Of what you came for and become like me,
Slave to a springtime passion for the earth.
How Love burns through the Putting in the Seed
On through the watching for that early birth
When, just as the soil tarnishes with weed,
The sturdy seedling with arched body comes
Shouldering its way and shedding the earth crumbs.

1916

The Oven Bird

There is a singer everyone has heard,
Loud, a mid-summer and a mid-wood bird,
Who makes the solid tree trunks sound again.
He says that leaves are old and that for flowers
Mid-summer is to spring as one to ten.
He says the early petal-fall is past,
When pear and cherry bloom went down in showers
On sunny days a moment overcast;
And comes that other fall we name the fall.
He says the highway dust is over all.
The bird would cease and be as other birds
But that he knows in singing not to sing.
The question that he frames in all but words
Is what to make of a diminished thing.

1916

"Out, Out —"

The buzz saw snarled and rattled in the yard
And made dust and dropped stove-length sticks of wood,
Sweet-scented stuff when the breeze drew across it.
And from there those that lifted eyes could count
Five mountain ranges one behind the other
Under the sunset far into Vermont.
And the saw snarled and rattled, snarled and rattled,
As it ran light, or had to bear a load.
And nothing happened: day was all but done.
Call it a day, I wish they might have said
To please the boy by giving him the half hour
That a boy counts so much when saved from work.
His sister stood beside them in her apron
To tell them "Supper." At the word, the saw,
As if to prove saws knew what supper meant,
Leaped out at the boy's hand, or seemed to leap —
He must have given the hand. However it was,
Neither refused the meeting. But the hand!
The boy's first outcry was a rueful laugh,
As he swung toward them holding up the hand,
Half in appeal, but half as if to keep
The life from spilling. Then the boy saw all —
Since he was old enough to know, big boy
Doing a man's work, though a child at heart —
He saw all spoiled. "Don't let him cut my hand off —
The doctor, when he comes. Don't let him, sister!"
So. But the hand was gone already.
The doctor put him in the dark of ether.
He lay and puffed his lips out with his breath.
And then — the watcher at his pulse took fright.
No one believed. They listened at his heart.
Little — less — nothing! — and that ended it.
No more to build on there. And they, since they
Were not the one dead, turned to their affairs.

1916

An Old Man's Winter Night

All out-of-doors looked darkly in at him
Through the thin frost, almost in separate stars,
That gathers on the pane in empty rooms.
What kept his eyes from giving back the gaze
Was the lamp tilted near them in his hand.
What kept him from remembering what it was

That brought him to that creaking room was age.
He stood with barrels round him — at a loss.
And having scared the cellar under him
In clomping here, he scared it once again
In clomping off — and scared the outer night,
Which has its sounds, familiar, like the roar
Of trees and crack of branches, common things,
But nothing so like beating on a box.
A light he was to no one but himself
Where now he sat, concerned with he knew what,
A quiet light, and then not even that.
He consigned to the moon — such as she was,
So late-arising — to the broken moon,
As better than the sun in any case
For such a charge, his snow upon the roof,
His icicles along the wall to keep;
And slept. The log that shifted with a jolt
Once in the stove, disturbed him and he shifted,
And eased his heavy breathing, but still slept.
One aged man — one man — can't keep a house,
A farm, a countryside, or if he can,
It's thus he does it of a winter night.

1916

Fire and Ice

Some say the world will end in fire,
Some say in ice.
From what I've tasted of desire
I hold with those who favor fire.
But if it had to perish twice,
I think I know enough of hate
To say that for destruction ice
Is also great
And would suffice.

1923

Dust of Snow

The way a crow
Shook down on me
The dust of snow
From a hemlock tree

Has given my heart
A change of mood
And saved some part
Of a day I had rued.

1923

Nothing Gold Can Stay

Nature's first green is gold,
Her hardest hue to hold.
Her early leaf's a flower;
But only so an hour.
Then leaf subsides to leaf,
So Eden sank to grief,
So dawn goes down to day,
Nothing gold can stay.

1923

For Once, Then, Something

Others taunt me with having knelt at well-curbs
Always wrong to the light, so never seeing
Deeper down in the well than where the water
Gives me back in a shining surface picture
Me myself in the summer heaven, godlike,
Looking out of a wreath of fern and cloud puffs.
Once, when trying with chin against a well-curb,
I discerned, as I thought, beyond the picture,
Through the picture, a something white, uncertain,
Something more of the depths — and then I lost it.
Water came to rebuke the too clear water.
One drop fell from a fern, and lo, a ripple
Shook whatever it was lay there at bottom,
Blurred it, blotted it out. What was that whiteness?
Truth? A pebble of quartz? For once, then, something.

1923

Stopping by Woods on a Snowy Evening

Whose woods these are I think I know.
His house is in the village, though;
He will not see me stopping here
To watch his woods fill up with snow.

My little horse must think it queer
To stop without a farmhouse near
Between the woods and frozen lake
The darkest evening of the year.

He gives his harness bells a shake
To ask if there is some mistake.
The only other sound's the sweep
Of easy wind and downy flake.

The woods are lovely, dark and deep,
But I have promises to keep,
And miles to go before I sleep,
And miles to go before I sleep.

1923

To Earthward

Love at the lips was touch
As sweet as I could bear;
And once that seemed too much;
I lived on air

That crossed me from sweet things,
The flow of — was it musk
From hidden grapevine springs
Downhill at dusk?

I had the swirl and ache
From sprays of honeysuckle
That when they're gathered shake
Dew on the knuckle.

I craved strong sweets, but those
Seemed strong when I was young;
The petal of the rose
It was that stung.

Now no joy but lacks salt,
That is not dashed with pain
And weariness and fault;
I crave the stain

Of tears, the aftermark
Of almost too much love,
The sweet of bitter bark
And burning clove.

When stiff and sore and scarred
I take away my hand
From leaning on it hard
In grass and sand,

The hurt is not enough:
I long for weight and strength
To feel the earth as rough
To all my length.

1923

Spring Pools

These pools that, though in forests, still reflect
The total sky almost without defect,
And like the flowers beside them, chill and shiver,
Will like the flowers beside them soon be gone,
And yet not out by any brook or river,
But up by roots to bring dark foliage on.

The trees that have it in their pent-up buds
To darken nature and be summer woods —
Let them think twice before they use their powers
To blot out and drink up and sweep away
These flowery waters and these watery flowers
From snow that melted only yesterday.

1928

Acquainted with the Night

I have been one acquainted with the night.
I have walked out in rain — and back in rain.
I have outwalked the furthest city light.

I have looked down the saddest city lane.
I have passed by the watchman on his beat
And dropped my eyes, unwilling to explain.

I have stood still and stopped the sound of feet
When far away an interrupted cry
Came over houses from another street,

But not to call me back or say good-by;
And further still at an unearthly height
One luminary clock against the sky

Proclaimed the time was neither wrong nor right.
I have been one acquainted with the night.

1928

Two Tramps in Mud Time

Out of the mud two strangers came
And caught me splitting wood in the yard.
And one of them put me off my aim
By hailing cheerily "Hit them hard!"
I knew pretty well why he dropped behind
And let the other go on a way.
I knew pretty well what he had in mind:
He wanted to take my job for pay.

Good blocks of oak it was I split,
As large around as the chopping block;
And every piece I squarely hit
Fell splinterless as a cloven rock.
The blows that a life of self-control
Spares to strike for the common good,
That day, giving a loose to my soul,
I spent on the unimportant wood.

The sun was warm but the wind was chill.
You know how it is with an April day
When the sun is out and the wind is still,
You're one month on in the middle of May.
But if you so much as dare to speak,
A cloud comes over the sunlit arch,
A wind comes off a frozen peak,
And you're two months back in the middle of March.

A bluebird comes tenderly up to alight
And turns to the wind to unruffle a plume,
His song so pitched as not to excite
A single flower as yet to bloom.
It is snowing a flake: and he half knew
Winter was only playing possum.
Except in color he isn't blue,
But he wouldn't advise a thing to blossom.

The water for which we may have to look
In summertime with a witching wand,
In every wheelrut's now a brook,
In every print of a hoof a pond.
Be glad of water, but don't forget

The lurking frost in the earth beneath
That will steal forth after the sun is set
And show on the water its crystal teeth.

The time when most I loved my task
These two must make me love it more
By coming with what they came to ask.
You'd think I never had felt before
The weight of an ax-head poised aloft,
The grip on earth of outspread feet.
The life of muscles rocking soft
And smooth and moist in vernal heat.

Out of the woods two hulking tramps
(From sleeping God knows where last night,
But not long since in the lumber camps).
They thought all chopping was theirs of right.
Men of the woods and lumberjacks,
They judged me by their appropriate tool.
Except as a fellow handled an ax
They had no way of knowing a fool.

Nothing on either side was said.
They knew they had but to stay their stay
And all their logic would fill my head:
As that I had no right to play
With what was another man's work for gain.
My right might be love but theirs was need.
And where the two exist in twain
Theirs was the better right — agreed.

But yield who will to their separation,
My object in living is to unite
My avocation and my vocation
As my two eyes make one in sight.
Only where love and need are one,
And the work is play for mortal stakes,
Is the deed ever really done
For Heaven and the future's sakes.

1936

Desert Places

Snow falling and night falling fast, oh, fast
In a field I looked into going past,
And the ground almost covered smooth in snow,
But a few weeds and stubble showing last.

The woods around it have it — it is theirs.
All animals are smothered in their lairs.
I am too absent-spirited to count;
The loneliness includes me unawares.

And lonely as it is, that loneliness
Will be more lonely ere it will be less —
A blanker whiteness of benighted snow
With no expression, nothing to express.

They cannot scare me with their empty spaces
Between stars — on stars where no human race is.
I have it in me so much nearer home
To scare myself with my own desert places.

1936

Neither Out Far Nor In Deep

The people along the sand
All turn and look one way.
They turn their back on the land.
They look at the sea all day.

As long as it takes to pass
A ship keeps raising its hull;
The wetter ground like glass
Reflects a standing gull.

The land may vary more;
But wherever the truth may be —
The water comes ashore,
And the people look at the sea.

They cannot look out far.
They cannot look in deep.
But when was that ever a bar
To any watch they keep?

1936

Design

I found a dimpled spider, fat and white,
On a white heal-all, holding up a moth
Like a white piece of rigid satin cloth —
Assorted characters of death and blight
Mixed ready to begin the morning right,

Like the ingredients of a witches' broth —
A snow-drop spider, a flower like a froth,
And dead wings carried like a paper kite.

What had that flower to do with being white,
The wayside blue and innocent heal-all?
What brought the kindred spider to that height,
Then steered the white moth thither in the night?
What but design of darkness to appall? —
If design govern in a thing so small.

1936

Provide, Provide

The witch that came (the withered hag)
To wash the steps with pail and rag
Was once the beauty Abishag,

The picture pride of Hollywood.
Too many fall from great and good
For you to doubt the likelihood.

Die early and avoid the fate.
Or if predestined to die late,
Make up your mind to die in state.

Make the whole stock exchange your own!
If need be occupy a throne,
Where nobody can call *you* crone.

Some have relied on what they knew,
Others on being simply true.
What worked for them might work for you.

No memory of having starred
Atones for later disregard
Or keeps the end from being hard.

Better to go down dignified
With boughten friendship at your side
Than none at all. Provide, provide!

1936

Come In

As I came to the edge of the woods,
Thrush music — hark!
Now if it was dusk outside,
Inside it was dark.

Too dark in the woods for a bird
By sleight of wing
To better its perch for the night,
Though it still could sing.

The last of the light of the sun
That had died in the west
Still lived for one song more
In a thrush's breast.

Far in the pillared dark
Thrush music went —
Almost like a call to come in
To the dark and lament.

But no, I was out for stars:
I would not come in.
I meant not even if asked,
And I hadn't been.

1942

The Most of It

He thought he kept the universe alone;
For all the voice in answer he could wake
Was but the mocking echo of his own
From some tree-hidden cliff across the lake.
Some morning from the boulder-broken beach
He would cry out on life, that what it wants
Is not its own love back in copy speech,
But counter-love, original response.
And nothing ever came of what he cried
Unless it was the embodiment that crashed
In the cliff's talus on the other side,
And then in the far-distant water splashed,
But after a time allowed for it to swim,
Instead of proving human when it neared
And someone else additional to him,
As a great buck it powerfully appeared,
Pushing the crumpled water up ahead,

And landed pouring like a waterfall,
And stumbled through the rocks with horny tread,
And forced the underbrush — and that was all.

1942

Never Again Would Birds' Song Be the Same

He would declare and could himself believe
That the birds there in all the garden round
From having heard the daylong voice of Eve
Had added to their own an oversound,
Her tone of meaning but without the words.
Admittedly an eloquence so soft
Could only have had an influence on birds
When call or laughter carried it aloft.
Be that as may be, she was in their song.
Moreover her voice upon their voices crossed
Had now persisted in the woods so long
That probably it never would be lost.
Never again would birds' song be the same.
And to do that to birds was why she came.

1942

The Gift Outright

The land was ours before we were the land's.
She was our land more than a hundred years
Before we were her people. She was ours
In Massachusetts, in Virginia,
But we were England's, still colonials,
Possessing what we still were unpossessed by,
Possessed by what we now no more possessed.
Something we were withholding made us weak
Until we found out that it was ourselves
We were withholding from our land of living,
And forthwith found salvation in surrender.
Such as we were we gave ourselves outright
(The deed of gift was many deeds of war)
To the land vaguely realizing westward,
But still unstoried, artless, unenhanced,
Such as she was, such as she would become.

1942

Directive

Back out of all this now too much for us,
Back in a time made simple by the loss
Of detail, burned, dissolved, and broken off
Like graveyard marble sculpture in the weather,
There is a house that is no more a house
Upon a farm that is no more a farm
And in a town that is no more a town.
The road there, if you'll let a guide direct you
Who only has at heart your getting lost,
May seem as if it should have been a quarry —
Great monolithic knees the former town
Long since gave up pretense of keeping covered.
And there's a story in a book about it:
Besides the wear of iron wagon wheels
The ledges show lines ruled southeast-northwest,
The chisel work of an enormous Glacier
That braced his feet against the Arctic Pole.
You must not mind a certain coolness from him
Still said to haunt this side of Panther Mountain.
Nor need you mind the serial ordeal
Of being watched from forty cellar holes
As if by eye pairs out of forty firkins.
As for the woods' excitement over you
That sends light rustle rushes to their leaves,
Charge that to upstart inexperience.
Where were they all not twenty years ago?
They think too much of having shaded out
A few old pecker-fretted apple trees.
Make yourself up a cheering song of how
Someone's road home from work this once was,
Who may be just ahead of you on foot
Or creaking with a buggy load of grain.
The height of the adventure is the height
Of country where two village cultures faded
Into each other. Both of them are lost.
And if you're lost enough to find yourself
By now, pull in your ladder road behind you
And put a sign up CLOSED to all but me.
Then make yourself at home. The only field
Now left's no bigger than a harness gall.
First there's the children's house of make-believe,
Some shattered dishes underneath a pine,
The playthings in the playhouse of the children.
Weep for what little things could make them glad.
Then for the house that is no more a house,
But only a belilaced cellar hole,
Now slowly closing like a dent in dough.

This was no playhouse but a house in earnest.
Your destination and your destiny's
A brook that was the water of the house,
Cold as a spring as yet so near its source,
Too lofty and original to rage.
(We know the valley streams that when aroused
will leave their tatters hung on barb and thorn.)
I have kept hidden in the instep arch
Of an old cedar at the waterside
A broken drinking goblet like the Grail
Under a spell so the wrong ones can't find it,
So can't get saved, as Saint Mark says they mustn't.
(I stole the goblet from the children's playhouse.)
Here are your waters and your watering place.
Drink and be whole again beyond confusion.

1947

AMY LOWELL (1874–1925)

Born into a famous American family, Amy Lowell was characterized by her younger relation, Robert Lowell, as "big and a scandal, as if Mae West were a cousin." Amy made headlines when she, the sister of Harvard University's president, was seen smoking a cigar one evening. "Before long, her notoriety would come from her vocal defense of 'the new poetry,' not from what she inhaled" (Honor Moore). She joined forces with Ezra Pound in London in 1913 and enthusiastically took up the imagist movement, which fired a salvo in the modernist revolution. The movement put a high value on precise imagery, common speech, the "*exact* word, not the nearly exact, nor the merely decorative word," freedom in choice of subject matter, and a goal of "poetry that is hard and clear, never blurred nor indefinite." After Lowell and Pound quarreled and he went his separate way, she became the movement's chief spokesperson; Pound ridiculed the result as "Amygism." Lowell's best poems are her erotic lyrics, such as "The Weather-Cock Points South." She also wrote prose poems and a biography of John Keats, the first by an American.

A Decade

When you came, you were like red wine and honey,
And the taste of you burnt my mouth with its sweetness.
Now you are like morning bread,
Smooth and pleasant.
I hardly taste you at all, for I know your savor;
But I am completely nourished.

1919

A Lover

If I could catch the green lantern of the firefly
I could see to write you a letter.

1919

The Weather-Cock Points South

I put your leaves aside,
One by one:
The stiff, broad outer leaves;
The smaller ones,
Pleasant to touch, veined with purple;
The glazed inner leaves.
One by one
I parted you from your leaves,
Until you stood up like a white flower
Swaying slightly in the evening wind.

White flower,
Flower of wax, of jade, of unstreaked agate;
Flower with surfaces of ice,
With shadows faintly crimson.
Where in all the garden is there such a flower?
The stars crowd through the lilac leaves
To look at you.
The low moon brightens you with silver.

The bud is more than the calyx.
There is nothing to equal a white bud,
Of no colour, and of all,
Burnished by moonlight,
Thrust upon by a softly-swinging wind.

1919

GERTRUDE STEIN (1874–1946)

Gertrude Stein was born in Allegheny, Pennsylvania, to wealthy German-Jewish immigrants. Her family moved to Vienna in 1875 and to Paris three years later. They returned to America in 1879 and settled in Oakland ("no there there"), California. Stein attended Radcliffe College, where she studied with William James. She settled in Paris in 1903, and her apartment at 27 rue de Fleurus became a legendary international avant-garde salon. Picasso, Matisse, Ezra Pound, Hemingway, and F. Scott Fitzgerald were among the writers and artists who paid court. In 1907, Stein met Alice B. Toklas, who became her lifelong companion. *The Autobiography of Alice B.*

Toklas (1933), which Stein wrote, became a best seller. Stein liked to say that she wrote "for myself and strangers." Of her own genius she was never in doubt. "It takes a lot of time to be a genius, you have to sit around so much doing nothing really doing nothing," she wrote. No other writer born in the nineteenth century still seems so formidably innovative today.

Guillaume Apollinaire

Give known or pin ware.
Fancy teeth, gas strips.
Elbow elect, sour stout pore, pore caesar, pour state at.
Leave eye lessons I. Leave I. Lessons. I. Leave I lessons, I.

1913

Cézanne

The Irish lady can say, that to-day is every day. Caesar can say that every day is to-day and they say that every day is as they say.

In this way we have a place to stay and he was not met because he was settled to stay. When I said settled I meant settled to stay. When I said settled to stay I meant settled to stay Saturday. In this way a mouth is a mouth. In this way if in as a mouth if in as a mouth where, if in as a mouth where and there. Believe they have water too. Believe they have that water too and blue when you see blue, is all blue precious too, is all that that is precious too is all that and they meant to absolve you. In this way Cézanne nearly did nearly in this way Cézanne nearly did nearly did and nearly did. And was I surprised. Was I very surprised. Was I surprised. I was surprised and in that patient, are you patient when you find bees. Bees in a garden make a specialty of honey and so does honey. Honey and prayer. Honey and there. There where the grass can grow nearly four times yearly.

1923

from *A Book Concluding with As a Wife Has a Cow A Love Story*

Key to Closet

There is a key.

There is a key to a closet that opens the drawer. And she keeps both so that neither money nor candy will go suddenly, Fancy, baby, new year. She keeps both so that neither money nor candy will go suddenly, Fancy baby New Year, fancy baby mine, fancy.

Fish

Can fish be wives and wives and wives and have as many as that. Can fish be wives and have as many as that.

Ten o' clock or earlier.

Had a Horse

If in place of a nose she had a horse and in place of a flower she had wax and in place of a melon she had a stone and in place of perfume buckles how many days would it be.

In Question

How large a mouth has a good singer. He knows. How much better is one colour than another. He knows. How far away is a city from a city. He knows. How often is it delayed. He knows.

Much Later

Elephants and birds of beauty and a gold-fish. Gold fish or a superstition. They always bring bad luck. He had them and he was not told. Gold fish and he was not old. Gold fish and he was not to scold. Gold fish all told. The result was that the other people never had them and he knows nothing of it.

Emily

Emily is admitted admittedly, Emily is admittedly Emily is admittedly.

Emily said Emily said, Emily is admittedly Emily. Emily said Emily is admittedly is Emily said Emily is admittedly Emily said Emily is Emily is admittedly.

There

There is an excuse for expecting success there is an excuse. There is an excuse for expecting success and there is an excuse for expecting success. And at once.

In English

Even in the midst and may be even in the midst and even in the midst and may be. Watched them.

Not Surprising

It is not at all surprising. Not at all surprising. If he gets it done at all. It is not at all surprising.

A Wish

And always not when absently enough and heard and said. He had a wish.

Fifty

Fifty fifty and fifty-one, she said she thought so and she was told that that was about what it was. Not in place considered as places. Julia was used only as cake, Julia cake was used only as Julia. In some countries cake is called candy. The next is as much as that. When do they is not the same as why do they.

1923

If I Told Him
A Completed Portrait of Picasso

If I told him would he like it. Would he like it if I told him.

Would he like it would Napoleon would Napoleon would would he like it.

If Napoleon if I told him if I told him if Napoleon. Would he like it if I told him if I told him if Napoleon. Would he like it if Napoleon if Napoleon if I told him. If I told him if Napoleon if Napoleon if I told him. If I told him would he like it would he like it if I told him.

Now.

Not now.

And now.

Now.

Exactly as as kings.

Feeling full for it.

Exactitude as kings.

So to beseech you as full as for it.

Exactly or as kings.

Shutters shut and open so do queens. Shutter shall and shutters and so shutters shut and shutters and so and so shutters and so shutters shut and so shutters shut and shutters and so. And so shutters shut and so and also. And also and so and so and also.

Exact resemblance. To exact resemblance the exact resemblance as exact as a resemblance, exactly as resembling, exactly resembling, exactly in resemblance exactly a resemblance, exactly and resemblance. For this is so. Because.

Now actively repeat at all, now actively repeat at all, now actively repeat at all.

Have hold and hear, actively repeat at all.

I judge judge.

As a resemblance to him.

Who comes first. Napoleon the first.

Who comes too coming coming too, who goes there, as they go they share, who shares all, all is as all as as yet or as yet.

Now to date now to date. Now and now and date and the date.

Who came first Napoleon at first. Who came first Napoleon the first. Who came first, Napoleon first.

Presently.

Exactly do they do.

First exactly.

Exactly do they do too.

First exactly.

And first exactly.

Exactly do they do.

And first exactly and exactly.

And do they do.

At first exactly and first exactly and do they do.

The first exactly.

And do they do.

The first exactly.

At first exactly.

First as exactly.

As first as exactly.

Presently

As presently.

As as presently.

He he he he and he and he and and he and he and he and and as and as he and as he and he. He is and as he is, and as he is and he is, he is and as he and he and as he is and he and he and and he and he.

Can curls rob can curls quote, quotable.

As presently.

As exactitude.

As trains.

Has trains.

Has trains.

As trains.

As trains.

Presently.

Proportions.

Presently.

As proportions as presently.

Father and farther.

Was the king or room.

Farther and whether.

Was there was there was there what was there was there what was there was there there was there.

Whether and in there.

As even say so.

One.

I land.

Two.

I land.

Three.

The land.

Three
The land.
Three
The land.
Two
I land.
Two
I land.
One
I land.
Two
I land.
As a so.
They cannot.
A note.
They cannot.
A float.
They cannot
They dote.
They cannot.
They as denote.
Miracles play.
Play fairly.
Play fairly well.
A well.
As well.
As or as presently.
Let me recite what history teaches. History teaches.

1924

TRUMBULL STICKNEY (1874–1904)

Trumbull Stickney was born in Geneva, Switzerland. He grew up in Europe and England but attended Harvard University. As a freshman he joined the editorial board of the *Harvard Monthly* and contributed to it almost exclusively for the rest of his life. The one collection of his poems that appeared in his lifetime was *Dramatic Verses* (1902). In 1950, F. O. Matthiessen wrote that the "nearly forgotten Stickney, who spent much of his life in France, is our closest approximation of the *fin de siecle* mood, the mood of [the French poet Paul] Verlaine." Stickney died of a brain tumor at the age of thirty.

Live Blindly

Live blindly and upon the hour. The Lord,
Who was the Future, died full long ago.

Knowledge which is the Past is folly. Go,
Poor child, and be not to thyself abhorred.
Around thine earth sun-wingèd winds do blow
And planets roll; a meteor draws his sword;
The rainbow breaks his seven-coloured chord
And the long strips of river-silver flow:
Awake! Give thyself to the lovely hours.
Drinking their lips, catch thou the dream in flight
About their fragile hairs' aërial gold.
Thou art divine, thou livest, — as of old
Apollo springing naked to the light,
And all his island shivered into flowers.

1898

He Said: "If in His Image I Was Made"

He said: "If in his image I was made,
I am his equal and across the land
We two should make our journey hand in hand
Like brothers dignified and unafraid."
And God that day was walking in the shade.
To whom he said: "The world is idly planned,
We cross each other, let us understand
Thou who thou art, I who I am," he said.
Darkness came down. And all that night was heard
Tremendous clamour and the broken roar
Of things in turmoil driven down before.
Then silence. Morning broke, and sang a bird.
He lay upon the earth, his bosom stirred;
But God was seen no longer any more.

1902

Six O'Clock

Now burst above the city's cold twilight
The piercing whistles and the tower-clocks:
For day is done. Along the frozen docks
The workmen set their ragged shirts aright.
Thro' factory doors a stream of dingy light
Follows the scrimmage as it quickly flocks
To hut and home among the snow's gray blocks. —
I love you, human labourers. Good-night!
Good-night to all the blackened arms that ache!
Good-night to every sick and sweated brow,
To the poor girl that strength and love forsake,

To the poor boy who can no more! I vow
The victim soon shall shudder at the stake
And fall in blood: we bring him even now.

1903

from *Dramatic Fragments*

IX

I hear a river thro' the valley wander
Whose water runs, the song alone remaining.
A rainbow stands and summer passes under.

1905

ADELAIDE CRAPSEY (1878–1914)

Adelaide Crapsey, a Vassar alumna who became a Smith College professor, invented the cinquain, a five-line stanza form containing twenty-two syllables, with the four, six, and eight syllables in its middle three lines sandwiched between opening and closing lines of two syllables each. Her life was marked by great sadness. In 1906, her father was defrocked after a public trial for heresy. Crapsey was diagnosed with tuberculosis of the brain lining, a diagnosis that she kept from her family until failing health forced her to reveal it.

Release

With swift
Great sweep of her
Magnificent arm my pain
Clanged back the doors that shut my soul
From life.

1915

Triad

These be
Three silent things:
The falling snow. . . the hour
Before the dawn. . . the mouth of one
Just dead.

1915

Trapped

Well and
If day on day
Follows, and weary year
On year. . . and ever days and years. . .
Well?

1915

Susanna and the Elders

"Why do
You thus devise
Evil against her?" "For that
She is beautiful, delicate;
Therefore."

1915

Amaze

I know
Not these my hands
And yet I think there was
A woman like me once had hands
Like these.

1915

CARL SANDBURG (1878–1967)

Carl Sandburg was born the son of Swedish immigrants in Galesburg, Illinois. In Milwaukee he met and married Lillian Steichen, sister of the photographer Edward Steichen. In Chicago he became an editorial writer for the *Daily News*. He won Pulitzer Prizes for his biography of Abraham Lincoln and for his *Complete Poems*. The self-sung poet of Chicago ("Hog Butcher for the World"), praiser of "the people," Sandburg once vied with Frost in popularity. Though his reputation has lagged far behind that of his slightly older contemporary (who despised him), Sandburg is remembered fondly for the straightforward free verse of his *Chicago Poems* (1916) and his muscular efforts to find genuine poetry in the *Smoke and Steel* (1920) of modern industrial life. Louise Bogan noted approvingly that he celebrated as well as described the "grime, stench, grinding, shriek, and clatter" of the city.

Chicago

Hog Butcher for the World,
Tool Maker, Stacker of Wheat,
Player with Railroads and the Nation's Freight Handler;
Stormy, husky, brawling,
City of the Big Shoulders:

They tell me you are wicked and I believe them, for I have seen your painted women under the gas lamps luring the farm boys.
And they tell me you are crooked and I answer: Yes, it is true I have seen the gunman kill and go free to kill again.
And they tell me you are brutal and my reply is: On the faces of women and children I have seen the marks of wanton hunger.
And having answered so I turn once more to those who sneer at this my city, and I give them back the sneer and say to them:
Come and show me another city with lifted head singing so proud to be alive and coarse and strong and cunning.
Flinging magnetic curses amid the toil of piling job on job, here is a tall bold slugger set vivid against the little soft cities;
Fierce as a dog with tongue lapping for action, cunning as a savage pitted against the wilderness,
Bareheaded,
Shoveling,
Wrecking,
Planning,
Building, breaking, rebuilding,
Under the smoke, dust all over his mouth, laughing with white teeth,
Under the terrible burden of destiny laughing as a young man laughs,
Laughing even as an ignorant fighter laughs who has never lost a battle,
Bragging and laughing that under his wrist is the pulse, and under his ribs the heart of the people,
Laughing!
Laughing the stormy, husky, brawling laughter of Youth, half-naked, sweating, proud to be Hog Butcher, Tool Maker, Stacker of Wheat, Player with Railroads and Freight Handler to the Nation.

1916

Grass

Pile the bodies high at Austerlitz and Waterloo.
Shovel them under and let me work —
I am the grass; I cover all.
And pile them high at Gettysburg
And pile them high at Ypres and Verdun.
Shovel them under and let me work.
Two years, ten years, and passengers ask the conductor:

What place is this?
Where are we now?

I am the grass.
Let me work.

1918

WALLACE STEVENS (1879–1955)

Born in Reading, Pennsylvania, Wallace Stevens spent most of his adult life in the employ of the Hartford [Connecticut] Accident and Indemnity Company, rising in 1934 to the rank of vice president. His wife, Elsie (whom he married in 1909), was the model for the figures on the Mercury dime and the Liberty half-dollar. Theirs was a gloomy marriage. Once, when asked how he had spent the afternoon, he replied, "Mrs. Stevens and I walked to the end of Westerly Terrace [where they lived], and she turned left and I turned right." Some of his poems can be understood as speculations on the poet's prerogatives in a godless universe; in other poems a metaphysical shoving match seems to be in progress between "the pressure of reality" and the force of the imagination pressing back on it. Under the heading "Adagia," Stevens wrote aphorisms of unusual pith, any of which might serve as the topic or title of a symposium, a lecture, a poem, or a book: "Money is a kind of poetry." "All poetry is experimental poetry." "All history is modern history." "Realism is a corruption of reality." "The death of one god is the death of all." "Poetry must be irrational." "Romanticism is to poetry what the decorative is to painting." "One's ignorance is one's chief asset." Stevens said that "The Emperor of Ice Cream" was his favorite among his poems because it "wears a deliberately commonplace costume, and yet seems to me to contain something of the essential gaudiness of poetry."

Disillusionment of Ten O'Clock

The houses are haunted
By white night-gowns.
None are green,
Or purple with green rings,
Or green with yellow rings,
Or yellow with blue rings.
None of them are strange,
With socks of lace
And beaded ceintures.
People are not going
To dream of baboons and periwinkles.
Only, here and there, an old sailor,
Drunk and asleep in his boots,
Catches tigers
In red weather.

1915

Sunday Morning

I

Complacencies of the peignoir, and late
Coffee and oranges in a sunny chair,
And the green freedom of a cockatoo
Upon a rug mingle to dissipate
The holy hush of ancient sacrifice.
She dreams a little, and she feels the dark
Encroachment of that old catastrophe,
As a calm darkens among water-lights.
The pungent oranges and bright, green wings
Seem things in some procession of the dead,
Winding across wide water, without sound.
The day is like wide water, without sound,
Stilled for the passing of her dreaming feet
Over the seas, to silent Palestine,
Dominion of the blood and sepulchre.

II

Why should she give her bounty to the dead?
What is divinity if it can come
Only in silent shadows and in dreams?
Shall she not find in comforts of the sun,
In pungent fruit and bright, green wings, or else
In any balm or beauty of the earth,
Things to be cherished like the thought of heaven?
Divinity must live within herself:
Passions of rain, or moods in falling snow;
Grievings in loneliness, or unsubdued
Elations when the forest blooms; gusty
Emotions on wet roads on autumn nights;
All pleasures and all pains, remembering
The bough of summer and the winter branch.
These are the measures destined for her soul.

III

Jove in the clouds had his inhuman birth.
No mother suckled him, no sweet land gave
Large-mannered motions to his mythy mind.
He moved among us, as a muttering king,
Magnificent, would move among his hinds,
Until our blood, commingling, virginal,
With heaven, brought such requital to desire
The very hinds discerned it, in a star.
Shall our blood fail? Or shall it come to be
The blood of paradise? And shall the earth
Seem all of paradise that we shall know?
The sky will be much friendlier then than now,

A part of labor and a part of pain,
And next in glory to enduring love,
Not this dividing and indifferent blue.

IV

She says, "I am content when wakened birds,
Before they fly, test the reality
Of misty fields, by their sweet questionings;
But when the birds are gone, and their warm fields
Return no more, where, then, is paradise?"
There is not any haunt of prophecy,
Nor any old chimera of the grave,
Neither the golden underground, nor isle
Melodious, where spirits gat them home,
Nor visionary south, nor cloudy palm
Remote on heaven's hill, that has endured
As April's green endures; or will endure
Like her remembrance of awakened birds,
Or her desire for June and evening, tipped
By the consummation of the swallow's wings.

V

She says, "But in contentment I still feel
The need of some imperishable bliss."
Death is the mother of beauty; hence from her,
Alone, shall come fulfilment to our dreams
And our desires. Although she strews the leaves
Of sure obliteration on our paths,
The path sick sorrow took, the many paths
Where triumph rang its brassy phrase, or love
Whispered a little out of tenderness,
She makes the willow shiver in the sun
For maidens who were wont to sit and gaze
Upon the grass, relinquished to their feet.
She causes boys to pile new plums and pears
On disregarded plate. The maidens taste
And stray impassioned in the littering leaves.

VI

Is there no change of death in paradise?
Does ripe fruit never fall? Or do the boughs
Hang always heavy in that perfect sky,
Unchanging, yet so like our perishing earth,
With rivers like our own that seek for seas
They never find, the same receding shores
That never touch with inarticulate pang?
Why set the pear upon those river-banks
Or spice the shores with odors of the plum?
Alas, that they should wear our colors there,

The silken weavings of our afternoons,
And pick the strings of our insipid lutes!
Death is the mother of beauty, mystical,
Within whose burning bosom we devise
Our earthly mothers waiting, sleeplessly.

VII

Supple and turbulent, a ring of men
Shall chant in orgy on a summer morn
Their boisterous devotion to the sun,
Not as a god, but as a god might be,
Naked among them, like a savage source.
Their chant shall be a chant of paradise,
Out of their blood, returning to the sky;
And in their chant shall enter, voice by voice,
The windy lake wherein their lord delights,
The trees, like serafin, and echoing hills,
That choir among themselves long afterward.
They shall know well the heavenly fellowship
Of men that perish and of summer morn.
And whence they came and whither they shall go
The dew upon their feet shall manifest.

VIII

She hears, upon that water without sound,
A voice that cries, "The tomb in Palestine
Is not the porch of spirits lingering.
It is the grave of Jesus, where he lay."
We live in an old chaos of the sun,
Or old dependency of day and night,
Or island solitude, unsponsored, free,
Of that wide water, inescapable.
Deer walk upon our mountains, and the quail
Whistle about us their spontaneous cries;
Sweet berries ripen in the wilderness;
And, in the isolation of the sky,
At evening, casual flocks of pigeons make
Ambiguous undulations as they sink,
Downward to darkness, on extended wings.

1915

Peter Quince at the Clavier

I

Just as my fingers on these keys
Make music, so the selfsame sounds
On my spirit make a music, too.

Music is feeling, then, not sound;
And thus it is that what I feel,
Here in this room, desiring you,

Thinking of your blue-shadowed silk,
Is music. It is like the strain
Waked in the elders by Susanna.

Of a green evening, clear and warm,
She bathed in her still garden, while
The red-eyed elders watching, felt

The basses of their beings throb
In witching chords, and their thin blood
Pulse pizzicati of Hosanna.

II

In the green water, clear and warm,
Susanna lay.
She searched
The touch of springs,
And found
Concealed imaginings.
She sighed,
For so much melody.

Upon the bank, she stood
In the cool
Of spent emotions.
She felt, among the leaves,
The dew
Of old devotions.

She walked upon the grass,
Still quavering.
The winds were like her maids,
On timid feet,
Fetching her woven scarves,
Yet wavering.

A breath upon her hand
Muted the night.
She turned —
A cymbal crashed,
And roaring horns.

III

Soon, with a noise like tambourines,
Came her attendant Byzantines.

They wondered why Susanna cried
Against the elders by her side;

And as they whispered, the refrain
Was like a willow swept by rain.

Anon, their lamps' uplifted flame
Revealed Susanna and her shame.

And then, the simpering Byzantines
Fled, with a noise like tambourines.

IV

Beauty is momentary in the mind —
The fitful tracing of a portal;
But in the flesh it is immortal.

The body dies; the body's beauty lives.
So evenings die, in their green going,
A wave, interminably flowing.
So gardens die, their meek breath scenting
The cowl of winter, done repenting.
So maidens die, to the auroral
Celebration of a maiden's choral.

Susanna's music touched the bawdy strings
Of those white elders; but, escaping,
Left only Death's ironic scraping.
Now, in its immortality, it plays
On the clear viol of her memory,
And makes a constant sacrament of praise.

1915

Domination of Black

At night, by the fire,
The colors of the bushes
And of the fallen leaves,
Repeating themselves,
Turned in the room,
Like the leaves themselves
Turning in the wind.

Yes: but the color of the heavy hemlocks
Came striding.
And I remembered the cry of the peacocks.

The colors of their tails
Were like the leaves themselves
Turning in the wind,
In the twilight wind.
They swept over the room,
Just as they flew from the boughs of the hemlocks
Down to the ground.
I heard them cry — the peacocks.
Was it a cry against the twilight
Or against the leaves themselves
Turning in the wind,
Turning as the flames
Turned in the fire,
Turning as the tails of the peacocks
Turned in the loud fire,
Loud as the hemlocks
Full of the cry of the peacocks?
Or was it a cry against the hemlocks?

Out of the window,
I saw how the planets gathered
Like the leaves themselves
Turning in the wind.
I saw how the night came,
Came striding like the color of the heavy hemlocks.
I felt afraid.
And I remembered the cry of the peacocks.

1916

Thirteen Ways of Looking at a Blackbird

I

Among twenty snowy mountains,
The only moving thing
Was the eye of the blackbird.

II

I was of three minds,
Like a tree
In which there are three blackbirds.

III

The blackbird whirled in the autumn winds.
It was a small part of the pantomime.

IV

A man and a woman
Are one.
A man and a woman and a blackbird
Are one.

V

I do not know which to prefer,
The beauty of inflections
Or the beauty of innuendoes,
The blackbird whistling
Or just after.

VI

Icicles filled the long window
With barbaric glass.
The shadow of the blackbird
Crossed it, to and fro.
The mood
Traced in the shadow
An indecipherable cause.

VII

O thin men of Haddam,
Why do you imagine golden birds?
Do you not see how the blackbird
Walks around the feet
Of the women about you?

VIII

I know noble accents
And lucid, inescapable rhythms;
But I know, too,
That the blackbird is involved
In what I know.

IX

When the blackbird flew out of sight,
It marked the edge
Of one of many circles.

X

At the sight of blackbirds
Flying in a green light,
Even the bawds of euphony
Would cry out sharply.

XI
He rode over Connecticut
In a glass coach.
Once, a fear pierced him,
In that he mistook
The shadow of his equipage
For blackbirds.

XII
The river is moving.
The blackbird must be flying.

XIII
It was evening all afternoon.
It was snowing
And it was going to snow.
The blackbird sat
In the cedar-limbs.

1917

The Death of a Soldier

Life contracts and death is expected,
As in a season of autumn.
The soldier falls.

He does not become a three-days personage,
Imposing his separation,
Calling for pomp.

Death is absolute and without memorial,
As in a season of autumn,
When the wind stops,

When the wind stops and, over the heavens,
The clouds go, nevertheless,
In their direction.

1918

Anecdote of the Jar

I placed a jar in Tennessee,
And round it was, upon a hill.
It made the slovenly wilderness
Surround that hill.

The wilderness rose up to it,
And sprawled around, no longer wild
The jar was round upon the ground
And tall and of a port in air.

It took dominion everywhere.
The jar was gray and bare.
It did not give of bird or bush,
Like nothing else in Tennessee.

1919

Tea at the Palaz of Hoon

Not less because in purple I descended
The western day through what you called
The loneliest air, not less was I myself.

What was the ointment sprinkled on my beard?
What were the hymns that buzzed beside my ears?
What was the sea whose tide swept through me there?

Out of my mind the golden ointment rained,
And my ears made the blowing hymns they heard.
I was myself the compass of that sea:

I was the world in which I walked, and what I saw
Or heard or felt came not but from myself;
And there I found myself more truly and more strange.

1921

The Snow Man

One must have a mind of winter
To regard the frost and the boughs
Of the pine-trees crusted with snow;

And have been cold a long time
To behold the junipers shagged with ice,
The spruces rough in the distant glitter

Of the January sun; and not to think
Of any misery in the sound of the wind,
In the sound of a few leaves,

Which is the sound of the land
Full of the same wind
That is blowing in the same bare place

For the listener, who listens in the snow,
And, nothing himself, beholds
Nothing that is not there and the nothing that is.

1921

The Bird with the Coppery, Keen Claws

Above the forest of the parakeets,
A parakeet of parakeets prevails,
A pip of life amid a mort of tails.

(The rudiments of tropics are around,
Aloe of ivory, pear of rusty rind.)
His lids are white because his eyes are blind.

He is not paradise of parakeets,
Of his gold ether, golden alguazil,
Except because he broods there and is still.

Panache upon panache, his tails deploy
Upward and outward, in green-vented forms,
His tip a drop of water full of storms.

But though the turbulent tinges undulate
As his pure intellect applies it laws,
He moves not on his coppery, keen claws.

He munches a dry shell while he exerts
His will, yet never ceases, perfect cock,
To flare, in the sun-pallor of his rock.

1921

A High-Toned Old Christian Woman

Poetry is the supreme fiction, madame.
Take the moral law and make a nave of it
And from the nave build haunted heaven. Thus,
The conscience is converted into palms,
Like windy citherns hankering for hymns.
We agree in principle. That's clear. But take
The opposing law and make a peristyle,
And from the peristyle project a masque
Beyond the planets. Thus, our bawdiness,
Unpurged by epitaph, indulged at last,
Is equally converted into palms,
Squiggling like saxophones. And palm for palm,

Madame, we are where we began. Allow,
Therefore, that in the planetary scene
Your disaffected flagellants, well-stuffed,
Smacking their muzzy bellies in parade,
Proud of such novelties of the sublime,
Such tink and tank and tunk-a-tunk-tunk,
May, merely may, madame, whip from themselves
A jovial hullabaloo among the spheres.
This will make widows wince. But fictive things
Wink as they will. Wink most when widows wince.

1922

The Emperor of Ice-Cream

Call the roller of big cigars,
The muscular one, and bid him whip
In kitchen cups concupiscent curds.
Let the wenches dawdle in such dress
As they are used to wear, and let the boys
Bring flowers in last month's newspapers.
Let be be finale of seem.
The only emperor is the emperor of ice-cream.

Take from the dresser of deal,
Lacking the three glass knobs, that sheet
On which she embroidered fantails once
And spread it so as to cover her face.
If her horny feet protrude, they come
To show how cold she is, and dumb.
Let the lamp affix its beam.
The only emperor is the emperor of ice-cream.

1922

Bantams in Pine-Woods

Chieftain Iffucan of Azcan in caftan
Of tan with henna hackles, halt!

Damned universal cock, as if the sun
Was blackamoor to bear your blazing tail.

Fat! Fat! Fat! Fat! I am the personal.
Your world is you. I am my world.

You ten-foot poet among inchlings. Fat!
Begone! An inchling bristles in these pines,

Bristles, and points their Appalachian tangs,
And fears not portly Azcan nor his hoos.

1922

The Man Whose Pharynx Was Bad

The time of year has grown indifferent.
Mildew of summer and the deepening snow
Are both alike in the routine I know.
I am too dumbly in my being pent.

The wind attendant on the solstices
Blows on the shutters of the metropoles,
Stirring no poet in his sleep, and tolls
The grand ideas of the villages.

The malady of the quotidian. . . .
Perhaps, if winter once could penetrate
Through all its purples to the final state,
Persisting bleakly in an icy haze,

One might in turn become less diffident,
Out of such mildew plucking neater mould
And spouting new orations of the cold.
One might. One might. But time will not relent.

1923

Autumn Refrain

The skreak and skritter of evening gone
And grackles gone and sorrows of the sun,
The sorrows of sun, too, gone . . . the moon and moon,
The yellow moon of words about the nightingale
In measureless measures, not a bird for me
But the name of a bird and the name of a nameless air
I have never — shall never hear. And yet beneath
The stillness that comes to me out of this, beneath
The stillness of everything gone, and being still,
Being and sitting still, something resides,
Some skreaking and skrittering residuum,
And grates these evasions of the nightingale
Though I have never — shall never hear that bird.
And the stillness is in the key, all of it is,
The stillness is all in the key of that desolate sound.

1931

The Idea of Order at Key West

She sang beyond the genius of the sea.
The water never formed to mind or voice,
Like a body wholly body, fluttering
Its empty sleeves; and yet its mimic motion
Made constant cry, caused constantly a cry,
That was not ours although we understood,
Inhuman, of the veritable ocean.

The sea was not a mask. No more was she.
The song and water were not medleyed sound
Even if what she sang was what she heard,
Since what she sang was uttered word by word.
It may be that in all her phrases stirred
The grinding water and the gasping wind;
But it was she and not the sea we heard.

For she was the maker of the song she sang.
The ever-hooded, tragic-gestured sea
Was merely a place by which she walked to sing.
Whose spirit is this? we said, because we knew
It was the spirit that we sought and knew
That we should ask this often as she sang.

If it was only the dark voice of the sea
That rose, or even colored by many waves;
If it was only the outer voice of sky
And cloud, of the sunken coral water-walled,
However clear, it would have been deep air,
The heaving speech of air, a summer sound
Repeated in a summer without end
And sound alone. But it was more than that,
More even than her voice, and ours, among
The meaningless plungings of water and the wind,
Theatrical distances, bronze shadows heaped
On high horizons, mountainous atmospheres
Of sky and sea.
It was her voice that made
The sky acutest at its vanishing.
She measured to the hour its solitude.
She was the single artificer of the world
In which she sang. And when she sang, the sea,
Whatever self it had, became the self
That was her song, for she was the maker. Then we,
As we beheld her striding there alone,
Knew that there never was a world for her
Except the one she sang and, singing, made.

Ramon Fernandez, tell me, if you know,
Why, when the singing ended and we turned
Toward the town, tell why the glassy lights,
The lights in the fishing boats at anchor there,
As the night descended, tilting in the air,
Mastered the night and portioned out the sea,
Fixing emblazoned zones and fiery poles,
Arranging, deepening, enchanting night.

Oh! Blessed rage for order, pale Ramon,
The maker's rage to order words of the sea,
Words of the fragrant portals, dimly-starred,
And of ourselves and of our origins,
In ghostlier demarcations, keener sounds.

1935

The American Sublime

How does one stand
To behold the sublime,
To confront the mockers,
The mickey mockers
And plated pairs?

When General Jackson
Posed for his statue
He knew how one feels.
Shall a man go barefoot
Blinking and blank?

But how does one feel?
One grows used to the weather,
The landscape and that;
And the sublime comes down
To the spirit itself,

The spirit and space,
The empty spirit
In a vacant space.
What wine does one drink?
What bread does one eat?

1935

The Poems of Our Climate

I

Clear water in a brilliant bowl,
Pink and white carnations. The light
In the room more like a snowy air,
Reflecting snow. A newly-fallen snow
At the end of winter when afternoons return.
Pink and white carnations — one desires
So much more than that. The day itself
Is simplified: a bowl of white,
Cold, a cold porcelain, low and round,
With nothing more than the carnations there.

II

Say even that this complete simplicity
Stripped one of all one's torments, concealed
The evilly compounded, vital I
And made it fresh in a world of white,
A world of clear water, brilliant-edged,
Still one would want more, one would need more,
More than a world of white and snowy scents.

III

There would still remain the never-resting mind,
So that one would want to escape, come back
To what had been so long composed.
The imperfect is our paradise.
Note that, in this bitterness, delight,
Since the imperfect is so hot in us,
Lies in flawed words and stubborn sounds.

1938

Study of Two Pears

I

Opusculum paedagogum.
The pears are not viols,
Nudes or bottles.
They resemble nothing else.

II

They are yellow forms
Composed of curves
Bulging toward the base.
They are touched red.

III

They are not flat surfaces
Having curved outlines.
They are round
Tapering toward the top.

IV

In the way they are modelled
There are bits of blue.
A hard dry leaf hangs
From the stem.

V

The yellow glistens.
It glistens with various yellows,
Citrons, oranges and greens
Flowering over the skin.

VI

The shadows of the pears
Are blobs on the green cloth.
The pears are not seen
As the observer wills.

1938

The Man on the Dump

Day creeps down. The moon is creeping up.
The sun is a corbeil of flowers the moon Blanche
Places there, a bouquet. Ho-ho . . . The dump is full
Of images. Days pass like papers from a press.
The bouquets come here in the papers. So the sun,
And so the moon, both come, and the janitor's poems
Of every day, the wrapper on the can of pears,
The cat in the paper-bag, the corset, the box
From Esthonia: the tiger chest, for tea.

The freshness of night has been fresh a long time.
The freshness of morning, the blowing of day, one says
That it puffs as Cornelius Nepos reads, it puffs
More than, less than or it puffs like this or that.
The green smacks in the eye, the dew in the green
Smacks like fresh water in a can, like the sea
On a cocoanut — how many men have copied dew
For buttons, how many women have covered themselves
With dew, dew dresses, stones and chains of dew, heads

Of the floweriest flowers dewed with the dewiest dew.
One grows to hate these things except on the dump.

Now, in the time of spring (azaleas, trilliums,
Myrtle, viburnums, daffodils, blue phlox),
Between that disgust and this, between the things
That are on the dump (azaleas and so on)
And those that will be (azaleas and so on),
One feels the purifying change. One rejects
The trash.

That's the moment when the moon creeps up
To the bubbling of bassoons. That's the time
One looks at the elephant-colorings of tires.
Everything is shed; and the moon comes up as the moon
(All its images are in the dump) and you see
As a man (not like an image of a man),
You see the moon rise in the empty sky.

One sits and beats an old tin can, lard pail.
One beats and beats for that which one believes.
That's what one wants to get near. Could it after all
Be merely oneself, as superior as the ear
To a crow's voice? Did the nightingale torture the ear,
Pack the heart and scratch the mind? And does the ear
Solace itself in peevish birds? Is it peace,
Is it a philosopher's honeymoon, one finds
On the dump? Is it to sit among mattresses of the dead,
Bottles, pots, shoes and grass and murmur *aptest eve*:
Is it to hear the blatter of grackles and say
Invisible priest; is it to eject, to pull
The day to pieces and cry *stanza my stone*?
Where was it one first heard of the truth? The the.

1938

The Sense of the Sleight-of-hand Man

One's grand flights, one's Sunday baths,
One's tootings at the weddings of the soul
Occur as they occur. So bluish clouds
Occurred above the empty house and the leaves
Of the rhododendrons rattled their gold,
As if someone lived there. Such floods of white
Came bursting from the clouds. So the wind
Threw its contorted strength around the sky.

Could you have said the bluejay suddenly
Would swoop to earth? It is a wheel, the rays

Around the sun. The wheel survives the myths.
The fire eye in the clouds survives the gods.
To think of a dove with an eye of grenadine
And pines that are cornets, so it occurs,
And a little island full of geese and stars:
It may be that the ignorant man, alone,
Has any chance to mate his life with life
That is the sensual, pearly spouse, the life
That is fluent in even the wintriest bronze.

1939

Of Modern Poetry

The poem of the mind in the act of finding
What will suffice. It has not always had
To find: the scene was set; it repeated what
Was in the script.

Then the theatre was changed
To something else. Its past was a souvenir.
It has to be living, to learn the speech of the place.
It has to face the men of the time and to meet
The women of the time. It has to think about war
And it has to find what will suffice. It has
To construct a new stage. It has to be on that stage
And, like an insatiable actor, slowly and
With meditation, speak words that in the ear,
In the delicatest ear of the mind, repeat,
Exactly, that which it wants to hear, at the sound
Of which, an invisible audience listens,
Not to the play, but to itself, expressed
In an emotion as of two people, as of two
Emotions becoming one. The actor is
A metaphysician in the dark, twanging
An instrument, twanging a wiry string that gives
Sounds passing through sudden rightnesses, wholly
Containing the mind, below which it cannot descend,
Beyond which it has no will to rise.

It must
Be the finding of a satisfaction, and may
Be of a man skating, a woman dancing, a woman
Combing. The poem of the act of the mind.

1940

The Motive for Metaphor

You like it under the trees in autumn,
Because everything is half dead.

The wind moves like a cripple among the leaves
And repeats words without meaning.

In the same way, you were happy in spring,
With the half colors of quarter-things,
The slightly brighter sky, the melting clouds,
The single bird, the obscure moon —

The obscure moon lighting an obscure world
Of things that would never be quite expressed,
Where you yourself were never quite yourself
And did not want nor have to be,

Desiring the exhilarations of changes:
The motive for metaphor, shrinking from
The weight of primary noon,
The A B C of being,

The ruddy temper, the hammer
Of red and blue, the hard sound —
Steel against intimation — the sharp flash;
The vital, arrogant, fatal, dominant X.

1943

The House Was Quiet and the World Was Calm

The house was quiet and the world was calm.
The reader became the book; and summer night

Was like the conscious being of the book.
The house was quiet and the world was calm.

The words were spoken as if there was no book,
Except that the reader leaned above the page,

Wanted to lean, wanted much most to be
The scholar to whom his book is true, to whom

The summer night is like a perfection of thought.
The house was quiet because it had to be.

The quiet was part of the meaning, part of the mind:
The access of perfection to the page.

And the world was calm. The truth in a calm world,
In which there is no other meaning, itself

Is calm, itself is summer and night, itself
Is the reader leaning late and reading there.

1945

The Plain Sense of Things

After the leaves have fallen, we return
To a plain sense of things. It is as if
We had come to an end of the imagination,
Inanimate in an inert savoir.

It is difficult even to choose the adjective
For this blank cold, this sadness without cause.
The great structure has become a minor house.
No turban walks across the lessened floors.

The greenhouse never so badly needed paint.
The chimney is fifty years old and slants to one side.
A fantastic effort has failed, a repetition
In a repetitiousness of men and flies.

Yet the absence of the imagination had
Itself to be imagined. The great pond,
The plain sense of it, without reflections, leaves,
Mud, water like dirty glass, expressing silence

Of a sort, silence of a rat come out to see,
The great pond and its waste of the lilies, all this
Had to be imagined as an inevitable knowledge,
Required, as a necessity requires.

1952

The Planet on the Table

Ariel was glad he had written his poems.
They were of a remembered time
Or of something seen that he liked.

Other makings of the sun
Were waste and welter
And the ripe shrub writhed.

His self and the sun were one
And his poems, although makings of his self,
Were no less makings of the sun.

It was not important that they survive.
What mattered was that they should bear
Some lineament or character,

Some affluence, if only half-perceived,
In the poverty of their words,
Of the planet of which they were part.

1953

Not Ideas About the Thing But the Thing Itself

At the earliest ending of winter,
In March, a scrawny cry from outside
Seemed like a sound in his mind.

He knew that he heard it,
A bird's cry, at daylight or before,
In the early March wind.

The sun was rising at six,
No longer a battered panache above snow . . .
It would have been outside.

It was not from the vast ventriloquism
Of sleep's faded papier-mâché . . .
The sun was coming from outside.

That scrawny cry — it was
A chorister whose c preceded the choir.
It was part of the colossal sun,

Surrounded by its choral rings,
Still far away. It was like
A new knowledge of reality.

1954

Reality Is an Activity of the Most August Imagination

Last Friday, in the big light of last Friday night,
We drove home from Cornwall to Hartford, late.

It was not a night blown at a glassworks in Vienna
Or Venice, motionless, gathering time and dust.

There was a crush of strength in a grinding going round,
Under the front of the westward evening star,

The vigor of glory, a glittering in the veins,
As things emerged and moved and were dissolved,

Either in distance, change or nothingness,
The visible transformations of summer night,

An argentine abstraction approaching form
And suddenly denying itself away.

There was an insolid billowing of the solid.
Night's moonlight lake was neither water nor air.

1954

A Clear Day and No Memories

No soldiers in the scenery,
No thoughts of people now dead,
As they were fifty years ago,
Young and living in a live air,
Young and walking in the sunshine,
Bending in blue dresses to touch something,
Today the mind is not part of the weather.

Today the air is clear of everything.
It has no knowledge except of nothingness
And it flows over us without meanings,
As if none of us had ever been here before
And are not now: in this shallow spectacle,
This invisible activity, this sense.

1954

Of Mere Being

The palm at the end of the mind,
Beyond the last thought, rises
In the bronze decor,

A gold-feathered bird
Sings in the palm, without human meaning,
Without human feeling, a foreign song.

You know then that it is not the reason
That makes us happy or unhappy.
The bird sings. Its feathers shine.

The palm stands on the edge of space.
The wind moves slowly in the branches.
The bird's fire-fangled feathers dangle down.

1955

Angelina Weld Grimké (1880–1958)

Angelina Weld Grimké was born in Boston, the daughter of a white abolitionist mother and a black father who was the vice president of the National Association for the Advancement of Colored People (NAACP). Grimké, who took classes at Harvard University, wrote the play *Rachel* in reaction to D. W. Griffith's film *Birth of a Nation* (1915) about the Ku Klux Klan. The play was produced with the following notice: "This is the first attempt to use the stage for race propaganda in order to enlighten the American people relating to the lamentable condition of ten millions of Colored citizens in this free republic." Not until 1991 was a volume of her poems published.

The Black Finger

I have just seen a beautiful thing
Slim and still,
Against a gold, gold sky,
A straight cypress,
Sensitive
Exquisite,
A black finger
Pointing upwards.
Why, beautiful, still finger are you black?
And why are you pointing upwards?

1925

Tenebris

There is a tree, by day,
That, at night,
Has a shadow,
A hand huge and black,
With fingers long and black.
All through the dark,
Against the white man's house,
In the little wind,
The black hand plucks and plucks
At the bricks.

The bricks are the color of blood and very small.
  Is it a black hand,
  Or is it a shadow?

1927

Fragment

I am the woman with the black black skin
I am the laughing woman with the black black face
I am living in the cellars and in every crowded place
  I am toiling just to eat
  In the cold and in the heat
    And I laugh
I am the laughing woman who's forgotten how to weep
I am the laughing woman who's afraid to go to sleep

c. 1930

MINA LOY (1882–1966)

Mina Loy was born Mina Lowry in London and lived in Florence from 1906 to 1916. She divorced her first husband and married expatriate American Arthur Cravan, a poet and boxer, in Mexico in January 1918. Less than a year into their marriage a pregnant Loy sailed for Buenos Aires, expecting Cravan to join her, but he disappeared, never to surface again. Loy settled among literary expatriates in Paris and published her book *Lunar Baedeker* in 1923. She died in Aspen, Colorado.

There is no Life or Death

There is no Life or Death,
Only activity
And in the absolute
Is no declivity.
There is no Love or Lust
Only propensity
Who would possess
Is a nonentity.
There is no First or Last
Only equality
And who would rule
Joins the majority.
There is no Space or Time

Only intensity,
And tame things
Have no immensity.

1914

One O'Clock at Night

Though you had never possessed me
I had belonged to you since the beginning of time
And sleepily I sat on your chair beside you
Leaning against your shoulder
And your careless arm across my back   gesticulated
As your indisputable male voice   roared
Through my brain and my body
Arguing dynamic decomposition
Of which I was understanding nothing
Sleepily
And the only less male voice of your brother pugilist of the
    intellect
Boomed   as it seemed to me   so sleepy
Across an interval of a thousand miles
An interim of a thousand years
But you who make more noise than any man in the world when
    you clear your throat
Deafening   woke me
And I caught the thread of the argument
Immediately assuming my personal mental attitude
And ceased to be a woman

Beautiful half-hour of being a mere woman
The animal woman
Understanding nothing of man
But mastery   and the security of imparted physical heat
Indifferent to cerebral gymnastics
Or regarding them as the self-indulgent play of children
Or the thunder of alien gods
But you woke me up
Anyhow   who am I that I should criticize your theories of
    plastic velocity

"Let us go home   she is tired   and wants to go to bed."

1914

Lunar Baedeker

A silver Lucifer
serves
cocaine in cornucopia

To some somnambulists
of adolescent thighs
draped
in satirical draperies

Peris in livery
prepare
Lethe
for posthumous parvenues

Delirious Avenues
lit
with the chandelier souls
of infusoria
from Pharoah's tombstones

lead
to mercurial doomsdays
Odious oasis
in furrowed phosphorous — — —

the eye-white sky-light
white-light district
of lunar lusts

— — — Stellectric signs
"Wing shows on Starway"
"Zodiac carrousel"

Cyclones
of ecstatic dust
and ashes whirl
crusaders
from hallucinatory citadels
of shattered glass
into evacuate craters

A flock of dreams
browse on Necropolis

From the shores
of oval oceans
in the oxidized Orient

Onyx-eyed Odalisques
and ornithologists
observe
the flight
of Eros obsolete

And "Immortality"
mildews . . .
in the museums of the moon

"Nocturnal cyclops"
"Crystal concubine"
— — — — — — — —
Pocked with personification
the fossil virgin of the skies
waxes and wanes — — — —

1923

Gertrude Stein

Curie
of the laboratory
of vocabulary
  she crushed
the tonnage
of consciousness
congealed to phrases
  to extract
a radium of the word

c. 1924

William Carlos Williams (1883–1963)

William Carlos Williams was born in Rutherford, New Jersey. The greatest modern master of free verse in "the American grain" studied medicine at the University of Pennsylvania, set up a private practice in Rutherford, and eventually became chief of pediatrics at the General Hospital in Paterson, New Jersey. Williams's poems are object lessons in the value of lining, enjambment, and word choice in free verse. In a letter to Robert Creeley in 1950, Williams argued that "to write badly is an offense to the state since the government can never be more than the government of the words." Williams tucked his most famous poetic pronouncement ("No ideas but in things") in a parenthesis within his multivolume poem *Paterson*. Poems from his Pulitzer-winning *Pictures from Brueghel* (1962) — such as "Landscape with the Fall of Icarus" and "The Hunters in the Snow" — might fruitfully be compared to poems by W. H. Auden ("Musee des Beaux Arts") and John Berryman ("Winter Landscape") on the same Brueghel paintings. "I write in the American idiom," Williams noted, "and for many years I have been using what I call the variable foot." One of the secrets of modern American poetry is that no one knows what "the variable foot" really is.

The Young Housewife

At ten A.M. the young housewife
moves about in négligé behind
the wooden walls of her husband's house.
I pass solitary in my car.

Then again she comes to the curb
to call the ice-man, fish-man, and stands
shy, uncorseted, tucking in
stray ends of hair, and I compare her
to a fallen leaf.

The noiseless wheels of my car
rush with a crackling sound over
dried leaves as I bow and pass smiling.

1916

Smell!

Oh strong-ridged and deeply hollowed
nose of mine! What will you not be smelling?
What tactless asses we are, you and I, boney nose,
always indiscriminate, always unashamed,
and now it is the souring flowers of the bedraggled
poplars: a festering pulp on the wet earth
beneath them. With what deep thirst
we quicken our desires
to that rank odor of a passing springtime!
Can you not be decent? Can you not reserve your ardors
for something less unlovely? What girl will care
for us, do you think, if we continue in these ways?
Must you taste everything? Must you know everything?
Must you have a part in everything?

1917

Danse Russe

If when my wife is sleeping
and the baby and Kathleen
are sleeping
and the sun is a flame-white disc
in silken mists
above shining trees, —
if I in my north room
dance naked, grotesquely
before my mirror
waving my shirt round my head
and singing softly to myself:
"I am lonely, lonely.
I was born to be lonely,
I am best so!"
If I admire my arms, my face,
my shoulders, flanks, buttocks
against the yellow drawn shades, —

Who shall say I am not
the happy genius of my household?

1917

Portrait of a Lady

Your thighs are appletrees
whose blossoms touch the sky.
Which sky? The sky
where Watteau hung a lady's
slipper. Your knees
are a southern breeze — or
a gust of snow. Agh! what
sort of man was Fragonard?
— as if that answered
anything. Ah, yes — below
the knees, since the tune
drops that way, it is
one of those white summer days,
the tall grass of your ankles
flickers upon the shore —
Which shore? —
the sand clings to my lips —
Which shore? —
Agh, petals maybe. How
should I know?

Which shore? Which shore?
I said petals from an appletree.

1920

A Coronal

New books of poetry will be written
New books and unheard of manuscripts
will come wrapped in brown paper
and many and many a time
the postman will blow
and sidle down the leaf-plastered steps
thumbing over other men's business

But we ran ahead of it all.
One coming after
could have seen her footprints
in the wet and followed us
among the stark chestnuts.

Anemones sprang where she pressed
and cresses
stood green in the slender source —
And new books of poetry
will be written, leather-colored oakleaves
many and many a time.

1920

Great Mullen

One leaves his leaves at home
being a mullen and sends up a lighthouse
to peer from: I will have my way,
yellow — A mast with a lantern, ten
fifty, a hundred, smaller and smaller
as they grow more — Liar, liar, liar!
You come from her! I can smell djer-kiss
on your clothes. Ha! You come to me,
you — I am a point of dew on a grass-stem.
Why are you sending heat down on me
from your lantern? — You are cowdung, a
dead stick with the bark off. She is
squirting on us both. She has had her
hand on you! — well? — She has defiled
ME. — Your leaves are dull, thick

and hairy. — Every hair on my body will
hold you off from me. You are a
dungcake, birdlime on a fencerail. —
I love you, straight, yellow
finger of God pointing to — her!
Liar, broken weed, dungcake, you have —
I am a cricket waving his antennae
and you are high, grey and straight. Ha!

1921

Queen Anne's Lace

Her body is not so white as
anemone petals nor so smooth — nor
so remote a thing. It is a field
of the wild carrot taking
the field by force; the grass
does not raise above it.
Here is no question of whiteness,
white as can be, with a purple mole
at the center of each flower.
Each flower is a hand's span
of her whiteness. Wherever
his hand has lain there is
a tiny purple blemish. Each part
is a blossom under his touch
to which the fibres of her being
stem one by one, each to its end,
until the whole field is a
white desire, empty, a single stem,
a cluster, flower by flower,
a pious wish to whiteness gone over —
or nothing.

1921

To Waken an Old Lady

Old age is
a flight of small
cheeping birds
skimming
bare trees
above a snow glaze.
Gaining and failing
they are buffeted
by a dark wind —

But what?
On harsh weedstalks
the flock has rested,
the snow
is covered with broken
seedhusks
and the wind tempered
by a shrill
piping of plenty.

1921

By the Road to the Contagious Hospital

By the road to the contagious hospital
under the surge of the blue
mottled clouds driven from the
northeast — a cold wind. Beyond, the
waste of broad, muddy fields
brown with dried weeds, standing and fallen

patches of standing water
the scattering of tall trees

All along the road the reddish
purplish, forked, upstanding, twiggy
stuff of bushes and small trees
with dead, brown leaves under them
leafless vines —

Lifeless in appearance, sluggish
dazed spring approaches —

They enter the new world naked,
cold, uncertain of all
save that they enter. All about them
the cold, familiar wind —

Now the grass, tomorrow
the stiff curl of wildcarrot leaf
One by one objects are defined —
It quickens: clarity, outline of leaf

But now the stark dignity of
entrance — Still, the profound change
has come upon them: rooted they
grip down and begin to awaken

1923

The Rose Is Obsolete

The rose is obsolete
but each petal ends in
an edge, the double facet
cementing the grooved
columns of air — The edge
cuts without cutting
meets — nothing — renews
itself in metal or porcelain —

whither? It ends —

But if it ends
the start is begun
so that to engage roses
becomes a geometry —

Sharper, neater, more cutting
figured in majolica —
the broken plate
glazed with a rose

Somewhere the sense
makes copper roses
steel roses —

The rose carried weight of love
but love is at an end — of roses

It is at the edge of the
petal that love waits

Crisp, worked to defeat
laboredness — fragile
plucked, moist, half-raised
cold, precise, touching

What

The place between the petal's
edge and the

From the petal's edge a line starts
that being of steel
infinitely fine, infinitely
rigid penetrates
the Milky Way
without contact — lifting
from it — neither hanging
nor pushing —

The fragility of the flower
unbruised
penetrates spaces

1923

Death the Barber

of death
the barber
the barber
talked to me

cutting my
life with
sleep to trim
my hair —

It's just
a moment
he said, we die
every night —

And of
the newest
ways to grow
hair on

bald death —
I told him
of the quartz
lamp

and of old men
with third
sets of teeth
to the cue

of an old man
who said
at the door —
Sunshine today!

for which
death shaves
him twice
a week

1923

To Elsie

The pure products of America
go crazy —
mountain folk from Kentucky

or the ribbed north end of
Jersey
with its isolate lakes and

valleys, its deaf-mutes, thieves
old names
and promiscuity between

devil-may-care men who have taken
to railroading
out of sheer lust of adventure —

and young slatterns, bathed
in filth
from Monday to Saturday

to be tricked out that night
with gauds
from imaginations which have no

peasant traditions to give them
character
but flutter and flaunt

sheer rags — succumbing without
emotion
save numbed terror

under some hedge of choke-cherry
or viburnum —
which they cannot express —

Unless it be that marriage
perhaps
with a dash of Indian blood

will throw up a girl so desolate
so hemmed round
with disease or murder

that she'll be rescued by an
agent —
reared by the state and

sent out at fifteen to work in
some hard-pressed
house in the suburbs —

some doctor's family, some Elsie —
voluptuous water
expressing with broken

brain the truth about us —
her great
ungainly hips and flopping breasts

addressed to cheap
jewelry
and rich young men with fine eyes

as if the earth under our feet
were
an excrement of some sky

and we degraded prisoners
destined
to hunger until we eat filth

while the imagination strains
after deer
going by fields of goldenrod in

the stifling heat of September
Somehow
it seems to destroy us

It is only in isolate flecks that
something
is given off

No one
to witness
and adjust, no one to drive the car

1923

The Red Wheelbarrow

so much depends
upon

a red wheel
barrow

glazed with rain
water

beside the white
chickens.

1923

Rapid Transit

Somebody dies every four minutes
in New York State —

To hell with you and your poetry —
You will rot and be blown
through the next solar system
with the rest of the gases —

What the hell do you know about it?

AXIOMS

Don't get killed

Careful Crossing Campaign
Cross Crossings Cautiously

THE HORSES	black
	&
PRANCED	white

What's the use of sweating over
this sort of thing, Carl; here
it is all set up —

Outings in New York City

Ho for the open country

Don't stay shut up in hot rooms
Go to one of the Great Parks
Pelham Bay for example

It's on Long Island Sound
with bathing, boating
tennis, baseball, golf, etc.

Acres and acres of green grass
wonderful shade trees, rippling brooks

Take the Pelham Bay Park Branch
of the Lexington Ave. (East Side)
Line and you are there in a few
Minutes

Interborough Rapid Transit Co.

1923

Rain

As the rain falls
so does
            your love

bathe every
                    open
object of the world —

In houses
the priceless dry
                            rooms
of illicit love
where we live
hear the wash of the
                              rain —

There
            paintings
and fine
            metalware
woven stuffs —
all the whorishness
of our
            delight
sees
from its window

the spring wash
of your love
                    the falling
rain —

The trees
are become
beasts fresh-risen
from the sea —
water

trickles
from the crevices of
their hides —

So my life is spent
                              to keep out love
with which
she rains upon

                        the world

of spring

                drips

so spreads

                  the words

far apart to let in

                              her love

And running in between

the drops

                  the rain

is a kind physician

                              the rain
of her thoughts over

the ocean
                every

where

          walking with
invisible swift feet
over

        the helpless
                              waves —

Unworldly love
that has no hope
                              of the world

                        and that
cannot change the world
to its delight —

          The rain
falls upon the earth
and grass and flowers

come
        perfectly

into form from its
                        liquid

clearness

               But love is
unworldly

               and nothing
comes of it but love

following
and falling endlessly
from
      her thoughts

1930

Nantucket

Flowers through the window
lavender and yellow

changed by white curtains —
Smell of cleanliness —

Sunshine of late afternoon —
On the glass tray

a glass pitcher, the tumbler
turned down, by which

a key is lying — And the
immaculate white bed

1930

Poem

As the cat
climbed over
the top of

the jamcloset
first the right
forefoot

carefully
then the hind
stepped down

into the pit of
the empty
flowerpot

1934

This Is Just To Say

I have eaten
the plums
that were in
the icebox

and which
you were probably
saving
for breakfast

Forgive me
they were delicious
so sweet
and so cold

1934

Proletarian Portrait

A big young bareheaded woman
in an apron

Her hair slicked back standing
on the street

One stockinged foot toeing
the sidewalk

Her shoe in her hand. Looking
intently into it

She pulls out the paper insole
to find the nail

That has been hurting her

1935

To a Poor Old Woman

munching a plum on
the street a paper bag
of them in her hand

They taste good to her
They taste good
to her. They taste
good to her

You can see it by
the way she gives herself
to the one half
sucked out in her hand

Comforted
a solace of ripe plums
seeming to fill the air
They taste good to her

1935

The Locust Tree in Flower

Among
of
green

stiff
old
bright

broken
branch
come

white
sweet
May

again

1935

Fine Work with Pitch and Copper

Now they are resting
in the fleckless light
separately in unison

like the sacks
of sifted stone stacked
regularly by twos

about the flat roof
ready after lunch
to be opened and strewn

The copper in eight
foot strips has been
beaten lengthwise

down the center at right
angles and lies ready
to edge the coping

One still chewing
picks up a copper strip
and runs his eye along it

1936

These

are the desolate, dark weeks
when nature in its barrenness
equals the stupidity of man.

The year plunges into night
and the heart plunges
lower than night

to an empty, windswept place
without sun, stars or moon
but a peculiar light as of thought

that spins a dark fire —
whirling upon itself until,
in the cold, it kindles

to make a man aware of nothing
that he knows, not loneliness
itself — Not a ghost but

would be embraced — emptiness,
despair — (They
whine and whistle) among

the flashes and booms of war;
houses of whose rooms
the cold is greater than can be thought,

the people gone that we loved,
the beds lying empty, the couches
damp, the chairs unused —

Hide it away somewhere
out of the mind, let it get roots
and grow, unrelated to jealous

ears and eyes — for itself.
In this mine they come to dig — all.
Is this the counterfoil to sweetest

music? The source of poetry that
seeing the clock stopped, says,
The clock has stopped

that ticked yesterday so well?
and hears the sound of lakewater
splashing — that is now stone.

1938

Landscape with the Fall of Icarus

According to Brueghel
when Icarus fell
it was spring

a farmer was ploughing
his field
the whole pageantry

of the year was
awake tingling
near

the edge of the sea
concerned
with itself

sweating in the sun
that melted
the wings' wax

unsignificantly
off the coast
there was

a splash quite unnoticed
this was
Icarus drowning

1962

The Hunters in the Snow

The over-all picture is winter
icy mountains
in the background the return

from the hunt it is toward evening
from the left
sturdy hunters lead in

their pack the inn-sign
hanging from a
broken hinge is a stag a crucifix

between his antlers the cold
inn yard is
deserted but for a huge bonfire

that flares wind-driven tended by
women who cluster
about it to the right beyond

the hill is a pattern of skaters
Brueghel the painter
concerned with it all has chosen

a winter-struck bush for his
foreground to
complete the picture.

1962

Ezra Pound (1885–1972)

The most controversial figure in modern poetry was born in Hailey, Idaho. Ezra Pound sparked a verse revolution, issuing proclamations: "Make it new." "Poetry must be at least as well written as prose." "Literature is news that stays news." Pound edited *The Waste Land*, performing major surgery, and T. S. Eliot dedicated the finished work to him (*il miglior fabbro*: "the better craftsman"). In a note to Eliot, Pound wrote, "Complimenti, you bitch. I am wracked by the seven jealousies." Pound befriended and assisted many poets besides Eliot. "Before meeting Pound is like B.C. and A.D.," wrote William Carlos Williams, a medical student at the University of Pennsylvania when he met Pound. When Pound translated from languages he did not know, or knew imperfectly, including Greek, Latin, Anglo-Saxon, and Chinese, he scandalized experts in the fields in question but caused a radical rethinking of what it was possible to do in verse translation and in poetry in general. The critic R. P. Blackmur observed that in such poems as "Homage to Sextus Propertius," Pound demonstrated the value in translation of "making a critical equivalent, rather than a duplicate, of the original." It may be useful to compare Pound's "Portrait d'une Femme" with two poems — one by T. S. Eliot, the other by William Carlos Williams — bearing the same title in English, "Portrait of a Lady." Each reveals its author's signature style. Pound's odious political activities — as an anti-Semitic propagandist for Mussolini and Fascism — eventually overshadowed, in many people's minds, his accomplishments as a poet, translator, editor, and literary agitator. "Usury is the cancer of the world, which only the surgeon's knife of Fascism can cut out of the life of the nations," he declared. In 1943 he was indicted for treason; he was arrested a year later and held prisoner in a stockade in Pisa, where he wrote the Pisan Cantos, parts of the ambitious long poem that he had begun in the early 1920s and never completed.

Sestina: Altaforte

LOQUITUR: *En* Bertrans de Born.
Dante Alighieri put this man in hell for that he was a
stirrer-up of strife.
Eccovi!
Judge ye!
Have I dug him up again?
The scene is at his castle, Altaforte. "Papiols" is his jongleur.
"The Leopard," the *device* of Richard Cœur de Lion.

I

Damn it all! all this our South stinks peace.
You whoreson dog, Papiols, come! Let's to music!
I have no life save when the swords clash.
But ah! When I see the standards gold, vair, purple, opposing
And the broad fields beneath them turn crimson,
Then howl I my heart nigh mad with rejoicing.

II

In hot summer have I great rejoicing
When the tempests kill the earth's foul peace,
And the lightnings from black heav'n flash crimson,
And the fierce thunders roar me their music
And the winds shriek through the clouds mad, opposing,
And through all the riven skies God's swords clash.

III

Hell grant soon we hear again the swords clash!
And the shrill neighs of destriers in battle rejoicing,
Spiked breast to spiked breast opposing!
Better one hour's stour than a year's peace
With fat boards, bawds, wine and frail music!
Bah! there's no wine like the blood's crimson!

IV

And I love to see the sun rise blood-crimson.
And I watch his spears through the dark clash
And it fills all my heart with rejoicing
And pries wide my mouth with fast music
When I see him so scorn and defy peace,
His lone might 'gainst all darkness opposing.

V

The man who fears war and squats opposing
My words for stour, hath no blood of crimson
But is fit only to rot in womanish peace
Far from where worth's won and the sword clash
For the death of such sluts I go rejoicing;
Yea, I fill all the air with my music.

VI

Papiols, Papiols, to the music!
There's no sound like to swords swords opposing,
No cry like the battle's rejoicing
When our elbows and swords drip the crimson
And our charges 'gainst "The Leopard's" rush clash.
May God damn for ever all who cry "Peace!"

VII

And let the music of the swords make them crimson!
Hell grant soon we hear again the swords clash!
Hell blot black for always the thought "Peace!"

1909

The Seafarer

From the Anglo-Saxon

May I for my own self song's truth reckon,
Journey's jargon, how I in harsh days
Hardship endured oft.
Bitter breast-cares have I abided,
Known on my keel many a care's hold,
And dire sea-surge, and there I oft spent
Narrow nightwatch nigh the ship's head
While she tossed close to cliffs. Coldly afflicted,
My feet were by frost benumbed.
Chill its chains are; chafing sighs
Hew my heart round and hunger begot
Mere-weary mood. Lest man know not
That he on dry land loveliest liveth,
List how I, care-wretched, on ice-cold sea,
Weathered the winter, wretched outcast
Deprived of my kinsmen;
Hung with hard ice-flakes, where hail-scur flew,
There I heard naught save the harsh sea
And ice-cold wave, at whiles the swan cries,
Did for my games the gannet's clamour,
Sea-fowls' loudness was for me laughter,
The mews' singing all my mead-drink.
Storms, on the stone-cliffs beaten, fell on the stern
In icy feathers; full oft the eagle screamed
With spray on his pinion.
                                        Not any protector
May make merry man faring needy.
This he little believes, who aye in winsome life
Abides 'mid burghers some heavy business,
Wealthy and wine-flushed, how I weary oft
Must bide above brine.
Neareth nightshade, snoweth from north,
Frost froze the land, hail fell on earth then,
Corn of the coldest. Nathless there knocketh now
The heart's thought that I on high streams
The salt-wavy tumult traverse alone.

Moaneth alway my mind's lust
That I fare forth, that I afar hence
Seek out a foreign fastness.
For this there's no mood-lofty man over earth's midst,
Not though he be given his good, but will have in his
youth greed;
Nor his deed to the daring, nor his king to the faithful
But shall have his sorrow for sea-fare
Whatever his lord will.
He hath not heart for harping, nor in ring-having
Nor winsomeness to wife, nor world's delight
Nor any whit else save the wave's slash,
Yet longing comes upon him to fare forth on the water.
Bosque taketh blossom, cometh beauty of berries,
Fields to fairness, land fares brisker,
All this admonisheth man eager of mood,
The heart turns to travel so that he then thinks
On flood-ways to be far departing.
Cuckoo calleth with gloomy crying,
He singeth summerward, bodeth sorrow,
The bitter heart's blood. Burgher knows not —
He the prosperous man — what some perform
Where wandering them widest draweth.
So that but now my heart burst from my breastlock,
My mood 'mid the mere-flood,
Over the whale's acre, would wander wide.
On earth's shelter cometh oft to me,
Eager and ready, the crying lone-flyer,
Whets for the whale-path the heart irresistibly,
O'er tracks of ocean; seeing that anyhow
My lord deems to me this dead life
On loan and on land, I believe not
That any earth-weal eternal standeth
Save there be somewhat calamitous
That, ere a man's tide go, turn it to twain.
Disease of oldness or sword-hate
Beats out the breath from doom-gripped body.
And for this, every earl whatever, for those speaking
after —
Laud of the living, boasteth some last word,
That he will work ere he pass onward,
Frame on the fair earth 'gainst foes his malice,
Daring ado, . . .
So that all men shall honour him after
And his laud beyond them remain 'mid the English,
Aye, for ever, a lasting life's-blast,
Delight 'mid the doughty.
Days little durable,
And all arrogance of earthen riches,

There come now no kings nor Cæsars
Nor gold-giving lords like those gone.
Howe'er in mirth most magnified,
Whoe'er lived in life most lordliest,
Drear all this excellence, delights undurable!
Waneth the watch, but the world holdeth.
Tomb hideth trouble. The blade is layed low.
Earthly glory ageth and seareth.
No man at all going the earth's gait,
But age fares against him, his face paleth,
Grey-haired he groaneth, knows gone companions,
Lordly men, are to earth o'ergiven,
Nor may he then the flesh-cover, whose life ceaseth,
Nor eat the sweet nor feel the sorry,
Nor stir hand nor think in mid heart,
And though he strew the grave with gold,
His born brothers, their buried bodies
Be an unlikely treasure hoard.

1912

The Return

See, they return; ah, see the tentative
          Movements, and the slow feet,
          The trouble in the pace and the uncertain
          Wavering!

See, they return, one, and by one,
With fear, as half-awakened;
As if the snow should hesitate
And murmur in the wind,
                    and half turn back;
These were the "Wing'd-with-Awe,"
                    Inviolable.

Gods of the wingéd shoe!
With them the silver hounds,
                    sniffing the trace of air!

Haie! Haie!
          These were the swift to harry;
These the keen-scented;
These were the souls of blood.

Slow on the leash,
                    pallid the leash-men!

1912

Portrait d'une Femme

Your mind and you are our Sargasso Sea,
London has swept about you this score years
And bright ships left you this or that in fee:
Ideas, old gossip, oddments of all things,
Strange spars of knowledge and dimmed wares of price.
Great minds have sought you — lacking someone else.
You have been second always. Tragical?
No. You preferred it to the usual thing:
One dull man, dulling and uxorious,
One average mind — with one thought less, each year.
Oh, you are patient, I have seen you sit
Hours, where something might have floated up.
And now you pay one. Yes, you richly pay.
You are a person of some interest, one comes to you
And takes strange gain away:
Trophies fished up; some curious suggestion;
Fact that leads nowhere; and a tale or two,
Pregnant with mandrakes, or with something else
That might prove useful and yet never proves,
That never fits a corner or shows use,
Or finds its hour upon the loom of days:
The tarnished, gaudy, wonderful old work;
Idols and ambergris and rare inlays,
These are your riches, your great store; and yet
For all this sea-hoard of deciduous things,
Strange woods half sodden, and new brighter stuff:
In the slow float of differing light and deep,
No! there is nothing! In the whole and all,
Nothing that's quite your own.
Yet this is you.

1912

The Garden

En robe de parade.
—Samain

Like a skein of loose silk blown against a wall
She walks by the railing of a path in Kensington Gardens,
And she is dying piece-meal
of a sort of emotional anæmia.

And round about there is a rabble
Of the filthy, sturdy, unkillable infants of the very poor.
They shall inherit the earth.

In her is the end of breeding.
Her boredom is exquisite and excessive.
She would like some one to speak to her,
And is almost afraid that I
will commit that indiscretion.

1913

Salutation

O generation of the thoroughly smug
and thoroughly uncomfortable,
I have seen fishermen picnicking in the sun,
I have seen them with untidy families,
I have seen their smiles full of teeth
and heard ungainly laughter.
And I am happier than you are,
And they were happier than I am;
And the fish swim in the lake
and do not even own clothing.

1913

Alba

When the nightingale to his mate
Sings day-long and night late
My love and I keep state
In bower,
In flower,
'Till the watchman on the tower
Cry:
"Up! Thou rascal, Rise,
I see the white
Light
And the night
Flies."

1915

The River-Merchant's Wife: A Letter

While my hair was still cut straight across my forehead
I played about the front gate, pulling flowers.
You came by on bamboo stilts, playing horse,
You walked about my seat, playing with blue plums.
And we went on living in the village of Chokan:
Two small people, without dislike or suspicion.

At fourteen I married My Lord you.
I never laughed, being bashful.
Lowering my head, I looked at the wall.
Called to, a thousand times, I never looked back.

At fifteen I stopped scowling,
I desired my dust to be mingled with yours
Forever and forever and forever.
Why should I climb the look out?

At sixteen you departed,
You went into far Ku-to-yen, by the river of swirling eddies,
And you have been gone five months.
The monkeys make sorrowful noise overhead.

You dragged your feet when you went out.
By the gate now, the moss is grown, the different mosses,
Too deep to clear them away!
The leaves fall early this autumn, in wind.
The paired butterflies are already yellow with August
Over the grass in the West garden;
They hurt me. I grow older.
If you are coming down through the narrows of the river Kiang,
Please let me know beforehand,
And I will come out to meet you
As far as Cho-fu-Sa.

1915

By Rihaku

In a Station of the Metro

The apparition of these faces in the crowd;
Petals on a wet, black bough.

1915

The Lake Isle

O God, O Venus, O Mercury, patron of thieves,
Give me in due time, I beseech you, a little tobacco-shop,
With the little bright boxes
piled up neatly upon the shelves
And the loose fragment cavendish
and the shag,
And the bright Virginia
loose under the bright glass cases,

And a pair of scales not too greasy,
And the whores dropping in for a word or two in passing,
For a flip word, and to tidy their hair a bit.

O God, O Venus, O Mercury, patron of thieves,
Lend me a little tobacco-shop,
                or install me in any profession
Save this damn'd profession of writing,
                where one needs one's brains all the time.

1916

from *Homage to Sextus Propertius*

I

Shades of Callimachus, Coan ghosts of Philetas
It is in your grove I would walk,
I who come first from the clear font
Bringing the Grecian orgies into Italy,
                                        and the dance into Italy.
Who hath taught you so subtle a measure,
                                in what hall have you heard it;
What foot beat out your time-bar,
            what water has mellowed your whistles?

Out-weariers of Apollo will, as we know, continue their Martian
      generalities,
            We have kept our erasers in order.
A new-fangled chariot follows the flower-hung horses:
A young Muse with young loves clustered about her
            ascends with me into the æther, . . .
And there is no high-road to the Muses.

Annalists will continue to record Roman reputations,
Celebrities from the Trans-Caucasus will belaud Roman celebrities
And expound the distentions of Empire,
But for something to read in normal circumstances?
For a few pages brought down from the forked hill unsullied?
I ask a wreath which will not crush my head.
                                        And there is no hurry about it;
I shall have, doubtless, a boom after my funeral,
Seeing that long standing increases all things
                                                regardless of quality.

And who would have known the towers
                                        pulled down by a deal-wood horse;
Or of Achilles withstaying waters by Simois
Or of Hector spattering wheel-rims,
Or of Polydmantus, by Scamander, or Helenus and Deiphoibos?

Their door-yards would scarcely know them, or Paris.
Small talk O Ilion, and O Troad
twice taken by Oetian gods,
If Homer had not stated your case!

And I also among the later nephews of this city
shall have my dog's day,
With no stone upon my contemptible sepulchre;
My vote coming from the temple of Phoebus in Lycia, at Patara,
And in the meantime my songs will travel,
And the devirginated young ladies will enjoy them
when they have got over the strangeness,
For Orpheus tamed the wild beasts —
and held up the Threician river;
And Citharaon shook up the rocks by Thebes
and danced them into a bulwark at his pleasure,
And you, O Polyphemus? Did harsh Galatea almost
Turn to your dripping horses, because of a tune, under Aetna?
We must look into the matter.
Bacchus and Apollo in favour of it,
There will be a crowd of young women doing homage to my palaver,
Though my house is not propped up by Taenarian columns from Laconia
(associated with Neptune and Cerberus),
Though it is not stretched upon gilded beams:
My orchards do not lie level and wide
as the forests of Phæcia
the luxurious and Ionian,
Nor are my caverns stuffed stiff with a Marcian vintage,
My cellar does not date from Numa Pompilius,
Nor bristle with wine jars,
Nor is it equipped with a frigidaire patent;
Yet the companions of the Muses
will keep their collective nose in my books,
And weary with historical data, they will turn to my dance tune.

Happy who are mentioned in my pamphlets,
the songs shall be a fine tomb-stone over their beauty.
But against this?
Neither expensive pyramids scraping the stars in their route,
Nor houses modelled upon that of Jove in East Elis,
Nor the monumental effigies of Mausolus,
are a complete elucidation of death.

Flame burns, rain sinks into the cracks
And they all go to rack ruin beneath the thud of the years.
Stands genius a deathless adornment,
a name not to be worn out with the years.

1919

from *Hugh Selwyn Mauberly*

IV

These fought in any case,
and some believing,
                    pro domo, in any case . . .
Some quick to arm,
some for adventure,
some from fear of weakness,
some from fear of censure,
some for love of slaughter, in imagination,
learning later . . .
some in fear, learning love of slaughter;

Died some, pro patria,
                    non "dulce" non "et decor" . . .
walked eye-deep in hell
believing in old men's lies, then unbelieving
came home, home to a lie,
home to many deceits,
home to old lies and new infamy;
usury age-old and age-thick
and liars in public places.

Daring as never before, wastage as never before.
Young blood and high blood,
fair cheeks, and fine bodies;

fortitude as never before

frankness as never before,
disillusions as never told in the old days,
hysterias, trench confessions,
laughter out of dead bellies.

V

There died a myriad,
And of the best, among them,
For an old bitch gone in the teeth,
For a botched civilization,

Charm, smiling at the good mouth,
Quick eyes gone under earth's lid,

For two gross of broken statues,
For a few thousand battered books.

1920

Canto XIII

Kung walked
            by the dynastic temple
and into the cedar grove,
            and then out by the lower river,
And with him Khieu Tchi
            and Tian the low speaking
And "we are unknown," said Kung,
"You will take up charioteering?
            "Then you will become known,
"Or perhaps I should take up charioteering, or archery?
"Or the practice of public speaking?"
And Tseu-lou said, "I would put the defences in order,"
And Khieu said, "If I were lord of a province
I would put it in better order than this is."
And Tchi said, "I would prefer a small mountain temple,
"With order in the observances,
            with a suitable performance of the ritual,"
And Tian said, with his hand on the strings of his lute
The low sounds continuing
            after his hand left the strings,
And the sound went up like smoke, under the leaves,
And he looked after the sound:
            "The old swimming hole,
"And the boys flopping off the planks,
"Or sitting in the underbrush playing mandolins."
            And Kung smiled upon all of them equally.
And Thseng-sie desired to know:
            "Which had answered correctly?"
And Kung said, "They have all answered correctly,
"That is to say, each in his nature."
And Kung raised his cane against Yuan Jang,
      Yuan Jang being his elder,
For Yuan Jang sat by the roadside pretending to
            be receiving wisdom.
And Kung said
            "you old fool, come out of it,
Get up and do something useful."
            And Kung said
"Respect a child's faculties
"From the moment it inhales the clear air,
"But a man of fifty who knows nothing
            Is worthy of no respect."
And "When the prince has gathered about him
"All the savants and artists, his riches will be fully employed."
And Kung said, and wrote on the bo leaves:
            If a man have not order within him
He can not spread order about him;

And if a man have not order within him
His family will not act with due order;
            And if the prince have not order within him
He can not put order in his dominions.
And Kung gave the words "order"
and "brotherly deference"
And said nothing of the "life after death."
And he said
            "Anyone can run to excesses,
It is easy to shoot past the mark,
It is hard to stand firm in the middle."

And they said: If a man commit murder
            Should his father protect him, and hide him?
And Kung said:
            He should hide him.

And Kung gave his daughter to Kong-Tchang
            Although Kong-Tchang was in prison.
And he gave his niece to Nan-Young
            although Nan-Young was out of office.
And Kung said "Wang ruled with moderation,
            In his day the State was well kept,
And even I can remember
A day when the historians left blanks in their writings,
I mean for things they didn't know,
But that time seems to be passing."
A day when the historians left blanks in their writings,
But that time seems to be passing."
And Kung said, "Without character you will
            be unable to play on that instrument
Or to execute the music fit for the Odes.
The blossoms of the apricot
            blow from the east to the west,
And I have tried to keep them from falling."

1930

Canto XLV

With *Usura*

With usura hath no man a house of good stone
each block cut smooth and well fitting
that design might cover their face,
with usura
hath no man a painted paradise on his church wall
harpes et luthes
or where virgin receiveth message

and halo projects from incision,
with usura
seeth no man Gonzaga his heirs and his concubines
no picture is made to endure nor to live with
but it is made to sell and sell quickly
with usura, sin against nature,
is thy bread ever more of stale rags
is thy bread dry as paper,
with no mountain wheat, no strong flour
with usura the line grows thick
with usura is no clear demarcation
and no man can find site for his dwelling.
Stone cutter is kept from his stone
weaver is kept from his loom
WITH USURA
wool comes not to market
sheep bringeth no gain with usura
Usura is a murrain, usura
blunteth the needle in the maid's hand
and stoppeth the spinner's cunning. Pietro Lombardo
came not by usura
Duccio came not by usura
nor Pier della Francesca; Zuan Bellin' not by usura
nor was "La Calunnia" painted.
Came not by usura Angelico; came not Ambrogio Praedis,
Came no church of cut stone signed: *Adamo me fecit.*
Not by usura St Trophime
Not by usura Saint Hilaire,
Usura rusteth the chisel
It rusteth the craft and the craftsman
It gnaweth the thread in the loom
None learned to weave gold in her pattern;
Azure hath a canker by usura; cramoisi is unbroidered
Emerald findeth no Memling
Usura slayeth the child in the womb
It stayeth the young man's courting
It hath brought palsey to bed, lyeth
between the young bride and her bridegroom
CONTRA NATURAM
They have brought whores for Eleusis
Corpses are set to banquet
at behest of usura.

1937

from *Canto LXXXI*

What thou lovest well remains,
                                        the rest is dross
What thou lov'st well shall not be reft from thee
What thou lov'st well is thy true heritage
Whose world, or mine or theirs
                                        or is it of none?
First came the seen, then thus the palpable
    Elysium, though it were in the halls of hell,
What thou lovest well is thy true heritage

The ant's a centaur in his dragon world.
Pull down thy vanity, it is not man
Made courage, or made order, or made grace,
    Pull down thy vanity, I say pull down.
Learn of the green world what can be thy place
In scaled invention or true artistry,
Pull down thy vanity,
                                Paquin pull down!
The green casque has outdone your elegance.

'Master thyself, then others shall thee beare'
    Pull down thy vanity
Thou art a beaten dog beneath the hail,
A swollen magpie in a fitful sun,
Half black half white
Nor knowst'ou wing from tail
Pull down thy vanity
                        How mean thy hates
Fostered in falsity,
                        Pull down thy vanity,
Rathe to destroy, niggard in charity,
Pull down thy vanity,
                        I say pull down.

But to have done instead of not doing
                        this is not vanity
To have, with decency, knocked
That a Blunt should open
            To have gathered from the air a live tradition
or from a fine old eye the unconquered flame
This is not vanity.
    Here error is all in the not done,
all in the diffidence that faltered.

1948

ELINOR WYLIE (1885–1928)

Beautiful, charming, and talented, Elinor Wylie was a figure of great allure in downtown New York in the 1920s, a time when glamour attached itself to bohemianism and liberated women celebrated their sexuality in sonnets. Wylie was often paired with the equally fashionable Edna St. Vincent Millay. Wylie preferred Percy Bysshe Shelley; Millay, John Keats — but on Wylie's death, Millay wrote, "I think that Keats and Shelley died with you," and dedicated a sonnet to her friend and rival. "Oh, she was beautiful in every part!" Millay exclaims, omitting neither her "lovely mouth" nor her "lively malice." Wylie — who would exert a strong influence on poets as different as Robert Hayden and James Merrill — was scandal-prone. She ran off to England with the married Horace Wylie in 1910, leaving her first husband and son; she divorced Wylie to marry the poet William Rose Benet in 1923. Sara Teasdale wrote cattily: "Elinor Wylie, Elinor Wylie, / What do I hear you say? / 'I wish it were Shelley / Astride my belly / Instead of poor Mr. Benet.'"

Sea Lullaby

The old moon is tarnished
With smoke of the flood,
The dead leaves are varnished
With colour like blood,

A treacherous smiler
With teeth white as milk,
A savage beguiler
In sheathings of silk,

The sea creeps to pillage,
She leaps on her prey;
A child of the village
Was murdered today.

She came up to meet him
In a smooth golden cloak,
She choked him and beat him
To death, for a joke.

Her bright locks were tangled,
She shouted for joy,
With one hand she strangled
A strong little boy.

Now in silence she lingers
Beside him all night
To wash her long fingers
In silvery light.

1921

Wild Peaches

I

When the world turns completely upside down
You say we'll emigrate to the Eastern Shore
Aboard a river-boat from Baltimore;
We'll live among wild peach trees, miles from town.
You'll wear a coonskin cap, and I a gown
Homespun, dyed butternut's dark gold color.
Lost, like your lotus-eating ancestor,
We'll swim in milk and honey till we drown.

The winter will be short, the summer long,
The autumn amber-hued, sunny and hot,
Tasting of cider and of scuppernong;
All seasons sweet, but autumn best of all.
The squirrels in their silver fur will fall
Like falling leaves, like fruit, before your shot.

II

The autumn frosts will lie upon the grass
Like bloom on grapes of purple-brown and gold.
The misted early mornings will be cold;
The little puddles will be roofed with glass.
The sun, which burns from copper into brass,
Melts these at noon, and makes the boys unfold
Their knitted mufflers; full as they can hold,
Fat pockets dribble chestnuts as they pass.

Peaches grow wild, and pigs can live in clover;
A barrel of salted herrings lasts a year;
The spring begins before the winter's over.
By February you may find the skins
Of garter snakes and water moccasins
Dwindled and harsh, dead-white and cloudy-clear.

III

When April pours the colors of a shell
Upon the hills, when every little creek
Is shot with silver from the Chesapeake
In shoals new-minted by the ocean swell,
When strawberries go begging, and the sleek
Blue plums lie open to the blackbird's beak,
We shall live well — we shall live very well.

The months between the cherries and the peaches
Are brimming cornucopias which spill
Fruits red and purple, somber-bloomed and black;
Then, down rich fields and frosty river beaches
We'll trample bright persimmons, while we kill
Bronze partridge, speckled quail, and canvasback.

IV

Down to the Puritan marrow of my bones
There's something in this richness that I hate.
I love the look, austere, immaculate,
Of landscapes drawn in pearly monotones.
There's something in my very blood that owns
Bare hills, cold silver on a sky of slate,
A thread of water, churned to milky spate
Streaming through slanted pastures fenced with stones.

I love those skies, thin blue or snowy gray,
Those fields sparse-planted, rendering meager sheaves;
That spring, briefer than apple-blossom's breath,
Summer, so much too beautiful to stay,
Swift autumn, like a bonfire of leaves,
And sleepy winter, like the sleep of death.

1921

Let No Charitable Hope

Now let no charitable hope
Confuse my mind with images
Of eagle and of antelope:
I am in nature none of these.

I was, being human, born alone;
I am, being woman, hard beset;
I live by squeezing from a stone
The little nourishment I get.

In masks outrageous and austere
The years go by in single file;
But none has merited my fear,
And none has quite escaped my smile.

1923

The Puritan's Ballad

My love came up from Barnegat,
    The sea was in his eyes;
He trod as softly as a cat
    And told me terrible lies.

His hair was yellow as new-cut pine
    In shavings curled and feathered;
I thought how silver it would shine
    By cruel winters weathered.

But he was in his twentieth year,
    This time I'm speaking of;
We were head over heels in love with fear
    And half a-feared of love.

His feet were used to treading a gale
    And balancing thereon;
His face was brown as a foreign sail
    Threadbare against the sun.

His arms were thick as hickory logs
    Whittled to little wrists;
Strong as the teeth of terrier dogs
    Were the fingers of his fists.

Within his arms I feared to sink
    Where lions shook their manes,
And dragons drawn in azure ink
    Leapt quickened by his veins.

Dreadful his strength and length of limb
    As the sea to foundering ships;
I dipped my hands in love for him
    No deeper than their tips.

But our palms were welded by a flame
    The moment we came to part,
And on his knuckles I read my name
    Enscrolled within a heart.

And something made our wills to bend
    As wild as trees blown over;
We were no longer friend and friend,
    But only lover and lover.

"In seven weeks or seventy years —
    God grant it may be sooner! —
I'll make a handkerchief for your tears
    From the sails of my captain's schooner.

"We'll wear our loves like wedding rings
    Long polished to our touch;
We shall be busy with other things
    And they cannot bother us much.

"When you are skimming the wrinkled cream
    And your ring clinks on the pan,
You'll say to yourself in a pensive dream,
    'How wonderful a man!'

"When I am slitting a fish's head
And my ring clanks on the knife,
I'll say with thanks, as a prayer is said,
'How beautiful a wife!'

"And I shall fold my decorous paws
In velvet smooth and deep,
Like a kitten that covers up its claws
To sleep and sleep and sleep.

"Like a little blue pigeon you shall bow
Your bright alarming crest;
In the crook of my arm you'll lay your brow
To rest and rest and rest."

Will he never come back from Barnegat
With thunder in his eyes,
Treading as soft as a tiger cat,
To tell me terrible lies?

1928

H.D. (Hilda Doolittle) (1886–1961)

Born in Bethlehem, Pennsylvania, Hilda Doolittle met Ezra Pound when she was fifteen. When Pound asked to marry her, Doolittle's donnish father responded, "Why, you're nothing but a nomad!" In London in 1910, Pound cajoled Hilda to join his modernist revolution; he sent her poems to *Poetry* (where they appeared in 1913 under the name H.D. Imagiste), and ever since she has been associated with the imagists. In 1912, she, the writer Richard Aldington (whom she married), and Pound laid out the central tenets of imagism. They called for "direct treatment of the thing," a strict economy of means, and the rhythm of the "musical phrase" rather than that of the metronome. H.D. went into psychoanalysis with Freud in 1933, corresponded with him, and wrote movingly about "the Professor" in *Tribute to Freud* (1944): "He said, 'My discoveries are not primarily a heal-all. My discoveries are a basis for a very grave philosophy. There are very few who understand this, *there are very few who are capable of understanding this.*' One day he said to me, 'You discovered for yourself what I discovered for the race.'" She died in Zurich, Switzerland, in 1961.

The Helmsman

O be swift —
we have always known you wanted us.

We fled inland with our flocks,
we pastured them in hollows,

cut off from the wind
and the salt track of the marsh.

We worshipped inland —
we stepped past wood-flowers,
we forgot your tang,
we brushed wood-grass.

We wandered from pine-hills
through oak and scrub-oak tangles,
we broke hyssop and bramble,
we caught flower and new bramble-fruit
in our hair: we laughed
as each branch whipped back,
we tore our feet in half-buried rocks
and knotted roots and acorn-cups.

We forgot — we worshipped,
we parted green from green,
we sought further thickets,
we dipped our ankles
through leaf-mold and earth,
and wood and wood-bank enchanted us —

and the feel of the clefts in the bark,
and the slope between tree and tree —
and a slender path strung field to field
and wood to wood
and hill to hill
and the forest after it.

We forgot for a moment;
tree-resin, tree-bark,
sweat of a torn branch
were sweet to the taste.

We were enchanted with the fields,
the tufts of coarse grass —
in the shorter grass —
we loved all this.

But now, our boat climbs — hesitates — drops —
climbs — hesitates — crawls back —
climbs — hesitates —
O, be swift —
we have always known you wanted us.

1916

Oread

Whirl up, sea —
whirl your pointed pines,
splash your great pines
on our rocks,
hurl your green over us,
cover us with your pools of fir.

1924

Helen

All Greece hates
the still eyes in the white face,
the lustre as of olives
where she stands,
and the white hands.

All Greece reviles
the wan face when she smiles,
hating it deeper still
when it grows wan and white,
remembering past enchantments
and past ills.

Greece sees, unmoved,
God's daughter, born of love,
the beauty of cool feet
and slenderest knees,
could love indeed the maid,
only if she were laid,
white ash amid funereal cypresses.

1924

Epitaph

So I may say,
"I died of living,
having lived one hour";

so they may say,
"she died soliciting
illicit fervour";

so you may say,
"Greek flower; Greek ecstasy
reclaims for ever

one who died
following
intricate songs' lost measure."

1931

The Moon in Your Hands

If you take the moon in your hands
and turn it round
(heavy, slightly tarnished platter)
you're there;

if you pull dry sea-weed from the sand
and turn it round
and wonder at the underside's bright amber,
your eyes

look out as they did here,
(you don't remember)
when my soul turned round,

perceiving the other-side of everything,
mullein-leaf, dogwood-leaf, moth-wing
and dandelion-seed under the ground.

1957

Fair the Thread

Fall the deep curtains,
delicate the weave,
fair the thread:

clear the colours,
apple-leaf green,
ox-heart blood-red:

rare the texture,
woven from wild ram,
sea-bred horned sheep:

the stallion and his mare,
unbridled, with arrow-pattern,
are worked on

the blue cloth
before the door
of religion and inspiration:

the scorpion, snake and hawk
are gold-patterned
as on a king's pall.

1957

ROBINSON JEFFERS (1887–1962)

Robinson Jeffers, the son of a theology professor, was born in Pittsburgh. He built Tor House, a stone cottage, and a forty-foot stone tower on the rocky cliff above Carmel Bay on the California coast, and took the side of nature in the perpetual conflict between nature and man. "Man would be better, more sane and more happy, if he devoted less attention and less passion (love, hate, etc.) to his own species, and more to non-human nature," he said; "the human race will cease after a while and leave no trace, but the great splendors of nature will go on." There is no getting around the noxiousness of Jeffers's political views: he felt that Churchill and Roosevelt were morally as culpable as Hitler and Mussolini. Yet the power of his poems has held a great appeal even for readers vehemently opposed to his politics. Gary Snyder sees in Jeffers's work a "humanism that goes beyond the human."

To the Stone-Cutters

Stone-cutters fighting time with marble, you foredefeated
Challengers of oblivion
Eat cynical earnings, knowing rock splits, records fall down,
The square-limbed Roman letters
Scale in the thaws, wear in the rain. The poet as well
Builds his monument mockingly;
For man will be blotted out, the blithe earth die, the brave sun
Die blind and blacken to the heart:
Yet stones have stood for a thousand years, and pained thoughts found
The honey of peace in old poems.

1924

Shine, Perishing Republic

While this America settles in the mould of its vulgarity, heavily
thickening to empire,
And protest, only a bubble in the molten mass, pops and sighs out, and
the mass hardens,

I sadly smiling remember that the flower fades to make fruit, the fruit
rots to make earth.
Out of the mother; and through the spring exultances, ripeness and
decadence; and home to the mother.

You making haste haste on decay: not blameworthy; life is good, be it
stubbornly long or suddenly
A mortal splendor: meteors are not needed less than mountains: shine,
perishing republic.

But for my children, I would have them keep their distance from the
thickening center; corruption
Never has been compulsory, when the cities lie at the monster's feet
there are left the mountains.

And boys, be in nothing so moderate as in love of man, a clever servant,
insufferable master.
There is the trap that catches noblest spirits, that caught — they say —
God, when he walked on earth.

1925

Credo

My friend from Asia has powers and magic, he plucks a blue
leaf from the young blue-gum
And gazing upon it, gathering and quieting
The God in his mind, creates an ocean more real than the
ocean, the salt, the actual
Appalling presence, the power of the waters.
He believes that nothing is real except as we make it. I humbler
have found in my blood
Bred west of Caucasus a harder mysticism.
Multitude stands in my mind but I think that the ocean in the
bone vault is only
The bone vault's ocean: out there is the ocean's;
The water is the water, the cliff is the rock, come shocks and
flashes of reality. The mind

Passes, the eye closes, the spirit is a passage;
The beauty of things was born before eyes and sufficient to
itself; the heart-breaking beauty
Will remain when there is no heart to break for it.

1927

Hurt Hawks

I

The broken pillar of the wing jags from the clotted shoulder,
The wing trails like a banner in defeat,
No more to use the sky forever but live with famine
And pain a few days: cat nor coyote
Will shorten the week of waiting for death, there is game without talons.
He stands under the oak-bush and waits
The lame feet of salvation; at night he remembers freedom
And flies in a dream, the dawns ruin it.
He is strong and pain is worse to the strong, incapacity is worse.
The curs of the day come and torment him
At distance, no one but death the redeemer will humble that head,
The intrepid readiness, the terrible eyes.
The wild God of the world is sometimes merciful to those
That ask mercy, not often to the arrogant.
You do not know him, you communal people, or you have forgotten him;
Intemperate and savage, the hawk remembers him;
Beautiful and wild, the hawks, and men that are dying, remember him.

II

I'd sooner, except the penalties, kill a man than a hawk; but the great
redtail
Had nothing left but unable misery
From the bone too shattered for mending, the wing that trailed under
his talons when he moved.
We had fed him six weeks, I gave him freedom,
He wandered over the foreland hill and returned in the evening, asking
for death,
Not like a beggar, still eyed with the old
Implacable arrogance. I gave him the lead gift in the twilight. What
fell was relaxed,
Owl-downy, soft feminine feathers; but what
Soared: the fierce rush: the night-herons by the flooded river cried fear
at its rising
Before it was quite unsheathed from reality.

1928

Fire on the Hills

The deer were bounding like blown leaves
Under the smoke in front of the roaring wave of the brushfire;
I thought of the smaller lives that were caught.
Beauty is not always lovely; the fire was beautiful, the terror
Of the deer was beautiful; and when I returned
Down the black slopes after the fire had gone by, an eagle
Was perched on the jag of a burnt pine,
Insolent and gorged, cloaked in the folded storms of his shoulders.
He had come from far off for the good hunting
With fire for his beater to drive the game; the sky was merciless
Blue, and the hills merciless black,
The sombre-feathered great bird sleepily merciless between them.
I thought, painfully, but the whole mind,
The destruction that brings an eagle from heaven is better than mercy.

1932

Rock and Hawk

Here is a symbol in which
Many high tragic thoughts
Watch their own eyes.

This gray rock, standing tall
On the headland, where the seawind
Lets no tree grow,

Earthquake-proved, and signatured
By ages of storms: on its peak
A falcon has perched.

I think, here is your emblem
To hang in the future sky;
Not the cross, not the hive,

But this; bright power, dark peace;
Fierce consciousness joined with final
Disinterestedness;

Life with calm death; the falcon's
Realist eyes and act
Married to the massive

Mysticism of stone,
Which failure cannot cast down
Nor success make proud.

1935

Ave Caesar

No bitterness: our ancestors did it.
They were only ignorant and hopeful, they wanted freedom but wealth
too.
Their children will learn to hope for a Caesar.
Or rather — for we are not aquiline Romans but soft mixed colonists —
Some kindly Sicilian tyrant who'll keep
Poverty and Carthage off until the Romans arrive.
We are easy to manage, a gregarious people,
Full of sentiment, clever at mechanics, and we love our luxuries.

1935

Marianne Moore (1887–1972)

Born in Kirkwood, Missouri, near St. Louis, Marianne Moore was educated at Bryn Mawr College, where she wrote her first poems. Later she lived with her mother in Brooklyn and worked as a librarian. From 1925 to 1929, she was editor of the literary journal *The Dial*. In later years she became something of a celebrity in her signature tricorn hat. She was an avid Brooklyn Dodgers fan and composed an ode to the 1955 World Championship team. Commissioned by the Ford Motor Company to help name a new model, she came up with "The Resilient Bullet," "Mongoose Civique," "Anticipator," "Varsity Stroke," "Andante con Moto," and "Utopian Turtletop." Ford declined her suggestions and called the car the Edsel; the car turned out to be the biggest lemon in American automotive history. Moore's "habit of using quotations not as illustrations, but as a means to extend and complete a poem's original intentions" (Louise Bogan) was a major innovation. The poet drastically revised (and reduced) her poem "Poetry" in her *Complete Poems* (1967), pointedly indicating in the epigraph to that volume that "omissions are not accidents." Both versions are below. In 1995, John Ashbery remarked that Moore's poem "An Octopus" is "as fine as anything written in this century." Elizabeth Bishop called Moore "the World's Greatest Living Observer."

The Past Is the Present

If external action is effete
and rhyme is outmoded,
I shall revert to you,
Habakkuk, as on a recent occasion I was goaded
into doing by XY, who was speaking of unrhymed
verse.
This man said — I think that I repeat
his identical words:
'Hebrew poetry is

prose with a sort of heightened consciousness.' Ecstasy
affords
the occasion and expediency determines the form.

1915

Poetry [original version]

I, too, dislike it: there are things that are important beyond all this fiddle.
Reading it, however, with a perfect contempt for it, one discovers in
it, after all, a place for the genuine.
Hands that can grasp, eyes
that can dilate, hair that can rise
if it must, these things are important not because a

high-sounding interpretation can be put upon them but because they are
useful. When they become so derivative as to become unintelligible,
the same thing may be said for all of us, that we
do not admire what
we cannot understand: the bat
holding on upside down or in quest of something to

eat, elephants pushing, a wild horse taking a roll, a tireless wolf under
a tree, the immovable critic twitching his skin like a horse that feels
a flea, the base-
ball fan, the statistician —
nor is it valid
to discriminate against "business documents and

school-books"; all these phenomena are important. One must make a
distinction
however: when dragged into prominence by half poets, the result is
not poetry,
nor till the poets among us can be
"literalists of
the imagination" — above
insolence and triviality and can present

for inspection, "imaginary gardens with real toads in them," shall we have
it. In the meantime, if you demand on the one hand,
the raw material of poetry in
all its rawness and
that which is on the other hand
genuine, you are interested in poetry.

1921

Poetry [revised version]

I, too, dislike it.
    Reading it, however, with a perfect contempt for it, one discovers in
    it, after all, a place for the genuine.

1967

The Fish

wade
through black jade.
    Of the crow-blue mussel-shells, one keeps
    adjusting the ash-heaps;
        opening and shutting itself like

an
injured fan.
    The barnacles which encrust the side
    of the wave, cannot hide
        there for the submerged shafts of the

sun,
split like spun
    glass, move themselves with spotlight swiftness
    into the crevices —
        in and out, illuminating

the
turquoise sea
    of bodies. The water drives a wedge
    of iron through the iron edge
        of the cliff; whereupon the stars,

pink
rice-grains, ink
    bespattered jelly-fish, crabs like green
    lilies, and submarine
        toadstools, slide each on the other.

All
external
    marks of abuse are present on this
    defiant edifice —
        all the physical features of

ac-
cident — lack
    of cornice, dynamite grooves, burns, and
    hatchet strokes, these things stand
        out on it; the chasm-side is

dead.
Repeated
    evidence has proved that it can live
    on what cannot revive
        its youth. The sea grows old in it.

1921

To a Steam Roller

The illustration
is nothing to you without the application.
    You lack half wit. You crush all the particles down
        into close conformity, and then walk back and forth
            on them.

Sparkling chips of rock
are crushed down to the level of the parent block.
    Were not 'impersonal judgment in aesthetic
        matters, a metaphysical impossibility,' you

might fairly achieve
It. As for butterflies, I can hardly conceive
    of one's attending upon you, but to question
        the congruence of the complement is vain, if it exists.

1921

To a Snail

If "compression is the first grace of style,"
you have it. Contractility is a virtue
as modesty is a virtue.
It is not the acquisition of any one thing
that is able to adorn,
or the incidental quality that occurs
as a concomitant of something well said,
that we value in style,
but the principle that is hid:

in the absence of feet, "a method of conclusions";
"a knowledge of principles,"
in the curious phenomenon of your occipital horn.

1924

Silence

My father used to say,
"Superior people never make long visits,
have to be shown Longfellow's grave
or the glass flowers at Harvard.
Self-reliant like the cat —
that takes its prey to privacy,
the mouse's limp tail hanging like a shoelace from its mouth —
they sometimes enjoy solitude,
and can be robbed of speech
by speech which has delighted them.
The deepest feeling always shows itself in silence;
not in silence, but restraint."
Nor was he insincere in saying, "Make my house your inn."
Inns are not residences.

1924

Critics and Connoisseurs

There is a great amount of poetry in unconscious
fastidiousness. Certain Ming
products, imperial floor coverings of coach-
wheel yellow, are well enough in their way but I have seen something
that I like better — a
mere childish attempt to make an imperfectly ballasted animal stand up,
similar determination to make a pup
eat his meat from the plate.

I remember a swan under the willows in Oxford,
with flamingo-colored, maple-
leaflike feet. It reconnoitered like a battle-
ship. Disbelief and conscious fastidiousness were
ingredients in its
disinclination to move. Finally its hardihood was
not proof against its
proclivity to more fully appraise such bits
of food as the stream

bore counter to it; it made away with what I gave it
to eat. I have seen this swan and
I have seen you; I have seen ambition without
understanding in a variety of forms. Happening to stand
by an ant-hill, I have
seen a fastidious ant carrying a stick north, south,
east, west, till it turned on
itself, struck out from the flower bed into the lawn,
and returned to the point

from which it had started. Then abandoning the stick as
useless and overtaxing its
jaws with a particle of whitewash — pill-like but
heavy — it again went through the same course of procedure.
What is
there in being able
to say that one has dominated the stream in an attitude of self-defense;
in proving that one has had the experience
of carrying a stick?

1924

Marriage

This institution,
perhaps one should say enterprise
out of respect for which
one says one need not change one's mind
about a thing one has believed in,
requiring public promises
of one's intention
to fulfil a private obligation:
I wonder what Adam and Eve
think of it by this time,
this fire-gilt steel
alive with goldenness;
how bright it shows —
"of circular traditions and impostures,
committing many spoils,"
requiring all one's criminal ingenuity
to avoid!
Psychology which explains everything
explains nothing,
and we are still in doubt.
Eve: beautiful woman —
I have seen her
when she was so handsome

she gave me a start,
able to write simultaneously
in three languages —
English, German, and French —
and talk in the meantime;
equally positive in demanding a commotion
and in stipulating quiet:
"I should like to be alone";
to which the visitor replies,
"I should like to be alone;
why not be alone together?"
Below the incandescent stars
below the incandescent fruit,
the strange experience of beauty;
its existence is too much;
it tears one to pieces
and each fresh wave of consciousness
is poison.
"See her, see her in this common world,"
the central flaw
in that first crystal-fine experiment,
this amalgamation which can never be more
than an interesting impossibility,
describing it
as "that strange paradise
unlike flesh, stones,
gold or stately buildings,
the choicest piece of my life:
the heart rising
in its estate of peace
as a boat rises
with the rising of the water";
constrained in speaking of the serpent —
shed snakeskin in the history of politeness
not to be returned to again —
that invaluable accident
exonerating Adam.
And he has beauty also;
it's distressing — the O thou
to whom from whom,
without whom nothing — Adam;
"something feline,
something colubrine" — how true!
a crouching mythological monster
in that Persian miniature of emerald mines,
raw silk — ivory white, snow white,
oyster white, and six others —
that paddock full of leopards and giraffes —

long lemon-yellow bodies
sown with trapezoids of blue.
Alive with words,
vibrating like a cymbal
touched before it has been struck,
he has prophesied correctly —
the industrious waterfall,
"the speedy stream
which violently bears all before it,
at one time silent as the air
and now as powerful as the wind."
"Treading chasms
on the uncertain footing of a spear,"
forgetting that there is in woman
a quality of mind
which as an instinctive manifestation
is unsafe,
he goes on speaking
in a formal customary strain,
of "past states, the present state,
seals, promises,
the evil one suffered,
the good one enjoys,
hell, heaven,
everything convenient
to promote one's joy."
In him a state of mind
perceives what it was not
intended that he should;
"he experiences a solemn joy
in seeing that he has become an idol."
Plagued by the nightingale
in the new leaves,
with its silence —
not its silence but its silences,
he says of it:
"It clothes me with a shirt of fire."
"He dares not clap his hands
to make it go on
lest it should fly off;
if he does nothing, it will sleep;
if he cries out, it will not understand."
Unnerved by the nightingale
and dazzled by the apple,
impelled by "the illusion of a fire
effectual to extinguish fire,"
compared with which
the shining of the earth

is but deformity — a fire
"as high as deep
as bright as broad
as long as life itself,"
he stumbles over marriage,
"a very trivial object indeed"
to have destroyed the attitude
in which he stood —
the ease of the philosopher
unfathered by a woman.
Unhelpful Hymen!
a kind of overgrown cupid
reduced to insignificance
by the mechanical advertising
parading as involuntary comment,
by that experiment of Adam's
with ways out but no way in —
the ritual of marriage,
augmenting all its lavishness;
its fiddlehead ferns,
lotus flowers, opuntias, white dromedaries,
its hippopotamus —
nose and mouth combined
in one magnificent hopper —
its snake and the potent apple.
He tells us
that "for love that will
gaze an eagle blind,
that is with Hercules
climbing the trees
in the garden of the Hesperides,
from forty-five to seventy
is the best age,"
commending it
as a fine art, as an experiment,
a duty or as merely recreation.
One must not call him ruffian
nor friction a calamity —
the fight to be affectionate:
"no truth can be fully known
until it has been tried
by the tooth of disputation."
The blue panther with black eyes,
the basalt panther with blue eyes,
entirely graceful —
one must give them the path —
the black obsidian Diana
who "darkeneth her countenance

as a bear doth,"
the spiked hand
that has an affection for one
and proves it to the bone,
impatient to assure you
that impatience is the mark of independence,
not of bondage.
"Married people often look that way" —
"seldom and cold, up and down,
mixed and malarial
with a good day and a bad."
"When do we feed?"
We Occidentals are so unemotional,
self lost, the irony preserved
in "the Ahasuerus *tête-à-tête* banquet"
with its small orchids like snakes' tongues,
with its "good monster, lead the way,"
with little laughter
and munificence of humor
in that quixotic atmosphere of frankness
in which "four o'clock does not exist,
but at five o'clock
the ladies in their imperious humility
are ready to receive you";
in which experience attests
that men have power
and sometimes one is made to feel it.
He says, "What monarch would not blush
to have a wife
with hair like a shaving brush?"
The fact of woman
is "not the sound of the flute
but very poison."
She says, "Men are monopolists
of 'stars, garters, buttons
and other shining baubles' —
unfit to be the guardians
of another person's happiness."
He says, "These mummies
must be handled carefully —
'the crumbs from a lion's meal,
a couple of shins and the bit of an ear';
turn to the letter M
and you will find
that 'a wife is a coffin,'
that severe object
with the pleasing geometry
stipulating space not people,

refusing to be buried
and uniquely disappointing,
revengefully wrought in the attitude
of an adoring child
to a distinguished parent."
She says, "This butterfly,
this waterfly, this nomad
that has 'proposed
to settle on my hand for life' —
What can one do with it?
There must have been more time
in Shakespeare's day
to sit and watch a play.
You know so many artists who are fools."
He says, "You know so many fools
who are not artists."
The fact forgot
that "some have merely rights
while some have obligations,"
he loves himself so much,
he can permit himself
no rival in that love.
She loves herself so much,
she cannot see herself enough —
a statuette of ivory on ivory,
the logical lost touch
to an expansive splendor
earned as wages for work done:
one is not rich but poor
when one can always seem so right.
What can one do for them —
these savages
condemned to disaffect
all those who are not visionaries
alert to undertake the silly task
of making people noble?
This model of petrine fidelity
who "leaves her peaceful husband
only because she has seen enough of him" —
that orator reminding you,
"I am yours to command."
"Everything to do with love is mystery;
it is more than a day's work
to investigate this science."
One sees that it is rare —
that striking grasp of opposites
opposed each to the other, not to unity,
which in cycloid inclusiveness

has dwarfed the demonstration
of Columbus with the egg —
a triumph of simplicity —
that charitive Euroclydon
of frightening disinterestedness
which the world hates,
admitting:

"I am such a cow,
if I had a sorrow
I should feel it a long time;
I am not one of those
who have a great sorrow
in the morning
and a great joy at noon";

which says: "I have encountered it
among those unpretentious
protégés of wisdom,
where seeming to parade
as the debater and the Roman,
the statesmanship
of an archaic Daniel Webster
persists to their simplicity of temper
as the essence of the matter:

'Liberty and union
now and forever';

the Book on the writing table;
the hand in the breast pocket."

1924

An Octopus

of ice. Deceptively reserved and flat,
it lies "in grandeur and in mass"
beneath a sea of shifting snow dunes;
dots of cyclamen-red and maroon on its clearly defined
pseudopodia
made of glass that will bend — a much needed invention —
comprising twenty-eight ice fields from fifty to five hundred
feet thick,
of unimagined delicacy.
"Picking periwinkles from the cracks"
or killing prey with the concentric crushing rigor of the python,

it hovers forward "spider fashion
on its arms" misleadingly like lace;
its "ghostly pallor changing
to the green metallic tinge of an anemone-starred pool."
The fir trees, in "the magnitude of their root systems,"
rise aloof from these maneuvers "creepy to behold,"
austere specimens of our American royal families,
"each like the shadow of the one beside it.
The rock seems frail compared with their dark energy of life,"
its vermilion and onyx and manganese-blue interior expensiveness
left at the mercy of the weather;
"stained transversely by iron where the water drips down,"
recognized by its plants and its animals.
Completing a circle,
you have been deceived into thinking that you have progressed,
under the polite needles of the larches
"hung to filter, not to intercept the sunlight" —
met by tightly wattled spruce twigs
"conformed to an edge like clipped cypress
as if no branch could penetrate the cold beyond its company";
and dumps of gold and silver ore enclosing The Goat's Mirror —
that ladyfinger-like depression in the shape of the left human foot,
which prejudices you in favor of itself
before you have had time to see the others;
its indigo, pea-green, blue-green, and turquoise,
from a hundred to two hundred feet deep,
"merging in irregular patches in the middle lake
where, like gusts of a storm
obliterating the shadows of the fir trees, the wind makes lanes of ripples."
What spot could have merits of equal importance
for bears, elk, deer, wolves, goats, and ducks?
Pre-empted by their ancestors,
this is the property of the exacting porcupine,
and of the rat "slipping along to its burrow in the swamp
or pausing on high ground to smell the heather";
of "thoughtful beavers
making drains which seem the work of careful men with shovels,"
and of the bears inspecting unexpectedly
ant-hills and berry bushes.
Composed of calcium gems and alabaster pillars,
topaz, tourmaline crystals and amethyst quartz,
their den is somewhere else, concealed in the confusion
of "blue forests thrown together with marble and jasper and agate
as if whole quarries had been dynamited."
And farther up, in stag-at-bay position
as a scintillating fragment of these terrible stalagmites,

stands the goat,
its eye fixed on the waterfall which never seems to fall —
an endless skein swayed by the wind,
immune to force of gravity in the perspective of the peaks.
A special antelope
acclimated to "grottoes from which issue penetrating draughts
which make you wonder why you came,"
it stands its ground
on cliffs the color of the clouds, of petrified white vapor —
black feet, eyes, nose, and horns, engraved on dazzling ice fields,
the ermine body on the crystal peak;
the sun kindling its shoulders to maximum heat like acetylene,
dyeing them white —
upon this antique pedestal,
"a mountain with those graceful lines which prove it a volcano,"
its top a complete cone like Fujiyama's
till an explosion blew it off.
Distinguished by a beauty
of which "the visitor dare never fully speak at home
for fear of being stoned as an impostor,"
Big Snow Mountain is the home of a diversity of creatures:
those who "have lived in hotels
but who now live in camps — who prefer to";
the mountain guide evolving from the trapper,
"in two pairs of trousers, the outer one older,
wearing slowly away from the feet to the knees";
"the nine-striped chipmunk
running with unmammal-like agility along a log";
the water ouzel
with "its passion for rapids and high-pressured falls,"
building under the arch of some tiny Niagara;
the white-tailed ptarmigan "in winter solid white,
feeding on heather-bells and alpine buckwheat";
and the eleven eagles of the west,
"fond of the spring fragrance and the winter colors,"
used to the unegoistic action of the glaciers
and "several hours of frost every midsummer night."
"They make a nice appearance, don't they,"
happy seeing nothing?
Perched on treacherous lava and pumice —
those unadjusted chimney pots and cleavers
which stipulate "names and addresses of persons to notify
in case of disaster" —
they hear the roar of ice and supervise the water
winding slowly through the cliffs,
the road "climbing like the thread
which forms the groove around a snail shell,
doubling back and forth until where snow begins, it ends."

No "deliberate wide-eyed wistfulness" is here
among the boulders sunk in ripples and white water
where "when you hear the best wild music of the forest
it is sure to be a marmot,"
the victim on some slight observatory,
of "a struggle between curiosity and caution,"
inquiring what has scared it:
a stone from the moraine descending in leaps,
another marmot, or the spotted ponies with glass eyes,
brought up on frosty grass and flowers
and rapid draughts of ice water.
Instructed none knows how, to climb the mountain,
by businessmen who require for recreation
three hundred and sixty-five holidays in the year,
these conspicuously spotted little horses are peculiar;
hard to discern among the birch trees, ferns, and lily pads,
avalanche lilies, Indian paintbrushes,
bear's ears and kittentails,
and miniature cavalcades of chlorophylless fungi
magnified in profile on the moss-beds like moonstones in the water;
the cavalcade of calico competing
with the original American menagerie of styles
among the white flowers of the rhododendron surmounting
rigid leaves
upon which moisture works its alchemy,
transmuting verdure into onyx.

"Like happy souls in Hell," enjoying mental difficulties,
the Greeks
amused themselves with delicate behavior
because it was "so noble and so fair";
not practised in adapting their intelligence
to eagle traps and snowshoes,
to alpenstocks and other toys contrived by those
"alive to the advantage of invigorating pleasures."
Bows, arrows, oars, and paddles, for which trees provide the
wood,
in new countries more eloquent than elsewhere —
augmenting the assertion that, essentially humane,
"the forest affords wood for dwellings and by its beauty
stimulates the moral vigor of its citizens."
The Greek liked smoothness, distrusting what was back
of what could not be clearly seen,
resolving with benevolent conclusiveness,
"complexities which still will be complexities
as long as the world lasts";
ascribing what we clumsily call happiness,
to "an accident or a quality,
a spiritual substance or the soul itself,

an act, a disposition, or a habit,
or a habit infused, to which the soul has been persuaded,
or something distinct from a habit, a power" —
such power as Adam had and we are still devoid of.
"Emotionally sensitive, their hearts were hard";
their wisdom was remote
from that of these odd oracles of cool official sarcasm,
upon this game preserve
where "guns, nets, seines, traps and explosives,
hired vehicles, gambling and intoxicants are prohibited;
disobedient persons being summarily removed
and not allowed to return without permission in writing."
It is self-evident
that it is frightful to have everything afraid of one;
that one must do as one is told
and eat rice, prunes, dates, raisins, hardtack, and tomatoes
if one would "conquer the main peak of Mount Tacoma,
this fossil flower concise without a shiver,
intact when it is cut,
damned for its sacrosanct remoteness" —
like Henry James "damned by the public for decorum";
not decorum, but restraint;
it is the love of doing hard things
that rebuffed and wore them out — a public out of sympathy
with neatness.
Neatness of finish! Neatness of finish!
Relentless accuracy is the nature of this octopus
with its capacity for fact.
"Creeping slowly as with meditated stealth,
its arms seeming to approach from all directions,"
it receives one under winds that "tear the snow to bits
and hurl it like a sandblast
shearing off twigs and loose bark from the trees."
Is "tree" the word for these things
"flat on the ground like vines"?
some "bent in a half circle with branches on one side
suggesting dust-brushes, not trees;
some finding strength in union, forming little stunted groves
their flattened mats of branches shrunk in trying to escape"
from the hard mountain "planed by ice and polished by the
wind" —
the white volcano with no weather side;
the lightning flashing at its base,
rain falling in the valleys, and snow falling on the peak —
the glassy octopus symmetrically pointed,
its claw cut by the avalanche
"with a sound like the crack of a rifle,
in a curtain of powdered snow launched like a waterfall."

1924

The Student

"In America," began
the lecturer, "everyone must have a
degree. The French do not think that
all can have it, they don't say everyone
must go to college." We
incline to feel
that although it may be unnecessary

to know fifteen languages,
one degree is not too much. With us, a
school — like the singing tree of which
the leaves were mouths singing in concert
is both a tree of knowledge
and of liberty —
seen in the unanimity of college

mottoes, *Lux et veritas*,
Christo et ecclesiae, *Sapient*
felici. It may be that we
have not knowledge, just opinions, that we
are undergraduates,
not students; we know
we have been told with smiles, by expatriates

of whom we had asked "When will
your experiment be finished?" "Science
is never finished." Secluded
from domestic strife, Jack Bookworm led a
college life, says Goldsmith;
and here also as
in France or Oxford, study is beset with

dangers — with bookworms, mildews,
and complaisancies. But someone in New
England has known enough to say
the student is patience personified,
is a variety
of hero, "patient
of neglect and of reproach" — who can "hold by

himself." You can't beat hens to
make them lay. Wolf's wool is the best of wool,
but it cannot be sheared because
the wolf will not comply. With knowledge as
with the wolf's surliness,
the student studies
voluntarily, refusing to be less

than individual. He
"gives his opinion and then rests on it";
he renders service when there is
no reward, and is too reclusive for
   some things to seem to touch
him, not because he
   has no feeling but because he has so much.

1932

No Swan So Fine

"No water so still as the
   dead fountains of Versailles." No swan,
with swart blind look askance
and gondoliering legs, so fine
   as the chintz china one with fawn-
brown eyes and toothed gold
collar on to show whose bird it was.

Lodged in the Louis Fifteenth
   candelabrum-tree of cockscomb-
tinted buttons, dahlias,
sea-urchins, and everlastings,
   it perches on the branching foam
of polished sculptured
flowers — at ease and tall. The king is dead.

1935

The Steeple-Jack

Dürer would have seen a reason for living
      in a town like this, with eight stranded whales
to look at; with the sweet sea air coming into your house
on a fine day, from water etched
      with waves as formal as the scales
on a fish.

One by one in two's and three's, the seagulls keep
      flying back and forth over the town clock,
or sailing around the lighthouse without moving their wings —
rising steadily with a slight
      quiver of the body — or flock
mewing where

a sea the purple of the peacock's neck is
    paled to greenish azure as Dürer changed
the pine green of the Tyrol to peacock blue and guinea
gray. You can see a twenty-five-
    pound lobster; and fish nets arranged
to dry. The

whirlwind fife-and-drum of the storm bends the salt
    marsh grass, disturbs stars in the sky and the
star on the steeple; it is a privilege to see so
much confusion. Disguised by what
    might seem the opposite, the sea-
side flowers and

trees are favored by the fog so that you have
    the tropics at first hand: the trumpet vine,
foxglove, giant snapdragon, a salpiglossis that has
spots and stripes; morning-glories, gourds,
    or moon-vines trained on fishing twine
at the back door:

cattails, flags, blueberries and spiderwort,
    striped grass, lichens, sunflowers, asters, daisies —
yellow and crab-claw ragged sailors with green bracts — toad-plant,
petunias, ferns; pink lilies, blue
    ones, tigers; poppies; black sweet-peas.
The climate

is not right for the banyan, frangipani, or
    jack-fruit trees; or for exotic serpent
life. Ring lizard and snakeskin for the foot, if you see fit;
but here they've cats, not cobras, to
    keep down the rats. The diffident
little newt

with white pin-dots on black horizontal spaced-
    out bands lives here; yet there is nothing that
ambition can buy or take away. The college student
named Ambrose sits on the hillside
    with his not-native books and hat
and sees boats

at sea progress white and rigid as if in
    a groove. Liking an elegance of which
the source is not bravado, he knows by heart the antique
sugar-bowl shaped summerhouse of
    interlacing slats, and the pitch
of the church

spire, not true, from which a man in scarlet lets
    down a rope as a spider spins a thread;
he might be part of a novel, but on the sidewalk a
sign says C. J. Poole, Steeple Jack,
    in black and white; and one in red
and white says

Danger. The church portico has four fluted
    columns, each a single piece of stone, made
modester by whitewash. This would be a fit haven for
waifs, children, animals, prisoners,
    and presidents who have repaid
sin-driven

senators by not thinking about them. The
    place has a schoolhouse, a post-office in a
store, fish-houses, hen-houses, a three-masted
    schooner on
the stocks. The hero, the student,
    the steeple-jack, each in his way,
is at home.

It could not be dangerous to be living
    in a town like this, of simple people,
who have a steeple-jack placing danger signs by the church
while he is gilding the solid-
    pointed star, which on a steeple
stands for hope.

1935

What Are Years?

  What is our innocence,
what is our guilt? All are
  naked, none is safe. And whence
is courage: the unanswered question,
the resolute doubt, —
dumbly calling, deafly listening — that
in misfortune, even death,
    encourages others
    and in its defeat, stirs

  the soul to be strong? He
sees deep and is glad, who
  accedes to mortality
and in his imprisonment rises
upon himself as

the sea in a chasm, struggling to be
free and unable to be,
      in its surrendering
      finds its continuing.

   So he who strongly feels,
behaves. The very bird,
   grown taller as he sings, steels
his form straight up. Though he is captive,
his mighty singing
says, satisfaction is a lowly
thing, how pure a thing is joy.
      This is mortality,
      this is eternity.

1941

T. S. ELIOT (1888–1965)

With the third line of "The Love Song of J. Alfred Prufrock," the romantic mood set by the opening couplet collapses, and modern poetry begins. Born in St. Louis, educated at Harvard and Oxford ("Oxford is very pretty, but I don't like to be dead," he wrote Conrad Aiken in 1914), Thomas Stearns Eliot worked in a bank, became a British subject, and wrote, in *The Waste Land* (1922), the most celebrated poem of the twentieth century and the first to require pages of footnotes. In his essay "Tradition and the Individual Talent," Eliot argued that "poetry is not a turning loose of emotion, but an escape from emotion; it is not an expression of personality, but an escape from personality. But, of course," he added, "only those who have personality and emotions know what it means to want to escape from these things." It is a profound irony that *The Waste Land*, which seems so impersonal and employs such abstract means, should turn out to be an obliquely autobiographical poem — and that a poem about the decay of Western civilization should turn out to be the product of a "personal and wholly insignificant grouse against life." (In William Carlos Williams's view, *The Waste Land* was nothing less than a "great catastrophe" interrupting the "rediscovery" of a native or "local" American tradition.) A self-described royalist, classicist, and Anglo-Catholic, Eliot gained eminence as a critic, and his precepts became orthodoxies.He formulated the concept of the "objective correlative" to support his view that *Hamlet* was a failure; he contended that a "dissociation of sensibility" has made it difficult for poets to amalgamate disparate phenomena and impose an order on the chaos of experience. A year after Eliot won the Nobel Prize in 1948, Delmore Schwartz called him an international literary dictator. He inspired many parodies. Henry Reed caught the later manner of the *Four Quartets*: "As we get older we do not get any younger." Wendy Cope reduced *The Waste Land* to five limericks, beginning "In April one seldom feels cheerful; / Dry stones, sun and dust make me fearful; / Clairvoyantes distress me, / Commuters depress me — / Met Stetson and gave him an earful."

The Love Song of J. Alfred Prufrock

S'io credessi che mia risposta fosse
a persona che mai tornasse al mondo,
questa fiamma staria senza più scosse.
Ma perciòche giammai di questo fondo
non tornò vivo alcun, s'i' odo il vero,
senza tema d'infarmia ti rispondo.*

Let us go then, you and I,
When the evening is spread out against the sky
Like a patient etherised upon a table;
Let us go, through certain half-deserted streets,
The muttering retreats
Of restless nights in one-night cheap hotels
And sawdust restaurants with oyster-shells:
Streets that follow like a tedious argument
Of insidious intent
To lead you to an overwhelming question . . .
Oh, do not ask, "What is it?"
Let us go and make our visit.

In the room the women come and go
Talking of Michelangelo.

The yellow fog that rubs its back upon the window-panes,
The yellow smoke that rubs its muzzle on the window-panes,
Licked its tongue into the corners of the evening,
Lingered upon the pools that stand in drains,
Let fall upon its back the soot that falls from chimneys,
Slipped by the terrace, made a sudden leap,
And seeing that it was a soft October night,
Curled once about the house, and fell asleep.

And indeed there will be time
For the yellow smoke that slides along the street
Rubbing its back upon the window-panes;
There will be time, there will be time
To prepare a face to meet the faces that you meet;
There will be time to murder and create,
And time for all the works and days of hands
That lift and drop a question on your plate;
Time for you and time for me,
And time yet for a hundred indecisions,
And for a hundred visions and revisions,
Before the taking of a toast and tea.

*If I believed I was speaking / to one who would return to the world, / this flame would shake no more. / But since no one has ever / gone back alive from this place, if what I hear is true, / without fear of infamy I answer you." (Dante, *Inferno*, 27: 61–66).

In the room the women come and go
Talking of Michelangelo.

And indeed there will be time
To wonder, "Do I dare?" and, "Do I dare?"
Time to turn back and descend the stair,
With a bald spot in the middle of my hair —
(They will say: "How his hair is growing thin!")
My morning coat, my collar mounting firmly to the chin,
My necktie rich and modest, but asserted by a simple pin —
(They will say: "But how his arms and legs are thin!")
Do I dare
Disturb the universe?
In a minute there is time
For decisions and revisions which a minute will reverse.

For I have known them all already, known them all —
Have known the evenings, mornings, afternoons,
I have measured out my life with coffee spoons;
I know the voices dying with a dying fall
Beneath the music from a farther room.
   So how should I presume?

And I have known the eyes already, known them all —
The eyes that fix you in a formulated phrase,
And when I am formulated, sprawling on a pin,
When I am pinned and, wriggling on the wall,
Then how should I begin
To spit out all the butt-ends of my days and ways?
   And how should I presume?

And I have known the arms already, known them all —
Arms that are braceleted and white and bare
(But in the lamplight, downed with light brown hair!)
Is it perfume from a dress
That makes me so digress?
Arms that lie along a table, or wrap about a shawl.
   And should I then presume?
   And how should I begin?

. . . . .

Shall I say, I have gone at dusk through narrow streets
And watched the smoke that rises from the pipes
Of lonely men in shirt-sleeves, leaning out of windows? . . .

I should have been a pair of ragged claws
Scuttling across the floors of silent seas.

. . . . .

And the afternoon, the evening, sleeps so peacefully!
Smoothed by long fingers,
Asleep . . . tired . . . or it malingers,
Stretched on the floor, here beside you and me.
Should I, after tea and cakes and ices,
Have the strength to force the moment to its crisis?
But though I have wept and fasted, wept and prayed,
Though I have seen my head (grown slightly bald)
  brought in upon a platter,
I am no prophet — and here's no great matter,
I have seen the moment of my greatness flicker,
And I have seen the eternal Footman hold my coat, and snicker,
And in short, I was afraid.

And would it have been worth it, after all,
After the cup, the marmalade, the tea,
Among the porcelain, among some talk of you and me,
Would it have been worth while,
To have bitten off the matter with a smile,
To have squeezed the universe into a ball
To roll it towards some overwhelming question,
To say: "I am Lazarus, come from the dead,
Come back to tell you all, I shall tell you all" —
If one, settling a pillow by her head,
  Should say: "That is not what I meant at all.
  That is not it, at all."

And would it have been worth it, after all,
Would it have been worth while,
After the sunsets and the dooryards and the sprinkled streets,
After the novels, after the teacups, after the skirts that trail along
  the floor —
And this, and so much more? —
It is impossible to say just what I mean!
But as if a magic lantern threw the nerves in patterns on a screen:
Would it have been worth while
If one, setting a pillow or throwing off a shawl,
And turning toward the window, should say:
  "That is not it at all,
  That is not what I meant, at all."

. . . . .

No! I am not Prince Hamlet, nor was meant to be;
Am an attendant lord, one that will do
To swell a progress, start a scene or two,
Advise the prince; no doubt, an easy tool,
Deferential, glad to be of use,
Politic, cautious, and meticulous;

Full of high sentence, but a bit obtuse;
At times, indeed, almost ridiculous —
Almost, at times, the Fool.

I grow old . . . I grow old . . .
I shall wear the bottom of my trousers rolled.

Shall I part my hair behind? Do I dare to eat a peach?
I shall wear white flannel trousers, and walk upon the beach.
I have heard the mermaids singing, each to each.

I do not think that they will sing to me.

I have seen them riding seaward on the waves
Combing the white hair of the wave blown back
When the wind blows the water white and black.

We have lingered in the chambers of the sea
By sea-girls wreathed with seaweed red and brown
Till human voices wake us, and we drown.

1917

Preludes

I

The winter evening settles down
With smell of steaks in passageways.
Six o' clock.
The burnt-out ends of smoky days.
And now a gusty shower wraps
The grimy scraps
Of withered leaves about your feet
And newspapers from vacant lots;
The showers beat
On broken blinds and chimney-pots,
And at the corner of the street
A lonely cab-horse steams and stamps.

And then the lighting of the lamps.

II

The morning comes to consciousness
Of faint stale smells of beer
From the sawdust-trampled street
With all its muddy feet that press
To early coffee-stands.

With the other masquerades
That time resumes,
One thinks of all the hands
That are raising dingy shades
In a thousand furnished rooms.

III

You tossed a blanket from the bed,
You lay upon your back, and waited;
You dozed, and watched the night revealing
The thousand sordid images
Of which your soil was constituted;
They flickered against the ceiling.
And when all the world came back
And the light crept up between the shutters
And you heard the sparrows in the gutters,
You had such a vision of the street
As the street hardly understands;
Sitting along the bed's edge, where
You curled the papers from your hair,
Or clasped the yellow soles of feet
In the palms of both soiled hands.

IV

His soul stretched tight across the skies
That fade behind a city block,
Or trampled by insistent feet
At four and five and six o'clock;
And short square fingers stuffing pipes,
And evening newspapers, and eyes
Assured of certain certainties,
The conscience of a blackened street
Impatient to assume the world.

I am moved by fancies that are curled
Around these images, and cling:
The notion of some infinitely gentle
Infinitely suffering thing.

Wipe your hand across your mouth, and laugh;
The worlds revolve like ancient women
Gathering fuel in vacant lots.

1917

Portrait of a Lady

> Thou hast committed —
> Fornication: but that was in another country,
> And besides, the wench is dead.
> — *The Jew of Malta*

I

Among the smoke and fog of a December afternoon
You have the scene arrange itself — as it will seem to do —
With "I have saved this afternoon for you";
And four wax candles in the darkened room,
Four rings of light upon the ceiling overhead,
An atmosphere of Juliet's tomb
Prepared for all the things to be said, or left unsaid.
We have been, let us say, to hear the latest Pole
Transmit the Preludes, through his hair and finger-tips.
"So intimate, this Chopin, that I think his soul
Should be resurrected only among friends
Some two or three, who will not touch the bloom
That is rubbed and questioned in the concert room."
— And so the conversation slips
Among velleities and carefully caught regrets
Through attenuated tones of violins
Mingled with remote cornets
And begins.

"You do not know how much they mean to me, my friends,
And how, how rare and strange it is, to find
In a life composed so much, so much of odds and ends,
(For indeed I do not love it . . . you knew? you are not blind!
How keen you are!)
To find a friend who has these qualities,
who has, and gives
Those qualities upon which friendship lives.
How much it means that I say this to you —
Without these friendships — life, what *cauchemar*!"
Among the windings of the violins
And the ariettes
Of cracked cornets
Inside my brain a dull tom-tom begins
Absurdly hammering a prelude of its own,
Capricious monotone
That is at least one definite "false note."
— Let us take the air, in a tobacco trance,
Admire the monuments,
Discuss the late events,
Correct our watches by the public clocks.
Then sit for half an hour and drink our bocks.

II

Now that lilacs are in bloom
She has a bowl of lilacs in her room
And twists one in her fingers while she talks.
"Ah, my friend, you do not know, you do not know
What life is, you who hold it in your hands";
(Slowly twisting the lilac stalks)
"You let it flow from you, you let it flow,
And youth is cruel, and has no remorse
And smiles at situations which it cannot see."
I smile, of course,
And go on drinking tea.
"Yet with these April sunsets, that somehow recall
My buried life, and Paris in the Spring,
I feel immeasurably at peace, and find the world
To be wonderful and youthful, after all."

The voice returns like the insistent out-of-tune
Of a broken violin on an August afternoon:
"I am always sure that you understand
My feelings, always sure that you feel,
Sure that across the gulf you reach your hand.

You are invulnerable, you have no Achilles' heel
You will go on, and when you have prevailed
You can say: at this point many a one has failed.

But what have I, but what have I, my friend,
To give you, what can you receive from me?
Only the friendship and the sympathy
Of one about to reach her journey's end.

I shall sit here, serving tea to friends. . . . "

I take my hat: how can I make a cowardly amends
For what she has said to me?
You will see me any morning in the park
Reading the comics and the sporting page.
Particularly I remark
An English countess goes upon the stage.
A Greek was murdered at a Polish dance,
Another bank defaulter has confessed.
I keep my countenance,
I remain self-possessed
Except when a street-piano, mechanical and tired
Reiterates some worn-out common song
With the smell of hyacinths across the garden
Recalling things that other people have desired.
Are these ideas right or wrong?

III

The October night comes down; returning as before
Except for a slight sensation of being ill at ease
I mount the stairs and turn the handle of the door
And feel as if I had mounted on my hands and knees.

"And so you are going abroad; and when do you return?
But that's a useless question.
You hardly know when you are coming back,
You will find so much to learn."
My smile falls heavily among the bric-à-brac

"Perhaps you can write to me."
My self-possession flares up for a second;
This is as I had reckoned.
"I have been wondering frequently of late
(But our beginnings never know our ends!)
Why we have not developed into friends."
I feel like one who smiles, and turning shall remark
Suddenly, his expression in a glass.
My self-possession gutters; we are really in the dark.

"For everybody said so, all our friends,
They all were sure our feelings would relate
So closely! I myself can hardly understand.
We must leave it now to fate.
You will write, at any rate.
Perhaps it is not too late.
I shall sit here, serving tea to friends."

And I must borrow every changing shape
To find expression . . . dance, dance
Like a dancing bear,
Cry like a parrot, chatter like an ape,
Let us take the air, in a tobacco trance —

Well! and what if she should die some afternoon,
Afternoon grey and smoky, evening yellow and rose;
Should die and leave me sitting pen in hand
With the smoke coming down above the housetops;
Doubtful, for a while
Not knowing what to feel or if I understand
Or whether wise or foolish, tardy or too soon …
Would she not have the advantage, after all?
This music is successful with a "dying fall"
Now that we talk of dying —
And should I have the right to smile?

1917

La Figlia Che Piange

O quam te memorem virgo . . .

Stand on the highest pavement of the stair —
Lean on a garden urn —
Weave, weave the sunlight in your hair —
Clasp your flowers to you with a pained surprise —
Fling them to the ground and turn
With a fugitive resentment in your eyes:
But weave, weave the sunlight in your hair.

So I would have had him leave,
So I would have had her stand and grieve,
So he would have left
As the soul leaves the body torn and bruised,
As the mind deserts the body it has used.
I should find
Some way incomparably light and deft,
Some way we both should understand,
Simple and faithless as a smile and shake of the hand.

She turned away, but with the autumn weather
Compelled my imagination many days,
Many days and many hours:
Her hair over her arms and her arms full of flowers.
And I wonder how they should have been together!
I should have lost a gesture and a pose.
Sometimes these cogitations still amaze
The troubled midnight and the noon's repose.

1917

The Waste Land

"Nam Sibyllam quidem Cumis ego ipse oculis meis vidi in ampulla pendere, et cum illi pueri dicerent: *Σίβυλλα τί θέλεις*; respondebat illa: "*άποθανεîν θέλω.*"*

For Ezra Pound
il miglior fabbro.

I. The Burial of the Dead

April is the cruellest month, breeding
Lilacs out of the dead land, mixing

*For I saw with my own eyes the Sibyl hanging in a jar at Cumae, and when the acolytes said, "Sibyl, what do you want?" she replied, "I want to die." (Petronius, *Satyricon*, chapter 48).

Memory and desire, stirring
Dull roots with spring rain.
Winter kept us warm, covering
Earth in forgetful snow, feeding
A little life with dried tubers.
Summer surprised us, coming over the Starnbergersee
With a shower of rain; we stopped in the colonnade,
And went on in sunlight, into the Hofgarten,
And drank coffee, and talked for an hour.
Bin gar keine Russin, stamm' aus Litauen, echt deutsch.
And when we were children, staying at the archduke's,
My cousin's, he took me out on a sled,
And I was frightened. He said, Marie,
Marie, hold on tight. And down we went.
In the mountains, there you feel free.
I read, much of the night, and go south in the winter.

What are the roots that clutch, what branches grow
Out of this stony rubbish? Son of man,
You cannot say, or guess, for you know only
A heap of broken images, where the sun beats,
And the dead tree gives no shelter, the cricket no relief,
And the dry stone no sound of water. Only
There is shadow under this red rock,
(Come in under the shadow of this red rock),
And I will show you something different from either
Your shadow at morning striding behind you
Or your shadow at evening rising to meet you;
I will show you fear in a handful of dust.
Frisch weht der Wind
Der Heimat zu
Mein Irisch Kind,
Wo weilest du?
"You gave me hyacinths first a year ago;
"They called me the hyacinth girl."
— Yet when we came back, late, from the Hyacinth garden,
Your arms full, and your hair wet, I could not
Speak, and my eyes failed, I was neither
Living nor dead, and I knew nothing,
Looking into the heart of light, the silence.
Oed' und leer das Meer.

Madame Sosostris, famous clairvoyante,
Had a bad cold, nevertheless
Is known to be the wisest woman in Europe,
With a wicked pack of cards. Here, said she,
Is your card, the drowned Phoenician Sailor,
(Those are pearls that were his eyes. Look!)
Here is Belladonna, the Lady of the Rocks,
The lady of situations.

Here is the man with three staves, and here the wheel,
And here is the one-eyed merchant, and this card,
Which is blank, is something he carries on his back,
Which I am forbidden to see. I do not find
The Hanged Man. Fear death by water.
I see crowds of people, walking round in a ring.
Thank you. If you see dear Mrs. Equitone,
Tell her I bring the horoscope myself:
One must be so careful these days.

Unreal City,
Under the brown fog of a winter dawn,
A crowd flowed over London Bridge, so many,
I had not thought death had undone so many.
Sighs, short and infrequent, were exhaled,
And each man fixed his eyes before his feet.
Flowed up the hill and down King William Street,
To where Saint Mary Woolnoth kept the hours
With a dead sound on the final stroke of nine.
There I saw one I knew, and stopped him, crying: "Stetson!
"You who were with me in the ships at Mylae!
"That corpse you planted last year in your garden,
"Has it begun to sprout? Will it bloom this year?
"Or has the sudden frost disturbed its bed?
"Oh keep the Dog far hence, that's friend to men,
"Or with his nails he'll dig it up again!
"You! Hypocrite lecteur! — mon semblable, — mon frère!"

II. A Game of Chess

The chair she sat in, like a burnished throne,
Glowed on the marble, where the glass
Held up by standards wrought with fruited vines
From which a golden Cupidon peeped out
(Another hid his eyes behind his wing)
Doubled the flames of sevenbranched candelabra
Reflecting light upon the table as
The glitter of her jewels rose to meet it,
From satin cases poured in rich profusion;
In vials of ivory and coloured glass
Unstoppered, lurked her strange synthetic perfumes,
Unguent, powdered, or liquid — troubled, confused
And drowned the sense in odours; stirred by the air
That freshened from the window, these ascended
In fattening the prolonged candle-flames,
Flung their smoke into the laquearia,
Stirring the pattern on the coffered ceiling.
Huge sea-wood fed with copper

Burned green and orange, framed by the coloured stone,
In which sad light a carvèd dolphin swam.
Above the antique mantel was displayed
As though a window gave upon the sylvan scene
The change of Philomel, by the barbarous king
So rudely forced; yet there the nightingale
Filled all the desert with inviolable voice
And still she cried, and still the world pursues,
"Jug Jug" to dirty ears.
And other withered stumps of time
Were told upon the walls; staring forms
Leaned out, leaning, hushing the room enclosed.
Footsteps shuffled on the stair.
Under the firelight, under the brush, her hair
Spread out in fiery points
Glowed into words, then would be savagely still.

  "My nerves are bad to-night. Yes, bad. Stay with me.
"Speak to me. Why do you never speak. Speak.
  "What are you thinking of? What thinking? What?
"I never know what you are thinking. Think."

I think we are in rats' alley
Where the dead men lost their bones.

"What is that noise?"
                              The wind under the door.
"What is that noise now? What is the wind doing?"
                                        Nothing again nothing.
                              "Do
"You know nothing? Do you see nothing? Do you remember
"Nothing?"

        I remember
Those are pearls that were his eyes.
"Are you alive, or not? Is there nothing in your head?"
                                                                                    But
O O O O that Shakespeherian Rag —
It's so elegant
So intelligent
"What shall I do now? What shall I do?"
"I shall rush out as I am, and walk the street
"With my hair down, so. What shall we do to-morrow?
"What shall we ever do?"
                                        The hot water at ten.
And if it rains, a closed car at four.
And we shall play a game of chess,
Pressing lidless eyes and waiting for a knock upon the door.

When Lil's husband got demobbed, I said —
I didn't mince my words, I said to her myself,
HURRY UP PLEASE ITS TIME
Now Albert's coming back, make yourself a bit smart.
He'll want to know what you done with that money he gave you
To get yourself some teeth. He did, I was there.
You have them all out, Lil, and get a nice set,
He said, I swear, I can't bear to look at you.
And no more can't I, I said, and think of poor Albert,
He's been in the army four years, he wants a good time,
And if you don't give it him, there's others will, I said.
Oh is there, she said. Something o' that, I said.
Then I'll know who to thank, she said, and give me a
    straight look.
HURRY UP PLEASE ITS TIME
If you don't like it you can get on with it, I said.
Others can pick and choose if you can't.
But if Albert makes off, it won't be for lack of telling.
You ought to be ashamed, I said, to look so antique.
(And her only thirty-one.)
I can't help it, she said, pulling a long face,
It's them pills I took, to bring it off, she said.
(She's had five already, and nearly died of young George.)
The chemist said it would be all right, but I've never been
    the same.
You *are* a proper fool I said.
Well, if Albert won't leave you alone, there it is, I said,
What you get married for if you don't want children?
HURRY UP PLEASE ITS TIME
Well, that Sunday Albert was home, they had a hot gammon,
And they asked me in to dinner, to get the beauty of it hot —
HURRY UP PLEASE ITS TIME
HURRY UP PLEASE ITS TIME
Goonight Bill. Goonight Lou. Goonight May. Goonight.
Ta ta. Goonight. Goonight.
Good night, ladies, good night, sweet ladies, good night,
    good night.

III. The Fire Sermon

The river's tent is broken: The last fingers of leaf
Clutch and sink into the wet bank. The wind
Crosses the brown land, unheard. The nymphs are departed.
Sweet Thames, run softly, till I end my song.
The river bears no empty bottles, sandwich papers,
Silk handkerchiefs, cardboard boxes, cigarette ends
Or other testimony of summer nights. The nymphs are departed.
And their friends, the loitering heirs of city directors;

Departed, have left no addresses.
By the waters of Leman I sat down and wept . . .
Sweet Thames, run softly till I end my song,
Sweet Thames, run softly, for I speak not loud or long.
But at my back in a cold blast I hear
The rattle of the bones, and chuckle spread from ear to ear.

A rat crept softly through the vegetation
Dragging its slimy belly on the bank
While I was fishing in the dull canal
On a winter evening round behind the gashouse
Musing upon the king my brother's wreck
And on the king my father's death before him.
White bodies naked on the low damp ground
And bones cast in a little low dry garret,
Rattled by the rat's foot only, year to year.
But at my back from time to time I hear
The sound of horns and motors, which shall bring
Sweeney to Mrs. Porter in the spring.
O the moon shone bright on Mrs. Porter
And on her daughter
They wash their feet in soda water
Et O ces voix d'enfants, chantant dans la coupole!

Twit twit twit
Jug jug jug jug jug jug
So rudely forc'd.
Tereu

  Unreal City
Under the brown fog of a winter noon
Mr. Eugenides, the Smyrna merchant
Unshaven, with a pocket full of currants
C.i.f. London: documents at sight,
Asked me in demotic French
To luncheon at the Cannon Street Hotel
Followed by a weekend at the Metropole.

  At the violet hour, when the eyes and back
Turn upward from the desk, when the human engine waits
Like a taxi throbbing waiting,
I Tiresias, though blind, throbbing between two lives,
Old man with wrinkled female breasts, can see
At the violet hour, the evening hour that strives
Homeward, and brings the sailor home from sea,
The typist home at teatime, clears her breakfast, lights
Her stove, and lays out food in tins.
Out of the window perilously spread
Her drying combinations touched by the sun's last rays,

On the divan are piled (at night her bed)
Stockings, slippers, camisoles, and stays.
I Tiresias, old man with wrinkled dugs
Perceived the scene, and foretold the rest —
I too awaited the expected guest.
He, the young man carbuncular, arrives,
A small house agent's clerk, with one bold stare,
One of the low on whom assurance sits
As a silk hat on a Bradford millionaire.
The time is now propitious, as he guesses,
The meal is ended, she is bored and tired,
Endeavours to engage her in caresses
Which still are unreproved, if undesired.
Flushed and decided, he assaults at once;
Exploring hands encounter no defence;
His vanity requires no response,
And makes a welcome of indifference.
(And I Tiresias have foresuffered all
Enacted on this same divan or bed;
I who have sat by Thebes below the wall
And walked among the lowest of the dead.)
Bestows one final patronising kiss,
And gropes his way, finding the stairs unlit . . .

She turns and looks a moment in the glass,
Hardly aware of her departed lover;
Her brain allows one half-formed thought to pass:
"Well now that's done: and I'm glad it's over."
When lovely woman stoops to folly and
Paces about her room again, alone,
She smoothes her hair with automatic hand,
And puts a record on the gramophone.

"This music crept by me upon the waters"
And along the Strand, up Queen Victoria Street.
O City city, I can sometimes hear
Beside a public bar in Lower Thames Street,
The pleasant whining of a mandoline
And a clatter and a chatter from within
Where fishmen lounge at noon: where the walls
Of Magnus Martyr hold
Inexplicable splendour of Ionian white and gold.

The river sweats
Oil and tar
The barges drift
With the turning tide
Red sails
Wide

To leeward, swing on the heavy spar.
The barges wash
Drifting logs
Down Greenwich reach
Past the Isle of Dogs.
                    Weialala leia
                    Wallala leialala

  Elizabeth and Leicester
Beating oars
The stern was formed
A gilded shell
Red and gold
The brisk swell
Rippled both shores
Southwest wind
Carried down stream
The peal of bells
White towers
                    Weialala leia
                    Wallala leialala

"Trams and dusty trees.
Highbury bore me. Richmond and Kew
Undid me. By Richmond I raised my knees
Supine on the floor of a narrow canoe."

"My feet are at Moorgate, and my heart
Under my feet. After the event
He wept. He promised 'a new start.'
I made no comment. What should I resent?"
"On Margate Sands.
I can connect
Nothing with nothing.
The broken fingernails of dirty hands.
My people humble people who expect
Nothing."
            la la

To Carthage then I came

Burning burning burning burning
O Lord Thou pluckest me out
O Lord Thou pluckest

burning

IV. Death by Water

Phlebas the Phoenician, a fortnight dead,
Forgot the cry of gulls, and the deep sea swell
And the profit and loss.
                                        A current under sea
Picked his bones in whispers. As he rose and fell
He passed the stages of his age and youth
Entering the whirpool.
                                        Gentile or Jew
O you who turn the wheel and look to windward,
Consider Phlebas, who was once handsome and tall as you.

V. What the Thunder Said

After the torchlight red on sweaty faces
After the frosty silence in the gardens
After the agony in stony places
The shouting and the crying
Prison and palace and reverberation
Of thunder of spring over distant mountains
He who was living is now dead
We who were living are now dying
With a little patience

Here is no water but only rock
Rock and no water and the sandy road
The road winding above among the mountains
Which are mountains of rock without water
If there were water we should stop and drink
Amongst the rock one cannot stop or think
Sweat is dry and feet are in the sand
If there were only water amongst the rock
Dead mountain mouth of carious teeth that cannot spit
Here one can neither stand nor lie nor sit
There is not even silence in the mountains
But dry sterile thunder without rain
There is not even solitude in the mountains
But red sullen faces sneer and snarl
From doors of mudcracked houses
                                        If there were water
    And no rock
    If there were rock
    And also water
    And water
    A spring
    A pool among the rock
    If there were the sound of water only

Not the cicada
And dry grass singing
But sound of water over a rock
Where the hermit-thrush sings in the pine trees
Drip drop drip drop drop drop drop
But there is no water

Who is the third who walks always beside you?
When I count, there are only you and I together
But when I look ahead up the white road
There is always another one walking beside you
Gliding wrapt in a brown mantle, hooded
I do not know whether a man or a woman
— But who is that on the other side of you?

What is that sound high in the air
Murmur of maternal lamentation
Who are those hooded hordes swarming
Over endless plains, stumbling in cracked earth
Ringed by the flat horizon only
What is the city over the mountains
Cracks and reforms and bursts in the violet air
Falling towers
Jerusalem Athens Alexandria
Vienna London
Unreal

A woman drew her long black hair out tight
And fiddled whisper music on those strings
And bats with baby faces in the violet light
Whistled, and beat their wings
And crawled head downward down a blackened wall
And upside down in air were towers
Tolling reminiscent bells, that kept the hours
And voices singing out of empty cisterns and exhausted wells.

In this decayed hole among the mountains
In the faint moonlight, the grass is singing
Over the tumbled graves, about the chapel
There is the empty chapel, only the wind's home.
It has no windows, and the door swings,
Dry bones can harm no one.
Only a cock stood on the rooftree
Co co rico co co rico
In a flash of lightning. Then a damp gust
Bringing rain

Ganga was sunken, and the limp leaves
Waited for rain, while the black clouds

Gathered far distant, over Himavant.
The jungle crouched, humped in silence.
Then spoke the thunder
DA
Datta: what have we given?
My friend, blood shaking my heart
The awful daring of a moment's surrender
Which an age of prudence can never retract
By this, and this only, we have existed
Which is not to be found in our obituaries
Or in memories draped by the beneficent spider
Or under seals broken by the lean solicitor
In our empty rooms
DA
Dayadhvam: I have heard the key
Turn in the door once and turn once only
We think of the key, each in his prison
Thinking of the key, each confirms a prison
Only at nightfall, aethereal rumours
Revive for a moment a broken Coriolanus
DA
Damyata: The boat responded
Gaily, to the hand expert with sail and oar
The sea was calm, your heart would have responded
Gaily, when invited, beating obedient
To controlling hands

I sat upon the shore
Fishing, with the arid plain behind me
Shall I at least set my lands in order?
London Bridge is falling down falling down falling down
Poi s'ascose nel foco che gli affina
Quando fiam uti chelidon — O swallow swallow
Le Prince d'Aquitaine à la tour abolie
These fragments I have shored against my ruins
Why then Ile fit you. Hieronymo's mad againe.
Datta. Dayadhvam. Damyata.
Shantih shantih shantih

1922

Notes on "The Waste Land"

Not only the title, but the plan and a good deal of the incidental symbolism of the poem were suggested by Miss Jessie L. Weston's book on the Grail legend: *From Ritual to Romance* (Cambridge). Indeed, so deeply am I indebted, Miss Weston's book will elucidate the difficulties of the poem much better than my notes can do; and I recommend it (apart from the great interest of the book itself) to any who think such elucidation of the poem worth the trouble. To another work of anthropology I am indebted in general, one which has influenced our generation profoundly; I mean *The Golden Bough;* I have used especially the two volumes *Adonis, Attis, Osiris.* Anyone who is acquainted with these works will immediately recognise in the poem certain references to vegetation ceremonies.

I. The Burial of the Dead

Line 20. Cf. Ezekiel II, i.

23. Cf. Ecclesiastes XII, v.

31. V. *Tristan und Isolde*, I, verses 5–8.

42. Id. III, verse 24.

46. I am not familiar with the exact constitution of the Tarot pack of cards, from which I have obviously departed to suit my own convenience. The Hanged Man, a member of the traditional pack, fits my purpose in two ways: because he is associated in my mind with the Hanged God of Frazer, and because I associate him with the hooded figure in the passage of the disciples to Emmaus in Part V. The Phoenician Sailor and the Merchant appear later; also the "crowds of people," and Death by Water is executed in Part IV. The Man with Three Staves (an authentic member of the Tarot pack) I associate, quite arbitrarily, with the Fisher King himself.

60. Cf. Baudelaire:

"Fourmillante cité, cité pleine de rêves,
"Où le spectre en plein jour raccroche le passant."

63. Cf. *Inferno* III, 55–57:

"si lunga tratta
di gente, ch'io non avrei mai creduto
che morte tanta n'avesse disfatta."

64. Cf. *Inferno* IV, 25–27:

"Quivi, secondo che per ascoltare,
"non avea pianto, ma' che di sospiri,
"che l'aura eterna facevan tremare"

68. A phenomenon which I have often noticed.

74. Cf. the Dirge in Webster's *White Devil.*

76. V. Baudelaire, preface to *Fleurs du Mal.*

II. A Game of Chess

77. Cf. *Antony and Cleopatra*, II, ii, l. 190.

92. Laquearia. *V. Aeneid*, I, 726:

dependent lychni laquearibus auries incensi, et noctem flammis funalia vincunt.

98. Sylvan scene V. Milton, *Paradise Lost*, IV, 140.

99. V. Ovid, *Metamorphoses*, VI, Philomela.

100. Cf. Part III, l. 204.

115. Cf. Part III, l. 195.

118. Cf. Webster: "Is the wind in that door still?"

126. Cf. Part I, l. 37, 48.

138. Cf. the game of chess in Middleton's *Women beware Women.*

III. The Fire Sermon

176. V. Spenser, *Prothalamion.*

192. Cf. *The Tempest*, I, ii.

196. Cf. Marvell, *To His Coy Mistress.*

197. Cf. Day, *Parliament of Bees*:

"When of the sudden, listening, you shall hear,
"A noise of horns and hunting, which shall bring
"Actaeon to Diana in the spring,
"Where all shall see her naked skin . . . "

199. I do not know the origin of the ballad from which these lines are taken: it was reported to me from Sydney, Australia.

202. V. Verlaine, *Parsifal.*

210. The currants were quoted at a price "carriage and insurance free to London"; and the Bill of lading etc. were to be handed to the buyer upon payment of the sight draft.

218. Tiresias, although a mere spectator and not indeed a "character," is yet the most important personage in the poem, uniting all the rest. Just as the one-eyed merchant, seller of currants, melts into the Phoenician Sailor, and the latter is not wholly distinct from Ferdinand Prince of Naples, so all the women are one woman, and the two sexes meet in Tiresias. What Tiresias *sees*, in fact, is the substance of the poem. The whole passage from Ovid is of great anthropological interest:

'. . . Cum Iunone iocos et maior vestra profecto est
Quam, quae contingit maribus,' dixisse, 'voluptas.'
Illa negat; placuit quae sit sententia docti
Quaerere Tiresiae: venus huic erat utraque nota.
Nam duo magnorum viridi coeuntia silva
Corpora serpentum baculi violaverat ictu
Deque viro factus, mirabile, femina septem
Egerat autumnos; octavo rursus eosdem
Vidit et 'est vestrae si tanta potentia plagae,'
Dixit 'ut auctoris sortem in contraria mutet,
Nunc quoque vos feriam!' percussis anguibus isdem
Forma prior rediit genetivaque venit imago.
Arbiter hic igitur sumptus de lite iocosa
Dicta Iovis firmat; gravius Saturnia iusto
Nec pro materia fertur doluisse suique
Iudicis aeterna damnavit lumina nocte,
At pater omnipotens (neque enim licet inrita cuiquam
Facta dei fecisse deo) pro lumine adempto
Scire futura dedit poenamque levavit honore.

221. This may not appear as exact as Sappho's lines, but I had in mind the "longshore" or "dory" fisherman, who returns at nightfall.

253. V. Goldsmith, the song in *The Vicar of Wakefield.*

257. V. *The Tempest*, as above.

264. The interior of St. Magnus Martyr is to my mind one of the finest among Wren's interiors. See *The Proposed Demolition of Nineteen City Churches*: (P. S. King & Son, Ltd.).

266. The song of the (three) Thames-daughters begins here. From line 292 to 306 inclusive they speak in turn. V. *Götterdämmerung*, III, i: the Rhine-daughters.

279. V. Froude, *Elizabeth*, Vol. I, ch. iv, letter of De Quadra to Philip of Spain: "In the afternoon we were in a barge, watching the games on the river. (The queen) was alone with Lord Robert and myself on the poop, when they began to talk nonsense, and went so far that Lord Robert at last said, as I was on the spot there was no reason why they should not be married if the queen pleased."

293. Cf. *Purgatorio*, V, 133:

"Ricorditi di me, che son la Pia;
"Siena mi fe', disfecemi Maremma."

307. V. St. Augustine's *Confessions*: "to Carthage then I came, where a cauldron of unholy loves sang all about mine ears."

308. The complete text of the Buddha's Fire Sermon (which corresponds in importance to the Sermon of the Mount) from which these words are taken, will be found translated in the late Henry Clarke Warren's *Buddhism in Translation* (Harvard Oriental Series). Mr. Warren was one of the great pioneers of Buddhist studies in the Occident.

309. From St. Augustine's *Confessions* again. The collocation of these two representatives of eastern and western asceticism, as the culmination of this part of the poem, is not an accident.

V. What the Thunder Said

In the first part of Part V three themes are employed: the journey to Emmaus, the approach to the Chapel Perilous (see Miss Weston's book) and the present decay of eastern Europe.

357. This is *Turdus aonalaschkae pallasii*, the hermit-thrush which I have heard in Quebec province. Chapman says (*Handbook of Birds of Eastern North America*) "it is most at home in secluded woodland and thickety retreats. . . . Its notes are not remarkable for variety or volume, but in purity and sweetness of tone and exquisite modulation they are unequalled." Its "water-dripping song" is justly celebrated.

360. The following lines were stimulated by the account of one of the Antarctic expeditions (I forget which, but I think one of Shackleton's): it was related that the party of explorers, at the extremity of their strength, had the constant delusion that there was *one more member* than could actually be counted.

367–77. Cf. Hermann Hesse, *Blick ins Chaos*: "Schon ist halb Europa, schon ist zumindest der halbe Osten Europas auf dem Wege zum Chaos, fährt betrunken im heiligem Wahn am Abgrund entlang und singt dazu, singt betrunken und hymnisch wie Dmitri Karamasoff sang. Ueber diese Lieder lacht der Bürger beleidigt, der Heilige und Seher hört sie mit Tränen."

402. "Datta, dayadhavam, damyata" (Give, sympathise, control). The fable of the meaning of the Thunder is found in the *Brihadaranayaka–Upanishad*, 5, 1. A translation is found in Deussen's *Sechzig Upanishads des Veda*, p. 489.

408. Cf. Webster, *The White Devil*, V, vi:

" . . . they'll remarry
Ere the worm pierce your winding-sheet, ere the spider
Make a thin curtain for your epitaphs."

412. Cf. *Inferno*, XXXIII, 46:

"ed io sentii chiavar l'uscio di sotto
all'orribile torre."

Also F. H. Bradley, *Appearance and Reality*, p. 346.

"My external sensations are no less private to myself than are my thoughts or my feelings. In either case my experience falls within my own circle, a circle closed on the outside; and, with all its elements alike, every sphere is opaque to the others which surround it. . . . In brief, regarded as an existence which appears in a soul, the whole world for each is peculiar and private to that soul."

425. V. Weston: *From Ritual to Romance*; chapter on the Fisher King.

428. V. *Purgatoriao*, XXVI, 148.

> "'Ara vos prec per aquella valor
> 'que vos guida al som de l'escalina,
> 'sovegna vos a temps de ma dolor.'
> Poi s'ascose nel foco gli affina."

429. V. *Pervilium Veneris*. Cf. Philomela in Parts II and III.

430. V. Gerard de Nerval, Sonnet *El Desdichado*.

432. V. Kyd's *Spanish Tragedy*.

434. Shantih. Repeated as here, a formal ending to an Upanishad. "The Peace which passeth understanding" is our equivalent to this word.

The Hollow Men

Mistah Kurtz — he dead.

A penny for the Old Guy

I

We are the hollow men
We are the stuffed men
leaning together
Headpiece filled with straw. Alas!
Our dried voices, when
We whisper together
Are quiet and meaningless
As wind in dry grass
or rats' feet over broken glass
in our dry cellar

Shape without form, shade without colour,
Paralysed force, gesture without motion;

Those who have crossed
With direct eyes, to death's other Kingdom
Remember us — if at all — not as lost
Violent souls, but only
As the hollow men
The stuffed men.

II

Eyes I dare not meet in dreams
In death's dream kingdom

These do not appear:
There, the eyes are
Sunlight on a broken column
There, is a tree swinging
And voices are
In the wind's singing
More distant and more solemn
Than a fading star.

Let me be no nearer
In death's dream kingdom
Let me also wear
Such deliberate disguises
Rat's coat, crowskin, crossed staves
In a field
Behaving as the wind behaves
No nearer —

Not that final meeting
in the twilight kingdom

III

This is the dead land
This is cactus land
Here the stone images
Are raised, here they receive
The supplication of a dead man's hand
Under the twinkle of a fading star.

Is it like this
In death's other kingdom
Waking alone
At the hour when we are
Trembling with tenderness
Lips that would kiss
Form prayers to broken stone.

IV

The eyes are not here
There are no eyes here
In this valley of dying stars
In this hollow valley
This broken jaw of our lost kingdoms

In this last of meeting places
We grope together
And avoid speech
Gathered on this beach of the tumid river

Sightless, unless
The eyes reappear
As the perpetual star
Multifoliate rose
Of death's twilight kingdom
The hope only
Of empty men.

V

Here we go round the prickly pear
Prickly pear prickly pear
Here we go round the prickly pear
At five o'clock in the morning.

Between the idea
And the reality
Between the motion
And the act
Falls the shadow
For Thine is the Kingdom

Between the conception
And the creation
Between the emotion
And the response
Falls the Shadow
Life is very long

Between the desire
And the spasm
Between the potency
And the existence
Between the essence
And the descent
Falls the Shadow
For Thine is the Kingdom

For Thine is
Life is
For Thine is the

This is the way the world ends
This is the way the world ends
This is the way the world ends
Not with a bang but a whimper.

1925

Journey of the Magi

"A cold coming we had of it,
Just the worst time of the year
For a journey, and such a long journey:
The ways deep and the weather sharp,
The very dead of winter."
And the camels galled, sore-footed, refractory,
Lying down in the melting snow.
There were times we regretted
The summer palaces on slopes, the terraces,
And the silken girls bringing sherbet.
Then the camel men cursing and grumbling
And running away, and wanting their liquor and women,
And the night-fires going out, and the lack of shelters,
And the cities hostile and the towns unfriendly
And the villages dirty and charging high prices:
A hard time we had of it.
At the end we preferred to travel all night,
Sleeping in snatches,
With the voices singing in our ears, saying
That this was all folly.

Then at dawn we came down to a temperate valley,
Wet, below the snow line, smelling of vegetation;
With a running stream and a water-mill beating the darkness,
And three trees on the low sky,
And an old white horse galloped away in the meadow.
Then we came to a tavern with vine-leaves over the lintel,
Six hands at an open door dicing for pieces of silver,
And feet kicking the empty wine-skins.
But there was no information, and so we continued
And arrived at evening, not a moment too soon
Finding the place; it was (you may say) satisfactory.

All this was a long time ago, I remember,
And I would do it again, but set down
This set down
This: were we led all that way for
Birth or Death? There was a Birth, certainly,
We had evidence and no doubt. I had seen birth and death,
But had thought they were different; this Birth was
Hard and bitter agony for us, like Death, our death.
We returned to our places, these Kingdoms,
But no longer at ease here, in the old dispensation,
With an alien people clutching their gods.
I should be glad of another death.

1927

Little Gidding

I

Midwinter spring is its own season
Sempiternal though sodden towards sundown,
Suspended in time, between pole and tropic.
When the short day is brightest, with frost and fire,
The brief sun flames the ice, on pond and ditches,
In windless cold that is the heart's heat,
Reflecting in a watery mirror
A glare that is blindness in the early afternoon.
And glow more intense than blaze of branch, or brazier,
Stirs the dumb spirit: no wind, but pentecostal fire
In the dark time of the year. Between melting and freezing
The soul's sap quivers. There is no earth smell
Or smell of living thing. This is the spring time
But not in time's covenant. Now the hedgerow
Is blanched for an hour with transitory blossom
Of snow, a bloom more sudden
Than that of summer, neither budding nor fading,
Not in the scheme of generation.
Where is the summer, the unimaginable
Zero summer?

If you came this way,
Taking the route you would be likely to take
From the place you would be likely to come from,
If you came this way in may time, you would find the hedges
White again, in May, with voluptuary sweetness.
It would be the same at the end of the journey,
If you came at night like a broken king,
If you came by day not knowing what you came for,
It would be the same, when you leave the rough road
And turn behind the pig-sty to the dull façade
And the tombstone. And what you thought you came for
Is only a shell, a husk of meaning
From which the purpose breaks only when it is fulfilled
If at all. Either you had no purpose
Or the purpose is beyond the end you figured
And is altered in fulfillment. There are other places
Which also are the world's end, some at the sea jaws,
Or over a dark lake, in a desert or a city —
But this is the nearest, in place and time,
Now and in England.

If you came this way,
Taking any route, starting from anywhere,
At any time or at any season,
It would always be the same: you would have to put off

Sense and notion. You are not here to verify,
Instruct yourself, or inform curiosity
Or carry report. You are here to kneel
Where prayer has been valid. And prayer is more
Than an order of words, the conscious occupation
Of the praying mind, or the sound of the voice praying.
And what the dead had no speech for, when living,
They can tell you, being dead: the communication
Of the dead is tongued with fire beyond the language of the living.
Here, the intersection of the timeless moment
Is England and nowhere. Never and always.

II

Ash on an old man's sleeve
Is all the ash the burnt roses leave.
Dust in the air suspended
Marks the place where a story ended.
Dust inbreathed was a house —
The wall, the wainscot and the mouse.
The death of hope and despair,
        This is the death of air.

        There are flood and drouth
Over the eyes and in the mouth,
Dead water and dead sand
Contending for the upper hand.
The parched eviscerate soil
Gapes at the vanity of toil,
Laughs without mirth.
        This is the death of earth.

    Water and fire succeed
The town, the pasture and the weed.
Water and fire deride
The sacrifice that we denied.
Water and fire shall rot
The marred foundations we forgot,
Of sanctuary and choir.
        This is the death of water and fire.

In the uncertain hour before the morning
    Near the ending of interminable night
    At the recurrent end of the unending
After the dark dove with the flickering tongue
    Had passed below the horizon of his homing
    While the dead leaves still rattled on like tin
Over the asphalt where no other sound was
    Between three districts whence the smoke arose
    I met one walking, loitering and hurried

As if blown towards me like the metal leaves
  Before the urban dawn wind unresisting.
  And as I fixed upon the down-turned face
That pointed scrutiny with which we challenge
  The first-met stranger in the waning dusk
  I caught the sudden look of some dead master
Whom I had known, forgotten, half recalled
  Both one and many; in the brown baked features
  The eyes of a familiar compound ghost
Both intimate and unidentifiable.
  So I assumed a double part, and cried
  And heard another's voice cry: "What! are *you* here?"
Although we were not. I was still the same,
  Knowing myself yet being someone other —
  And he a face still forming; yet the words sufficed
To compel the recognition they preceded.
  And so, compliant to the common wind,
  Too strange to each other for misunderstanding,
In concord at this intersection time
  Of meeting nowhere, no before and after,
  We trod the pavement in a dead patrol.
I said: "The wonder that I feel is easy,
  Yet ease is cause of wonder. Therefore speak:
  I may not comprehend, may not remember."
And he: "I am not eager to rehearse
  My thought and theory which you have forgotten.
  These things have served their purpose: let them be.
So with your own, and pray they be forgiven
  By others, as I pray you to forgive
  Both bad and good. Last season's fruit is eaten
And the fullfed beast shall kick the empty pail.
  For last year's words belong to last year's language
  And next year's words await another voice.
But, as the passage now presents no hindrance
  To the spirit unappeased and peregrine
  Between two worlds become much like each other,
So I find words I never thought to speak
  In streets I never thought I should revisit
  When I left my body on a distant shore.
Since our concern was speech, and speech impelled us
  To purify the dialect of the tribe
  And urge the mind to aftersight and foresight,
Let me disclose the gifts reserved for age
  To set a crown upon your lifetime's effort.
  First, the cold friction of expiring sense
Without enchantment, offering no promise
  But bitter tastelessness of shadow fruit
  As body and soul begin to fall asunder.

Second, the conscious impotence of rage
  At human folly, and the laceration
  Of laughter at what ceases to amuse.
And last, the rending pain of re-enactment
  Of all that you have done, and been; the shame
  Of motives late revealed, and the awareness
Of things ill done and done to others harm
  Which once you took for exercise of virtue.
  The fools' approval stings, and honour stains.
From wrong to wrong the exasperated spirit
  Proceeds, unless restored by that refining fire
  Where you must move in measure, like a dancer."
The day was breaking. In the disfigured street
  He left me, with a kind of valediction,
  And faded on the blowing of the horn.

III

There are three conditions which often look alike
Yet differ completely, flourish in the same hedgerow:
Attachment to self and to things and to persons, detachment
From self and from things and from persons; and, growing between
    them, indifference
Which resembles the others as death resembles life,
Being between two lives — unflowering, between
The live and the dead nettle. This is the use of memory:
For liberation — not less of love but expanding
Of love beyond desire, and so liberation
From the future as well as the past. Thus, love of a country
Begins as attachment to our own field of action
And comes to find that action of little importance
Though never indifferent. History may be servitude,
History may be freedom. See, now they vanish,
The faces and places, with the self which, as it could, loved them,
To become renewed, transfigured, in another pattern.
Sin is Behovely, but
All shall be well, and
All manner of thing shall be well.
If I think, again, of this place,
And of people, not wholly commendable,
Of no immediate kin or kindness,
But some of peculiar genius,
All touched by a common genius,
United in the strife which divided them;
If I think of a king at nightfall,
Of three men, and more, on the scaffold
And a few who died forgotten
In other places, here and abroad,
And of one who died blind and quiet,
Why should we celebrate
These dead men more than the dying?

It is not to ring the bell backward
Nor is it an incantation
To summon the spectre of a Rose.
We cannot revive old factions
We cannot restore old policies
Or follow an antique drum.
These men, and those who opposed them
And those whom they opposed
Accept the constitution of silence
And are folded in a single party.
Whatever we inherit from the fortunate
We have taken from the defeated
What they had to leave us — a symbol:
A symbol perfected in death.
And all shall be well and
All manner of thing shall be well
By the purification of the motive
In the ground of our beseeching.

IV

The dove descending breaks the air
With flame of incandescent terror
Of which the tongues declare
The one discharge from sin and error.
The only hope, or else despair
   Lies in the choice of pyre or pyre —
   To be redeemed from fire by fire.

   Who then devised the torment? Love.
Love is the unfamiliar Name
Behind the hands that wove
The intolerable shirt of flame
Which human power cannot remove.
   We only live, only suspire
   Consumed by either fire or fire.

V

What we call the beginning is often the end
And to make an end is to make a beginning.
The end is where we start from. And every phrase
And sentence that is right (where every word is at home,
Taking its place to support the others,
The word neither diffident nor ostentatious,
An easy commerce of the old and the new,
The common word exact without vulgarity,
The formal word precise but not pedantic,
The complete consort dancing together)
Every phrase and every sentence is an end and a beginning,
Every poem an epitaph. And any action

Is a step to the block, to the fire, down the sea's throat
Or to an illegible stone: and that is where we start.
We die with the dying:
See, they depart, and we go with them.
We are born with the dead:
See, they return, and bring us with them.
The moment of the rose and the moment of the yew-tree
Are of equal duration. A people without history
Is not redeemed from time, for history is a pattern
Of timeless moments. So, while the light fails
On a winter's afternoon, in a secluded chapel
History is now and England.

With the drawing of this Love and the voice of this Calling

We shall not cease from exploration
And the end of all our exploring
Will be to arrive where we started
And know the place for the first time.
Through the unknown, remembered gate
When the last of earth left to discover
Is that which was the beginning;
At the source of the longest river
The voice of the hidden waterfall
And the children in the apple-tree
Not known, because not looked for
But heard, half-heard, in the stillness
Between two waves of the sea.
Quick now, here, now, always —
A condition of complete simplicity
(Costing not less than everything)
And all shall be well and
All manner of thing shall be well
When the tongues of flame are in-folded
Into the crowned knot of fire
And the fire and the rose are one.

1942

JOHN CROWE RANSOM (1888–1974)

A leader of the Southern Agrarians, and among the most influential proponents of the New Criticism, John Crowe Ransom, a native of Pulaski, Tennessee, began teaching at Vanderbilt in 1914. There he joined with other "Fugitives," such as Allen Tate and Robert Penn Warren. Ransom went in 1937 to Kenyon College in Gambier, Ohio, to teach, and founded the *Kenyon Review* two years later. Under his editorship it became one of the nation's most important literary journals. He remained its editor until his retirement in 1959. In John Berryman's view,

Ransom's "Captain Carpenter" is "a fantasia on bruised Southern gentility and the prototype of bruised Christian chivalry, Don Quixote. Just who the female enemy is is not clear."

Agitato ma non troppo

I have a grief
(It was not stolen like a thief)
Albeit I have no bittern by the lake
To cry it up and down the brake.

None there hath been like Dante's fury
When Beatrice was given him to bury;
Except, when the young heart was hit, you know
How Percy Shelley's reed sang tremolo.

'If grief be in his mind,
Where is his fair child moaning in the wind?
Where is the white frost snowing on his head?
When did he stalk and weep and not loll in his bed?'

I will be brief,
Assuredly I have a grief,
And I am shaken; but not as a leaf.

1924

Bells for John Whiteside's Daughter

There was such speed in her little body,
And such lightness in her footfall,
It is no wonder her brown study
Astonishes us all.

Her wars were bruited in our high window.
We looked among orchard trees and beyond
Where she took arms against her shadow,
Or harried unto the pond

The lazy geese, like a snow cloud
Dripping their snow on the green grass,
Tricking and stopping, sleepy and proud,
Who cried in goose, Alas,

For the tireless heart within the little
Lady with rod that made them rise
From their noon apple-dreams and scuttle
Goose-fashion under the skies!

But now go the bells, and we are ready,
In one house we are sternly stopped
To say we are vexed at her brown study,
Lying so primly propped.

1924

Captain Carpenter

Captain Carpenter rose up in his prime
Put on his pistols and went riding out
But had got wellnigh nowhere at that time
Till he fell in with ladies in a rout.

It was a pretty lady and all her train
That played with him so sweetly but before
An hour she'd taken a sword with all her main
And twined him of his nose for evermore.

Captain Carpenter mounted up one day
And rode straightway into a stranger rogue
That looked unchristian but be that as may
The Captain did not wait upon prologue.

But drew upon him out of his great heart
The other swung against him with a club
And cracked his two legs at the shinny part
And let him roll and stick like any tub.

Captain Carpenter rode many a time
From male and female took he sundry harms
He met the wife of Satan crying "I'm
The she-wolf bids you shall bear no more arms."

Their strokes and counters whistled in the wind
I wish he had delivered half his blows
But where she should have made off like a hind
The bitch bit off his arms at the elbows.

And Captain Carpenter parted with his ears
To a black devil that used him in this wise
O Jesus ere his threescore and ten years
Another had plucked out his sweet blue eyes.

Captain Carpenter got up on his roan
And sallied from the gate in hell's despite
I heard him asking in the grimmest tone
If any enemy yet there was to fight?

"To any adversary it is fame
If he risk to be wounded by my tongue
Or burnt in two beneath my red heart's flame
Such are the perils he is cast among.

"But if he can he has a pretty choice
From an anatomy with little to lose
Whether he cut my tongue and take my voice
Or whether it be my round red heart he choose."

It was the neatest knave that ever was seen
Stepping in perfume from his lady's bower
Who at this word put in his merry mien
And fell on Captain Carpenter like a tower.

I would not knock old fellows in the dust
But there lay Captain Carpenter on his back
His weapons were the old heart in his bust
And a blade shook between rotten teeth alack.

The rogue in scarlet and grey soon knew his mind
He wished to get his trophy and depart
With gentle apology and touch refined
He pierced him and produced the Captain's heart.

God's mercy rest on Captain Carpenter now
I thought him Sirs an honest gentleman
Citizen husband soldier and scholar enow
Let jangling kites eat of him if they can.

But God's deep curses follow after those
That shore him of his goodly nose and ears
His legs and strong arms at the two elbows
And eyes that had not watered seventy years.

The curse of hell upon the sleek upstart
That got the Captain finally on his back
And took the red red vitals of his heart
And made the kites to whet their beaks clack clack.

1924

Piazza Piece

— I am a gentleman in a dustcoat trying
To make you hear. Your ears are soft and small
And listen to an old man not at all,
They want the young men's whispering and sighing.

But see the roses on your trellis dying
And hear the spectral singing of the moon;
For I must have my lovely lady soon,
I am a gentleman in a dustcoat trying.

— I am a lady young in beauty waiting
Until my truelove comes, and then we kiss.
But what grey man among the vines is this
Whose words are dry and faint as in a dream?
Back from my trellis, Sir, before I scream!
I am a lady young in beauty waiting.

1924

Vision by Sweetwater

Go and ask Robin to bring the girls over
To Sweetwater, said my Aunt; and that was why
It was like a dream of ladies sweeping by
The willows, clouds, deep meadowgrass, and river.

Robin's sisters and my Aunt's lily daughter
Laughed and talked, and tinkled light as wrens
If there were a little colony all hens
To go walking by the steep turn of Sweetwater.

Let them alone, dear Aunt, just for one minute
Till I go fishing in the dark of my mind:
Where have I seen before, against the wind,
These bright virgins, robed and bare of bonnet,

Flowing with music of their strange quick tongue
And adventuring with delicate paces by the stream, —
Myself a child, old suddenly at the scream
From one of the white throats which it hid among?

1927

Conrad Aiken (1889–1973)

Conrad Aiken was born in Savannah, Georgia, the son of a doctor. When he was eleven years old, he heard pistol shots in the next room, rushed in, and found the dead bodies of his parents; his father had killed his wife and then himself. At Harvard, Aiken began a lifelong friendship with T. S. Eliot, whom he dubbed "Tsetse." The prolific Aiken edited Emily Dickinson's *Selected Poems* (1924), giving her reputation a boost. Denis Donoghue in *Reading America* (1987) notes that "Everybody, or nearly everybody, liked him. Allen Tate, Blackmur, all sorts of people warmed to Aiken, but when they had finished complaining about the neglect of his poetry they went on their several ways without adverting to it. When his name comes up, people agree that he has been shamefully neglected, but nobody has been able to think of any compelling reason for changing that situation." Harold Bloom edited a new edition of Aiken's *Selected Poems* in 2003 and praised the "cognitive music" of Aiken's poetry, "free of all ideology, and courageous in confronting family madness, solitude, death-as-annihilation, chaos."

Music I heard with you

Music I heard with you was more than music,
And bread I broke with you was more than bread;
Now that I am without you, all is desolate;
All that was once so beautiful is dead.

Your hands once touched this table and this silver,
And I have seen your fingers hold this glass.
These things do not remember you, belovèd, —
And yet your touch upon them will not pass.

For it was in my heart you moved among them,
And blessed them with your hands and with your eyes;
And in my heart they will remember always, —
They knew you once, O beautiful and wise.

1916

from *Preludes*

I

Winter for a moment takes the mind; the snow
Falls past the arclight; icicles guard a wall;
The wind moans through a crack in the window;
A keen sparkle of frost is on the sill.
Only for a moment; as spring too might engage it,
With a single crocus in the loam, or a pair of birds;
Or summer with hot grass; or autumn with a yellow leaf.
Winter is there, outside, is here in me:
Drapes the planets with snow, deepens the ice on the moon,
Darkens the darkness that was already darkness.
The mind too has its snows, its slippery paths,
Walls bayonetted with ice, leaves ice-encased.
Here is the in-drawn room, to which you return
When the wind blows from Arcturus: here is the fire
At which you warm your hands and glaze your eyes;
The piano, on which touch the cold treble;
Five notes like breaking icicles; and then silence.

The alarm-clock ticks, the pulse keeps time with it,
Night and the mind are full of sounds. I walk
From the fire-place, with its imaginary fire,
To the window, with its imaginary view.
Darkness, and snow ticking the window: silence,
And the knocking of chains on a motor-car, the tolling
Of a bronze bell, dedicated to Christ.
And then the uprush of angelic wings, the beating
Of wings demonic, from the abyss of the mind:
The darkness filled with a feathery whistling, wings
Numberless as the flakes of angelic snow,
The deep void swarming with wings and sound of wings,
The winnowing of chaos, the aliveness
Of depth and depth and depth dedicated to death.

Here are the bickerings of the inconsequential,
The chatterings of the ridiculous, the iterations
Of the meaningless. Memory, like a juggler,
Tosses its colored balls into the light, and again
Receives them into darkness. Here is the absurd,
Grinning like an idiot, and the omnivorous quotidian,
Which will have its day. A handful of coins,
Tickets, items from the news, a soiled handkerchief,
A letter to be answered, notice of a telephone call,
The petal of a flower in a volume of Shakspere,
The program of a concert. The photograph, too,
Propped on the mantel, and beneath it a dry rosebud;
The laundry bill, matches, an ash-tray, Utamaro's
Pearl-fishers. And the rug, on which are still the crumbs
Of yesterday's feast. These are the void, the night,
And the angelic wings that make it sound.

What is the flower? It is not a sigh of color,
Suspiration of purple, sibilation of saffron,
Nor aureate exhalation from the tomb.
Yet it is these because you think of these,
An emanation of emanations, fragile
As light, or glisten, or gleam, or coruscation,
Creature of brightness, and as brightness brief.
What is the frost? It is not the sparkle of death,
The flash of time's wing, seeds of eternity;
Yet it is these because you think of these.
And you, because you think of these, are both
Frost and flower, the bright ambiguous syllable
Of which the meaning is both no and yes.

Here is the tragic, the distorting mirror
In which your gesture becomes grandiose;
Tears form and fall from your magnificent eyes,

The brow is noble, and the mouth is God's.
Here is the God who seeks his mother, Chaos, —
Confusion seeking solution, and life seeking death.
Here is the rose that woos the icicle; the icicle
That woos the rose. Here is the silence of silences
Which dreams of becoming a sound, and the sound
Which will perfect itself in silence. And all
These things are only the uprush from the void,
The wings angelic and demonic, the sound of the abyss
Dedicated to death. And this is you.

XIX

Watch long enough, and you will see the leaf
Fall from the bough. Without a sound it falls:
And soundless meets the grass . . . And so you have
A bare bough, and a dead leaf in dead grass.
Something has come and gone. And that is all.

But what were all the tumults in this action?
What wars of atoms in the twig, what ruins,
Fiery and disastrous, in the leaf?
Timeless the tumult was, but gave no sign.
Only, the leaf fell, and the bough is bare.

This is the world: there is no more than this.
The unseen and disastrous prelude, shaking
The trivial act from the terrific action.
Speak: and the ghosts of change, past and to come,
Throng the brief word. The maelstrom has us all.

XXXIII

Then came I to the shoreless shore of silence,
Where never summer was nor shade of tree,
Nor sound of water, nor sweet light of sun,
But only nothing and the shore of nothing,
Above, below, around, and in my heart:

Where day was not, not night, nor space, nor time,
Where no bird sang, save him of memory,
Nor footstep marked upon the marl, to guide
My halting footstep; and I turned for terror,
Seeking in vain the Pole Star of my thought;

Where it was blown among the shapeless clouds,
And gone as soon as seen, and scarce recalled,
Its image lost and I directionless;
Alone upon the brown sad edge of chaos,
In the wan evening that was evening always;

Then closed my eyes upon the sea of nothing
While memory brought back a sea more bright,
With long, long waves of light, and the swift sun,
And the good trees that bowed upon the wind;
And stood until grown dizzy with that dream;

Seeking in all that joy of things remembered
One image, one the dearest, one most bright,
One face, one star, one daisy, one delight,
One hour with wings most heavenly and swift,
One hand the tenderest upon my heart;

But still no image came, save of that sea,
No tenderer thing than thought of tenderness,
No heart or daisy brighter than the rest;
And only sadness at the bright sea lost,
And mournfulness that all had not been praised.

O lords of chaos, atoms of desire,
Whirlwind of fruitfulness, destruction's seed,
Hear now upon the void my late delight,
The quick brief cry of memory, that knows
At the dark's edge how great the darkness is.

1931

CLAUDE MCKAY (1889–1948)

Born in Sunny Ville, Jamaica, Claude McKay figured prominently in the Harlem Renaissance. He lived for a time in England, spent a year in the Soviet Union, and met Trotsky. Disillusioned with Communism, McKay converted to Catholicism after returning to the United States in 1934. He wrote his most famous poem, "If We Must Die," in response to the race riots in New York City, Chicago, and other cities in the summer of 1919. Winston Churchill declaimed the poem in the House of Commons during World War II.

If We Must Die

If we must die, let it not be like hogs
Hunted and penned in an inglorious spot,
While round us bark the mad and hungry dogs,
Making their mock at our accursed lot.
If we must die, O let us nobly die,
So that our precious blood may not be shed
In vain; then even the monsters we defy
Shall be constrained to honor us though dead!

O kinsmen! we must meet the common foe!
Though far outnumbered let us show us brave,
And for their thousand blows deal one death-blow!
What though before us lies the open grave?
Like men we'll face the murderous, cowardly pack,
Pressed to the wall, dying, but fighting back!

1922

America

Although she feeds me bread of bitterness,
And sinks into my throat her tiger's tooth,
Stealing my breath of life, I will confess
I love this cultured hell that tests my youth!
Her vigor flows like tides into my blood,
Giving me strength erect against her hate.
Her bigness sweeps my being like a flood.
Yet as a rebel fronts a king in state,
I stand within her walls with not a shred
Of terror, malice, not a word of jeer.
Darkly I gaze into the days ahead,
And see her might and granite wonders there,
Beneath the touch of Time's unerring hand,
Like priceless treasures sinking in the sand.

1922

The White City

I will not toy with it nor bend an inch.
Deep in the secret chambers of my heart
I muse my life-long hate, and without flinch
I bear it nobly as I live my part.
My being would be a skeleton, a shell,
If this dark Passion that fills my every mood,
And makes my heaven in the white world's hell,
Did not forever feed me vital blood.
I see the mighty city through a mist —
The strident trains that speed the goaded mass,
The poles and spires and towers vapor-kissed,
The fortressed port through which the great ships pass,
The tides, the wharves, the dens I contemplate,
Are sweet like wanton loves because I hate.

1922

The Harlem Dancer

Applauding youths laughed with young prostitutes
And watched her perfect, half-clothed body sway;
Her voice was like the sound of blended flutes
Blown by black players upon a picnic day.
She sang and danced on gracefully and calm,
The light gauze hanging loose about her form;
To me she seemed a proudly-swaying palm
Grown lovelier for passing through a storm.
Upon her swarthy neck black shiny curls
Luxuriant fell; and tossing coins in praise,
The wine-flushed, bold-eyed boys, and even the girls,
Devoured her shape with eager, passionate gaze;
But looking at her falsely-smiling face,
I knew her self was not in that strange place.

1922

The Tropics in New York

Bananas ripe and green, and ginger-root
    Cocoa in pods and alligator pears,
And tangerines and mangoes and grape fruit,
    Fit for the highest prize at parish fairs,

Set in the window, bringing memories
    Of fruit-trees laden by low-singing rills,
And dewy dawns, and mystical blue skies
    In benediction over nun-like hills.

My eyes grow dim, and I could no more gaze;
    A wave of longing through my body swept.
And, hungry for the old, familiar ways,
    I turned aside and bowed my head and wept.

1922

ARCHIBALD MACLEISH (1892–1982)

Archibald MacLeish, who was born in Glencoe, Illinois, went to Hotchkiss, played football at Yale, served in World War I, attended Harvard Law School, joined a Boston law firm, then abandoned a promising legal career for Paris and the bohemian life in 1923. During the 1930s he wrote for *Fortune*. Franklin D. Roosevelt appointed him Librarian of Congress in 1939. He contributed to

FDR's speeches, headed a government office devoted to pro-U.S. propaganda, and became an assistant secretary of state in 1944. The English poet Philip Larkin, himself a professional librarian, wrote admiringly that MacLeish "had taken the Library of Congress, beaten the dust out of it, shaken it into a new pattern, and made it newsworthy." In later years, MacLeish admired Bob Dylan. For an ill-fated play entitled *Scratch* (1971), which he based on Stephen Vincent Benet's "The Devil and Daniel Webster," MacLeish asked Dylan to write songs. "There was no way I could make its purpose mine," Dylan writes in *Chronicles (Volume One)*, "but it was great meeting him, a man who had reached the moon when most of us scarcely make it off the ground. In some ways, he taught me how to swim the Atlantic." In his lifetime MacLeish's reputation rested on his forays in verse drama and his large public utterances, which now seem dated, though his "Invocation to the Social Muse" remains a valuable exposition of a liberal point of view. (See the headnote on Allen Tate for that poet's conservative reply.) The aphoristic conclusion of MacLeish's "Ars Poetica" is often quoted: "A poem should not mean / But be."

Ars Poetica

A poem should be palpable and mute
As a globed fruit,

Dumb
As old medallions to the thumb,

Silent as the sleeve-worn stone
Of casement ledges where the moss has grown —

A poem should be wordless
As the flight of birds.

*

A poem should be motionless in time
As the moon climbs,

Leaving, as the moon releases
Twig by twig the night-entangled trees,

Leaving, as the moon behind the winter leaves,
Memory by memory the mind —

A poem should be motionless in time
As the moon climbs.

*

A poem should be equal to:
Not true.

For all the history of grief
An empty doorway and a maple leaf.

For love
The leaning grasses and two lights above the sea —

A poem should not mean
But be.

1926

Invocation to the Social Muse

Señora it is true the Greeks are dead:

It is true also that we here are Americans:
That we use the machines: that a sight of the god is
unusual:
That more people have more thoughts: that there are

Progress and science and tractors and revolutions and
Marx and the wars more antiseptic and murderous
And music in every home: there is also Hoover:

Does the lady suggest we should write it out in The Word?
Does Madame recall our responsibilities? We are
Whores Fräulein: poets Fräulein are persons of

Known vocation following troops: they must sleep with
Stragglers from either prince and of both views:
The rules permit them to further the business of neither:

It is also strictly forbidden to mix in maneuvers:
Those that infringe are inflated with praise on the plazas —
Their bones are resultantly afterwards found under newspapers:

Preferring life with the sons to death with the fathers
We also doubt on the record whether the sons
Will still be shouting around with the same huzzas —

For we hope Lady to live to lie with the youngest:
There are only a handful of things a man likes
Generation to generation hungry or

Well fed: the earth's one: life's
One: Mister Morgan is not one:

There is nothing worse for our trade than to be in style:

He that goes naked goes farther at last than another:
Wrap the bard in a flag or a school and they'll jimmy his
Door down and be thick in his bed — for a month:

(Who recalls the address now of the Imagists?)
But the naked man has always his own nakedness:
People remember forever his live limbs:

They may drive him out of the camps but one will take him:
They may stop his tongue on his teeth with a rope's argument —
He will lie in a house and be warm when they are shaking:

Besides Tovarishch how to embrace an army?
How to take to one's chamber a million souls?
How to conceive in the name of a column of marchers?

The things of the poet are done to a man alone
As the things of love are done — or of death when he hears the
Step withdraw on the stair and the clock tick only:

Neither his class nor his kind nor his trade may come near him
There where he lies on his left arm and will die:
Nor his class nor his kind nor his trade when the blood is jeering

And his knee's in the soft of the bed where his love lies:

I remind you Barinya the life of the poet is hard —
A hardy life with a boot as quick as a fiver:

Is it just to demand of us also to bear arms?

1932

What Any Lover Learns

Water is heavy silver over stone.
Water is heavy silver over stone's
Refusal. It does not fall. It fills. It flows
Every crevice, every fault of the stone,
Every hollow. River does not run.
River presses its heavy silver self
Down into stone and stone refuses.

What runs,
Swirling and leaping into sun, is stone's
Refusal of the river, not the river.

1952

EDNA ST. VINCENT MILLAY (1892–1950)

Born in Rockland, Maine, Edna St. Vincent Millay graduated from Vassar College in 1917, published her first book of poems, and moved to Greenwich Village, then emerging as a bohemian paradise. Millay, whose friends called her "Vincent," lived in a nine-foot-wide attic, wrote journalism, joined the Provincetown Theatre Group, and acted in, directed, and wrote plays the group produced. She and her fellow writers were, she wrote, "very, very poor and very, very merry." In 1923 she was the first woman to win the Pulitzer Prize for poetry. Her poems, expressing pleasure in their author's sexual freedom and erotic desire, won her a devoted following, unusual popularity, and the possibly inevitable backlash that followed it. A sonneteer of great skill and a blithe spirit of much charm, she was able to "put chaos into fourteen lines."

If I should learn, in some quite casual way

If I should learn, in some quite casual way,
    That you were gone, not to return again —
Read from the back-page of a paper, say,
    Held by a neighbor in a subway train,
How at the corner of this avenue
    And such a street (so are the papers filled)
A hurrying man, who happened to be you,
    At noon to-day had happened to be killed —
I should not cry aloud — I could not cry
    Aloud, or wring my hands in such a place —
I should but watch the station lights rush by
    With a more careful interest on my face;
Or raise my eyes and read with greater care
Where to store furs and how to treat the hair.

1917

First Fig

My candle burns at both ends;
  It will not last the night;
But ah, my foes, and oh, my friends —
  It gives a lovely light!

1920

Pity me not because the light of day

Pity me not because the light of day
At close of day no longer walks the sky;
Pity me not for beauties passed away

From field and thicket as the year goes by;
Pity me not the waning of the moon,
Nor that the ebbing tide goes out to sea,
Nor that a man's desire is hushed so soon,
And you no longer look with love on me.
This have I known always: Love is no more
Than the wide blossom which the wind assails,
Than the great tide that treads the shifting shore,
Strewing fresh wreckage gathered in the gales:
Pity me that the heart is slow to learn
What the swift mind beholds at every turn.

1923

What lips my lips have kissed, and where, and why

What lips my lips have kissed, and where, and why,
I have forgotten, and what arms have lain
Under my head till morning; but the rain
Is full of ghosts tonight, that tap and sigh
Upon the glass and listen for reply,
And in my heart there stirs a quiet pain
For unremembered lads that not again
Will turn to me at midnight with a cry.
Thus in the winter stands the lonely tree,
Nor knows what birds have vanished one by one,
Yet knows its boughs more silent than before:
I cannot say what loves have come and gone,
I only know that summer sang in me
A little while, that in me sings no more.

1923

Love is not all: it is not meat nor drink

Love is not all: it is not meat nor drink
Nor slumber nor a roof against the rain;
Nor yet a floating spar to men that sink
And rise and sink and rise and sink again;
Love can not fill the thickened lung with breath,
Nor clean the blood, nor set the fractured bone;
Yet many a man is making friends with death
Even as I speak, for lack of love alone.
It well may be that in a difficult hour,
Pinned down by pain and moaning for release,
Or nagged by want past resolution's power,

I might be driven to sell your love for peace,
Or trade the memory of this night for food.
It well may be. I do not think I would.

1931

Rendezvous

Not for these lovely blooms that prank your chambers did I
 come. Indeed,
I could have loved you better in the dark;
That is to say, in rooms less bright with roses, rooms more
 casual, less aware
Of History in the wings about to enter with benevolent air
On ponderous tiptoe, at the cue "Proceed."
Not that I like the ash-trays over-crowded and the place in a mess,
Or the monastic cubicle too unctuously austere and stark,
But partly that these formal garlands for our Eighth Street
 Aphrodite are a bit too Greek,
And partly that to make the poor walls rich with our unaided
 loveliness
Would have been more *chic*.

Yet here I am, having told you of my quarrel with the taxi-driver
 over a line of Milton, and you laugh; and you are you,
 none other.
Your laughter pelts my skin with small delicious blows.
But I am perverse: I wish you had not scrubbed — with pumice,
 I suppose —
The tobacco stains from your beautiful fingers. And I wish I did
 not feel like your mother.

1939

SAMUEL GREENBERG (1893–1917)

Samuel Greenberg was born in Vienna. His devoutly Jewish family emigrated to America when the boy was seven. He grew up on the Lower East Side of Manhattan, dropping out of school in the seventh grade to work twelve-hour days in factories. Greenberg developed tuberculosis in 1913 and wrote reams of poetry in the hospital. His poems might not have survived had Hart Crane not liked several of them enough to copy them out. Crane's "Emblems of Conduct" is, in fact, a rewriting of Greenberg's "Conduct." Greenberg, the self-taught boy genius, died miserably at age 23.

East River's Charm

Is this the river East I heard? —
Where the ferries, tugs and sailboats stirred
And the reaching wharves from the inner land
Ourstretched, like the harmless receiving hand —

And the silvery tinge that sparkles aloud
Like brilliant white demons, which a tide has towed
From the rays of the morning sun
Which it doth ceaselessly shine upon.

But look at the depth of the drippling tide
That dripples, reripples like locusts astride;
As the boat turns upon the silvery spread
It leaves — strange — a shadow dead.

And the very charms from the reflective river
And from the stacks of the floating boat —
There seemeth the quality ne'er to dissever
Like the ruffles from the mystified smoke.

1913

Conduct

By a peninsula the painter sat and
Sketched the uneven valley groves.
The apostle gave alms to the
Meek. The volcano burst
In fusive sulphur and hurled
Rocks and ore into the air —
Heaven's sudden change at
The drawing tempestuous,
Darkening shade of dense clouded hues.
The wanderer soon chose
His spot of rest; they bore the
Chosen hero upon their shoulders,
Whom they strangely admired, as
The beach-tide summer of people desired.

c. 1915

The Glass Bubbles

The motion of gathering loops of water
Must either burst or remain in a moment.
The violet colors through the glass

Throw up little swellings that appear
And spatter as soon as another strikes
And is born; so pure are they of colored
Hues, that we feel the absent strength
Of its power. When they begin they gather
Like sand on the beach: each bubble
Contains a complete eye of water.

c. 1916

Dorothy Parker (1893–1967)

Dorothy Parker was born Dorothy Rothschild to a Scottish mother and a Jewish father. Celebrated for her acid tongue, urbane sophistication, and sometimes self-lacerating humor, Parker was the only female founding member of the Algonquin Round Table, that circle of writers and wits where she kept company with Robert Benchley, Robert Sherwood, James Thurber, George S. Kaufman, and Alexander Woolcott. She began contributing drama reviews and poems to the *New Yorker* in 1925 and became the magazine's book critic two years later. She wrote stories and plays and, in 1937, won an Academy Award for her part of the screenplay of *A Star Is Born*. For many years she lived in the Algonquin Hotel. "Miss Millay remains lyrically, of course far superior to Mrs. Parker," said the poet Genevieve Taggard. "But there are moods when Dorothy Parker is more acceptable, whiskey straight, not champagne." She died of a heart attack in New York City in 1967.

Résumé

Razors pain you;
Rivers are damp;
Acids stain you;
And drugs cause cramp.
Guns aren't lawful;
Nooses give;
Gas smells awful;
You might as well live.

1926

Unfortunate Coincidence

By the time you swear you're his,
   Shivering and sighing,
And he vows his passion is
   Infinite, undying —
Lady, make a note of this:
   One of you is lying.

1926

Observation

If I don't drive around the park,
I'm pretty sure to make my mark.
If I'm in bed each night by ten,
I may get back my looks again,
If I abstain from fun and such,
I'll probably amount to much,
But I shall stay the way I am,
Because I do not give a damn.

1926

News Item

Men seldom make passes
At girls who wear glasses.

1928

E. E. CUMMINGS (1894–1962)

Born in Cambridge, Massachusetts, E. E. Cummings was celebrated for his oddities of punctuation and his bias in favor of lowercase letters; he contended that English was the only language in which the pronoun "I" is written as a capital letter. Randall Jarrell wrote that "inexperienced or unwilling" readers of modern poetry feel towards Cummings's poems "the same gratitude that the gallery-goer feels when, his eyes blurred with corridors of analytical cubism, he comes into a little room full of the Pink and Blue periods of Picasso." But Jarrell also accused Cummings of complacency and lack of a tragic sense: "He has hidden his talent under a flower, and there it has gone on reproducing, by parthenogenesis, poem after poem after poem." Beneath the veneer of his modernity there beats a romantic heart, but Cummings is also capable of fierce satire, as in the poem beginning "next to of course god america i." In Cummings "the language emancipated itself from uppercase, danced around the page, called attention to its shapes, did nonphonetic tricks, made obscene jokes, and transcribed in literal phonemes the demotic sounds made by American speakers," Helen Vendler wrote in 1992.

All in green went my love riding

All in green went my love riding
on a great horse of gold
into the silver dawn.

four lean hounds crouched low and smiling
the merry deer ran before.

Fleeter be they than dappled dreams
the swift sweet deer
the red rare deer.

Four red roebuck at a white water
the cruel bugle sang before.

Horn at hip went my love riding
riding the echo down
into the silver dawn.

four lean hounds crouched low and smiling
the level meadows ran before.

Softer be they than slippered sleep
the lean lithe deer
the fleet flown deer.

Four fleet does at a gold valley
the famished arrow sang before.

Bow at belt went my love riding
riding the mountain down
into the silver dawn.

four lean hounds crouched low and smiling
the sheer peaks ran before.

Paler be they than daunting death
the sleek slim deer
the tall tense deer.

Four tall stags at a green mountain
the lucky hunter sang before.

All in green went my love riding
on a great horse of gold
into the silver dawn.

four lean hounds crouched low and smiling
my heart fell dead before.

Buffalo Bill's

Buffalo Bill's
defunct
            who used to
            ride a watersmooth-silver
                                                            stallion

and break onetwothreefourfive pigeonsjustlikethat
                                                                                    Jesus

he was a handsome man
                                                  and what i want to know is
how do you like your blueeyed boy
Mister Death

1923

"next to of course god america i"

"next to of course god america i
love you land of the pilgrims' and so forth oh
say can you see by the dawn's early my
country 'tis of centuries come and go
and are no more what of it we should worry
in every language even deafanddumb
thy sons acclaim your glorious name by gorry
by jingo by gee by gosh by gum
why talk of beauty what could be more beaut-
iful than these heroic happy dead
who rushed like lions to the roaring slaughter
they did not stop to think they died instead
then shall the voice of liberty be mute?"

He spoke. And drank rapidly a glass of water

1926

may i feel said he

may i feel said he
(i'll squeal said she
just once said he)
it's fun said she

(may i touch said he
how much said she
a lot said he)
why not said she

(let's go said he
not too far said she
what's too far said he
where you are said she)

may i stay said he
(which way said she

like this said he
if you kiss said she

may i move said he
is it love said she)
if you're willing said he
(but you're killing said she

but it's life said he
but your wife said she
now said he)
ow said she

(tiptop said he
don't stop said she
oh no said he)
go slow said she

(cccome?said he
ummm said she)
you're divine!said he
(you are Mine said she)

1935

the boys i mean are not refined

the boys i mean are not refined
they go with girls who buck and bite
they do not give a fuck for luck
they hump them thirteen times a night

one hangs a hat upon her tit
one carves a cross on her behind
they do not give a shit for wit
the boys i mean are not refined

they come with girls who bite and buck
who cannot read and cannot write
who laugh like they would fall apart
and masturbate with dynamite

the boys i mean are not refined
they cannot chat of that and this
they do not give a fart for art
they kill like you would take a piss

they speak whatever's on their mind
they do whatever's in their pants
they boys i mean are not refined
they shake the mountains when they dance

1935

anyone lived in a pretty how town

anyone lived in a pretty how town
(with up so floating many bells down)
spring summer autumn winter
he sang his didn't he danced his did.

Women and men(both little and small)
cared for anyone not at all
they sowed their isn't they reaped their same
sun moon stars rain

children guessed(but only a few
and down they forgot as up they grew
autumn winter spring summer)
that noone loved him more by more

when by now and tree by leaf
she laughed his joy she cried his grief
bird by snow and stir by still
anyone's any was all to her

someones married their everyones
laughed their cryings and did their dance
(sleep wake hope and then)they
said their nevers they slept their dream

stars rain sun moon
(and only the snow can begin to explain
how children are apt to forget to remember
with up so floating many bells down)

one day anyone died i guess
(and noone stooped to kiss his face)
busy folk buried them side by side
little by little and was by was

all by all and deep by deep
and more by more they dream their sleep
noone and anyone earth by april
wish by spirit and if by yes.

Women and men(both dong and ding)
summer autumn winter spring
reaped their sowing and went their came
sun moon stars rain

1940

my father moved through dooms of love

my father moved through dooms of love
through sames of am through haves of give,
singing each morning out of each night
my father moved through depths of height

this motionless forgetful where
turned at his glance to shining here;
that if(so timid air is firm)
under his eyes would stir and squirm

newly as from unburied which
floats the first who,his april touch
drove sleeping selves to swarm their fates
woke dreamers to their ghostly roots

and should some why completely weep
my father's fingers brought her sleep:
vainly no smallest voice might cry
for he could feel the mountains grow.

Lifting the valleys of the sea
my father moved through griefs of joy;
praising a forehead called the moon
singing desire into begin

joy was his song and joy so pure
a heart of star by him could steer
and pure so now and now so yes
the wrists of twilight would rejoice

keen as midsummer's keen beyond
conceiving mind of sun will stand,
so strictly(over utmost him
so hugely)stood my father's dream

his flesh was flesh his blood was blood:
no hungry man but wished him food;
no cripple wouldn't creep one mile
uphill to only see him smile.

Scorning the pomp of must and shall
my father moved through dooms of feel;
his anger was as right as rain
his pity was as green as grain

septembering arms of year extend
less humbly wealth to foe and friend
than he to foolish and to wise
offered immeasurable is

proudly and(by octobering flame
beckoned)as earth will downward climb,
so naked for immortal work
his shoulders marched against the dark

his sorrow was as true as bread:
no liar looked him in the head;
if every friend became his foe
he'd laugh and build a world with snow.

My father moved through theys of we,
singing each new leaf out of each tree
(and every child was sure that spring
danced when she heard my father sing)

then let men kill which cannot share,
let blood and flesh be mud and mire,
scheming imagine,passion willed,
freedom a drug that's bought and sold

giving to steal and cruel kind,
a heart to fear, to doubt a mind,
to differ a disease of same,
conform the pinnacle of am

though dull were all we taste as bright,
bitter all utterly things sweet,
maggoty minus and dumb death
all we inherit,all bequeath

and nothing quite so least as truth
— i say though hate were why men breathe —
because my father lived his soul
love is the whole and more than all

1940

plato told

plato told

him:he couldn't
believe it (jesus

told him;he
wouldn't believe
it)lao

tsze
certainly told
him, and general
(yes

mam)
sherman;
and even
(believe it
or

not)you
told him:i told
him;we told him
(he didn't believe it,no

sir)it took
a nipponized bit of
the old sixth

avenue
el;in the top of his head: to tell

him

1944

poem

l(a

le
af
fa

ll

s)
one
l

iness

1958

Charles Reznikoff (1894–1976)

Charles Reznikoff was born in Brooklyn and went to New York University Law School. He loved walking in the city, routinely covering five or six miles a day. His legal training enters his poetry, which sometimes resembles evidence or testimony, as in the volumes entitled *Testimony* (1965) and *Holocaust* (1975), which are based on court records. An Objectivist poet, he worked by example rather than by metaphor. His poems are sometimes anecdotal, sometimes epigrammatic, always rooted in Jewish moral seriousness and sometimes evincing a blend of gallows humor and streetwise sarcasm.

Beggar Woman

When I was four years old my mother led me to the park.
The spring sunshine was not too warm. The street was almost
  empty.
The witch in my fairy-book came walking along.
She stooped to fish some mouldy grapes out of the gutter.

1921

from *Testimony*

Outside the night was cold, the snow was deep
on sill and sidewalk; but in our kitchen
it was bright and warm.
I smelt the damp clothes
as my mother lifted them from the basket,
the pungent smell of melting wax
as she rubbed it on the iron,
and the good lasting smell of meat and potatoes
in the black pot that simmered on the stove.
The stove was so hot it was turning red.
My mother lifted the lid of the pot
to stir the roast with a long wooden spoon:
Father would not be home for another hour.
I tugged at her skirts. Tell me a story!

Once upon a time (the best beginning!)
there was a rich woman, a baroness, and a poor woman, a beggar.
The poor woman came every day to beg and every day
the rich woman gave her a loaf of bread
until the rich woman was tired of it.
I will put poison in the next loaf, she thought,
to be rid of her.
The beggar woman thanked the baroness for that loaf
and went to her hut,
but, as she was going through the fields,
she met the rich woman's son coming out of the forest.
"Hello, hello, beggar woman!" said the young baron,
"I have been away for three days hunting
and am very hungry.
I know you are coming from my mother's
and that she has given you a loaf of bread;
let me have it — she will give you another."
"Gladly, gladly," said the beggar woman,
and, without knowing it was poisoned, gave him the loaf.
But, as he went on, he thought, I am nearly home —
I will wait.
You may be sure that his mother was glad to see him,
and she told the maids to bring a cup of wine
and make his supper — quickly, quickly!
"I met the beggar woman," he said,
"and was so hungry I asked for the loaf you gave her."
"Did you eat it, my son?" the baroness whispered.
"No, I knew you had something better for me
than this dry bread."
She threw it right into the fire,
and every day, after that, gave the beggar woman a loaf
and never again tried to poison her.
So, my son, if you try to harm others,
you may only harm yourself.

And, Mother, if you are a beggar, sooner or later,
there is poison in your bread.

1941

The Bridge

In a cloud bones of steel.

1941

Te Deum

Not because of victories
I sing,

having none,
but for the common sunshine,
the breeze,
the largess of the spring.

Not for victory
but for the day's work done
as well as I was able;
not for a seat upon the dais
but at the common table.

1959

The Old Man

The fish has too many bones
and the watermelon too many seeds.

1969

Similes

Indifferent as a statue
to the slogan
scribbled on its pedestal.

The way an express train
snubs the passengers at a local station.

Like a notebook forgotten on the seat in the bus,
full of names, addresses and telephone numbers:
important no doubt, to the owner —
and of no interest whatever
to anyone else

Words like drops of water on a stove —
a hiss and gone.

1969

Epitaph

Not the five feet of water to your chin
but the inch above the tip of your nose.

1969

H. Phelps Putnam (1894–1948)

Howard Phelps Putnam was born in Allston, Massachusetts, and was educated at Phillips Exeter Academy and Yale. Edmund Wilson characterized Putnam as "fatally irresistible to women"; he was a "woman's ideal poet, attractive and unreliable." He had a relationship with the actress Katharine Hepburn, among others. Putnam's second book, *The Five Seasons* (1931), chronicled episodes in the life of the fictitious Bill Williams. In an earlier, vastly different version of "Bill Gets Burned," which appeared under the title "Bill and *Les Enfants Pendus*" (1927), three young men (one of them Putnam himself) hang by the neck, the tree is blossoming, and the city is identified as Boston. In the 1931 version given here, "Bill Gets Burned" is printed with Putnam's prose gloss: "There are many constituents of Hell, and one of them is that murky and defenseless sympathy into which Bill fell during his sojourn in that place." Gone from the later version are these lines: "He saw the smarter eunuchs learn the tricks / Of emulating minor anthropoids, / To pick up dollars for the organ-man, / And in their eyes he saw that they were sick."

Bill Gets Burned

Bill Williams was in Hell without a guide
And wandering around alone and cold,
Hoping for fires, for he said, "The name
Of Hell is not enough to keep the old
Place dignified without a flame."
Bill was a hero, so he wandered on.

Then, near a city, where the apartments thinned
To suburbs, and the trolley-cars
Moved jerkily along the oily street
By clustered corners selling drugs and meat
And real-estate and tailoring and tinned
Denatured food, and by the hutches where
The rabbits bred the images of God,
Bill found a playground near a school, and there
Erect against the dusk was raised a tree,
Not blossoming, a three-armed gallows-tree.
Its fruit was only this — one empty noose,
And on the other arms two women hung
Not quite alive and yet not very dead.
"Sweet Christ, what savagery," Bill said.

And then he saw there was a troubled girl
Standing beneath the rope which dangled loose
And reaching for it with her feverish hands.
She heard Bill's step. "Come, lift me up," she cried,
Her smile was like destructive drink, "I too
Will hang, I shall be sisterly.
There is no other way, and you
Are strong and maybe good and not so wise
As I — why, you might even hang with me."

And Bill was dazed; he spoke to one of them
Who hung. "Please, tortured lady, tell
This girl that she is mad in Hell."
Which woman had no guile and answered, "No,
I cannot say it. When he kept from me
My house, my lovely garden, and my child
I suffered much; but that was long ago."
She closed her honest eyes, her hand caressed
Her noose, she said, "Oh, excellent and mild
My pain that keeps my love for me."
Bill touched her other hand and found her rings
Were hot and seared his fingers horribly.

Bill nursed his hand and would have soothed his
mind,
When she, the other woman hanging there,
On whose exquisite face such great despair
Had walked as never came to Bill, said, "Boy,
They do not know, they have not been like me,
A prize producer of the race, a cow,
And served to a lusty male, to be a bed
And board and servant in his house;
For which my pay is sometimes puppy-love.
There are no flowers in Hell;
Instead of flowers each one a constant bell
Saying that time has gone and I am here,
Still young, my belly ripe with slavery.
And all this body once was like a soul,
And now my soul is only common flesh;
Thought after thought he undermined the frail
Delight, and in its place has given me
These nervous heats which are not passionate
But now most unavoidable are mine
And raise my blood to empty bawdiness."
"Enough," said Bill and closed her mouth with his,
Holding her swinging body to himself,
And murmured unheard pitying words beneath
The unlikely delicacy of his kiss.
Her hands caressed his head, her face became
Translucent with a small suffocated flame —
But suddenly was turned away from hope
And was not light; "No, go away," she said,
"For solace only tightens at my rope."

And Bill had found some fires in Hell;
His brain was scorched and all his flesh
Was cowardly with burns. And now
The female moon appeared, whose calendar
Is marked with blood, and lighted him away.
He left the unhung girl, forgetting her,

And took a taxi to the city where
He had a room engaged by telegraph,
And lay awake all night and suffered there.

1931

Sonnets to Some Sexual Organs

I

Female

Mother of Men, and bearded like a male;
Loose lips that smile and smile without a face;
Mistress of vision, paths which cannot fail,
If rightly trod, to save the human race —

O, queenly hole, it is most wisely done
That you like oracles are kept from sight
And only show yourself when one by one
Man's wits have to his blood lost their delight.

So, perfumed high and finely diapered
And coyly hidden in the fat of thighs,
You shall be mystic still, and your absurd
And empty grin shall mock no lover's eyes.

For love of you, for love of you, old hole,
Man made the dream of woman and her soul.

II

Male

O, ludicrous and pensive trinity;
O, jest dependent from the loins of man;
Symbolic pink and white futility,
From which let him escape who thinks he can —

Whether in throbbing hope you raise your head,
One-eyed and hatless, peering from the bush,
Or if you dangle melancholy dead,
A battered hose, long-punished in the push,

It matters not; you are the potent lord,
The hidden spinner of our magic schemes,
The master of the arts, the captain sword,
The source of all our attitudes and dreams.

You lead us, master, sniffing to the hunt,
In quest forever of the perfect cunt.

1971

Ship of State and Grandpa

Whitman is dead and his thought
Died with him in my youth: —
The tall people free and happy
In their love, the commanding crew,
Died and the ship slewed
With defeated sails, slatting
Into the old marsh where
Grandpa would always raise the duck.
So Grandpa shot the sail, being half
A blind man, hearing the sails
As if they were the wings of duck.

1971

Bessie Smith (1894–1937)

Bessie Smith was born in Chattanooga, Tennessee. She sang on street corners at the age of seven, and at eighteen she danced and sang on tour with Pa and Ma Rainey. In the 1920s, the "Empress of the Blues" was the highest-paid black artist in the country and could afford to purchase her own traveling railway car. In the 1930s, when interest in the blues waned, she had to relive some of the hardships of her youth. Bessie Smith wrote many of her blues and is credited with the authorship of "Empty Bed Blues" in the Library of America's two-volume anthology, *American Poetry: The Twentieth Century* (2000). There is, however, ample evidence to suggest that the song was written by J. C. Johnson (1896–1981), a pianist and songwriter not to be confused with James P. Johnson. (J. C. Johnson worked productively with Fats Waller and, in the late 1930s, with Chick Webb's band, in addition to writing songs that Bessie Smith recorded.) Smith's singing was a model and an inspiration for Billie Holiday. On 27 September 1937, she died in a car crash in Clarkesdale, Mississippi.

Empty Bed Blues

I woke up this mornin' with an awful achin' head
I woke up this mornin' with a awful achin' head
My new man had left me just a room and a empty bed

Bought me a coffee grinder, got the best one I could find
Bought me a coffee grinder, got the best one I could find
So he could grind my coffee, 'cause he had a brand new grind

He's a deep sea diver with a stroke that can't go wrong
He's a deep sea diver with a stroke that can't go wrong
He can touch the bottom and his wind holds out so long

He knows how to thrill me and he thrills me night and day
Lord, he knows how to thrill me, he thrills me night and day
He's got a new way of lovin' almost takes my breath away

Lord, he's got that sweet somethin', and I told my gal friend
Lou
He's got that sweet somethin', and I told my gal friend Lou
From the way she's ravin', she must have gone and tried it
too.

When my bed get empty, make me feel awful mean and blue
When my bed get empty, make me feel awful mean and blue
My springs are gettin' rusty, sleepin' single like I do

Bought him a blanket, pillow for his head at night
Bought him a blanket, pillow for his head at night
Then I bought him a mattress so he could lay just right

He came home one evening with his spirit way up high
He came home one evening with his spirit way up high
What he had to give me made me wring my hands and cry

He give me a lesson that I never had before
He give me a lesson that I never had before
When he got through teachin' me, from my elbow down was
sore

He boiled my first cabbage and he made it awful hot
He boiled my first cabbage and he made it awful hot
Then he put in the bacon, it overflowed the pot

When you get good lovin', never go and spread the news
Yeah, it will double cross you and leave you with them empty
bed blues.

1928

JEAN TOOMER (1894–1967)

Jean Toomer was born and raised in Washington, D.C. Married twice, in each case to a white woman, the light-skinned black man passed as white for certain periods in his life. It has been argued that his "ambivalence toward his blackness" was the crucial element in his work and life, although his most enduring achievement, *Cane* (1923), may be read as an affirmation of his identity as a black man. About the people and landscape of Georgia, *Cane* consists of stories and sketches with poems and prose poems interspersed and concludes with a one-act play. Commenting on "Georgia Dusk," Robert Pinsky praises "the richness of old pentameter eloquence made richer by the untamed, cane-lipped genius of the specific American place, the sexual, heavily atmospheric silence that settles, in a brilliant image, like pollen."

November Cotton Flower

Boll-weevil's coming, and the winter's cold,
Made cotton-stalks look rusty, seasons old,
And cotton, scarce as any southern snow,
Was vanishing; the branch, so pinched and slow,
Failed in its function as the autumn rake;
Drouth fighting soil had caused the soil to take
All water from the streams; dead birds were found
In wells a hundred feet below the ground —
Such was the season when the flower bloomed.
Old folks were startled, and it soon assumed
Significance. Superstition saw
Something it had never seen before:
Brown eyes that loved without a trace of fear,
Beauty so sudden for that time of year.

1923

Beehive

Within this black hive to-night
There swarm a million bees;
Bees passing in and out the moon,
Bees escaping out the moon,
Bees returning through the moon,
Silver bees intently buzzing,
Silver honey dripping from the swarm of bees
Earth is a waxen cell of the world comb,
And I, a drone,
Lying on my back,
Lipping honey,
Getting drunk with silver honey,
Wish that I might fly out past the moon
And curl forever in some far-off farmyard flower.

1923

Reapers

Black reapers with the sound of steel on stones
Are sharpening scythes. I see them place the hones

In their hip-pockets as a thing that's done,
And start their silent swinging, one by one.
Black horses drive a mower through the weeds,
And there, a field rat, startled, squealing bleeds,
His belly close to ground. I see the blade,
Blood-stained, continue cutting weeds and shade.

1923

Georgia Dusk

The sky, lazily disdaining to pursue
  The setting sun, too indolent to hold
  A lengthened tournament for flashing gold,
Passively darkens for night's barbecue,

A feast of moon and men and barking hounds,
  An orgy for some genius of the South
  With blood-hot eyes and cane-lipped scented mouth,
Surprised in making folk-songs from soul sounds.

The sawmill blows its whistle, buzz-saws stop,
  And silence breaks the bud of knoll and hill,
  Soft settling pollen where plowed lands fulfill
Their early promise of a bumper crop.

Smoke from the pyramidal sawdust pile
  Curls up, blue ghosts of trees, tarrying low
  Where only chips and stumps are left to show
The solid proof of former domicile.

Meanwhile, the men, with vestiges of pomp,
  Race memories of king and caravan,
  High-priests, an ostrich, and a juju-man,
Go singing through the footpaths of the swamp.

Their voices rise . . . the pine trees are guitars,
  Strumming, pine-needles fall like sheets of rain . . .
  Their voices rise . . . the chorus of the cane
Is caroling a vesper to the stars . . .

O singers, resinous and soft your songs
  Above the sacred whisper of the pines,
  Give virgin lips to cornfield concubines,
Bring dreams of Christ to dusky cane-lipped throngs.

1923

The Gods Are Here

This is no mountain
But a house,
No rock of solitude
But a family chair,
No wilds
But life appearing
As life anywhere domesticated,
Yet I know the gods are here,
And that if I touch them
I will arise
And take majesty into the kitchen.

1939

MARK VAN DOREN (1894–1972)

The poet and Columbia professor Mark Van Doren was born in Hope, Illinois, a place "hard to find in any atlas" — Van Doren wrote in his *Autobiography* in 1958 — "though it still exists as Faith and Charity, its sister villages named a century ago, do not." At Columbia his students included Louis Zukofsky, John Berryman, Allen Ginsberg, John Hollander, Richard Howard, and Louis Simpson, to name only those poets represented in this volume; Jack Kerouac quit the Columbia football team and took up literature after getting an A in Van Doren's Shakespeare course. Van Doren put his genius into his teaching, which informs his great critical books *Shakespeare* (1939) and *The Noble Voice* (1946), the latter a study of epic poems by such as Homer, Virgil, Dante, Milton, Wordsworth, and Byron.

My Brother Lives Too Far Away

My brother lives too far away
For me to see him when I would;
Which is now; is every day;
Is always, always; so I say
When I remember our boyhood.

So close together, long ago,
And he the one that knew me best;
He the one that loved me so,
Himself was nothing; this I know
Too late for my own love to rest.

It runs to tell him I have learned
At last the secret: he was I.
And still he is, though the time has turned

Us back to back, and age has burned
This difference in us till we die.

1973

Orbit

The silence of it takes my breath,
Considering, believing; blinds
My eyes, that cannot hope to see
Six hundred million miles ahead
To where I'll be twelve months from now —
Here, only here, but oh, meanwhile
The necessary swiftness of it
Dizzies me; the smoothness, too,
As of a perfect engine rounding
Curve on curve then straight away
As if forever; yet not so,
For the swinging is incessant — soft
The turning, light the going, slow
The moving after all, if seen
From nowhere: thistledown, suspended,
Floating come to rest in my
Own mind that cannot feel or hear
The wind — there is no wind — O endless
World out there, O emptiness,
Receive the roundness that I ride on,
Save it, save it, as you save
The sun its master, save the circling,
Let the speed of it not falter,
Let the swiftness not diminish,
Though the terror of it slay me.

1973

LOUISE BOGAN (1897–1970)

Louise Bogan was born in Livermore Falls, Maine, the daughter of a mill-town foreman. Her childhood memories of her parents' quarrels and her mother's frequent absences troubled her. For thirty-eight years beginning in 1931, she reviewed poetry regularly for the *New Yorker*. An astringent critic, she despised the confessional aesthetic of the 1960s and had a limited tolerance for surrealism, but was warmly supportive of such poets as Theodore Roethke, to whom she wrote in 1935: "The difficulty with you now, as I see it, is that you are afraid to suffer, or to feel in any way. And that is what you'll have to get over, lamb pie, before you can toss off the masterpieces." Bogan's *Achievement in American Poetry* (1951) succinctly tells how American poetry changed in the first half of the twentieth century. Her own poems are characteristically melancholy in tone, fastidious of craft. "Evening in the Sanitarium," written in imitation of

Auden, draws on her experience of being hospitalized for a nervous breakdown. Marianne Moore wrote that "Louise Bogan's art is compactness compacted."

Last Hill in a Vista

Come, let us tell the weeds in ditches
How we are poor, who once had riches,
And lie out in the sparse and sodden
Pastures that the cows have trodden,
The while an autumn night seals down
The comforts of the wooden town.

Come, let us counsel some cold stranger
How we sought safety, but loved danger.
So, with stiff walls about us, we
Chose this more fragile boundary:
Hills, where light poplars, the firm oak,
Loosen into a little smoke.

1922

Juan's Song

When beauty breaks and falls asunder
I feel no grief for it, but wonder.
When love, like a frail shell, lies broken,
I keep no chip of it for token.
I never had a man for friend
Who did not know that love must end.
I never had a girl for lover
Who could discern when love was over.
What the wise doubt, the fool believes —
Who is it, then, that love deceives?

1923

Men Loved Wholly Beyond Wisdom

Men loved wholly beyond wisdom
Have the staff without the banner.
Like a fire in a dry thicket
Rising within women's eyes
Is the love men must return.
Heart, so subtle now, and trembling,
What a marvel to be wise,
To love never in this manner!
To be quiet in the fern
Like a thing gone dead and still,

Listening to the prisoned cricket
Shake its terrible, dissembling
Music in the granite hill.

1923

Winter Swan

It is a hollow garden, under the cloud;
Beneath the heel a hollow earth is turned;
Within the mind the live blood shouts aloud;
Under the breast the willing blood is burned,
Shut with the fire passed and the fire returned.
But speak, you proud!
Where lies the leaf-caught world once thought abiding,
Now but a dry disarray and artifice?
Here, to the ripple cut by the cold, drifts this
Bird, the long throat bent back, and the eyes in hiding.

1929

*Evening in the Sanitarium**

The free evening fades, outside the windows fastened
with decorative iron grilles.
The lamps are lighted; the shades drawn; the nurses
are watching a little.
It is the hour of the complicated knitting on the safe
bone needles; of the games of anagrams and bridge;
The deadly game of chess; the book held up like a mask.

The period of the wildest weeping, the fiercest delusion, is
over.
The women rest their tired half-healed hearts; they are
almost well.
Some of them will stay almost well always: the blunt-faced
woman whose thinking dissolved
Under academic discipline; the manic-depressive girl
Now leveling off; one paranoiac afflicted with jealousy.
Another with persecution. Some alleviation has been
possible.

O fortunate bride, who never again will become elated
after childbirth!
O lucky older wife, who has been cured of feeling
unwanted!
To the suburban railway station you will return, return,
To meet forever Jim home on the 5:35.
You will be again as normal and selfish and heartless as
anybody else.

There is life left: the piano says it with its octave smile.
The soft carpets pad the thump and splinter of the suicide
to be.
Everything will be splendid: the grandmother will not
drink habitually.
The fruit salad will bloom on the plate like a bouquet
And the garden produce the blue-ribbon aquilegia.
The cats will be glad; the fathers feel justified; the
mothers relieved.
The sons and husbands will no longer need to pay the
bills.
Childhoods will be put away, the obscene nightmare
abated.

At the ends of the corridors the baths are running.
Mrs. C. again feels the shadow of the obsessive idea.
Miss R. looks at the mantel-piece, which must mean
something.

*This poem was originally published with the subtitle "Imitated from Auden."

1938

JOHN WHEELWRIGHT (1897–1940)

Born in Milton, Massachusetts, John Wheelwright was a Boston Brahmin, a dandy and an eccentric, characteristically attired in top hat and tails and raccoon coat. He joined the Socialist Labor Party and, as Ron Horning notes, published his first book *Rock and Shell* in 1933 "at a time when similarities between the sacrament of communion and the ritual of the breadline, and between the persecution of a new faith and government-sanctioned strike-beating, would be apparent even to readers who weren't steeped in Marxist doctrine and the history of primitive Christianity." Still, it was Wheelwright's less tendentious poems that held the greatest appeal for such of his admirers as John Ashbery, who has written appreciatively of the poet's humor, satire, and "peculiarly elliptical turn of mind which convolutes and compresses clarities to the point of opacity." Wheelwright was killed by a drunken driver at the intersection of Massachusetts Avenue and Beacon Street in Boston in 1940.

Why Must You Know?

for Ethel Ripley Thayer

— "What was that sound we heard
fall on the snow?"
— "It was a frozen bird.
Why must you know?
All the dull earth knows the good
that the air, with claws and wings
tears to the scattered questionings

which burn in fires of our blood."
— "Let the air's beak and claws
   carry my deeds
far, where no springtime thaws
   the frost for their seeds."
— "One could fathom every sound
that the circling blood can tell
who heard the diurnal syllable,
while lying close against the ground."
— "My flesh, bone and sinew
   now would discern
hidden waters in you
   Earth, waters that burn."
— "One who turns to earth again
finds solace in its weight; and deep
hears the blood forever keep
the silence between drops of rain."

1933

Would You Think?

for Ethel Ripley Thayer

Does the sound or the silence make
music? When no ripples pass
over watery trees; like painted glass
lying beneath a quiet lake;
   would you think the real forest lay
   only in the reflected
   trees, which are protected
   by non-existence from the air of day?
Our blood gives voice to earth and shell,
they speak but in refracted sounds.
The silence of the dead resounds,
but what they say we cannot tell.
   Only echoes of what they taught
   are heard by living ears.
   The tongue tells what it hears
   and drowns the silence which the dead besought.
The questioning, circumambient light
the answering, luminiferous doubt
listen, and whisper it about
until the mocking stars turn bright.
   Tardy flowers have bloomed long
   but they have long been dead.
   Now on the ice, like lead
   hailstones drop loud, with a rattlesnake's song.

1933

There Is No Opera Like "Lohengrin"

But one Apocalyptic Lion's whelp (in flesh
called William Lyon Phelps) purrs: After all,
there is no opera like "Lohengrin"!
My father, a Baptist preacher, a good man,
is now with God — and every day is Christmas.
Apart from questions of creative genius,
there are no gooder men than our good writers.
Lyman Abbott and I, who never can read Dante,
still find cathedrals beautifully friendly.
Hell is O.K.; Purgatory bores me; Heaven's dull.
There is no opera like "Lohengrin"!
Miss Lulu Bett's outline is a Greek statue.
Augustus Thomas' "Witching Hour"'s a masterpiece;
Housman's Second Volume is a masterpiece;
Anglo-Americans well know Ollivant's
masterpiece, "Bob, Son of Battle," that masterpiece!
There is no opera like "Lohengrin"!
In verse, these masterpieces are worth reading:
"The Jar of Dreams," by Lilla Cabot Perry;
"Waves of Unrest," by Bernice Lesbia Kenyon.
(O Charlotte Endymion Porter! Percy Bysshe Shelley?
Helen Archibald Clark! O women with three names!)
Ann Hempstead Branch read all the Bible
through in a few days. Speaking of Milton,
bad manners among critics are too common,
but gentlemen should not grow obsolete.
Often we fall asleep — not when we're bored,
but when we think we are most interesting.
There is no opera like "Lohengrin"!
I sometimes think there are no persons who
can do more good than good librarians can.
American books grow easier to hold;
dull paper and light weight is the ideal.

1939

Train Ride

for Horace Gregory

After rain, through afterglow, the unfolding fan
of railway landscape sidled on the pivot
of a larger arc into the green of evening;
I remembered that noon I saw a gradual bud
still white; though dead in its warm bloom;
always the enemy is the foe at home.
    And I wondered what surgery could recover
our lost, long stride of indolence and leisure

which is labor in reverse; what physic recall the smile
not of lips, but of eyes as of the sea bemused.
    We, when we disperse from common sleep to several
tasks, we gather to despair; we, who assembled
once for hopes from common toil to dreams
or sickish and hurting or triumphal rapture;
always our enemy is our foe at home.
    We, deafened with far scattered city rattles
to the hubbub of forest birds (never having
"had time" to grieve or to hear through vivid sleep
the sea knock on its cracked and hollow stones)
so that the stars, almost, and birds comply,
and the garden-wet; the trees retire; We are
a scared patrol, fearing the guns behind;
always the enemy is the foe at home
    What wonder that we fear our own eyes' look
and fidget to be at home alone, and pitifully
put off age by some change in brushing the hair
and stumble to our ends like smothered runners at their tape;
    We follow our shreds of fame into an ambush.

    Then (as while the stars herd to the great trough
the blind, in the always-only-outward of their dismantled
archways, awake at the smell of warmed stone
or to the sound of reeds, lifting from the dim
into their segment of green dawn) *always*
our enemy is our foe at home, more
certainly than through spoken words or from grief-
twisted writing on paper, unblotted by tears
the thought came:
                    There is no physic
for the world's ill, nor surgery; it must
(hot smell of tar on wet salt air)
burn in a fever forever, an incense pierced
with arrows, whose name is Love and another name
Rebellion (the twinge, the gulf, split seconds,
the very raindrop, render, and instancy
of Love).
    All Poetry to this not-to-be-looked-upon sun
of Passion is the moon's cupped light; all
Politics to this moon, a moon's reflected
cupped light, like the moon of Rome, after
the deep wells of Grecian light sank low;
always the enemy is the foe at home.
    But these three are friends whose arms twine
without words; as, in a still air,
the great grove leans to wind, past and to come.

1940

A Poem by David McCord

A poem by David McCord from the Boston Transcript
deals with Orson Welles' radio War between the Worlds,
during which the Communists (no doubt) placed their hopes
upon a pact of Collective Security
with the hidden face of the moon:
The original author of that radio play (H. G. Wells) washed his hands
surgically clean
from the social repercussions of his imaginative conception.
Bernard Shaw would not have done so.
He would have risen to such an occasion had it been given him.

Americans are still a nation of boobs (he might have said).
But Americans are more sophisticated than any other Europeans.
The so-called Europeans
who have been duped out of a United States of Europe
abandoned themselves to the delights of a war scare
under the blandishments of fact. But the dupes of the United States
of America, that land of hoax, that nation of kidders,
remained calm through the fact, and took fright
only from the creative imagination. I devoutly hope
that your great President Roosevelt
who is good enough at acting to engage in drama
will not take his cue from this experience.

But I despair to approximate the wit of a Bernard Shaw
and seek refuge in David McCord's poem from the Boston Transcript.

1940

STEPHEN VINCENT BENET (1898–1943)

Stephen Vincent Benet was born in Bethlehem, Pennsylvania, the son of an Army colonel and the grandson of a brigadier general. He won the Pulitzer Prize twice and chose, as judge of the Yale Younger Poets Series, the first books by James Agee and Muriel Rukeyser. (His brother William Rose Benet, who married Elinor Wylie, also won a Pulitzer.) Stephen Vincent Benet remains best known perhaps for his story "The Devil and Daniel Webster." When World War II began, he wrote radio scripts — *They Burned the Books, Your Army, Dear Adolf* — to further the U.S. war effort.

American Names

I have fallen in love with American names,
The sharp names that never get fat,
The snakeskin-titles of mining-claims,
The plumed war-bonnet of Medicine Hat,
Tucson and Deadwood and Lost Mule Flat.

Seine and Piave are silver spoons,
But the spoonbowl-metal is thin and worn,
There are English counties like hunting-tunes
Played on the keys of a postboy's horn,
But I will remember where I was born.

I will remember Carquinez Straits,
Little French Lick and Lundy's Lane,
The Yankee ships and the Yankee dates
And the bullet-towns of Calamity Jane.
I will remember Skunktown Plain.

I will fall in love with a Salem tree
And a rawhide quirt from Santa Cruz,
I will get me a bottle of Boston sea
And a blue-gum nigger to sing me blues.
I am tired of loving a foreign muse.

Rue des Martyrs and Bleeding-Heart-Yard,
Senlis, Pisa, and Blindman's Oast,
It is a magic ghost you guard
But I am sick for a newer ghost,
Harrisburg, Spartanburg, Painted Post.

Henry and John were never so
And Henry and John were always right?
Granted, but when it was time to go
And the tea and the laurels had stood all night,
Did they never watch for Nantucket Light?

I shall not rest quiet in Montparnasse.
I shall not lie easy at Winchelsea.
You may bury my body in Sussex grass,
You may bury my tongue at Champmédy.
I shall not be there. I shall rise and pass.
Bury my heart at Wounded Knee.

1927

MELVIN B. TOLSON (1898–1966)

Melvin B. Tolson was born in Moberly, Missouri, the eldest son of a Methodist preacher. His first published poem, about the sinking of the *Titanic*, appeared in an Iowa newspaper when Tolson was fourteen. In 1947, he was named poet laureate of Liberia and wrote *Libretto for the Republic of Liberia* to celebrate the centennial of the small African republic founded by freed American slaves. He called for a "New Negro Poetry" suitable to the modern "age of T. S. Eliot." He also said, wryly, "My poetry is of the proletariat, by the proletariat, and for the bourgeoisie." *Harlem Gallery* was published in 1965, a year before Tolson died of an abdominal cancer.

Sootie Joe

The years had rubbed out his youth,
But his fellows ranked him still
As a chimney sweep without a peer . . .
Whether he raced a weighted corset
Up and down the throat of a freakish flue,
Or, from a chair of rope,
His eyes goggled and his mouth veiled,
He wielded his scraping knife
Through the walled-in darkness.

The soot from ancient chimneys
Had wormed itself into his face and hands.
The four winds had belabored the grime on him.
The sun had trifled with his ebony skin
And left ashen spots.

Sometimes Sootie Joe's wealthy customers
Heard his singing a song that gave them pause:

I's a chimney sweeper, a chimney sweeper,
I's black as the blackest night.
I's a chimney sweeper, a chimney sweeper,
And the world don't treat me right.
But somebody hasta black hisself
For somebody else to stay white.

1935

Mu (from *Harlem Gallery*)

Hideho Heights
and I, like the brims of old hats,
slouched at a sepulchered table in the Zulu Club.
Frog Legs Lux and his Indigo Combo
spoke with tongues that sent their devotees
out of this world!

Black and brown and yellow fingers flashed,
like mirrored sunrays of a heliograph,
on clarinet and piano keys, on cornet valves.

Effervescing like acid on limestone,
Hideho said:
"O White Folks, O Black Folks,
the dinosaur imagined its extinction meant
the death of the piss ants."

Cigarette smoke
— opaque veins in Carrara marble —
magicked the habitués into
humoresques and grotesques.
Lurid lights
spraying African figures on the walls
ecstasied maids and waiters,
pickups and stevedores —
with delusions
of Park Avenue grandeur.

Once, twice,
Hideho sneaked a swig.
"On the house," he said, proffering the bottle
as he lorded it under the table.
Glimpsing the harpy eagle at the bar,
I grimaced,
"I'm not the house snake of the Zulu Club."

A willow of a woman,
bronze as knife money,
executed, near our table, the Lenox Avenue Quake.
Hideho winked at me and poked
that which
her tight Park Avenue skirt vociferously advertised.
Peacocking herself, she turned like a ballerina,
her eyes blazing drops of rum on a crêpe suzette.
"Why, you —"
A sanitary decree, I thought. "Don't *you* me!" he fumed.
The lips of a vixen exhibited a picadill flare.
"*What* you smell isn't cooking," she said.
Hideho sniffed.
"Chanel No. 5," he scoffed,
"from Sugar Hill."
I laughed and clapped him on the shoulder.
"A bad metaphor, *poet*."
His jaws closed
like an alligator squeezer.
"She's a willow," I emphasized,
"a willow by a cesspool."
Hideho mused aloud,
"Do I hear The Curator rattle Eliotic bones?"

Out of the Indigo Combo
flowed rich and complex polyrhythms.
Like surfacing bass,
exotic swells and softening
of the veld vibrato
emerged.

. . .

Was that Snakehips Briskie
gliding out of the aurora australis of the Zulu Club
into the kaleidoscopic circle?

. . .

Etnean gasps!
Vesuvian acclamations!

. . .

Snakehips poised himself—
Giovanni Gabrieli's
Single violin against his massed horns.

. . .

The silence of the revelers was the arrested
hemorrhage of an artery
grasped by bull forceps.
I felt Hideho's breath against my ear.
"The penis act in the Garden of Eden," he confided.

. . .

Convulsively, unexampledly,
Snakehips' body and soul
began to twist and untwist like a gyrating rawhide—
began to coil, to writhe
like a prismatic-hued python
in the throes of copulation.

Eyes bright as the light
at Eddystone Rock,
an ebony Penthesilea
grabbed her tiger's-eye yellow-brown
beanpole Sir Testiculus of the evening
and gave him an Amazonian hug.
He wilted in her arms
like a limp morning-glory.
"The Zulu Club is in the groove," chanted Hideho,
"and the cats, the black cats, are *gone!*"

In the *ostinato*
of stamping feet and clapping hands,
the Promethean bard of Lenox Avenue became a
lost loose-leaf
as memory vignetted

Rabelaisian I's of the Boogie-Woogie dynasty
in barrel houses, at rent parties,
on riverboats, at wakes:
The Toothpick, Funky Five, and Tippling Tom!
Ma Rainey, Countess Willie V., and Aunt Harriet!
Speckled Red, Skinny Head Pete, and Stormy Weather!
Listen, Black Boy.
Did the High Priestess at 27 rue de Fleurus
assert, "The Negro suffers from nothingness"?
Hideho confided like a neophyte on the Walk,
"Jazz is the marijuana of the Blacks."
In the *tribulum* of dialectics, I juggled the idea;
then I observed,
"Jazz is the philosophers' egg of the Whites."

Hideho laughed from below the Daniel Boone rawhide belt
he'd redeemed, in a Dallas pawn shop,
with part of the black-market
loot set loose
in a crap game
by a Yangtze ex-coolie who,
in a Latin Quarter dive below Telegraph Hill,
out-Harvarded his Alma Mater.

. . .

Frog Legs Lux and his Indigo Combo
let go
with a wailing pedal point
that slid into
Basin Street Blues
like Ty Cobb stealing second base:
Zulu,
King of the Africans,
arrives on Mardi Gras morning;
the veld drum of Baby Dodds'
great-grandfather
in Congo Square
pancakes the first blue note
in a callithump of the USA.
And now comes the eve of Ash Wednesday.
Comus on parade!
All God's children revel
like a post-Valley Forge
charivari in Boston celebrating the nuptials of
a gay-old-dog minuteman with a lusty maid.

. . .

Just as
the bourgeois adopted
the lyric-winged piano of Liszt in the court at Weimar
for the solitude of his

aeried apartment,
Harlem chose
for its cold-water flat
the hot-blues corner of King Oliver
in his cart
under the
El pillars of the Loop.

. . .

The yanking fishing rod
of Hideho's voice
jerked me out of my bird's-foot voilet romanticism.
He mixed Shakespeare's image with his own
and caricatured me:
"Yonder Curator has a lean and hungry look;
he thinks too much.
Such blackmoors are dangerous to
the Great White World!"

. . .

With a dissonance
from the Weird Sisters,
the jazz diablerie
boiled down and away
in the vaccum pan
of the Indigo Combo.

1965

Leonie Adams (1899–1988)

Leonie Adams was born in Brooklyn. She entered Barnard College in 1917 and began writing poems in secret. Her most important books are *Those Not Elect* (1925) and *High Falcon* (1929). She and Hart Crane, born the same year, became friends; Crane's poem "The Broken Tower" can be viewed as his response to Adams's "Bell Tower," his favorite of her poems.

Magnificat in Little

I was enriched, not casting after marvels,
But as one walking in a usual place,
Without desert but common eyes and ears,
No recourse to hear, power but to see,
Got to love you of grace.

Subtle musicians, that could body wind,
Or contrive strings to anguish, in conceit

Random and artless strung a branch with bells,
Fixed in one silver whim, which at a touch
Shook and were sweet.

And you, you lovely and unpurchased note,
One run distraught, and vexing hot and cold
To give to the heart's poor confusion tongue,
By chance caught you, and henceforth all unlearned
Repeats you gold.

1929

The Horn

While coming to the feast I found
A venerable silver-throated horn,
Which were I brave enough to sound,
Then all, as from that moment born,
Would breathe the honey of this clime,
And three times merry in their time
Would praise the virtue of the horn.

The mist is risen like thin breath;
The young leaves of the ground smell chill,
So faintly are they strewn on death,
The road I came down a west hill;
But none can name as I can name
A little golden-bright thing, flame,
Since bones have caught their marrow chill.

And in a thicket passed me by,
In the black brush, a running hare,
Having a spectre in his eye,
That sped in darkness to the snare;
And who but I can know in pride
The heart, set beating in the side,
Has but the wisdom of a hare?

1929

The Figurehead

This that is washed with weed and pebblestone
Curved once a dolphin's length before the prow,
And I who read the land to which we bore
In its grave eyes, question my idol now,
What cold and marvelous fancy it may keep,
Since the salt terror swept us from our course,
Or if a wisdom later than the storm,

For old green ocean's tinctured it so deep;
And with some reason to me on this strand
The waves, the ceremonial waves have come
And stooped their barbaric heads, and all spread out
Their lovely arms before them, and are gone,
Leaving their murderous tribute on the sand.

1929

Bell Tower

I have seen, O desolate one, the voice has its tower,
The voice also, builded at secret cost,
Its temple of precious tissue. Not silent then
Forever — casting silence in your hour.

There marble boys are leant from the light throat,
Thick locks that hang with dew and eyes dewlashed,
Dazzled with morning, angels of the wind,
With ear a-point to the enchanted note.

And these at length shall tip the hanging bell,
And first the sound must gather in deep bronze,
Till, rarer than ice, purer than a bubble of gold,
It fill the sky to beat on an airy shell.

1929

Hart Crane (1899–1932)

Hart Crane was born in Garrettsville, Ohio, the son of a candy manufacturer who tried to dissuade him from writing poetry. Crane came to New York in 1916, moved there permanently in 1923, and lived in the Columbia Heights section of Brooklyn. From his building he could see a vista dominated by the Brooklyn Bridge: "It is everything from mountains to the walls of Jerusalem and Nineveh." He wrote *The Bridge* (1930) and other celebrated poems characterized by visionary intensity and an ecstatic lyricism. Densely packed and difficult to comprehend in any conventional sense, his work provides proof that the enjoyment of poetry precedes (and does not require) the understanding of it. Quizzed about his poems, Crane had ready answers. He wrote that his poem "For the Marriage of Faustus and Helen" is a "kind of fusion of our own time with the past. Almost every symbol of current significance is matched by a correlative, suggested or actually stated, 'of ancient days.' Helen the symbol of this abstract 'sense of beauty,' Faustus the symbol of myself, the poetic or imaginative man of all times. The street car device is the most concrete symbol I could find for the transition of the imagination from quotidian details to the universal consideration of beauty — the body still 'centered in traffic,' the imagination eluding its daily nets and self-consciousness." Volatile and self-destructive, Crane drank heavily. He committed suicide in 1932, at the age of thirty-three, by jumping from the deck of a steamship sailing back to New York from Mexico.

Emblems of Conduct

By a peninsula the wanderer sat and sketched
The uneven valley graves. While the apostle gave
Alms to the meek the volcano burst
With sulphur and aureate rocks . . .
For joy rides in stupendous coverings
Luring the living into spiritual gates.

Orators follow the universe
And radio the complete laws to the people.
The apostle conveys thought through discipline.
Bowls and cups fill historians with adorations, —
Dull lips commemorating spiritual gates.

The wanderer later chose this spot of rest
Where marble clouds support the sea
And where was finally borne a chosen hero.
By that time summer and smoke were past.
Dolphins still played, arching the horizons,
But only to build memories of spiritual gates.

1926

Chaplinesque

We make our meek adjustments,
Contented with such random consolations
As the wind deposits
In slithered and too ample pockets.

For we can still love the world, who find
A famished kitten on the step, and know
Recesses for it from the fury of the street,
Or warm torn elbow coverts.

We will sidestep, and to the final smirk
Dally the doom of that inevitable thumb
That slowly chafes its puckered index toward us,
Facing the dull squint with what innocence
And what surprise!

And yet these fine collapses are not lies
More than the pirouettes of any pliant cane;
Our obsequies are, in a way, no enterprise.
We can evade you, and all else but the heart:
What blame to us if the heart live on.

The game enforces smirks; but we have seen
The moon in lonely alleys make

A grail of laughter of an empty ash can,
And through all sound of gaiety and quest
Have heard a kitten in the wilderness.

1926

My Grandmother's Love Letters

There are no stars to-night
But those of memory.
Yet how much room for memory there is
In the loose girdle of soft rain.

There is even room enough
For the letters of my mother's mother,
Elizabeth,
That have been pressed so long
Into a corner of the roof
That they are brown and soft,
And liable to melt as snow.

Over the greatness of such space
Steps must be gentle.
It is all hung by an invisible white hair.
It trembles as birch limbs webbing the air.

And I ask myself:

"Are your fingers long enough to play
Old keys that are but echoes:
Is the silence strong enough
To carry back the music to its source
And back to you again
As though to her?"
Yet I would lead my grandmother by the hand
Through much of what she would not understand;
And so I stumble. And the rain continues on the roof
With such a sound of gently pitying laughter.

1926

Repose of Rivers

The willows carried a slow sound,
A sarabande the wind mowed on the mead.
I could never remember
That seething, steady leveling of the marshes
Till age had brought me to the sea.

Flags, weeds. And remembrance of steep alcoves
Where cypresses shared the noon's
Tyranny; they drew me into hades almost.
And mammoth turtles climbing sulphur dreams
Yielded, while sun-silt rippled them
Asunder . . .

How much I would have bartered! the black gorge
And all the singular nestings in the hills
Where beavers learn stitch and tooth.
The pond I entered once and quickly fled —
I remember now its singing willow rim.

And finally, in that memory all things nurse;
After the city that I finally passed
With scalding unguents spread and smoking darts
The monsoon cut across the delta
At gulf gates . . . There, beyond the dykes

I heard wind flaking sapphire, like this summer,
And willows could not hold more steady sound.

1926

At Melville's Tomb

Often beneath the wave, wide from this ledge
The dice of drowned men's bones he saw bequeath
An embassy. Their numbers as he watched,
Beat on the dusty shore and were obscured.

And wrecks passed without sound of bells,
The calyx of death's bounty giving back
A scattered chapter, livid hieroglyph,
The portent wound in corridors of shells.

Then in the circuit calm of one vast coil,
Its lashings charmed and malice reconciled,
Frosted eyes there were that lifted altars;
And silent answers crept across the stars.

Compass, quadrant and sextant contrive
No farther tides . . . High in the azure steeps
Monody shall not wake the mariner.
This fabulous shadow only the sea keeps.

1926

For the Marriage of Faustus and Helen

And so we may arrive by Talmud skill
And profane Greek to raise the building up
Of Helen's house against the Ismaelite,
King of Thogarma, and his habergeons
Brimstony, blue and fiery; and the force
Of king Abaddon, and the beast of Cittim;
Which Rabbi David Kimchi, Onkelos,
And Aben Ezra do interpret Rome.

— THE ALCHEMIST

I

The mind has shown itself at times
Too much the baked and labeled dough
Divided by accepted multitudes.
Across the stacked partitions of the day —
Across the memoranda, baseball scores,
The stenographic smiles and stock quotations
Smutty wings flash out equivocations.

The mind is brushed by sparrow wings;
Numbers, rebuffed by asphalt, crowd
The margins of the day, accent the curbs,
Convoying divers dawns on every corner
To druggist, barber and tobacconist,
Until the graduate opacities of evening
Take them away as suddenly to somewhere
Virginal perhaps, less fragmentary, cool.

There is the world dimensional for
those untwisted by the love of things
irreconcilable. . .

And yet, suppose some evening I forgot
The fare and transfer, yet got by that way
Without recall, — lost yet poised in traffic,
Then I might find your eyes across an aisle,
Still flickering with those prefigurations —
Prodigal, yet uncontested now,
Half-riant before the jerky window frame.

There is some way, I think, to touch
Those hands of yours that count the nights
Stippled with pink and green advertisements.
And now, before its arteries turn dark,
I would have you meet this bartered blood.
Imminent in his dream, none better knows
The white wafer cheek of love, or offers words
Lightly as moonlight on the eaves meets snow.

Reflective conversion of all things
At your deep blush, when ecstasies thread
The limbs and belly, when rainbows spread
Impinging on the throat and sides . . .
Inevitable, the body of the world
Weeps in inventive dust for the hiatus
That winks above it, bluet in your breasts.

The earth may glide diaphanous to death;
But if I lift my arms it is to bend
To you who turned away once, Helen, knowing
The press of troubled hands, too alternate
With steel and soil to hold you endlessly.
I meet you, therefore, in that eventual flame
You found in final chains, no captive then —
Beyond their million brittle, bloodshot eyes;
White, through white cities passed on to assume
That world which comes to each of us alone.

Accept a lone eye riveted to your plane,
Bent axle of devotion along companion ways
That beat, continuous, to hourless days —
One inconspicuous, glowing orb of praise.

II

Brazen hypnotics glitter here;
Glee shifts from foot to foot,
Magnetic to their tremolo.
This crashing opéra bouffe,
Blest excursion! this ricochet
From roof to roof —
Know, Olympians, we are breathless
While nigger cupids scour the stars!

A thousand light shrugs balance us
Through snarling hails of melody.
White shadows slip across the floor
Splayed like cards from a loose hand;
Rhythmic ellipses lead into canters
Until somewhere a rooster banters.

Greet naïvely — yet intrepidly
New soothings, new amazements
That cornets introduce at every turn —
And you may fall downstairs with me
With perfect grace and equanimity.
Or, plaintively scud past shores
Where, by strange harmonic laws
All relatives, serene and cool,
Sit rocked in patent armchairs.

O, I have known metallic paradises
Wher cuckoos clucked to finches
Above the deft catastrophes of drums.
While titters hailed the groans of death
Beneath gyrating awnings I have seen
The incunabula of the divine grotesque.
This music has a reassuring way.

The siren of the springs of guilty song —
Let us take her on the incandescent wax
Striated with nuances, nervosities
That we are heir to: she is still so young,
We cannot frown upon her as she smiles,
Dipping here in this cultivated storm
Among slim skaters of the gardened skies.

III

Capped arbiter of beauty in this street
That narrows darkly into motor dawn, —
You, here beside me, delicate ambassador
Of intricate slain numbers that arise
In whispers, naked of steel;
religious gunman!
Who faithfully, yourself, will fall too soon,
And in other ways than as the wind settles
On the sixteen thrifty bridges of the city:
Let us unbind our throats of fear and pity.

We even,
Who drove speediest destruction
In corymbulous formations of mechanics, —
Who hurried the hill breezes, spouting malice
Plangent over meadows, and looked down
On rifts of torn and empty houses
Like old women with teeth unjubilant
That waited faintly, briefly and in vain:

We know, eternal gunman, our flesh remembers
The tensile boughs, the nimble blue plateaus,
The mounted, yielding cities of the air!

That saddled sky that shook down vertical
Repeated play of fire — no hypogeum
Of wave or rock was good against one hour.

We did not ask for that, but have survived,
And will persist to speak again before
All stubble streets that have not curved
To memory, or known the ominous lifted arm

That lowers down the arc of Helen's brow
To saturate with blessing and dismay.

A goose, tobacco and cologne —
Three-winged and gold-shod prophecies of heaven,
The lavish heart shall always have to leaven
And spread with bells and voices, and atone
The abating shadows of our conscript dust.

Anchises' navel, dripping of the sea, —
The hands Erasmus dipped in gleaming tides,
Gathered the voltage of blown blood and vine;
Delve upward for the new and scattered wine,
O brother-thief of time, that we recall.
Laugh out the meager penance of their days
Who dare not share with us the breath released,
The substance drilled and spent beyond repair
For golden, or the shadow of gold hair.

Distinctly praise the years, whose volatile
Blamed bleeding hands extend and thresh the height
The imagination spans beyond despair,
Outpacing bargain, vocable and prayer.

1926

from *Voyages*

I

Above the fresh ruffles of the surf
Bright striped urchins flay each other with sand.
They have contrived a conquest for shell shucks,
And their fingers crumble fragments of baked weed
Gaily digging and scattering.

And in answer to their treble interjections
The sun beats lightning on the waves,
The waves fold thunder on the sand;
And could they hear me I would tell them:

O brilliant kids, frisk with your dog,
Fondle your shells and sticks, bleached
By time and the elements; but there is a line
You must not cross nor ever trust beyond it
Spry cordage of your bodies to caresses
Too lichen-faithful from too wide a breast.
The bottom of the sea is cruel.

II

— And yet this great wink of eternity,
Of rimless floods, unfettered leewardings,
Samite sheeted and processioned where
Her undinal vast belly moonward bends,
Laughing the wrapt inflections of our love;

Take this Sea, whose diapason knells
On scrolls of silver snowy sentences,
The sceptred terror of whose sessions rends
As her demeanors motion well or ill,
All but the pieties of lovers' hands.

And onward, as bells off San Salvador
Salute the crocus lustres of the stars,
In these poinsettia meadows of her tides, —
Adagios of islands, O my Prodigal,
Complete the dark confessions her veins spell.

Mark how her turning shoulders wind the hours,
And hasten while her penniless rich palms
Pass superscription of bent foam and wave, —
Hasten, while they are true, — sleep, death, desire,
Close round one instant in one floating flower.

Bind us in time, O Seasons clear, and awe.
O minstrel galleons of Carib fire,
Bequeath us to no earthly shore until
Is answered in the vortex of our grave
The seal's wide spindrift gaze toward paradise.

1926

from *The Bridge*

To Brooklyn Bridge

How many dawns, chill from his rippling rest
The seagull's wings shall dip and pivot him,
Shedding white rings of tumult, building high
Over the chained bay waters Liberty —

Then, with inviolate curve, forsake our eyes
As apparitional as sails that cross
Some page of figures to be filed away;
— Till elevators drop us from our day . . .

I think of cinemas, panoramic sleights
With multitudes bent toward some flashing scene
Never disclosed, but hastened to again,
Foretold to other eyes on the same screen;

And Thee, across the harbor, silver-paced
As though the sun took step of thee, yet left
Some motion ever unspent in thy stride, —
Implicitly thy freedom staying thee!

Out of some subway scuttle, cell or loft
A bedlamite speeds to thy parapets,
Tilting there momently, shrill shirt ballooning,
A jest falls from the speechless caravan.

Down Wall, from girder into street noon leaks,
A rip-tooth of the sky's acetylene;
All afternoon the cloud-flown derricks turn . . .
Thy cables breathe the North Atlantic still.

And obscure as that heaven of the Jews,
Thy guerdon . . . Accolade thou dost bestow
Of anonymity time cannot raise:
Vibrant reprieve and pardon thou dost show.

O harp and altar, of the fury fused,
(How could mere toil align thy choiring strings!)
Terrific threshold of the prophet's pledge,
Prayer of pariah, and the lover's cry, —

Again the traffic lights that skim thy swift
Unfractioned idiom, immaculate sigh of stars,
Beading thy path — condense eternity:
And we have seen night lifted in thine arms.

Under thy shadow by the piers I waited;
Only in darkness is thy shadow clear.
The City's fiery parcels all undone,
Already snow submerges an iron year . . .

O Sleepless as the river under thee,
Vaulting the sea, the prairies' dreaming sod,
Unto us lowliest sometime sweep, descend
And of the curveship lend a myth to God.

The Harbor Dawn

400 years and more . . . or is it from the soundless shore of sleep that time

Insistently through sleep — a tide of voices —
They meet you listening midway in your dream,
The long, tired sounds, fog-insulated noises:
Gongs in white surplices, beshrouded wails,
Far strum of fog horns . . . signals dispersed in veils.

And then a truck will lumber past the wharves
As winch engines begin throbbing on some deck;
Or a drunken stevedore's howl and thud below
Comes echoing alley-upward through dim snow.

And if they take your sleep away sometimes
They give it back again. Soft sleeves of sound
Attend the darkling harbor, the pillowed bay;
Somewhere out there in blankness steam

Spills into steam, and wanders, washed away
— Flurried by keen fifings, eddied
Among distant chiming buoys — adrift. The sky,
Cool feathery fold, suspends, distills
This wavering slumber . . . Slowly —
Immemorially the window, the half-covered chair,
Ask nothing but this sheath of pallid air.

recalls you to your love, there in a waking dream to merge your seed

And you beside me, blessèd now while sirens
Sing to us, stealthily weave us into day —
Serenely now, before day claims our eyes
Your cool arms murmurously about me lay.

While myriad snowy hands are clustering at
the panes —

your hands within my hands are deeds;
my tongue upon your throat — singing
arms close; eyes wide, undoubtful
dark
drink the dawn —
a forest shudders in your hair!

— with whom?

The window goes blond slowly. Frostily clears.
From Cyclopean towers across Manhattan waters
— Two — three bright window-eyes aglitter, disk

Who is the woman with us in the dawn? . . . whose is the flesh our feet have moved upon?

The sun, released — aloft with cold gulls hither.

The fog leans one last moment on the sill.
Under the misletoe of dreams, a star —
As though to join us at some distant hill —
Turns in the waking west and goes to sleep.

The River

. . . and past the din and slogans of the year —

Stick your patent name on a signboard
brother — all over — going west — young man
Tintex — Japalac — Certain-teed Overalls ads
and lands sakes! under the new playbill ripped
in the guaranteed corner — see Bert Williams what?
Minstrels when you steal a chicken just
save me the wing for if it isn't
Erie it ain't for miles around a
Mazda — and the telegraphic night coming on Thomas

a Ediford — and whistling down the tracks
a headlight rushing with the sound — can you
imagine — while an EXPRESS makes time like
SCIENCE — COMMERCE and the HOLYGHOST
RADIO ROARS IN EVERY HOME WE HAVE THE NORTHPOLE
WALLSTREET AND VIRGINBIRTH WITHOUT STONES OR
WIRES OR EVEN RUNning brooks connecting ears
and no more sermons windows flashing roar
Breathtaking — as you like it . . . eh?

So the 20th Century — so
whizzed the Limited — roared by and left
three men, still hungry on the tracks, ploddingly
watching the tail lights wizen and converge, slip-
ping gimleted and neatly out of sight.

*

to those whose addresses are never near

The last bear, shot drinking in the Dakotas
Loped under wires that span the mountain stream.
Keen instruments, strung to a vast precision
Bind town to town and dream to ticking dream.
But some men take their liquor slow — and count
— Though they'll confess no rosary nor clue —
The river's minute by the far brook's year.
Under a world of whistles, wires and steam
Caboose-like they go ruminating through
Ohio, Indiana — blind baggage —
To Cheyenne tagging . . . Maybe Kalamazoo.

Time's rendings, time's blendings they construe
As final reckonings of fire and snow;
Strange bird-wit, like the elemental gist
Of unwalled winds they offer, singing low
My Old Kentucky Home and *Casey Jones*,
Some Sunny Day. I heard a road-gang chanting so.
And afterwards, who had a colt's eyes — one said,
"Jesus! Oh I remember watermelon days!" And sped
High in a cloud of merriment, recalled
"— And when my Aunt Sally Simpson smiled," he drawled —
"It was almost Louisiana, long ago."
"There's no place like Booneville though, Buddy,"
One said, excising a last burr from his vest,
"— For early trouting." Then peering in the can,
"— But I kept on the tracks." Possessed, resigned,
He trod the fire down pensively and grinned,
Spreading dry shingles of a beard. . . .

Behind
My father's cannery works I used to see
Rail-squatters ranged in nomad raillery,
The ancient men — wifeless or runaway
Hobo-trekkers that forever search
An empire wilderness of freight and rails.
Each seemed a child, like me, on a loose perch,
Holding to childhood like some termless play.
John, Jake or Charley, hopping the slow freight
— Memphis to Tallahassee — riding the rods,
Blind fists of nothing, humpty-dumpty clods.

but who have touched her, knowing her without name

Yet they touch something like a key perhaps.
From pole to pole across the hills, the states
— They know a body under the wide rain;
Youngsters with eyes like fjords, old reprobates
With racetrack jargon, — dotting immensity
They lurk across her, knowing her yonder breast
Snow-silvered, sumac-stained or smoky blue —
Is past the valley-sleepers, south or west.
— As I have trod the rumorous midnights, too,

And past the circuit of the lamp's thin flame
(O Nights that brought me to her body bare!)
Have dreamed beyond the print that bound her name.
Trains sounding the long blizzards out — I heard
Wail into distances I knew were hers.
Papooses crying on the wind's long mane
Screamed redskin dynasties that fled the brain,
— Dead echoes! But I knew her body there,
Time like a serpent down her shoulder, dark,
And space, an eaglet's wing, laid on her hair.

nor the myths of her fathers . . .

Under the Ozarks, domed by Iron Mountain,
The old gods of the rain lie wrapped in pools
Where eyeless fish curvet a sunken fountain
And re-descend with corn from querulous crows.
Such pilferings make up their timeless eatage,
Propitiate them for their timber torn
By iron, iron — always the iron dealt cleavage!
They doze now, below axe and powder horn.

And Pullman breakfasters glide glistening steel
From tunnel into field — iron strides the dew —
Straddles the hill, dance of wheel on wheel.
You have a half-hour's wait at Siskiyou,
Or stay the night and take the next train through.
Southward, near Cairo passing, you can see
The Ohio merging, — borne down Tennessee;
And if it's summer and the sun's in dusk
Maybe the breeze will lift the River's musk
— As though the waters breathed that you might know
Memphis Johnny, Steamboat Bill, Missouri Joe.
Oh, lean from the window, if the train slows down,
As though you touched hands with some ancient clown,
— A little while gaze absently below
And hum *Deep River* with them while they go.

Yes, turn again and sniff once more — look see,
O Sheriff, Brakeman and Authority —
Hitch up your pants and crunch another quid,
For you, too, feed the River timelessly.
And few evade full measure of their fate;
Always they smile out eerily what they seem.
I could believe he joked at heaven's gate —
Dan Midland — jolted from the cold brake-beam.

Down, down — born pioneers in time's despite,
Grimed tributaries to an ancient flow —
They win no frontier by their wayward plight,
But drift in stillness, as from Jordan's brow.

You will not hear it as the sea; even stone
Is not more hushed by gravity . . . But slow,
As loth to take more tribute — sliding prone
Like one whose eyes were buried long ago

The River, spreading, flows — and spends your dream.
What are you, lost within this tideless spell?
You are your father's father, and the stream —
A liquid theme that floating niggers swell.

Damp tonnage and alluvial march of days —
Nights turbid, vascular with silted shale
And roots surrendered down of moraine clays:
The Mississippi drinks the farthest dale.

O quarrying passion, undertowed sunlight!
The basalt surface drags a jungle grace
Ochreous and lynx-barred in lengthening might;
Patience! and you shall reach the biding place!

Over De Soto's bones the freighted floors
Throb past the City storied of three thrones.
Down two more turns the Mississippi pours
(Anon tall ironsides up from salt lagoons)

And flows within itself, heaps itself free.
All fades but one thin skyline 'round . . . Ahead
No embrace opens but the stinging sea;
The River lifts itself from its long bed,

Poised wholly on its dream, a mustard glow
Tortured with history, its one will — flow!
— The Passion spreads in wide tongues, choked and slow,
Meeting the Gulf, hosannas silently below.

The Tunnel

To Find the Western path
Right thro' the Gates of Wrath.
— Blake

Performances, assortments, résumés —
Up Times Square to Columbus Circle lights
Channel the congresses, nightly sessions,
Refractions of the thousand theatres, faces —
Mysterious kitchens. . . . You shall search them all.
Someday by heart you'll learn each famous sight
And watch the curtain lift in hell's despite;
You'll find the garden in the third act dead,
Finger your knees — and wish yourself in bed
With tabloid crime-sheets perched in easy sight.

Then let you reach your hat
and go.
As usual, let you — also
walking down — exclaim
to twelve upward leaving

a subscription praise
for what time slays.

Or can't you quite make up your mind to ride;
A walk is better underneath the L a brisk
Ten blocks or so before? But you find yourself
Preparing penguin flexions of the arms, —
As usual you will meet the scuttle yawn:
The subway yawns the quickest promise home.

Be minimum, then, to swim the hiving swarms
Out of the Square, the Circle burning bright —
Avoid the glass doors gyring at your right,
Where boxed alone a second, eyes take fright
— Quite unprepared rush naked back to light:
And down beside the turnstile press the coin
Into the slot. The gongs already rattle.

And so
of cities you bespeak
subways, rivered under streets
and rivers. . . . In the car
the overtone of motion
underground, the monotone
of motion is the sound
of other faces, also underground —

"Let's have a pencil Jimmy — living now
at Floral Park
Flatbush — on the fourth of July —
like a pigeon's muddy dream — potatoes
to dig in the field — travlin the town — too —
night after night — the Culver line — the
girls all shaping up — it used to be —"

Our tongues recant like beaten weather vanes.
This answer lives like verdigris, like hair
Beyond extinction, surcease of the bone;
And repetition freezes — "What

"what do you want? getting weak on the links?
fandaddle daddy don't ask for change — IS THIS
FOURTEENTH? it's half past six she said — if
you don't like my gate why did you
swing on it, why *didja*
swing on it
anyhow — "

And somehow anyhow swing —

The phonographs of hades in the brain
Are tunnels that re-wind themselves, and love
A burnt match skating in a urinal —
Somewhere above Fourteenth TAKE THE EXPRESS
To brush some new presentiment of pain —

"But I want service in this office SERVICE
I said — after
the show she cried a little afterwards but —"

Whose head is swinging from the swollen strap?
Whose body smokes along the bitten rails,
Bursts from a smoldering bundle far behind
In back forks of the chasms of the brain, —
Puffs from a riven stump far out behind
In interborough fissures of the mind . . . ?

And why do I often meet your visage here,
Your eyes like agate lanterns — on and on
Below the toothpaste and the dandruff ads?
— And did their riding eyes right through your side,
and did their eyes like unwashed platters ride?
And Death, aloft, — gigantically down
Probing through you — toward me, O evermore!
And when they dragged your retching flesh,
Your trembling hands that night through Baltimore —
That last night on the ballot rounds, did you
Shaking, did you deny the ticket, Poe?

For Gravesend Manor change at Chambers Street.
The platform hurries along to a dead stop.

The intent escalator lifts a serenade
Stilly
Of shoes, umbrellas, each eye attending its shoe, then
Blotting outright somewhere above where streets
Burst suddenly in rain. . . . The gongs recur:
Elbows and levers, guard and hissing the door.
Thunder is galvothermic here below. . . . The car
Wheels off. The train rounds, bending to a scream,
Taking the final lever for the dive
Under the river —
And somewhat emptier than before,
Demented for a hitching second, humps; then
Lets go. . . . Toward the corners of the floor
Newspapers wing, revolve and wing.
Blank windows gargle signals through the roar.

And does the Dæmon take you home, also,
Wop washerwoman, with the bandaged hair?
After the corridors are swept, the cuspidors —
The gaunt sky-barracks cleanly now, and bare,
O Genoese, do you bring mother eyes and hands
Back home to children and to golden hair?

Dæmon, demurring and the eventful yawn!
Whose hideous laugher is bellows mirth
— Or the muffled slaughter of a day in birth —
O cruelly to inoculate the brinking dawn
With antennæ toward worlds that glow and sink; —
To spoon us out more liquid than the dim
Locution of the eldest star, and pack
The conscience navelled in the plunging wind,
Umbilical to call — and straightway die!

O caught like pennies beneath soot and steam,
Kiss of our agony thou gatherest;
Condensed, thou takest all — shrill ganglia
Impassioned with some song we fail to keep.
And yet, like Lazarus, to feel the slope,
The sod and billow breaking, — lifting ground,
— A sound of waters bending astride the sky
Unceasing with some Word that will not die . . . !

. . . .

A tugboat, wheezing wreaths of steam,
Lunged past, with one galvanic blare stove up the River.
I counted the echoes, assembling, one after one,
Searching, thumbing the midnight on the piers.
Lights coasting, left the oily tympanum of waters;
The blackness somewhere gouged glass on a sky.
And this thy harbor, O my City, I have driven under,
Tossed from the coil tricking towers. . . . Tomorrow,
And to be. . . . Here by the River that is East —
Here at the waters' edge the hands drop memory;
Shadowless in that abyss they unaccounting lie.
How far away the star has pooled the sea —
Or shall the hands to be drawn away, to die?

Kiss of our agony Thou gatherest,
O Hand of Fire
gatherest —

1930

O Carib Isle!

The tarantula rattling at the lily's foot
Across the feet of the dead, laid in white sand
Near the coral beach — nor zigzag fiddle crabs
Side-stilting from the path (that shift, subvert
And anagrammatize your name) — No, nothing here
Below the palsy that one eucalyptus lifts
In wrinkled shadows — mourns.

And yet suppose
I count these nacreous frames of tropic death,
Brutal necklaces of shells around each grave
Squared off so carefully. Then

To the white sand I may speak a name, fertile
Albeit in a stranger tongue. Tree names, flower names
Deliberate, gainsay death's brittle crypt. Meanwhile
The wind that knots itself in one great death —
Coils and withdraws. So syllables want breath.

But where is the Captain of this doubloon isle
Without a turnstile? Who but catchword crabs
Patrols the dry groins of the underbrush?
What man, or What
Is Commissioner of mildew throughout the ambushed senses?
His Carib mathematics web the eyes' baked lenses!

Under the poinciana, of a noon or afternoon
Let fiery blossoms clot the light, render my ghost
Sieved upward, white and black along the air
Until it meets the blue's comedian host.

Let not the pilgrim see himself again
For slow evisceration bound like those huge terrapin
Each daybreak on the wharf, their brine caked eyes;
— Spiked, overturned; such thunder in their strain!
And clenched beaks coughing for the surge again!

Slagged of the hurricane — I, cast within its flow,
Congeal by afternoons here, satin and vacant.
You have given me the shell, Satan, — carbonic amulet
Sere of the sun exploded in the sea.

1930

— And Bees of Paradise

I had come all the way here from the sea,
Yet met the wave again between your arms
Where cliff and citadel — all verily
Dissolved within a sky of beacon forms —

Sea gardens lifted rainbow-wise through eyes
I found.

            Yes, tall, inseparably our days
Pass sunward. We have walked the kindled skies
Inexorable and girded with your praise,

By the dove filled, and bees of Paradise.

1933

To Emily Dickinson

You who desired so much — in vain to ask —
Yet fed your hunger like an endless task,
Dared dignify the labor, bless the quest —
Achieved that stillness ultimately best,

Being, of all, least sought for: Emily, hear!
O sweet, dead silencer, most suddenly clear
When singing that Eternity possessed
And plundered momently in every breast;

— Truly no flower yet withers in your hand,
The harvest you descried and understand
Needs more than wit to gather, love to bind.
Some reconcilement of remotest mind —

Leaves Ormus rubyless, and Ophir chill.
Else tears heap all within one clay-cold hill.

1933

The Broken Tower

The bell-rope that gathers God at dawn
Dispatches me as though I dropped down the knell
Of a spent day — to wander the cathedral lawn
From pit to crucifix, feet chill on steps from hell.

Have you not heard, have you not seen that corps
Of shadows in the tower, whose shoulders sway
Antiphonal carillons launched before
The stars are caught and hived in the sun's ray?

The bells, I say, the bells break down their tower;
And swing I know not where. Their tongues engrave
Membrane through marrow, my long-scattered score
Of broken intervals. . . . And I, their sexton slave!

Oval encyclicals in canyons heaping
The impasse high with choir. Banked voices slain!
Pagodas, campaniles with reveilles outleaping —
O terraced echoes prostrate on the plain! . . .

And so it was I entered the broken world
To trace the visionary company of love, its voice
An instant in the wind (I know not whither hurled)
But not for long to hold each desperate choice.

My word I poured. But was it cognate, scored
Of that tribunal monarch of the air
Whose thigh embronzes earth, strikes crystal Word
In wounds pledged once to hope — cleft to despair?

The steep encroachments of my blood left me
No answer (could blood hold such a lofty tower
As flings the question true?) — or is it she
Whose sweet mortality stirs latent power? —

And through whose pulse I hear, counting the strokes
My veins recall and add, revived and sure
The angelus of wars my chest evokes:
What I hold healed, original now, and pure . . .

And builds, within, a tower that is not stone
(Not stone can jacket heaven) — but slip
Of pebbles — visible wings of silence sown
In azure circles, widening as they dip

The matrix of the heart, lift down the eye
That shrines the quiet lake and swells a tower . . .
The commodious, tall decorum of the sky
Unseals her earth, and lifts love in its shower.

1933

ALLEN TATE (1899–1979)

Born in Winchester, Kentucky, Allen Tate joined John Crowe Ransom and Robert Penn Warren as mainstays of the Southern Agrarians (also known as the Fugitive movement, after the magazine of that name). Tate wrote "Aeneas at New York" as a verse rebuttal of his friend Archibald MacLeish's "Invocation to the Social Muse." The liberal MacLeish, speaking for himself and fellow poets, had asked rhetorically, "Is it just to demand of us also to bear arms?" The conservative Tate answered yes, it was: "The use of arms is ownership / Of the appropriate gun. It is ownership that brings / Victory that is not hinted at in *Das Kapital.* / I think there is never but one true war / So let us as you desire perfect our trade." Of his poem "The Mediterranean," Tate wrote, "the poem is in iambic pentameter, but I made a point of not writing any two lines in the same rhythm. This is a little like the man who either avoids or steps upon all the cracks in the sidewalk. A great many of my poems have had to conform to a similar preconceived technical requirement which does not necessarily have any relation to the subject about to be explored. Even most serious poems are partly a game, not unlike a children's game, the rules of which are arbitrarily made in advance."

Ode to the Confederate Dead

Row after row with strict impunity
The headstones yield their names to the element,
The wind whirrs without recollection;
In the riven troughs the splayed leaves
Pile up, of nature the casual sacrament
To the seasonal eternity of death;
Then driven by the fierce scrutiny
Of heaven to their election in the vast breath,
They sough the rumour of mortality.

Autumn is desolation in the plot
Of a thousand acres where these memories grow
From the inexhaustible bodies that are not
Dead, but feed the grass row after rich row.
Think of the autumns that have come and gone! —
Ambitious November with the humors of the year,
With a particular zeal for every slab,
Staining the uncomfortable angels that rot
On the slabs, a wing chipped here, an arm there:
The brute curiosity of an angel's stare
Turns you, like them, to stone,
Transforms the heaving air
Till plunged to a heavier world below
You shift your sea-space blindly
Heaving, turning like the blind crab.

Dazed by the wind, only the wind
The leaves flying, plunge

You know who have waited by the wall
The twilight certainty of an animal,
Those midnight restitutions of the blood
You know — the immitigable pines, the smoky frieze
Of the sky, the sudden call: you know the rage,
The cold pool left by the mounting flood,
Of muted Zeno and Parmenides.
You who have waited for the angry resolution
Of those desires that should be yours tomorrow,
You know the unimportant shrift of death
And praise the vision
And praise the arrogant circumstance
Of those who fall
Rank upon rank, hurried beyond decision —
Here by the sagging gate, stopped by the wall.

Seeing, seeing only the leaves
Flying, plunge and expire

Turn your eyes to the immoderate past,
Turn to the inscrutable infantry rising
Demons out of the earth — they will not last.
Stonewall, Stonewall, and the sunken fields of hemp,
Shiloh, Antietam, Malvern Hill, Bull Run,
Lost in that orient of the thick-and-fast
You will curse the setting sun.

Cursing only the leaves crying
Like an old man in a storm

You hear the shout, the crazy hemlocks point
With troubled fingers to the silence which
Smothers you, a mummy, in time.

The hound bitch
Toothless and dying, in a musty cellar
Hears the wind only.

Now that the salt of their blood
Stiffens the saltier oblivion of the sea,
Seals the malignant purity of the flood,
What shall we who count our days and bow
Our heads with a commemorial woe
In the ribboned coats of grim felicity,
What shall we say of the bones, unclean,
Whose verdurous anonymity will grow?
The ragged arms, the ragged heads and eyes
Lost in these acres of the insane green?
The gray lean spiders come, they come and go;

In a tangle of willows without light
The singular screech-owl's tight
Invisible lyric seeds the mind
With the furious murmur of their chivalry.

We shall say only the leaves
Flying, plunge and expire

We shall say only the leaves whispering
In the improbable mist of nightfall
That flies on multiple wing;
Night is the beginning and the end
And in between the ends of distraction
Waits mute speculation, the patient curse
That stones the eyes, or like the jaguar leaps
For his own image in a jungle pool, his victim.
What shall we say who have knowledge
Carried to the heart? Shall we take the act
To the grave? Shall we, more hopeful, set up the grave
In the house? The ravenous grave?

Leave now
The shut gate and the decomposing wall:
The gentle serpent, green in the mulberry bush,
Riots with his tongue through the hush —
Sentinel of the grave who counts us all!

1928

The Wolves

There are wolves in the next room waiting
With heads bent low, thrust out, breathing
At nothing in the dark; between them and me
A white door patched with light from the hall
Where it seems never (so still is the house)
A man has walked from the front door to the stair.
It has all been forever. Beasts claw the floor.
I have brooded on angels and archfiends
But no man has ever sat where the next room's
Crowded with wolves, and for the honor of man
I affirm that never have I before. Now while
I have looked for the evening star at a cold window
And whistled when Arcturus spilt his light,
I've heard the wolves scuffle, and said: So this
Is man; so — what better conclusion is there —
The day will not follow night, and the heart

Of man has a little dignity, but less patience
Than a wolf's, and a duller sense that cannot
Smell its own mortality. (This and other
Meditations will be suited to other times
After dog silence howls his epitaph.)
Now remember courage, go to the door,
Open it and see whether coiled on the bed
Or cringing by the wall, a savage beast
Maybe with golden hair, with deep eyes
Like a bearded spider on a sunlit floor
Will snarl — and man can never be alone.

1932

The Mediterranean

Quem das finem, rex magne, dolorum?

Where we went in the boat was a long bay
A slingshot wide, walled in by towering stone —
Peaked margin of antiquity's delay,
And we went there out of time's monotone:

Where we went in the black hull no light moved
But a gull white-winged along the feckless wave,
The breeze, unseen but fierce as a body loved,
That boat drove onward like a willing slave:

Where we went in the small ship the seaweed
Parted and gave to us the murmuring shore,
And we made feast and in our secret need
Devoured the very plates Aeneas bore:

Where derelict you see through the low twilight
The green coast that you, thunder-tossed, would win,
Drop sail, and hastening to drink all night
Eat dish and bowl to take that sweet land in!

Where we feasted and caroused on the sandless
Pebbles, affecting our day of piracy,
What prophecy of eaten plates could landless
Wanderers fulfil by the ancient sea?

We for that time might taste the famous age
Eternal here yet hidden from our eyes
When lust of power undid its stuffless rage;
They, in a wineskin, bore earth's paradise.

Let us lie down once more by the breathing side
Of Ocean, where our live forefathers sleep
As if the Known Sea still were a month wide —
Atlantis howls but is no longer steep!

What country shall we conquer, what fair land
Unman our conquest and locate our blood?
We've cracked the hemispheres with careless hand!
Now, from the Gates of Hercules we flood

Westward, westward till the barbarous brine
Whelms us to the tired land where tasseling corn,
Fat beans, grapes sweeter than muscadine
Rot on the vine: in that land were we born.

1933

The Ivory Tower

Let us begin to understand the argument.
There is a solution to everything: Science.
Separate those evils strictly social
From other evils that are eventually social.
It ends in all evils being social: Deduction.
Is not marriage a social institution,
Un contra social? Is not prostitution
An institution? Abolish (1) marriage, (2) poverty.
We understand everything: Dialectic
We who get plenty to eat and get it
Advertising the starvation of others
Understand everything not including
Ourselves: we have enough to eat. Oedipus
Was necessarily an example — everything
Is an example — of capitalism pooped
By decay; King Lear, of neurotic senility
Bred of tyrannous escape from reality;
Cleopatra, of the unadjusted girl.
Everybody but us is an example of capitalism.
We are understanding the argument
That we have got to make men slaves
Of their bellies in order to get them fed.

The sole problem is the problem of hunger
(Or the distribution of commodities)
And a beast came out of the sea
And a fire came out of the night
To them that were not hungry
The commodities being well distributed

And the prostate thrives a little, then delays,
The hour of light is brief, then decays;
But light must be a social institution
Even if we are not sure what the other
Is (*pro*, forth; *stare*, to stand).
We know everything to know on sea or land.
And on the mountains by the sea
There was enacted tragedy
(Or maybe in a hollow by a tree),
Both man and woman were well-fed
When he had brought her hot to bed
But he was largely make-believe
And she no better than a sieve.
Soon the uneconomic woe
That love engenders crushed them, so
That every time they drank or ate
They cursed the board where food was set.

Axel's Castle, the text they took,
Was a most remarkable book
But yet in spite of Mr. Wilson
Beef and cheese washed down by Pilsen
Did not adjust the sexual act
To truths of economic fact,
So was produced this tragedy
In a far tower of ivory
Where, O young men, late in the night
All you who drink light and stroke the air
Come back, seeking the night, and cry
To strict Rapunzel to let down her hair.

1936

YVOR WINTERS (1900–1968)

Yvor Winters was born in Chicago. At the age of eighteen he was diagnosed with tuberculosis and moved to Santa Fe, New Mexico, for treatment. In 1922 he met the poet Janet Lewis, herself a Chicago native who suffered from the same ailment. They married in 1926. As a Stanford professor, Winters became an eminence. He was "the most exciting teacher I ever had," wrote Thom Gunn. "Even to disagree with him was exciting." Winters wrote "in defense of reason" and against the doctrine that madness is genius. He passionately advocated "the tougher poets" of Elizabethan and seventeenth-century England, naming them in his poem "Time and the Garden" as "Gascoigne, Ben Jonson, Greville, Raleigh, Donne." Winters took exception to the whole American tradition. "The doctrine of Emerson and Whitman, if really put into practice, should naturally lead to suicide," he wrote. "In the first place, if the impulses are indulged systematically and passionately, they can lead only to madness; in the second place, death, according to the doctrine, is not only a release from suffering but its also and inevitably the way to beatitude." Richard Wilbur, who studied with Winters, was asked what the professor was like. "Well," Wilbur said, "I asked him why he raised Airedales. He said, 'Because they can kill any other dog.'"

Before Disaster

Evening traffic homeward burns
Swift and even on the turns,
Drifting weight in triple rows,
Fixed relation and repose.
This one edges out and by,
Inch by inch with steady eye.
But should error be increased,
Mass and moment are released;
Matter loosens, flooding blind,
Levels drivers to its kind.
   Ranks of nation thus descend,
Watchful to a stormy end.
By a moment's calm beguiled,
I have got a wife and child.
Fool and scoundrel guide the State.
Peace is whore to Greed and Hate.
Nowhere may I turn to flee:
Action is security.
Treading change with savage heel,
We must live or die by steel.

1934

A Summer Commentary

When I was young, with sharper sense,
The farthest insect cry I heard
Could stay me; through the trees, intense,
I watched the hunter and the bird.

Where is the meaning that I found?
Or was it but a state of mind,
Some old penumbra of the ground,
In which to be but not to find?

Now summer grasses, brown with heat,
Have crowded sweetness through the air;
The very roadside dust is sweet;
Even the unshadowed earth is fair.

The soft voice of the nesting dove,
And the dove in soft erratic flight

Like a rapid hand within a glove,
Caress the silence and the light.

Amid the rubble, the fallen fruit,
Fermenting in its rich decay,
Smears brandy on the trampling boot
And sends it sweeter on its way.

1938

Much in Little

Amid the iris and the rose,
The honeysuckle and the bay,
The wild earth for a moment goes
In dust or weed another way.

Small though its corner be, the weed
Will yet intrude its creeping beard;
The harsh blade and the hairy seed
Recall the brutal earth we feared.

And if no water touch the dust
In some far corner, and one dare
To breathe upon it, one may trust
The spectre on the summer air:

The risen dust alive with fire,
The fire made visible, a blur
Interrate, the pervasive ire
Of foxtail and of hoarhound burr.

1940

At the San Francisco Airport

To my daughter, 1954

This is the terminal: the light
Gives perfect vision, false and hard;
The metal glitters, deep and bright.
Great planes are waiting in the yard —
They are already in the night.

And you are here beside me, small,
Contained and fragile, and intent
On things that I but half recall —
Yet going whither you are bent.
I am the past, and that is all.

But you and I in part are one:
The frightened brain, the nervous will,
The knowledge of what must be done,
The passion to acquire the skill
To face that which you dare not shun.

The rain of matter upon sense
Destroys me momently. The score:
There comes what will come. The expense
Is what one thought, and something more —
One's being and intelligence.

This is the terminal, the break.
Beyond this point, on lines of air,
You take the way that you must take;
And I remain in light and stare —
In light, and nothing else, awake.

1954

STERLING A. BROWN (1901–1989)

Sterling A. Brown was born in Washington, D.C., the son of a religion professor at Howard University. He attended Williams College, received a master's degree at Harvard, and taught at Howard University from 1929 until he retired forty years later. *Southern Road*, his book of poems, was published in 1932. He wrote several critical studies, including *The Negro in American Fiction* and *Negro Poetry and Drama* (both 1937). Brown saw his poetry as exploring qualities of character submerged beneath racial stereotypes: "tonic shrewdness, the ability to take it, and the double-edged humor built up of irony and shrewd observation." Of his place in American society and literature, he wrote: "I want to be in the best American traditions. I want to be accepted as a whole man. My standards are not white. My standards are not black. My standards are human."

Bitter Fruit of the Tree

They said to my grandmother: "Please do not be bitter,"
When they sold her first-born and let the second die,
When they drove her husband till he took to the swamplands,
And brought him home bloody and beaten at last.
They told her, "It is better you should not be bitter,
Some must work and suffer so that we, who must, can live,
Forgiving is noble, you must not be heathen bitter;
These are your orders: you *are* not to be bitter."
And they left her shack for their porticoed house.

They said to my father: "Please do not be bitter,"
When he ploughed and planted a crop not his,
When he weatherstripped a house that he would not enter,
And stored away a harvest he could not enjoy.
They answered his questions: "It does not concern you,
It is not for you to know, it is past your understanding,
All you need know is: you must not be bitter."

1936

Master and Man

The yellow ears are crammed in Mr. Cromartie's bin
The wheat is tight sacked in Mr. Cromartie's barn.
The timothy is stuffed in Mr. Cromartie's loft.
The ploughs are lined up in Mr. Cromartie's shed.
The cotton has gone to Mr. Cromartie's factor.
The money is in Mr. Cromartie's bank.
Mr. Cromartie's son made his frat at the college.
Mr. Cromartie's daughter has got her new car.
The veranda is old, but the fireplace is rosy.
Well done, Mr. Cromartie. Time now for rest.

Blackened sticks line the furrows that Uncle Ned laid.
Bits of fluff are in the corners where Uncle Ned ginned.
The mules he ploughed are sleek in Mr. Cromartie's pastures.
The hoes grow dull in Mr. Cromartie's shed.
His winter rations wait on the commissary shelves;
Mr. Cromartie's ledger is there for his service.
Uncle Ned daubs some mortar between the old logs.
His children have traipsed off to God knows where.
His old lady sits patching the old, thin denims;
She's got a new dress, and his young one a doll,
He's got five dollars. The year has come round.
The harvest is over: Uncle Ned's harvesting,
Mr. Cromartie's harvest. Time now for rest.

1936

Southern Cop

Let us forgive Ty Kendricks.
The place was Darktown. He was young.
His nerves were jittery. The day was hot.
The Negro ran out of the alley.
And so he shot.

Let us understand Ty Kendricks.
The Negro must have been dangerous,
Because he ran;
And here was a rookie with a chance
To prove himself a man.

Let us condone Ty Kendricks
If we cannot decorate.
When he found what the Negro was running for,
It was too late;
And all we can say for the Negro is
It was unfortunate.

Let us pity Ty Kendricks,
He has been through enough,
Standing there, his big gun smoking,
Rabbit-scared, alone,
Having to hear the wenches wail
And the dying Negro moan.

1938

Harlem Happiness

I think there is in this the stuff for many lyrics: — the
A dago fruit stand at three A.M.; the wop asleep, his woman
Knitting a tiny garment, laughing when we approached her,
Flashing a smile from white teeth, then weighing out the grapes,
Grapes large as plums, and tart and sweet as — well we know the lady
And purplish red and firm, quite as this lady's lips are. . . .
We laughed, all three when she awoke her swarthy, snoring Pietro
To make us change, which we, rich paupers, left to help the garment.
We swaggered off; while they two stared, and laughed in understanding,
And thanked us lovers who brought back an old Etrurian springtide.
Then, once beyond their light, a step beyond their pearly smiling
We tasted grapes and tasted lips, and laughed at sleepy Harlem,
And when the huge Mick cop stomped by, a'swingin' of his billy
You nodded to him gaily, and I kissed you with him looking,
Beneath the swinging light that weakly fought against the mist
That settled on Eighth Avenue, and curled around the houses.
And he grinned too and understood the wisdom of our madness.
That night at least the world was ours to spend, nor were we misers.
Ah, Morningside with Maytime awhispering in the foliage!
Alone, atop the city, — the tramps were still in shelter —
And moralizing lights that peered up from the murky distance
Seemed soft as our two cigarette ends burning slowly, dimly,
And careless as the jade stars that winked upon our gladness. . . .

And when I flicked my cigarette, and we watched it falling, falling,
It seemed a shooting meteor, that we, most proud creators
Sent down in gay capriciousness upon a trivial Harlem —

And then I madly quoted lyrics from old kindred masters,
Who wrote of you, unknowing you, for far more lucky me —
And you sang broken bits of song, and we both slept in snatches,
And so the night sped on too swift, with grapes, and words and kisses,
And numberless cigarette ends glowing in the darkness
Old Harlem slept regardless, but a motherly old moon —
Shone down benevolently on two happy wastrel lovers. . . .

1980

Legend

The old black man was stood on the block
The old white man looked into his mouth
The old white man held up his fingers
"I own you, nigger,"
Said the old white man.

The old black man drove his plough afield
From sun-come-up until sun-go-down,
His hut was leaky, and the food was scarce,
"I'm grateful for these favors,"
Said the old black man.

The old black man had a pretty wife
The old white man took her to his house
The wife came back with a half-white baby.
"I'm glad to be of service,"
Said the old black man.

The old black man heard talk of his freedom
The old black man saw his mates take flight
He rushed the news to his old white master
"I thought it best you know it,"
Said the old black man.

The old black man lost his half-white daughter
Down the river, and a son in the swamp.
The old black man lost his wife in the grave.
"I've still got my master,"
Said the old black man.

The old black man saw his son grow sturdy
Saw his eyes taking stock of the old white man

Heard him say things past all believing,
"You're on the road to ruin,"
Said the old black man.

The old black man was hung by his thumbs
To the smokehouse rafters while the old cat lashed
He rubbed salt and water upon the welts
"I must have deserved it,"
Said the old black man.

The young black man got to asking questions
Why corn and cotton were his own for working
But not his at all in the shocks and the bales.
"You're a fool blasphemer,"
Said the old black man.

The old black man had talk with his master
The old white man was near to a stroke
The young black man would not be grateful
"After all you've done for him,"
Said the old black man.

The old white man took his whip from the wall,
The old black man brought the trace-chains from the barn,
The two old man bared their old men's muscles,
"Let me whip him into reason,"
Said the old black man.

The young black man faced his old black father.
The young black man faced the old white man.
He straightened his shoulders, and threw back his head,
"I wish you both in hell,"
Said the young black man.

The young black man broke the whipstock to pieces,
The young black man cut the lash into bits.
Then chained the old men together with the traces,
"Your fine day is over,"
Said the young black man.

1980

Laura Riding (1901–1991)

Laura Riding was born in New York City to poor Jewish parents, her father a tailor. She went to Cornell University, married Louis Gottschalk, and changed her name from Reichenthal to Riding. She lived in Europe from 1926 to 1939, much of that time with Robert Graves as her lover and literary collaborator in Majorca. She may be the model of Graves's "white goddess." In 1939 she renounced poetry. Famous for her cantankerousness — she would fire off long angry letters to the editor even when the article she was responding to was an utter rave — she married Schuyler B. Jackson in 1941 and took Laura (Riding) Jackson as her official name. Hart Crane nicknamed her "Laura Riding Roughshod."

Postponement of Self

I took another day,
I moved to another city,
I opened a new door to me.
Then again a last night came.
My bed said: 'To sleep and back again?'
I said: 'This time go forward.'

Arriving, arriving, not yet, not yet,
Yet yet arriving, till I am met.
For what would be her disappointment
Coming late ('She did not wait').
I wait. And meet my mother.
Such is accident.
She smiles: long afterwards.
I sulk: long before.
I grow to six.
At six little girls in love with fathers.
He lifts me up.
See. Is this Me?
Is this Me I think
In all the different ways till twenty.
At twenty I say She.
Her face is like a flower.
In a city we have no flower-names, forgive me.
But flower-names not necessary
To diary of identity.

1938

Opening of Eyes

Thought looking out on thought
Makes one an eye.
One is the mind self-blind,

The other is thought gone
To be seen from afar and not known.
Thus is a universe very soon.

The immense surmise swims round and round,
And heads grow wise
Of marking bigness,
And idiot size
Spaces out Nature,

And ears report echoes first,
Then sounds, distinguish words
Of which the sense comes last —
From mouths spring forth vocabularies
As if by charm.
And thus do false horizons claim pride
For distance in the head
The head conceives outside.

Self-wonder, rushing from the eyes,
Returns lesson by lesson.
The all, secret at first,
Now is the knowable,
The view of flesh, mind's muchness.

But what of secretness,
Thought not divided, thinking
A single whole of seeing?
That mind dies ever instantly
Of too plain sight foreseen
Within too suddenly,
While mouthless lips break open
Mutely astonished to rehearse
The unutterable simple verse.

1938

The Unthronged Oracle

Not to ask, not to be answered,
Not to fall down from last of breath,
Not to be raised — the stricken mouth
Though fit uniquely to make shape
Of unique plaint for stricken mind:
Never to this final cave and mouth of mouths
Have you, are you come, contestant race
That boastfully flew birds of tiding here
So long — from extinct monster-wing,

That never flew, to the etherealest feather
That floated back from far, forgetting
What too-heavy auspices were hung
There on its thin prophetic claw.
Birds, birds, all bird-like were your reaches,
Minds quicker than your minds, vain flights
Of consolation. ('It will be as time tells,
As we attempt, as thoughts anticipate
Against exhaustion and straggle of feet.')

Your coming, asking, seeing, knowing,
Was a fleeing from and stumbling
Into only mirrors, and behind which,
Behind all mirrors, dazzling pretences,
The general light of fortune
Keeps wrapt in sleeping unsleep,
All-mute of time, self-muttering like mute:
Fatality like lone wise-woman
Her unbought secrets counting over
That stink of hell, from fuming in her lap.

Is this to be alone?
When, when the day when votary ghosts unpale
And shriek rebellion at themselves
So dumbly death-loyal serving her
In acquiescent guile — since never came
A word of angry flesh or impious meaning
Through that hushed screen of priding world?
When, when the day? Is this to be alone?

Newspapers, mirrors, birds and births and clocks
Divide you from her by a trembling film
That never may dissolve between.
Perhaps even as you were will you remain
Such other manufactures of yourselves —
While round her storm unwillingly
Your empty spirits like better selves
You dared not be or gainsay — arguing,
'That ancient mystery-monger grows
By times of ours more and more ancient,
More deaf and slow in deeper company
Of omens private to her distance,
And love of talking lone in unheard bodement.'

But when, when the day? Is this to be alone?

1938

The World and I

This is not exactly what I mean
Any more than the sun is the sun.
But how to mean more closely
If the sun shines but approximately?
What a world of awkwardness!
What hostile implements of sense!
Perhaps this is as close a meaning
As perhaps becomes such knowing.
Else I think the world and I
Must live together as strangers and die —
A sour love, each doubtful whether
Was ever a thing to love the other.
No, better for both to be nearly sure
Each of each — exactly where
Exactly I and exactly the world
Fail to meet by a moment, and a word.

1938

Because of Clothes

Without dressmakers to connect
The good-will of the body
With the purpose of the head,
We should be two worlds
Instead of a world and its shadow
The flesh.

The head is one world
And the body is another —
The same, but somewhat slower
And more dazed and earlier,
The divergence being corrected
In dress.

There is an odour of Christ
In the cloth: below the chin
No harm is meant. Even, immune
From capital test, wisdom flowers
Out of the shaded breast, and the thighs
Are meek.

The union of matter with mind
By the method of raiment
Destroys not our nakedness
Nor muffles the bell of thought.
Merely the moment to its dumb hour
Is joined.

Inner is the glow of knowledge
And outer is the gloom of appearance.
But putting on the cloak and cap
With only the hands and the face showing,
We turn the gloom in and the glow forth
Softly.

Wherefore, by the neutral grace
Of the needle, we posses our triumphs
Together with our defeats
In a single balanced couplement:
We pause between sense and foolishness,
And live.

1938

Kenneth Fearing (1902–1961)

Kenneth Fearing was born in Oak Park, Illinois. He worked as a journalist for both *Time* and *Newsweek* and wrote several notable murder mysteries, including *Dagger of the Mind* (1941) and *The Big Clock* (1946), which was made into a movie with Charles Laughton and Ray Milland in 1948; Fearing based the character of the eccentric painter in *The Big Clock* on his friend the artist Alice Neel. Fearing was considered a "proletarian poet," or a "Depression poet," but that oversimplifies his case. Weldon Kees writes that Fearing "gathers up-to-the-minute horrors with all the eager thoroughness of a bibliophile cackling over pagination errors."

Green Light

Bought at the drug store, very cheap; and later pawned.
  After a while, heard on the street; seen in the park.
  Familiar but not quite recognized.
  Followed and taken home and slept with.
  Traded or sold. Or lost.
Bought again at the corner drug store,
  At the green light, at the patient's demand, at nine o'clock.
  Re-read and memorized and re-wound.
  Found unsuitable.
  Smashed, put together, and pawned.
Heard on the street, seen in a dream, heard in the park,
        seen by the light of day,
  Carefully observed one night by a secret agent of the
        Greek Hydraulic Mining Commission, in
        Plain clothes, off duty.
  The agent, in broken English, took copious notes.
        Which he lost.

Strange and yet ordinary.
Sad, but true.
True; or exaggerated; or true;
As the people laugh and the sparrows fly;
As the people change and the sea stays;
As the people go;
As the lights go on and it is night, and it is serious, and it is just the same;
As some one dies and it is serious and just the same;
As a girl knows and it is small; and true;
As a butcher knows and it is true; and pointless;
As an old man knows and it is comical; and true;
As the people laugh, as the people think, as the people change,
It is serious and the same; exaggerated; or true.
Bought at the drug store on the corner
Where the wind blows and the motors go by and it is night or day.
Bought for the hero's pride.
Bought to instruct the animals in the zoo.
Bought to impress the statuary in the park.
Bought for the spirit of the nation's splendid cultural heritage.
Bought to use as a last resort.
Bought at a cut rate, at a cheap demand, at the green light, at nine o'clock.
Borrowed or bought, to look well. To ennoble. To prevent disease. To have.
Broken or sold. Or given away.

1929

Dirge

1-2-3 was the number he played but today the number came 3-2-1;
bought his Carbide at 30 and it went to 29; had the favorite at Bowie but the track was slow —

O, executive type, would you like to drive a floating power, knee-action, silk-upholstered six? Wed a Hollywood star? Shoot the course in 58? Draw to the ace, king, jack?
O, fellow with a will who won't take no, watch out for three cigarettes on the same, single match; O, democratic voter born in August under Mars, beware of liquidated rails —

Denouement to denouement, he took a personal pride
in the certain, certain way he lived his own,
private life,
but nevertheless, they shut off his gas; nevertheless,
the bank foreclosed; nevertheless, the landlord
called; nevertheless, the radio broke,

And twelve o'clock arrived just once too often,
just the same he wore one grey tweed suit, bought
one straw hat, drank one straight Scotch,
walked one short step, took one long look,
drew one deep breath,
just one too many,

And wow he died as wow he lived,
going whop to the office and blooie home to sleep
and biff got married and bam had children and
oof got fired,
zowie did he live and zowie did he die,

With who the hell are you at the corner of his casket,
and where the hell we going on the right-hand
silver knob, and who the hell cares walking
second from the end with an American Beauty
wreath from why the hell not,

Very much missed by the circulation staff of the New
York Evening Post; deeply, deeply mourned by
the B.M.T.,

Wham, Mr. Roosevelt; pow, Sears Roebuck; awk, big
dipper; bop, summer rain;
bong, Mr., bong, Mr., bong, Mr., bong.

1935

X Minus X

Even when your friend, the radio, is still; even when her
dream, the magazine, is finished; even when
his life, the ticker, is silent; even when their
density, the boulevard, is bare,
and after that paradise, the dancehall, is closed; after
that theatre, the clinic, is dark,

Still there will be your desire, and her desire, and his
desire, and their desire,
your laughter, their laughter,

your curse and his curse, her reward and their reward,
their dismay and his dismay and her dismay
and yours —
Even when your enemy, the collector, is dead; even
when your counsellor, the salesman, is
sleeping; even when your sweetheart, the
movie queen, has spoken; even when your
friend, the magnate, is gone.

1935

LANGSTON HUGHES (1902–1967)

Langston Hughes was born in Joplin, Missouri. He grew up in various midwestern towns and attended Columbia University briefly in the early 1920s. A leading figure of the Harlem Renaissance, he adapted the blues to his poetic purposes, remarking, "The mood of the Blues is almost always despondency, but when they are sung, people laugh." *The Weary Blues* appeared in 1926, his book-length poem *Montage of a Dream Deferred* in 1951. Hughes spent one winter in Mexico City, sharing digs with the French photographer Henri Cartier-Bresson; he covered the Spanish Civil War for the Baltimore *Afro-American*. He bought a home in Harlem, and a stretch of East 127th Street in New York City has been renamed Langston Hughes Place.

The Weary Blues

Droning a drowsy syncopated tune,
Rocking back and forth to a mellow croon,
I heard a Negro play.
Down on Lenox Avenue the other night
By the pale dull pallor of an old gas light
He did a lazy sway. . . .
He did a lazy sway. . . .
To the tune o' those Weary Blues.
With his ebony hands on each ivory key
He made that poor piano moan with melody.
O Blues!
Swaying to and fro on his rickety stool
He played that sad raggy tune like a musical fool.
Sweet Blues!
Coming from a black man's soul.
O Blues!
In a deep song voice with melancholy tone
I heard that Negro sing, that old piano moan —
"Ain't got nobody in all this world,
Ain't got nobody but ma self.
I's gwine to quit ma frownin'
And put ma troubles on the shelf."

Thump, thump, thump, went his foot on the floor.
He played a few chords then he sang some more —
  "I got the Weary Blues
  And I can't be satisfied.
  Got the Weary Blues
  And can't be satisfied —
  I ain't happy no mo'
  And I wish that I had died."
And far into the night he crooned that tune.
The stars went out and so did the moon.
The singer stopped playing and went to bed
While the Weary Blues echoed through his head.
He slept like a rock or a man that's dead.

1926

Juke Box Love Song

I could take the Harlem night
and wrap around you,
Take the neon lights and make a crown,
Take the Lenox Avenue busses,
Taxis, subways,
And for your love song tone their rumble down.
Take Harlem's heartbeat,
Make a drumbeat,
Put it on a record, let it whirl,
And while we listen to it play,
Dance with you till day —
Dance with you, my sweet brown Harlem girl.

1950

from *Montage of a Dream Deferred*

Dream Boogie

Good morning, daddy!
Ain't you heard
The boogie-woogie rumble
Of a dream deferred?

Listen closely:
You'll hear their feet
Beating out and beating out a —

You think
It's a happy beat?

Listen to it closely:
Ain't you heard
something underneath
like a —

What did I say?

Sure,
I'm happy!
Take it away!

Hey, pop!
Re-bop!
Mop!

Y-e-a-h!

1951

Passing

On sunny summer Sunday afternoons in Harlem
when the air is one interminable ball game
and grandma cannot get her gospel hymns
from the Saints of God in Christ
on account of the Dodgers on the radio,
on sunny Sunday afternoons
when the kids look all new
and far too clean to stay that way,
and Harlem has its
washed-and-ironed-and-cleaned-best out,
the ones who've crossed the line
to live downtown
miss you,
Harlem of the bitter dream,
since their dream has
come true.

1951

Nightmare Boogie

I had a dream
and I could see
a million faces
black as me!
A nightmare dream:
Quicker than light

All them faces
Turned dead white!
Boogie-woogie,
Rolling bass,
Whirling treble
of cat-gut lace.

1951

Neighbor

Down home
he sets on a stoop
and watches the sun go by.
In Harlem
when his work is done
he sets in a bar with a beer.
He looks taller than he is
and younger than he ain't.
He looks darker than he is, too.
And he's smarter than he looks,

He ain't smart.
That cat's a fool.

Naw, he ain't neither.
He's a good man,
Except that he talks too much.
In fact, he's a great cat.
But when he drinks,
he drinks fast.

Sometimes
he don't drink.

True,
he just
lets his glass
set there.

1951

Chord

Shadow faces
In the shadow night
Before the early dawn
Bops bright.

1951

Fact

There's been an eagle on a nickel,
An eagle on a quarter, too.
But there ain't no eagle
On a dime.

1951

Hope

He rose up on his dying bed
and asked for fish.
His wife looked it up in her dream book
and played it.

1951

Dream Boogie: Variation

Tinkling treble,
Rolling bass,
High noon teeth
In a midnight face,
Great long fingers
On great big hands,
Screaming pedals
Where his twelve-shoe lands,
Looks like his eyes
Are teasing pain,
A few minutes late
For the Freedom Train.

1951

Harlem

What happens to a dream deferred?

Does it dry up
like a raisin in the sun?
Or fester like a sore —
And then run?
Does it stink like rotten meat?
Or crust and sugar over —
like a syrupy sweet?

Maybe it just sags
like a heavy load.

Or does it explode?

1951

Good Morning

Good morning, daddy!
I was born here, he said,
watched Harlem grow
until colored folks spread
from river to river
across the middle of Manhattan
out of Penn Station
dark tenth of a nation,
planes from Puerto Rico,
and holds of boats, chico,
up from Cuba Haiti Jamaica,
in buses marked New York
from Georgia Florida Louisiana
to Harlem Brooklyn the Bronx
but most of all to Harlem
dusky sash across Manhattan
I've seen them come dark
    wondering
    wide-eyed
    dreaming
out of Penn Station —
but the trains are late.
The gates open —
Yet there're bars
at each gate.

    What happens
    to a dream deferred?

Daddy, ain't you heard?

1951

Same in Blues

I said to my baby,
Baby, take it slow.
I can't, she said, I can't!
I got to go!

There's a certain
amount of traveling
in a dream deferred.

Lulu said to Leonard,
I want a diamond ring.
Leonard said to Lulu,
You won't get a goddamn thing!

A certain
amount of nothing
in a dream deferred.

Daddy, daddy, daddy,
All I want is you.
You can have me, baby —
but my lovin' days is through.

A certain
amount of impotence
in a dream deferred.

Three parties
On my party line —
but that third party,
Lord, ain't mine!

There's liable
to be confusion
in a dream deferred.

From river to river,
Uptown and down,
There's liable to be confusion
when a dream gets kicked around.

1951

Comment on Curb

You talk like
they don't kick
dreams around
downtown.

I expect they do —
But I'm talking about
Harlem to you!

1951

Dream Variations

To fling my arms wide
In some place of the sun,
To whirl and to dance
Till the white day is done.
Then rest at cool evening
Beneath a tall tree
While night comes on gently,
      Dark like me —
That is my dream!

To fling my arms wide
In the face of the sun,
Dance! Whirl! Whirl!
Till the quick day is done.
Rest at pale evening . . .
A tall, slim tree . . .
Night coming tenderly
      Black like me.

1926

Luck

Sometimes a crumb falls
From the tables of joy,
Sometimes a bone
Is flung.

To some people
Love is given,
To others
Only heaven.

1959

OGDEN NASH (1902–1971)

Born in Rye, New York, to wealthy parents, Ogden Nash joined the staff of the *New Yorker* in 1929. He contributed poems regularly to the magazine, appeared often on radio programs, wrote screenplays for MGM, and collaborated with S. J. Perelman and Kurt Weill on the musical *One Touch of Venus* in 1943. A satirist of the "minor idiocies of humanity," Nash said he would rather be "a good bad poet, rather than a bad good poet." He used long lines, shameless puns, and polysyllabic rhymes in his signature brand of light verse. His poems seem intent on not taking themselves (or anything else) too seriously. They affect a nonchalance that their own baroque cleverness belies. At the same time they advance the notion that the better part of sophistication is skepticism.

Long Time No See, 'Bye Now

Let us all point an accusing finger at Mr. Latour.
Mr. Latour is an illiterate boor.
He watches horse racing, instead of the sport of kings, when at the track,
And to him first base is simply first base, instead of the initial sack.
He eats alligator pear, instead of avocado;
He says fan, or enthusiast, instead of aficionado.
He has none of the feeling for words that Ouida and Spinoza felt.
Instead of Eleanor, he says Mrs. Roosevelt.
Sometimes he speaks even more bluntly and rashly,
And says the former Mrs. Douglas Fairbanks Senior, instead of Sylvia,
   Lady Ashley.
He drinks his drinks in a saloon, instead of a tavern or grill,
And pronounces "know-how" "skill."
He calls poor people poor, instead of underprivileged,
Claiming that the English language is becoming overdrivileged.
He says the English language ought to get out of the nursery and leave the
   toys room,
So he goes to the bathroom, instead of the little boys' room.
I will offer the hand of my daughter and half my income tax to he who
   will bring me the head of Mr. Latour on a saucer
Before he has everybody else talking as illiterate as Defoe and Chaucer.

1949

Just How Low Can a Highbrow Go When a Highbrow Lowers His Brow?

Take the intellectual prig;
For his pretensions I do not care a whit or a fig.
I am content that he should know what name Achilles assumed
   among the women, and do his crosswords in Esperanto,
And ostentatiously comprehend the inner meaning of Pound's
   obscurest canto.
It does not disturb me that he can distinguish between "flaunt" and
   "flout," and "costive" and "costate,"
What does disturb me is his black-sheep brother, the intellectual prig
   apostate.
Such a one is so erudite that he frequently thinks in Aramaic,
But he expresses himself in slang long passé in Passaic.
His signature is purple ink in an illegible curlicue,
And he compares baseball to ballet, and laments the passing of
   burlesque, which he refers to as burlicue.

He has a folksy approach to the glory that was Greece,
And professes to find more social and sociological significance in
"Li'l Abner" than in "War and Peace."
For the most part, my feelings about him I silently conceal,
But when he comments that "The Power of Positive Thinking" burns
with a hard, gemlike flame, I can only cry that he is robbing
Pater to paw Peale.

1958

COUNTEE CULLEN (1903–1946)

Countee Cullen's exact place of birth is unknown. He was adopted by a Harlem preacher and his wife at age fifteen, and he regarded himself as a New Yorker. He went to New York University and taught in public schools, where his students included James Baldwin. Cullen's marriage to W. E. B. DuBois's daughter seemed a symbolic union of the generations, but it was a troubled marriage and ended in divorce. His satirical novel *One Way to Heaven* (1934) presents a window into the Harlem Renaissance.

Colored Blues Singer

Some weep to find the Golden Pear
Feeds maggots at the core,
And some grow cold as ice, and bear
Them prouder than before.

But you go singing like the sea
Whose lover turns to land;
You make your grief a melody
And take it by the hand.

Such songs the mellow-bosomed maids
Of Africa intone
For lovers dead in hidden glades,
Slow rotting flesh and bone.

Such keenings tremble from the kraal,
Where sullen-browed abides
The second wife whose dark tears fail
To draw him to her sides.

Somewhere Jeritza breaks her heart
On symbols Verdi wrote;
You tear the strings of your soul apart,
Blood dripping note by note.

1925

To John Keats, Poet at Spring Time

I cannot hold my peace, John Keats;
There never was a spring like this;
It is an echo, that repeats
My last year's song and next year's bliss.
I know, in spite of all men say
Of Beauty, you have felt her most.
Yea, even in your grave her way
Is laid. Poor, troubled, lyric ghost,
Spring never was so fair and dear
As Beauty makes her seem this year.

I cannot hold my peace, John Keats,
I am as helpless in the toil
Of Spring as any lamb that bleats
To feel the solid earth recoil
Beneath his puny legs. Spring beats
Her tocsin call to those who love her,
And lo! The dogwood petals cover
Her breast with drifts of snow, and sleek
White gulls fly screaming to her, and hover
About her shoulders, and kiss her cheek,
While white and purple lilacs muster
A strength that bears them to a cluster
Of color and odor; for her sake
All things that slept are now awake.

And you and I, shall we lie still,
John Keats, while Beauty summons us?
Somehow I feel your sensitive will
Is pulsing up some tremulous
Sap road of a maple tree, whose leaves
Grow music as they grow, since your
Wild voice is in them, a harp that grieves
For life that opens death's dark door.
Though dust, your fingers still can push
The Vision Splendid to a birth,
Though now they work as grass in the hush
Of the night on the broad sweet page of the earth.

"John Keats is dead," they say, but I
Who hear your full insistent cry
In bud and blossom, leaf and tree,
Know John Keats still writes poetry.
And while my head is earthward bowed
To read new life sprung from your shroud,
Folks seeing me must think it strange
That merely spring should so derange

My mind. They do not know that you,
John Keats, keep revel with me, too.

1925

EDWIN DENBY (1903–1983)

Edwin Denby was born in Tienstin, China, the son of an American diplomat. The family returned to the United States at the outbreak of World War I. A trained dancer and gymnast, Denby became a dance critic for the *New York Herald Tribune* and is widely considered the finest dance critic of his time. Of the function of criticism, he wrote, "It is not the critic's historic function to have the right opinions but to have interesting ones. He talks but he has nothing to sell. His social value is that of a man standing on a street corner talking so intently about his subject that he doesn't realize how peculiar he looks doing it. The intentness of his interest makes people who don't know what he's talking about believe that whatever it is, it must be real somehow — that the art of dancing must be a real thing to some people some of the time. That educates citizens who didn't know it and cheers up those who do."

Summer

I stroll on Madison in expensive clothes, sour.
Ostrich-legg'd or sweet-chested, the loping clerks
Slide me a glance nude as oh in a tiled shower
And lope on dead-pan, large male and female jerks.

Later from the open meadow in the Park
I watch a bulging pea-soup storm lie midtown;
Here the high air is clear, there buildings are murked,
Manhattan absorbs the cloud like a sage-brush plain.

In the grass sleepers sprawl without attraction:
Some large men who turned sideways, old ones on papers,
A soldier, face handkerchiefed, an erection
In his pants — only men, the women don't nap here.

Can these wide spaces suit a particular man?
They can suit whomever man's intestines can.

1948

The Silence at Night

(The designs on the sidewalk Bill pointed out)

The sidewalk cracks, gumspots, the water, the bits of refuse,
They reach out and bloom under arclight, neonlight —

Luck has uncovered this bloom as a by-produce
Having flowered too out behind the frightful stars of night.
And these cerise and lilac strewn fancies, open to bums
Who lie poisoned in vast delivery portals,
These pictures, sat on by the cats that watch the slums,
Are a bouquet luck has dropped here suitable to mortals.
So honey, it's lucky how we keep throwing away
Honey, it's lucky how it's no use anyway
Oh honey, it's lucky no one knows the way
Listen chum, if there's that much luck then it don't pay.
The echoes of a voice in the dark of a street
Roar when the pumping heart, bop, stops for a beat.

1948

On the Home Front — 1942

Because Jim insulted Harry eight years previous
By taking vengeance for a regular business loss
Forwardlooking Joe hints that Leslie's devious
Because who stands to lose by it, why you yourself boss.
Figures can't lie so it's your duty to keep control
You've got to have people you can trust, look at em smile
That's why we're going to win this war, I read a man's soul
Like a book, intuition, that's how I made my pile.
Anybody can make it, that's democracy, sure
The hard part's holding on, keeping fit, world of difference
You know war, mass hysteria, makes things insecure
Yep a war of survival, frankly I'm off the fence.
The small survivor has a difficult task
Answering the questions great historians ask.

1948

Alex Katz Paints His North Window

Alex Katz paints his north window
A bed and across the street, glare
City day that I within know
Like wide as high and near as far
New York School friends, you paint glory
Itself crowding closer further
Lose your marbles making it
What's in a name — it regathers
From within, a painting's silence
Resplendent, the silent roommate
Watch him, not a pet, long listen

Before glory, the stone heartbeat
When he's painted himself out of it
De Kooning says his picture's finished

1975

LORINE NIEDECKER (1903–1970)

Lorine Niedecker was born in Ford Atkinson, Wisconsin. She grew up and lived most of her life in grim circumstances on marshy Black Hawk Island nearby. Her close friendship with Louis Zukofsky began after she read the Zukosky-edited Objectivist issue of *Poetry* in 1931. She held a variety of jobs ("a job does not necessarily sustain life"), including that of cleaning woman at the Fort Atkinson Memorial Hospital from 1957 through 1962. She walked the five miles to work and back to her small cabin lacking plumbing on the bank of the Rock River. "If we knew more chemistry and physics I'd have more faith," she said. She had a fierce material grasp on reality, as even her analogies reveal: "People of all nationalities and color have changed the language like weather and pressure have changed the rocks." A posthumous boom in her reputation is in progress.

If I Were a Bird

I'd be a dainty contained cool
Greek figurette
on a morning shore —
H.D.

I'd flitter and feed and delouse myself
close to Williams' house
and his kind eyes

I'd be a never-museumed tinted glass
breakable from the shelves of Marianne Moore.

On Stevens' fictive sibilant hibiscus flower
I'd poise myself, a cuckoo, flamingo-pink.

I'd plunge the depths with Zukofsky
and all that means — stirred earth,
cut sky, organ-sounding, resounding
anew, anew.

I'd prick the sand in cunning, lean,
Cummings irony, a little drunk dead sober.
Man, that walk down the beach!

I'd sit on a quiet fence
and sing a quiet thing: sincere, sincere.
And that would be Reznikoff.

1956

Poet's Work

Grandfather
  advised me:
    Learn a trade

I learned
  to sit at desk
    and condense

No layoff
  from this
    condensery

1962

Who Was Mary Shelley?

What was her name
before she married?

She eloped with this Shelley
She rode a donkey
till the donkey had to be carried.

Mary was Frankenstein's creator
his yellow eye
before her husband was to drown

Created the monster nights
after Byron, Shelley
talked the candle down.

Who was Mary Shelley?
She read Greek, Italian
She bore a child

Who died
and yet another child
who died.

1964

My Life by Water

My life
  by water —
    Hear

spring's
  first frog
    or board

out on the cold
  ground
    giving

to wild green
  arts and letters
    Rabbits

raided
  my lettuce
    One boat

two —
  pointed toward
    my shore

thru birdstart
  wingdrip
    weed-drift

of the soft
  and serious —
    Water

1967

Lake Superior

In every part of every living thing
is stuff that once was rock

In blood the minerals
of the rock

Iron the common element of earth
in rocks and freighters

Sault Sainte Marie — big boats
coal-black and iron-ore-red
topped with what white castlework

The waters working together
    internationally
Gulls playing both sides

Radisson:
'a labyrinth of pleasure'
this world of the Lake

Long hair, long gun

Fingernails pulled out
by Mohawks

(*The long*
canoes)

'Birch Bark
    and white Seder
        for the ribs'

Through all this granite land
the sign of the cross

Beauty: impurities in the rock

And at the blue ice superior spot
priest-robed Marquette grazed
azoic rock, hornblende granite
basalt the common dark
in all the Earth

And his bones of such is coral
raised up out of his grave
were sunned and birch bark-floated
to the straits

Joliet

Entered the Mississippi
Found there the paddlebill catfish
come down from The Age of Fishes

At Hudson Bay he conversed in Latin
with an Englishman

To Labrador and back to vanish
His funeral gratis — he'd played
Quebec's Cathedral organ
so many winters

Ruby of corundum
lapis lazuli
from changing limestone
glow-apricot red-brown
carnelian sard

Greek named
Exodus-antique
kicked up in America's
Northwest
you have been in my mind
between my toes
agate

Wild pigeon

Did not man
    maimed by no
        stone-fall

mash the cobalt
    and carnelian
        of that bird

Schoolcraft left the Soo — canoes
US pennants, masts, sails
Chanting canoemen, barge
Soldiers — for Minnesota

Their South Shore journey
        as if Life's —
The Chocolate River
        The Laughing Fish
and The River of the Dead

Passed peaks of volcanic thrust
Hornblende in massed granite
Wave-cut Cambrian rock
painted by soluble mineral oxides
wave-washed and the rains
did their work and a green
running as from copper

Sea-roaring caverns —
Chippewas threw deermeat
to the savage maws
'*Voyageurs* crossed themselves
tossed a twist of tobacco in'

Inland then
beside the great granite
gneiss and the schists

to the redolent pondy lakes'
lilies, flag and Indian reed
'through which we successfully
passed'

The smooth black stone
I picked up in true source park
the leaf beside it
once was stone

Why should we hurry
home

I'm sorry to have missed
Sand Lake
My dear one tells me
we did not
We watched a gopher there

1968

I Married

I married
in the world's black night
for warmth
if not repose.
At the close —
someone.

I hid with him
from the long range guns.
We lay leg
in the cupboard, head
in closet.

A slit of light
at no bird dawn —
Untaught
I thought
he drank

too much.
I say

I married
and lived unburied.
I thought —

1968

Wilderness

You are the man
You are my other country
and I find it hard going

You are the prickly pear
You are the sudden violent storm

the torrent to raise the river
to float the wounded doe

2002

Louis Zukofsky (1904–1978)

Born to Yiddish-speaking Russian immigrants on the Lower East Side of New York City, Louis Zukofsky attended Stuyvesant High School and Columbia College, where his best friend (and classmate) was Whittaker Chambers. As a Columbia student, Zukofsky was a "subtle poet" with an "inarticulate soul," wrote his professor, Mark Van Doren. Zukofsky edited the February 1931 issue of *Poetry* devoted to the "Objectivists," a Zukofsky coinage to describe the ways and means of such poets as William Carlos Williams, George Oppen, Carl Rakosi, and Charles Reznikoff. Zukofsky later met and formed close ties to Lorine Niedecker. "Louis Zukofsky, whose name may well be the best known of our time when the dust has settled around the year 2050, remains unknown and unread," Guy Davenport lamented in 1987.

"A" 11

for Celia and Paul

River that must turn full after I stop dying
Song, my song, raise grief to music
Light as my loves' thought, the few sick
So sick of wrangling: thus weeping,
Sounds of light, stay in her keeping
And my son's face — this much for honor.

Freed by their praises who make honor dearer
Whose losses show them rich and you no poorer
Take care, song, that what stars' imprint you mirror
Grazes their tears; draw speech from their nature or
Love in you — faced to your outer stars — purer
Gold than tongues make without feeling
Art new, hurt old: revealing
The slackened bow as the stinging
Animal dies, thread gold stringing
The fingerboard pressed in my honor.

Honor, song, sang the blest is delight knowing
We overcome ills by love. Hurt, song, nourish
Eyes, think most of whom you hurt. For the flowing
River's poison where what rod blossoms. Flourish
By love's sweet lights and sing *in them I flourish.*
No, song, not any one power
May recall or forget, our
Love to see your love flows into
Us. If Venus lights, your words spin, to
Live our desires lead us to honor.

Graced, your heart in nothing less than in death, go —
I, dust — raise the great hem of the extended
World that nothing can leave; having had breath go
Face my son, say: 'If your father offended
You with mute wisdom, my words have not ended
His second paradise where
His love was in her eyes where
They turn, quick for you two — sick
Or gone cannot make music
You set less than all. Honor

His voice in me, the river's turn that finds the
Grace in you, four notes first too full for talk, leaf
Lighting stem, stems bound to the branch that binds the
Tree, and then as from the same root we talk, leaf
After leaf of your mind's music, page, walk leaf
Over leaf of his thought, sounding
His happiness: song sounding
The grace that comes from knowing
Things, her love our own showing
Her love in all her honor.'

1966

To My Wash-stand

To my wash-stand
in which I wash
my left hand
and my right hand

To my wash-stand
whose base is Greek
whose shaft
is marble and is fluted

To my wash-stand
whose wash-bowl
is an oval
in a square

To my wash-stand
whose square is marble
and inscribes two
smaller ovals to left and right for soap

Comes a song of
water from the right faucet and the left
my left and my
right hand mixing hot and cold

Comes a flow which
if I have called a song
is a song
entirely in my head

a song out of imagining
modillions described above
my head a frieze
of stone completing what no longer

is my wash-stand
since its marble has completed
my getting up each morning
my washing before going to bed

my look into a mirror
to glimpse half an oval
as if its half
were half-oval in my head and the

climates of many
inscriptions human heads shapes'
horses' elephants' (tusks) others'
scratched in marble tile

so my wash-stand
in one particular breaking of the
tile at which I have
looked and looked

has opposed to my head
the inscription of a head
whose coinage is the
coinage of the poor

observant in waiting
in their getting up mornings
and in their waiting
going to bed

carefully attentive
to what they have
and to what they do not
have

when a flow of water
doubled in narrow folds
occasions invertible counterpoints
over a head and

an age in a wash-stand
and in their own heads

1966

No it was no dream of coming death

No it was no dream of coming death,
Those you love will live long.
If light hurried my dream, I saw none:
Stepped from my bed and to the sill,
From a window looked down
On the river I knew set forth
To rise toward me — full after rain.
People watched, crowded the banks, thought
As with old words to a river:
(whose waters seemed unwillingly
to glide like friends who linger while
they sever.) Soon, as expected!

A coffin launched like a ship's hull
Sped as from a curtain afire
Draped to the keystone of an arch
And — as at a burial at sea —
Sank. The displaced water rose,
Made the heart sound the coffin's grave,
Woke under the stream and in me
A set of furtive bells, muted
And jangling by rote "What does this say?
What loss will make the world different?
Are they gathered to further war?
What sorrow do you fear?
Ask, will you, is it here
Distrust is cast off, all
Cowardice dies. Eyes, looking out,
Without the good of intellect,
Rouse as you are used to:
It is the bad fallen away,
And the sorrow in the good.
You saw now for your book, *Anew*."

1966

Stanley Kunitz (1905–2006)

Stanley Kunitz was born in Worcester, Massachusetts, and educated at Harvard. During World War II he served in the Air Transport Command of the U.S. Army. He taught for many years at Columbia University, where his students revered him. As judge of the Yale Younger Poets series he chose the first books of Robert Hass and Carolyn Forché. In 2000, at the age of 95, Kunitz succeeded Robert Pinsky in a one-year stint as the nation's poet laureate.

Three Small Parables for My Poet Friends

I

Certain saurian species, notably the skink, are capable of shedding their tails in self-defense when threatened. The detached appendage diverts attention to itself by taking on a life of its own and thrashing furiously about. As soon as the stalking wildcat pounces on the wriggler, snatching it up from the sand to bite and maul it, the free lizard scampers off. A new tail begins to grow in place of the one that has been sacrificed.

II

The larva of the tortoise beetle has the neat habit of collecting its droppings and exfoliated skin into a little packet that it carries over its back when it is out in the open. If it were not for this fecal shield, it would lie naked before its enemies.

III

Among the Bedouins, the beggar poets of the desert are held in contempt because of their greed, their thievery and venality. Everyone in the scattered encampments knows that poems of praise can be bought, even by the worst of scoundrels, for food or money. Furthermore, these wandering minstrels are notorious for stealing the ideas, lines, and even whole songs of others. Often the recitation is interrupted by the shouts of the squatters around the campfire: "Thou liest. Thou stolest it from So-and-so!" When the poet tries to defend himself, calling for witnesses to vouch for his probity or, in extremity, appealing to Allah, his hearers hoot him down, crying, "Kassad, kaddab! A poet is a liar."

1985

Kenneth Rexroth (1905–1982)

Kenneth Rexroth was born in South Bend, Indiana. Like Robert Lowell and William Stafford, he was a conscientious objector during World War II. *Time* magazine dubbed Rexroth "the Daddy of the Beat Generation." He was the master of ceremonies at Allen Ginsberg's celebrated public declamation of "Howl" on 13 October 1955 at the Six Gallery in San Francisco. In 1957 he wrote in the *Evergreen Review*, "Poets come to San Francisco for the same reason so many Hungarians have been going to Austria recently." He felt the urgent need to escape from "the world of poet-professors, Southern Colonels and ex-Left Social Fascists" and ridiculed the editors of the *Partisan Review* as "Brooks Brothers Boys who got an overdose of T. S. Eliot at some Ivy League fog factory." In addition to his many translations of poems from the Japanese and the Chinese, Rexroth wrote a popular "great books" column in which he discussed the virtues of Homer, Apuleius, Lady Murasaki, Montaigne, Cervantes, and Tolstoy. The columns appeared in the *Saturday Review* and were collected in a book entitled *Classics Revisited.* An academic critic once charged that Rexroth belonged, with Gary Snyder and Philip Whalen, to the "bear-shit-on-the-trail school of poetry," which Rexroth took as a compliment.

Delia Rexroth

Died June, 1916

Under your illkempt yellow roses,
Delia, today you are younger
Than your son. Two and a half decades —
The family monument sagged askew,
And he overtook your half-a-life.
On the other side of the country,
Near the willows by the slow river,
Deep in the earth, the white ribs retain
The curve of your fervent, careful breast;
The fine skull, the ardor of your brain.
And in the fingers the memory
Of Chopin études, and in the feet

Slow waltzes and champagne twosteps sleep.
And the white full moon of midsummer,
That you watched awake all that last night,
Watches history fill the deserts
And oceans with corpses once again;
And looks in the east window at me,
As I move past you to middle age
And knowledge past your agony and waste.

1944

Vitamins and Roughage

Strong ankled, sun burned, almost naked,
The daughters of California
Educate reluctant humanists;
Drive into their skulls with tennis balls
The unhappy realization
That nature is still stronger than man.
The special Hellenic privilege
Of the special intellect seeps out
At last in this irrigated soil.
Sweat of athletes and juice of lovers
Are stronger than Socrates' hemlock;
And the games of scrupulous Euclid
Vanish in the gymnopaedia.

1944

The Signature of All Things

I

My head and shoulders, and my book
In the cool shade, and my body
Stretched bathing in the sun, I lie
Reading beside the waterfall —
Boehme's 'Signature of All Things.'
Through the deep July day the leaves
Of the laurel, all the colors
Of gold, spin down through the moving
Deep laurel shade all day. They float
On the mirrored sky and forest
For a while, and then, still slowly
Spinning, sink through the crystal deep
Of the pool to its leaf gold floor.
The saint saw the world as streaming
In the electrolysis of love.
I put him by and gaze through shade

Folded into shade of slender
Laurel trunks and leaves filled with sun.
The wren broods in her moss domed nest.
A newt struggles with a white moth
Drowning in the pool. The hawks scream,
Playing together on the ceiling
Of heaven. The long hours go by.
I think of those who have loved me,
Of all the mountains I have climbed,
Of all the seas I have swum in.
The evil of the world sinks.
My own sin and trouble fall away
Like Christian's bundle, and I watch
My forty summers fall like falling
Leaves and falling water held
Eternally in summer air.

II

Deer are stamping in the glades,
Under the full July moon.
There is a smell of dry grass
In the air, and more faintly,
The scent of a far off skunk.
As I stand at the wood's edge,
Watching the darkness, listening
To the stillness, a small owl
Comes to the branch above me,
On wings more still than my breath.
When I turn my light on him,
His eyes glow like drops of iron,
And he perks his head at me,
Like a curious kitten.
The meadow is bright as snow.
My dog prowls the grass, a dark
Blur in the blur of brightness.
I walk to the oak grove where
The Indian village was once.
There, in blotched and cobwebbed light
And dark, dim in the blue haze,
Are twenty Holstein heifers,
Black and white, all lying down,
Quietly together, under
The huge trees rooted in the graves.

III

When I dragged the rotten log
From the bottom of the pool,
It seemed heavy as stone.
I let it lie in the sun
For a month; and then chopped it

Into sections, and split them
For kindling, and spread them out
To dry some more. Late that night;
After reading for hours,
While moths rattled at the lamp,
The saints and the philosophers
On the destiny of man;
I went out on my cabin porch,
And looked up through the black forest
At the swaying islands of stars.
Suddenly I saw at my feet,
Spread on the floor of night, ingots
Of quivering phosphorescence,
And all about were scattered chips
Of pale cold light that was alive.

1949

Empty Mirror

As long as we are lost
In the world of purpose
We are not free. I sit
In my ten foot square hut.
The birds sing. The bees hum.
The leaves sway. The water
Murmurs over the rocks.
The canyon shuts me in.
If I moved, Basho's frog
Would splash in the pool.
All summer long the gold
Laurel leaves fell through space.
Today I was aware
Of a maple leaf floating
On the pool. In the night
I stare into the fire.
Once I saw fire cities,
Towns, palaces, wars,
Heroic adventures,
In the campfires of youth.
Now I see only fire.
My breath moves quietly.
The stars move overhead.
In the clear darkness
Only a small red glow
Is left in the ashes.
On the table lies a cast
Snake skin and an uncut stone.

1952

Robert Penn Warren (1905–1989)

Robert Penn Warren was born in Guthrie, Kentucky. He achieved great acclaim as a poet and novelist, professor and critic. He was coeditor (with Cleanth Brooks) of *Understanding Poetry* (1938), the widely used textbook that did much to promote the New Criticism and particularly the then-revolutionary notion that poems can be read, analyzed, and appreciated on textual terms without reference to the author's biography or to the social circumstances surrounding the poem's composition. Nicknamed "Red," Warren won three Pulitzer Prizes: one for his novel *All the King's Men* (1946) and the other two for poetry collections. He had served as poetry consultant to the Library of Congress in 1944–1945, and in 1986, when the name of the position was officially changed to poet laureate, Warren was the first to be appointed to the post.

Watershed

From this high place all things flow:
Land of divided streams, of water spilled
Eastward, westward without memento;
Land where the morning mist is curled
Like smoke about the ridgepole of the world.
The mist is furled.

The sunset hawk now rides
The tall light up the climbing deep of air.
Beneath him swings the rooftree that divides
The east and west. His gold eyes scan
The crumpled shade on gorge and crest,
And streams that creep and disappear, appear,
Past fingered ridges and their shrivelling span.
Under the broken eaves men take their rest.

Forever, should they stir, their thought would keep
This place. Not love, happiness past, constrains,
But certitude. Enough, and it remains;
Though they who thread the flood and neap
Of earth itself have felt the earth creep,
In pastures hung against the rustling gorge
Have felt the shudder and the sweat of stone,
Knowing thereby no constant moon
Sustains the hill's lost granite surge.

1932

Brotherhood in Pain

Fix your eyes on any chance object. For instance,
The leaf, prematurely crimson, of the swamp maple

That dawdles down gold air to the velvet-black water
Of the moribund beaver-pond. Or the hunk

Of dead chewing gum in the gutter with the mark of a molar
Yet distinct on it, like the most delicate Hellenistic chisel-work.

Or a black sock you took off last night and by mistake
Left lying, to be found in the morning, on the bathroom tiles.

Or pick up a single stone from the brookside, inspect it
Most carefully, then throw it back in. You will never

See it again. By the next spring flood, it may have been hurled
A mile downstream. Fix your gaze on any of these objects,

Or if you think me disingenuous in my suggestions,
Whirl around three times like a child, or a dervish, with eyes shut,

Then fix on the first thing seen when they open.
In any case, you will suddenly observe an object in the obscene
moment of birth.

It does not know what it is. It has no name. The matrix from which
it is torn
Bleeds profusely. It has not yet begun to breathe. Its experience

Is too terrible to recount. Only when it has completely forgotten
Everything, will it smile shyly, and try to love you,

For somehow it knows that you are lonely, too.
It pityingly knows that you are more lonely than it is, for

You exist only in the delirious illusion of language.

1975

The Whole Question

You'll have to rethink the whole question. This
Getting born business is not as simple as it seemed,
Or the midwife thought, or doctor deemed. It is,
Time shows, more complicated than either — or you — ever dreamed.

If it can be said that you dreamed anything
Before what's called a hand slapped blazing breath
Into you, snatched your dream's lulling nothing-
ness into what — was it Calvin? — called the body of this death.

You had not, for instance, provisioned the terrible thing called love,
Which began with a strange, sweet taste and bulbed softness while
Two orbs of tender light leaned there above.
Sometimes your face got twisted. They called it a smile.

You noticed how faces from outer vastness might twist, too.
But sometimes different twists, with names unknown,
And there were noises with no names you knew,
Or times of dark silence when you seemed nothing — or gone.

Years passed, but sometimes seemed nothing except the same.
You knew more words, but they were words only, only —
Metaphysical midges that plunged at the single flame
That centered the inward dark of your skull, or lonely, lonely.

You woke in the dark of real night to hear the breath
That seemed to promise reality in the vacuum
Of the sleepless dream beginning when underneath
The curtain dawn seeps, and on wet asphalt first tires hum.

Yes, you must try to rethink what is real. Perhaps
It is only a matter of language that traps you. You
May find a new way in which experience overlaps
Words. Or find some words that make the Truth come true.

1982

W. H. Auden (1907–1973)

Wystan Hugh Auden, who was born in York, England, moved to New York City in 1939. The most prominent English poet of his generation, he had discovered his vocation as a student at Oxford University, where he found himself at the center of a literary circle that included Stephen Spender, C. Day Lewis, Christopher Isherwood, and Louis MacNeice. He collaborated with Isherwood on such plays as *The Dog Beneath the Skin* (1935) and with MacNeice on a travelogue, *Letters from Iceland* (1937). Many in Britain never forgave him for his "defection" to the United States on the eve of a global conflict. Others felt that Auden began to decline as a poet from the time he set foot in America. On the other hand, it is also possible to regard the metaphorical trade of the American T. S. Eliot for the English Auden as that rare deal that enriches both teams. Auden, who became an American citizen in 1946, was a major presence in New York City. He wrote some of the most enduring poems of the twentieth century, brilliant critical essays (*The Dyer's Hand*), masterly light verse (*Academic Graffiti*); he was also an accomplished anthologist and editor, with great funds of knowledge and bons mots. In later years, when his countenance was as cracked with lines as the limestone landscapes he loved, he quipped that his face looked "like a wedding-cake left out in the rain." Auden compulsively rewrote (and sometimes weakened) or even renounced some of his signature poems, including both "September 1, 1939" and "In Memory of William Butler Yeats," both of which are given here in their original, unexpurgated versions.

It's no use raising a shout

It's no use raising a shout.
No, Honey, you can cut that right out.
I don't want any more hugs;
Make me some fresh tea, fetch me some rugs.
Here am I, here are you:
But what does it mean? What are we going to do?

A long time ago I told my mother
I was leaving home to find another:
I never answered her letter
But I never found a better.
Here am I, here are you:
But what does it mean? What are we going to do?

It wasn't always like this?
Perhaps it wasn't, but it is.
Put the car away; when life fails,
What's the good of going to Wales?
Here am I, here are you:
But what does it mean? What are we going to do?

In my spine there was a base,
And I knew the general's face:
But they've severed all the wires,
And I can't tell what the general desires.
Here am I, here are you:
But what does it mean? What are we going to do?

In my veins there is a wish,
And a memory of fish:
When I lie crying on the floor,
It says, 'you've often done this before,'
Here am I, here are you:
But what does it mean? What are we going to do?

A bird used to visit this shore:
It isn't going to come any more.
I've come a very long way to prove
No land, no water, and no love.
Here am I, here are you:
But what does it mean? What are we going to do?

1929

As I walked out one evening

As I walked out one evening,
Walking down Bristol Street,
The crowds upon the pavement
Were fields of harvest wheat.

And down by the brimming river
I heard a lover sing
Under an arch of the railway:
'Love has no ending.

'I'll love you, dear, I'll love you
Till China and Africa meet
And the river jumps over the mountain
And the salmon sing in the street.

'I'll love you till the ocean
Is folded and hung up to dry
And the seven stars go squawking
Like geese about the sky.

'The years shall run like rabbits
For in my arms I hold
The Flower of the Ages
And the first love of the world.'

But all the clocks in the city
Began to whirr and chime:
'O let not Time deceive you,
You cannot conquer Time.

'In the burrows of the Nightmare
Where Justice naked is,
Time watches from the shadow
And coughs when you would kiss.

'In headaches and in worry
Vaguely life leaks away,
And Time will have his fancy
To-morrow or to-day.

'Into many a green valley
Drifts the appalling snow;
Time breaks the threaded dances
And the diver's brillant bow.

'O plunge your hands in water,
Plunge them in up to the wrist;

Stare, stare in the basin
　　And wonder what you've missed.

'The glacier knocks in the cupboard,
　　The desert sighs in the bed,
And the crack in the tea-cup opens
　　A lane to the land of the dead.

'Where the beggars raffle the banknotes
　　And the Giant is enchanting to Jack,
And the Lily-white Boy is a Roarer
　　And Jill goes down on her back.

'O look, look in the mirror,
　　O look in your distress;
Life remains a blessing
　　Although you cannot bless.

'O stand, stand at the window
　　As the tears scald and start;
You shall love your crooked neighbour
　　With your crooked heart.'

It was late, late in the evening,
　　The lovers they were gone;
The clocks had ceased their chiming
　　And the deep river ran on.

1937

Musée des Beaux Arts

About suffering they were never wrong,
The Old Masters: how well they understood
Its human position: how it takes place
While someone else is eating or opening a window or just
　　walking dully along:
How, when the aged are reverently, passionately waiting
For the miraculous birth, there always must be
Children who did not specially want it to happen, skating
On a pond at the edge of the wood:
They never forgot
That even the dreadful martyrdom must run its course
Anyhow in a corner, some untidy spot
Where the dogs go on with their doggy
　　life and the torturer's horse
Scratches its innocent behind on a tree.

In Brueghel's *Icarus*, for instance: how everything turns away
Quite leisurely from the disaster; the ploughman may
Have heard the splash, the forsaken cry,
But for him it was not an important failure; the sun shone
As it had to on the white legs disappearing into the green
Water; and the expensive delicate ship that must have seen
Something amazing, a boy falling out of the sky,
Had somewhere to get to and sailed calmly on.

1938

In Memory of W. B. Yeats

(d. January 1939)

I

He disappeared in the dead of winter:
The brooks were frozen, the air-ports almost deserted,
And snow disfigured the public statues;
The mercury sank in the mouth of the dying day.
O all the instruments agree
The day of his death was a dark cold day.

Far from his illness
The wolves ran on through the evergreen forests,
The peasant river was untempted by the fashionable quays;
By mourning tongues
The death of the poet was kept from his poems.

But for him it was his last afternoon as himself,
An afternoon of nurses and rumours;
The provinces of his body revolted,
The squares of his mind were empty,
Silence invaded the suburbs,
The current of his feeling failed: he became his admirers.

Now he is scattered among a hundred cities
And wholly given over to unfamiliar affections;
To find his happiness in another kind of wood
And be punished under a foreign code of conscience.
The words of a dead man
Are modified in the guts of the living.

But in the importance and noise of to-morrow
When the brokers are roaring like beasts on the
floor of the Bourse,
And the poor have the sufferings to which
they are fairly accustomed,

And each in the cell of himself is almost
    convinced of his freedom;
A few thousand will think of this day
As one thinks of a day when one did something
    slightly unusual.

O all the instruments agree
The day of his death was a dark cold day.

II

You were silly like us: your gift survived it all;
The parish of rich women, physical decay,
Yourself; mad Ireland hurt you into poetry.
Now Ireland has her madness and her weather still,
For poetry makes nothing happen: it survives
In the valley of its saying where executives
Would never want to tamper; it flows south
From ranches of isolation and the busy griefs,
Raw towns that we believe and die in; it survives,
A way of happening, a mouth.

III

Earth, receive an honoured guest;
William Yeats is laid to rest:
Let the Irish vessel lie
Emptied of its poetry.

Time that is intolerant
Of the brave and innocent,
And indifferent in a week
To a beautiful physique,

Worships language and forgives
Everyone by whom it lives;
Pardons cowardice, conceit,
Lays its honours at their feet.

Time that with this strange excuse
Pardoned Kipling and his views,
And will pardon Paul Claudel,
Pardons him for writing well.

In the nightmare of the dark
All the dogs of Europe bark,
And the living nations wait,
Each sequestered in its hate;

Intellectual disgrace
Stares from every human face,
And the seas of pity lie
Locked and frozen in each eye.

Follow, poet, follow right
To the bottom of the night,
With your unconstraining voice
Still persuade us to rejoice;

With the farming of a verse
Make a vineyard of the curse,
Sing of human unsuccess
In a rapture of distress;

In the deserts of the heart
Let the healing fountain start,
In the prison of his days
Teach the free man how to praise.

1939

September 1, 1939

I sit in one of the dives
On Fifty-Second Street
Uncertain and afraid
As the clever hopes expire
Of a low dishonest decade:
Waves of anger and fear
Circulate over the bright
And darkened lands of the earth,
Obsessing our private lives;
The unmentionable odour of death
Offends the September night.

Accurate scholarship can
Unearth the whole offence
From Luther until now
That has driven a culture mad,
Find what occurred at Linz,
What huge imago made
A psychopathic god:
I and the public know
What all schoolchildren learn,
Those to whom evil is done
Do evil in return.

Exiled Thucydides knew
All that a speech can say
About Democracy,
And what dictators do,
The elderly rubbish they talk
To an apathetic grave;
Analysed all in his book,
The enlightenment driven away,
The habit-forming pain,
Mismanagement and grief:
We must suffer them all again.

Into this neutral air
Where blind skyscrapers use
Their full height to proclaim
The strength of Collective Man,
Each language pours its vain
Competitive excuse:
But who can live for long
In an euphoric dream;
Out of the mirror they stare,
Imperialism's face
And the international wrong.

Faces along the bar
Cling to their average day:
The lights must never go out,
The music must always play,
All the conventions conspire
To make this fort assume
The furniture of home;
Lest we should see where we are,
Lost in a haunted wood,
Children afraid of the night
Who have never been happy or good.

The windiest militant trash
Important persons shout
Is not so crude as our wish:
What mad Nijinsky wrote
About Diaghilev
Is true of the normal heart;
For the error bred in the bone
Of each woman and each man
Craves what it cannot have,
Not universal love
But to be loved alone.

From the conservative dark
Into the ethical life
The dense commuters come,
Repeating their morning vow,
"I *will* be true to the wife,
I'll concentrate more on my work,"
And helpless governors wake
To resume their compulsory game:
Who can release them now,
Who can reach the deaf,
Who can speak for the dumb?

All I have is a voice
To undo the folded lie,
The romantic lie in the brain
Of the sensual man-in-the-street
And the lie of Authority
Whose buildings grope the sky:
There is no such thing as the State
And no one exists alone;
Hunger allows no choice
To the citizen or the police;
We must love one another or die.

Defenceless under the night
Our world in stupor lies;
Yet, dotted everywhere,
Ironic points of light
Flash out wherever the Just
Exchange their messages:
May I, composed like them
Of Eros and of dust,
Beleaguered by the same
Negation and despair,
Show an affirming flame.

1939

Law, say the gardeners, is the sun

Law, say the gardeners, is the sun,
Law is the one
All gardeners obey
To-morrow, yesterday, to-day.

Law is the wisdom of the old
The impotent grandfathers shrilly scold;
The grandchildren put out a treble tongue,
Law is the senses of the young.

Law, says the priest with a priestly look,
Expounding to an unpriestly people,
Law is the words in my priestly book,
Law is my pulpit and my steeple.

Law, says the judge as he looks down his nose,
Speaking clearly and most severely,
Law is as I've told you before,
Law is as you know I suppose,
Law is but let me explain it once more,
Law is The Law.

Yet law-abiding scholars write:
Law is neither wrong nor right,
Law is only crimes
Punished by places and by times,
Law is the clothes men wear.
Anytime, anywhere,
Law is Good-morning and Good-night.

Others say, Law is our Fate;
Others say, Law is our State;
Others say, others say
Law is no more
Law has gone away.

And always the loud angry crowd
Very angry and very loud
Law is We,
And always the soft idiot softly Me.

If we, dear, know we know no more
Than they about the law,
If I no more than you
Know what we should and should not do
Except that all agree
Gladly or miserably
That the law is
And that all know this,
If therefore thinking it absurd
To identify Law with some other word,
Unlike so many men
I cannot say Law is again,
No more than they can we suppress
The universal wish to guess
Or slip out of our own position
Into an unconcerned condition.
Although I can at least confine
Your vanity and mine

To stating timidly
A timid similarity,
We shall boast anyway:
Like love I say.

Like love we don't know where or why
Like love we can't compel or fly
Like love we often weep
Like love we seldom keep.

1939

In Memory of Sigmund Freud

(d. September 1939)

When there are so many we shall have to mourn,
When grief has been made so public, and exposed
    To the critique of a whole epoch
    The frailty of our conscience and anguish,

Of whom shall we speak? For every day they die
Among us, those who were doing us some good,
    And knew it was never enough but
    Hoped to improve a little by living.

Such was this doctor: still at eighty he wished
To think of our life, from whose unruliness
    So many plausible young futures
    With threats or flattery ask obedience.

But his wish was denied him; he closed his eyes
Upon that last picture common to us all,
    Of problems like relatives standing
    Puzzled and jealous about our dying.

For about him at the very end were still
Those he had studied, the nervous and the nights,
    And shades that still waited to enter
    The bright circle of his recognition

Turned elsewhere with their disappointment as he
Was taken away from his old interest
    To go back to the earth in London,
    An important Jew who died in exile.

Only Hate was happy, hoping to augment
His practice now, and his shabby clientele

Who think they can be cured by killing
And covering the gardens with ashes.

They are still alive but in a world he changed
Simply by looking back with no false regrets;
All that he did was to remember
Like the old and be honest like children.

He wasn't clever at all: he merely told
The unhappy Present to recite the Past
Like a poetry lesson till sooner
Or later it faltered at the line where

Long ago the accusations had begun,
And suddenly knew by whom it had been judged,
How rich life had been and how silly,
And was life-forgiven and more humble,

Able to approach the Future as a friend
Without a wardrobe of excuses, without
A set mask of rectitude or an
Embarrassing over-familiar gesture.

No wonder the ancient cultures of conceit
In his technique of unsettlement foresaw
The fall of princes, the collapse of
Their lucrative patterns of frustration.

If he succeeded, why, the Generalised Life
Would become impossible, the monolith
Of State be broken and prevented
The co-operation of avengers.

Of course they called on God: but he went his way,
Down among the Lost People like Dante, down
To the stinking fosse where the injured
Lead the ugly life of the rejected.

And showed us what evil is: not as we thought
Deeds that must be punished, but our lack of faith,
Our dishonest mood of denial,
The concupiscence of the oppressor.

And if something of the autocratic pose,
The paternal strictness he distrusted, still
Clung to his utterance and features,
It was a protective imitation

For one who lived among enemies so long:
If often he was wrong and at times absurd,
        To us he is no more a person
        Now but a whole climate of opinion

Under whom we conduct our differing lives:
Like weather he can only hinder or help,
        The proud can still be proud but find it
        A little harder, and the tyrant tries

To make him do but doesn't care for him much.
He quietly surrounds all our habits of growth;
        He extends, till the tired in even
        The remotest most miserable duchy

Have felt the change in their bones and are cheered,
And the child unlucky in his little State,
        Some hearth where freedom is excluded,
        A hive whose honey is fear and worry,

Feels calmer now and somehow assured of escape;
While as they lie in the grass of our neglect,
        So many long-forgotten objects
        Revealed by his undiscouraged shining

Are returned to us and made precious again;
Games we had thought we must drop as we grew up,
        Little noises we dared not laugh at,
        Faces we made when no one was looking.

But he wishes us more than this: to be free
Is often to be lonely; he would unite
        The unequal moieties fractured
        By our own well-meaning sense of justice,

Would restore to the larger the wit and will
The smaller possesses but can only use
        For arid disputes, would give back to
        The son the mother's richness of feeling.

But he would have us remember most of all
To be enthusiastic over the night
        Not only for the sense of wonder
        It alone has to offer, but also

Because it needs our love: for with sad eyes
Its delectable creatures look up and beg
        Us dumbly to ask them to follow;
        They are exiles who long for the future

That lies in our power. They too would rejoice
If allowed to serve enlightenment like him,
Even to bear our cry of "Judas,"
As he did and all must bear who serve it.

One rational voice is dumb: over a grave
The household of Impulse mourns one dearly loved.
Sad is Eros, builder of cities,
And weeping anarchic Aphrodite.

1939

But I Can't

Time will say nothing but I told you so,
Time only knows the price we have to pay;
If I could tell you I would let you know.

If we should weep when clowns put on their show,
If we should stumble when musicians play,
Time will say nothing but I told you so.

There are no fortunes to be told, although,
Because I love you more than I can say,
If I could tell you I would let you know.

The winds must come from somewhere when they blow,
There must be reasons why the leaves decay;
Time will say nothing but I told you so.

Perhaps the roses really want to grow,
The vision seriously intends to stay;
If I could tell you I would let you know.

Suppose the lions all get up and go,
And all the brooks and soldiers run away;
Will Time say nothing but I told you so?
If I could tell you I would let you know.

1940

Jumbled in the common box

Jumbled in the common box
Of their dark stupidity,
Orchid, swan, and Caesar lie;
Time that tires of everyone

Has corroded all the locks,
Thrown away the key for fun.

In its cleft the torrent mocks
Prophets who in days gone by
Made a profit on each cry,
Persona grata now with none;
And a jackass language shocks
Poets who can only pun.

Silence settles on the clocks;
Nursing mothers point a sly
Index finger at a sky,
Crimson with the setting sun;
In the valley of the fox
Gleams the barrel of a gun.

Once we could have made the docks,
Now it is too late to fly;
Once too often you and I
Did what we should not have done;
Round the rampant rugged rocks
Rude and ragged rascals run.

1941

A Healthy Spot

They're nice — one would never dream of going over
Any contract of theirs with a magnifying
Glass, or of locking up one's letters — also
Kind and efficient — one gets what one asks for.
Just what is wrong, then, that, living among them,
One is constantly struck by the number of
Happy marriages and unhappy people?
They attend all the lectures on Post-War Problems,
For they do mind, they honestly want to help; yet,
As they notice the earth in their morning papers,
What sense do they make of its folly and horror
Who have never, one is convinced, felt a sudden
Desire to torture the cat or do a strip-tease
In a public place? Have they ever, one wonders,
Wanted so much to see a unicorn, even
A dead one? Probably. But they won't say so,
Ignoring by tacit consent our hunger
For eternal life, that caged rebuked question
Occasionally let out at clambakes or

College reunions, and which the smoking-room story
Alone, ironically enough, stands up for.

1944

Under Which Lyre
A Reactionary Tract For The Times

(Phi Beta Kappa Poem, Harvard, 1946)

Ares at last has quit the field,
The bloodstains on the bushes yield
        To seeping showers,
And in their convalescent state
The fractured towns associate
        With summer flowers.

Encamped upon the college plain
Raw veterans already train
        As freshman forces;
Instructors with sarcastic tongue
Shepherd the battle-weary young
        Through basic courses.

Among bewildering appliances
For mastering the arts and sciences
        They stroll or run,
And nerves that steeled themselves to slaughter
Are shot to pieces by the shorter
        Poems of Donne.

Professors back from secret missions
Resume their proper eruditions,
        Though some regret it;
They liked their dictaphones a lot,
They met some big wheels, and do not
        Let you forget it.

But Zeus' inscrutable decree
Permits the will-to-disagree
        To be pandemic,
Ordains that vaudeville shall preach
And every commencement speech
        Be a polemic.

Let Ares doze, that other war
Is instantly declared once more
        'Twixt those who follow

Precocious Hermes all the way
And those who without qualms obey
        Pompous Apollo.

Brutal like all Olympic games,
Though fought with smiles and Christian names
        And less dramatic,
This dialectic strife between
The civil gods is just as mean,
        And more fanatic.

What high immortals do in mirth
Is life and death on Middle Earth;
        Their a-historic
Antipathy forever gripes
All ages and somatic types,
        The sophomoric

Who face the future's darkest hints
With giggles or with prairie squints
        As stout as Cortez,
And those who like myself turn pale
As we approach with ragged sail
        The fattening forties.

The sons of Hermes love to play,
And only do their best when they
        Are told they oughtn't;
Apollo's children never shrink
From boring jobs but have to think
        Their work important.

Related by antithesis,
A compromise between us is
        Impossible;
Respect perhaps but friendship never:
Falstaff the fool confronts forever
        The prig Prince Hal.

If he would leave the self alone,
Apollo's welcome to the throne,
        Fasces and falcons;
He loves to rule, has always done it;
The earth would soon, did Hermes run it,
        Be like the Balkans.

But jealous of our god of dreams,
His common-sense in secret schemes
        To rule the heart;

Unable to invent the lyre,
Creates with simulated fire
Official art.

And when he occupies a college,
Truth is replaced by Useful Knowledge;
He pays particular
Attention to Commercial Thought,
Public Relations, Hygiene, Sport,
In his curricula.

Athletic, extrovert and crude,
For him, to work in solitude
Is the offence,
The goal a populous Nirvana:
His shield bears this device: *Mens sana*
Qui mal y pense.

Today his arms, we must confess,
From Right to Left have met success,
His banners wave
From Yale to Princeton, and the news
From Broadway to the Book Reviews
Is very grave.

His radio Homers all day long
In over-Whitmanated song
That does not scan,
With adjectives laid end to end,
Extol the doughnut and commend
The Common Man.

His, too, each homely lyric thing
On sport or spousal love or spring
Or dogs or dusters,
Invented by some court-house bard
For recitation by the yard
In filibusters.

To him ascend the prize orations
And sets of fugal variations
On some folk-ballad,
While dietitians sacrifice
A glass of prune-juice or a nice
Marsh-mallow salad.

Charged with his compound of sensational
Sex plus some undenominational
Religious matter,

Enormous novels by co-eds
Rain down on our defenceless heads
        Till our teeth chatter.

In fake Hermetic uniforms
Behind our battle-line, in swarms
        That keep alighting,
His existentialists declare
That they are in complete despair,
        Yet go on writing.

No matter; He shall be defied;
White Aphrodite is on our side:
        What though his threat
To organize us grow more critical?
Zeus willing, we, the unpolitical,
        Shall beat him yet.

Lone scholars, sniping from the walls
Of learned periodicals,
        Our facts defend,
Our intellectual marines,
Landing in little magazines
        Capture a trend.

By night our student Underground
At cocktail parties whisper round
        From ear to ear;
Fat figures in the public eye
Collapse next morning, ambushed by
        Some witty sneer.

In our morale must lie our strength:
So, that we may behold at length
        Routed Apollo's
Battalions melt away like fog,
Keep well the Hermetic Decalogue,
        Which runs as follows: —

Thou shalt not do as the dean pleases,
Thou shalt not write thy doctor's thesis
        On education,
Thou shalt not worship projects nor
Shalt thou or thine bow down before
        Administration.

Thou shalt not answer questionnaires
Or quizzes upon World-Affairs,
        Nor with compliance

Take any test. Thou shalt not sit
With statisticians nor commit
        A social science.

Thou shalt not be on friendly terms
With guys in advertising firms,
        Nor speak with such
As read the Bible for its prose,
Nor, above all, make love to those
        Who wash too much.

Thou shalt not live within thy means
Nor on plain water and raw greens.
        If thou must choose
Between the chances, choose the odd:
Read *The New Yorker*, trust in God;
        And take short views.

1946

In Praise of Limestone

If it form the one landscape that we the inconstant ones
    Are consistently homesick for, this is chiefly
Because it dissolves in water. Mark these rounded slopes
    With their surface fragrance of thyme and beneath
A secret system of caves and conduits; hear these springs
    That spurt out everywhere with a chuckle
Each filling a private a pool for its fish and carving
    Its own little ravine whose cliffs entertain
The butterfly and the lizard; examine this region
    Of short distances and definite places:
What could be more like Mother or a fitter background
    For her son, for the nude young male who lounges
Against a rock displaying his dildo, never doubting
    That for all his faults he is loved, whose works are but
Extensions of his power to charm? From weathered outcrop
    To hill-top temple, from appearing waters to
Conspicuous fountains, from a wild to a formal vineyard,
    Are ingenious but short steps that a child's wish
To receive more attention than his brothers, whether
    By pleasing or teasing, can easily take.

Watch, then, the band of rivals as they climb up and down
    Their steep stone gennels in twos and threes, sometimes
Arm in arm, but never, thank God, in step; or engaged
    On the shady side of a square at midday in

Voluble discourse, knowing each other too well to think
There are any important secrets, unable
To conceive a god whose temper-tantrums are moral
And not to be pacified by a clever line
Or a good lay: for, accustomed to a stone that responds,
They have never had to veil their faces in awe
Of a crater whose blazing fury could not be fixed;
Adjusted to the local needs of valleys
Where everything can be touched or reached by walking,
Their eyes have never looked into infinite space
Through the lattice-work of a nomad's comb; born lucky,
Their legs have never encountered the fungi
And insects of the jungle, the monstrous forms and lives
With which we have nothing, we like to hope, in common.
So, when one of them goes to the bad, the way his mind works
Remains comprehensible: to become a pimp
Or deal in fake jewelry or ruin a fine tenor voice
For effects that bring down the house could happen to all
But the best and the worst of us . . .
That is why, I suppose,
The best and worst never stayed here long but sought
Immoderate soils where the beauty was not so external,
The light less public and the meaning of life
Something more than a mad camp. "Come!" cried the granite wastes,
"How evasive is your humor, how accidental
Your kindest kiss, how permanent is death." (Saints-to-be
Slipped away sighing.) "Come!" purred the clays and gravels
"On our plains there is room for armies to drill; rivers
Wait to be tamed and slaves to construct you a tomb
In the grand manner: soft as the earth is mankind and both
Need to be altered." (Intendant Caesars rose and
Left, slamming the door.) But the really reckless were fetched
By an older colder voice, the oceanic whisper:
"I am the solitude that asks and promises nothing;
That is how I shall set you free. There is no love;
There are only the various envies, all of them sad."

They were right, my dear, all those voices were right
And still are; this land is not the sweet home that it looks,
Nor its peace the historical calm of a site
Where something was settled once and for all: A backward
And dilapidated province, connected
To the big busy world by a tunnel, with a certain
Seedy appeal, is that all it is now? Not quite:
It has a worldly duty which in spite of itself
It does not neglect, but calls into question
All the Great Powers assume; it disturbs our rights. The poet
Admired for his earnest habit of calling

The sun the sun, his mind Puzzle, is made uneasy
By these solid statues which so obviously doubt
His antimythological myth; and these gamins,
Pursuing the scientist down the tiled colonnade
With such lively offers, rebuke his concern for Nature's
Remotest aspects: I, too, am reproached, for what
And how much you know. Not to lose time, not to get caught
Not to be left behind, not, please! to resemble
The beasts who repeat themselves, or a thing like water
Or stone whose conduct can be predicted, these
Are our Common Prayer, whose greatest comfort is music
Which can be made anywhere, is invisible,
And does not smell. In so far as we have to look forward
To death as a fact, no doubt we are right: But if
Sins can be forgiven, if bodies rise from the dead,
These modifications of matter into
Innocent athletes and gesticulating fountains,
Made solely for pleasure, make a further point:
The blessed will not care what angle they are regarded from,
Having nothing to hide. Dear, I know nothing of
Either, but when I try to imagine a faultless love
Or the life to come, what I hear is the murmur
Of underground streams, what I see is a limestone landscape.

1948

The Shield of Achilles

She looked over his shoulder
For vines and olive trees,
Marble well-governed cities,
And ships upon untamed seas,
But there on the shining metal
His hands had put instead
An artificial wilderness
And a sky like lead.

A plain without a feature, bare and brown,
No blade of grass, no sign of neighborhood,
Nothing to eat and nowhere to sit down,
Yet, congregated on its blankness, stood
An unintelligible multitude,
A million eyes, a million boots in line,
Without expression, waiting for a sign.

Out of the air a voice without a face
Proved by statistics that some cause was just

In tones as dry and level as the place:
No one was cheered and nothing was discussed;
Column by column in a cloud of dust
They marched away enduring a belief
Whose logic brought them, somewhere else, to grief.

She looked over his shoulder
For ritual pieties,
White flower-garlanded heifers,
Libation and sacrifice,
But there on the shining metal
Where the altar should have been,
She saw by his flickering forge-light
Quite another scene.

Barbed wire enclosed an arbitrary spot
Where bored officials lounged (one cracked a joke)
And sentries sweated, for the day was hot:
A crowd of ordinary decent folk
Watched from without and neither moved nor spoke
As three pale figures were led forth and bound
To three posts driven upright in the ground.

The mass and majesty of this world, all
That carries weight and always weighs the same,
Lay in the hands of others; they were small
And could not hope for help and no help came:
What their foes liked to do was done, their shame
Was all the worst could wish; they lost their pride
And died as men before their bodies died.

She looked over his shoulder
For athletes at their games,
Men and women in a dance
Moving their sweet limbs
Quick, quick, to music,
But there on the shining shield
His hands had set no dancing-floor
But a weed-choked field.

A ragged urchin, aimless and alone,
Loitered about that vacancy; a bird
Flew up to safety from his well-aimed stone:
That girls are raped, that two boys knife a third,
Were axioms to him, who'd never heard
Of any world where promises were kept
Or one could weep because another wept.

The thin-lipped armorer,
   Hephaestos, hobbled away;
Thetis of the shining breasts
   Cried out in dismay
At what the god had wrought
   To please her son, the strong
Iron-hearted man-slaying Achilles
   Who would not live long.

1952

The More Loving One

Looking up at the stars, I know quite well
That, for all they care, I can go to hell,
But on earth indifference is the least
We have to dread from man or beast.

How should we like it were stars to burn
With a passion for us we could not return?
If equal affection cannot be,
Let the more loving one be me.

Admirer as I think I am
Of stars that do not give a damn,
I cannot, now I see them, say
I missed one terribly all day.

Were all stars to disappear or die,
I should learn to look at an empty sky
And feel its total dark sublime,
Though this might take me a little time.

1957

LINCOLN KIRSTEIN (1907–1996)

Lincoln Kirstein was born in Rochester, New York. While still an undergraduate at Harvard, he was a founding editor of the literary magazine *Hound and Horn.* In partnership with the great choreographer George Balanchine he founded the New York City Ballet in 1946. He served as its general director, and he wrote many books on dance. He served in the U.S. Third Army from 1943 to 1945. W. H. Auden said that *Rhymes of a PFC* (1964) contained the best writing he had read about World War II. "Underneath the foolery runs a relentless note of savage sarcasm" (Kenneth Rexroth). Kirstein: "I was never in combat, nor fired a weapon in anger or fear. This vexed me, and made me take irresponsible risks." "To me, already thirty-six, war was largely didactic. I'd had Harvard, spoke French, some German, and held no rank." He said he wanted "to witness enough action to be able to write about it."

Rank

Differences between rich and poor, king and queen,
Cat and dog, hot and cold, day and night, now and then,
Are less clearly distinct than all those between
Officers and us: enlisted men.

Not by brass may you guess nor their private latrine
Since distinctions obtain in any real well-run war;
It's when off duty, drunk, one acts nice or mean
In a sawdust-strewn bistro-type bar.

Ours was on a short street near the small market square;
Farmers dropped by for some beer or oftener to tease
The Gargantuan bartender Jean-Pierre
About his sweet wife, Marie-Louise.

GI's got the habit who liked French movies or books,
Tried to talk French or were happy to be left alone;
It was our kinda club; we played chess in nooks
With the farmers. We made it our own.

To this haven one night came an officer bold;
Crocked and ugly, he'd had it in five bars before.
A lurid luster glazed his eye which foretold
He'd better stay out of our shut door,

But did not. He barged in, slung his cap on the zinc:
"Dewbelle veesky," knowing well there was little but
beer.
Jean-Pierre showed the list of what one could drink:
"What sorta jerk joint you running here?"

Jean-Pierre had wine but no whisky to sell.
Wine loves the soul. Hard liquor hots up bloody fun,
And it's our rule noncommissioned personnel
Must keep by them their piece called a gun.

As well we are taught, enlisted soldiers may never
Ever surrender this piece — M1, carbine, or rifle —
With which no mere officer whomsoever
May freely or foolishly trifle.

A porcelain stove glowed in its niche, white and warm.
Jean-Pierre made jokes with us French-speaking boys.
Marie-Louise lay warm in bed far from harm;
Upstairs, snored through the ensuing noise.

This captain swilled beer with minimal grace. He began:
"Shit. What you-all are drinkin's not liquor. It's piss."
Two privates (first class) now consider some plan
To avoid what may result from this.

Captain Stearnes is an Old Army joe. Eighteen years
In the ranks, man and boy; bad luck, small promotion;
Without brains or cash, not the cream of careers.
Frustration makes plenty emotion.

"Now, Mac," Stearnes grins (Buster's name is not Mac; it is Jack),
"Toss me your gun an' I'll show you an old army trick;
At forty feet, with one hand, I'll crack that stove, smack."
"Let's not," drawls Jack back, scared of this prick.

"You young punk," Stearnes now storms, growing moody but mean,
"Do you dream I daren't pull my superior rank?"
His hand snatches Jack's light clean bright carbine.
What riddles the roof is no blank.

The rifle is loaded as combat zones ever require.
His arm kicks back without hurt to a porcelain stove.
Steel drilling plaster and plank, thin paths of fire
Plug Marie-Louise sleeping above.

Formal enquiry subsequent to this shootin'
Had truth and justice separately demanded.
Was Stearnes found guilty? You are darned tootin':
Fined, demoted. More: reprimanded.

The charge was not murder, mayhem, mischief malicious,
Yet something worse, and this they brought out time and again:
Clearly criminal and caddishly vicious
Was his: Drinking With Enlisted Men.

I'm serious. It's what the Judge Advocate said:
Strict maintenance of rank or our system is sunk.
Stearnes saluted. Jean-Pierre wept his dead.
Jack and I got see-double drunk.

1964

JOSEPHINE JACOBSEN (1908–2003)

Josephine Jacobsen was born in Boboury, Ontario. With her family she moved to New York City and then Maryland, where she lived for more than eighty years. Her first poem appeared in print when she was ten. From 1971 to 1973 she served as poetry consultant to the Library of Congress. Jacobsen has characterized the imagination as "the active, secret subterranean life" and likened poetry to walking along a "narrow ridge up on a precipice. You never know the next step, whether there's going to be a plunge. I think poetry is dangerous. There's nothing mild and predictable about poetry."

The Monosyllable

One day
she fell
in love with its
heft and speed.
Tough, lean,

fast as light
slow
as a cloud.
It took care
of rain, short

noon, long dark.
It had rough kin;
did not stall.
With it, she said,
I may,

if I can,
sleep; since I must,
die.
Some say,
rise.

1981

The Birthday Party

The sounds are the sea, breaking out of sight,
and down the green slope the children's voices
that celebrate the fact of being eight.

One too few chairs are for desperate forces:
when the music hushes, the children drop
into their arms, except for one caught by choices.

In a circle gallops the shrinking crop
to leave a single sitter in hubris
when the adult finger tells them: stop.

There is a treasure, somewhere easy to miss.
In the blooms? by the pineapple-palms' bark?
somewhere, hidden, the shape of bliss.

Onto the pitted sand comes highwater mark.
Waves older than eight begin a retreat;
they will come, the children gone, the slope dark.

One of the gifts was a year, complete.
There will be others: those not eight
will come to be eight, bar a dire defeat.

On the green grass there is a delicate
change; there is a change in the sun
though certainly it is not truly late,

and still caught up in the scary fun,
like a muddle of flowers blown around.
For treasure, for triumph, the children run

and the wind carries the steady pound,
and salty weight that falls, and dies,
and falls. The wind carries the sound

of the children's light high clear cries.

1995

The Blue-Eyed Exterminator

The exterminator has arrived. He has not intruded. He was summoned.
At the most fruitless spot, a regiment
of the tiniest of ants, obviously deluded,
have a jetty ferment of undisclosed intent.

The blue-eyed exterminator is friendly and fair;
one can tell he knows exactly what he is about.
He is young as the day that makes the buds puff out,
grass go rampant, big bees ride the air;

it seems the spring could drown him in its flood.
But though he appears modest as what he was summoned for,
he will prove himself more potent than grass or bud,
being a scion of the greatest emperor.

His success is total: no jet platoon on the wall.
At the door he calls good-bye and hitches his thumb.
For an invisible flick, grass halts, buds cramp, bees stall
in air. He has called, and what has been called has come.

1995

George Oppen (1908–1984)

George Oppen was born in New Rochelle, New York, the son of a prosperous businessman. When George was four, his mother committed suicide. After the poet and his future wife, Mary Colby, were expelled from Oregon State University in 1926, the couple hitchhiked across the country, eventually settling in Brooklyn, where they fell in with Louis Zukosky and Charles Reznikoff and formed the nucleus of the Objectivist movement. For twenty-five years, from 1934 to 1958, Oppen stopped writing poetry. He joined the Communist Party. In World War II he served in the 103rd Antitank Division, saw action in the Battle of the Bulge, and was later wounded in Alsace and awarded the Purple Heart. Oppen is "bold, severe, intense, mysterious, serene and fiercely economical" (Louise Glück).

Chartres

The bulk of it
In air

Is what they wanted. Compassion
Above the doors, the doorways

Mary the woman and the others
The lesser

Are dreams on the structure. But that a stone
Supports another

That the stones
Stand where the masons locked them

Above the farmland
Above the will

Because a hundred generations
Back of them and to another people

The world cried out above the mountain

1962

The Undertaking in New Jersey

Beyond the Hudson's
Unimportant water lapping
In the dark against the city's shores
Are the small towns, remnants
Of forge and coal yard. The bird's voice in their streets
May not mean much: a bird the age of a child chirping
At curbs and curb gratings,
At barber shops and townsmen
Born of girls —
Of girls! Girls gave birth . . . But the interiors
Are the women's: curtained,
Lit, the fabric
To which the men return. Surely they imagine
Some task beyond the window glass
And the fabrics as if an eventual brother
In the fields were nourished by all this in country
Torn by the trucks where towns
And the flat boards of homes
Visibly move at sunrise and the trees
Carry quickly into daylight the excited birds.

1962

Boy's Room

A friend saw the rooms
Of Keats and Shelley
At the lake, and saw 'they were just
Boys' rooms' and was moved

By that. And indeed a poet's room
Is a boy's room
And I suppose that women know it.

Perhaps the unbeautiful banker
Is exciting to a woman, a man
Not a boy gasping
For breath over a girl's body.

1965

The Gesture

The question is: how does one hold an apple
Who likes apples

And how does one handle
Filth? The question is

How does one hold something
In the mind which he intends

To grasp and how does the salesman
Hold a bauble he intends

To sell? The question is
When will there not be a hundred

Poets who mistake that gesture
For a style.

1965

Psalm

Veritas sequitur . . .

In the small beauty of the forest
The wild deer bedding down —
That they are there!

Their eyes
Effortless, the soft lips
Nuzzle and the alien small teeth
Tear at the grass

The roots of it
Dangle from their mouths
Scattering earth in the strange woods.
They who are there.

Their paths
Nibbled thru the fields, the leaves that shade them
Hang in the distances
Of sun

The small nouns
Crying faith
In this in which the wild deer
Startle, and stare out.

1965

The Building of the Skyscraper

The steel worker on the girder
Learned not to look down, and does his work
And there are words we have learned
Not to look at,
Not to look for substance
Below them. But we are on the verge
Of vertigo.

There are words that mean nothing
But there is something to mean.
Not a declaration, which is truth
But a thing
Which is. It is the business of the poet
'To suffer the things of the world
And to speak them and himself out.'

O, the tree, growing from the sidewalk —
It has a little life, sprouting
Little green buds
Into the culture of the streets.
We look back
Three hundred years and see bare land.
And suffer vertigo.

1965

THEODORE ROETHKE (1908–1963)

Theodore Roethke was born in Saginaw, Michigan. His father owned what one visitor from Holland called "the finest greenhouse in America." When Roethke was fourteen, the greenhouse—Roethke's "symbol for the whole of life, a womb, a heaven-on-earth"—was sold after a bitter dispute between Otto, the poet's father, and Otto's brother Charles. In the aftermath, Charles committed suicide; Otto died of bowel cancer mere months later. Roethke, who had a history of mental breakdowns, taught for many years at the University of Washington, where his devoted students included Richard Hugo, Carolyn Kizer, David Wagoner, and James Wright. "Write like someone else" was Roethke's best pedagogic advice. Of his 1948 book *The Lost Son*, the author said, "In spite of all the muck and welter, the dark, the *dreck* of these poems, I count myself among the happy poets." He suffered a fatal heart attack in a friend's swimming pool in 1963.

The Minimal

I study the lives on a leaf: the little
Sleepers, numb nudgers in cold dimensions,

Beetles in caves, newts, stone-deaf fishes,
Lice tethered to long limp subterranean weeds,
Squirmers in bogs,
And bacterial creepers
Wriggling through wounds
Like elvers in ponds,
Their wan mouths kissing the warm sutures,
Cleaning and caressing,
Creeping and healing.

1948

My Papa's Waltz

The whiskey on your breath
Could make a small boy dizzy;
But I hung on like death:
Such waltzing was not easy.

We romped until the pans
Slid from the kitchen shelf;
My mother's countenance
Could not unfrown itself.

The hand that held my wrist
Was battered on one knuckle;
At every step you missed
My right ear scraped a buckle.

You beat time on my head
With a palm caked hard by dirt,
Then waltzed me off to bed
Still clinging to your shirt.

1948

Root Cellar

Nothing would sleep in that cellar, dank as a ditch,
Bulbs broke out of boxes hunting for chinks in the dark,
Shoots dangled and drooped,
Lolling obscenely from mildewed crates,
Hung down long yellow evil necks, like tropical snakes.
And what a congress of stinks! —
Roots ripe as old bait,

Pulpy stems, rank, silo-rich,
Leaf-mould, manure, lime, piled against slippery planks.
Nothing would give up life:
Even the dirt kept breathing a small breath.

1948

Dolor

I have known the inexorable sadness of pencils,
Neat in their boxes, dolor of pad and paper-weight,
All the misery of manilla folders and mucilage,
Desolation in immaculate public places,
Lonely reception room, lavatory, switchboard,
The unalterable pathos of basin and pitcher,
Ritual of multigraph, paper-clip, comma,
Endless duplication of lives and objects.
And I have seen dust from the walls of institutions,
Finer than flour, alive, more dangerous than silica,
Sift, almost invisible, through long afternoons of tedium,
Dropping a fine film on nails and delicate eyebrows,
Glazing the pale hair, the duplicate grey standard faces.

1948

The Lost Son

1. The Flight

At Woodlawn I heard the dead cry:
I was lulled by the slamming of iron,
A slow drip over stones,
Toads brooding wells.
All the leaves stuck out their tongues;
I shook the softening chalk of my bones,
Saying,
Snail, snail, glister me forward,
Bird, soft-sigh me home,
Worm, be with me.
This is my hard time.

Fished in an old wound,
The soft pond of repose;
Nothing nibbled my line,
Not even the minnows came.

Sat in an empty house
Watching shadows crawl,
Scratching.
There was one fly.

Voice, come out of the silence.
Say something.
Appear in the form of a spider
Or a moth beating the curtain.

Tell me:
Which is the way I take;
Out of what door do I go,
Where and to whom?

Dark hollows said, lee to the wind,
The moon said, back of an eel,
The salt said, look by the sea,
Your tears are not enough praise,
You will find no comfort here,
In the kingdom of bang and blab.

Running lightly over spongy ground,
Past the pasture of flat stones,
The three elms,
The sheep strewn on a field,
Over a rickety bridge
Toward the quick-water, wrinkling and rippling.

Hunting along the river,
Down among the rubbish, the bug-riddled foliage,
By the muddy pond-edge, by the bog-holes,
By the shrunken lake, hunting, in the heat of summer.

The shape of a rat?
It's bigger than that.
It's less than a leg
And more than a nose,
Just under the water
It usually goes.

Is it soft like a mouse?
Can it wrinkle its nose?
Could it come in the house
On the tips of its toes?

Take the skin of a cat
And the back of an eel,

Then roll them in grease, —
That's the way it would feel.

It's sleek as an otter
With wide webby toes
Just under the water
It usually goes.

2. The Pit

Where do the roots go?
        Look down under the leaves.
Who put the moss there?
        These stones have been here too long.
Who stunned the dirt into noise?
        Ask the mole, he knows.
I feel the slime of a wet nest.
        Beware Mother Mildew.
Nibble again, fish nerves.

3. The Gibber

At the wood's mouth,
By the cave's door,
I listened to something
I had heard before.

Dogs of the groin
Barked and howled,
The sun was against me,
The moon would not have me.

The weeds whined,
The snakes cried,
The cows and briars
Said to me: Die.

What a small song. What slow clouds. What dark water.
Hath the rain a father? All the caves are ice. Only the snow's here.
I'm cold. I'm cold all over. Rub me in father and mother.
Fear was my father, Father Fear.
His look drained the stones.

What gliding shape
Beckoning through halls,
Stood poised on the stair,
Fell dreamily down?

From the mouths of jugs
Perched on many shelves,
I saw substance flowing
That cold morning.

Like a slither of eels
That watery cheek
As my own tongue kissed
My lips awake.

Is this the storm's heart? The ground is unstilling itself.
My veins are running nowhere. Do the bones cast out their fire?
Is the seed leaving the old bed? These buds are live as birds.
Where, where are the tears of the world?
Let the kisses resound, flat like a butcher's palm;
Let the gestures freeze; our doom is already decided.
All the windows are burning! What's left of my life?
I want the old rage, the last of primordial milk!
Goodbye, goodbye, old stones, and time-order is going,
I have married my hands to perpetual agitation,
I run, I run to the whistle of money.

Money money money
Water water water

How cool the grass is.
Has the bird left?
The stalk still sways.
Has the worm a shadow?
What do the clouds say?

These sweeps of light undo me.
Look, look, the ditch is running white!
I've more veins than a tree!
Kiss me, ashes, I'm falling through a dark swirl.

4. *The Return*

The way to the boiler was dark,
Dark all the way,
Over slippery cinders
Through the long greenhouse.

The roses kept breathing in the dark.
They had many mouths to breathe with.
My knees made little winds underneath
Where the weeds slept.

There was always a single light
Swinging by the fire-pit,
Where the fireman pulled out roses,
The big roses, the big bloody clinkers.

Once I stayed all night.
The light in the morning came slowly over the white
Snow.
There were many kinds of cool
Air.
Then came steam.

Pipe-knock.

Scurry of warm over small plants.
Ordnung! ordnung!
Papa is coming!

A fine haze moved off the leaves;
Frost melted on far panes;
The rose, the chrysanthemum turned toward the light.
Even the hushed forms, the bent yellowy weeds
Moved in a slow up-sway.

5. "*It was beginning winter*"

It was beginning winter,
An in-between time,
The landscape still partly brown:
The bones of weeds kept swinging in the wind,
Above the blue snow.

It was beginning winter,
The light moved slowly over the frozen field,
Over the dry seed-crowns,
The beautiful surviving bones
Swinging in the wind.

Light traveled over the wide field;
Stayed.
The weeds stopped swinging.
The mind moved, not alone,
Through the clear air, in the silence.

Was it light?
Was it light within?
Was it light within light?
Stillness becoming alive,
Yet still?

A lively understandable spirit
Once entertained you.
It will come again.
Be still.
Wait.

1948

The Waking

I strolled across
An open field;
The sun was out;
Heat was happy.

This way! This way!
The wren's throat shimmered,
Either to other,
The blossoms sang.

The stones sang,
The little ones did,
And flowers jumped
Like small goats.

A ragged fringe
Of daisies waved;
I wasn't alone
In a grove of apples.

Far in the wood
A nestling sighed;
The dew loosened
Its morning smells.

I came where the river
Ran over stones:
My ears knew
An early joy.

And all the waters
Of all the streams
Sang in my veins
That summer day.

1948

The Waking

I wake to sleep, and take my waking slow.
I feel my fate in what I cannot fear.
I learn by going where I have to go.

We think by feeling. What is there to know?
I hear my being dance from ear to ear.
I wake to sleep, and take my waking slow.

Of those so close beside me, which are you?
God bless the Ground! I shall walk softly there,
And learn by going where I have to go.

Light takes the Tree; but who can tell us how?
The lowly worm climbs up a winding stair;
I wake to sleep, and take my waking slow.

Great Nature has another thing to do
To you and me; so take the lively air,
And, lovely, learn by going where to go.

This shaking keeps me steady. I should know.
What falls away is always. And is near.
I wake to sleep, and take my waking slow.
I learn by going where I have to go.

1953

I Knew a Woman

I knew a woman, lovely in her bones,
When small birds sighed, she would sigh back at them;
Ah, when she moved, she moved more ways than one:
The shapes a bright container can contain!
Of her choice virtues only gods should speak,
Or English poets who grew up on Greek
(I'd have them sing in chorus, cheek to cheek).

How well her wishes went! She stroked my chin,
She taught me Turn, and Counter-turn, and Stand;
She taught me Touch, that undulant white skin;
I nibbled meekly from her proffered hand;
She was the sickle; I, poor I, the rake,
Coming behind her for her pretty sake
(But what prodigious mowing we did make).

Love likes a gander, and adores a goose:
Her full lips pursed, the errant note to seize;
She played it quick, she played it light and loose;
My eyes, they dazzled at her flowing knees;
Her several parts could keep a pure repose,
Or one hip quiver with a mobile nose
(She moved in circles, and those circles moved).

Let seed be grass, and grass turn into hay:
I'm martyr to a motion not my own;
What's freedom for? To know eternity.
I swear she cast a shadow white as stone.
But who would count eternity in days?
These old bones live to learn her wanton ways:
(I measure time by how a body sways).

1958

In a Dark Time

In a dark time, the eye begins to see,
I meet my shadow in the deepening shade;
I hear my echo in the echoing wood —
A lord of nature weeping to a tree.
I live between the heron and the wren,
Beasts of the hill and serpents of the den.

What's madness but nobility of soul
At odds with circumstance? The day's on fire!
I know the purity of pure despair,
My shadow pinned against a sweating wall.
That place among the rocks — is it a cave,
Or winding path? The edge is what I have.

A steady storm of correspondences!
A night flowing with birds, a ragged moon,
And in broad day the midnight come again!
A man goes far to find out what he is —
Death of the self in a long, tearless night,
All natural shapes blazing unnatural light.

Dark, dark my light, and darker my desire.
My soul, like some heat-maddened summer fly,
Keeps buzzing at the sill. Which I is *I*?
A fallen man, I climb out of my fear.
The mind enters itself, and God the mind,
And one is One, free in the tearing wind.

1964

Charles Olson (1910–1970)

Charles Olson was born in Worcester, Massachusetts, less than two months before Elizabeth Bishop was born in the same city. A graduate of Wesleyan University, he published *Call Me Ishmael*, a study of Herman Melville, in 1947. In 1951, Olson succeeded the painter Josef Albers as the rector of Black Mountain College, which was a school in two senses: an experimental college of the arts in North Carolina and a movement of like-minded poets, including Robert Creeley and Robert Duncan. Olson advocated what he called "projective or open verse," also known as "composition by field." He felt that poems should be organized not around the line, the stanza, or the verse form but around a free flow of perceptions, and he developed the idea that the breath of an utterance can serve as an adequate measure in place of traditional meter. Like Cummings, Olson saw the potential of the typewriter keyboard for producing or altering the sense or look of a poem. Olson chose the slash mark because he wanted "a pause so light it hardly separates the words" instead of a comma, "which is an interruption of the meaning rather than the sounding of the line."

The Kingfishers

I

1
What does not change / is the will to change

He woke, fully clothed, in his bed. He
remembered only one thing, the birds, how
when he came in, he had gone around the rooms
and got them back in their cage, the green one first,
she with the bad leg, and then the blue,
the one they had hoped was a male

Otherwise? Yes, Fernand, who had talked lispingly of Albers & Angkor Vat.
He had left the party without a word. How he got up, got into his coat,
I do not know. When I saw him, he was at the door, but it did not matter,
he was already sliding along the wall of the night, losing himself
in some crack of the ruins. That it should have been he who said, "The
kingfishers?

who cares
for their feathers
now?"

His last words had been, "The pool is slime." Suddenly everyone,
ceasing their talk, sat in a row around him, watched
they did not so much hear, or pay attention, they
wondered, looked at each other, smirked, but listened,
he repeated and repeated, could not go beyond his thought
"The pool   the kingfishers' feathers were wealth   why
did the export stop?"

It was then he left

2
I thought of the E on the stone, and of what Mao said
"la lumiere"
                but the kingfisher
"de l'aurore"
                but the kingfisher flew west
est devant nous!
                he got the color of his breast
                from the heat of the setting sun!

The features are, the feebleness of the feet (syndactylism of the 3rd & 4th digit)
the bill, serrated, sometimes a pronounced beak, the wings
where the color is, short and round, the tail
inconspicuous.

But not these things are the factors. Not the birds.
The legends are
legends. Dead, hung up indoors, the kingfisher
will not indicate a favoring wind,
or avert the thunderbolt. Nor, by its nesting,
still the waters, with the new year, for seven days.
It is true, it does nest with the opening year, but not on the waters.
It nests at the end of a tunnel bored by itself on a bank. There,
six or eight white and translucent eggs are laid, on fishbones,
not on bare clay, on bones thrown up in pellets by the birds.

                                            On these rejectamenta
(as they accumulate they form a cup-shaped structure) the young are born
And, as they are fed and grow, this nest of excrement and decayed fish becomes
                                                        a dripping, fetid mass
Mao concluded
                nous devons
                                nous lever
                                                et agir!

3
When the attentions change / the jungle
leaps in
                even the stones are split
                                        they rive
Or,
enter
that other conqueror we more naturally recognize
he so resembles ourselves

But the E
cut so rudely on that oldest stone
sounded otherwise,
was differently heard

as, in another time, were treasures used:
(and, later, much later, a fine ear thought
a scarlet coat)

"of green feathers feet, beaks and eyes
of gold

"animals likewise,
resembling snails

"a large wheel, gold with figures of unknown four-foots,
and worked with tufts of leaves, weight
3800 ounces

"last, two birds of thread and featherwork, the quills
gold, the feet
gold, the two birds perched on two reeds
gold, the reeds arising from two embroidered mounds,
one yellow, the other
white.
"And from each reed hung
seven feathered tassels.

In this instance, the priests
(in dark cotton robes, and dirty,
their disheveled hair matted with blood, and flowing wildly
over their shoulders)
rush in among the people, calling on them
to protect their gods

And all now is war
Where so lately there was peace,
and the sweet brotherhood, the use
of tilled fields.

4
Not one death but many,
not accumulation but change, the feed-back proves, the feed-back is
the law

Into the same river no man steps twice
When fire dies air dies
No one remains, nor is, one

Around an appearance, one common model, we grow up
many. Else how is it,
if we remain the same,
we take pleasure now

in what we did not take pleasure before? love
contrary objects? admire and/or find fault? use
other words, feel other passions, have
nor figure, appearance, disposition, tissue
the same?

To be in different states without a change
is not a possibility

We can be precise. The factors are
in the animal and/or the machine the factors are
communication and/or control, both involve
the message. And what is the message? The message is
a discrete or continuous sequence of measurable events distributed in time

is the birth of air, is
the birth of water, is
a state between
the origin and
the end, between
birth and the beginning of
another fetid nest

is change, presents
no more than itself

And the too strong grasping of it,
When it is pressed together and condensed,
loses it

This very thing you are

II

They buried their dead in a sitting posture
serpent cane razor ray of the sun

And she sprinkled water on the head of the child, crying
"Cioa-coatl! Cioa-coatl!"
with her face to the west

Where the bones are found, in each personal heap
with what each enjoyed, there is always
the Mongolian louse

The light is in the east. Yes. And we must rise, act. Yet
in the west, despite the apparent darkness (the whiteness
which covers all), if you look, if you can bear, if you can, long enough

as long as it was necessary for him, my guide
to look into the yellow of that longest-lasting rose

so you must, and in that whiteness, into that face, with what candor, look

and, considering the dryness of the place
the long absence of an adequate race
(of the two who first came, each a conquistador, one healed, the other
tore the eastern idols down, toppled
the temple walls, which, says the excuser
were black from human gore)

hear
hear, where the dry blood talks
where the old appetite walks

la piu saporita et migliore
che si possa truovar al mondo

where it hides, look
in the eye how it runs
in the flesh / chalk
but under these petals
in the emptiness
regard the light, contemplate
the flower

whence it arose

with what violence benevolence is bought
what cost in gesture justice brings
what wrongs domestic rights involve
what stalks
this silence

what pudor pejorocracy affronts
how awe, night-rest and neighbourhood can rot
what breeds where dirtiness is law
what crawls
below

III

I am no Greek, hath not th'advantage.
And of course, no Roman:
he can take no risk that matters,
the risk of beauty least of all.

But I have my kin, if for no other reason than
(as he said, next of kin) I commit myself, and
given my freedom, I'd be a cad
if I didn't. Which is more true.

It works out this way, despite the disadvantage.
I offer, in explanation, a quote:
si j'ai du gout, ce n'est gueres
Que pour la terre et les pierres

Despite the discrepancy (an ocean courage age)
this is also true: if I have any taste
it is only because I have interested myself
in what was slain in the sun

        I pose you your question:

shall you uncover honey / where maggots are?

        I hunt among stones

1950

Winfield Townley Scott (1910–1968)

Winfield Townley Scott was born in Haverhill, Massachusetts. The author of a memorable poem about the savagery of combat in World War II was a mild-mannered civilian, a Brown University graduate who became the book editor of the *Providence Journal*. "The sailor is a type of the conquering hero, and the decapitated object he carries close to himself is a Medusa head that gradually turns him to stone," writes Laurence Goldstein in his comment on "The U.S. Sailor with the Japanese Skull."

The U.S. Sailor with the Japanese Skull

Bald-bare, bone-bare, and ivory yellow: skull
Carried by a thus two-headed U.S. sailor
Who got it from a Japanese soldier killed
At Guadalcanal in the ever-present war: our

Bluejacket, I mean, aged 20, in August strolled
Among the little bodies on the sand and hunted
Souvenirs: teeth, tags, diaries, boots; but bolder still
Hacked off this head and under a Ginkgo tree skinned it:

Peeled with a lifting knife the jaw and cheeks, bared
The nose, ripped off the black-haired scalp and gutted
The dead eyes to these thoughtful hollows: a scarred
But bloodless job, unless it be said brains bleed.

Then, his ship underway, dragged this aft in a net
Many days and nights — the cold bone tumbling
Beneath the foaming wake, weed-worn and salt-cut
Rolling safe among fish and washed with Pacific;

Till on a warm and level-keeled day hauled in
Held to the sun and the sailor, back to a gun-rest,
Scrubbed the cured skull with lye, perfecting this:
Not foreign as he saw it first: death's familiar cast.

Bodiless, fleshless, nameless, it and sun
Offend each other in strange fascination
As though one of the two were mocked; but nothing is in
This head, or it fills with what another imagines

As: here were love and hate and the will to deal
Death or to kneel before it, death emperor,
Recorded orders without reasons, bomb-blast, still
A child's morning, remembered moonlight on Fujiyama:

All scoured out now by the keeper of this skull
Made elemental, historic, parentless by our
Sailor boy who thinks of home, voyages laden, will
Not say, "Alas! I did not know him at all."

1945

ELIZABETH BISHOP (1911–1979)

Elizabeth Bishop was born in Worcester, Massachusetts. Her father died when she was eight months old; her mother was placed in a mental institution when Bishop was five, and Bishop never saw her again. Brought up in New England and Nova Scotia, she went to Vassar (class of 1934) and was the prototype for a character in Mary McCarthy's novel *The Group*. She spent substantial amounts of time in New York City and in Key West, Florida ("the state with the prettiest name," she wrote). In 1951 she went to Brazil and lived there for fifteen years with her lover, Lota de Macedo Soares, a landscape architect, who committed suicide shortly after she and Bishop moved to New York City in 1967. Bishop settled in Boston and taught at Harvard from 1970 to 1977. She was impatient with what she called "our-beautiful-old-silver" school of female writing and steadfastly refused to let her work appear in anthologies devoted exclusively to women or feminism. In 1948 she told Robert Lowell, "When you write my epitaph, you must say I was the loneliest person who ever lived." Always admired by her fellow poets ("I don't know of any other poet with so high a proportion of good poems," wrote Randall Jarrell), she has enjoyed a steady climb in reputation. Helen Vendler has called Bishop's "Roosters" "the most excellent and complex war poem by a woman poet." The reader may wish to consider her "Crusoe in England" alongside William Wordsworth's "I Wandered Lonely as a Cloud," which it quotes, and to speculate on why Bishop's narrator blanks out where he does when reciting Wordsworth's famous lines from memory. It is possible that the key to Bishop's "One Art" lies concealed in the pun within the parenthesis of the villanelle's last line.

A Miracle for Breakfast

At six o'clock we were waiting for coffee,
waiting for coffee and the charitable crumb
that was going to be served from a certain balcony
— like kings of old, or like a miracle.
It was still dark. One foot of the sun
steadied itself on a long ripple in the river.

The first ferry of the day had just crossed the river.
It was so cold we hoped that the coffee
would be very hot, seeing that the sun
was not going to warm us; and that the crumb
would be a loaf each, buttered, by a miracle.
At seven a man stepped out on the balcony.

He stood for a minute alone on the balcony
looking over our heads toward the river.
A servant handed him the makings of a miracle,
consisting of one lone cup of coffee
and one roll, which he proceeded to crumb,
his head, so to speak, in the clouds — along with the sun.

Was the man crazy? What under the sun
was he trying to do, up there on his balcony!
Each man received one rather hard crumb,
which some flicked scornfully into the river,
and, in a cup, one drop of the coffee.
Some of us stood around, waiting for the miracle.

I can tell what I saw next; it was not a miracle.
A beautiful villa stood in the sun
and from its doors came the smell of hot coffee.
In front, a baroque white plaster balcony
added by birds, who nest along the river,
— I saw it with one eye close to the crumb —

and galleries and marble chambers. My crumb
my mansion, made for me by a miracle,
through ages, by insects, birds, and the river
working the stone. Every day, in the sun,
at breakfast time I sit on my balcony
with my feet up, and drink gallons of coffee.

We licked up the crumb and swallowed the coffee.
A window across the river caught the sun
as if the miracle were working, on the wrong balcony.

1946

Seascape

This celestial seascape, with white herons got up as angels,
flying high as they want and as far as they want sidewise
in tiers and tiers of immaculate reflections;
the whole region, from the highest heron
down to the weightless mangrove island
with bright green leaves edged neatly with bird-droppings
like illumination in silver,
and down to the suggestively Gothic arches of the mangrove roots
and the beautiful pea-green back-pasture
where occasionally a fish jumps, like a wild-flower
in an ornamental spray of spray;
this cartoon by Raphael for a tapestry for a Pope:
it does look like heaven.
But a skeletal lighthouse standing there
in black and white clerical dress,
who lives on his nerves, thinks he knows better.
He thinks that hell rages below his iron feet,
that that is why the shallow water is so warm,
and he knows that heaven is not like this.
Heaven is not like flying or swimming,
but has something to do with blackness and a strong glare
and when it gets dark he will remember something
strongly worded to say on the subject.

1946

Roosters

At four o'clock
in the gun-metal blue dark
we hear the first crow of the first cock

just below
the gun-metal blue window
and immediately there is an echo

off in the distance,
then one from the back-yard fence,
then one, with horrible insistence,

grates like a wet match
from the broccoli patch,
flares, and all over town begins to catch.

Cries galore
come from the water-closet door,
from the dropping-plastered henhouse floor,

where in the blue blur
their rustling wives admire,
the roosters brace their cruel feet and glare

with stupid eyes
while from their beaks there rise
the uncontrolled, traditional cries.

Deep from protruding chests
in green-gold medals dressed,
planned to command and terrorize the rest,

the many wives
who lead hens' lives
of being courted and despised;

deep from raw throats
a senseless order floats
all over town. A rooster gloats

over our beds
from rusty iron sheds
and fences made from old bedsteads,

over our churches
where the tin rooster perches,
over our little wooden northern houses,

making sallies
from all the muddy alleys,
marking out maps like Rand McNally's:

glass headed pins,
oil-golds and copper greens,
anthracite blues, alizarins,

each one an active
displacement in perspective;
each screaming, "This is where I live!"

Each screaming
"Get up! Stop dreaming!"
Roosters, what are you projecting?

You, whom the Greeks elected
to shoot at on a post, who struggled
when sacrificed, you whom they labeled

"Very combative . . . "
what right have you to give
commands and tell us how to live,

cry 'Here!' and 'Here!'
and wake us here where are
unwanted love, conceit and war?

The crown of red
set on your little head
is charged with all your fighting blood.

Yes, that excrescence
makes a most virile presence,
plus all that vulgar beauty of iridescence.

Now in mid-air
by twos they fight each other.
Down comes a first flame-feather,

and one is flying,
with raging heroism defying
even the sensation of dying.

And one has fallen,
but still above the town
his torn-out, bloodied feathers drift down;

and what he sung
no matter. He is flung
on the gray ash-heap, lies in dung

with his dead wives
with open, bloody eyes,
while those metallic feathers oxidize.

St. Peter's sin
was worse than that of Magdalen
whose sin was of the flesh alone;

of spirit, Peter's,
falling, beneath the flares,
among the "servants and officers."

Old holy sculpture
could set it all together
in one small scene, past and future:

Christ stands amazed,
Peter, two fingers raised
to surprised lips, both as if dazed.

But in between
a little cock is seen
carved on a dim column in the travertine,

explained by *gallus canit*;
flet Petrus underneath it.
There is inescapable hope, the pivot;

yes, and there Peter's tears
run down our chanticleer's
sides and gem his spurs.

Tear-encrusted thick
as a medieval relic
he waits. Poor Peter, heart-sick,

still cannot guess
those cock-a-doodles yet might bless,
his dreadful rooster come to mean forgiveness,

a new weathervane
on basilica and barn,
and that outside the Lateran

there would always be
a bronze cock on a porphyry
pillar so the people and the Pope might see

that even the Prince
of the Apostles long since
had been forgiven, and to convince

all the assembly
that "Deny deny deny,"
is not all the roosters cry.

In the morning
a low light is floating
in the backyard, and gilding

from underneath
the broccoli, leaf by leaf;
how could the night have come to grief?

gilding the tiny
floating swallow's belly
and lines of pink cloud in the sky,

the day's preamble
like wandering lines in marble.
The cocks are now almost inaudible.

The sun climbs in,
following 'to see the end,'
faithful as enemy, or friend.

1946

Over 2,000 Illustrations and a Complete Concordance

Thus should have been our travels:
serious, engravable.
The Seven Wonders of the World are tired
and a touch familiar, but the other scenes,
innumerable, though equally sad and still,
are foreign. Often the squatting Arab,
or group of Arabs, plotting, probably,
against our Christian Empire,
while one apart, with outstretched arm and hand
points to the Tomb, the Pit, the Sepulcher.
The branches of the date-palms look like files.
The cobbled courtyard, where the Well is dry,
is like a diagram, the brickwork conduits
are vast and obvious, the human figure
far gone in history or theology,
gone with its camel or its faithful horse.
Always the silence, the gesture, the specks of birds
suspended on invisible threads above the Site,
or the smoke rising solemnly, pulled by threads.
Granted a page alone or a page made up
of several scenes arranged in cattycornered rectangles.
or circles set on stippled gray,
granted a grim lunette,
caught in the toils of an initial letter,

when dwelt upon, they all resolve themselves.
The eye drops, weighted, through the lines
the burin made, the lines that move apart
like ripples above sand,
dispersing storms, God's spreading fingerprint,
and painfully, finally, that ignite
in watery prismatic white-and-blue.

Entering the Narrows at St. Johns
the touching bleat of goats reached to the ship.
We glimpsed them, reddish, leaping up the cliffs
among the fog-soaked weeds and butter-and-eggs.
And at St. Peter's the wind blew and the sun shone madly.
Rapidly, purposefully, the Collegians marched in lines,
crisscrossing the great square with black, like ants.
In Mexico the dead man lay
in a blue arcade; the dead volcanoes
glistened like Easter lilies.
The jukebox went on playing "Ay, Jalisco!"
And at Volubilis there were beautiful poppies
splitting the mosaics; the fat old guide made eyes.
In Dingle harbor a golden length of evening
the rotting hulks held up their dripping plush.
The Englishwoman poured tea, informing us
that the Duchess was going to have a baby.
And in the brothels of Marrakesh
the little pockmarked prostitutes
balanced their tea-trays on their heads
and did their belly-dances; flung themselves
naked and giggling against our knees,
asking for cigarettes. It was somewhere near there
I saw what frightened me most of all:
A holy grave, not looking particularly holy,
one of a group under a keyhole-arched stone baldaquin
open to every wind from the pink desert.
An open, gritty, marble trough, carved solid
with exhortation, yellowed
as scattered cattle-teeth;
half-filled, with dust, not even the dust
of the poor prophet paynim who once lay there.
In a smart burnoose Khadour looked on amused.

Everything only connected by "and" and "and."
Open the book. (The gilt rubs off the edges
of the pages and pollinates the fingertips.)
Open the heavy book. Why couldn't we have seen

this old Nativity while we were at it?
— the dark ajar, the rocks breaking with light,
an undisturbed, unbreathing flame,
colorless, sparkless, freely fed on straw,
and, lulled within, a family with pets,
— and looked and looked our infant sight away.

1955

At the Fishhouses

Although it is a cold evening,
down by one of the fishhouses
an old man sits netting,
his net, in the gloaming almost invisible,
a dark purple-brown,
and his shuttle worn and polished.
The air smells so strong of codfish
it makes one's nose run and one's eyes water.
The five fishhouses have steeply peaked roofs
and narrow, cleated gangplanks slant up
to storerooms in the gables
for the wheelbarrows to be pushed up and down on.
All is silver: the heavy surface of the sea,
swelling slowly as if considering spilling over,
is opaque, but the silver of the benches,
the lobster pots, and masts, scattered
among the wild jagged rocks,
is of an apparent translucence
like the small old buildings with an emerald moss
growing on their shoreward walls.
The big fish tubs are completely lined
with layers of beautiful herring scales
and the wheelbarrows are similarly plastered
with creamy iridescent coats of mail,
with small iridescent flies crawling on them.
Up on the little slope behind the houses,
set in the sparse bright sprinkle of grass,
is an ancient wooden capstan,
cracked, with two long bleached handles
and some melancholy stains, like dried blood,
where the ironwork has rusted.
The old man accepts a Lucky Strike.
He was a friend of my grandfather.
We talk of the decline in the population
and of codfish and herring
while he waits for a herring boat to come in.
There are sequins on his vest and on his thumb.

He has scraped the scales, the principal beauty,
from unnumbered fish with that black old knife,
The blade of which is almost worn away.

Down at the water's edge, at the place
Where they haul up the boats, up the long ramp
descending into the water, thin silver
tree trunks are laid horizontally
across the gray stones, down and down
at intervals of four or five feet.

Cold dark deep and absolutely clear,
element bearable to no mortal,
to fish and to seals . . . One seal particularly
I have seen here evening after evening.
He was curious about me. He was interested in music;
like me a believer in total immersion,
so I used to sing him Baptist hymns.
I also sang "A Mighty Fortress Is Our God."
He stood up in the water and regarded me
steadily, moving his head a little.
Then he would disappear, then suddenly emerge
almost in the same spot, with a sort of shrug
as if it were against his better judgment.
Cold dark deep and absolutely clear,
the clear gray icy water . . . Back, behind us,
the dignified tall firs begin.
Bluish, associating with their shadows,
a million Christmas trees stand
waiting for Christmas. The water seems suspended
above the rounded gray arid blue-gray stones.
I have seen it over and over, the same sea, the same,
slightly, indifferently swinging above the stones,
icily free above the stones,
above the stones and then the world.
If you should dip your hand in,
your wrist would ache immediately,
your bones would begin to ache and your hand would burn
as if the water were a transmutation of fire
that feeds on stones and burns with a dark gray flame.
If you tasted it, it would first taste bitter,
then briny, then sorely burn your tongue.
It is like what we imagine knowledge to be:
dark, salt, clear, moving, utterly free,
drawn from the cold hard mouth
of the world, derived from the rocky breasts
forever, flowing and drawn, and since
our knowledge is historical, flowing, and flown.

1955

Rain Towards Morning

The great light cage has broken up in the air,
freeing, I think, about a million birds
whose wild ascending shadows will not be back,
and all the wires come falling down.
No cage, no frightening birds; the rain
is brightening now. The face is pale
that tried the puzzle of their prison
and solved it with an unexpected kiss,
whose freckled unsuspected hands alit.

1955

The Shampoo

The still explosions on the rocks,
the lichens, grow
by spreading, gray, concentric shocks.
They have arranged
to meet the rings around the moon, although
within our memories they have not changed.

And since the heavens will attend
as long on us,
you've been, dear friend,
precipitate and pragmatical;
and look what happens. For Time is
nothing if not amenable.

The shooting stars in your black hair
in bright formation
are flocking where,
so straight, so soon?
— Come, let me wash it in this big tin basin,
battered and shiny like the moon.

1955

Exchanging Hats

Unfunny uncles who insist
in trying on a lady's hat,
— oh, even if the joke falls flat,
we share your slight transvestite twist

in spite of our embarrassment.
Costume and custom are complex.

The headgear of the other sex
inspires us to experiment.

Anandrous aunts, who, at the beach
with paper plates upon your laps,
keep putting on the yachtsmen's caps
with exhibitionistic screech,

the visors hanging o'er the ear
so that the golden anchors drag,
— the tides of fashion never lag.
Such caps may not be worn next year.

Or you who don the paper plate
itself, and put some grapes upon it,
or sport the Indian's feather bonnet,
— perversities may aggravate

the natural madness of the hatter.
And if the opera hats collapse
and crowns grow draughty, then, perhaps,
he thinks what might a miter matter?

Unfunny uncle, you who wore a
hat too big, or one too many,
tell us, can't you, are there any
stars inside your black fedora?

Aunt exemplary and slim,
with avernal eyes, we wonder
what slow changes they see under
their vast, shady, turned-down brim.

1956

Questions of Travel

There are too many waterfalls here; the crowded streams
hurry too rapidly down to the sea,
and the pressure of so many clouds on the mountaintops
makes them spill over the sides in soft slow-motion,
turning to waterfalls under our very eyes.
— For if those streaks, those mile-long, shiny, tearstains,
aren't waterfalls yet,
in a quick age or so, as ages go here,
they probably will be.
But if the streams and clouds keep travelling, travelling,
the mountains look like the hulls of capsized ships,
slime-hung and barnacled.

Think of the long trip home.
Should we have stayed at home and thought of here?
Where should we be today?
Is it right to be watching strangers in a play
in this strangest of theatres?
What childishness is it that while there's a breath of life
in our bodies, we are determined to rush
to see the sun the other way around?
The tiniest green hummingbird in the world?
To stare at some inexplicable old stonework,
inexplicable and impenetrable,
at any view,
instantly seen and always, always delightful?
Oh, must we dream our dreams
and have them, too?
And have we room
for one more folded sunset, still quite warm?

But surely it would have been a pity
not to have seen the trees along this road,
really exaggerated in their beauty,
not to have seen them gesturing
like noble pantomimists, robed in pink,
— Not to have had to stop for gas and heard
the sad, two-noted, wooden tune
of disparate wooden clogs
carelessly clacking over
a grease-stained filling-station floor.
(In another country the clogs would all be tested.
Each pair there would have identical pitch.)
— A pity not to have heard
the other, less primitive music of the fat brown bird
who sings above the broken gasoline pump
in a bamboo church of Jesuit baroque:
three towers, five silver crosses.
— Yes, a pity not to have pondered,
blurr'dly and inconclusively,
on what connection can exist for centuries
between the crudest wooden footwear
and, careful and finicky,
the whittled fantasies of wooden cages.
— Never to have studied history in
the weak calligraphy of songbirds' cages.
— And never to have had to listen to rain
so much like politicians' speeches:
two hours of unrelenting oratory
and then a sudden golden silence
in which the traveller takes a notebook, writes:

"Is it lack of imagination that makes us come
to imagined places, not just stay at home?
Or could Pascal have been not entirely right
about just sitting quietly in one's room?

Continent, city, country, society:
the choice is never wide and never free.
And here, or there . . . No. Should we have stayed at home,
wherever that may be?"

1965

Sestina

September rain falls on the house.
In the failing light, the old grandmother
sits in the kitchen with the child
beside the Little Marvel Stove,
reading the jokes from the almanac,
laughing and talking to hide her tears.

She thinks that her equinoctial tears
and the rain that beats on the roof of the house
were both foretold by the almanac,
but only known to a grandmother.
The iron kettle sings on the stove.
She cuts some bread and says to the child,

It's time for tea now; but the child
is watching the teakettle's small hard tears
dance like mad on the hot black stove,
the way the rain must dance on the house.
Tidying up, the old grandmother
hangs up the clever almanac

on its string. Bird like, the almanac
hovers half open above the child,
hovers above the old grandmother
and her teacup full of dark brown tears.
She shivers and says she thinks the house
feels chilly, and puts more wood in the stove.

It was to be, says the Marvel Stove.
I know what I know, says the almanac.
With crayons the child draws a rigid house
and a winding pathway. Then the child
puts in a man with buttons like tears
and shows it proudly to the grandmother.

But secretly, while the grandmother
busies herself about the stove,
the little moons fall down like tears
from between the pages of the almanac
into the flower bed the child
has carefully placed in the front of the house.

Time to plant tears, says the almanac.
The grandmother sings to the marvellous stove
and the child draws another inscrutable house.

1965

In the Waiting Room

In Worcester, Massachusetts,
I went with Aunt Consuelo
to keep her dentist's appointment
and sat and waited for her
in the dentist's waiting room.
It was winter. It got dark
early. The waiting room
was full of grown-up people,
arctics and overcoats,
lamps and magazines.
My aunt was inside
what seemed like a long time
and while I waited I read
the *National Geographic*
(I could read) and carefully
studied the photographs:
The inside of a volcano,
black, and full of ashes;
then it was spilling over
in rivulets of fire.
Osa and Martin Johnson
dressed in riding breeches,
laced boots, and pith helmets.
A dead man slung on a pole
— "Long Pig," the caption said.
Babies with pointed heads
wound round and round with string;
black, naked women with necks
wound round and round with wire
like the necks of light bulbs.
Their breasts were horrifying.
I read it right straight through.
I was too shy to stop.
And then I looked at the cover:
the yellow margins, the date.

Suddenly, from inside,
came an *oh*! of pain
— Aunt Consuelo's voice —
not very loud or long.
I wasn't at all surprised;
even then I knew she was
a foolish, timid woman.
I might have been embarrassed,
but wasn't. What took me
completely by surprise
was that it was *me*:
my voice, in my mouth.
Without thinking at all
I was my foolish aunt,
I — we — were falling, falling,
our eyes glued to the cover
of the *National Geographic*,
February, 1918.

I said to myself: three days
and you'll be seven years old.
I was saying it to stop
the sensation of falling off
the round, turning world
into cold, blue-black space.
But I felt: you are an *I*,
you are an *Elizabeth*,
you are one of *them*.
Why should you be one, too?
I scarcely dared to look
to see what it was I was.
I gave a sidelong glance
— I couldn't look any higher —
at shadowy gray knees,
trousers and skirts and boots
and different pairs of hands
lying under the lamps.
I knew that nothing stranger
had ever happened, that nothing
stranger could ever happen.
Why should I be my aunt,
or me, or anyone?
What similarities —
boots, hands, the family voice
I felt in my throat, or even
the *National Geographic*
and those awful hanging breasts —
held us all together

or made us all just one?
How — I didn't know any
word for it — how "unlikely" . . .
How had I come to be here,
like them, and overhear
a cry of pain that could have
got loud and worse but hadn't?

The waiting room was bright
and too hot. It was sliding
beneath a big black wave,
another, and another.

Then I was back in it.
The War was on. Outside,
in Worcester, Massachusetts,
were night and slush and cold,
and it was still the fifth
of February, 1918.

1976

Crusoe in England

A new volcano has erupted,
the papers say, and last week I was reading
where some ship saw an island being born:
at first a breath of steam, ten miles away;
and then a black fleck — basalt, probably —
rose in the mate's binoculars
and caught on the horizon like a fly.
They named it. But my poor old island's still
un-rediscovered, un-renamable.
None of the books has ever got it right.

Well, I had fifty-two
miserable, small volcanoes I could climb
with a few slithery strides —
volcanoes dead as ash heaps.
I used to sit on the edge of the highest one
and count the others standing up,
naked and leaden, with their heads blown off.
I'd think that if they were the size
I thought volcanoes should be, then I had
become a giant;
and if I had become a giant,
I couldn't bear to think what size
the goats and turtles were,
or the gulls, or the overlapping rollers

— a glittering hexagon of rollers
closing and closing in, but never quite,
glittering and glittering, though the sky
was mostly overcast.

My island seemed to be
a sort of cloud-dump. All the hemisphere's
left-over clouds arrived and hung
above the craters — their parched throats
were hot to touch.
Was that why it rained so much?
And why sometimes the whole place hissed?
The turtles lumbered by, high-domed,
hissing like teakettles.
(And I'd have given years, or taken a few,
for any sort of kettle, of course.)
The folds of lava, running out to sea,
would hiss. I'd turn. And then they'd prove
to be more turtles.
The beaches were all lava, variegated,
black, red, and white, and gray;
the marbled colors made a fine display.
And I had waterspouts. Oh,
half a dozen at a time, far out,
they'd come and go, advancing and retreating,
their heads in cloud, their feet in moving patches
of scuffed-up white.
Glass chimneys, flexible, attenuated,
sacerdotal beings of glass . . . I watched
the water spiral up in them like smoke.
Beautiful, yes, but not much company.

I often gave way to self-pity.
"Do I deserve this? I suppose I must.
I wouldn't be here otherwise. Was there
a moment when I actually chose this?
I don't remember, but there could have been."
What's wrong about self-pity, anyway?
With my legs dangling down familiarly
over a crater's edge, I told myself
"Pity should begin at home." So the more
pity I felt, the more I felt at home.

The sun set in the sea; the same odd sun
rose from the sea,
and there was one of it and one of me.
The island had one kind of everything:
one tree snail, a bright violet-blue
with a thin shell, crept over everything,

over the one variety of tree,
a sooty, scrub affair.
Snail shells lay under these in drifts
and, at a distance,
you'd swear that they were beds of irises.
There was one kind of berry, a dark red.
I tried it, one by one, and hours apart.
Sub-acid, and not bad, no ill effects;
and so I made home-brew. I'd drink
the awful, fizzy, stinging stuff
that went straight to my head
and play my home-made flute
(I think it had the weirdest scale on earth)
and, dizzy, whoop and dance among the goats.
Home-made, home-made! But aren't we all?
I felt a deep affection for
the smallest of my island industries.
No, not exactly, since the smallest was
a miserable philosophy.

Because I didn't know enough.
Why didn't I know enough of something?
Greek drama or astronomy? The books
I'd read were full of blanks;
the poems — well, I tried
reciting to my iris-beds,
"They flash upon that inward eye,
which is the bliss . . ." The bliss of what?
One of the first things that I did
when I got back was look it up.

The island smelled of goat and guano.
The goats were white, so were the gulls,
and both too tame, or else they thought
I was a goat, too, or a gull.
Baa, baa, baa and *shriek, shriek, shriek,*
baa . . . shriek . . . baa . . . I still can't shake
them from my ears; they're hurting now.
The questioning shrieks, the equivocal replies
over a ground of hissing rain
and hissing, ambulating turtles
got on my nerves.

When all the gulls flew up at once, they sounded
like a big tree in a strong wind, its leaves.
I'd shut my eyes and think about a tree,
an oak, say, with real shade, somewhere.
I'd heard of cattle getting island-sick.
I thought the goats were.

One billy-goat would stand on the volcano
I'd christened *Mont d'Espoir* or *Mount Despair*
(I'd time enough to play with names),
and bleat and bleat, and sniff the air.
I'd grab his beard and look at him.
His pupils, horizontal, narrowed up
and expressed nothing, or a little malice.
I got so tired of the very colors!
One day I dyed a baby goat bright red
with my red berries, just to see
something a little different.
And then his mother wouldn't recognize him.

Dreams were the worst. Of course I dreamed of food
and love, but they were pleasant rather
than otherwise. But then I'd dream of things
like slitting a baby's throat, mistaking it
for a baby goat. I'd have
nightmares of other islands
stretching away from mine, infinities
of islands, islands spawning islands,
like frogs' eggs turning into polliwogs
of islands, knowing that I had to live
on each and every one, eventually,
for ages, registering their flora,
their fauna, their geography.

Just when I thought I couldn't stand it
another minute longer, Friday came.
(Accounts of that have everything all wrong.)
Friday was nice.
Friday was nice, and we were friends.
If only he had been a woman!
I wanted to propagate my kind,
and so did he, I think, poor boy.
He'd pet the baby goats sometimes,
and race with them, or carry one around.
— Pretty to watch; he had a pretty body.

And then one day they came and took us off.

Now I live here, another island,
that doesn't seem like one, but who decides?
My blood was full of them; my brain
bred islands. But that archipelago
has petered out. I'm old.
I'm bored, too, drinking my real tea,
surrounded by uninteresting lumber.
The knife there on the shelf —

it reeked of meaning, like a crucifix.
It lived. How many years did I
beg it, implore it, not to break?
I knew each nick and scratch by heart,
the bluish blade, the broken tip,
the lines of wood-grain on the handle . . .
Now it won't look at me at all.
The living soul has dribbled away.
My eyes rest on it and pass on.

The local museum's asked me to
leave everything to them:
the flute, the knife, the shrivelled shoes,
my shedding goatskin trousers
(moths have got in the fur),
the parasol that took me such a time
remembering the way the ribs should go.
It still will work but, folded up,
looks like a plucked and skinny fowl.
How can anyone want such things?
— And Friday, my dear Friday, died of measles
seventeen years ago come March.

1976

One Art

The art of losing isn't hard to master;
so many things seem filled with the intent
to be lost that their loss is no disaster.

Lose something every day. Accept the fluster
of lost door keys, the hour badly spent.
The art of losing isn't hard to master.

Then practice losing farther, losing faster:
places, and names, and where it was you meant
to travel. None of these will bring disaster.

I lost my mother's watch. And look! my last, or
next-to-last, of three loved houses went.
The art of losing isn't hard to master.

I lost two cities, lovely ones. And, vaster,
some realms I owned, two rivers, a continent.
I miss them, but it wasn't a disaster.

— Even losing you (the joking voice, a gesture
I love) I shan't have lied. It's evident
the art of losing's not too hard to master
though it may look like (*Write* it!) like disaster.

1976

Five Flights Up

Still dark.
The unknown bird sits on his usual branch.
The little dog next door barks in his sleep
inquiringly, just once.
Perhaps in his sleep, too, the bird inquires
once or twice, quavering.
Questions — if that is what they are —
answered directly, simply,
by day itself.

Enormous morning, ponderous, meticulous;
gray light streaking each bare branch,
each single twig, along one side,
making another tree, of glassy veins . . .
The bird still sits there. Now he seems to yawn.

The little black dog runs in his yard.
His owner's voice arises, stern,
"You ought to be ashamed!"
What has he done?
He bounces cheerfully up and down;
he rushes in circles in the fallen leaves.

Obviously, he has no sense of shame.
He and the bird know everything is answered,
all taken care of,
no need to ask again.
— Yesterday brought to today so lightly!
(A yesterday I find almost impossible to lift.)

1976

J. V. CUNNINGHAM (1911–1985)

Born in Cumberland, Maryland, J. V. Cunningham was a student and protégé of Yvor Winters at Stanford University. He is a poet of wit and witty insults, a specialist in epigrams and epitaphs, practicing a severe commitment to the plain style. He was vehemently opposed to modernism in its various forms. Asked once to explain why he liked an epitaph he had written, he replied with an abbreviated version of his poetics: "because it is all denotation and no connotation; because it has only one level of meaning; because it is not ironic, paradoxical, complex, or subtle; and because the meter is monotonously regular."

For My Contemporaries

How time reverses
The proud in heart!
I now make verses
Who aimed at art.

But I sleep well.
Ambitious boys
Whose big lines swell
With spiritual noise,

Despise me not,
And be not queasy
To praise somewhat:
Verse is not easy.

But rage who will.
Time that procured me
Good sense and skill
Of madness cured me.

1942

Montana Pastoral

I am no shepherd of a child's surmises.
I have seen fear where the coiled serpent rises,

Thirst where the grasses burn in early May
And thistle, mustard, and the wild oat stay.

There is dust in this air. I saw in the heat
Grasshoppers busy in the threshing wheat.

So to this hour. Through the warm dusk I drove
To blizzards sifting on the hissing stove,

And found no images of pastoral will,
But fear, thirst, hunger, and this huddled chill.

1942

from *Epigrams*

An Epitaph for Anyone

An old dissembler who lived out his lie
Lies here as if he did not fear to die.

1942

Lip was a man who used his head

Lip was a man who used his head.
He used it when he went to bed
With his friend's wife, or with his friend,
With either sex, at either end.

1950

In a few days now when two memories meet

In a few days now when two memories meet
In that place of disease, waste, and desire
Where forms receptive, featureless, and vast
Find occupation, in that narrow dark,
That warm sweat of a carnal tenderness,
What figure in the pantheon of lust,
What demon is our god? What name subsumes
That act external to our sleeping selves?
Not pleasure — it is much too broad and narrow —,
Not sex, not for the moment love, but pride,
And not in prowess, but pride undefined,
Autonomous in its unthought demands,
A bit of vanity, but mostly pride.

1964

Jack and Jill

She said he was a man who cheated.
He said she didn't play the game.
She said an expletive deleted.
He said the undeleted same.
And so they ended their relation
With meaningful communication.

1981

Paul Goodman (1911–1972)

Paul Goodman, a native New Yorker and graduate of City College, was at the center of the radical bohemian literary circle Delmore Schwartz satirized in his story "The World Is a Wedding" (1948). Goodman is "Rudyard Bell," described as the "leader and captain of all hearts," who lives with his sister in Washington Heights and writes plays that are regularly rejected by Broadway producers. Nevertheless his sister maintains "that Rudyard was a genius and ought not to be required to earn a living." Goodman, a lay psychotherapist, became well known for his books of social commentary, such as *Growing Up Absurd* (1960) and *Compulsory Mis-Education* (1964), but his poems (neglected except for "The Lordly Hudson") and his novel *The Empire City* (1959) have not yet received their due.

The Lordly Hudson

"Driver, what stream is it?" I asked, well knowing
it was our lordly Hudson hardly flowing,
"It is our lordly Hudson hardly flowing,"
he said, "under the green-grown cliffs."

Be still, heart! no one needs your passionate
suffrage to select this glory,
this is our lordly Hudson hardly flowing
under the green-grown cliffs.

"Driver! has this a peer in Europe or the East?"
"No no!" he said. Home! home!
be quiet, heart! this is our lordly Hudson
and has no peer in Europe or the East,

this is our lordly Hudson hardly flowing
under the green-grown cliffs
and has no peer in Europe or the East.
Be quiet, heart! home! home!

1962

I planned to have a border of lavender

I planned to have a border of lavender
but planted the bank too of lavender
and now my whole crazy garden
    is grown in lavender

it smells so sharp heady and musky
of lavender, and the hue of only

lavender is all my garden up
   into the gray rocks.

When forth I go from here the heedless lust
I squander — and in vain for I am stupid
and miss the moment — it has blest me silly
   when forth I go

and when, sitting as gray as these gray rocks
among the lavender, I breathe the lavender's
tireless squandering, I liken it
   to my silly lusting,

I liken my silly indefatigable
lusting to the lavender which has grown over
all my garden, banks and borders, up
   into the gray rocks.

1962

A Chess Game

   The chessboard was reflected in her eyes.
Eager to beat her, first I looked in her eyes.
   I made a Spanish move, an ancient one,
and broken was the red rank of pawns in her light eyes.
   Then I lowered my eyes from that chessboard
and Love said, "Oh not her; conquer the king if you can."

   My eyes I lowered to the checkerboard
planted with lords in particolored fiefs.
   My red soul hated the black chesspieces
and first my knights flew forth, to dominate.
   I hovered over the pattern like a hawk
and Art said, "Do not win. The pattern is enough."

   Then the chess-game became luminous
and then I was not and then we were again,
   and suddenly into the center came
of that luminous crisscross of mathematical
   possibilities the Angel Fame
whose left wing was love and his right wing was death.

1962

Josephine Miles (1911–1985)

Josephine Miles was born in Chicago and raised in California. From an early age she suffered from rheumatoid arthritis so severe that it confined her to a wheelchair. She received her doctorate at Berkeley in 1938 and taught there from 1940 until her retirement in 1978; her students included A. R. Ammons and Jack Spicer. Kenneth Rexroth, a rival in San Francisco poetry circles, disparaged her early work as "small, very neat holes cut in the paper." But her gift for compression and her riddling intelligence make her an authentic heir of Emily Dickinson. Miles singled out "Reason" as a favorite of her poems, "because I like the idea of speech — not images, not ideas, not music, but people talking — as the material from which poetry is made."

Center

What they had at their window was earth's own shadow,
What they had on their garden, bloom's intermission,
Slept in the car the graceful far.

Slept in the breast a city and statewide rest,
Ran at the wrist time strapped and glassed,
They had eyes closed tight in a central standard night.

1939

Government Injunction Restraining Harlem Cosmetic Co.

They say La Jac Brite Pink Skin Bleach avails not,
They say its Orange Beauty Glow does not glow,
Nor the face grow five shades lighter nor the heart
Five shades lighter. They say no.

They deny good luck, love, power, romance, and inspiration
From La Jac Brite ointment and incense of all kinds,
And condemn in writing skin brightening and whitening
And whitening of minds.

There is upon the federal trade commission a burden of glory
So to defend the fact, so to impel
The plucking of hope from the hand, honor from the complexion,
Sprite from the spell.

1941

Dec. 7, 1941

On the war day, mainly the soldiers got going.
Around some corners with which I was familiar
The steps were still mostly up and down,
Meditative, and not widely directed.

The little wars still raged, of crutch with stair,
Beard with crumb, buyer with incantation,
Trouble with peace, the awkwardest
Fights, and freest of origin.

1941

Ride

It's not my world, I grant, but I made it.
It's not my ranch, lean oak, buzzard crow,
Not my fryers, mixmaster, well-garden.
And now it's down the road and I made it.

It's not your rackety car but you drive it.
It's not your four-door, top-speed, white-wall tires,
Not our state, not even I guess, our nation,
But now it's down the road, and we're in it.

1955

Reason

Said, Pull her up a bit will you, Mac, I want to unload there.
Said, Pull her up my rear end, first come first serve.
Said, Give her the gun, Bud, he needs a taste of his own bumper.
Then the usher came out and got into the act:

Said, Pull her up, pull her up a bit, we need this space, sir.
Said, For God's sake, is this still a free country or what?
You go back and take care of Gary Cooper's horse
And leave me handle my own car.

Saw them unloading the lame old lady,
Ducked out under the wheel and gave her an elbow,
Said, All you needed to do was just explain;
Reason, Reason is my middle name.

1955

The Doctor Who Sits at the Bedside of a Rat

The doctor who sits at the bedside of a rat
Obtains real answers — a paw twitch,
An ear tremor, a gain or loss of weight,
No problem as to which

Is temper and which is true.
What a rat feels, he will do.

Concomitantly then, the doctor who sits
At the bedside of a rat
Asks real questions, as befits
The place, like where did that potassium go, not what
Do you think of Willie Mays or the weather?
So rat and doctor may converse together.

1960

As Difference Blends into Identity

As difference blends into identity
Or blurs into obliteration, we give
To zero our position at the center,
Withdraw our belief and baggage.

As rhyme at the walls lapses, at frontiers
Customs scatter like a flight of snow,
And boundaries moonlike draw us out, our opponents
Join us, we are their refuge.

As barriers between us melt, I may treat you
Unkindly as myself, I may forget
Your name as my own. Then enters
Our anonymous assailant.

As assonance by impulse burgeons
And that quaver shakes us by which we are spent,
We may move to consume another with us,
Stir into parity another's cyphers.

Then when our sniper steps to a window
In the brain, starts shooting, and we fall surprised,
Of what we know not do we seek forgiveness
From ourselves, for ourselves?

1967

Conception

Death did not come to my mother
Like an old friend.
She was a mother, and she must
Conceive him.

Up and down the bed she fought crying
Help me, but death
Was a slow child
Heavy. He

Waited. When he was born
We took and tired him, now he is ready
To do his good in the world.

He has my mother's features.
He can go among strangers
To save lives.

1974

ANNE PORTER (b. 1911)

Anne Porter was born in Sherborn, Massachusetts. She married the painter Fairfield Porter in 1932, and she and their five children often appeared in his paintings. The Porters were close to the poets at the center of the "New York school." James Schuyler lived with the Porter family in their Southampton (Long Island) and Penobscot Bay homes for many years; Anne Porter quipped that Schuyler had come to lunch one day and stayed for eleven years. Though she had toiled in virtual secrecy for most of her life, when *An Altogether Different Language*, a retrospective gathering of her poems, was published in 1994 it was promptly short-listed for the National Book Award in poetry. David Shapiro wrote that "For My Son Johnny" is "filled with the audacious Pop-Art vividness of unembarrassed life."

For My Son Johnny

July 11th, 1980

The maker of worlds and tender father of sparrows
Who told us what's done to the smallest is done to him,
Told us also, the least will be greatest in heaven,
And since it was he who told us we know it's true.
So Johnny, now you're one of the greatest,
Because here on earth you were certainly one of the least.

You called yourself "a man without money or power,"
You seemed only to ask to drink countless cans of soda,
Though it did have to be one special brand.
You seemed only to ask
To tell your difficult puns with a delighted smile
To friends and acquaintances and even strangers,
And to stand in front of your house and rock and wave your arms
And sing, varying it with whoops and growls
Of wild ecstatic joy,

And later to inquire of shopkeepers and policemen
If they could hear you at the other end of town.
You seemed to ask only to spend hours in the woods and fields
Alone, "talking to God."

But you also loved to go swimming
Especially in thunderstorms,
Especially in autumn "under the colored leaves"
And if the leaves weren't there you pretended they were there.
You loved napping in the "messy attic
With filing cabinets and old comic books
And empty cartons saying B&M BAKED BEANS."
And passionately you loved the thunder
With all its "fancy sounds"
In which you detected all kinds of subtleties.
"Did it sound like a subway train?
Did it say Relinquish Relinquish?
Did it shake the ground?"

And you loved women, most of whom you admired
Quite regardless of age,
And whom you hugged with great abandon,
Particularly the ones in flowered dresses
And the ones with curly hair,
Knowing you'd never marry because
"A wife might be hard to please."
This may have hurt.
Perhaps that's why you asked to be excused from weddings,
Saying that they were boring.

A little girl once asked you, "Johnny,
How does it feel to be retarded?"
And you answered gently,
"I don't know dear, I'm not retarded."
Which you were not.

Though light-heartedly you described your outbursts of temper
As "just a little jump and a babyish roar,"
Far oftener, your scruples attacked you:
"Am I the worst person in the world?"

Though your shoelaces were hardly ever tied
And you seldom wore matching socks
You tried to behave with dignity in the village
"So as not to embarrass my little sisters."

There was a father in you too somewhere
Though you never corrected other people's children
"I don't want to act like a staff member!"

If you saw a baby in town you'd smile
And with just the tip of one finger
You'd carefully touch the tiny hands and feet.
With the Child in the Christmas manger you did the same.

You told us that "In heaven the angels kid and joke."
Quite casually you'd mention
  seeing St. Michael the Archangel,
"That's who I just waved to."
We couldn't see him, so we asked what he was like.
You told us, "Just a friendly man in a business suit,"
And said "Next time I see an Archangel
Would it be all right to ask him his name?"

Often you visited our parish church,
First splashing on much holy water.
Inside the church you went down hard on both knees
And then, dropping a lot of flaming matches,
You lighted almost a full row of candles
To pray for "blind and deaf and crippled children."

"And when the church is locked," you said,
"I just go up to it and touch the wall."

Your family sent you away to live on a farm in Vermont,
And for years your times at home were so short
    and so far apart
That hearing them once called "visits" you turned white,
So deep was your speechless fear
That you might be only a guest at home, and have no home.
But in your humility you knew how to forgive,
Growing kinder and kinder as you grew older.

"I'm not afraid of dying," you said, "just of getting hurt."
Johnny, now you're a staff member!
And now you're home.
Now you're with Mary, whose starry veil you loved,
And of whom you said, "She won't get bored with my puns,"
And, "She won't mind if I touch her dress."
While your mother, who sometimes did
    get bored with your puns,
Cries here on earth

And asks you, now that you're one of the greatest,
To grant her a portion of your littleness.

1980

ROBERT JOHNSON (1911–1938)

Born in Hazelhurst, Mississippi, Robert Johnson made only forty-two recordings, but these exerted a major influence on rock artists including Bob Dylan, Eric Clapton, and the Rolling Stones. Johnson's strum style was revolutionary. His "Me and the Devil" and "Cross Road" blues fueled the legend that he had sold his soul to the devil in exchange for musical genius. In 1938, Johnson died when a jook joint owner poisoned his whiskey in a dispute over a woman.

Me and the Devil Blues

Early this morning
when you knocked upon my door
Early this morning oooooo
when you knocked upon my door
And I said, Hello Satan
I believe it's time to go

Me and the Devil
was walking side by side
Me and the Devil oooooo
was walking side by side
I'm going to beat my woman
until I get satisfied

She said you knows the way
that I always dog her 'round
(now baby you know
you ain't doing me right now)
She said you knows the way oooooo
that I be dog her 'round
It must be that old evil spirit
so deep down in the ground

You may bury my body
down by the highway side
(now baby I don't care where
you bury my body
when I'm dead and gone)
You may bury my body oooooo
down by the highway side
So my old evil spirit
can get a Greyhound Bus and ride

1937

JEAN GARRIGUE (1912–1972)

Jean Garrigue was born Gertrude Louise Garrigus in Evansville, Indiana. She was educated at the University of Chicago and the Iowa Writers' Workshop and settled in New York City's Greenwich Village. She writes about the amorous lives and sometimes conflicting priorities of women and men in a manner Lee Upton characterizes as "elaborate, doubly-tongued, highly stylized." Garrigue herself described her work as a "dialogue of self with soul, the quarrel of self with world." She died of Hodgkin's disease in 1972.

Dialog

Dreams, said the dog,
Suffice us not.
We strain at eels and catch a gnat instead.
Who'll have Red Rabbit
And his riding wood
And my lady moon in a simpled hood?

It's perfectly true
Said the fat cat,
I dream no more but stare at a hole
For the mouse, fiction, to come out.
Succulent taster!
Amorous waster!
All my appetite's in my paunch.

Then to your eyes he smiling said
That when we meet do shock our blood,
Here's rabbit and here's dog and cat
And which is which for all of that?

The wise mistress in settled fur
Knows what original attared myrrh
Brings lovers from afar.
It is in nature, not in art,
She only has to do her part
It's done and both being satisfied
Cease, a family's started.

As for the dog in a net
It knows its heart
When made to quake.
Propinquity's a moment's fit.

When sun and moon were one?
Cried she,

Out of white nights grown
The wildest lightness known?

Sap of wood
And beast of blood,
World run from this
If I am wrong
When down we put our arms at dawn.

Said he,
It all depends on a lasting net
If you'd fish for eternity.

Said she,
Love's besetting property!

1971

Movie Actors Scribbling Letters Very Fast in Crucial Scenes

The velocity with which they write —
Don't you know it? It's from the heart!
They are acting the whole part out.
Love! has taken them up —
Like writing to god in the night.
Meet me! I'm dying! Come at once!
The crisis is on them, the shock
Drives from the nerve to the pen,
Pours from the blood into ink.

1972

Song in Sligo

I had a bear that danced,
A monkey on a stick,
A dog that begged,
A cat that moused,
And, slouching by a ditch,
A rook in black of silk.
I had those birds that rode
Upon the levels of the cove
At late long twilight in the north
When the brand of sun still burned
Above the shoddy bridges of the Garavogue.
I had a boat that beat
Up levels of the reed-flagged shore

And rock-grained, rack-ruined battlements.
I had a boat and traveled with the birds
That flew against me in the breath of winds,
To each bend of the river its own mews
Of samite-backed and sable-legged young swans
Who winter from the Bay of Rosses here.
I had an island for my own one want,
A ring of prophecy and scent,
Where trees were sloped upon a moss of turf,
One ruined wall that I could sit against
And dip a ragged net to catch a fish
Of rainbowed armor in the scales of night.
I had a love who spoke to me of wars.
It was the summer of the fires.
Blackout by desolating energy.
You silken tatters of the sliding flow,
I had your voices and your leafy pools,
I have these poisons we must choose.

1973

Grenoble Café

At breakfast they are sober, subdued.
It is early. They have not much to say
Or with declamations fit only for whisper
Keep under pressure the steam of their joy.
She listens, usually. It is he who talks,
Surrounding her with the furious smoke
Of his looking that simply feeds,
Perhaps, her slightly traveling-away dreams
That, if you judge from her cheek,
Young and incomparably unbroken,
Are rich with the unknowing knowing
Of what he has said the time before
And with the smiles coming down the corridor
Of how it will be for year on year,
Nights as they'll be in his rough arms.

1973

Bad Times Song

Where is my cat, my rake,
My poultry seasoning and my stick?
Where is the heart I had who flung your hat
Over the millstream years back?

Where is my tail and purpose strait
For which I fought and won with luck
And where my kin of shining hue
The dark put up?

How do I live and by whose right?
When the war goes on, the price goes up.
Whose treasuries may I sack
And who would give me ransom should I try?

To ask such questions is a childish rote.
Besides, they do not fit
The answers given by the great.
A snake under every stone,

In every suitcase and in every bed,
The thing to do is not to ask but act.

1992

ROBERT HAYDEN (1913–1980)

Robert Hayden was born Asa Bundy Sheffey in Detroit and was brought up by foster parents. He studied with W. H. Auden at the University of Michigan in 1941 and returned to Ann Arbor as a professor in 1969. Much honored in later years, Hayden declared that he opposed "the chauvinistic and the doctrinaire" and saw no reason why "a Negro poet should be limited to 'racial utterance' or to having his writing judged by standards different from those applied to the work of other poets." He said he wanted to be a black poet "the same way Yeats is an Irish poet," feeling free to make use of black history without "narrow, racial, propagandistic implications," as in "Middle Passage," which treats the subject of the slave trade. Singling out "Those Winter Sundays" as a favorite poem, David Huddle writes that this "loose" sonnet transforms a "son's remorse over never thanking his father" into a "permanent expression of gratitude." The "Empress of the Blues" in Hayden's "Homage" is Bessie Smith.

Those Winter Sundays

Sundays too my father got up early
and put his clothes on in the blueblack cold
then with cracked hands that ached
from labor in the weekday weather made
banked fires blaze. No one ever thanked him.

I'd wake and hear the cold splintering, breaking.
When the rooms were warm, he'd call,
and slowly I would rise and dress,
fearing the chronic angers of that house,

Speaking indifferently to him,
who had driven out the cold
and polished my good shoes as well.
What did I know, what did I know
of love's austere and lonely offices?

1962

Middle Passage

I

Jesús, Estrella, Esperanza, Mercy:

Sails flashing to the wind like weapons,
sharks following the moans the fever and the dying;
horror the corposant and compass rose.

Middle Passage:
voyage through death
to life upon these shores.

"10 April 1800 —
Blacks rebellious. Crew uneasy. Our linguist says
their moaning is a prayer for death,
ours and their own. Some try to starve themselves.
Lost three this morning leaped with crazy laughter
to the waiting sharks, sang as they went under."

Desire, Adventure, Tartar, Ann:

Standing to America, bringing home
black gold, black ivory, black seed.

Deep in the festering hold thy father lies,
of his bones New England pews are made,
those are altar lights that were his eyes.

Jesus Saviour Pilot Me
Over Life's Tempestuous Sea

We pray that Thou wilt grant, O Lord,
safe passage to our vessels bringing
heathen souls unto Thy chastening.

Jesus Saviour

"8 bells. I cannot sleep, for I am sick
with fear, but writing eases fear a little
since still my eyes can see these words take shape

upon the page & so I write, as one
would turn to exorcism. 4 days scudding,
but now the sea is calm again. Misfortune
follows in our wake like sharks (our grinning
tutelary gods). Which one of us
has killed an albatross? A plague among
our blacks — Ophthalmia: blindness — & we
have jettisoned the blind to no avail.
It spreads, the terrifying sickness spreads.
Its claws have scratched sight from the Capt.'s eyes
& there is blindness in the fo'c'sle
& we must sail 3 weeks before we come
to port."

What port awaits us, Davy Jones'
or home? I've heard of slavers drifting, drifting,
playthings of wind and storm and chance, their crews
gone blind, the jungle hatred
crawling up on deck.

Thou Who Walked On Galilee

"Deponent further sayeth *The Bella J*
left the Guinea Coast
with cargo of five hundred blacks and odd
for the barracoons of Florida:

"That there was hardly room 'tween-decks for half
the sweltering cattle stowed spoon-fashion there;
that some went mad of thirst and tore their flesh
and sucked the blood:

"That Crew and Captain lusted with the comeliest
of the savage girls kept naked in the cabins;
that there was one they called The Guinea Rose
and they cast lots and fought to lie with her:

"That when the Bo's'n piped all hands, the flames
spreading from starboard already were beyond
control, the negroes howling and their chains
entangled with the flames:

"That the burning blacks could not be reached,
that the Crew abandoned ship,
leaving their shrieking negresses behind,
that the Captain perished drunken with the wenches:

"Further Deponent sayeth not."

Pilot Oh Pilot Me

II

Aye, lad, and I have seen those factories,
Gambia, Rio Pongo, Calabar;
have watched the artful mongos baiting traps
of war wherein the victor and the vanquished

Were caught as prizes for our barracoons.
Have seen the nigger kings whose vanity
and greed turned wild black hides of Fellatah,
Mandingo, Ibo, Kru to gold for us.

And there was one — King Anthracite we named him —
fetish face beneath French parasols
of brass and orange velvet, impudent mouth
whose cups were carven skulls of enemies:

He'd honor us with drum and feast and conjo
and palm-oil-glistening wenches deft in love,
and for tin crowns that shone with paste,
red calico and German-silver trinkets

Would have the drums talk war and send
his warriors to burn the sleeping villages
and kill the sick and old and lead the young
in coffles to our factories.

Twenty years a trader, twenty years,
for there was wealth aplenty to be harvested
from those black fields, and I'd be trading still
but for the fevers melting down my bones.

III

Shuttles in the rocking loom of history,
the dark ships move, the dark ships move,
their bright ironical names
like jests of kindness on a murderer's mouth;
plough through thrashing glister toward
fata morgana's lucent melting shore,
weave toward New World littorals that are
mirage and myth and actual shore.

Voyage through death,
                                        voyage whose chartings are unlove.

A charnel stench, effluvium of living death
spreads outward from the hold,
where the living and the dead, the horribly dying,
lie interlocked, lie foul with blood and excrement.

Deep in the festering hold thy father lies,
the corpse of mercy rots with him,
rats eat loves rotten gelid eyes.

But, oh, the living look at you
with human eyes whose suffering accuses you,
whose hatred reaches through the swill of dark
to strike you like a leper's claw.

You cannot stare that hatred down
or chain the fear that stalks the watches
and breathes on you its fetid scorching breath;
cannot kill the deep immortal human wish,
the timeless will

"But for the storm that flung up barriers
of wind and wave, The Amistad, señores,
would have reached the port of Príncipe in two,
three days at most; but for the storm we should
have been prepared for what befell.
Swift as the puma's leap it came. There was
that interval of moonless calm filled only
with the water's and the rigging's usual sounds,
then sudden movement, blows and snarling cries
and they had fallen on us with machete
and marlinspike. It was as though the very
air, the night itself were striking us.
Exhausted by the rigors of the storm,
we were no match for them. Our men went down
before the murderous Africans. Our loyal
Celestino ran from below with gun
and lantern and I saw, before the cane-
knife's wounding flash, Cinquez,
that surly brute who calls himself a prince,
directing, urging on the ghastly work.
He hacked the poor mulatto down, and then
he turned on me. The decks were slippery
when daylight finally came. It sickens me
to think of what I saw, of how these apes
threw overboard the butchered bodies of
our men, true Christians all, like so much jetsam.
Enough, enough. The rest is quickly told:
Cinquez was forced to spare the two of us
you see to steer the ship to Africa,
and we like phantoms doomed to rove the sea
voyaged east by day and west by night,
deceiving them, hoping for rescue,
prisoners on our own vessel, till
at length we drifted to the shores of this

your land, America, where we were freed
from our unspeakable misery. Now we
demand, good sirs, the extradition of
Cinquez and his accomplices to La
Havana. And it distresses us to know
there are so many here who seem inclined
to justify the mutiny of these blacks.
We find it paradoxical indeed
that you whose wealth, whose tree of liberty
are rooted in the labor of your slaves
should suffer the august John Quincy Adams
to speak with so much passion of the right
of chattel slaves to kill their lawful masters
and with his Roman rhetoric weave a hero's
garland for Cinquez. I tell you that
we are determined to return to Cuba
with our slaves and there see justice done. Cinquez —
or let us say 'the Prince' — Cinquez shall die."

The deep immortal human wish,
the timeless will:

Cinquez its deathless primaveral image,
Life that transfigures many lives.

Voyage through death
to life upon these shores.

1962

Homage to the Empress of the Blues

Because there was a man somewhere in a candystripe silk shirt,
gracile and dangerous as a jaguar and because a woman moaned
for him in sixty-watt gloom and mourned him Faithless Love
Twotiming Love Oh Love Oh Careless Aggravating Love,

She came out on the stage in yards of pearls, emerging like
a favorite scenic view, flashed her golden smile and sang.

Because grey laths began somewhere to show from underneath
torn hurdygurdy lithographs of dollfaced heaven;
and because there were those who feared alarming fists of snow
on the door and those who feared the riot-squad of statistics,

She came out on the stage in ostrich feathers, beaded satin,
and shone that smile on us and sang.

1966

MURIEL RUKEYSER (1913–1980)

Muriel Rukeyser was born in New York City, the daughter of secular Jewish parents. Passionately political, she took part in the People's Olympiad in Barcelona in 1936, an event held in protest of the Nazi Olympics in Berlin, and she was present at the outbreak of the Spanish Civil War, championing the Loyalists against the Fascists. In 1944, Rukeyser described herself as "poet, woman, American, and Jew," each identity in her view strengthening the others. To be Jewish was her proud choice: "To be a Jew in the twentieth century / Is to be offered a gift. If you refuse, / Wishing to be invisible, you choose / Death of the spirit, the stone insanity. / Accepting, take full life." Rukeyser was vulnerable to the charge, leveled by Louise Bogan, that "her style, an amalgam of modern styles, was almost wholly unrelieved by moments of clarity, or her seriousness by moments of lightness." Rukeyser famously asked, "What would happen if one woman told the truth about her life?" She answered, "The world would split open."

Waiting for Icarus

He said he would be back and we'd drink wine together
He said that everything would be better than before
He said we were on the edge of a new relation
He said he would never again cringe before his father
He said that he was going to invent full-time
He said he loved me that going into me
He said was going into the world and the sky
He said all the buckles were very firm
He said the wax was the best wax
He said Wait for me here on the beach
He said Just don't cry

I remember the gulls and the waves
I remember the islands going dark on the sea
I remember the girls laughing
I remember they said he only wanted to get away from me
I remember mother saying: Inventors are like poets,
a trashy lot
I remember she told me those who try out inventions are
worse
I remember she added: Women who love such are the worst
of all
I have been waiting all day, or perhaps longer.
I would have liked to try those wings myself.
It would have been better than this.

1973

Myth

Long afterward, Oedipus, old and blinded, walked the
roads. He smelled a familiar smell. It was
the Sphinx. Oedipus said, 'I want to ask one question.
Why didn't I recognize my mother?' 'You gave the
wrong answer,' said the Sphinx. 'But that was what
made everything possible,' said Oedipus. 'No,' she said.
'When I asked, What walks on four legs in the morning,
two at noon, and three in the evening, you answered,
Man. You didn't say anything about woman.'
'When you say Man,' said Oedipus, 'you include women
too. Everyone knows that.' She said, 'That's what
you think.'

1973

DAVID SCHUBERT (1913–1946)

David Schubert was born in Brooklyn and grew up in Detroit. When he was about twelve, his father abandoned the family, and his mother killed herself shortly after; David discovered the body. He was raised by various relatives and won a scholarship to Amherst College, where he neglected his studies and concentrated on his poems. Supported by his wife, Judith, a schoolteacher, he suffered from mental illness and was ultimately diagnosed as a paranoid schizophrenic. He died of tuberculosis. Not until 1961 did his collection *Initial A* appear in print. Speaking of Schubert's poem "Midston House," John Ashbery, an admirer, credits the poem's "multiple points of view and the multiplicity of possible situations" with the power to transform "a job interview into one of life's major turning points."

Kind Valentine

She hugs a white rose to her heart —
The petals flare — in her breath blown;
She'll catch the fruit on her death day —
The flower rooted in the bone.
The face at evening comes for love;
Reeds in the river meet below.
She sleeps small child, her face a tear;
The dream comes in with stars to go
Into the window, feigning snow.
This is the book that no one knows.
The paper wall holds mythic oaks,
Behind the oaks a castle grows.
Over the door, and over her

(She dies! she wakes!) the steeds gallop.
The child stirs, hits the dumb air, weeps,
Afraid of night's long loving-cup.

Into yourself, live, Joanne!
And count the buttons — how they run
To doctor, red chief, lady's man!
Most softly pass, on the stairs down,
The stranger in your evening gown.
Hearing white, inside your grief,
An insane laughter up the roof.
O little wind, come in with dawn —
It is your shadow on the lawn.

Break the pot! and let carnations —
Smell them! they're the very first.
Break the sky and let come magic
Rain! Let earth come pseudo-tragic
Roses — blossom, unrehearsed.
Head, break! is broken. Dream, so small,
Come in to her. O little child,
Dance on squills where the winds run wild.

The candles rise in the warm night
Back and forth, the tide is bright.
Slowly, slowly, the waves retreat
Under her wish and under feet.
And over tight breath, tighter eyes,
The mirror ebbs, it ebbs and flows.
And the intern, the driver, speed
To gangrene! But — who knows — suppose
He was beside her! Please, star-bright,
First I see, while in the night
A soft-voiced, like a tear, guitar —
It calls a palm coast from afar.
And oh, so far the stars were there
For him to hang upon her hair
Like the white rose he gave, white hot,
While the low sobbing band — it wept
Violets and forget-me-nots.

1936

Peter and Mother

"A hand is writing these lines
On your eyes for journeys
You'll never start for. They're

Transparencies. Wear rubbers
And you will be wise."

In dreams initial A and in the parlor
The chandelier was bright with small toy tears;
At evening the door opened on clematis
And his mother with a shawl ran down the years
To meet someone with an empty lunch-box.
As they returned across the lot —
He listened — in her head was truth
Hansel and Gretel and a bar
Of sweetest song.

Where the word
Is shadow of the deed and hard
Upon it like first crocuses
In snow . . . "grow up and be
My tenement house, my brick building!"

This paper representation imperfectly made,
Be like words at a railway station still
Speaking though the train has gone —
The pity strong enough
To tear the four walls down, scatter the children,
The picture of the cow on the wall
Grazing a different pasture.

Talking her trite ghost, the smell
Of lilac is fainter and fainter;
Thinking her worn face is like a face
A whiteness on the brush of some eternal painter.
And always growing farther, trying to hear
Something that was never expressed very
Clearly.

Her journey ended that was hidden
In the blindness of his naïve skin.

1938

Midston House

What is needed is a technique
Of conversation, I think, as I put on the
Electric light. But not the limited
Vocabulary of our experience, the
Surface irritations which pile up,
Accumulate a city, — but the expression,

Metamorphosed, of what they are the
Metaphor of; — and their conversion into light.

    On the bus toward Midston House
I survey the people in their actions. Placid
And relaxed are they; this is the humdrum
Claptrap costume of girls and food, men
And work and house. The insurance
Of habit is circular, as
Democracy has interlocking duties,
Circular obediences.

    Yet how to transform
The continual failing clouds of
Energy, into light? The vital
Intelligence of the man whom I am
Going to visit — does he know? I
Think how the sharp severing of
My life's task — severed associations,
Produced in me almost a
Lypothymia of grief and a hiatus of
Days, which grew fangs of anger, my
Lycanthropy — thank god, it's over!

    I am fired from my job by flames, big
As angry consciences; I can do
Nothing; I have not one ability! This man
Whom I am waiting to see in the lobby —
All my life I am waiting for something that
Does not eventuate — will he
Exist?

    The law of life, like an abstract
Rigorous lawyer, passes a terrifying judg-
Ment on poor little me, in a strange foreign
Syllogism. He is cheating me! He will not
Keep the appointment!

                    His probity
Rebukes my suspicion. What can I say, that
I love him; that I am un-
Worthy? My doubt makes me feel,
— Even as we discuss another's dishonesty —
Ugly, irate, and damned avid, a cunning
Rascal, like that ugly bird of the White
Nile.

    But the poem is just this
Speaking of what cannot be said

To the person I want to say it.
I am sleepy with subtlety; the room strikes me as
Dark, so cold, so lonely. There is
No one in it. I will put on all the lights.
I wish I could go
On a long, on a long long journey
To a place where life is simple and decent, not
Too demanding.

No! On the vehicle, Tomorrow, I will see
That man, whose handshake was happiness.

1961

DELMORE SCHWARTZ (1913–1966)

The volatile life of Brooklyn-born Delmore Schwartz prompted his friend Robert Lowell to replace "gladness" with "sadness" in the famous couplet from Wordsworth's "Resolution and Independence": "We poets in our youth begin in sadness, / But thereof in the end come despondency and madness." When he was twenty-one, Schwartz wrote "In Dreams Begin Responsibilities," a marvelous story that gained him immediate entrée into the family circle of New York City Jewish intellectuals centered on the *Partisan Review*. In Schwartz's "Coriolanus and His Mother," a long poem devoted to one performance of the Shakespeare tragedy with Freud, Marx, and illustrious others in the audience, "Pleasure" is one of five prose speeches punctuating the verse. Schwartz died paranoid and miserable in a squalid midtown Manhattan hotel in 1966. He was eulogized movingly by John Berryman in a group of his *Dream Songs* ("one solid block of agony") and was the model for the title character in Saul Bellow's novel *Humboldt's Gift*.

Far Rockaway

"the cure of souls." Henry James

The radiant soda of the seashore fashions
Fun, foam, and freedom. The sea laves
The shaven sand. And the light sways forward
On the self-destroying waves.

The rigor of the weekday is cast aside with shoes,
With business suits and the traffic's motion;
The lolling man lies with the passionate sun,
Or is drunken in the ocean.

A socialist health takes hold of the adult,
He is stripped of his class in the bathing-suit,

He returns to the children digging at summer,
A melon-like fruit.

O glittering and rocking and bursting and blue
— Eternities of sea and sky shadow no pleasure:
Time unheard moves and the heart of man is eaten
Consummately at leisure.

The novelist tangential on the boardwalk overhead
Seeks his cure of souls in his own anxious gaze.
"Here," he says, "With whom?" he asks, "This?" he questions,
"What tedium, what blaze?"

"What satisfaction, fruit? What transit, heaven?
Criminal? justified? arrived at what June?"
That nervous conscience amid the concessions
Is a haunting, haunted moon.

1938

All Clowns Are Masked and All Personae

All clowns are masked and all *personae*
Flow from choices; sad and gay, wise,
Moody and humorous are: chosen faces,
And yet not so! For all are circumstances,
Given, like a tendency
To colds or like blond hair and wealth,
Or war and peace or gifts for mathematics,
Fall from the sky, rise from the ground, stick to us
In time, surround us: Socrates is mortal.

Gifts and choices! All men are masked,
And we are clowns who think to choose our faces
And we are taught in time of circumstances
And we have colds, blond hair and mathematics,
For we have gifts which interrupt our choices,
And all our choices grasp in Blind Man's Buff:
"My wife was very different, after marriage,"
"I practise law, but botany's my pleasure,"
Save postage stamps or photographs,
But save your soul! Only the past is immortal.

Decide to take a trip, read books of travel,
Go quickly! Even Socrates is mortal.
Mention the name of happiness: it is
Atlantis, Ultima Thule, or the limelight,
Cathay or Heaven. But go quickly

And remember: there are circumstances,
And he who chooses chooses what is given,
He who chooses is ignorant of Choice
— Choose love, for love is full of children,
Full of choices, children choosing
Botany, mathematics, law and love,
So full of choices! So full of children!
And the past is immortal, the future is inexhaustible!

1938

Pleasure

I come, I said, to be useful and to entertain. What else can one do? Between the acts something must be done to occupy our minds or we become too aware of our great emptiness. It is true, we might converse with one another. But then we would learn again how little all of us have to say to each other. Love is not American. Neither is conversation, but that is not exactly what I mean.

One ought to be amusing, but unfortunately I know very few witty sayings, entertaining stories. I find that my idea of the comical is not, as they say, objective. I have tried for some time to invent a good story for this occasion, but the best I could do is this new wrinkle, entitled "Turning the Tables": ABC says to DEF: "Who was that lady I saw you with last night? Some fun, hey, boy!" DEF, offended by the lightness with which his passion is regarded, replies: "That was no lady, that was *your* wife." A good story too, at least to me, is Stendhal's remark on first eating ice cream: "What a pity it is not a sin!" Becoming more serious in order to approach nearer to my true subject, I recall the fact that Fichte drank champagne for the first time when his infant boy said "I" for the first time. Let me continue with two more quotations bearing on this Laocoön-like process and presentation which we are here to see. "I can hire half the working class to fight the other half." So said Jay Gould at about the same time that Engels, intimate friend of a member of the audience, was observing with the most perfect justice that the most appalling evil produced by class conflict was its corruption and degradation of the *ruling class* — barbarism, inexorable cynicism, contempt for all values on the part of those who enjoy the greatest benefits of society. Sophocles observes that man is the most admirable of beings. It is true. The most disgusting also, one ought to add. It is dialectical. The possibility of the one means the possibility of the other.

Now take this world's champion of men, Coriolanus, whose life we passively suffer to step over our faces (as we sit here, in the prepared darkness). All things are tied together, though sometimes loosely. Hence, more and more facts are dragged on the stage, as this moving individual passes before the footlights. Who knows if there will, indeed, be sufficient room? No doubt that I am an intruder, but try to eject me. The sky cannot be excluded. It is the greatest natural object. The state cannot be omitted. It is the greatest artificial object. The individual requires our focused gaze. He is the greatest subject, natural and artificial. Then there is his mother, his wife, his child, all his fathers, all his children. What an enormous crowd it may become! And the audience is already so complex, so full of foreigners.

Besides, there are questions of emphasis. "The individual is the only verifiable actuality, the individual, his experience from moment to moment." So said one in French at about the same time as Lev Davidovich, better known as Trotzky, justly remarked that "The individual — is an abstraction!" He is right and yet you know and so do I as we sit here in this theatre — the essential stareotorium, one might say — we both know that we cannot regard the warm identity beneath our faces as being no more than an abstraction. Man is always in the world, yes! inconceivable apart from being surrounded by a greater whole than himself. And yet he is at the same time himself and in and by himself and by traveling here and there may separate himself from any particular interior in which he finds himself. There is a thought which will take a considerable amount of chewing and then you will only have to spit it out again. As I said, all this bears upon what is taking place here. Also on Coriolanus the individual. Food, for example, improves the spirit, coffee consoles the soul. Most men, to quote again, lead lives of quiet desperation, the victims, all of them, of innumerable intentions. Hence the enormous *spiritual* and emotional quality of food and drink. There is also tobacco and alcohol, although wine too is not American.

Why be desperate, even quietly? Thus one might ask. Because one end merely leads to another one, one activity to another one, one activity to another in an inexhaustible *endlessnessness* which is exasperating, metaphysically speaking, although such speech is not the fashion. Do not, however, be disconsolate nor given over to unutterable despair. Consider the nature of pleasure. It is a maligned word, meaning merely the innocence and intrinsicality of being, each thing and each state taken as final and for itself. A cup of coffee destroys your sadness. To be born, we are told, is the greatest of all pains — all else a dilution and weakening which offends the masochist. Though this be but a gynecologist's truth, yet let us remember it. Pleasure is what it is as is the rose. It justifies itself. To have pleasure, to be pleased, to enjoy oneself, that is sufficient, and only the Philistine asks: What for? Although there is a question of the permanent, the intermittent, the conflicting, and the exclusive, but let us not discuss this now.

Pleasure has a hundred thousand obvious forms, plentiful variety for the most fickle spirit. Pleasure of convalescence (how voluptuous weakness can be); pleasure of need (a dry crust of bread); pleasure of the first time and the last time; pleasure of mere looking (as the sunlight delights itself upon the tumbling fountain, as the small morning makes the metropolis unreal); pleasure of being a child (mixture of curiosity, wantonness, and the gradual stages); pleasure of having a child (O my son Absalom, graduating from high school!); pleasure of discovery and pleasure of memory, freshness and nostalgic sweetness, surprise and return. Pleasure of arising, the keenness of breakfast; pleasure of sleeping (there one is Caesar); the pleasure of the old, a stronger tobacco, to possess the time that is past; the pleasure of the young, who are not yet tired; the pleasure of marriage—the mystery of being called Mrs. for the first time; the pleasure, do not deny it, of the funeral (that, after all, the conclusion should have a certain sublimity and repose); pleasure of the grandchild (a difficult pleasure, needing so much strength to last that long and so many refusals, year after year); the pleasure of ritual, the gloves drawn on precisely; the pleasure of spontaneity, kissed by the overjoyed, the wave's foaming white head, touched at the lips.

Delight in the silver, delight in the rock, delight in the soft silk, delight in the stubble, delight in the thimble, delight in the mountain, happiness of the virgin, the satisfaction of custom, joy in denial (the firmness of the soldier, the rigor of the surgeon, the formal athlete, the painstaking scholar), and the sweetness of saying yes.

Eating too is a fine thing, though it makes difficulties (do not laugh; economy and original sin may in fact be inseparable): and there is the pleasure at the conclusion of effort, the best of all delights, as the swimmer returned to the sunlight, his being flowing in the warmth responsive to the shocking chill of the waters (surrounded by them, he understood his body). Or the pleasure of the idle who, prone, full-length, made almost unknowingly a few exact perceptions, especially of those who hurry. And the satisfaction of the guilty (thus to have an identity not dissipated by their weakness); the delight of the famous, their self-regard coming from the outside; the joy of narration, thus to invent and, inventing, understand; the sweetness of the musician, from thunder and whisper tone's moving constellations; and also the pleasure of small pains, the sweetness of anger, as Homer observes; the delight of the game (from out of the scrimmage came the tall and plunging figure and ran to a touchdown!); the pleasure of the task, the pleasure of the opus (the span, the parts, the detail, the conclusion); the delight, dear as fresh water, of theory and knowing (O lucid mathematics!). To each age and each stage a special quality of satisfaction, enough for everyone, and enough for all time, no need to compete. States of being suffice. Let the handsome be familiar with the looking-glass, and let the ugly be gourmets (since so many cannot be beautiful, let eating be socially superior to portraits). Let this unwarranted sadness come to an end, sound and fury signify a multitude of enjoyments, the pleasure of pain, the pleasure indeed of pleasure. Pleasure believes in friends, pleasure creates communities, pleasure crumbles faces into smiles, pleasure links hand in hand, pleasure restores, pain is the most selfish thing. And yet, I know, all this is nothing, nothing consoles one, and our problem and pain are still before us.

Let us continue to gaze upon it. Let us, I say, make a few sharp clear definite observations before we die. Let us judge all things according to the measure of our hearts (otherwise we cannot live). Let us require of ourselves the strength and power to view our selves and the heart of man *with* disgust.

1938

KARL SHAPIRO (1913–2000)

Karl Shapiro was born in Baltimore, Maryland. As a soldier assigned to a medical unit in the South Pacific during World War II, Shapiro wrote *Essay on Rime* — a book-length tour de force — during a three-month period in which he was without access to a library. The entire book, from the foreword to the acknowledgments, is in blank verse. The Pulitzer Prize that Shapiro won for *V-Letter* in 1945 confirmed his status as a wunderkind. Interest in his work has waned, but many of his early poems are imbued with the spirit of the 1940s and retain their appeal. An inveterate controversialist, Shapiro was the sole panelist on the 1948 Bollingen Prize committee who voted against awarding Ezra Pound the prestigious award.

Buick

As a sloop with a sweep of immaculate wing on her delicate spine
And a keel as steel as a root that holds in the sea as she leans,
Leaning and laughing, my warm-hearted beauty, you ride, you ride,
You tack on the curves with parabola speed and a kiss of goodbye,
Like a thoroughbred sloop, my new high-spirited spirit, my kiss.

As my foot suggests that you leap in the air with your hips of a girl,
My finger that praises your wheel and announces your voices of song,
Flouncing your skirts, you blueness of joy, you flirt of politeness,
You leap, you intelligence, essence of wheelness with silvery nose,
And your platinum clocks of excitement stir like the hairs of a fern.

But how alien you are from the booming belts of your birth and the smoke
Where you turned on the stinging lathes of Detroit and Lansing at night
And shrieked at the torch in your secret parts and the amorous tests,
But now with your eyes that enter the future of roads you forget;
You are all instinct with your phosphorous glow and your streaking hair.

And now when we stop it is not as the bird from the shell that I leave
Or the leathery pilot who steps from his bird with a sneer of delight,
And not as the ignorant beast do you squat and watch me depart,
But with exquisite breathing you smile, with satisfaction of love,
And I touch you again as you tick in the silence and settle in sleep.

1942

Troop Train

It stops the town we come through. Workers raise
Their oily arms in good salute and grin.
Kids scream as at a circus. Business men
Glance hopefully and go their measured way.
And women standing at their dumbstruck door
More slowly wave and seem to warn us back,
As if a tear blinding the course of war
Might once dissolve our iron in their sweet wish.

Fruit of the world, O clustered on ourselves
We hang as from a cornucopia
In total friendliness, with faces bunched
To spray the streets with catcalls and with leers.
A bottle smashes on the moving ties
And eyes fixed on a lady smiling pink
Stretch like a rubber-band and snap and sting
The mouth that wants the drink-of-water kiss.

And on through crummy continents and days,
Deliberate, grimy, slightly drunk we crawl,
The good-bad boys of circumstance and chance,
Whose bucket-helmets bang the empty wall
Where twist the murdered bodies of our packs
Next to the guns that only seem themselves.
And distance like a strap adjusted shrinks,
Tightens across the shoulder and holds firm.

Here is a deck of cards; out of this hand
Dealer, deal me my luck, a pair of bulls,
The right draw to a flush, the one-eyed jack.
Diamonds and hearts are red but spades are black,
And spades are spades and clubs are clovers — black.
But deal me winners, souvenirs of peace.
This stands to reason and arithmetic,
Luck also travels and not all come back.

Trains lead to ships and ships to death or trains,
And trains to death or trucks, and trucks to death,
Or trucks lead to the march, the march to death,
Or that survival which is all our hope;
And death leads back to trucks and trains and ships,
But life leads to the march, O flag! at last
The place of life found after trains and death
— Nightfall of nations brilliant after war.

1944

The Funeral of Poetry

The password of the twentieth century: Communications (as if we had to invent them). Animals and cannibals have communications; birds and bees and even a few human creatures called artists (generally held to be insane). But the bulk of humanity had to invent Communications. The Romans had the best roads in the world, but had nothing to communicate over them except other Romans. Americans have conquered world-time and world-space and chat with the four corners of the earth at breakfast. The entire solar system is in the hands of cartoonists.

I am sitting in the kitchen in Nebraska and watching a shrouded woman amble down the market in Karachi. She is going to get her morning smallpox shot. It's cold and mental love they want. It's the mystic sexuality of Communications. The girl hugs the hi-fi speaker to her belly: it pours into her openings like gravy. Money was love. Power was love. Communications now are love. In the spring Hitler arises. This is the rime of trampling.

A man appears at the corner of the street; I prepare myself for hospitality. Man or angel, welcome! But I am afraid and double-lock the door. On the occasion of the death of a political party, I send an epitaph by Western Union. I didn't go to the funeral of poetry. I stayed home and watched it on television.

1964

MAY SWENSON (1913–1989)

May Swenson was born in Logan, Utah, the daughter of Swedish immigrants. She went to Utah State, worked on a Salt Lake City daily for a year, then came east, to New York City, where she settled in 1936. She had a long and emotionally complicated friendship with Elizabeth Bishop, sometimes suspecting the Vassar-educated Bishop of condescension. Swenson detested being confused with May Sarton. "One May S. is a weak poet with a big rep.; the other is the opposite," she noted in a letter to Bishop. "Not to need illusion — to dare to see and say how things really are, is the emancipation I would like to attain," she wrote in another letter to Bishop. Swenson's formal experiments — a poem consisting exclusively of four-word lines, a poem whose organizing principle requires the hyphenation of most end words — are undertaken in a bravura spirit that mingles the poet's self-delight with the belief that such displays of wit and craft may lead to sublime ends, as in the "elation" reached in her subway love poem, "Riding the A."

Question

Body my house
my horse my hound
what will I do
when you are fallen

Where will I sleep
How will I ride
What will I hunt

Where can I go
without my mount
all eager and quick
How will I know
in thicket ahead
is danger or treasure
when Body my good
bright dog is dead

How will it be
to lie in the sky
without roof or door
and wind for an eye

With cloud for shift
how will I hide?

1954

Riding the A

I ride
the "A" train
and feel
like a ball-
bearing in a roller skate.
I have on a gray
rain-
coat. The hollow
of the car
is gray.
My face
a negative in the slate
window,
I sit
in a lit
corridor that races
through a dark
one. Strok-
ing steel,
what a smooth rasp — it feels
like the newest of knives
slicing
along
a long
black crust loaf
from West 4th to 168th.
Wheels
and rails
in their prime
collide,
make love in a glide
of slickness
and friction.
It is an elation
I wish to pro-
long.
The station
is reached
too soon.

1963

The Wave and the Dune

The wave-shaped dune is still.
Its curve does not break,
though it looks as if it will,

like the head of the dune-
shaped wave advancing,
its ridge strewn

with white shards flaking.
A sand-faced image of the wave
is always in the making.

Opposite the sea's rough glass
cove, the sand's smooth-whittled cave,
under the brow of grass,

is sunny and still. Rushing
to place its replica
on the shore, the sea is pushing

sketches of itself
incessantly into the foreground.
All the models smash upon the shelf,

but grain by grain the creeping sand
reërects their profiles
and makes them stand.

1964

Four-Word Lines

Your eyes are just
like bees, and I
feel like a flower.
Their brown power makes
a breeze go over
my skin. When your
lashes ride down and
rise like brown bees'
legs, your pronged gaze
makes my eyes gauze.
I wish we were
in some shade and
no swarm of other
eyes to know that

I'm a flower breathing
bare, laid open to
your bees' warm stare.
I'd let you wade
in me and seize
with your eager brown
bees' power a sweet
glistening at my core.

1967

Waterbird

Part otter, part snake, part bird the bird Anhinga,
jalousie wings, draped open, dry. When slack-
hinged, the wind flips them shut. Her cry,
a slatted clatter, inflates her chin-
pouch; it's like a fish's swim-
bladder. Anhinga's body, otter-
furry, floats, under water-
mosses, neck a snake with white-
rimmed blue round roving eyes. Those long feet stilt-
paddle the only bird of the marsh that flies
submerged. Otter-
quick over bream that hover in water-
shade, she feeds, finds fillets among the water-
weeds. Her beak, ferrule of a folded black
umbrella, with neat thrust impales her prey.
She flaps up to dry on the crooked, look-
dead-limb of the Gumbo Limbo, her tan-
tipped wing fans spread, tail a shut fan dangled.

1971

Staring at the Sea on the Day of the Death of Another

The long body of the water fills its hollow,
slowly rolls upon its side,
and in the swaddlings of the waves,
their shadowed hollows falling forward with the tide,

like folds of Grecian garments molded to cling
around some classic immemorial marble thing,
I see the vanished bodies of friends who have died.

Each form is furled into its hollow,
white in the dark curl,
the sea a mausoleum, with countless shelves,
cradling the prone effigies of our unearthly selves,

some of the hollows empty, long niches in the tide.
One of them is mine
and gliding forward, gaping wide.

1972

JOHN BERRYMAN (1914–1972)

John Berryman was born John Allyn Smith in MacAlester, Oklahoma. When he was eleven, his father (whose restaurant business had gone under) was found shot to death. The death was ruled a suicide, and the boy was renamed John Allyn Berryman when his mother remarried mere months later. The incident haunted Berryman, who wrote many poems devoted to suicide: his father's, Hemingway's, predictions of his own. Berryman characterized his early "Winter Landscape" (1939)—based on Brueghel's painting *Hunters in the Snow*—as a war poem of an unusual kind. In his *Dream Songs*, Berryman fashioned a form that retains traditional elements (rhymes, stanzas) but uses a diction that wanders up and down the register. It is as if the poet were a sophisticated sort of vaudeville artist. The subject and speaker of his dream songs, Berryman announced, is "not the poet, not me," but Henry, a white middle-aged American male "sometimes in blackface, who has suffered an irreversible loss," and has an unnamed friend who calls him "Mister Bones." Berryman felt that the "artist is extremely lucky who is presented with the worst possible ordeal which will not actually kill him. At that point, he's in business." On 7 January 1972, he jumped to his death off the Washington Avenue bridge between St. Paul and Minneapolis.

Winter Landscape

The three men coming down the winter hill
In brown, with tall poles and a pack of hounds
At heel, through the arrangement of the trees,
Past the five figures at the burning straw,
Returning cold and silent to their town,

Returning to the drifted snow, the rink
Lively with children, to the older men,
The long companions they can never reach,
The blue light, men with ladders, by the church
The sledge and shadow in the twilit street,

Are not aware that in the sandy time
To come, the evil waste of history
Outstretched, they will be seen upon the brow
Of that same hill: when all their company
Will have been irrecoverably lost,

These men, this particular three in brown
Witnessed by birds will keep the scene and say
By their configuration with the trees,
The small bridge, the red houses and the fire,
What place, what time, what morning occasion

Sent them into the wood, a pack of hounds
At heel and the tall poles upon their shoulders,
Thence to return as now we see them and
Ankle-deep in snow down the winter hill
Descend, while three birds watch and the fourth flies.

1948

The Traveler

They pointed me out on the highway, and they said
"That man has a curious way of holding his head."

They pointed me out on the beach; they said "That man
Will never become as we are, try as he can."

They pointed me out at the station, and the guard
Looked at me twice, thrice, thoughtfully & hard.

I took the same train that the others took,
To the same place. Were it not for that look
And those words, we were all of us the same.
I studied merely maps. I tried to name
The effects of motion on the travelers,
I watched the couple I could see, the curse
And blessings of that couple, their destination,
The deception practised on them at the station,
Their courage. When the train stopped and they knew
The end of their journey, I descended too.

1948

from *The Dream Songs*

God Bless Henry (13)

God bless Henry. He lived like a rat,
with a thatch of hair on his head
in the beginning.
Henry was not a coward. Much.
He never deserted anything; instead
he stuck, when things like pity were thinning.

So may be Henry was a human being.
Let's investigate that.
. . . We did; okay.
He is a human American man.
That's true. My lass is braking.
My brass is aching. Come & diminish me, & map my way.

God's Henry's enemy. We're in business . . . Why,
what business must be clear.
A cornering.
I couldn't feel more like it. — Mr Bones,
as I look on the saffron sky,
you strikes me as ornery.

1964

Life, Friends, Is Boring. We Must Not Say So (14)

Life, friends, is boring. We must not say so.
After all, the sky flashes, the great sea yearns,
we ourselves flash and yearn,
and moreover my mother told me as a boy
(repeatingly) "Ever to confess you're bored
means you have no

Inner Resources." I conclude now I have no
inner resources, because I am heavy bored.
Peoples bore me,
literature bores me, especially great literature,
Henry bores me, with his plights & gripes
as bad as achilles,

who loves people and valiant art, which bores me.
And the tranquil hills, & gin, look like a drag
and somehow a dog
has taken itself & its tail considerably away
into mountains or sea or sky, leaving
behind: me, wag.

1964

The Lay of Ike (23)

This is the lay of Ike.
Here's to the glory of the Great White — awk —
who has been running — er — er — things in recent — ech —

in the United — If your screen is black,
ladies & gentlemen, we — I like —
at the Point he was already terrific — sick

to a second term, having done no wrong —
no right — no right — having let the Army — bang —
defend itself from Joe, let venom' Strauss
bile Oppenheimer out of use — use Robb,
who'll later fend for Goldfine — Breaking no laws,
he lay in the White House — sob!! —

who never understood his own strategy — whee —
so Monty's memoirs — nor any strategy,
wanting the ball bulled thro' all parts of the line
at once — proving, by his refusal to take Berlin,
he misread even Clauswitz — wide empty grin
that never lost a vote (O Adlai mine).

1964

There Sat Down, Once, a Thing on Henry's Heart (29)

There sat down, once, a thing on Henry's heart
so heavy, if he had a hundred years
& more, & weeping, sleepless, in all them time
Henry could not make good.
Starts again always in Henry's ears
the little cough somewhere, an odour, a chime.

And there is another thing he has in mind
like a grave Sienese face a thousand years
would fail to blur the still profiled reproach of. Ghastly,
with open eyes, he attends, blind.
All the bells say: too late. This is not for tears;
thinking.

But never did Henry, as he thought he did,
end anyone and hacks her body up
and hide the pieces, where they may be found.
He knows: he went over everyone, & nobody's missing.
Often he reckons, in the dawn, them up.
Nobody is ever missing.

1964

Full Moon. Our Narragansett Gales Subside (61)

Full moon. Our Narragansett gales subside
and the land is celebrating men of war
more or less, less or more.
In valleys, thin on headlands, narrow & wide
our targets rest. In us we trust. Far, near,
the bivouacs of fear

are solemn in the moon somewhere tonight,
in turning time. It's late for gratitude,
an annual, rude
roar of a moment's turkey's 'Thanks'. Bright & white
their ordered markers undulate away
awaiting no day.

Away from us, from Henry's feel or fail,
campaigners lie with mouldered toes, disarmed,
out of order,
with whom we will one. The war is real,
and a sullen glory pauses over them harmed,
incident to murder.

1964

Henry's Mind Grew Blacker the More He Thought (147)

Henry's mind grew blacker the more he thought.
He looked onto the world like the act of an aged whore.
Delmore, Delmore.
He flung to pieces and they hit the floor.
Nothing was true but what Marcus Aurelius taught,
'All that is foul smell & blood in a bag.'

He lookt on the world like the leavings of a hag.
Almost his love died from him, any more.
His mother & William
were vivid in the same mail Delmore died.
The world is lunatic. This is the last ride.
Delmore, Delmore.

High in the summer branches the poet sang.
His throat ached, and he could sing no more.
All ears closed
across the heights where Delmore & Gertrude sprang
so long ago, in the goodness of which it was composed.
Delmore, Delmore!

1968

Tears Henry Shed for Poor Old Hemingway (235)

Tears Henry shed for poor old Hemingway
Hemingway in despair, Hemingway at the end,
the end of Hemingway,
tears in a diningroom in Indiana
and that was years ago, before his marriage say,
God to him no worse luck send.

Save us from shotguns & fathers' suicides.
It all depends on who you're the father *of*
if you want to kill yourself —
a bad example, murder of oneself,
the final death, in a paroxysm, of love
for which good mercy hides?

A girl at the door: 'A few coppers pray'
But to return, to return to Hemingway
that cruel & gifted man.
Mercy! my father; do not pull the trigger
or all my life I'll suffer from your anger
killing what you began

1968

Henry's Understanding

He was reading late, at Richard's, down in Maine,
aged 32? Richard & Helen long in bed,
my good wife long in bed.
All I had to do was strip & get into my bed,
putting the marker in the book, & sleep,
& wake to a hot breakfast.

Off the coast was an island, P'tit Manaan,
the bluff from Richard's lawn was almost sheer.
A chill at four o'clock.
It only takes a few minutes to make a man.
A concentration upon now & here.
Suddenly, unlike Bach,

& horribly, unlike Bach, it occurred to me
that *one* night, instead of warm pajamas,
I'd take off all my clothes
& cross the damp cold lawn & down the bluff
into the terrible water & walk forever
under it out toward the island.

1972

RANDALL JARRELL (1914–1965)

Born in Nashville, Tennessee, Randall Jarrell studied with John Crowe Ransom at Vanderbilt University and Kenyon College. In the 1940s he wrote poems about the men who flew the Flying Fortresses in World War II, and in the 1950s and 1960s he wrote poems from an aging woman's point of view. *Pictures from an Institution*, a comic academic novel set at the imaginary Benton College, is a masterpiece of its kind. Jarrell wrote magnificent criticism in such volumes as *Poetry and the Age;* he was possibly the best, and certainly the most pleasure-giving, of the critics in the era he himself dubbed "the age of criticism." Robert Lowell said Jarrell was "the only man I have ever met who could make other writers feel that their work was more important to him than his own." In some ways a magnanimous critic, as Lowell's encomium implies, he could also be a devastating one, as in his essays on W. H. Auden, whom he once compared to "someone who keeps showing how well he can hold his liquor until he becomes a drunkard." (To which Auden replied: "Randall must be in love with me.") On an October evening in 1965, Jarrell was hit by a car while he was walking to the hospital in Chapel Hill, North Carolina, where he had been receiving physical therapy for a wrist he had injured in a suicide attempt earlier that year. Lowell among others suspected that Jarrell had deliberately stepped in front of the moving car.

The Death of the Ball Turret Gunner

From my mother's sleep I fell into the State,
And I hunched in its belly till my wet fur froze.
Six miles from earth, loosed from its dream of life,
I woke to black flak and the nightmare fighters.
When I died they washed me out of the turret with a hose.

1945

A Sick Child

The postman comes when I am still in bed.
"Postman, what do you have for me today?"
I say to him. (But really I'm in bed.)
Then he says — what shall I have him say?

"This letter says that you are president
Of — this word here; it's a republic."
Tell them I can't answer right away.
"It's your duty." No, I'd rather just be sick.

Then he tells me there are letters saying everything
That I can think of that I want for them to say.
I say, "Well, thank you very much. Good-bye."
He is ashamed, and turns and walks away.

If I can think of it, it isn't what I want.
I want . . . I want a ship from some near star

To land in the yard, and beings to come out
And think to me: "So this is where you are!

Come." Except that they won't do,
I thought of them. . . . And yet somewhere there must be
Something that's different from everything.
All that I've never thought of — think of me!

1949

The Woman at the Washington Zoo

The saris go by me from the embassies.

Cloth from the moon. Cloth from another planet.
They look back at the leopard like the leopard.

And I. . . .
                this print of mine, that has kept its color
Alive through so many cleanings; this dull null
Navy I wear to work, and wear from work, and so
To my bed, so to my grave, with no
Complaints, no comment: neither from my chief,
The Deputy Chief Assistant, nor his chief —
Only I complain. . . . this serviceable
Body that no sunlight dyes, no hand suffuses
But, dome-shadowed, withering among columns,
Wavy beneath fountains — small, far-off, shining
In the eyes of animals, these beings trapped
As I am trapped but not, themselves, the trap,
Aging, but without knowledge of their age,
Kept safe here, knowing not of death, for death —
Oh, bars of my own body, open, open!

The world goes by my cage and never sees me.
And there come not to me, as come to these,
The wild beasts, sparrows pecking the llamas' grain,
Pigeons settling on the bears' bread, buzzards
Tearing the meat the flies have clouded. . . .
                                                                Vulture,
When you come for the white rat that the foxes left,
Take off the red helmet of your head, the black
Wings that have shadowed me, and step to me as man:
The wild brother at whose feet the white wolves fawn,
To whose hand of power the great lioness
Stalks, purring. . . .
                                You know what I was,
You see what I am: change me, change me!

1960

The Lost Children

Two little girls, one fair, one dark,
One alive, one dead, are running hand in hand
Through a sunny house. The two are dressed
In red and white gingham, with puffed sleeves and sashes.
They run away from me . . . But I am happy;
When I wake I feel no sadness, only delight.
I've seen them again, and I am comforted
That, somewhere, they still are.

It is strange
To carry inside you someone else's body;
To know it before it's born;
To see at last that it's a boy or girl, and perfect;
To bathe it and dress it; to watch it
Nurse at your breast, till you almost know it
Better than you know yourself — better than it knows itself.
You own it as you made it.
You are the authority upon it.

But as the child learns
To take care of herself, you know her less.
Her accidents, adventures are her own,
You lose track of them. Still, you know more
About her than anyone *except* her.

Little by little the child in her dies.
You say, "I have lost a child, but gained a friend."
You feel yourself gradually discarded.
She argues with you or ignores you
Or is kind to you. She who begged to follow you
Anywhere, just so long as it was you,
Finds follow the leader no more fun.
She makes few demands; you are grateful for the few.

The young person who writes once a week
Is the authority upon herself.
She sits in my living room and shows her husband
My albums of her as a child. He enjoys them
And makes fun of them. I look too
And I realize the girl in the matching blue
Mother-and-daughter dress, the fair one carrying
The tin lunch box with the half-pint thermos bottle
Or training her pet duck to go down the slide
Is lost just as the dark one, who is dead, is lost.
But the world in which the two wear their flared coats
And the hats that match, exists so uncannily
That, after I've seen its pictures for an hour,
I believe in it: the bandage coming loose

One has in the picture of the other's birthday,
The castles they are building, at the beach for asthma.
I look at them and all the old sure knowledge
Floods over me, when I put the album down
I keep saying inside: "I *did* know those children.
I braided those braids. I was driving the car
The day that she stepped in the can of grease
We were taking to the butcher for our ration points.
I *know* those children. I know all about them.
Where are they?"

I stare at her and try to see some sign
Of the child she was. I can't believe there isn't any.
I tell her foolishly, pointing at the picture,
That I keep wondering where she is.
She tells me, "Here I am."
                                        Yes, and the other
Isn't dead, but has everlasting life . . .

The girl from next door, the borrowed child,
Said to me the other day, "You like children so much,
Don't you want to have some of your own?"
I couldn't believe that she could say it.
I thought: "Surely you can look at me and see them."

When I see them in my dreams I feel such joy.
If I could dream of them every night!

When I think of my dream of the little girls
It's as if we were playing hide-and-seek.
The dark one
Looks at me longingly, and disappears;
The fair one stays in sight, just out of reach
No matter where I reach. I am tired
As a mother who's played all day, some rainy day.
I don't want to play it any more, I don't want to,
But the child keeps on playing, so I play.

1965

The Player Piano

I ate pancakes one night in a Pancake House
Run by a lady my age. She was gay.
When I told her that I came from Pasadena
She laughed and said, "I lived in Pasadena
When Fatty Arbuckle drove the El Molino bus."

I felt that I had met someone from home.
No, not Pasadena, Fatty Arbuckle.
Who's that ? Oh, something that we had in common
Like — like — the false armistice. Piano rolls.
She told me her house was the first Pancake House

East of the Mississippi, and I showed her
A picture of my grandson. Going home —
Home to the hotel — I began to hum,
"Smile a while, I bid you sad adieu,
When the clouds roll back I'll come to you."

Let's brush our hair before we go to bed,
I say to the old friend who lives in my mirror.
I remember how I'd brush my mother's hair
Before she bobbed it. How long has it been
Since I hit my funnybone? had a scab on my knee?

Here are Mother and Father in a photograph,
Father's holding me. . . . They both look so *young*.
I'm so much older than they are. Look at them,
Two babies with their baby. I don't blame you,
You weren't old enough to know any better;

If I could I'd go back, sit down by you both,
And sign our true armistice: you weren't to blame.
I shut my eyes and there's our living room.
The piano's playing something by Chopin,
And Mother and Father and their little girl

Listen. Look, the keys go down by themselves!
I go over, hold my hands out, play I play —
If only, somehow, I had learned to live!
The three of us sit watching, as my waltz
Plays itself out a half-inch from my fingers.

1965

WELDON KEES (1914–1955)

Weldon Kees was born in Beatrice, Nebraska. In addition to writing poetry, he played jazz piano, composed songs, wrote for *Time* magazine, made movies, painted in the abstract expressionist mode and was good enough to have a number of one-man shows in New York City galleries. In his poetry he made cunning use of forms derived from music (the round, the fugue) and mass culture (the detective story, the obituary), and satirized mordantly what struck him as phony. Kees's alter ego in several poems is called Robinson — fittingly, for his loneliness recalls that of Robinson Crusoe. On 18 July 1955, Kees's car was found abandoned on the entry ramp to the Golden Gate Bridge. In the issue of the *New Republic* bearing that date, a piece by Kees — in which he characterized the "present atmosphere" as one of "distrust, violence, and irrationality" — was printed under the heading "How to Be Happy: Installment 1053." He was forty-one when he disappeared. Donald Justice edited Kees's *Collected Poems* in 1962, helping to rescue this poet of desolation and darkness from unwarranted obscurity.

For My Daughter

Looking into my daughter's eyes I read
Beneath the innocence of morning flesh
Concealed, hintings of death she does not heed.
Coldest of winds have blown this hair, and mesh
Of seaweed snarled these miniatures of hands;
The night's slow poison, tolerant and bland,
Has moved her blood. Parched years that I have seen
That may be hers appear: foul, lingering
Death in certain war, the slim legs green.
Or, fed on hate, she relishes the sting
Of others' agony; perhaps the cruel
Bride of a syphilitic or a fool.
These speculations sour in the sun.
I have no daughter. I desire none.

1943

Crime Club

No butler, no second maid, no blood upon the stair.
No eccentric aunt, no gardener, no family friend
Smiling among the bric-a-brac and murder.
Only a suburban house with the front door open
And a dog barking at a squirrel, and the cars
Passing. The corpse quite dead. The wife in Florida.

Consider the clues: the potato masher in a vase,
The torn photograph of a Wesleyan basketball team,
Scattered with check stubs in the hall;
The unsent fan letter to Shirley Temple,
The Hoover button on the lapel of the deceased,
The note: "To be killed this way is quite all right with me."

Small wonder that the case remains unsolved,
Or that the sleuth, Le Roux, is now incurably insane,
And sits alone in a white room in a white gown,
Screaming that all the world is mad, that clues
Lead nowhere, or to walls so high their tops cannot be seen;

Screaming all day of war, screaming that nothing can be
solved.

1947

Robinson

The dog stops barking after Robinson has gone.
His act is over. The world is a gray world,
Not without violence, and he kicks under the grand piano,
The nightmare chase well under way.

The mirror from Mexico, stuck to the wall,
Reflects nothing at all. The glass is black.
Robinson alone provides the image Robinsonian.

Which is all of the room — walls, curtains,
Shelves, bed, the tinted photograph of Robinson's first wife,
Rugs, vases, panatellas in a humidor.
They would fill the room if Robinson came in.

The pages in the books are blank,
The books that Robinson has read. That is his favorite chair,
Or where the chair would be if Robinson were here.

All day the phone rings. It could be Robinson
Calling. It never rings when he is here.

Outside, white buildings yellow in the sun.
Outside, the birds circle continuously
Where trees are actual and take no holiday.

1947

River Song

By the public hook for the private eye,
Near the neutral river where the children were,
I was hung for the street, to watch the sky.

When they strung me there, I waved like a flag
Near the bright blue river where the children played,
And my smile became part of the cultural lag.

I named three martyrs. My mother came
To the grayish river where the children stared:
"My son, you have honored the family name."

I was happy. Then a parade went by
Near the shadowy river where the children waved,
And the uniforms made me shiver and cry.

I tried to get down. What I had learned
Near the sunless river where the children screamed
Was only pain. My ropemarks burned.

But I couldn't move. Had I been thrown
By the darkening river where the children failed,
Or had I come there quite alone?

The bands were playing when they cut me down
By the dirty river where the children cried,
And a man made a speech in a long black gown.

He called me a hero. I didn't care.
The river ran blood and the children died.
And I wanted to die, but they left me there.

1947

Round

"Wondrous life!" cried Marvell at Appleton House.
Renan admired Jesus Christ "wholeheartedly."
But here dried ferns keep falling to the floor,
And something inside my head
Flaps like a worn-out blind. Royal Cortissoz is dead.
A blow to the *Herald-Tribune.* A closet mouse
Rattles the wrapper on the breakfast food. Renan
Admired Jesus Christ "wholeheartedly."

Flaps like a worn-out blind. Cézanne
Would break out in the quiet streets of Aix
And shout, "Le monde, c'est terrible!" Royal
Cortissoz is dead. And something inside my head
Flaps like a worn-out blind. The soil
In which the ferns are dying needs more Vigoro.
There is no twilight on the moon, no mist or rain,
No hail or snow, no life. Here in this house

Dried ferns keep falling to the floor, a mouse
Rattles the wrapper on the breakfast food. Cézanne
Would break out in the quiet streets and scream. Renan
Admired Jesus Christ "wholeheartedly." And something inside my head
Flaps like a worn-out blind. Royal Cortissoz is dead.
There is no twilight on the moon, no hail or snow.

One notes fresh desecrations of the portico.
"Wondrous life!" cried Marvell at Appleton House.

1954

1926

The porchlight coming on again,
Early November, the dead leaves
Raked in piles, the wicker swing
Creaking. Across the lots
A phonograph is playing *Ja-Da.*

An orange moon. I see the lives
Of neighbors, mapped and marred
Like all the wars ahead, and R.
Insane, B. with his throat cut,
Fifteen years from now, in Omaha.

I did not know them then.
My airedale scratches at the door.
And I am back from seeing Milton Sills
And Doris Kenyon. Twelve years old.
The porchlight coming on again.

1954

Aspects of Robinson

Robinson at cards at the Algonquin; a thin
Blue light comes down once more outside the blinds.
Gray men in overcoats are ghosts blown past the door.
The taxis streak the avenues with yellow, orange, and red.
This is Grand Central, Mr. Robinson.

Robinson on a roof above the Heights; the boats
Mourn like the lost. Water is slate, far down.
Through sounds of ice cubes dropped in glass, an osteopath,
Dressed for the links, describes an old Intourist tour.
— Here's where old Gibbons jumped from, Robinson.

Robinson walking in the Park, admiring the elephant.
Robinson buying the *Tribune*, Robinson buying the *Times*.
  Robinson
Saying, "Hello. Yes, this is Robinson. Sunday
At five? I'd love to. Pretty well. And you?"
Robinson alone at Longchamps, staring at the wall.

Robinson afraid, drunk, sobbing Robinson
In bed with a Mrs. Morse. Robinson at home;
Decisions: Toynbee or luminol? Where the sun
Shines, Robinson in flowered trunks, eyes toward
The breakers. Where the night ends, Robinson in East Side
  bars.

Robinson in Glen plaid jacket, Scotch-grain shoes,
Black four-in-hand and oxford button-down,
The jeweled and silent watch that winds itself, the brief-
Case, covert topcoat, clothes for spring, all covering
His sad and usual heart, dry as a winter leaf.

1954

William Stafford (1914–1993)

A native of Hutchinson, Kansas, William Stafford declared himself a conscientious objector in World War II and spent four years in work camps in Arkansas and California. His first book of poems, *West of Your City*, came out in 1960, when the poet was 46. He advocated the habit of daily writing and each day before dawn practiced what he preached, lying "partly propped up, / the way Thomas Jefferson did when he slept / at Monticello." When the muse visits Stafford in a poem, it is to identify herself as "your own / way of looking at things." There were never mornings that he could not write; the poet disarmingly told an interviewer, "I think that anybody could write if he would have standards as low as mine." Stafford died in Oregon in 1993.

Traveling Through the Dark

Traveling through the dark I found a deer
dead on the edge of the Wilson River road.
It is usually best to roll them into the canyon:
that road is narrow; to swerve might make more dead.

By glow of the tail-light I stumbled back of the car
and stood by the heap, a doe, a recent killing;
she had stiffened already, almost cold.
I dragged her off; she was large in the belly.

My fingers touching her side brought me the reason —
her side was warm; her fawn lay there waiting,
alive, still, never to be born.
Beside that mountain road I hesitated.

The car aimed ahead its lowered parking lights;
under the hood purred the steady engine.

I stood in the glare of the warm exhaust turning red;
around our group I could hear the wilderness listen.

I thought hard for us all — my only swerving — ,
then pushed her over the edge into the river.

1962

Ask Me

Some time when the river is ice ask me
mistakes I have made. Ask me whether
what I have done is my life. Others
have come in their slow way into
my thought, and some have tried to help
or to hurt: ask me what difference
their strongest love or hate has made.

I will listen to what you say.
You and I can turn and look
at the silent river and wait. We know
the current is there, hidden; and there
are comings and goings from miles away
that hold the stillness exactly before us.
What the river says, that is what I say.

1977

An Archival Print

God snaps your picture — don't look away —
this room right now, your face titled
exactly as it is before you can think
or control it. Go ahead, let it betray
all the secret emergencies and still hold
that partial disguise you call your character.

Even your lip, they say, the way it curves
or doesn't, or can't decide, will deliver
bales of evidence. The camera, wide open,
stands ready; the exposure is thirty-five years
or so — after that you have become
whatever the veneer is, all the way through.

Now you want to explain. Your mother
was a certain — how to express it? — *influence.*

Yes. And your father, whatever he was,
you couldn't change that. No. And your town
of course had its limits. Go on, keep talking —
Hold it. Don't move. That's you forever.

1991

RUTH STONE (b. 1915)

Ruth Stone was born in Roanoke, Virginia. The subject of much of her poetry is her widowhood: her second husband, the novelist Walter Stone, committed suicide in 1959. Stone seems committed to disproving the notion that a poet's powers decline with age. She has received national recognition for her books *Ordinary Words* (1999) and *In the Next Century* (2002), both published after she turned eighty. Roger Gilbert points out that in "For My Dead Red-Haired Mother" the irregular rhyming "subtly shapes the poem from beginning to end" and that if the poet had wanted a smoother finish, the last line would read "but first must die" instead of the "more emphatic dissymmetry that grimly hammers the poem shut": "but must first die."

Winter

The ten o'clock train to New York,
coaches like loaves of bread powdered with snow.
Steam wheezes between the couplings.
Stripped to plywood, the station's cement standing room
imitates a Russian novel. It is now that I remember you.
Your profile becomes the carved handle of a letter knife.
Your heavy-lidded eyes slip under the seal of my widowhood.
It is another raw winter. Stray cats are suffering.
Starlings crowd the edges of chimneys.
It is a drab misery that urges me to remember you.
I think about the subjugation of women and horses;
brutal exposure; weather that forces, that strips.
In our time we met in ornate stations
arching up with nineteenth-century optimism.
I remember you running beside the train waving good-bye.
I can produce a facsimile of you standing
behind a column of polished oak to surprise me.
Am I going toward you or away from you on this train?
Discarded junk of other minds is strewn beside the tracks:
mounds of rusting wire, grotesque pop art of dead motors,
senile warehouses. The train passes a station;
fresh people standing on the platform,
their faces expecting something.
I feel their entire histories ravish me.

1987

The Latest Hotel Guest Walks Over Particles That Revolve in Seven Other Dimensions Controlling Latticed Space

It is an old established hotel.
She is here for two weeks.
Sitting in the room
toward the end of October,
she turns on three lamps
each with a sixty watt bulb.
The only window opens
on a dark funnel of brick and cement.
Tiny flakes of paint glitter
between the hairs on her arms.
Paint disintegrates from a ceiling
that has surely looked down on the bed beneath it
during World War Two,
the Korean War, Vietnam,
the Cuban crisis, little difficulties
with the Shah, covert action, and presently,
projected Star Wars.
In fact, within that time,
this home away from home, room 404,
probably now contains the escaped molecules,
radiation photons and particulate particles
of the hair and skin of all its former guests.
It would be a kind of queeze mixture of body fluids
and polyester fibers which if assembled,
might be sculptured into an android,
even programmed to weep and beat its head
and shout, "Which war? . . . How much?"
She feels its presence in the dim artificial light.
It is standing in the closet.
There is an obsolete rifle, a bayonet.
It is an antihero composed of all the lost neutrinos.
Its feet are bandaged with the lint of old sheets.
It is the rubbish of all the bodies who sweated here.
She hears it among her blouses and slacks
and she knows at this moment it is, at last,
counting from ten to zero.

1987

Resonance

The universe is sad.
I heard it when Artur Rubinstein played the piano.

He was a little man with small hands.
We were bombing Germany by then.
I went to see him in a dark warehouse
where a piano had been placed for his practice —
or whatever he did before a recital.
He signed the book I had with me —
it was called *Warsaw Ghetto.*
I later heard about about him —
his affairs with young women —
if only I had known — but I was
in love with you.
Artur is dead;
and you, my darling,
the imprint of your face, alert like a deer —
oh god, it is eaten away —
the earth has taken it back
but I listen to Artur —
he springs out of the grave —
his genius wired to this tape —
a sad trick of the neural pathways, resonating flesh
and my old body remembers the way you touched me.

1993

For My Dead Red-Haired Mother

I loved a red-haired girl.
Freud knew it was a wicked thing to do.
This is how all poems begin.
Sometime after the age of two
1 beat the Adam in me black and blue.
Infant, wicked infant!
I threw my love outside
and grew into a bride.

You and I reflecting in our bones
the sea and sky,
we dressed ourselves as flesh,
we learned to lie.

Dearly beloved,
forgive me for that mean and meager self,
that now would mingle
but must first die.

1995

Train Ride

All things come to an end;
small calves in Arkansas,
the bend of the muddy river.
Do all things come to an end?
No, they go on forever.
They go on forever, the swamp,
the vine-choked cypress, the oaks
rattling last year's leaves,
the thump of the rails, the kite,
the still white stilted heron.
All things come to an end.
The red clay bank, the spread hawk,
the bodies riding this train,
the stalled truck, pale sunlight, the talk;
the talk goes on forever,
the wide dry field of geese,
a man stopped near his porch
to watch. Release, release;
between cold death and a fever,
send what you will, I will listen.
All things come to an end.
No, they go on forever.

2002

GWENDOLYN BROOKS (1917–2000)

Gwendolyn Brooks was born in Topeka, Kansas, and grew up on Chicago's South Side. Her first poem appeared in print when she was thirteen. She received encouragement from James Weldon Johnson and Langston Hughes, and wrote poems about the predicaments of black people in Chicago; her subjects include abortion, poverty, and racial prejudice in the military. She won the Pulitzer Prize in 1950 — the first African-American poet to do so. Her most famous poem, "We Real Cool," was banned in Mississippi and West Virginia schools because of the supposed sexual connotations of the word "jazz." Art, Brooks remarked, "hurts. Art urges voyages — and it is easier to stay at home."

a song in the front yard

I've stayed in the front yard all my life.
I want a peek at the back
Where it's rough and untended and hungry weed grows.
A girl gets sick of a rose.

I want to go in the back yard now
And maybe down the alley,
To where the charity children play.
I want a good time today.

They do some wonderful things.
They have some wonderful fun.
My mother sneers, but I say it's fine
How they don't have to go in at quarter to nine.
My mother, she tells me that Johnnie Mae
Will grow up to be a bad woman.
That George'll be taken to Jail soon or late
(On account of last winter he sold our back gate).

But I say it's fine. Honest, I do.
And I'd like to be a bad woman, too,
And wear the brave stockings of night-black lace
And strut down the streets with paint on my face.

1945

the mother

Abortions will not let you forget.
You remember the children you got that you did not get,
The damp small pulps with a little or with no hair,
The singers and workers that never handled the air.
You will never neglect or beat
Them, or silence or buy with a sweet.
You will never wind up the sucking-thumb
Or scuttle off ghosts that come.
You will never leave them, controlling your luscious sigh,
Return for a snack of them, with gobbling mother-eye.

I have heard in the voices of the wind the voices of my dim killed children.
I have contracted. I have eased
My dim dears at the breasts they could never suck.
I have said, Sweets, if I sinned, if I seized
Your luck
And your lives from your unfinished reach,
If I stole your births and your names,
Your straight baby tears and your games,
Your stilted or lovely loves, your tumults, your marriages, aches,
    and your deaths,
If I poisoned the beginnings of your breaths,
Believe that even in my deliberateness I was not deliberate.
Though why should I whine,

Whine that the crime was other than mine? –
Since anyhow you are dead.
Or rather, or instead,
You were never made.
But that too, I am afraid,
Is faulty: oh, what shall I say, how is the truth to be said?
You were born, you had body, you died.
It is just that you never giggled or planned or cried.

Believe me, I loved you all.
Believe me, I knew you, though faintly, and I loved, I loved you
All.

1945

Negro Hero

to suggest Dorie Miller

I had to kick their law into their teeth in order to save them.
However I have heard that sometimes you have to deal
Devilishly with drowning men in order to swim them to shore.
Or they will haul themselves and you to the trash and the fish
        beneath.
(When I think of this, I do not worry about a few
Chipped teeth.)

It is good I gave glory, it is good I put gold on their name.
Or there would have been spikes in the afterward hands.
But let us speak only of my success and the pictures in the
        Caucasian dailies
As well as the Negro weeklies. For I am a gem.
(They are not concerned that it was hardly The Enemy my fight
        was against
But them.)

It was a tall time. And of course my blood was
Boiling about in my head and straining and howling and
        singing me on.
Of course I was rolled on wheels of my boy itch to get at the
        gun.
Of course all the delicate rehearsal shots of my childhood
        massed in mirage before me.
Of course I was child
And my first swallow of the liquor of battle bleeding black air
        dying and demon noise
Made me wild.

It was kinder than that, though, and I showed like a banner my
kindness.
I loved. And a man will guard when he loves.
Their white-gowned democracy was my fair lady.
With her knife lying cold, straight, in the softness of her sweet-
flowing sleeve.
But for the sake of the dear smiling mouth and the stuttered
promise I toyed with my life.
I threw back! — I would not remember
Entirely the knife.

Still — am I good enough to die for them, is my blood bright
enough to be spilled,
Was my constant back-question — are they clear
On this? Or do I intrude even now?
Am I clean enough to kill for them, do they wish me to kill
For them or is my place while death licks his lips and strides to
them
In the galley still?

(In a southern city a white man said
Indeed, I'd rather be dead;
Indeed, I'd rather be shot in the head
Or ridden to waste on the back of a flood
Than saved by the drop of a black man's blood.)

Naturally, the important thing is, I helped to save them, them
and a part of their democracy.
Even if I had to kick their law into their teeth in order to do
that for them.
And I am feeling well and settled in myself because I believe it
was a good job,
Despite this possible horror: that they might prefer the
Preservation of their law in all its sick dignity and their knives
To the continuation of their creed
And their lives.

1945

still do I keep my look, my identity . . .

Each body has its art, its precious prescribed
Pose, that even in passion's droll contortions, waltzes,
Or push of pain — or when a grief has stabbed,
Or hatred hacked — is its, and nothing else's.
Each body has its pose. No other stock
That is irrevocable, perpetual
And its to keep. In castle or in shack.

With rags or robes. Through good, nothing, or ill.
And even in death a body, like no other
On any hill or plain or crawling cot
Or gentle for the lilyless hasty pall
(Having twisted, gagged, and then sweet-ceased to bother),
Shows the old personal art, the look. Shows what
It showed at baseball. What it showed in school.

1945

We Real Cool

The Pool Players.
Seven at the Golden Shovel.

We real cool. We
Left school. We

Lurk late. We
Strike straight. We

Sing sin. We
Thin gin. We

Jazz June. We
Die soon.

1960

Ruth Herschberger (b. 1917)

Ruth Herschberger was born in Philipse Manor, New York, the daughter of an all-American fullback and an officer of the University of Chicago's Renaissance Society. She grew up in Chicago and attended the University of Chicago and Black Mountain College. In 1948, *A Way of Happening* — the title a reference to Auden's "In Memory of William Butler Yeats" — was published, Herschberger's first and only book of poems. The same year saw the publication of her nonfiction book, *Adam's Rib*, an important (and proleptic) feminist text. (The British and other foreign editions were published under the pseudonym Josephine Langstaff.) In her poem "Mentor," she issues these instructions: "Be rude, and true, devise the early tear, / Explain the emmet's laughter and be kind. / Be sweet, and tart, explode the hobbling heart. / When entering necessity, be blind."

The Virgin

O were it but a venial sin, and I asleep
And he, so strong and right, a very rogue,
And we exchange some small and wooly joke,
Then enter actions that are rough to reap.

O were I but a roe-deer, roe, and he
A very panther, brown (as is the sea!)
And he would come — and I — that is, then we
Would roam the wilds with bestiality.

O were the midnight darker, and the moon
Absconded neath a cloud, and he and I
But sitting helpless with a spring nearby
Till faint and pallored, both indulgent swoon.

But O that mortal criminal, the eye,
Still stares straight out, and will not faint nor sleep,
And he is far, and I — my gloom is deep —
For O how weary-grown is chastity.

Life seems the mortal sin on such a night,
And love but small transgression. O were I
A man who strode and ranted, I would fly
To my own arms and there all sins recite.

1948

Page Torn from a Notebook

Not as though storks were sorry that they'd brought the child
But just as summer clouds gather and gray
So did the friendship waver, so did time delay
Its final shot too long, and play too hardily the witch.
Finally, as we know, the whole world broke and fell,
The soldiers mutinied like salts; the kings invaded
Heads of queens, queens drank dull-flavored poisons,
Pages fell from inanition, and the crowds maligned their loved.
Trouble with its deep truths and rights caught privilege
From administrative hands, and used its knowledge
To inflict its pain. All was disorganized, the circling vultures
Wrongly chose their dead from life, and plucked confusedly
The blinking eyes of babes, the drooping ears of thoughtful men.
How could this happen, how could life desert
Its office of reward, judicious punishment,
For such far-reaching unaccountable disease and misery?
Far beyond estimate, the crucified had grown:
Who could make pertinent to God the horizontal woe,
Stretching its miles of agony over the heads and through the hearts

Of feast days once hurrahed and known?
People were anxious only to know death. At once!
Without delay, Death! Only to be within the analgesic rot
Of fallen flesh, not looking on at peace in others'
Gaping jaw, those careless of unfastened lip,
Jointed or undone limb; those dead bereaved forever
And bereaved of care, man's well-lost relative.

The child was not without dismay at all this sloth;
The blood was bright, with blood's bright ruddiness,
The skies were battened blue, and touched with mitigated self
The open ponds, but parks, alas, were ravaged:
Shrubbery burnt, turf dug with heels; cadavers: dung upon
the lawn,
The odors heady. What could a child do in a soundless room?
Whom could it quarrel with? Not its pot of stew
Pushed gravely through the door-trap, led by water
And a piece of bread, not with the glass-men fighting past the pane,
Who made such fierce grimaces, dropped unwillingly,
Jerked angrily at death, but lay as still as cloverbloom
Thereafter. No, the scene was slothful, but not active
In the little-knowing child's frame: dull recurrence,
Over-played, it thought; I'd like another game.
Another room, too; yes, another room. Another
Set of poplars blocking the good sun; another play
Of praying-mantis men, there where the curb gives foothold
And their raised arms fall, ill-favoredly, undone.

O well, for children there must be pretense, protection,
The glass pane, misleading lack of salt in stew,
That finally in some blurred way, in unacclimated doom
The childish destiny may come, seasoned, decided,
As no mother ever knew.

1948

The Huron

I swam the Huron of love, and am not ashamed,
It was many saw me do it, scoffing, scoffing,
They said it was foolish, winter and all,
But I dove in, greaselike, and swam,
And came up where Erie verges.
I would say for the expenditure of love,
And the atrophy of longing, there is no cure
So swift, so sleek, so fine, so draining
As a swim through the Huron in the wintertime.

1953

ROBERT LOWELL (1917–1977)

The scion of a famous old American family, always willful, Robert Lowell dropped out of Harvard to study with John Crowe Ransom and Allen Tate at Kenyon College. He converted to Catholicism, grew chummy with Randall Jarrell and John Berryman, married Jean Stafford, divorced Stafford, renounced Catholicism, considered proposing to Elizabeth Bishop, married Elizabeth Hardwick, and helped found the *New York Review of Books*. His life was a curious kind of highbrow page-turner. In 1943, with the United States in the thick of World War II, he wrote a letter to President Roosevelt that he would later (accurately) characterize as "a rather humorless bombastic statement," declining the opportunity to serve in the armed forces. He served five months in prison as a result. In 1965 he wrote an open letter to President Johnson, refusing an invitation to the White House on account of his opposition to the war in Vietnam. The letter was printed in the *New York Times*. Lowell landed on the cover of *Time* and is one of the heroes in *Armies of the Night*, Norman Mailer's chronicle of a major antiwar demonstration on the steps of the Pentagon in 1967. Lowell's tightly controlled early poetry underwent a major transformation when he relaxed his rhetoric and focused his lens on his suffering self. The "confessional" style or movement was initiated by Lowell's *Life Studies* (1959). Jarrell wrote admiringly, "You feel before reading any new poem of his the uneasy expectation of perhaps encountering a masterpiece." Asked by Frederick Seidel if he revised a lot, Lowell replied: "Endlessly."

Colloquy in Black Rock

Here the jack-hammer jabs into the ocean;
My heart, you race and stagger and demand
More blood-gangs for your nigger-brass percussions,
Till I, the stunned machine of your devotion,
Clanging upon this cymbal of a hand,
Am rattled screw and footloose. All discussions

End in the mud-flat detritus of death.
My heart, beat faster, faster. In Black Mud
Hungarian workmen give their blood
For the martyre Stephen, who was stoned to death.

Black Mud, a name to conjure with: O mud
For watermelons gutted to the crust,
Mud for the mole-tide harbor, mud for mouse,
Mud for the armored Diesel fishing tubs that thud
A year and a day to wind and tide; the dust
Is on this skipping heart that shakes my house,

House of our Savior who was hanged till death.
My heart, beat faster, faster. In Black Mud
Stephen the martyre was broken down to blood:
Our ransom is the rubble of his death.

Christ walks on the black water. In Black Mud
Darts the kingfisher. On Corpus Christi, heart,
Over the drum-beat of St. Stephen's choir
I hear him, *Stupor Mundi*, and the mud
Flies from his hunching wings and beak — my heart,
The blue kingfisher dives on you in fire.

1946

Memories of West Street and Lepke

Only teaching on Tuesdays, book-worming
in pajamas fresh from the washer each morning,
I hog a whole house on Boston's
"hardly passionate Marlborough Street,"
where even the man
scavenging filth in the back alley trash cans,
has two children, a beach wagon, a helpmate,
and is "a young Republican."
I have a nine months' daughter,
young enough to be my granddaughter.
Like the sun she rises in her flame-flamingo infants' wear.

These are the tranquillized *Fifties*,
and I am forty. Ought I to regret my seedtime?
I was a fire-breathing Catholic C.O.,
and made my manic statement,
telling off the state and president, and then
sat waiting sentence in the bull pen
beside a negro boy with curlicues
of marijuana in his hair.

Given a year,
I walked on the roof of the West Street Jail, a short
enclosure like my school soccer court,
and saw the Hudson River once a day
through sooty clothesline entanglements
and bleaching khaki tenements.
Strolling, I yammered metaphysics with Abramowitz,
a jaundice-yellow ("it's really tan")
and fly-weight pacifist,
so vegetarian,
he wore rope shoes and preferred fallen fruit.
He tried to convert Bioff and Brown,
the Hollywood pimps, to his diet.
Hairy, muscular, suburban,
wearing chocolate double-breasted suits,
they blew their tops and beat him black and blue.

I was so out of things, I'd never heard
of the Jehovah's Witnesses.
"Are you a C.O.?" I asked a fellow jailbird.
"No," he answered, "I'm a J.W."
He taught me the hospital "tuck,"
and pointed out the T-shirted back
of *Murder Incorporated*'s Czar Lepke,
there piling towels on a rack,
or dawdling off to his little segregated cell full
of things forbidden the common man:
a portable radio, a dresser, two toy American
flags tied together with a ribbon of Easter palm.
Flabby, bald, lobotomized,
he drifted in a sheepish calm,
where no agonizing reappraisal
jarred his concentration on the electric chair —
hanging like an oasis in his air
of lost connections . . .

1959

Skunk Hour

for Elizabeth Bishop

Nautilus Island's hermit
heiress still lives through winter in her Spartan cottage;
her sheep still graze above the sea.
Her son's a bishop. Her farmer
is first selectman in our village,
she's in her dotage.

Thirsting for
the hierarchic privacy
of Queen Victoria's century,
she buys up all
the eyesores facing her shore,
and lets them fall.

The season's ill —
we've lost our summer millionaire,
who seemed to leap from an L. L. Bean
catalogue. His nine-knot yawl
was auctioned off to lobstermen.
A red fox stain covers Blue Hill.

And now our fairy
decorator brightens his shop for fall,
his fishnet's filled with orange cork,

orange, his cobbler's bench and awl,
there is no money in his work,
he'd rather marry.

One dark night,
my Tudor Ford climbed the hill's skull,
I watched for love-cars. Lights turned down,
they lay together, hull to hull,
where the graveyard shelves on the town. . . .
My mind's not right.

A car radio bleats,
"Love, O careless Love . . . " I hear
my ill-spirit sob in each blood cell,
as if my hand were at its throat . . .
I myself am hell,
nobody's here —

only skunks, that search
In the moonlight for a bite to eat.
They march on their soles up Main Street:
white stripes, moonstruck eyes' red fire
under the chalk-dry and spar spire
of the Trinitarian Church.

I stand on top
of our back steps and breathe the rich air —
a mother skunk with her column of kittens swills the garbage pail
She jabs her wedge head in a cup
of sour cream, drops her ostrich tail,
and will not scare.

1959

Night Sweat

Work-table, litter, books and standing lamp,
plain things, my stalled equipment, the old broom —
but I am living in a tidied room,
for ten nights now I've felt the creeping damp
float over my pajamas' wilted white . . .
Sweet salt embalms me and my head is wet,
everything streams and tells me this is right;
my life's fever is soaking in night sweat —
one life, one writing! But the downward glide
and bias of existing wrings us dry —
always inside me is the child who died,
always inside me is his will to die —

one universe, one body . . . in this urn
the animal night sweats of the spirit burn.

Behind me! You! Again I feel the light
lighten my leaded eyelids, while the gray
skulled horses whinny for the soot of night.
I dabble in the dapple of the day,
a heap of wet clothes, seamy, shivering,
I see my flesh and bedding washed with light,
my child exploding into dynamite,
my wife . . . your lightness alters everything,
and tears the black web from the spider's sack,
as your heart hops and flutters like a hare.
Poor turtle, tortoise, if I cannot clear
the surface of these troubled waters here,
absolve me, help me, Dear Heart, as you bear
this world's dead weight and cycle on your back.

1964

For the Union Dead

Relinquunt Omnia Servare Rem Publicam.

The old South Boston Aquarium stands
in a Sahara of snow now. Its broken windows are boarded.
The bronze weathervane cod has lost half its scales.
The airy tanks are dry.

Once my nose crawled like a snail on the glass;
my hand tingled
to burst the bubbles
drifting from the noses of the cowed, compliant fish.

My hand draws back. I often sigh still
for the dark downward and vegetating kingdom
of the fish and reptile. One morning last March,
I pressed against the new barbed and galvanized

fence on the Boston Common. Behind their cage,
yellow dinosaur steamshovels were grunting
as they cropped up tons of mush and grass
to gouge their underworld garage.

Parking spaces luxuriate like civic
sandpiles in the heart of Boston.
A girdle of orange, Puritan-pumpkin colored girders
braces the tingling Statehouse,

shaking over the excavations, as it faces Colonel Shaw
and his bell-cheeked Negro infantry
on St. Gaudens' shaking Civil War relief,
propped by a plank splint against the garage's earthquake.

Two months after marching through Boston,
half the regiment was dead;
at the dedication,
William James could almost hear the bronze Negroes breathe.

Their monument sticks like a fishbone
in the city's throat.
Its Colonel is as lean
as a compass-needle.

He has an angry wrenlike vigilance,
a greyhound's gentle tautness;
he seems to wince at pleasure,
and suffocate for privacy.

He is out of bounds now. He rejoices in man's lovely,
peculiar power to choose life and die —
when he leads his black soldiers to death,
he cannot bend his back.

On a thousand small town New England greens,
the old white churches hold their air
of sparse, sincere rebellion; frayed flags
quilt the graveyards of the Grand Army of the Republic.

The stone statues of the abstract Union Soldier
grow slimmer and younger each year —
wasp-wasted, they doze over muskets
and muse through their sideburns . . .

Shaw's father wanted no monument
except the ditch,
where his son's body was thrown
and lost with his "niggers."

The ditch is nearer.
There are no statues for the last war here;
on Boylston Street, a commercial photograph
shows Hiroshima boiling

over a Mosler Safe, the "Rock of Ages"
that survived the blast. Space is nearer.
When I crouch to my television set,
the drained faces of Negro school-children rise like balloons

Colonel Shaw
is riding on his bubble,
he waits
for the blesséd break.

The Aquarium is gone. Everywhere,
giant finned cars nose forward like fish;
a savage servility
slides by on grease.

1964

Fall 1961

Back and forth, back and forth
goes the tock, tock, tock
of the orange, bland ambassadorial
face of the moon
on the grandfather clock.

All autumn, the chafe and jar
of nuclear war;
we have talked our extinction to death.
I swim like a minnow
behind my studio window.

Our end drifts nearer,
the moon lifts,
radiant with terror.
The state
is a diver under a glass bell.

A father's no shield
for his child.
We are like a lot of wild
spiders crying together,
but without tears.

Nature holds up a mirror.
One swallow makes a summer.
It's easy to tick
off the minutes,
but the clockhands stick.

Back and forth!
Back and forth, back and forth —
my one point of rest
is the orange and black
oriole's swinging nest!

1964

Waking Early Sunday Morning

O to break loose, like the chinook
salmon jumping and falling back,
nosing up to the impossible
stone and bone-crushing waterfall —
raw-jawed, weak-fleshed there, stopped by ten
steps of the roaring ladder, and then
to clear the top on the last try,
alive enough to spawn and die.

Stop, back off. The salmon breaks
water, and now my body wakes
to feel the unpolluted joy
and criminal leisure of a boy —
no rainbow smashing a dry fly
in the white run is free as I,
here squatting like a dragon on
time's hoard before the day's begun!

Vermin run for their unstopped holes;
in some dark nook a fieldmouse rolls
a marble, hours on end, then stops;
the termite in the woodwork sleeps —
listen, the creatures of the night
obsessive, casual, sure of foot,
go on grinding, while the sun's
daily remorseful blackout dawns.

Fierce, fireless mind, running downhill.
Look up and see the harbor fill:
business as usual in eclipse
goes down to the sea in ships —
wake of refuse, dacron rope,
bound for Bermuda or Good Hope,
all bright before the morning watch
the wine-dark hulls of yawl and ketch.

I watch a glass of water wet
with a fine fuzz of icy sweat,
silvery colors touched with sky,
serene in their neutrality —
yet if I shift, or change my mood,
I see some object made of wood,
background behind it of brown grain,
to darken it, but not to stain.

O that the spirit could remain
tinged but untarnished by its strain!
Better dressed and stacking birch,

or lost with the Faithful at Church —
anywhere, but somewhere else!
And now the new electric bells,
clearly chiming, "Faith of our fathers,"
and now the congregation gathers.

O Bible chopped and crucified
in hymns we hear but do not read,
none of the milder subtleties
of grace or art will sweeten these
stiff quatrains shovelled out four-square —
they sing of peace, and preach despair;
yet they gave darkness some control,
and left a loophole for the soul.

No, put old clothes on, and explore
the corners of the woodshed for
its dregs and dreck: tools with no handle,
ten candle-ends not worth a candle,
old lumber banished from the Temple,
damned by Paul's precept and example,
cast from the kingdom, banned in Israel,
the wordless sign, the tinkling cymbal.

When will we see Him face to face?
Each day, He shines through darker glass —
In this small town where everything
is known, I see His vanishing
emblems, His white spire and flag-
pole sticking out above the fog,
like old white china doorknobs, sad,
slight, useless things to calm the mad.

Hammering military splendor,
top-heavy Goliath in full armor —
little redemption in the mass
liquidations of their brass,
elephant and phalanx moving
with the times and still improving,
when that kingdom hit the crash:
a million foreskins stacked like trash . . .

Sing softer! But what if a new
diminuendo brings no true
tenderness, only restlessness,
excess, the hunger for success,
sanity of self-deception
fixed and kicked by reckless caution,
while we listen to the bells —
anywhere, but somewhere else!

O to break loose. All life's grandeur
is something with a girl in summer . . .
elated as the President
girdled by his establishment
this Sunday morning, free to chaff
his own thoughts with his bear-cuffed staff,
swimming nude, unbuttoned, sick
of his ghost-written rhetoric!

No weekends for the gods now. Wars
flicker, earth licks its open sores,
fresh breakage, fresh promotions, chance
assassinations, no advance.
Only man thinning out his kind
sounds through the Sabbath noon, the blind
swipe of the pruner and his knife
busy about the tree of life . . .

Pity the planet, all joy gone
from this sweet volcanic cone;
peace to our children when they fall
in small war on the heels of small
war — until the end of time
to police the earth, a ghost
orbiting forever lost
in our monotonous sublime.

1967

Dolphin

My Dolphin, you only guide me by surprise,
a captive as Racine, the man of craft,
drawn through his maze of iron composition
by the incomparable wandering voice of Phèdre.
When I was troubled in mind, you made for my body
caught in its hangman's-knot of sinking lines,
the glassy bowing and scraping of my will . . .
I have sat and listened to too many
words of the collaborating muse,
and plotted perhaps too freely with my life,
not avoiding injury to others,
not avoiding injury to myself —
to ask compassion . . . this book, half fiction,
an eelnet made by man for the eel fighting —

my eyes have seen what my hand did.

1973

Epilogue

Those blessèd structures, plot and rhyme —
why are they no help to me now
I want to make
something imagined, not recalled?
I hear the noise of my own voice:
The painter's vision is not a lens,
it trembles to caress the light.
But sometimes everything I write
with the threadbare art of my eye
seems a snapshot,
lurid, rapid, garish, grouped,
heightened from life,
yet paralyzed by fact.
All's misalliance.
Yet why not say what happened?
Pray for the grace and accuracy
Vermeer gave to the sun's illumination
stealing like the tide across a map
to his girl solid with yearning.
We are poor passing facts,
warned by that to give
each figure in the photograph
his living name.

1977

JOAN MURRAY (1917–1942)

Born to Canadian parents in London during a dirigible air raid in World War I, Joan Murray suffered as a teenager from rheumatic fever, which left her heart seriously damaged. She studied acting and dancing but did not take up poetry until she took a class with W. H. Auden at the New School in New York City in 1940. She wrote all of her poems in the following year before contracting the heart valve infection that ended her life in January 1942, a month shy of her twenty-fifth birthday. In 1947, the year that began Auden's celebrated reign as judge of the Yale Younger Poets series, he chose Murray's posthumous *Poems* as the winning title. (Auden went on to pick the first books of Ashbery, Hollander, Merwin, Rich, and James Wright.) Though not well known, Murray's poems represent, as George Bradley notes in the *Yale Younger Poets Anthology*, "one of the high points in the series."

Lullaby

Sleep, little architect. It is your mother's wish
That you should lave your eyes and hang them up in dreams.

Into the lowest sea swims the great sperm fish.
If I should rock you, the whole world would rock within my arms.

Your father is a greater architect than even you.
His structure falls between high Venus and far Mars.
He rubs the magic of the old and then peers through
The blueprint where lies the night, the plan the stars.

You will place mountains too, when you are grown.
The grass will not be so insignificant, the stone so dead.
You will spiral up the mansions we have sown.
Drop your lids, little architect. Admit the bats of wisdom into your head.

1947

You Talk of Art

You talk of art, of work, of books.
Have you ever sat down, thought all that's to do?
That book to read, that book to write,
Sat down, stood up, walked back and forth,
Because not an action you could do would
Fill the gap that's wanting action to the chin?

Look. Look into the past one damned moment,
And on that you ask me to work, to dream, to do?
Try it yourself on nothing. I can't.

Every confounded one has had so much of life
That left them gasping in a stinking or a lighter air,
Left out of breath and glad to think at last,
Higher or lower, their there and there and there.

And where am I? Where I began, and where I'll end:
Sitting, sitting, with the last grain of will
Rotting in time, and there's no time or tide in me.

You talk of art, of work, of books.
I'll talk of nothing in its lowest state,
Talk till my jaw hangs limply at the joint,
And the talk that's one big yawn in the face of all of you,
Empty as head, empty as mood, and weak.
And I can hear all the watery wells of desolation
Lapping a numbing sleep within the head.

1947

Men and Women Have Meaning Only as Man and Woman

Men and women have meaning only as man and woman.
The moon is itself and it is lost among stars.
The days are individual, and in the passage
The nights are each sleep, but the dreams vary.
A repeated action is upon its own feet.
We who have spoken there speak here.
A world turns and walks away.
The timing of independent objects
Permits them to live and move and admit their space
And entity and various attitudes of life.
All things are cool in themselves and complete.

1947

Even the Gulls of the Cool Atlantic

The gulls of the cool Atlantic tip the foam.
The boats that warn me of fog warn me of their motion.
I have looked for my childhood among pebbles, and my home
Within the lean cupboards of Mother Hubbard and neat Albion.

A wind whose freshness blows over the cape to me
Has made me laugh at the thought of a friend whose hair is
 blond.
Still I laugh and place my hands across the sea
From the farthest stretch of lands to the end of the end.

I had so often run down to these shores to stare out.
If I took an island for a lover and Atlantic for my sheet,
There was no one to tell me that loving across distance would
 turn about
And make the here and now an elsewhere of defeat.

In my twenty-first year to have the grubby hand and slums,
Be the small child at my knee, my knee the glistening chalk
That sails to meet the stationary boat, the water sloping as it comes,
And all the Devon coast of grey and abrupt rock.

By gazing across water I have flicked many gulls from my eyes,
Shuffled small shells and green crabs to my feet.
The day is cool; the sun bright; the piper cries
Shrilly, tempering the untouched sand in delicate retreat.

Up beyond the height and over the bank, I have a friend.
How is your winter night and summer action?

There need be little more than a teacup hour to make us both
comprehend
A mature man's simplicity or grave child's sweet reaction.

1947

WILLIAM BRONK (1918–1999)

William Bronk was born in Hudson Falls, New York, into the old Dutch patrician family after whom the borough of the Bronx was named. Bronk went to Dartmouth, served in World War II, took over his family's lumber business, and ran it until his retirement in 1978. His poetry is concerned almost obsessively with epistemological questions.

I Thought It Was Harry

Excuse me. I thought for a moment you were someone I know.
It happens to me. One time at *The Circle in the Square*
when it *was* still in the Square, I turned my head
when the lights went up and saw me there with a girl
and another couple. Out in the lobby, I looked
right at him and he looked away. I was no one he knew.
Well, it takes two, as they say, and I don't know what
it would prove anyway. Do we know who we are,
do you think? Kids seem to know. One time I asked
a little girl. She said she'd been sick. She said
she'd looked different and felt different. I said,
"Maybe it wasn't you. How do you know?"
"Oh, I was me," she said, "I know I was."

That part doesn't bother me anymore
or not the way it did. I'm nobody else
and nobody anyway. It's all the rest
I don't know. I don't know anything.
It hit me. I thought it was Harry when I saw you
and thought, "I'll ask Harry." I don't suppose
he knows, though. It's not that I get confused.
I don't mean that. If someone appeared and said,
"Ask me questions," I wouldn't know where to start.
I don't have questions even. It's the way I fade
as though I were someone's snapshot left in the light.
And the background fades the way it might if we woke
in the wrong twilight and things got dim and grey
while we waited for them to sharpen. Less and less
is real. No fixed point. Questions fix
a point, as answers do. Things move again

and the only place to move is away. It was wrong:
questions and answers are what to be without
and all we learn is how sound our ignorance is.
That's what I wanted to talk to Harry about.
You looked like him. Thank you anyway.

1971

The Ignorant Lust After Knowledge

I come in from the canal. I don't know anything.
It is well and good to ask what we need to know
as if it were all, as if we didn't need.

Well, I need. I may never know anything
but I need. One sees desire not
as something to satisfy but to live with.

A light, this side of the hills toward Argyle,
flowed like fog through the hollows, rose to the depth
of the hills, illumined me. I faded in it
as the world faded in me, dissolved in the light.
No one to know and nothing knowable.
Oh, we know that knowing is not our way;

but, the choice ours, would make it our way, would leave
the world for the same world made knowable.

1972

Robert Duncan (1919–1988)

Robert Duncan was born in Oakland, California. His mother died in childbirth, and his father could not afford to raise him; he was adopted while still an infant. Educated at Berkeley, he was drafted in 1941 and sent to San Antonio for training but was discharged after disclosing that he was a homosexual. In August 1944, his article "The Homosexual in Society" appeared in Dwight Macdonald's magazine *Politics*. One result of the article was that John Crowe Ransom backed out of printing one of Duncan's poems, which had earlier been accepted for publication in the *Kenyon Review*. In 1951 Duncan met the painter Jess, his companion, with whom he lived in San Francisco. He taught at Black Mountain College in 1956 and is commonly grouped with Charles Olson and Robert Creeley as a Black Mountain poet; he is also identified as a major figure in the San Francisco Renaissance. In "My Mother Would Be a Falconress," the images of the mother as falconress and the poet as "the obedient little falcon who is later to break away from her enable Duncan to dramatize the whole series of conflicts involving possessiveness and love on the one hand and freedom and the need for identity on the other" (Thom Gunn). "Working in words I am an escapist," Duncan said. "But I want every part of the actual world involved in my escape."

The Temple of the Animals

The temple of the animals has fallen into disrepair
The pad of feet has faded.
The panthers flee the shadows of the day.
The smell of musk has faded but lingers there . . .
lingers, lingers. Ah, bitterly in my room.
Tired, I recall the animals of last year —
the altars of the bear, tribunals of the ape,
solitudes of elephantine gloom, rare
zebra-striped retreats, prophecies of dog,
sanctuaries of the pygmy deer.

Were there rituals I had forgotten? animal calls
to which those animal voices replied,
calld and calld until the jungle stirrd?
Were there voices that I heard?
Love was the very animal made his lair,
slept out his winter in my heart.
Did he seek my heart or ever
sleep there?

I have seen the animals depart,
forgotten their voices, or barely remembered
— like the last speech when the company goes
or the beloved face that the heart knows,
forgets and knows —
I have heard the dying footsteps fall.
The sound has faded, but lingers here.
Ah, bitterly I recall
the animals of last year.

1960

Often I Am Permitted to Return to a Meadow

as if it were a scene made-up by the mind,
that is not mine, but is a made place,

that is mine, it is so near to the heart,
an eternal pasture folded in all thought
so that there is a hall therein

that is a made place, created by light
wherefrom the shadows that are forms fall.

Wherefrom fall all architectures I am
I say are likenesses of the First Beloved
whose flowers are flames lit to the Lady.

She it is Queen Under The Hill
whose hosts are a disturbance of words within words
that is a field folded.

It is only a dream of the grass blowing
and against the source of the sun
in an hour before the sun's going down

whose secret we see in a children's game
of ring a round of roses told.

Often I am permitted to return to a meadow
as if it were a given property of the mind
that certain bounds hold against chaos,

that is a place of first permission,
everlasting omen of what is.

1960

Poetry, a Natural Thing

      Neither our vices nor our virtues
further the poem. "They came up
      and died
just like they do every year
      on the rocks."

      The poem
feeds upon thought, feeling, impulse,
      to breed itself,
a spiritual urgency at the dark ladders leaping.

This beauty is an inner persistence
      toward the source
striving against (within) down-rushet of the river,
      a call we heard and answer
in the lateness of the world
      primordial bellowings
from which the youngest world might spring,

salmon not in the well where the
    hazelnut falls
but at the falls battling, inarticulate,
    blindly making it.

This is one picture apt for the mind.

A second: a moose painted by Stubbs,
where last year's extravagant antlers
    lie on the ground.
The forlorn moosey-faced poem wears
    new antler-buds,
    the same,
"a little heavy, a little contrived."

his only beauty to be
    all moose.

1960

My Mother Would Be a Falconress

My mother would be a falconress,
And I, her gay falcon treading her wrist,
would fly to bring back
from the blue of the sky to her, bleeding, a prize,
where I dream in my little hood with many bells
jangling when I'd turn my head.

My mother would be a falconress,
and she sends me as far as her will goes.
She lets me ride to the end of her curb
where I fall back in anguish.
I dread that she will cast me away,
for I fall, I mis-take, I fail in her mission.

She would bring down the little birds.
And I would bring down the little birds.
When will she let me bring down the little birds,
pierced from their flight with their necks broken,
their heads like flowers limp from the stem?

I tread my mother's wrist and would draw blood.
Behind the little hood my eyes are hooded.
I have gone back into my hooded silence,
talking to myself and dropping off to sleep.

For she has muffled my dreams in the hood she has made me,
sewn round with bells, jangling when I move.
She rides with her little falcon upon her wrist.
She uses a barb that brings me to cower.
She sends me abroad to try my wings
and I come back to her. I would bring down
the little birds to her
I may not tear into, I must bring back perfectly.

I tear at her wrist with my beak to draw blood,
and her eye holds me, anguisht, terrifying.
She draws a limit to my flight.
Never beyond my sight, she says.
She trains me to fetch and to limit myself in fetching.
She rewards me with meat for my dinner.
But I must never eat what she sends me to bring her.

Yet it would have been beautiful, if she would have carried me,
always, in a little hood with the bells ringing,
at her wrist, and her riding
to the great falcon hunt, and me
flying up to the curb of my heart from her heart
to bring down the skylark from the blue to her feet,
straining, and then released for the flight.

My mother would be a falconress,
and I her gerfalcon, raised at her will,
from her wrist sent flying, as if I were her own
pride, as if her pride
knew no limits, as if her mind
sought in me flight beyond the horizon.

Ah, but high, high in the air I flew.
And far, far beyond the curb of her will,
were the blue hills where the falcons nest.
And then I saw west to the dying sun —
it seemd my human soul went down in flames.

I tore at her wrist, at the hold she had for me,
until the blood ran hot and I heard her cry out,
far, far beyond the curb of her will

to horizons of stars beyond the ringing hills of the world where
 the falcons nest
I saw, and I tore at her wrist with my savage beak.
I flew, as if sight flew from the anguish in her eye beyond her sight,
sent from my striking loose, from the cruel strike at her wrist,
striking out from the blood to be free of her.

My mother would be a falconress,
and even now, years after this,
when the wounds I left her had surely heald,
and the woman is dead,
her fierce eyes closed, and if her heart
were broken, it is stilld.

I would be a falcon and go free.
I tread her wrist and wear the hood,
talking to myself, and would draw blood.

1968

The Torso (Passage 18)

Most beautiful! the red-flowering eucalyptus,
the madrone, the yew

Is he . . .

So thou wouldst smile, and take me in thine arms
The sight of London to my exiled eyes
Is as Elysium to a new-come soul

If he be Truth
I would dwell in the illusion of him

His hands unlocking from chambers of my male body

such an idea in man's image

rising tides that sweep me towards him

. . . *homosexual*?

and at the treasure of his mouth

pour forth my soul

his soul commingling

I thought a Being more than vast, His body leading
into Paradise, his eyes
quickening a fire in me, a trembling

hieroglyph: At the root of the neck

the clavicle, for the neck is the stem of the great artery
upward into his head that is beautiful

At the rise of the pectoral muscles

the nipples, for the breasts are like sleeping fountains
of feeling in man, waiting above the beat of his heart,
shielding the rise and fall of his breath, to be
awakend

At the axis of his mid hriff

the navel, for in the pit of his stomach the chord from
which first he was fed has its temple

At the root of the groin

the pubic hair, for the torso is the stem in which the man
flowers forth and leads to the stamen of flesh in which
his seed rises

a wave of need and desire over   taking me

cried out my name

(This was long ago.   It was another life)

and said,

What do you want of me?

I do not know, I said.   I have fallen in love.   He
has brought me into heights and depths my heart
would fear   without him.   His look

pierces my side • fire eyes •

I have been waiting for you, he said:
I know what you desire

you do not yet know   but through me •

And I am with you everywhere.   In your falling

I have fallen from a high place.   I have raised myself

from darkness in your   rising

wherever you are

my hand in your hand   seeking   the locks, the keys

I am there.   Gathering me, you gather

your Self ·

For my Other is not a woman but a man

the King upon whose bosom let me lie.

1968

CHARLES BUKOWSKI (1920–1994)

Charles Bukowski was born in Andernach, Germany. He came to the United States at the age of two, grew up in Los Angeles, and worked many menial jobs including a fourteen-year stint as a postal worker, the subject of his 1971 novel, *Post Office.* Robert Frost described himself as one who was "acquainted with the night." In the same sense Bukowski was "acquainted" with prostitutes, bars, racetracks, bums, skid row, and wage slavery. He wrote, he once said, for "the defeated, the demented, and the damned." He had a gift for being (or simulating being) honest and spontaneous in poems and stories whose artistry conceals itself behind brash talk, profanity, and general misanthropy. No one was more antiacademic than Bukowski, who was quick to expose the pretensions of "phonies" (as in his poem excoriating "The Beats"). Mickey Rourke played him — opposite Faye Dunaway — in the 1987 fictional account of his life, *Barfly*, and in 2003, Bukowski was the subject of the documentary *Born Into This.* According to unofficial bookstore records, more of his books are stolen than any other writer's.

my old man

16 years old
during the depression
I'd come home drunk
and all my clothing —
shorts, shirts, stockings —
suitcase, and pages of
short stories
would be thrown out on the
front lawn and about the
street.

my mother would be
waiting behind a tree:
"Henry, Henry, don't
go in . . . he'll
kill you, he's read
your stories. . . "

"I can whip his
ass. . . "
"Henry, please take
this . . . and
find yourself a room."

but it worried him
that I might not
finish high school
so I'd be back
again.

one evening he walked in
with pages of
one of my short stories
(which I had never submitted
to him)
and he said, "this is
a great short story."
I said, "o.k.,"
and he handed it to me
and I read it.
it was a story about
a rich man
who had a fight with
his wife and had
gone out into the night
for a cup of coffee
and had observed
the waitress and the spoons
and forks and the
salt and pepper shakers
and the neon sign
in the window
and then had gone back
to his stable
to see and touch his
favorite horse
who then
kicked him in the head
and killed him.

somehow
the story held
meaning for him
though
when I had written it
I had no idea

of what I was
writing about.

so I told him,
"o.k., old man, you can
have it."

and he took it
and walked out
and closed the door.
I guess that's
as close
as we ever got.

1977

freaky time

the lady down at the end of the bar keeps looking at
me, I put my head down, I look away, I light
a cigarette, glance again: she's still staring at me, she's
charmingly dressed and she, herself, well, you might
say she's beautiful.
her eyes meld with mine; I am
elated and nervous, then
she gets up, goes to the ladies' room:
such a behind!
such grace!
what a gazelle!

I glance at my face in the bar mirror, look
away.

she's back; then the barkeep comes down: "a drink
from the lady at the end of the bar."

I nod thanks to her, lift my drink, smile, have a
hit.

she is looking again, what a strange and pleasur-
able experience.

I look forward, examine the backs of my hands — not
bad hands as far as hands go.

then, at once, it occurs to me:
she has mistaken me for somebody
else.

I leave my stool and slowly walk to the exit,
and out into the night; I walk half a block down the
boulevard, feel the need for a smoke, slip the
pack of cigarettes out of my coat pocket, look
curiously at the brand name (I did *not* purchase
these): DEATH, it
says.

I curse, hurl the pack into the street, move toward
the next bar: knew it all along: she was a
whore.

1989

comments upon my last book of poesy:

you're better than ever.
you've sold out.
you suck.
my mother hates you.
you're rich.
you're the best writer in the English language.
can I come see you?
I write just like you do, only better.
why do you drive a BMW?
why don't you give more readings?
can you still get it up?
do you know Allen Ginsberg?
what do you think of Henry Miller?
will you write a foreword to my next book?
I enclose a photograph of Céline.
I enclose my grandfather's pocket watch.
the enclosed jacket was knitted by my wife in Bavarian style.
have you been drunk with Mickey Rourke?
I am a young girl 19 years old and I will come and clean your house.
you are a stinking bastard to tell people that Shakespeare is not readable.
what do you think of Norman Mailer?
why do you put down Hemingway?
why do you steal from Hemingway?
why do you knock Tolstoy?
I'm doing hard time and when I get out I'm coming to see you.
I think you suck ass.
you've saved my god-damned life.
why do you hate women?
I love you.
I read your poems at parties.

did all those things really happen to you?
why do you drink?
I saw you at the racetrack but I didn't bother you.
I'd like to renew our relationship.
do you really stay up all night?
I can out-drink you.
you stole it from Sherwood Anderson.
did you ever meet Ezra?
I am alone and I think of you every night.
who the hell do you think you're fooling?
my tits aren't much but I've got great legs.
fuck you, man.
my wife hates you.
will you please read the enclosed poems and comment?
I am going to publish all those letters you wrote me.
you jack-off motherfuck, you're not fooling anybody.

1989

me against the world

when I was a kid
one of the questions asked was,
would you rather eat a bucket of shit
or drink a bucket of piss?
I thought that was easy.
"that's easy," I said, "I'll take the
piss."
"maybe we'll make you do both,"
they told me.
I was the new kid in the
neighborhood.
"oh yeah," I said.
"yeah!" they said.
there were 4 of them.
"yeah," I said, "you and whose
army?"
"we won't need no army," the
biggest one said.
I slammed my fist into his
stomach.
then all 5 of us were down on
the ground fighting.
they got in each other's way
but there were still too many
of them.
I broke free and started
running.

"sissy! sissy!" they yelled.
"going home to mama?"
I kept running.
they were right.
I ran all the way to my house,
up the driveway and onto the
porch and into the
house
where my father was beating
up my mother.
she was screaming.
things were broken on the floor.
I charged my father and started swinging.
I reached up but he was too tall,
all I could hit were his
legs.
then there was a flash of red and
purple and green
and I was on the floor.
"you little prick!" my father said,
"you stay out of this!"
"don't you hit my boy!" my mother
screamed.
but I felt good because my father
was no longer hitting my
mother.
to make sure, I got up and charged
him again, swinging.
there was another flash of colors
and I was on the floor
again.
when I got up again
my father was sitting in one chair
and my mother was sitting in
another chair
and they both just sat there
looking at me.
I walked down the hall and into
my bedroom and sat on the
bed.
I listened to make sure there
weren't any more sounds of
beating and screaming
out there.
there weren't.
then I didn't know what to
do.
it wasn't any good outside
and it wasn't any good

inside.
so I just sat there.
then I saw a spider making a web
across a window.
I found a match, walked over,
lit it and burned the spider to
death.
then I felt better.
much better.

1994

so you want to be a writer?

if it doesn't come bursting out of you
in spite of everything,
don't do it.
unless it comes unasked out of your
heart and your mind and your mouth
and your gut,
don't do it.
if you have to sit for hours
staring at your computer screen
or hunched over your
typewriter
searching for words,
don't do it.
if you're doing it for money or
fame,
don't do it.
if you're doing it because you want
women in your bed,
don't do it.
if you have to sit there and
rewrite it again and again,
don't do it.
if it's hard work just thinking about doing it,
don't do it.
if you're trying to write like somebody
else,
forget about it.

if you have to wait for it to roar out of
you,
then wait patiently.
if it never does roar out of you,
do something else.

if you first have to read it to your wife
or your girlfriend or your boyfriend
or your parents or to anybody at all,
you're not ready.

don't be like so many writers,
don't be like so many thousands
of people who call themselves writers,
don't be dull and boring and
pretentious, don't be consumed with self-
love.
the libraries of the world have
yawned themselves to
sleep
over your kind.
don't add to that.
don't do it.
unless it comes out of
your soul like a rocket,
unless being still would
drive you to madness or
suicide or murder,
don't do it.
unless the sun inside you is
burning your gut,
don't do it.

when it is truly time,
and if you have been chosen,
it will do it by
itself and it will keep on doing it
until you die or it dies in
you

there is no other way.

and there never was.

2002

AMY CLAMPITT (1920–1994)

Amy Clampitt was born in New Providence, Iowa. She worked in publishing and as a librarian before enjoying a belated but meteoric rise as a poet. When her first book, *The Kingfisher*, was published in 1983, the critic Helen Vendler in the *New York Review of Books* wrote ecstatically that "a century from now, this volume will still offer a rare window into a rare mind, it will still offer beautiful objects of delectation; but it will have taken on as well the documentary value of what, in the twentieth century, made up the stuff of culture." Vendler describes "Marine Surface, Low Overcast" as "a one-sentence fifty-line poem on fog, named, as a painting might be," and with the painterly aim of representing a variety of "lusters and hues and transitions."

Marine Surface, Low Overcast

Out of churned aureoles
this buttermilk, this
herringbone of albatross,
floss of mercury,
déshabille of spun
aluminum, furred with a velouté
of looking-glass,

a stuff so single
it might almost be lifted,
folded over, crawled underneath
or slid between, as nakedness-
caressing sheets, or donned
and worn, the train-borne
trapping of an unrepeatable
occasion,

this wind-silver
rumpling as of oatfields,
a suede of meadow,
a nub, a nap, a mane of lustre
lithe as the slide
of muscle in its
sheath of skin,

laminae of living tissue,
mysteries of flex,
affinities of texture,
subtleties of touch, of pressure
and release, the suppleness
of long and intimate
association,

new synchronies of fingertip,
of breath, of sequence,
entities that still can rouse,
can stir or solder,
whip to a froth, or force
to march in strictly
hierarchical formation

down galleries of sheen, of flux,
cathedral domes that seem to hover
overturned and shaken like a basin
to the noise of voices,
from a rustle to the jostle
of such rush-hour
conglomerations

no loom, no spinneret, no forge, no factor,
no process whatsoever, patent
applied or not applied for,
no five-year formula, no fabric
for which pure imagining,
except thus prompted,
can invent the equal.

1938

The Sun Underfoot Among the Sundews

An ingenuity too astonishing
to be quite fortuitous is
this bog full of sundews, sphagnum-
lined and shaped like a teacup.
                                        A step
down and you're into it; a
wilderness swallows you up:
ankle-, then knee-, then midriff-
to-shoulder-deep in wetfooted
understory, an overhead
spruce-tamarack horizon hinting
you'll never get out of here.
                                        But the sun
among the sundews, down there,
is so bright, an underfoot
webwork of carnivorous rubies,
a star-swarm thick as the gnats
they're set to catch, delectable
double-faced cockleburs, each
hair-tip a sticky mirror
afire with sunlight, a million
of them and again a million,
each mirror a trap set to
unhand unbelieving,
                              that either
a First Cause said once, "Let there
be sundews," and there were, or they've

made their way here unaided
other than by that backhand, round-
about refusal to assume responsibility
known as Natural Selection.
                                        But the sun
underfoot is so dazzling
down there among the sundews,
there is so much light
in the cup that, looking,
you start to fall upward.

1983

Palm Sunday

Neither the wild tulip, poignant
and sanguinary, nor the dandelion
blowsily unbuttoning, answers
the gardener's imperative, if need be,
to maim and hamper in the name of order,
or the taste for rendering adorable
the torturer's implements — never mind
what entrails, not yet trampled under
by the feet of choirboys (sing,
my tongue, the glorious battle),
mulch the olive groves, the flowering
of apple and almond, the boxwood
corridor, the churchyard yew,
the gallows tree.

1983

Barbara Guest (1920–2006)

Barbara Guest was born in Wilmington, North Carolina. She grew up in Los Angeles, graduated from the University of California at Berkeley, and lived for many years in New York City. She has written twenty-three volumes of poetry — most recently *The Red Gaze* in 2005. The author of a biography of H.D., *Herself Defined*, she has been associated with the poets of the "New York school" and more recently with the Language poets.

Parachutes, My Love, Could Carry Us Higher

I just said I didn't know
And now you are holding me

In your arms,
How kind.
Parachutes, my love, could carry us higher.
Yet around the net I am floating
Pink and pale blue fish are caught in it,
They are beautiful,
But they are not good for eating.
Parachutes, my love, could carry us higher
Than this mid-air in which we tremble,
Having exercised our arms in swimming,
Now the suspension, you say,
Is exquisite. I do not know.
There is coral below the surface,
There is sand, and berries
Like pomegranates grow.
This wide net, I am treading water
Near it, bubbles are rising and salt
Drying on my lashes, yet I am no nearer
Air than water. I am closer to you
Than land and I am in a stranger ocean
Than I wished.

1960

On the Verge of the Path

What inspires me?
                    Picasso!
He's there on the right in the photo
Where are we?
                    In Mougins, Cannes
tributary states and rivers. Yes!
Here I am in Penthouse A rue Ninety Fourth
                    thinking about Picasso.
I detest this pencil. I wish I had a 'crayon'
or a cactus or my life were being consumed
by villas called Jacqueline.
                    It was a summer evening
in the 1950's when I attended a performance
it was something like "people and animals
in their habitats in Montparnasse"
                    by Picasso
The dog was played by Frank and John
I had not yet made their acquaintance
but I lived on a nearby rue
                    Picasso!
Yourselves consider me in profile
when I am awakened from a dream of pottery
rattling like candle sticks in the factory

of Apollinaire and Eluard a century
looking up at me from the shelves of O'Hara and Ashbery
those odd tables where we mixed our cement

1973

Words

The simple contact with a wooden spoon and the word
recovered itself, began to spread as grass, forced
as it lay sprawling to consider the monument where
patience looked at grief, where warfare ceased
eyes curled outside themes to search the paper
now gleaming and potent, wise and resilient, word
entered its continent eager to find another as
capable as a thorn. The nearest possession would
house them both, they being then two might glide
into this house and presently create a rather larger
mansion filled with spoons and condiments, gracious
as a newly laid table where related objects might gather
to enjoy the interplay of gravity upon facetious hints,
the chocolate dish presuming an endowment, the ladle
of galactic rhythm primed as a relish dish, curved
knives, finger bowls, morsel carriages words might
choose and savor before swallowing so much was the
sumptuousness and substance of a rented house where words
placed dressing gowns as rosemary entered their scent
percipient as elder branches in the night where words
gathered, warped, then straightened, marking new wands.

1989

HOWARD NEMEROV (1920–1991)

Howard Nemerov was born in New York City. After graduating from Harvard, he flew bombing missions for the Royal Canadian Air Force and the U.S. Army Air Force during World War II. A poet of urbanity and epigrammatic wit, he has written on subjects ranging from lawn sprinklers and Santa Claus ("an overstuffed confidence man") to the *Challenger* disaster and "the good war, the one we won."

Brainstorm

The house was shaken by a rising wind
That rattled window and door. He sat alone
In an upstairs room and heard these things: a blind

Ran up with a bang, a door slammed, a groan
Came from some hidden joist, and a leaky tap,
At any silence of the wind, walked like
A blind man through the house. Timber and sap
Revolt, he thought, from washer, baulk and spike.
Bent to his book, continued unafraid
Until the crows came down from their loud flight
To walk along the rooftree overhead.
Their horny feet, so near but out of sight,
Scratched on the slate; when they were blown away
He heard their wings beat till they came again,
While the wind rose, and the house seemed to sway,
And window panes began to blind with rain.
The house was talking, not to him, he thought,
But to the crows; the crows were talking back
In their black voices. The secret might be out:
Houses are only trees stretched on the rack.
And once the crows knew, all nature would know.
Fur, leaf and feather would invade the form,
Nail rust with rain and shingle warp with snow,
Vine tear the wall, till any straw-borne storm
Could rip both roof and rooftree off and show
Naked to nature what they had kept warm.

He came to feel the crows walk on his head
As if he were the house, their crooked feet
Scratched, through the hair, his scalp. He might be dead
It seemed, and all the noises underneath
Be but the cooling of the sinews, veins,
Juices, and sodden sacks suddenly let go;
While in his ruins of wiring, his burst mains,
The rainy wind had been set free to blow
Until the green uprising and mob rule
That ran the world had taken over him,
Split him like seed, and set him in the school
Where any crutch can learn to be a limb.

Inside his head he heard the stormy crows.

1958

Style

Flaubert wanted to write a novel
About nothing. It was to have no subject
And be sustained upon style alone,
Like the Holy Ghost cruising above
The abyss, or like the little animals

In Disney cartoons who stand upon a branch
That breaks, but do not fall
Till they look down. He never wrote that novel,
And neither did he write another one
That would have been called *La Spirale*,
Wherein the hero's fortunes were to rise
In dreams, while his waking life disintegrated.

Even so, for these two books
We thank the master. They can be read,
With difficulty, in the spirit alone,
Are not so wholly lost as certain works
Burned at Alexandria, flooded at Florence,
And are never taught at universities.
Moreover, they are not deformed by style,
That fire that eats what it illuminates.

1967

Because You Asked About the Line Between Prose and Poetry

Sparrows were feeding in a freezing drizzle
That while you watched turned into pieces of snow
Riding a gradient invisible
From silver aslant to random, white, and slow.

There came a moment that you couldn't tell.
And then they clearly flew instead of fell.

1980

MONA VAN DUYN (1921–2004)

Mona Van Duyn was born in Waterloo, Iowa, in 1921. When Van Duyn was appointed the first female U.S. poet laureate in 1992, Judith Hall defined "quintessential Van Duyn" as "narrative draped around a rumination; accentual stanzaic pattern with end rhymes, slanted and supported by internal assonance. Suburbia; a friend; a garden, but with dog's penises in it and wounds."

Open Letter from a Constant Reader

To all who carve their love on a picnic table
or scratch it on smoked glass panes of a public toilet,

I send my thanks for each plain and perfect fable
of how the three pains of the body, surfeit,

hunger, and chill (or loneliness), create
a furniture and art of their own easing.
And I bless two public sites and, like Yeats,
two private sites where the body receives its blessing.

Nothing is banal or lowly that tells us how well
the world, whose highways proffer table and toilet
as signs and occasions of comfort for belly and bowel,
can comfort the heart too, somewhere in secret.

Where so much constant news of good has been put,
both fleeting and lasting lines compel belief.
Not by talent or riches or beauty, but
by the world's grace, people have found relief

from the worst pain of the body, loneliness,
and say so with a simple heart as they sit
being relieved of one of the others. I bless
all knowledge of love, all ways of publishing it.

1970

Relationships

The legal children of a literary man
remember his ugly words to their mother.
He made them keep quiet and kissed them later.
He made them stop fighting and finish their supper.
His stink in the bathroom sickened their noses.
He left them with sitters in lonesome houses.
He mounted their mother and made them wear braces.
He fattened on fame and raised them thin.

But the secret sons of the same man
spring up like weeds from the seed of his word.
They eat from his hand and it is not hard.
They unravel his sweater and swing from his beard.
They smell in their sleep his ferns and roses.
They hunt the fox on his giant horses.
They slap their mother, repeating his phrases,
and swell in his sight and suck him thin.

1970

Causes

"Questioned about why she had beaten her spastic child to death, the mother told police, 'I hit him because he kept falling off his crutches.'" News Item

Because one's husband is different from one's self,
the pilot's last words were "Help, my God, I'm shot!"
Because the tip growth on a pine looks like Christmas tree candles,
cracks appear in the plaster of old houses.

And because the man next door likes to play golf,
a war started up in some country where it is hot,
and whenever a maid waits at the bus-stop with her bundles,
the fear of death comes over us in vacant places.

It is all foreseen in the glassy eye on the shelf,
woven in the web of notes that sprays from a trumpet,
announced by a salvo of crackles when the fire kindles,
printed on the nature of things when a skin bruises.

And there's never enough surprise at the killer in the self,
nor enough difference between the shooter and the shot,
nor enough melting down of stubs to make new candles
as the earth rolls over, inverting billions of houses.

1970

RICHARD WILBUR (b. 1921)

Richard Wilbur was born in New York City. An Amherst graduate, he served in the infantry in World War II, seeing action in Italy, France, and Germany. He did graduate work at Harvard, taught there, and later joined the faculty of Wesleyan University. A poet of rare finesse and humane intelligence, cheerfully out of step with many of his contemporaries, he favors traditional forms, rhyme, and meter on the grounds that "limitation makes for power: the strength of the genie comes from his being confined in a bottle." In addition to poetry, he has written lyrics (for Leonard Bernstein's *Candide*) and is responsible for acclaimed translations of Molière's plays (*The Misanthrope* and *Tartuffe*). His is the voice of the civilized man, affirming the possibility of an aesthetically pleasing order in a world of accident and chaos. He wrote "A Baroque Wall-Fountain in the Villa Sciarra" in Rome, where he would pass "a charming sixteenth- or seventeenth-century fountain" on his daily walk: "This fountain appeared to me the very symbol or concretion of Pleasure; I felt reproached by it for my Puritanical industry; and at last I compromised with it by making it the subject of a poem." Of "Lying," he has commented that "there are 'lies' or fictions which are ways of telling the truth," and that the poem ends with "three fictions having one burden." Though Wilbur, as Randall Jarrell observed, "obsessively sees, and shows, the bright underside of every dark thing," he also writes with great clarity on common moral concerns, as in "Advice to a Prophet."

The Beautiful Changes

One wading a Fall meadow finds on all sides
The Queen Anne's Lace lying like lilies
On water; it glides
So from the walker, it turns
Dry grass to a lake, as the slightest shade of you
Valleys my mind in fabulous blue Lucernes.

The beautiful changes as a forest is changed
By a chameleon's tuning his skin to it;
As a mantis, arranged
On a green leaf, grows
Into it, makes the leaf leafier, and proves
Any greenness is deeper than anyone knows.

Your hands hold roses always in a way that says
They are not only yours; the beautiful changes
In such kind ways,
Wishing ever to sunder
Things and things' selves for a second finding, to lose
For a moment all that it touches back to wonder.

1947

Love Calls Us to the Things of This World

The eyes open to a cry of pulleys,
And spirited from sleep, the astounded soul
Hangs for a moment bodiless and simple
As false dawn.
Outside the open window
The morning air is all awash with angels.

Some are in bed-sheets, some are in blouses,
Some are in smocks: but truly there they are.
Now they are rising together in calm swells
Of halcyon feeling, filling whatever they wear
With the deep joy of their impersonal breathing;

Now they are flying in place, conveying
The terrible speed of their omnipresence, moving
And staying like white water; and now of a sudden
They swoon down in so rapt a quiet
That nobody seems to be there. The soul shrinks

From all that it is about to remember,
From the punctual rape of every blessèd day,

And cries,
"Oh, let there be nothing on earth but laundry,
Nothing but rosy hands in the rising steam
And clear dances done in the sight of heaven."

Yet, as the sun acknowledges
With a warm look the world's hunks and colors,
The soul descends once more in bitter love
To accept the waking body, saying now
In a changed voice as the man yawns and rises,

"Bring them down from their ruddy gallows;
Let there be clean linen for the backs of thieves;
Let lovers go fresh and sweet to be undone,
And the heaviest nuns walk in a pure floating
Of dark habits,
keeping their difficult balance."

1956

Mind

Mind in its purest play is like some bat
That beats about in caverns all alone,
Contriving by a kind of senseless wit
Not to conclude against a wall of stone.

It has no need to falter or explore;
Darkly it knows what obstacles are there,
And so may weave and flitter, dip and soar
In perfect courses through the blackest air.

And has this simile a like perfection?
The mind is like a bat. Precisely. Save
That in the very happiest intellection
A graceful error may correct the cave.

1956

Boy at the Window

Seeing the snowman standing all alone
In dusk and cold is more than he can bear.
The small boy weeps to hear the wind prepare
A night of gnashings and enormous moan.
His tearful sight can hardly reach to where
The pale-faced figure with bitumen eyes
Returns him such a god-forsaken stare
As outcast Adam gave to Paradise.

The man of snow is, nonetheless, content,
Having no wish to go inside and die.
Still, he is moved to see the youngster cry.
Though frozen water is his element,
He melts enough to drop from one soft eye
A trickle of the purest rain, a tear
For the child at the bright pane surrounded by
Such warmth, such light, such love, and so much fear.

1956

A Baroque Wall-Fountain in the Villa Sciarra

for Dore and Adja

Under the bronze crown
Too big for the head of the stone cherub whose feet
A serpent has begun to eat,
Sweet water brims a cockle and braids down

Past spattered mosses, breaks
On the tipped edge of a second shell, and fills
The massive third below. It spills
In threads then from the scalloped rim, and makes

A scrim or summery tent
For a faun-ménage and their familiar goose.
Happy in all that ragged, loose
Collapse of water, its effortless descent

And flatteries of spray,
The stocky god upholds the shell with ease,
Watching, about his shaggy knees,
The goatish innocence of his babes at play;

His fauness all the while
Leans forward, slightly, into a clambering mesh
Of water-lights, her sparkling flesh
In a sæcular ecstasy, her blinded smile

Bent on the sand floor
Of the trefoil pool, where ripple-shadows come
And go in swift reticulum,
More addling to the eye than wine, and more

Interminable to thought
Than pleasure's calculus. Yet since this all
Is pleasure, flash, and waterfall,
Must it not be too simple? Are we not

More intricately expressed
In the plain fountains that Maderna set
Before St. Peter's — the main jet
Struggling aloft until it seems at rest

In the act of rising, until
The very wish of water is reversed,
That heaviness borne up to burst
In a clear, high, cavorting head, to fill

With blaze, and then in gauze
Delays, in a gnatlike shimmering, in a fine
Illumined version of itself, decline,
And patter on the stones its own applause?

If that is what men are
Or should be, if those water-saints display
The patterm of our areté,
What of these showered fauns in their bizarre,

Spangled, and plunging house?
They are at rest in fulness of desire
For what is given, they do not tire
Of the smart of the sun, the pleasant water-douse

And riddled pool below,
Reproving our disgust and our ennui
With humble insatiety.
Francis, perhaps, who lay in sister snow

Before the wealthy gate
Freezing and praising, might have seen in this
No trifle, but a shade of bliss —
That land of tolerable flowers, that state

As near and far as grass
Where eyes become the sunlight, and the hand
Is worthy of water: the dreamt land
Toward which all hungers leap, all pleasures pass.

1956

Advice to a Prophet

When you come, as you soon must, to the streets of our city,
Mad-eyed from stating the obvious,
Not proclaiming our fall but begging us
In God's name to have self-pity,

Spare us all word of the weapons, their force and range,
The long numbers that rocket the mind;
Our slow, unreckoning hearts will be left behind,
Unable to fear what is too strange.

Nor shall you scare us with talk of the death of the race.
How should we dream of this place without us? —
The sun mere fire, the leaves untroubled about us,
A stone look on the stone's face?

Speak of the world's own change. Though we cannot conceive
Of an undreamt thing, we know to our cost
How the dreamt cloud crumbles, the vines are blackened by frost,
How the view alters. We could believe,

If you told us so, that the white-tailed deer will slip
Into perfect shade, grown perfectly shy,
The lark avoid the reaches of our eye,
The jack-pine lose its knuckled grip

On the cold ledge, and every torrent burn
As Xanthus once, its gliding trout
Stunned in a twinkling. What should we be without
The dolphin's arc, the dove's return,

These things in which we have seen ourselves and spoken?
Ask us, prophet, how we shall call
Our natures forth when that live tongue is all
Dispelled, that glass obscured or broken

In which we have said the rose of our love and the clean
Horse of our courage, in which beheld
The singing locust of the soul unshelled,
And all we mean or wish to mean.

Ask us, ask us whether with the worldless rose
Our hearts shall fail us; come demanding
Whether there shall be lofty or long standing
When the bronze annals of the oak-tree close.

1961

Shame

It is a cramped little state with no foreign policy,
Save to be thought inoffensive. The grammar of the language
Has never been fathomed, owing to the national habit
Of allowing each sentence to trail off in confusion.

Those who have visited Scusi, the capital city,
Report that the railway-route from Schuldig passes
Through country best described as unrelieved.
Sheep are the national product. The faint inscription
Over the city gates may perhaps be rendered,
"I'm afraid you won't find much of interest here."
Census-reports which give the population
As zero are, of course, not to be trusted,
Save as reflecting the natives' flustered insistence
That they do not count, as well as their modest horror
Of letting one's sex be known in so many words.
The uniform grey of the nondescript buildings, the absence
Of churches or comfort-stations, have given observers
An odd impression of ostentatious meanness,
And it must be said of the citizens (muttering by
In their ratty sheepskins, shying at cracks in the sidewalk)
That they lack the peace of mind of the truly humble.
The tenor of life is careful, even in the stiff
Unsmiling carelessness of the border-guards
And *douaniers*, who admit, whenever they can,
Not merely the usual carloads of deodorant
But gypsies, g-strings, hasheesh, and contraband pigments.
Their complete negligence is reserved, however,
For the hoped-for invasion, at which time the happy people
(Sniggering, ruddily naked, and shamelessly drunk)
Will stun the foe by their overwhelming submission,
Corrupt the generals, infiltrate the staff,
Usurp the throne, proclaim themselves to be sun-gods,
And bring about the collapse of the whole empire.

1961

A Shallot

The full cloves
Of your buttocks, the convex
Curve of your belly, the curved
Cleft of your sex —

Out of this corm
That's planted in strong thighs
The slender stem and radiant
Flower rise.

1976

Lying

To claim, at a dead party, to have spotted a grackle
When in fact you haven't of late, can do no harm.
Your reputation for saying things of interest
Will not be marred, if you hasten to other topics,
Nor will the delicate web of human trust
Be ruptured by that airy fabrication.
Later, however, talking with toxic zest
Of golf, or taxes, or the rest of it
Where the beaked ladle plies the chuckling ice,
You may enjoy a chill of severance, hearing
Above your head the shrug of unreal wings.
Not that the world is tiresome in itself:
We know what boredom is: it is a dull
Impatience or a fierce velleity,
A champing wish, stalled by our lassitude,
To make or do. In the strict sense, of course,
We invent nothing, merely bearing witness
To what each morning brings again to light:
Gold crosses, cornices, astonishment
Of panes, the turbine-vent which natural law
Spins on the grill-end of the diner's roof,
Then grass and grackles or, at the end of town
In sheen-swept pastureland, the horse's neck
Clothed with its usual thunder, and the stones
Beginning now to tug their shadows in
And track the air with glitter. All these things
Are there before us; there before we look
Or fail to look; there to be seen or not
By us, as by the bee's twelve thousand eyes,
According to our means and purposes.
So too with strangeness not to be ignored,
Total eclipse or snow upon the rose,
And so with that most rare conception, nothing.
What is it, after all, but something missed?
It is the water of a dried-up well
Gone to assail the cliffs of Labrador.
There is what galled the arch-negator, sprung
From Hell to probe with intellectual sight
The cells and heavens of a given world
Which he could take but as another prison:
Small wonder that, pretending not to be,
He drifted through the bar-like boles of Eden
In a *black mist low creeping*, dragging down
And darkening with moody self-absorption
What, when he left it, lifted and, if seen
From the sun's vantage, seethed with vaulting hues.
Closer to making than the deftest fraud

Is seeing how the catbird's tail was made
To counterpoise, on the mock-orange spray,
Its light, up-tilted spine; or, lighter still,
How the shucked tunic of an onion, brushed
To one side on a backlit chopping-board
And rocked by trifling currents, prints and prints
Its bright, ribbed shadow like a flapping sail.
Odd that a thing is most itself when likened:
The eye mists over, basil hints of clove,
The river glazes toward the dam and spills
To the drubbed rocks below its crashing cullet,
And in the barnyard near the sawdust-pile
Some great thing is tormented. Either it is
A tarp torn loose and in the groaning wind
Now puffed, now flattened, or a hip-shot beast
Which tries again, and once again, to rise.
What, though for pain there is no other word,
Finds pleasure in the cruellest simile?
It is something in us like the catbird's song
From neighbor bushes in the grey of morning
That, harsh or sweet, and of its own accord,
Proclaims its many kin. It is a chant
Of the first springs, and it is tributary
To the great lies told with the eyes half-shut
That have the truth in view: the tale of Chiron
Who, with sage head, wild heart, and planted hoof
Instructed brute Achilles in the lyre,
Or of the garden where we first mislaid
Simplicity of wish and will, forgetting
Out of what cognate splendor all things came
To take their scattering names; and nonetheless
That matter of a baggage-train surprised
By a few Gascons in the Pyrenees
Which, having worked three centuries and more
In the dark caves of France, poured out at last
The blood of Roland, who to Charles his king
And to the dove that hatched the dove-tailed world
Was faithful unto death, and shamed the Devil.

1987

Man Running

Whatever he has done
Against our law and peace of mind,
Our mind's eye looks with pity of a kind
At the scared, stumbling fellow on the run

Who hears a siren scream
As through the thickets we conceive
He plows with fending arms, and to deceive
The snuffling dogs now flounders up a stream

Until he doubles back,
Climbing at length a rocky rise
To where he crumples and, exhausted, lies
In the scorched brush beside a railroad track.

*

If then he hops a freight
And clatteringly rides as far
As the next county in a cattle car,
We feel our sense of him disintegrate

In rumors, warnings, claims
That here or there he has appeared —
Tall, short, fierce, furtive, with or without a beard.
Still, in fidelity to childhood games

And outlaws of romance,
We darkly cheer him, whether or not
He robbed that store, or bank, or fired that shot,
And wish him, guiltily, a sporting chance.

*

Ditching the stolen truck,
He disappears into a vast
Deep-wooded wilderness, and is at last
Beyond the reach of law, and out of luck,

And we are one with him,
Sharing with him that eldest dread
Which, when it gathers in a sleeping head,
Is a place mottled, ominous, and dim

Remembered from the day
When we descended from the trees
Into the shadow of our enemies,
Not lords of nature yet, but naked prey.

2003

HOWARD MOSS (1922–1987)

Howard Moss was born in New York City. He became the poetry editor of the *New Yorker* in 1950 and held the position until his death thirty-seven years later. He once estimated that he had spent the equivalent of three months of his life in the elevators of the magazine's old mid-town headquarters. His poem "King Midas" led Richard Howard to propound his theory that the poets of their common generation were "children of Midas," who had grown up wishing for the touch that turned things into gold but later renounced the gift and dissolved it in a flowing stream. Perhaps because of his stature as an editor or because of resentment of his influence, Moss's well-made lyric poems are seriously undervalued.

King Midas

My food was pallid till I heard it ring
Against fine china. Every blessed thing
I touch becomes a work of art that baits
Its goldsmith's appetite: My bread's too rich,
My butter much too golden, and my meat
A nugget on my plate, as cold as ice;
Fresh water in my throat turns precious there,
Where every drop becomes a millionaire.

My hands leak gold into the flower's mouth,
Whose lips in tiers of rigid foliage
Make false what flowers are supposed to be.
I did not know I loved their warring thorns
Until they flowered into spikes so hard
My blood made obdurate the rose's stem.
My God was generous. But when I bleed,
It clogs the rosebed and cements the seed.

My dog was truly witty while he breathed.
I saw the tiny hairs upon his skin
Grow like a lion's into golden down.
I plucked them by the handfuls off of him,
And, now he is pure profit, my sculpturing
Might make a King go mad, for it was I
Who made those lively muscles stiffly pose —
This jaundice is relentless, and it grows.

I hate the glint of stars, the shine of wheat,
And when I walk, the tracings of my feet
Are affluent and litter where I go
With money that I sweat. I bank the slow
Gold-leaf of everything and, in my park,
A darkness shimmers that is not the dark,
A daylight glitters that is not the day —
All things are much less darling gilt this way.

Princess, come no closer; my tempered kiss,
Though it is royal still, will make you this
Or that kind of a statue. And my Queen,
Be armed against this gold paralysis,
Or you will starve and thinly bed alone,
And when you dream, a gold mine in your brain
Will have both eyes release their golden ore
And cry for tears they could not cry before.

I would be nothing but the dirt made loud,
A clay that ripples with the worm, decay
In ripeness of the weeds, a timid sun,
Or oppositely be entirely cloud,
Absolved of matter, dissolving in the rain.
Before gold kills me as it kills all men,
Dear Dionysus, give me back again
Ten fingertips that leave the world alone.

1960

The Long Island Night

Nothing as miserable has happened before.
The Long Island night has refused its moon.
La belle dame sans merci's next door.
The Prince of Darkness is on the phone.

Certain famous phrases of our time
Have taken on the glitter of poems,
Like "Catch me before I kill again,"
And "Why are you sitting in the dark alone?"

1979

The Summer Thunder

Now the equivocal lightning flashes
Come too close for comfort and the thunder
Sends the trembling dog under the table,
I long for the voice that is never shaken.

Above the sideboard, representation
Takes its last stand: a small rectangle
Of oak trees dripping with a painted greenness,
And in the foreground, a girl asleep

In a field who speaks for a different summer
From the one the thunder is mulling over —

How calm the sensuous is! How saintly!
Undersea light from a lit-up glen

Lends perspective to an arranged enchantment,
As peaceful as a Renaissance courtyard
Opened for tourists centuries after
Knights have bloodied themselves with doctrine.

1984

Making a Bed

I know how to make a bed
While still lying in it, and
Slip out of an imaginary hole
As if I were squeezed out of a tube:
Tug, smooth — the bed is made.
And if resurrections are this easy,
Why then I believe in all of them:
Lazarus rising from his tomb,
Elijah at the vertical —
Though death, I think, has more than clever
Household hints in mind and wants
The bed made, once, and for good.

1984

ANTHONY HECHT (1923–2004)

Anthony Hecht was born in New York City. After graduating from Bard College in 1944, he served in the infantry in World War II and witnessed the liberation of concentration camps, a searing experience that informs his work. A master of meter and form, he taught for many years at the University of Rochester. In conjunction with John Hollander he edited *Jiggery-Pokery* (1967), a compendium of double dactyls, the light-verse form that Hecht invented. In 1979, Daniel Hoffman wrote that "at the core of [Hecht's] poetry there is a Hebraic stoicism in the presence of immitigable fate." Hoffman places Hecht "among those who write determinedly as though the breaking of form and meter had not occurred, or had happened in some place like Bulgaria." Glyn Maxwell expresses a similar sentiment more reverently: Hecht's work "shatters the cozy notion that a fragmented, fractured age should be reflected in the forms of its art, that ugliness and shapelessness demand payment in kind."

The Dover Bitch

A Criticism of Life

for Andrews Wanning

So there stood Matthew Arnold and this girl
With the cliffs of England crumbling away behind them,

And he said to her, "Try to be true to me,
And I'll do the same for you, for things are bad
All over, etc., etc."
Well now, I knew this girl. It's true she had read
Sophocles in a fairly good translation
And caught that bitter allusion to the sea,
But all the time he was talking she had in mind
The notion of what his whiskers would feel like
On the back of her neck. She told me later on
That after a while she got to looking out
At the lights across the channel, and really felt sad,
Thinking of all the wine and enormous beds
And blandishments in French and the perfumes.
And then she got really angry. To have been brought
All the way down from London, and then be addressed
As a sort of mournful cosmic last resort
Is really tough on a girl, and she was pretty.
Anyway, she watched him pace the room
And finger his watch-chain and seem to sweat a bit,
And then she said one or two unprintable things.
But you mustn't judge her by that. What I mean to say is,
She's really all right. I still see her once in a while
And she always treats me right. We have a drink
And I give her a good time, and perhaps it's a year
Before I see her again, but there she is,
Running to fat, but dependable as they come.
And sometimes I bring her a bottle of *Nuit d'Amour*.

1967

A Hill

In Italy, where this sort of thing can occur,
I had a vision once — though you understand
It was nothing at all like Dante's, or the visions of saints,
And perhaps not a vision at all. I was with some friends,
Picking my way through a warm sunlit piazza
In the early morning. A clear fretwork of shadows
From huge umbrellas littered the pavement and made
A sort of lucent shallows in which was moored
A small navy of carts. Books, coins, old maps,
Cheap landscapes and ugly religious prints
Were all on sale. The colors and noise
Like the flying hands were gestures of exultation,
So that even the bargaining
Rose to the ear like a voluble godliness.
And then, where it happened, the noises suddenly stopped,

And it got darker; pushcarts and people dissolved
And even the great Farnese Palace itself
Was gone, for all its marble; in its place
Was a hill, mole-colored and bare. It was very cold,
Close to freezing, with a promise of snow.
The trees were like old ironwork gathered for scrap
Outside a factory wall. There was no wind,
And the only sound for a while was the little click
Of ice as it broke in the mud under my feet.
I saw a piece of ribbon snagged on a hedge,
But no other sign of life. And then I heard
What seemed the crack of a rifle. A hunter, I guessed;
At least I was not alone. But just after that
Came the soft and papery crash
Of a great branch somewhere unseen falling to earth.

And that was all, except for the cold and silence
That promised to last forever, like the hill.

Then prices came through, and fingers, and I was restored
To the sunlight and my friends. But for more than a week
I was scared by the plain bitterness of what I had seen.
All this happened about ten years ago,
And it hasn't troubled me since, but at last, today,
I remembered that hill; it lies just to the left
Of the road north of Poughkeepsie; and as a boy
I stood before it for hours in wintertime.

1967

Third Avenue in Sunlight

Third Avenue in sunlight. Nature's error.
Already the bars are filled and John is there.
Beneath a plentiful lady over the mirror
He tilts his glass in the mild mahogany air.

I think of him when he first got out of college,
Serious, thin, unlikely to succeed;
For several months he hung around the Village,
Boldly T-shirted, unfettered but unfreed.

Now he confides to a stranger, "I was first scout,
And kept my glimmers peeled till after dark.
Our outfit had as its sign a bloody knout,
We met behind the museum in Central Park.

Of course, we were kids." But still those savages,
War-painted, a flap of leather at the loins,

File silently against him. Hostages
Are never taken. One summer, in Des Moines,

They entered his hotel room, tomahawks
Flashing like barracuda. He tried to pray.
Three years of treatment. Occasionally he talks
About how he almost didn't get away.

Daily the prowling sunlight whets its knife
Along the sidewalk. We almost never meet.
In the Rembrandt dark he lifts his amber life.
My bar is somewhat further down the street.

1967

The Book of Yolek

Wir haben ein Gesetz,
Und nach dem Gesetz soll er sterben.

The dowsed coals fume and hiss after your meal
Of grilled brook trout, and you saunter off for a walk
Down the fern trail, it doesn't matter where to,
Just so you're weeks and worlds away from home,
And among midsummer hills have set up camp
In the deep bronze glories of declining day.

You remember, peacefully, an earlier day
In childhood, remember a quite specific meal:
A corn roast and bonfire in summer camp.
That summer you got lost on a Nature Walk;
More than you dared admit, you thought of home;
No one else knows where the mind wanders to.

The fifth of August, 1942.
It was morning and very hot. It was the day
They came at dawn with rifles to The Home
For Jewish Children, cutting short the meal
Of bread and soup, lining them up to walk
In close formation off to a special camp.

How often you have thought about that camp,
As though in some strange way you were driven to,
And about the children, and how they were made to walk,
Yolek who had bad lungs, who wasn't a day
Over five years old, commanded to leave his meal
And shamble between armed guards to his long home.

We're approaching August again. It will drive home
The regulation torments of that camp
Yolek was sent to, his small, unfinished meal,
The electric fences, the numeral tattoo,
The quite extraordinary heat of the day
They all were forced to take that terrible walk.

Whether on a silent, solitary walk
Or among crowds, far off or safe at home,
You will remember, helplessly, that day,
And the smell of smoke, and the loudspeakers of the camp.
Wherever you are, Yolek will be there, too.
His unuttered name will interrupt your meal.

Prepare to receive him in your home some day.
Though they killed him in the camp they sent him to,
He will walk in as you're sitting down to a meal.

1990

To Fortuna Parvulorum

> Young men have strong passions, and tend to gratify them indiscriminately . . . they show absence of self-control . . . they are hot tempered. Their lives are mainly spent not in memory but in expectation . . . The character of Elderly Men [is different]. They have lived many years; they have often been taken in, and often made mistakes; and life on the whole is a bad business.
>
> ARISTOTLE, *Rhetoric*, II, 12.

As a young man I was headstrong, willful, rash,
    Determined to amaze,
Grandly indifferent to comfort as to cash,
Past Envy's sneer, past Age's toothless gnash,
    Boldly I went my ways.

Then I matured. I sacrificed the years
    Lost in impetuous folly
To calm Prudentia, paying my arrears
For heedlessness in the cautious coin of fears
    And studious melancholy.

Now, having passed the obligatory stations,
    I turn in turn to you,
Divinity of diminished expectations,

To whom I direct these tardy supplications,
    Having been taught how few

Are blessed enough to encounter on their way
    The least chipped glint of joy,
And learned in what altered tones I hear today
The remembered words, "*Messieurs, les jeux sont faits,*"
    That stirred me as a boy.

1996

RICHARD HUGO (1923–1982)

Richard Hugo was born in White Center, Washington, a suburb of Seattle. He flew thirty-five missions as a bombardier in the Army Air Corps during World War II. In 1972 he met Charles Simic, whose native Belgrade he had bombed. In his "Letter to Simic from Boulder," he wrote, "We were after a bridge on the Danube / hoping to cut the German armies off as they fled north / from Greece. We missed." After the war, Hugo worked for Boeing for twelve years as a technical writer, composing poetry on his own time. In 1964 he joined the faculty of the University of Montana. His signature poems are set in desolate ghost towns of the Pacific Northwest. He died of leukemia in October 1982.

Montesano Unvisited

With houses hung that slanted and remote
the road that goes there if you found it
would be dangerous and dirt. Dust would cake
the ox you drive by and you couldn't meet
the peasant stare that drills you black. Birds
might be at home but rain would feel rejected
in the rapid drain and wind would bank off
fast without a friend to stars. Inside
the convent they must really mean those prayers.

You never find the road. You pass the cemetery,
military, British, World War Two and huge.
Maybe your car will die and the garage
you go to will be out of parts. The hotel
you have to stay in may have postcard shots,
deep focus stuff, of graves close up
and far off, just as clear, the bright town
that is someone's grave. Towns are bad things happening,
a spear elected mayor, a whip ordained.
You know in that town there's a beautiful girl
you'd rescue if your horse could run.

When your car is fixed you head on north
sticking with the highway, telling yourself
if you'd gone it would have been no fun.
Mountain towns are lovely, hung way away
like that, throbbing in light. But stay in one
two hours. You pat your car and say
let's go, friend. You drive off never hearing
the bruised girl in the convent screaming
take me with you. I am not a nun.

1969

Degrees of Gray in Philipsburg

You might come here Sunday on a whim.
Say your life broke down. The last good kiss
you had was years ago. You walk these streets
laid out by the insane, past hotels
that didn't last, bars that did, the tortured try
of local drivers to accelerate their lives.
Only churches are kept up. The jail
turned 70 this year. The only prisoner
is always in, not knowing what he's done.

The principal supporting business now
is rage. Hatred of the various grays
the mountain sends, hatred of the mill,
The Silver Bill repeal, the best liked girls
who leave each year for Butte. One good
restaurant and bars can't wipe the boredom out.
The 1907 boom, eight going silver mines,
a dance floor built on springs —
all memory resolves itself in gaze,
in panoramic green you know the cattle eat
or two stacks high above the town,
two dead kilns, the huge mill in collapse
for fifty years that won't fall finally down.

Isn't this your life? That ancient kiss
still burning out your eyes? Isn't this defeat
so accurate, the church bell simply seems
a pure announcement: ring and no one comes?
Don't empty houses ring? Are magnesium
and scorn sufficient to support a town,
not just Philipsburg, but towns
of towering blondes, good jazz and booze
the world will never let you have
until the town you came from dies inside?

Say no to yourself. The old man, twenty
when the jail was built, still laughs
although his lips collapse. Someday soon,
he says, I'll go to sleep and not wake up.
You tell him no. You're talking to yourself.
The car that brought you here still runs.
The money you buy lunch with,
no matter where it's mined, is silver
and the girl who serves you food
is slender and her red hair lights the wall.

1973

DENISE LEVERTOV (1923–1997)

Denise Levertov was born in Ilford, Essex, England. Her father and mother were descendants of a Hassidic rabbi and a Welsh mystic, a dual heritage Levertov acknowledges in her poem "Illustrious Ancestors." She served as a nurse in London during World War II, married an American, moved to the United States, and eventually became a naturalized American citizen. She took an active part in leftist political causes and argued, in poetry, for "organic form" rather than received verse structures. "I read the end of a line, the line break, as roughly equivalent to half a comma," she said. Levertov died from complications of lymphoma in December 1997.

Illustrious Ancestors

The Rav
of Northern White Russia declined,
in his youth, to learn the
language of birds, because
the extraneous did not interest him; nevertheless
when he grew old it was found
he understood them anyway, having
listened well, and as it is said, "prayed
                                        with the bench and the floor." He used
what was at hand — as did
Angel Jones of Mold, whose meditations
were sewn into coats and britches.
                                        Well, I would like to make,
thinking some line still taut between me and them,
poems direct as what the birds said,
hard as a floor, sound as a bench,
mysterious as the silence when the tailor
would pause with his needle in the air.

1961

The Ache of Marriage

The ache of marriage:

thigh and tongue, beloved,
are heavy with it,
it throbs in the teeth

We look for communion
and are turned away, beloved,
each and each

It is leviathan and we
in its belly
looking for joy, some joy
not to be known outside it

two by two in the ark of
the ache of it.

1964

The Mutes

Those groans men use
passing a woman on the street
or on the steps of the subway

to tell her she is a female
and their flesh knows it,

are they a sort of tune,
an ugly enough song, sung
by a bird with a slit tongue

but meant for music?

Or are they the muffled roaring
of deafmutes trapped in a building that is
slowly filling with smoke?

Perhaps both.
Such men most often

look as if groan were all they could do,
yet a woman, in spite of herself,

knows it's a tribute:
if she were lacking all grace
they'd pass her in silence:

so it's not only to say she's
a warm hole. It's a word

in grief-language, nothing to do with
primitive, not an ur-language;
language stricken, sickened, cast down

in decrepitude. She wants to
throw the tribute away, dis-
gusted, and can't,

it goes on buzzing in her ear,
it changes the pace of her walk,
the torn posters in echoing corridors

spell it out, it
quakes and gnashes as the train comes in.
Her pulse sullenly

had picked up speed,
but the cars slow down and
jar to a stop while her understanding

keeps on translating:
"Life after life after life goes by

without poetry,
without seemliness,
without love."

1967

Abel's Bride

Woman fears for man, he goes
out alone to his labors. No mirror
nests in his pocket. His face
opens and shuts with his hopes.
His sex hangs unhidden
or rises before him
blind and questing.

She thinks herself
lucky. But sad. When she goes out

she looks in the glass, she remembers
herself. Stones, coal,
the hiss of water upon the kindled
branches — her being
is a cave, there are bones at the hearth.

1967

JAMES SCHUYLER (1923–1991)

James Schuyler was born in Chicago. A key figure in the "New York school," he wrote two novels and collaborated with John Ashbery on a third. In a statement written in 1959 for Donald Allen's anthology *New American Poetry*, Schuyler noted that New York City poets "are affected most by the floods of paint in whose crashing surf we all scramble." He also argued that "the best American writing is French rather than English oriented." Reviewing Schuyler's book *The Morning of the Poem* (1980), Howard Moss observed that "the title poem, in particular, is the work of a persistent romantic, and as American as apple pie; in fact, it sometimes reads like a perverse underground commentary on *Our Town.*" Not until 1988, when he was sixty-five, did the shy and emotionally unstable Schuyler give his first poetry reading. When Jorie Graham chose "Haze" for *The Best American Poetry 1990,* Schuyler wrote, "Like many other of my poems, this is about what can be seen out the window: except here, though nothing is said about it, the poem combines the view from two windows, and several times of day. I do not usually take such license."

A White City

My thoughts turn south
a white city
we will wake in one another's arms.
I wake
and hear the steampipe knock
like a metal heart
and find it has snowed.

1969

Things to Do

Balance checkbook.
Rid lawn of onion grass.
"this patented device"
"this herbicide"
"Sir, We find none of these
killers truly satisfactory. Hand weed
for onion grass." Give

old clothes away, "such as you
yourself would willingly wear."
Impasse. Walk three miles
a day beginning tomorrow.
Alphabetize.
Purchase nose-hair shears.
Answer letters.
Elicit others.
Write Maxine.
Move to Maine.
Give up NoCal.
See more movies.
Practice long-distance dialing.
Ditto gymnastics:
The Beast with Two Backs
and, The Fan.
Complain to laundry
any laundry. Ask for borrowed books back.
Return
junk mail to sender
marked, Return to Sender.
Condole. Congratulate.
" . . . this sudden shock . . . "
" . . . this swift surprise . . . "
Send. Keep. Give. Destroy.
Brush rub polish burn
mend scratch foil evert
emulate surpass. Remember
"to write three-act play"
and lead "a full and active life."

1977

Korean mums

beside me in this garden
are huge and daisy-like
(why not? are not
oxeye daisies a chrysanthemum?),
shrubby and thick-stalked,
the leaves pointing up
the stems from which
the flowers burst in
sunbursts. I love
this garden in all its moods,
even under its winter coat
of salt hay, or now,
in October, more than

half gone over: here
a rose, there a clump
of aconite. This morning
one of the dogs killed
a barn owl. Bob saw
it happen, tried to
intervene. The airedale
snapped its neck and left
it lying. Now the bird
lies buried by an apple
tree. Last evening
from the table we saw
the owl, huge in the dusk,
circling the field
on owl-silent wings.
The first one ever seen
here: now it's gone,
a dream you just remember.

The dogs are barking. In
the studio music plays
and Bob and Darragh paint.
I sit scribbling in a little
notebook at a garden table,
too hot in a heavy shirt
in the mid-October sun
into which the Korean mums
all face. There is a
dull book with me,
an apple core, cigarettes,
an ashtray. Behind me
the rue I gave Bob
flourishes. Light on leaves,
so much to see, and
all I really see is that
owl, its bulk troubling
the twilight. I'll
soon forget it: what
is there I have not forgot?
Or one day will forget:
this garden, the breeze
in stillness, even
the words, Korean mums.

1980

Dec. 28, 1974

The plants against the light
which shines in (it's four o'clock)
right on my chair: I'm in my chair:
are silhouettes, barely green,
growing black as my eyes move right,
right to where the sun is.
I am blinded by a fiery circle:
I can't see what I write. A man
comes down iron stairs (I
don't look up) and picks up brushes
which, against a sonata of Scriabin's,
rattle like wind in a bamboo clump.
A wooden sound, and purposeful footsteps
softened by a drop-cloth-covered floor.
To be encubed in flaming splendor,
one foot on a Chinese rug, while
the mad emotive music
tears at my heart. Rip it open:
I want to cleanse it in an icy wind.
And what kind of tripe is that?
Still, last night I did wish —
no, that's my business and I
don't wish it now. "Your poems,"
a clunkhead said, "have grown
more open." I don't want to be open,
merely to say, to see and say, things
as they are. That at my elbow
there is a wicker table. *Hortus*
Second says a book. The fields
beyond the feeding sparrows are
brown, palely brown yet with an inward glow
like that of someone of a frank good nature
whom you trust. I want to hear the music
hanging in the air and drink my
Coca-Cola. The sun is off me now,
the sky begins to color up, the air
in here is filled with wildly flying notes.
Yes, the sun moves off to the right
and prepares to sink, setting,
beyond the dunes, an ocean on fire.

1980

Dining Out with Doug and Frank

for Frank Polach

Not quite yet. First,
around the corner for a visit

to the Bella Landauer Collection
of printed ephemera:
luscious lithos and why did
Fairy Soap vanish and
Crouch and Fitzgerald survive?
Fairy Soap was once a
household word! I've been living
at Broadway and West 74th
for a week and still haven't
ventured on a stroll in
Central Park, two bizarre blocks
away. (Bizarre is for the ex-
town houses, mixing Byzantine
with Gothic and Queen Anne.)
My abstention from the Park
is for Billy Nichols who went
bird-watching there and, for
his binoculars, got his
head beat in. Streaming blood,
he made it to an avenue
where no cab would pick him up
until one did and at
Roosevelt Hospital he waited
several hours before any
doctor took him in hand. A
year later he was dead. But
I'll make the park: I carry
more cash than I should and
walk the street at night
without feeling scared unless
someone scary passes.

II

Now it's tomorrow,
as usual. Turned out that
Doug (Douglas Crase, the poet)
had to work (he makes his bread
writing speeches): thirty pages
explaining why Eastman Kodak's
semi-slump (?) is just what
the stockholders ordered. He
looked glum, and declined
a drink. By the by did you know
that John Ashbery's grandfather
was offered an investment-in
when George Eastman founded his
great corporation? He turned it

down. Eastman Kodak will survive.
"Yes" and where would our
John be now? I can't imagine him
any different than he is,
a problem which does not arise,
so I went with Frank (the poet,
he makes his dough as a librarian,
botanical librarian at Rutgers
and as a worker he's a beaver:
up at 5:30, home after 7, but
over striped bass he said he
had begun to see the unwisdom
of his ways and next week will
revert to the seven-hour day
for which he's paid. Good. Time
and energy to write. Poetry
takes it out of you, or you
have to have a surge to bring
to it. Words. So useful and
pleasant) to dine at McFeely's
at West 23rd and Eleventh Avenue
by the West River, which is
the right name for the Hudson
when it bifurcates from
the East River to create
Manhattan "an isle of joy."
Take my word for it, don't
(shall I tell you about my
friend who effectively threw
himself under a train in
the Times Square station?
No. Too tender to touch. In
fact, at the moment I've blocked
out his name. No I haven't:
Peter Kemeny, gifted and tormented
fat man) listen to anyone
else.

III

Oh. At the Battery all
that water becomes the
North River, which seems
to me to make no sense
at all. I always thought
Castle Garden faced Calais.

IV

Peconic Bay scallops, the
tiny, the real ones and cooked

in butter, not breaded and
plunged in deep grease. The food
is good and reasonable (for these
days) but the point is McFeely's
itself — the owner's name or
was it always called that? It's
the bar of the old Terminal Hotel
and someone (McFeely?) has had
the wit to restore it to what
it was: all was there, under
layers of paint and abuse, neglect.
You, perhaps, could put a date
on it: I'll vote for 1881
or the 70's. The ceiling
is florid glass, like the cabbage-rose
runners in the grand old hotels
at Saratoga: when were they built?
The bar is thick and long and
sinuous, virile. Mirrors: are
the decorations on them cut
or etched? I do remember that
above the men's room door the
word Toilet is etched
on a transom. Beautiful lettering,
but nothing to what lurks
within: the three most
splendid urinals I've ever
seen. Like Roman steles. I
don't know what I was going
to say. Yes. Does the Terminal Hotel
itself still function? (Did you
know that "they" sold all the
old mirror glass out of Gage
and Tollner's? Donald Droll has
a fit every time he eats there.)
"Terminal," I surmise, because
the hotel faced the terminal
of the 23rd Street ferry, a
perfect sunset sail to Hoboken
and the yummies of the Clam
Broth House, which, thank God,
still survives. Not many do:
Gage and Tollner's, the Clam Broth House,
McSorley's and now McFeely's. Was
that the most beautiful of the
ferry houses or am I thinking
of Christopher Street? And there
was another uptown that crossed
to Jersey and back but docking

further downtown: it sailed
on two diagonals. And wasn't
there one at 42nd? It couldn't
matter less, they're gone, all
gone and we are left with just
the Staten Island ferry, all
right in its way but how often
do you want to pass Miss Liberty
and see that awesome spiky postcard
view? The river ferryboats were
squat and low like tugs, old
and wooden and handsome, you
were *in* the water, *in* the shipping:
Millay wrote a lovely poem about
it all. I cannot accept their
death, or any other death. Bill
Aalto, my first lover (five tumultuous
years found Bill chasing me around
the kitchen table — in Wystan Auden's
house in Forio d'Ischia — with
a carving knife. He was serious
and so was I and so I wouldn't go
when he wanted to see me when
he was dying of leukemia. Am I
sorry? Not really. The fear had
gone too deep. The last time I
saw him was in the City Center lobby
and he was jolly — if he just
stared at you and the tears began
it was time to cut and run —
and the cancer had made him lose
a lot of weight and he looked
young and handsome as the night
we picked each other up
in Pop Tunick's long-gone gay bar.
Bill never let me forget that
on the jukebox I kept playing
Lena Horne's "Mad about the Boy."
Why the nagging teasing? It's
a great performance but he
thought it was East Fifties queen
taste. Funny — or, funnily enough —
in dreams, and I dream about him
a lot, he's always the nice guy
I first knew and loved, not
the figure of terror he became.
Oh well. Bill had his hour: he
was a hero, a major in the
Abraham Lincoln Brigade. A dark

Finn who looked not unlike
a butch version of Valentino.
Watch out for Finns. They're
murder when they drink) used
to ride the ferries all the
time, doing the bars along
the waterfront: did you know
that Hoboken has — or had —
more bars to the square inch
(Death. At least twice when
someone I knew and hated
died I felt the joy of vengeance:
I mean I smiled and laughed out
loud: a hateful feeling.
It passes.) to the square inch
than any other city? "Trivia,
Goddess . . . " Through dinner
I wanted to talk more than we
did about Frank's poems. All it
came down to was "experiment
more," "try collages," and "write
some skinny poems" but I like
where he's heading now and
Creative Writing has never
been my trip although I understand
the fun of teaching someone
something fun to do although most people
simply have not got the gift
and where's the point? What
puzzles me is what my friends
find to say. Oh forget it. Reading,
writing, knowing other poets
will do it, if there is
anything doing. The reams
of shit I've read. It would
have been so nice after dinner
to take a ferry boat with Frank
across the Hudson (or West River,
if you prefer). To be on
the water in the dark and
the wonder of electricity —
the real beauty of Manhattan.
Oh well. When they tore down
the Singer Building,
and when I saw the Bogardus building
rusty and coming unstitched in
a battlefield of rubble I deliberately
withdrew my emotional investments
in loving old New York. Except

you can't. I really like
dining out and last night was
especially fine. A full moon
when we parted hung over
Frank and me. Why is this poem
so long? And full of death?
Frank and Doug are young and
beautiful and have nothing
to do with that. Why is this poem
so long? "Enough is as good
as a feast" and I'm a Herrick fan.
I'd like to take that plunge
into Central Park, only I'm
waiting for Darragh Park to phone.
Oh. Doug and Frank. One is light,
the other dark.
Doug is the tall one.

1980

Haze

hangs heavy
down into trees: dawn
doesn't break today,
the morning
seeps into being, one
bird, maybe
two, chipping
away at it. A white dahlia,
big
as Baby Bumstead's head,
leans
its folded petals
at a window, a lesson
in origami.
Frantically, God
knows what
machine: oh no,
just Maggio's
garbage truck.
Staring
at all the roughage
that hides an estuary,
such urbanity
seems inapt: the endless city
builds on and on

thinning out, here and there,
for the wet green velvet towels
("slight imperfections")
of summer
("moderately priced")
and a hazy morning
in August,
even that
we may grow to love.

1989

LOUIS SIMPSON (b. 1923)

Louis Simpson was born in Jamaica, the West Indies. He interrupted his studies at Columbia University to serve with the 101st Airborne Division on active duty in France, Holland, Belgium, and Germany during World War II. A paratrooper, he received two Purple Hearts and a Bronze Star for valor in battle. "The aim of military training is not just to prepare men for battle, but to make them long for it," he reflected. In 1957 he was coeditor with Donald Hall and Robert Pack of *The New Poets of England and America*, which, in the battle of the anthologies that helped define the direction of American poetry, represented the mainstream and was countered by Donald Allen's *The New American Poetry, 1945–1960*, which embraced the experimental, the rebellious, and the avant-garde. Simpson "caught the malaise of his contemporaries of the post war decade in a brief poem that gave it, and them, a name: 'The Silent Generation'" (Daniel Hoffman). Simpson began teaching at Berkeley in 1959, and later taught for many years at Stony Brook, Long Island.

The Silent Generation

When Hitler was the Devil
He did as he had sworn
With such enthusiasm
That even, *donnerwetter*,
The Germans say, "Far better
Had he been never born!"

It was my generation
That put the Devil down
With great enthusiasm.
But now our occupation
Is gone. Our education
Is wasted on the town.

We lack enthusiasm.
Life seems a mystery;

It's like the play a lady
Told me about: "It's not . . .
It doesn't *have* a plot,"
She said, "It's history."

1959

To the Western World

A siren sang, and Europe turned away
From the high castle and the shepherd's crook.
Three caravels went sailing to Cathay
On the strange ocean, and the captains shook
Their banners out across the Mexique Bay.

And in our early days we did the same.
Remembering our fathers in their wreck
We crossed the sea from Palos where they came
And saw, enormous to the little deck,
A shore in silence waiting for a name.

The treasures of Cathay were never found.
In this America, this wilderness
Where the axe echoes with a lonely sound,
The generations labor to possess
And grave by grave we civilize the ground.

1959

My Father in the Night Commanding No

My father in the night commanding No
Has work to do. Smoke issues from his lips;
    He reads in silence.
The frogs are croaking and the streetlamps glow.

And then my mother winds the gramophone;
The Bride of Lammermoor begins to shriek —
    Or reads a story
About a prince, a castle, and a dragon.

The moon is glittering above the hill.
I stand before the gateposts of the King —
    So runs the story —
Of Thule, at midnight when the mice are still.

And I have been in Thule! It has come true —
The journey and the danger of the world,

All that there is
To bear and to enjoy, endure and do.

Landscapes, seascapes . . . where have I been led?
The names of cities — Paris, Venice, Rome —
Held out their arms.
A feathered god, seductive, went ahead.

Here is my house. Under a red rose tree
A child is swinging; another gravely plays.
They are not surprised
That I am here; they were expecting me.

And yet my father sits and reads in silence,
My mother sheds a tear, the moon is still,
And the dark wind
Is murmuring that nothing ever happens.

Beyond his jurisdiction as I move
Do I not prove him wrong? And yet, it's true
They will not change
There, on the stage of terror and of love.

The actors in that playhouse always sit
In fixed positions — father, mother, child
With painted eyes.
How sad it is to be a little puppet!

Their heads are wooden. And you once pretended
To understand them! Shake them as you will,
They cannot speak.
Do what you will, the comedy is ended.

Father, why did you work? Why did you weep,
Mother? Was the story so important?
"*Listen!*" the wind
Said to the children, and they fell asleep.

1963

DONALD JUSTICE (1925–2004)

Donald Justice was born and grew up in Florida, where he studied music with the composer Carl Ruggles. In Justice's *Collected Poems*, published by some cosmic coincidence in the month of his death, you can hear the piano keys. An accomplished painter who composed music for his own pleasure, Justice balanced the demands of traditional stanzas and forms (including the extravagant sestina and the rigorous villanelle) with the attractions of the American idiom. In his work, desire has turned into nostalgia; many of his poems live or lurk "in the shadows," as he puts it at the close of his elegy "On the Death of Friends in Childhood." At the University of Iowa Writers' Workshop, where Justice taught for many years, his students included Mark Strand, Charles Wright, and Jorie Graham. Strand recalled that Justice was "courtly and controlled" when running a workshop and "emotional and competitive" when playing ping-pong, softball, or cards. "The games might last all right," Strand said. "And all the while we were writing poems."

On the Death of Friends in Childhood

We shall not ever meet them bearded in heaven,
Nor sunning themselves among the bald of hell;
If anywhere, in the deserted schoolyard at twilight,
Forming a ring, perhaps, or joining hands
In games whose very names we have forgotten.
Come, memory, let us seek them there in the shadows.

1960

But That Is Another Story

I do not think the ending can be right.
How can they marry and live happily
Forever, these who were so passionate
At chapter's end? Once they are settled in
The quiet country house, what will they do,
So many miles from anywhere?
Those blond ancestral ghosts crowding the stair,
Surely they disapprove? Ah me,
I fear love will catch cold and die
From pacing naked through those drafty halls
Night after night. Poor Frank! Poor Imogene!
Before them now their lives
Stretch empty as great Empire beds
After the lovers rise and the damp sheets
Are stripped by envious chambermaids.

And if the first night passes brightly enough,
What with the bonfires lit with old love letters,
That is no inexhaustible fuel, perhaps?
God knows how it must end, not I.
Will Frank walk out one day
Alone through the ruined orchard with his stick,
Strewing the path with lissome heads
Of buttercups? Will Imogene
Conceal in the crotches of old trees
Love notes for beardless gardeners and such?
Meanwhile they quarrel and make it up
Only to quarrel again. A sudden storm

Pulls the last fences down. Now moonstruck sheep
Stray through the garden all night peering in
At the exhausted lovers where they sleep.

1967

Men at Forty

Men at forty
Learn to close softly
The doors to rooms they will not be
Coming back to.

At rest on a stair landing,
They feel it moving
Beneath them now like the deck of a ship,
Though the swell is gentle.

And deep in mirrors
They rediscover
The face of the boy as he practices tying
His father's tie there in secret,

And the face of that father,
Still warm with the mystery of lather.
They are more fathers than sons themselves now.
Something is filling them, something

That is like the twilight sound
Of the crickets, immense,
Filling the woods at the foot of the slope
Behind their mortgaged houses.

1967

The Tourist From Syracuse

One of those men who can be a car salesman or a tourist from Syracuse or a hired assassin. —John D. Macdonald

You would not recognize me.
Mine is the face which blooms in
The dank mirrors of washrooms
As you grope for the light switch.

My eyes have the expression
Of the cold eyes of statues
Watching their pigeons return
From the feed you have scattered,

And I stand on my corner
With the same marble patience.
If I move at all, it is
At the same pace precisely

As the shade of the awning
Under which I stand waiting
And with whose blackness it seems
I am already blended.

I speak seldom, and always
In a murmur as quiet
As that of crowds which surround
The victims of accidents.

Shall I confess who I am?
My name is all names and none.
I am the used-car salesman,
The tourist from Syracuse,

The hired assassin, waiting.
I will stand here forever
Like one who has missed his bus —
Familiar, anonymous —

On my usual corner,
The corner at which you turn
To approach that place where now
You must not hope to arrive.

1967

Self-Portrait as Still Life

The newspaper on the table,
Confessing its lies.
The melon beside it,
Plump, unspoiled,

Trying to forget
That it was ever wrapped up
In anything so
Scandalous, so banal.

Already out, the knife,
Confident lover.
It smiles. It knows
How attractive it is

To sunlight. On the wall,
A guitar, in shadow,
Remembering hands . . .
I don't come into the picture.

Poets, O fellow exiles,
It's your scene now, and welcome.
You take up the guitar.
You cut up the melon.

But when are you going to
Roll up the newspaper, swat
The flies, take out all the garbage?
Mañana? Always mañana.

1973

In the Attic

There's a half hour toward dusk when flies,
Trapped by the summer screens, expire
Musically in the dust of sills;
And ceilings slope toward remembrance.

The same crimson afternoons expire
Over the same few rooftops repeatedly;
Only, being stored up for remembrance,
They somehow escape the ordinary.

Childhood is like that, repeatedly
Lost in the very longueurs it redeems.
One forgets how small and ordinary
The world looked once by dusklight from above . . .

But not the moment which redeems
The drowsy arias of the flies —
And the chin settles onto palms above
Numbed elbows propped on rotting sills.

1979

Villanelle at Sundown

Turn your head. Look. The light is turning yellow.
The river seems enriched thereby, not to say deepened.
Why this is, I'll never be able to tell you.

Or are Americans half in love with failure?
One used to say so, reading Fitzgerald, as it happened.
(That Viking Portable, all water-spotted and yellow —

Remember?) Or does mere distance lend a value
To things? — false it may be, but the view is hardly cheapened.
Why this is, I'll never be able to tell you.

The smoke, those tiny cars, the whole urban milieu —
One can like *any*thing diminishment has sharpened.
Our painter friend, Lang, might show the whole thing yellow

And not be much off. It's nuance that counts, not color —
As in some late James novel, saved up for the long weekend
And vivid with all the Master simply won't tell you.

How frail our generation has got, how sallow
And pinched with just surviving! We all go off the deep end
Finally, gold beaten thinly out to yellow.
And why this is, I'll never be able to tell you.

1987

CAROLYN KIZER (b. 1925)

Born in Spokane, Washington, and educated at Sarah Lawrence College, Carolyn Kizer became a fellow of the Chinese government at Columbia University and subsequently went to China, where her father directed Chinese relief. She was a founder of the poetry quarterly *Poetry Northwest*, and was the first director of literature for the National Endowment for the Arts. When Robert Bly chose "The Erotic Philosophers" for *The Best American Poetry 1999*, Kizer said that she had recently read a biography of Saint Augustine and was sitting in her Paris apartment when the phone rang. The caller asked if she was busy. "I'm just sitting here drinking kir and reading Kierkegaard," she recalls having replied, adding: "When I find myself talking pentameter — with rhymes — I know I'm in the throes of a poem."

Bitch

Now, when he and I meet, after all these years,
I say to the bitch inside me, don't start growling.
He isn't a trespasser anymore,
Just an old acquaintance tipping his hat.
My voice says, "Nice to see you,"
As the bitch starts to bark hysterically.
He isn't an enemy now,
Where are your manners, I say, as I say,

"How are the children? They must be growing up."
At a kind word from him, a look like the old days,
The bitch changes her tone: she begins to whimper.
She wants to snuggle up to him, to cringe.
Down, girl! Keep your distance
Or I'll give you a taste of the choke-chain.
"Fine, I'm just fine," I tell him.
She slobbers and grovels.
After all, I am her mistress. She is basically loyal.
It's just that she remembers how she came running
Each evening, when she heard his step;
How she lay at his feet and looked up adoringly
Though he was absorbed in his paper;
Or, bored with her devotion, ordered her to the kitchen
Until he was ready to play.
But the small careless kindnesses
When he'd had a good day, or a couple of drinks,
Come back to her now, seem more important
Than the casual cruelties, the ultimate dismissal.
"It's nice to know you are doing so well," I say.
He couldn't have taken you with him;
You were too demonstrative, too clumsy,
Not like the well-groomed pets of his new friends.
"Give my regards to your wife," I say. You gag
As I drag you off by the scruff,
Saying, "Good-bye! Good-bye! Nice to have seen you again."

1971

The Erotic Philosophers

It's a spring morning; sun pours in the window
As I sit here drinking coffee, reading Augustine.
And finding him, as always, newly minted
From when I first encountered him in school.
Today I'm overcome with astonishment
At the way we girls denied all that was mean
In those revered philosophers we studied;
Who found us loathsome, loathsomely seductive;
Irrelevant at best to noble discourse
Among the sex, the only sex that counted.
Wounded, we pretended not to mind it
And wore tight sweaters to tease our shy professor.

We sat in autumn sunshine "as the clouds arose
From slimy desires of the flesh, and from
Youth's seething spring." Thank you, Augustine.

Attempting to seem blasé, our cheeks on fire,
It didn't occur to us to rush from the room.
Instead, we brushed aside "the briars of unclean desire"
And struggled on through mires of misogyny
Till we arrived at Kierkegaard, and began to see
That though Saint A. and Søren had much in common
Including fear and trembling before women,
The Saint scared himself, while Søren was scared of *us*.
Had we, poor girls, been flattered by their thralldom?

Yes, it was always us, the rejected feminine
From whom temptation came. It was our flesh
With its deadly sweetness that led them on.
Yet how could we not treasure Augustine,
"stuck fast in the birdlime of pleasure"?
That roomful of adolescent poets manqué
Assuaged, bemused by music, let the meaning go.
Swept by those psalmic cadences, we were seduced!
Some of us tried for awhile to be well-trained souls
And pious seekers, enmeshed in the Saint's dialectic:
Responsible for our actions, yet utterly helpless.
A sensible girl would have barked like a dog before God.

We students, children still, were shocked to learn
The children these men desired were younger than we!
Augustine fancied a girl about eleven,
The age of Adeodatus, Augustine's son.
Søren, like Poe, eyed his girl before she was sixteen.
To impose his will on a malleable child, when
She was not equipped to withstand or understand him.
Ah, the Pygmalion instinct! Mold the clay!
Create the compliant doll that can only obey,
Expecting to be abandoned, minute by minute.
It was then I abandoned philosophy,
A minor loss, although I majored in it.

But we were a group of sunny innocents.
I don't believe we knew what evil meant.
Now I live with a well-trained soul who deals with evil,
Including error, material or spiritual,
Easily, like changing a lock on the kitchen door.
He prays at set times and in chosen places
(at meals, in church), while I
Pray without thinking how or when to pray,
In a low mumble, several times a day,
Like running a continuous low fever;
The sexual impulse for the most part being over.
Believing I believe. Not banking on it ever.

It's afternoon. I sit here drinking kir
And reading Kierkegaard: "All sin begins with fear."
(True. We lie first from terror of our parents.)
In, I believe, an oblique crack at Augustine,
Søren said by denying the erotic
It was brought to the attention of the world.
The rainbow curtain rises on the sensual:
Christians must admit it before they can deny it.
He reflected on his father's fierce repression
Of the sexual, which had bent him out of shape:
Yet he had to pay obeisance to that power:
He chose his father when he broke with his Regina.

Søren said by denying the erotic
It is brought to the attention of the world.
You must admit it before you can deny it.
So much for "Repetition" — another theory
Which some assume evolved from his belief
He could replay his courtship of Regina
With a happy ending. Meanwhile she'd wait for him,
Eternally faithful, eternally seventeen.
Instead, within two years, the bitch got married.
In truth, he couldn't wait till he got rid of her,
To create from recollection, not from living;
To use the material, not the material girl.

I sip my kir, thinking of *Either/Or*,
Especially *Either*, starring poor Elvira.
He must have seen *Giovanni* a score of times,
And Søren knew the score.
He took Regina to the opera only once,
And as soon as Mozart's overture was over,
Kierkegaard stood up and said, "Now we are leaving.
You have heard the best: the expectation of pleasure."
In his interminable aria on the subject
SK insisted the performance *was* the play.
Was the overture then the foreplay? Poor Regina
Should have known she'd be left waiting in the lurch.

Though he chose a disguise in which to rhapsodize,
It was his voice too: Elvira's beauty
Would perish soon; the deflowered quickly fade:
A night-blooming cereus after Juan's one-night stand.
Søren, eyes clouded by romantic mist,
Portrayed Elvira always sweet sixteen.
SK's interpretation seems naive.
He didn't realize that innocent sopranos
Who are ready to sing Elvira, don't exist.
His diva may have had it off with Leporello

Just before curtain time, believing it freed her voice
(so backstage legend has it), and weakened his.

I saw La Stupenda sing Elvira once.
Her cloak was larger than an army tent.
Would Giovanni be engulfed when she inhaled?
Would the boards shiver when she stamped her foot?
Her voice of course was great. Innocent it was not.
Søren, long since, would have fallen in a faint.
When he, or his doppelgänger, wrote
That best-seller, "The Diary of a Seducer,"
He showed how little he knew of true Don Juans:
Those turgid letters, machinations and excursions,
Those tedious conversations with dull aunts,
Those convoluted efforts to get the girl!

Think of the worldly European readers
Who took Søren seriously, did not see
His was the cynicism of the timid virgin.
Once in my youth I knew a real Don Juan
Or he knew me. He didn't need to try,
The characteristic of a true seducer.
He seems vulnerable, shy; he hardly speaks.
Somehow you know he will never speak of you.
You trust him — and you thrust yourself at him.
He responds with an almost absent-minded grace.
Even before the consummation he's looking past you
For the next bright yearning pretty face.

Relieved at last of anxieties and tensions
When your terrible efforts to capture him are over,
You overflow with happy/unhappy languor.
But SK's alter ego believes the truly terrible
Is for you to be consoled by the love of another.
We women, deserted to a woman, have a duty
Rapidly to lose our looks, decline and die,
Our only chance of achieving romantic beauty.
So Augustine was sure, when Monica, his mother,
Made him put aside his nameless concubine
She'd get her to a nunnery, and pine.
He chose his mother when he broke with his beloved.

In Søren's long replay of his wrecked romance,
"Guilty/Not Guilty," he says he must tear himself away
From earthly love, and suffer to love God.
Augustine thought better: love, human therefore flawed,
Is the way to the love of God. To deny this truth
Is to be "left outside, breathing into the dust,
Filling the eyes with earth." We women,
Outside, breathing dust, are still the Other.

The evening sun goes down; time to fix dinner.
"*You women have no major philosophers.*" We know.
But we remain philosophic, and say with the Saint,
"Let me enter my chamber and sing my songs of love."

2001

KENNETH KOCH (1925–2002)

Kenneth Koch was born in Cincinnati, went to Harvard, and became a charter member of the "New York school" of poets. At Columbia, where he taught for nearly forty years, Koch's course in imaginative writing proved a college highlight for many future writers. He adapted his teaching techniques to the needs of elementary school children and elderly residents of nursing homes, and worked a minor revolution in pedagogy through such influential books as *Rose, Where Did You Get That Red?* (1973) and *I Never Told Anybody* (1977). When Koch's book *Straits* appeared in 1998, Tom Disch wrote that "the context in which Koch's poetry is to be read is not the Mainstream of Contemporary American Poetry, in which his conspicuous virtues scarcely figure: ribaldry and wit, musicianship, pitch-perfect mimicry of the Great Tradition, and the celebration of pleasure for its own sunlit sake." Of "To World War Two," Koch commented that he had not been able to write about his service as an infantryman in the Pacific until he thought of "the device of talking to World War Two as if it were a person — or at least someone or something that could understand what I said."

You Were Wearing

You were wearing your Edgar Allan Poe printed cotton blouse.
In each divided up square of the blouse was a picture of Edgar Allan Poe.
Your hair was blonde and you were cute. You asked me, "Do most boys think
  that most girls are bad?"
I smelled the mould of your seaside resort hotel bedroom on your hair held
  in place by a John Greenleaf Whittier clip.
"No," I said, "it's girls who think that boys are bad." Then we read
  Snowbound together.
And ran around in an attic, so that a little of the blue enamel was scraped off
  my George Washington, Father of His Country, shoes.

Mother was walking in the living room, her Strauss Waltzes comb in her hair.
We waited for a time and then joined her, only to be served tea in cups
  painted with pictures of Herman Melville.
As well as with illustrations from his book *Moby Dick* and from his novella,
  Benito Cereno.
Father came in wearing his Dick Tracy necktie: "How about a drink,
  everyone?"
I said, "Let's go outside a while." Then we went onto the porch and sat on
  the Abraham Lincoln swing.
You sat on the eyes, mouth, and beard part, and I sat on the knees.
In the yard across the street we saw a snowman holding a garbage can lid

smashed into a likeness of the mad English king, George the Third.

1962

Permanently

One day the Nouns were clustered in the street.
An Adjective walked by, with her dark beauty.
The Nouns were struck, moved, changed.
The next day a Verb drove up, and created the Sentence.

Each Sentence says one thing — for example, "Although it was a dark rainy day when the Adjective walked by, I shall remember the pure and sweet expression on her face until the day I perish from the green, effective earth."
Or, "Will you please close the window, Andrew?"
Or, for example, "Thank you, the pink pot of flowers on the window sill has changed color recently to a light yellow, due to the heat from the boiler factory which exists nearby."

In the springtime the Sentences and the Nouns lay silently on the grass.
A lonely Conjunction here and there would call, "And! But!"
But the Adjective did not emerge.

As the adjective is lost in the sentence,
So I am lost in your eyes, ears, nose, and throat —
You have enchanted me with a single kiss
Which can never be undone
Until the destruction of language.

1962

The Railway Stationery

The railway stationery lay upon
The desk of the railway clerk, from where he could see
The springtime and the tracks. Engraved upon
Each page was an inch-and-a-half-high T
And after that an H and then an E
And then, slightly below it to the right,
There was COLUMBUS RAILWAY COMPANY
In darker ink as the above was light.
The print was blue. And just beneath it all
There was an etching — not in blue, but black —
Of a real railway engine half-an-inch tall
Which, if you turned the paper on its back,
You could see showing through, as if it ran
To one edge of the sheet then back again.

To one edge of the sheet then back again!
The springtime comes while we're still drenched in snow
And, whistling now, snow-spotted Number Ten
Comes up the track and stops, and we must go
Outside to get its cargo, with our hands
Cold as the steel they touch. Inside once more
Once we have shut the splintery wooden door
Of the railway shack, the stationery demands
Some further notice. For the first time the light,
Reflected from the snow by the bright spring sun,
Shows that the engine wheel upon the right
Is slightly darker than the left-side one
And slightly lighter than the one in the center,
Which may have been an error of the printer.

Shuffling through many sheets of it to establish
Whether this difference is consistent will
Prove that it is not. Probably over-lavish
At the beginning with the ink, he still
(The printer) had the presence of mind to change
His operating process when he noticed
That on the wheels the ink had come out strange.
Because the windows of the shack are latticed
The light that falls upon the stationery
Is often interrupted by straight lines
Which shade the etching. Now the words "Dear Mary"
Appear below the engine on one sheet
Followed by a number of other conventional signs,
Among which are "our love," "one kiss," and "sweet."

The clerk then signs his name — his name is Johnson,
But all he signs is Bill, with a large B
Which overflows its boundaries like a Ronson
With too much fluid in it, which you see
Often, and it can burn you, though the *i*
Was very small and had a tiny dot.
The *l*'s were different — the first was high,
The second fairly low. And there was a spot
Of ink at the end of the signature which served
To emphasize that the letter was complete.
On the whole, one could say his writing swerved
More than the average, although it was neat.
He'd used a blue-black ink, a standing pen,
Which now he stuck back in its stand again.

Smiling and sighing, he opened up a drawer
And took an envelope out, which then he sealed
After he'd read the letter three times more
And folded it and put it in. A field

Covered with snow, untouched by man, is what
The envelope resembled, till he placed
A square with perforated edges that
Pictured a white-haired President, who faced
The viewer, in its corner, where it stuck
After he'd kissed its back and held it hard
Against the envelope. Now came the truck
Of the postman "Hello, Jim." "Hello there, Bill."
"I've got this — can you take it?" "Sure, I will!"

Now the snow fell down gently from the sky.
Strange wonder — snow in spring! Bill walked into
The shack again and wrote the letter *I*
Idly upon a sheet of paper. New
Ideas for writing Mary filled his mind,
But he resisted — there was work to do.
For in the distance he could hear the grind
Of the Seventy-Eight, whose engine was half blue;
So, putting on a cap, he went outside
On the tracks side, to wait for it to come.
It was the Seventy-Eight which now supplied
The city with most of its produce, although some
Came in by truck and some was grown in town.
Now it screams closer, and he flags it down.

1962

Variations on a Theme by William Carlos Williams

I

I chopped down the house that you had been saving to live in next summer.
I am sorry, but it was morning, and I had nothing to do
and its wooden beams were so inviting.

II

We laughed at the hollyhocks together
and then I sprayed them with lye.
Forgive me. I simply do not know what I am doing.

III

I gave away the money that you had been saving to live on for the
next ten years.
The man who asked for it was shabby
and the firm March wind on the porch was so juicy and cold.

IV

Last evening we went dancing and I broke your leg.

Forgive me. I was clumsy, and
I wanted you here in the wards, where I am the doctor!

1962

The Circus

I

We will have to go away, said the girls in the circus
And never come back any more. There is not enough of an audience
In this little town. Waiting against the black, blue sky
The big circus chariots took them into their entrances.
The light rang out over the hill where the circus wagons dimmed away.
Underneath their dresses the circus girls were sweating,
But then, an orange tight sticking to her, one spoke with
Blue eyes, she was young and pretty, blonde
With bright eyes, and she spoke with her mouth open when she sneezed
Lightly against the backs of the other girls waiting in line
To clock the rope, or come spinning down with her teeth on the line,
And she said that the circus might leave — and red posters
Stuck to the outside of the wagon, it was beginning to
Rain — she said might leave but not her heart would ever leave
Not that town but just any one where they had been, risking their lives,
And that each place they were should be celebrated by blue rosemary
In a patch, in the town. But they laughed and said Sentimental
Blonde, and she laughed, and they all, circus girls, clinging
To each other as the circus wagons rushed through the night.

II

In the next wagon, the one forward of theirs, the next wagon
Was the elephants' wagon. A grey trunk dragged on the floor . . .

III

Orville the Midget tramped up and down. Paul the Separated Man
Leaped forward. It rained and rained. Some people in the cities
Where they passed through were sitting behind thick glass
Windows, talking about their brats and drinking chocolate syrup.

IV

Minnie the Rabbit fingered her machine gun.
The bright day was golden.
She aimed the immense pine needle at the foxes
Thinking Now they will never hurt my tribe any more.

V

The circus wagons stopped during the night

For eighteen minutes in a little town called Rosebud, Nebraska.
It was after dinner it was after bedtime it was after nausea it was
After lunchroom. The girls came out and touched each other and had fun
And just had time to get a breath of the fresh air of the night in
Before the ungodly procession began once more down the purple highway.

VI

With what pomp and ceremony the circus arrived orange and red in the dawn!
It was exhausted, cars and wagons, and it lay down and leaped
Forward a little bit, like a fox. Minnie the Rabbit shot a little woolen bullet at it,
And just then the elephant man came to his doorway in the sunlight and stood still.

VII

The snoring circus master wakes up, he takes it on himself to arrange the circus.
Soon the big tent floats high. Birds sing on the tent.
The parade girls and the living statue girls and the trapeze girls
Cover their sweet young bodies with phosphorescent paint.
Some of the circus girls are older women, but each is beautiful.
They stand, waiting for their cues, at the doorway of the tent.
The sky-blue lion tamer comes in, and the red giraffe manager.
They are very brave and wistful, and they look at the girls.
Some of the circus girls feel a hot sweet longing in their bodies.
But now is it time for the elephants!
Slowly the giant beasts march in. Some of their legs are clothed in papier-mâché ruffles.
One has a red eye. The elephant man is at the peak of happiness.
He speaks, giddily, to every one of the circus people he passes,
He does not know what he is saying, he does not care —
His elephants are on display! They walk into the sandy ring . . .

VIII

Suddenly a great scream breaks out in the circus tent!
It is Aileen the trapeze artist, she has fallen into the dust and dirt
From so high! She must be dead! The stretcher bearers rush out,
They see her lovely human form clothed in red and white and orange wiry net,
And they see that she does not breathe any more.
The circus doctor leaves his tent, he runs out to care for Aileen.
He traverses the circus grounds and the dusty floor of the circus entrance and he comes
Where she is, now she has begun to move again, she is not dead,

But the doctor tells her he does not know if she will ever be able to perform on the trapeze again,
And he sees the beautiful orange and red and white form shaken with sobs,
And he puts his hand on her forehead and tells her she must lie still.

IX

The circus girls form a cortege, they stand in file in the yellow and white sunlight.
"What is death in the circus? That depends on if it is spring.
Then, if elephants are there, *mon père,* we are not completely lost.
Oh the sweet strong odor of beasts which laughs at decay!
Decay! decay! We are like the elements in a kaleidoscope,
But such passions we feel! bigger than beaches and
Rustier than harpoons." After his speech the circus practitioner sat down.

X

Minnie the Rabbit felt the blood leaving her little body
As she lay in the snow, orange and red and white,
A beautiful design. The dog laughs, his tongue hangs out, he looks at the sky.
It is white. The master comes. He laughs. He picks up Minnie the Rabbit
And ties her to a pine tree bough, and leaves.

XI

Soon through the forest came the impassioned bumble bee.
He saw the white form on the bough. "Like rosebuds when you are thirteen," said Elmer.
Iris noticed that he didn't have any cap on.
"You must be polite when mother comes," she said.
The sky began to get grey, then the snow came.
The two tots pressed together. Elmer opened his mouth and let the snow fall in it. Iris felt warm and happy.

XII

Bang! went the flyswatter. Mr. Watkins, the circus manager, looked around the room.
"Damn it, damn these flies!" he said. Mr. Loftus, the circus clerk, stared at the fly interior he had just exposed.
The circus doctor stood beside the lake. In his hand he had a black briefcase.
A wind ruffled the surface of the lake and slightly rocked the boats.

Red and green fish swam beneath the surface of the water.
The doctor went into the lunchroom and sat down. No, he said, he didn't care for anything to eat.
The soft wind of summer blew in the light green trees.

1962

The Circus

I remember when I wrote The Circus
I was living in Paris, or rather we were living in Paris
Janice, Frank was alive, the Whitney Museum
Was still on 8th Street, or was it still something else?
Fernand Léger lived in our building
Well it wasn't really our building it was the building we lived in
Next to a Grand Guignol troupe who made a lot of noise
So that one day I yelled through a hole in the wall
Of our apartment I don't know why there was a hole there
Shut up! And the voice came back to me saying something
I don't know what. Once I saw Léger walk out of the building
I think. Stanley Kunitz came to dinner. I wrote The Circus
In two tries, the first getting most of the first stanza;
That fall I also wrote an opera libretto called Louisa or Matilda.
Jean-Claude came to dinner. He said (about "cocktail sauce")
It should be good on something but not on these (oysters).
By that time I think I had already written The Circus.
Part of the inspiration came while walking to the post office one night
And I wrote a big segment of The Circus
When I came back, having been annoyed to have to go
I forget what I went there about
You were back in the apartment what a dump actually we liked it
I think with your hair and your writing and the pans
Moving strummingly about the kitchen and I wrote The Circus
It was a summer night no it was an autumn one summer when
I remember it but actually no autumn that black dusk toward the post office
And I wrote many other poems then but The Circus was the best
Maybe not by far the best Geography was also wonderful
And the Airplane Betty poems (inspired by you) but The Circus was the best.

Sometimes I feel I actually am the person
Who did this, who wrote that, including that poem The Circus
But sometimes on the other hand I don't.
There are so many factors engaging our attention!
At every moment the happiness of others, the health of those we know and our own!
And the millions upon millions of people we don't know and their well-being to think about
So it seems strange I found time to write The Circus
And even spent two evenings on it, and that I have also the time
To remember that I did it, and remember you and me then, and write this poem about it.
At the beginning of The Circus
The Circus girls are rushing through the night

In the circus wagons and tulips and other flowers will be picked
A long time from now this poem wants to get off on its own
Someplace like a painting not held to a depiction of composing The
Circus.

Noel Lee was in Paris then but usually out of it
In Germany or Denmark giving a concert
As part of an endless activity
Which was either his career or his happiness or a combination of both
Or neither I remember his dark eyes looking he was nervous
With me perhaps because of our days at Harvard.

It is understandable enough to be nervous with anybody!

How softly and easily one feels when alone
Love of one's friends when one is commanding the time and space
syndrome
If that's the right word which I doubt but together how come one is so
nervous?
One is not always but what was I then and what am I now attempting
to create
If create is the right word
Out of this combination of experience and aloneness
And who are you telling me it is or is not a poem (not you)? Go back
with me though
To those nights I was writing The Circus.
Do you like that poem? have you read it? It is in my book Thank You
Which Grove just reprinted. I wonder how long I am going to live
And what the rest will be like I mean the rest of my life.

John Cage said to me the other night How old are you? and I told him
forty-six
(Since then I've become forty-seven) he said
Oh that's a great age I remember.
John Cage once told me he didn't charge much for his mushroom
identification course (at the New School)
Because he didn't want to make a profit from nature.

He was ahead of his time I was behind my time we were both in time
Brilliant go to the head of the class and "time is a river"
It doesn't seem like a river to me it seems like an unformed plan
Days go by and still nothing is decided about
What to do until you know it never will be and then you say "time"
But you really don't care much about it any more
Time means something when you have the major part of yours ahead of
you
As I did in Aix-en-Provence that was three years before I wrote The
Circus

That year I wrote Bricks and The Great Atlantic Rainway
I felt time surround me like a blanket endless and soft
I could go to sleep endlessly and wake up and still be in it
But I treasured secretly the part of me that was individually changing
Like Noel Lee I was interested in my career
And still am but now it is like a town I don't want to leave
Not a tower I am climbing opposed by ferocious enemies.

I never mentioned my friends in my poems at the time I wrote The
Circus
Although they meant almost more than anything to me
Of this now for some time I've felt an attenuation
So I'm mentioning them maybe this will bring them back to me
Not them perhaps but what I felt about them
John Ashbery Jane Freilicher Larry Rivers Frank O'Hara
Their names alone bring tears to my eyes
As seeing Polly did last night.
It is beautiful at any time but the paradox is leaving it
In order to feel it when you've come back the sun has declined
And the people are merrier or else they've gone home altogether
And you are left alone well you put up with that your sureness is like
the sun
While you have it but when you don't its lack's a black and icy night. I
came home

And wrote The Circus that night, Janice. I didn't come and speak to you
And put my arm around you and ask you if you'd like to take a walk
Or go to the Cirque Medrano though that's what I wrote poems about
And am writing about that now, and now I'm alone

And this is not as good a poem as The Circus
And I wonder if any good will come of either of them all the same.

1975

One Train May Hide Another

(sign at a railroad crossing in Kenya)

In a poem, one line may hide another line,
As at a crossing, one train may hide another train.
That is, if you are waiting to cross
The tracks, wait to do it for one moment at
Least after the first train is gone. And so when you read
Wait until you have read the next line —
Then it is safe to go on reading.
In a family one sister may conceal another,
So, when you are courting, it's best to have them all in view

Otherwise in coming to find one you may love another.
One father or one brother may hide the man,
If you are a woman, whom you have been waiting to love.
So always standing in front of something the other
As words stand in front of objects, feelings, and ideas.
One wish may hide another. And one person's reputation may hide
The reputation of another. One dog may conceal another
On a lawn, so if you escape the first one you're not necessarily safe;
One lilac may hide another and then a lot of lilacs and on the Appia
Antica one tomb
May hide a number of other tombs. In love, one reproach may hide
another
One small complaint may hide a great one.
One injustice may hide another — one Colonial may hide another,
One blaring red uniform another, and another, a whole column. One
bath may hide another bath
As when, after bathing, one walks out into the rain
One idea may hide another: Life is simple
Hide Life is incredibly complex, as in the prose of Gertrude Stein
One sentence hides another and is another as well. And in the
laboratory
One invention may hide another invention,
One evening may hide another, one shadow, a nest of shadows.
One dark red, or one blue, or one purple — this is a painting
By someone after Matisse. One waits at the tracks until they pass,
These hidden doubles or, sometimes, likenesses. One identical twin
May hide the other. And there may be even more in there! The
obstetrician
Gazes at the Valley of the Var. We used to live there, my wife and I,
but
One life hid another life. And now she is gone and I am here.
A vivacious mother hides a gawky daughter. The daughter hides
Her own vivacious daughter in turn. They are in
A railway station and the daughter is holding a bag
Bigger than her mother's bag and successfully hides it.
In offering to pick up the daughter's bag one finds oneself confronted
by the mother's
And has to carry that one, too. So one hitchhiker
May deliberately hide another and one cup of coffee
Another, too, until one is over-excited. One love may hide another
love or the same love
As when "I love you" suddenly rings false and one discovers
The better love lingering behind, as when "I'm full of doubts"
Hides "I'm certain about something and it is that"
And one dream may hide another as is well known, always, too. In
the Garden of Eden
Adam and Eve may hide the real Adam and Eve.
Jerusalem may hide another Jerusalem.
When you come to something, stop to let it pass

So you can see what else is there. At home, no matter where,
Internal tracks pose dangers, too; one memory
Certainly hides another, that being what memory is all about,
The eternal reverse succession of contemplated entities. Reading
A Sentimental Journey look around
When you have finished, for *Tristam Shandy*, to see
If it is standing there, it should be, stronger
And more profound and theretofore hidden as Santa Maria Maggiore
May be hidden by similar churches inside Rome. One sidewalk
May hide another, as when you're asleep there, and
One song hide another song: for example "Stardust"
Hide "What Have They Done to the Rain?" Or vice versa. A
pounding upstairs
Hide the beating of drums. One friend may hide another, you sit at
the foot of a tree
With one and when, you get up to leave there is another
Whom you'd have preferred to talk to all along. One teacher,
One doctor, one ecstasy, one illness, one woman, one man
May hide another. Pause to let the first one pass.
You think, Now it is safe to cross and you are hit by the next one.
It can be important
To have waited at least a moment to see what was already there.

1994

To World War Two

Early on you introduced me to young women in bars
You were large, and with a large hand
You presented them in different cities,
Made me in San Luis Obispo, drunk
On French seventy-fives, in Los Angeles, on pousse-cafés.
It was a time of general confusion
Of being a body hurled at a wall.
I didn't do much fighting. I sat, rather I stood, in a foxhole.
I stood while the typhoon splashed us into morning.
It felt unusual
Even if for a good cause
To be part of a destructive force
With my rifle in my hands
And in my head
My serial number
The entire object of my existence
To eliminate Japanese soldiers
By killing them
With a rifle or with a grenade

And then, many years after that,
I could write poetry
Fall in love
And have a daughter
And think
About these things
From a great distance
If I survived
I was "paying my debt
To society" a paid
Killer. It wasn't
Like anything I'd done
Before, on the paved
Streets of Cincinnati
Or on the ballroom floor
At Mr. Vathé's dancing class
What would Anne Marie Goldsmith
Have thought of me
If instead of asking her to dance
I had put my BAR to my shoulder
And shot her in the face
I thought about her in my foxhole —
One, in a foxhole near me, has his throat cut during the night
We take more precautions but it is night and it is you.
The typhoon continues and so do you.
"I can't be killed — because of my poetry. I have to live on in order to write it."
I thought — even crazier thought, or just as crazy —
"If I'm killed while thinking of lines, it will be too corny
When it's reported" (I imagined it would be reported!)
So I kept thinking of lines of poetry. One that came to me on the beach in Leyte
Was "The surf comes in like masochistic lions."
I loved this terrible line. It was keeping me alive. My Uncle Leo wrote to me,
"You won't believe this, but someday you may wish
You were footloose and twenty on Leyte again." I have never wanted
To be on Leyte again,
With you, whispering into my ear,
"Go on and win me! Tomorrow you may not be alive,
So do it today!" How could anyone ever win you?
How many persons would I have had to kill
Even to begin to be a part of winning you?
You were too much for me, though I
Was older than you were and in camouflage. But for you
Who threw everything together, and had all the systems
Working for you all the time, this was trivial. If you could use me
You'd use me, and then forget. How else
Did I think you'd behave?
I'm glad you ended. I'm glad I didn't die. Or lose my mind.
As machines make ice

We made dead enemy soldiers, in
Dark jungle alleys, with weapons in our hands
That produced fire and kept going straight through
I was carrying one,
I who had gone about for years as a child
Praying God don't let there ever be another war
Or if there is, don't let me be in it. Well, I was in you.
All you cared about was existing and being won.
You died of a bomb blast in Nagasaki, and there were parades.

2000

Proverb

Les morts vont vite, the dead go fast, the next day absent!
Et les vivants sont dingues, the living are haywire.
Except for a few who grieve, life rapidly readjusts itself
The milliner trims the hat not thinking of the departed
The horse sweats and throws his stubborn rider to the earth
Uncaring if he has killed him or not
The thrown man rises. But now he knows that he is not going,
Not going fast, though he was close to having been gone.
The day after Caesar's death, there was a new, bustling Rome
The moment after the racehorse's death, a new one is sought for
 the stable
The second after a moth's death there are one or two hundred other
 moths
The month after Einstein's death the earth is inundated with new
 theories
Biographies are written to cover up the speed with which we go:
No more presence in the bedroom or waiting in the hall
Greeting to say hello with mixed emotions. The dead go quickly
Not knowing why they go or where they go. To die is human,
To come back divine. Roosevelt gives way to Truman
Suddenly in the empty White House a brave new voice resounds
And the wheelchaired captain has crossed the great divide.
Faster than memories, faster than old mythologies, faster than the
 speediest train.
Alexander of Macedon, on time!
Prudhomme on time, Gorbachev on time, the beloved and the lover
 on time!
Les morts vont vite. We living stand at the gate
And life goes on.

2002

JACK SPICER (1925–1965)

Born in Hollywood, Jack Spicer was a friend of Robert Duncan and, like him, was an important presence in the lively San Francisco poetry scene of the 1950s and 1960s. In 1957, in a "Letter to Federico Garcia Lorca" — the Spanish poet of *duende* who was killed two decades earlier during the Spanish Civil War — Spicer wrote, "A poet is a time mechanic not an embalmer." And, "I yell 'Shit' down a cliff at an ocean. Even in my lifetime the immediacy of that word will fade. It will be dead as 'Alas.' But if I put the real cliff and the real ocean into the poem, the word 'Shit' will ride along with them, travel the time-machine until cliffs and oceans disappear." At "The Place," a San Francisco bar, Spicer took part in "babble" competitions in which rival bards had to improvise their work into a microphone. He died an alcoholic. His last words were, "My vocabulary did this to me."

Improvisations on a Sentence by Poe

"Indefiniteness is an element of the true music."
The grand concord of what
Does not stoop to definition. The seagull
Alone on the pier cawing its head off
Over no fish, no other seagull,
No ocean. As absolutely devoid of meaning
As a French horn.
It is not even an orchestra. Concord
Alone on a pier. The grand concord of what
Does not stoop to definition. No fish
No other seagull, no ocean — the true
Music.

1958

A Book of Music

Coming at an end, the lovers
Are exhausted like two swimmers. Where
Did it end? There is no telling. No love is
Like an ocean with the dizzy procession of the waves' boundaries
From which two can emerge exhausted, nor long goodbye
Like death.
Coming at an end. Rather, I would say, like a length
Of coiled rope
Which does not disguise in the final twists of its lengths
Its endings.
But, you will say, we loved
And some parts of us loved
And the rest of us will remain

Two persons. Yes,
Poetry ends like a rope.

1958

Thing Language

This ocean, humiliating in its disguises
Tougher than anything.
No one listens to poetry. The ocean
Does not mean to be listened to. A drop
Or crash of water. It means
Nothing.
It
Is bread and butter
Pepper and salt. The death
That young men hope for. Aimlessly
It pounds the shore. White and aimless signals. No
One listens to poetry.

1965

Sporting Life

The trouble with comparing a poet with a radio is that radios don't develop scar tissue. The tubes burn out, or with a transistor, which most souls are, the battery or diagram burns out replaceable or not replaceable, but not like that punchdrunk fighter in the bar. The poet
Takes too many messages. The right to the ear that floored him in New Jersey. The right to say that he stood six rounds with a champion.
Then they sell beer or go on sporting commissions, or, if the scar tissue is too heavy, demonstrate in a bar where the invisible champions might not have hit him. Too many of them.
The poet is a radio. The poet is a liar. The poet is a counterpunching radio.
And those messages (God would not damn them) do not even know they are champions.

1965

A Red Wheelbarrow

Rest and look at this goddamned wheelbarrow. Whatever

It is. Dogs and crocodiles, sunlamps. Not
For their significance.
For their significant. For being human
The signs escape you. You, who aren't very bright
Are a signal for them. Not,
I mean, the dogs and crocodiles, sunlamps. Not
Their significance.

1968

A. R. Ammons (1926–2001)

Born and raised in rural North Carolina, the youngest of a tobacco farmer's three surviving children, Archie Randolph Ammons started writing poetry aboard a U.S. Navy destroyer escort in the South Pacific. He worked briefly as the principal of an elementary school in Cape Hatteras and later managed a biological glass factory in southern New Jersey. Beginning in 1964 he taught at Cornell University. Drawn to the philosophical question of the one and the many, he is constantly on the lookout for a unifying principle among minute and divergent particulars. "Corsons Inlet" is characteristically peripatetic, chronicling the poet's thoughts as he walks along the shore, where he celebrates fluid forms and disdains artificial enclosures. In many poems Ammons uses the colon as an all-purpose punctuation mark, with the effect that closure is continually postponed. In a review of Ammons's *Collected Poems* in 1973, John Ashbery contended that Ammons's poetry seemed "a much closer and more successful approximation of 'Action Painting' or art as process" than the work of "New York school" poets. Ammons writes in the American idiom, switches rapidly from high to low diction, and in one mood may remind his readers that "magnificent" in North Carolina comes out "maggie-went-a-fishing." But his sly wit does not obscure the visionary nature of his poetry, the aim to affirm the magnificence of creation, however lowly in appearance and dark in design. Asked what moved him to write poetry, Ammons commented tersely, "anxiety."

So I Said I Am Ezra

So I said I am Ezra
and the wind whipped my throat
gaming for the sounds of my voice
      I listened to the wind
go over my head and up into the night
Turning to the sea I said
            I am Ezra
but there were no echoes from the waves
The words were swallowed up
      in the voice of the surf
or leaping over swells

lost themselves oceanward
      Over the bleached and broken fields
I moved my feet and turning from the wind
      that ripped sheets of sand
      from the beach and threw them
      like seamists across the dunes
swayed as if the wind were taking me away
and said
            I am Ezra
As a word too much repeated
falls out of being
so I Ezra went out into the night
like a drift of sand
and splashed among the windy oats
that clutch the dunes
of unremembered seas

1955

Mansion

So it came time
      for me to cede myself
and I chose
the wind
      to be delivered to

The wind was glad
      and said it needed all
the body
it could get
      to show its motions with

and wanted to know
      willingly as I hoped it would
if it could do
something in return
      to show its gratitude

When the tree of my bones
      rises from the skin I said
come and whirlwinding
stroll my dust
      around the plain

so I can see
      how the ocotillo does
and how saguaro-wren is
and when you fall
      with evening

fall with me here
      where we can watch
the closing up of day
and think how morning breaks

1955

Still

I said I will find what is lowly
      and put the roots of my identity
      down there:
each day I'll wake up
and find the lowly nearby,
      a handy focus and reminder,
a ready measure of my significance,
the voice by which I would be heard,
the wills, the kinds of selfishness
      I could
freely adopt as my own:

but though I have looked everywhere,
      I can find nothing
      to give myself to:
      everything is

magnificent with existence, is in
surfeit of glory:
nothing is diminished,
nothing has been diminished for me:

I said what is more lowly than the grass:
      ah, underneath,
      a ground-crust of dry-burnt moss:
      I looked at it closely
and said this can be my habitat: but
nestling in I
found
      below the brown exterior
      green mechanisms beyond the intellect
awaiting resurrection in rain: so I got up

and ran saying there is nothing lowly in the universe:
I found a beggar:
he had stumps for legs: nobody was paying
him any attention: everybody went on by:
      I nestled in and found his life:
there, love shook his body like a devastation:

I said
    though I have looked everywhere
    I can find nothing lowly
    in the universe:

I whirled though transfigurations up and down,
transfigurations of size and shape and place:

    at one sudden point came still,
    stood in wonder:
moss, beggar, weed, tick, pine, self, magnificent
    with being!

1963

Corsons Inlet

I went for a walk over the dunes again this morning
to the sea,
then turned right along
  the surf
                rounded a naked headland
                and returned

  along the inlet shore:

it was muggy sunny, the wind from the sea steady and high,
crisp in the running sand,
    some breakthroughs of sun
  but after a bit

continuous overcast:

the walk liberating, I was released from forms,
from the perpendiculars,
    straight lines, blocks, boxes, binds
of thought
into the hues, shadings, rises, flowing bends and blends
        of sight:

                I allow myself eddies of meaning:
yield to a direction of significance
running
like a stream through the geography of my work:
  you can find
in my sayings

swerves of action
like the inlet's cutting edge:
there are dunes of motion,
organizations of grass, white sandy paths of remembrance
in the overall wandering of mirroring mind:

but Overall is beyond me: is the sum of these events
I cannot draw, the ledger I cannot keep, the accounting
beyond the account:

in nature there are few sharp lines: there are areas of
primrose
more or less dispersed;

disorderly orders of bayberry; between the rows
of dunes,
irregular swamps of reeds,
though not reeds alone, but grass, bayberry, yarrow, all . . .
predominantly reeds:

I have reached no conclusions, have erected no boundaries,
shutting out and shutting in, separating inside
from outside: I have
drawn no lines:
as

manifold events of sand
change the dune's shape that will not be the same shape
tomorrow,

so I am willing to go along, to accept
the becoming
thought, to stake off no beginnings or ends, establish
no walls:

by transitions the land falls from grassy dunes to creek
to undercreek: but there are no lines, though
change in that transition is clear
as any sharpness: but "sharpness" spread out,
allowed to occur over a wider range
than mental lines can keep:

the moon was full last night: today, low tide was low:
black shoals of mussels exposed to the risk
of air
and, earlier, of sun,
waved in and out with the waterline, waterline inexact,

caught always in the event of change:
    a young mottled gull stood free on the shoals
    and ate
to vomiting: another gull, squawking possession, cracked a crab,
picked out the entrails, swallowed the soft-shelled legs, a ruddy
turnstone running in to snatch leftover bits:

risk is full: every living thing in
siege: the demand is life, to keep life: the small
white blacklegged egret, how beautiful, quietly stalks and spears
  the shallows, darts to shore
            to stab — what? I couldn't
    see against the black mudflats — a frightened
    fiddler crab?

        the news to my left over the dunes and
reeds and bayberry clumps was
        fall: thousands of tree swallows
        gathering for flight:
        an order held
        in constant change: a congregation
rich with entropy: nevertheless, separable, noticeable
      as one event,
          not chaos: preparations for
flight from winter,
cheet, cheet, cheet, cheet, wings rifling the green clumps,
beaks
at the bayberries
  a perception full of wind, flight, curve,
  sound:
  the possibility of rule as the sum of rulelessness:
the "field" of action
with moving, incalculable center:

in the smaller view, order tight with shape:
blue tiny flowers on a leafless weed: carapace of crab:
snail shell:
      pulsations of order
      in the bellies of minnows: orders swallowed,
broken down, transferred through membranes
to strengthen larger orders: but in the large view, no
lines or changeless shapes: the working in and out, together
      and against, of millions of events: this,
            so that I make
            no form
            formlessness:

orders as summaries, as outcomes of actions override

or in some way result, not predictably (seeing me gain
the top of a dune,
the swallows
could take flight — some other fields of bayberry
        could enter fall
        berryless) and there is serenity:
        no arranged terror: no forcing of image, plan,
or thought:
no propaganda, no humbling of reality to precept:

terror pervades but is not arranged, all possibilities
of escape open: no route shut, except in
  the sudden loss of all routes:

        I see narrow orders, limited tightness, but will
not run to that easy victory:
        still around the looser, wider forces work:
        I will try
      to fasten into order enlarging grasps of disorder, widening
scope, but enjoying the freedom that
scope eludes my grasp, that there is no finality of vision,
that I have perceived nothing completely,
        that tomorrow a new walk is a new walk.

1965

Reflective

I found a
weed
that had a

mirror in it
and that
mirror

looked in at
a mirror
in

me that
had a
weed in it

1966

Cascadilla Falls

I went down by Cascadilla
Falls this
evening, the
stream below the falls,
and picked up a
handsized stone
kidney-shaped, testicular, and

thought all its motions into it,
the 800 mph earth spin,
the 190-million-mile yearly
displacement around the sun,
the overriding
grand
haul

of the galaxy with the 30,000
mph of where
the sun's going:
thought all the interweaving
motions
into myself: dropped

the stone to dead rest:
the stream from other motions
broke
rushing over it:
shelterless,
I turned

to the sky and stood still:
Oh
I do
not know where I am going
that I can live my life
by this single creek.

1970

Mountain Talk

I was going along a dusty highroad
when the mountain
across the way
turned me to its silence:

oh I said how come
I don't know your
massive symmetry and rest:
nevertheless, said the mountain,
would you want
to be
lodged here with
a changeless prospect, risen
to an unalterable view:
so I went on
counting my numberless fingers.

1970

The City Limits

When you consider the radiance, that it does not withhold
itself but pours its abundance without selection into every
nook and cranny not overhung or hidden; when you consider

that birds' bones make no awful noise against the light but
lie low in the light as in a high testimony; when you consider
the radiance, that it will look into the guiltiest

swervings of the weaving heart and bear itself upon them,
not flinching into disguise or darkening; when you consider
the abundance of such resource as illuminates the glow-blue

bodies and gold-skeined wings of flies swarming the dumped
guts of a natural slaughter or the coil of shit and in no
way winces from its storms of generosity; when you consider

that air or vacuum, snow or shale, squid or wolf, rose or lichen,
each is accepted into as much light as it will take, then
the heart moves roomier, the man stands and looks about, the

leaf does not increase itself above the grass, and the dark
work of the deepest cells is of a tune with May bushes
and fear lit by the breadth of such calmly turns to praise.

1971

Triphammer Bridge

I wonder what to mean by *sanctuary*, if a real or
apprehended place, as of a bell rung in a gold
surround, or as of silver roads along the beaches

of clouds seas don't break or black mountains
overspill; jail: ice here's shapelier than anything,
on the eaves massive, jawed along gorge ledges, solid

in the plastic blue boat fall left water in: if I
think the bitterest thing I can think of that seems like
reality, slickened back, hard, shocked by rip-high wind:

sanctuary, *sanctuary*, I say it over and over and the
word's sound is the one place to dwell: that's it, just
the sound, and the imagination of the sound — a place.

1972

Ballad

I want to know the unity in all things and the difference
between one thing and another
    I said to the willow
and asked what it wanted to know: the willow said it
wanted to know how to get rid of the wateroak
that was throwing it into shade every afternoon at 4 o'clock:
        that is a real problem I said I suppose
and the willow, once started, went right on saying
I can't take you for a friend because while you must
be interested in willowness, which you could find nowhere
    better than right here,
        I'll bet you're just as interested in wateroakness
which you can find in a pure form right over there,
a pure form of evil and death to me:
I know I said I want to be friends with you both but the
willow sloughed into a deep grief
and said
if you could just tie back some of those oak branches
until I can get a little closer to mastering that domain
of space up there — see it? how empty it is
and how full of light:
        why I said don't I ask the wateroak if he would mind
withholding himself until you're more nearly even: after
all I said you are both trees and you both need water and
light and space to unfold into, surely the wateroak will
understand that commonness:
    not so you could tell it, said the willow:
        that I said is cynical and uncooperative: what could
you give the wateroak in return for his withholding:

what could I give him, said the willow, nothing
that he hasn't already taken:
    well, I said, but does he know about the unity in
all things, does he understand that all things have a
common source and end: if he could be made
to see that rather deeply, don't you think he might
        give you a little way:
    no said the willow he'd be afraid I would take all:
would you I said:
or would you, should the need come, give him a little way
back:
    I would said the willow but my need is greater than
his
and the trade would not be fair:
maybe not I said but let's approach him with our powerful
concept that all things are in all
    and see if he will be moved

1975

Easter Morning

I have a life that did not become,
that turned aside and stopped,
astonished:
I hold it in me like a pregnancy or
as on my lap a child
not to grow or grow old but dwell on

it is to his grave I most
frequently return and return
to ask what is wrong, what was
wrong, to see it all by
the light of a different necessity
but the grave will not heal
and the child,
stirring, must share my grave
with me, an old man having
gotten by on what was left

when I go back to my home country in these
fresh far-away days, it's convenient to visit
everybody, aunts and uncles, those who used to say,
look how he's shooting up, and the
trinket aunts who always had a little
something in their pocketbooks, cinnamon bark
or a penny or nickel, and uncles who

were the rumored fathers of cousins
who whispered of them as of great, if
troubled, presences, and school
teachers, just about everybody older
(and some younger) collected in one place
waiting, particularly, but not for
me, mother and father there, too, and others
close, close as burrowing
under skin, all in the graveyard
assembled, done for, the world they
used to wield, have trouble and joy
in, gone

the child in me that could not become
was not ready for others to go,
to go on into change, blessings and
horrors, but stands there by the road
where the mishap occurred, crying out for
help, come and fix this or we
can't get by, but the great ones who
were to return, they could not or did
not hear and went on in a flurry and
now, I say in the graveyard, here
lies the flurry, now it can't come
back with help or helpful asides, now
we all buy the bitter
incompletions, pick up the knots of
horror, silently raving, and go on
crashing into empty ends not
completions, not rondures the fullness
has come into and spent itself from

I stand on the stump
of a child, whether myself
or my little brother who died, and
yell as far as I can, I cannot leave this place, for
for me it is the dearest and the worst,
it is life nearest to life which is
life lost: it is my place where
I must stand and fail,
calling attention with tears
to the branches not lofting
boughs into space, to the barren
air that holds the world that was my world

though the incompletions
(& completions) burn out
standing in the flash high-burn
momentary structure of ash, still it

is a picture-book, letter-perfect
Easter morning: I have been for a
walk: the wind is tranquil: the brook
works without flashing in an abundant
tranquility: the birds are lively with
voice: I saw something I had
never seen before: two great birds,
maybe eagles, blackwinged, whitenecked
and -headed, came from the south oaring
the great wings steadily; they went
directly over me, high up, and kept on
due north: but then one bird,
the one behind, veered a little to the
left and the other bird kept on seeming
not to notice for a minute: the first
began to circle as if looking for
something, coasting, resting its wings
on the down side of some of the circles:
the other bird came back and they both
circled, looking perhaps for a draft;
they turned a few more times, possibly
rising — at least, clearly resting —
then flew on falling into distance till
they broke across the local bush and
trees: it was a sight of bountiful
majesty and integrity: the having
patterns and routes, breaking
from them to explore other patterns or
better ways to routes, and then the
return: a dance sacred as the sap in
the trees, permanent in its descriptions
as the ripples round the brook's
ripplestone: fresh as this particular
flood of burn breaking across us now
from the sun.

1981

Anxiety's Prosody

Anxiety clears meat chunks out of the stew, carrots, takes
the skimmer to floats of greasy globules and with cheesecloth

filters the broth, looking for the transparent, the colorless
essential, the unbeginning and unending of consommé: the

open anxiety breezes through thick conceits, surface congestions
(it likes metaphors deep-lying, out of sight, their airs misting

up into, lighting up consciousness, unidentifiable presences),
it distills consonance and assonance, glottal thickets, brush

clusters, it thins the rhythms, rushing into longish gaits, more
distance in less material time: it hates clots, its stump-fires

level fields: patience and calm define borders and boundaries,
hedgerows, and sharp whirls: anxiety burns instrumentation

matterless, assimilates music into motion, sketches the high
suasive turnings, mild natures tangled still in knotted clumps.

1989

Their Sex Life

One failure on
Top of another

1990

In View of the Fact

The people of my time are passing away: my
wife is baking for a funeral, a 60-year-old who

died suddenly, when the phone rings, and it's
Ruth we care so much about in intensive care:

it was once weddings that came so thick and
fast, and then, first babies, such a hullabaloo:

now, it's this that and the other and somebody
else gone or on the brink: well, we never

thought we would live forever (although we did)
and now it looks like we won't: some of us

are losing a leg to diabetes, some don't know
what they went downstairs for, some know that

a hired watchful person is around, some like
to touch the cane tip into something steady,

so nice: we have already lost so many,
brushed the loss of ourselves ourselves: our

address books for so long a slow scramble now
are palimpsests, scribbles and scratches: our

index cards for Christmases, birthdays,
halloweens drop clean away into sympathies:

at the same time we are getting used to so
many leaving, we are hanging on with a grip

to the ones left: we are not giving up on the
congestive heart failures or brain tumors, on

the nice old men left in empty houses or on
the widows who decide to travel a lot: we

think the sun may shine someday when we'll
drink wine together and think of what used to

be: until we die we will remember every
single thing, recall every word, love every

loss: then we will, as we must, leave it to
others to love, love that can grow brighter

and deeper till the very end, gaining strength
and getting more precious all the way. . . .

1996

ROBERT BLY (b. 1926)

Robert Bly was born in Madison, Minnesota. In the late 1950s he rebelled against the mainstream poetry of the time, which struck him as polite and lacking in anguish. "During most poems the poet is visiting Italy on a grant, admiring paintings, trying to get into the poems stuff about the Netherlands or Greek history that he had learned in graduate school, trying to decide whether the infants just born were noble savages or not — that sort of thing," Bly said. Through his translations Bly helped secure an American readership for such poets as Cesar Vallejo, Pablo Neruda, and Tomas Transtromer. He labored to alert a generation of poets to the possibilities of surrealism — what he called "leaping poetry" — and the value of storytelling and myth in a laconic American idiom. In his own first book, *Silence in the Snowy Fields* (1962), Bly introduced the "deep image" poem, in which images are imbued with "great spiritual energy" and can bring to the surface forgotten or repressed material from the unconscious; James Wright and W. S. Merwin were among those attracted to this nexus of ideas. Bly's second book, *The Light Around the Body* (1967), was a fierce outcry against the Vietnam War, and Bly has remained politically active and socially conscious. He wrote *Iron John* (1990) and fathered the men's movement in the United States.

Johnson's Cabinet Watched by Ants

I

It is a clearing deep in a forest: overhanging boughs
Make a low place. Here the citizens we know during the day,
The ministers, the department heads,
Appear changed: the stockholders of large steel companies
In small wooden shoes: here are the generals dressed as gamboling lambs,

II

Tonight they burn the rice-supplies; tomorrow
They lecture on Thoreau; tonight they move around the trees,
Tomorrow they pick the twigs from their clothes;
Tonight they throw the fire-bombs, tomorrow
They read the Declaration of Independence; tomorrow they are in
church.

III

Ants are gathered around an old tree.
In a choir they sing, in harsh and gravelly voices,
Old Etruscan songs on tyranny.
Toads nearby clap their small hands, and join
The fiery songs, their five long toes trembling in the soaked earth.

1967

After the Industrial Revolution, All Things Happen at Once

Now we enter a strange world, where the Hessian Christmas
Still goes on, and Washington has not reached the other shore;
The Whiskey Boys
Are gathering again on the meadows of Pennsylvania
And the Republic is still sailing on the open sea.

I saw a black angel in Washington dancing
On a barge, saying, "Let us now divide kennel dogs
And hunting dogs"; Henry Cabot Lodge, in New York,
Talking of sugarcane in Cuba; Ford,
In Detroit, drinking mother's milk;
Henry Cabot Lodge, saying, "Remember the *Maine*!"
Ford, saying, "History is bunk!"
And Wilson saying, "What is good for General Motors . . . "

Who is it, singing? Don't you hear singing?
It is the dead of Cripple Creek;
Coxey's army
Like turkeys are singing from the tops of trees!
And the Whiskey Boys are drunk outside Philadelphia.

1967

After Long Busyness

I start out for a walk at last after weeks at the desk.
Moon gone, plowing underfoot, no stars; not a trace of light!
Suppose a horse were galloping toward me in this open field?
Every day I did not spend in solitude was wasted.

1971

My Father at 85

His large ears hear
everything.
A hermit wakes
and sleeps
in a hut underneath
his gaunt cheeks.
His eyes blue,
alert, dis-
appointed and suspicious
complain
I do not bring him
the same sort of jokes
the nurses do.
He is a small bird
waiting to be fed,
mostly beak,
an eagle or a vulture
or the Pharoah's servant
just before death.
My arm on the bedrail
rests there,
relaxed, with new love.
All I know of the Troubadours
I bring
to this bed.
I do not want
or need
to be shamed
by him
any longer.
The general of shame
has discharged him
and left him in this
small provincial
Egyptian town.
If I do not wish
to shame him, then
why not
love him?

His long hands,
large, veined, capable,
can still retain
hold of what he wanted.
But is that
what he desired?
Some powerful
river of desire
goes on flowing
through him.
He never phrased
what he desired,
and I am
his son.

1989

The Resemblance Between Your Life and a Dog

I never intended to have this life, believe me —
It just happened. You know how dogs turn up
At a farm, and they wag but can't explain.

It's good if you can accept your life — you'll notice
Your face has become deranged trying to adjust
To it. Your face thought your life would look

Like your bedroom mirror when you were ten.
That was a clear river touched by mountain wind.
Even your parents can't believe how much you've changed.

Sparrows in winter, if you've ever held one, all feather:
Burst out of your hand with a fiery glee.
You see them later in hedges. Teachers praise you,

But you can't quite get back to the winter sparrow.
Your life is a dog. He's been hungry for miles,
Doesn't particularly like you, but gives up, and comes in.

1997

The Night Abraham Called to the Stars

Do you remember the night Abraham first saw
The stars? He cried to Saturn: "You are my Lord!"
How happy he was! When he saw the Dawn Star,

He cried, ""You are my Lord!" How destroyed he was
When he watched them set. Friends, he is like us:
We take as our Lord the stars that go down.

We are faithful companions to the unfaithful stars.
We are diggers, like badgers; we love to feel
The dirt flying out from behind our back claws.

And no one can convince us that mud is not
Beautiful. It is our badger soul that thinks so.
We are ready to spend the rest of our life

Walking with muddy shoes in the wet fields.
We resemble exiles in the kingdom of the serpent.
We stand in the onion fields looking up at the night.

My heart is a calm potato by day, and a weeping
Abandoned woman by night. Friend, tell me what to do,
Since I am a man in love with the setting stars.

2001

ROBERT CREELEY (1926–2005)

Robert Creeley was born in Arlington, Massachusetts. He met Charles Olson in 1950, a signal event in both men's lives. They sought to create a new poetics. "Form is never more than an extension of content," Creeley asserted. (Denise Levertov proposed substituting "a revelation" for "an extension" in that sentence.) Creeley joined Olson on the faculty of Black Mountain College in 1954. Even poets on the other end of the poetic spectrum admire Creeley as, in Donald Hall's phrase, the "master of the strange, stuttering line-break." Hall observes that if you took a sentence from a late Henry James novel like *The Ambassadors* and arranged it in two-word lines, you would "have a Creeley poem worrying out its self-consciousness." Creeley seems often to substitute speech rhythms for imagery as the engine of a poem.

I Know a Man

As I sd to my
friend, because I am
always talking, —John, I

sd, which was not his
name, the darkness sur-
rounds us, what

can we do against
it, or else, shall we &
why not, buy a goddamn big car,

drive, he sd, for
Christ's sake, look
out where yr going.

1954

Heroes

In all those stories the hero
is beyond himself into the next
thing, be it those labors
of Hercules, or Aeneas going into death.

I thought the instant of the one humanness
in Virgil's plan of it
was that it was of course human enough to die,
yet to come back, as he said, *hoc opus, hic labor est.*

That was the Cumaean Sibyl speaking.
This is Robert Creeley, and Virgil
is dead now two thousand years, yet Hercules
and the *Aeneid*, yet all that industrious wis-
dom lives in the way the mountains
and the desert are waiting
for the heroes, and death also
can still propose the old labors.

1959

After Lorca

for M. Marti

The church is a business, and the rich
are the business men.
When they pull on the bells, the
poor come piling in and when a poor man dies, he has a wooden
cross, and they rush through the ceremony.

But when a rich man dies, they
drag out the Sacrament
and a golden Cross, and go *doucement, doucement*
to the cemetery.

And the poor love it
and think it's crazy.

1962

The Dishonest Mailmen

They are taking all my letters, and they
put them into a fire.

                                        I see the flames, etc.
But do not care, etc.

They burn everything I have, or what little
I have. I don't care, etc.

The poem supreme, addressed to
emptiness — this is the courage

necessary. This is something
quite different.

1962

Like They Say

Underneath the tree on some
soft grass I sat, I

watched two happy
woodpeckers be

disturbed by my presence. And
why not, I thought to

myself, why
not.

1962

Kore

As I was walking
  I came upon
chance walking
  the same road upon.

As I sat down
  by chance to move

later
  if and as I might,

light the wood was,
  light and green,
and what I saw
  before I had not seen.

It was a lady
  accompanied
by goat men
  leading her.

Her hair held earth.
  Her eyes were dark.
A double flute
  made her move.

'O love,
  where are you
leading
  me now?'

1962

To And

To and
back and forth,
direction
is a third

or simple fourth
of the intention
like it
goes and goes.

No
more snow this
winter?
No more snow.

Then what replaces
all the faces,
wasted,
wasted.

1962

I Keep to Myself Such Measures . . .

I keep to myself such
measures as I care for,
daily the rocks
accumulate position.

There is nothing
but what thinking makes
it less tangible. The mind,
fast as it goes, loses

pace, puts in place of it
like rocks simple markers,
for a way only to
hopefully come back to

where it cannot. All
forgets. My mind sinks.
I hold in both hands such weight
it is my only description.

1967

Kitchen

The light in the morning
comes in the front windows,
leaving a lace-like pattern
on the table and floor.

* * *

In the silence now
of this high square room
the clock's tick adjacent
seems to mark old time.

* * *

Perpetually sweeping
this room, I want it
to be like it was.

1974

Other

Having begun in thought there
in that factual embodied wonder
what was lost in the emptied lovers
patience and mind I first felt there
wondered again and again what for
myself so meager and finally singular
despite all issued therefrom whether
sister or mother or brother and father
come to love's emptied place too late
to feel it again see again first there
all the peculiar wet tenderness the care
of her for whom to be other was first fate.

1993

ALLEN GINSBERG (1926–1997)

Allen Ginsberg was born in Newark, New Jersey. He attended Columbia College, where he studied with Lionel Trilling, Mark Van Doren, and Meyer Schapiro. In *On the Road*, Jack Kerouac based the character of Carlo Marx on Ginsberg. When Ginsberg read "Howl" at the Six Gallery in San Francisco's North Beach in 1955, he uttered the battle cry of the Beat movement. The poem, banned, became a cause célèbre. "Ideally each line of 'Howl' is a single breath unit," Ginsberg said on recording "Howl" in 1959. "Let it be raw, there is beauty." Once, at a reading, a heckler shouted, "What do you mean, nakedness?" Ginsberg stripped off his clothes in response. "Under all this self-revealing candor is purity of heart," says the narrator of Saul Bellow's *Him with His Foot in His Mouth*. "And the only authentic living representative of American Transcendentalism is that fat-breasted, bald, bearded homosexual in smeared goggles, innocent in his uncleanness." Ginsberg quoted the Tibetan Buddhist teacher Chogyam Trungpa Rinpoche's maxim, "First thought, best thought," to express his philosophy of composition. In addition to many books of poetry, several volumes of Ginsberg's photographs have been published, including *Snapshot Poetics* (1993). Ginsberg died of a heart attack on 5 April 1997.

A Supermarket in California

What thoughts I have of you tonight, Walt Whitman, for I walked down the sidestreets under the trees with a headache self-conscious looking at the full moon.

In my hungry fatigue, and shopping for images, I went into the neon fruit supermarket, dreaming of your enumerations!

What peaches and what penumbras! Whole families shopping at night! Aisles full of husbands! Wives in the avocados, babies in the tomatoes! — and you, Garcia Lorca, what were you doing down by the watermelons?

I saw you, Walt Whitman, childless, lonely old grubber poking among the meats in the refrigerator and eyeing the grocery boys.

I heard you asking questions of each: Who killed the pork chops? What price bananas? Are you my Angel?

I wandered in and out of the brilliant stacks of cans following you and followed in my imagination by the store detective.

We strode down the open corridors together in out solitary fancy tasting artichokes, possessing every frozen delicacy, and never passing the cashier.

Where are we going, Walt Whitman? The doors close in an hour. Which way does your beard point tonight?

(I touch your book and dream of our odyssey in the supermarket and feel absurd.)

Will we walk all night through solitary streets? The trees add shade to shade, lights out in the houses, we'll both be lonely.

Will we stroll dreaming of the lost America of love past blue automobiles in driveways, home to our silent cottage?

Ah, dear father, graybeard, lonely old courage-teacher, what America did you have when Charon quit poling his ferry and you got out on a smoking bank and stood watching the boat disappear on the black waters of Lethe?

1955

from *Kaddish*

for Naomi Ginsberg 1894–1956

I

Strange now to think of you, gone without corsets & eyes, while I walk
    on the sunny pavement of Greenwich Village.
downtown Manhattan, clear winter noon, and I've been up all night.
    taking, talking, reading the Kaddish aloud, listening to Ray Charles
    blues shout blind on the phonograph
the rhythm the rhythm — and your memory in my head three years
    after — And read Adonais' last triumphant stanzas aloud — wept,
    realizing how we suffer —
And how Death is that remedy all singers dream of, sing, remember,
    prophesy as in the Hebrew Anthem, or the Buddhist Book of
    Answers — and my own imagination of a withered leaf — at
    dawn —
Dreaming back thru life, Your time — and mine accelerating toward
    Apocalypse,

the final moment — the flower burning in the Day — and what comes after,
looking back on the mind itself that saw an American city
a flash away, and the great dream of Me or China, or you and a phantom Russia, or a crumpled bed that never existed —
like a poem in the dark — escaped back to Oblivion —
No more to say, and nothing to weep for but the Beings in the Dream, trapped in its disappearance,
sighing, screaming with it, buying and selling pieces of phantom, worshipping each other,
worshipping the God included in it all — longing or inevitability? — while it lasts, a Vision — anything more?
It leaps about me, as I go out and walk the street, look back over my shoulder. Seventh Avenue, the battlements of window office buildings shouldering each other high, under a cloud, tall as the sky an instant — and the sky above — an old blue place.
or down the Avenue to the South, to — as I walked toward the Lower East Side — where you walked 50 years ago, little girl — from Russia, eating the first poisonous tomatoes of America — frightened on the dock —
then struggling in the crowds of Orchard Street toward what? — toward Newark
toward candy store, first home-made sodas of the century, hand-churned ice cream in backroom on musty brownfloor boards —
Toward education marriage nervous breakdown, operation, teaching school, and learning to be mad, in a dream — what is this life?
Toward the Key in the window — and the great Key lays its head of light on top of Manhattan, and over the floor, and lays down on the sidewalk — in a single vast beam, moving, as I walk down First toward the Yiddish Theater — and the place of poverty
you knew, and I know, but without caring now — Strange to have moved thru Paterson, and the West, and Europe and here again,
with the cries of Spaniards now in the doorstoops doors and dark boys on the street, fire escapes old as you
— Tho you're not old now, that's left here with me —
Myself, anyhow, maybe as old as the universe — and I guess that dies with us — enough to cancel all that comes — What came is gone forever every time —
That's good! That leaves it open for no regret — no fear radiation, lacklove, torture even toothache in the end —
Though while it comes it is a lion that eats the soul — and the lamb the soul, in us, alas, offering itself in sacrifice to change's fierce hanger — hair and teeth — and the roar of bonepain, skull bare, break rib rot-skin, braintricked Implacability.
Ai! ai! we do worse! We are in a fix! And you're out, Death let you out. Death had the Mercy, you're done with your century, done with God, done with the path thru it — Done with yourself at last —

Pure — Back to the Babe dark before your Father, before us all — before the world —
There, rest. No more suffering for you. I know where you've gone, it's good.
No more flowers in the summer fields of New York, no joy now, no more fear of Louis,
and no more of his sweetness and glasses, his high school decade debts loves, frightened telephone calls, conception beds, relative, hands —
No more of sister Elanor, — she gone before you — we kept it secret you killed her — or she killed herself to bear with you — an arthritic heart — But Death's killed you both — No matter —
Nor your memory of your mother, 1915 tears in silent movie weeks and weeks — forgetting, agrieve watching Marie Dressler address humanity, Chaplin dance in youth,
or Boris Godunov, Chaliapin's at the Met, hailing his voice of a weeping Czar — by standing room with Elanor & Max — watching also the Capitalists take seats in Orchestra, white furs, diamonds,
with the YPSL's hitch-hiking thru Pennsylvania, in black baggy gym skirts pants, photograph of 4 girls holding each other round the waste, and laughing eye, too coy, virginal solitude of 1920
all girls grown old, or dead, now, and that long hair in the grave — lucky to have husbands later —
You made it — I came too — Eugene my brother before (still grieving now and will gream on to his last stiff hand, as he goes thru his cancer — or kill — later perhaps — soon he will think —)
And it's the last moment I remember, which I see them all, thru myself, now — tho not you
I didn't foresee what you felt — what more hideous gape of bad mouth came first — to you — and were you prepared?
To go where? In that Dark — that — in that God? a radiance? A Lord in the Void? Like an eye in the black cloud in a dream? Adonoi at last, with you?
Beyond my remembrance! Incapable to guess! Not merely the yellow skull in the grave, or a box of worm dust, and a stained ribbon — Deathshead with Halo? can you believe it?
Is it only the sun that shines once for the mind, only the flash of existence, than none ever was?
Nothing beyond what we have — what you had — that so pitiful — yet Triumph,
to have been here, and changed, like a tree, broken, or flower — fed to the ground — but mad, with its petals, colored, thinking Great Universe, shaken, cut in the head, leaf stript, hid in an egg crate hospital, cloth wrapped, sore — freaked in the moon brain, Naughtless.
No flower like that flower, which knew itself in the garden, and fought the knife — lost
Cut down by an idiot Snowman's icy — even in the Spring — strange ghost thought — some Death — Sharp icicle in his hand — crowned

with old roses — a dog in his eyes — cock of a sweatshop — heart of electric irons.
All the accumulations of life, that wear us out — clocks, bodies, consciousness, shoe, breasts — begotten sons — your Communism — "Paranoia" into hospitals.
You once kicked Elanor in the leg, she died of heart failure later. You of stroke. Asleep? within a year, the two of you, sisters in death. Is Elanor happy?
Max grieves alive in an office on Lower Broadway, lone large mustache over midnight Accountings, not sure. His life passes — as he sees — and what does he doubt now? Still dream of making money, or that might have made money, hired nurse, had children, found even your Immortality, Naomi?
I'll see him soon. Now I've got to cut through — to talk to you — as I didn't when you had a mouth.
Forever. And we're bound for that, Forever — like Emily Dickinson's horses — headed to the End.
They know the way — These Steeds — run faster than we think — it's our own life they cross — and take with them.

Magnificent, mourned no more, marred of heart, mind behind, married dreamed, mortal changed — Ass and face done with murder.

In the world, given, flower maddened, made no Utopia, shut under pine, aimed in Earth, balmed in Lone, Jehovah, accept.

Nameless, One Faced, Forever beyond me, beginningless, endless, Father in death. Tho I am not there for this Prophecy, I am unmarried, I'm hymnless, I'm Heavenless, headless in blisshood I would still adore

Thee, Heaven, after Death, only One blessed in Nothingness, not light or darkness, Dayless Eternity —

Take this, this Psalm, from me, burst from my hand in a day, some of my Time, now given to Nothing — to praise Thee — But Death

This is the end, the redemption from Wilderness, way for the Wonderer, House sought for All, black handkerchief washed clean by weeping — page beyond Psalm — Last change of mine and Naomi — to God's perfect Darkness — Death, stay thy phantoms!

III

Only to have not forgotten the beginning in which she drank cheap sodas in the morgues of Newark,
only to have seen her weeping on grey tables in long wards of her universe
only to have known the weird ideas of Hitler at the door, the wires in her head, the three big sticks
rammed down her back, the voices in the ceiling shrieking out her ugly early lays for 30 years,
only to have seen the time-jumps, memory lapse, the crash of wars, the roar and silence of a vast electric shock,
only to have seen her painting crude pictures of Elevateds running over the rooftops of the Bronx

her brothers dead in Riverside or Russia, her lone in Long
Island writing a last letter — and her image in the sun-
light at the window
'The key is in the sunlight at the window in the bars the key
is in the sunlight,'
only to have come to that dark night on iron bed by stroke when
the sun gone down on Long Island
and the vast Atlantic roars outside the great call of Being to
its own
to come back out of the Nightmare — divided creation — with
her head lain on a pillow of the hospital to die
— in one last glimpse — all Earth one everlasting Light in the
familiar blackout — no tears for this vision —
But that the key should be left behind — at the window — the
key in the sunlight — to the living — that can take
that slice of light in hand — and turn the door — and look
back see
Creation glistening backwards to the same grave, size of universe,
size of the tick of the hospital's clock on the archway over the
white door —

IV

O mother
what have I left out
O mother
what have I forgotten
O mother
farewell
with a long black shoe
farewell
with Communist Party and a broken stocking
farewell
with six dark hairs on the wen of your breast
farewell
with your old dress and a long black beard around the vagina
farewell
with your sagging belly
with your fear of Hitler
with your mouth of bad short stories
with your fingers of rotten mandolines
with your arms of fat Paterson porches
with your belly of strikes and smokestacks
with your chin of Trotsky and the Spanish War
with your voice singing for the decaying overbroken workers
with your nose of bad lay with your nose of the smell of the
pickles of Newark
with your eyes
with your eyes of Russia
with your eyes of no money

with your eyes of false China
with your eyes of Aunt Elanor
with your eyes of starving India
with your eyes pissing in the park
with your eyes of America taking a fall
with your eyes of your failure at the piano
with your eyes of your relatives in California
with your eyes of Ma Rainey dying in an ambulance
with your eyes of Czechoslovakia attacked by robots
with your eyes going to painting class at night in the Bronx
with your eyes of the killer Grandma you see on the horizon
from the Fire-Escape
with your eyes running naked out of the apartment screaming
into the hall
with your eyes being led away by policemen to an ambulance
with your eyes strapped down on the operating table
with your eyes with the pancreas removed
with your eyes of appendix operation
with your eyes of abortion
with your eyes of ovaries removed
with your eyes of shock
with your eyes of lobotomy
with your eyes of divorce
with your eyes of stroke
with your eyes alone
with your eyes
with your eyes
with your Death full of Flowers

V

Caw caw caw crows shriek in the white sun over grave stones
in Long Island
Lord Lord Lord Naomi underneath this grass my halflife and
my own as hers
caw caw my eye be buried in the same Ground where I stand
in Angel
Lord Lord great Eye that stares on All and moves in a black
cloud
caw caw strange cry of Beings flung up into sky over the waving
trees
Lord Lord O Grinder of giant Beyonds my voice in a boundless
field in Sheol
Caw caw the call of Time rent out of foot and wing an instant
in the universe
Lord Lord an echo in the sky the wind through ragged leaves
the roar of memory
caw caw all years my birth a dream caw caw New York the bus
the broken shoe the vast highschool caw caw all Visions
of the Lord

Lord Lord Lord caw caw caw Lord Lord Lord caw caw caw
Lord

1959

America

America I've given you all and now I'm nothing.
America two dollars and twentyseven cents January 17, 1956.
I can't stand my own mind.
America when will we end the human war?
Go fuck yourself with your atom bomb
I don't feel good don't bother me.
I won't write my poem till I'm in my right mind.
America when will you be angelic?
When will you take off your clothes?
When will you look at yourself through the grave?
When will you be worthy of your million Trotskyites?
America why are your libraries full of tears?
America when will you send your eggs to India?
I'm sick of your insane demands.
When can I go into the supermarket and buy what I need with my good looks?
America after all it is you and I who are perfect not the next world.
Your machinery is too much for me.
You made me want to be a saint.
There must be some other way to settle this argument.
Burroughs is in Tangiers I don't think he'll come back it's sinister.
Are you being sinister or is this some form of practical joke?
I'm trying to come to the point.
I refuse to give up my obsession.
America stop pushing I know what I'm doing.
America the plum blossoms are falling.
I haven't read the newspapers for months, everyday somebody goes on trial for murder.
America I feel sentimental about the Wobblies.
America I used to be a communist when I was a kid I'm not sorry.
I smoke marijuana every chance I get.
I sit in my house for days on end and stare at the roses in the closet.
When I go to Chinatown I get drunk and never get laid.
My mind is made up there's going to be trouble.
You should have seen me reading Marx.
My psychoanalyst thinks I'm perfectly right.
I won't say the Lord's Prayer.
I have mystical visions and cosmic vibrations.
America I still haven't told you what you did to Uncle Max after he came over from Russia.
I'm addressing you.

Are you going to let our emotional life be run by Time Magazine?
I'm obsessed by Time Magazine.
I read it every week.
Its cover stares at me every time I slink past the corner candystore.
I read it in the basement of the Berkeley Public Library.
It's always telling me about responsibility. Businessmen are serious. Movie producers are serious. Everybody's serious but me.
It occurs to me that I am America.
I am talking to myself again.

Asia is rising against me.
I haven't got a chinaman's chance.
I'd better consider my national resources.
My national resources consist of two joints of marijuana millions of genitals an unpublishable private literature that jetplanes 1400 miles an hour and twentyfive-thousand mental institutions.
I say nothing about my prisons nor the millions of underpriviliged who live in my flowerpots under the light of five hundred suns.
I have abolished the whorehouses of France, Tangiers is the next to go.
My ambition is to be President despite the fact that I'm a Catholic.

America how can I write a holy litany in your silly mood?
I will continue like Henry Ford my strophes are as individual as his automobiles more so they're all different sexes
America I will sell you strophes $2500 apiece $500 down on your old strophe
America free Tom Mooney
America save the Spanish Loyalists
America Sacco & Vanzetti must not die
America I am the Scottsboro boys.
America when I was seven momma took me to Communist Cell meetings they sold us garbanzos a handful per ticket a ticket costs a nickel and the speeches were free everybody was angelic and sentimental about the workers it was all so sincere you have no idea what a good thing the party was in 1935 Scott Nearing was a grand old man a real mensch Mother Bloor the Silk-strikers' Ewig-Weibliche made me cry I once saw the Yiddish orator Israel Amter plain. Everybody must have been a spy.
America you don't really want to go to war.
America it's them bad Russians.
Them Russians them Russians and them Chinamen. And them Russians.
The Russia wants to eat us alive. The Russia's power mad. She wants to take our cars from out our garages.
Her wants to grab Chicago. Her needs a Red *Reader's Digest*. Her wants our auto plants in Siberia. Him big bureaucracy running our fillingstations.
That no good. Ugh. Him make Indians learn read. Him need big black niggers. Hah. Her make us all work sixteen hours a day. Help.
America this is quite serious.
America this is the impression I get from looking in the television set.
America is this correct?

I'd better get right down to the job.
It's true I don't want to join the Army or turn lathes in precision parts
factories, I'm nearsighted and psychopathic anyway.
America I'm putting my queer shoulder to the wheel.

1956

To Aunt Rose

Aunt Rose — now — might I see you
with your thin face and buck tooth smile and pain
of rheumatism — and a long black heavy shoe
for your bony left leg
limping down the long hall in Newark on the running carpet
past the black grand piano
in the day room
where the parties were
and I sang Spanish loyalist songs
in a high squeaky voice
(hysterical) the committee listening
while you limped around the room
collected the money —
Aunt Honey, Uncle Sam, a stranger with a cloth arm
in his pocket
and huge young bald head
of Abraham Lincoln Brigade

— your long sad face
your tears of sexual frustration
(what smothered sobs and bony hips
under the pillows of Osborne Terrace)
— the time I stood on the toilet seat naked
and you powdered my thighs with Calomine
against the poison ivy — my tender
and shamed first black curled hairs
what were you thinking in secret heart then
knowing me a man already —
and I an ignorant girl of family silence on the thin pedestal
of my legs in the bathroom — Museum of Newark.
Aunt Rose
Hitler is dead, Hitler is in Eternity; Hitler is with
Tamburlane and Emily Brontë

Though I see you walking still, a ghost on Osborne Terrace
down the long dark hall to the front door
limping a little with a pinched smile
in what must have been a silken
flower dress

welcoming my father, the Poet, on his visit to Newark
— see you arriving in the living room
dancing on your crippled leg
and clapping hands his book
had been accepted by Liveright

Hitler is dead and Liveright's gone out of business
The Attic of the Past and *Everlasting Minute* are out of print
Uncle Harry sold his last silk stocking
Claire quit interpretive dancing school
Buba sits a wrinkled monument in Old
Ladies Home blinking at new babies

last time I saw you was the hospital
pale skull protruding under ashen skin
blue veined unconscious girl
in an oxygen tent
the war in Spain has ended long ago
Aunt Rose

1958

City Midnight Junk Strains

for Frank O'Hara

Switch on lights yellow as the sun
in the bedroom . . .
The gaudy poet dead   Frank O'Hara's bones
under cemetery grass
An emptiness at 8 PM in the Cedar Bar
Throngs of drunken
guys talking about paint
& lofts, and Pennsylvania youth.
Kline attacked by his heart
& chattering Frank
stopped forever —
Faithful drunken adorers, mourn.
The busfare's a nickle more
past his old apartment 9th Street by the park.
Delicate Peter loved his praise,
I wait for the things he says
about me —
Did he think me an Angel
as angel I am still talking into earth's microphone
willy nilly
— to come back as words ghostly hued
by early death

but written so bodied
mature in another decade.
Chatty prophet
of yr own loves, personal
memory feeling fellow
Poet of building-glass
I see you walking you said with your tie
flopped over your shoulder in the wind down 5th Ave
under the handsome breasted workmen
on their scaffolds ascending Time
& washing the windows of Life
— off to a date with Martinis & a blond
beloved poet far from home
— with thee and Thy sacred Metropolis
in the enormous bliss of a long afternoon
where death is the shadow
cast by Rockefeller Center
over your intimate street.
Who were you, black suited, hurrying to meet,
Unsatisfied one?
Unmistakable,
Darling date
for the charming solitary young poet with a big cock
who could fuck you all night long
till you never came,
trying your torture on his obliging fond body
eager to satisfy god's whim that made you
Innocent, as you are.
I tried your boys and found them ready
sweet and amiable
collected gentlemen
with large sofa apartments
lonesome to please for pure language;
and you mixed with money
because you knew enough language to be rich
if you wanted your walls to be empty —
Deep philosophical terms dear Edwin Denby serious as Herbert Read
with silvery hair announcing your dead gift
to the grave crowd whose historic op art frisson was
the new sculpture your big blue wounded body made in the
Universe
when you went away to Fire Island for the weekend
tipsy with a family of decade-olden friends

Peter stares out the window at robbers
the Lower East Side distracted in Amphetamine
I stare into my head & look for your/ broken roman nose
your wet mouth-smell of martinis

& a big artistic tipsy kiss.
40's only half a life to have filled
with so many fine parties and evenings'
interesting drinks together with one
faded friend or new
understanding social cat . . .
I want to be there in your garden party in the clouds
all of us naked
strumming our harps and reading each other new poetry
in the boring celestial
friendship Committee Museum.
You're in a bad mood?
Take an Asprin.
In the Dumps?
I'm falling asleep
safe in your thoughtful arms.
Someone uncontrolled by History would have to own Heaven,
on earth as it is.
I hope you satisfied your childhood love
Your puberty fantasy your sailor punishment on your knees
your mouth-suck
Elegant insistency
on the honking self-prophetic Personal
as Curator of funny emotions to the mob,
Trembling One, whenever possible. I see New York thru your eyes
and hear of one funeral a year nowadays —
From Billie Holiday's time
appreciated more and more
a common ear
for our deep gossip.

1966

JAMES MERRILL (1926–1995)

James Merrill was born in New York City, the son of Charles E. Merrill, a founder of the major investment firm Merrill Lynch. Educated at Amherst College, where he wrote an honors thesis on Marcel Proust, he lived in Stonington, Connecticut, and Key West, Florida, and spent sizable amounts of time in Athens, Greece. Merrill's poetry is characterized by diabolically clever puns, lyrical intensity sometimes put to the service of narrative aims, and formal virtuosity. In "Syrinx," a poem about music whose title denotes a "panpipe" or primitive wind instrument, Merrill riffs on the musical "scale of love and dread." The next four words — "O ramify, sole antidote!" — combined with the final "d" of "dread," spell out a homophonic approximation of the succession of tones from "do" to "ti." Merrill's seemingly effortless fluency has led critics to compare him to Mozart or Fred Astaire, but such comparisons risk obscuring vital other aspects of his achievement: the relentless investigation of the self as life turns into autobiography, and his engagement with public events ranging from rocket flight to violent student protesters. He appropriated the "Days of . . ." conceit from the great Greek poet Constantine Cavafy. The epic poem begun in *Divine Comedies* (1976), extended in two subsequent volumes, and published in its entirety and with a coda as *The Changing Light at Sandover* (1983) owes its origin to nights that Merrill and his companion, David Jackson, spent playing with a homemade Ouija board. The parlor game turned into a way of generating material; among the otherworldly voices in the poem are those of W. H. Auden and Gertrude Stein.

A Dedication

Hans, there are moments when the whole mind
Resolves into a pair of brimming eyes, or lips
Parting to drink from the deep spring of a death
That freshness they do not yet need to understand.
These are the moments, if ever, an angel steps
Into the mind, as kings into the dress
Of a poor goatherd, for their acts of charity.
There are moments when speech is but a mouth pressed
Lightly and humbly against the angel's hand.

1959

Charles on Fire

Another evening we sprawled about discussing
Appearances. And it was the consensus
That while uncommon physical good looks
Continued to launch one, as before, in life
(Among its vaporous eddies and false claims),
Still, as one of us said into his beard,
"Without your intellectual and spiritual
Values, man, you are sunk." No one but squared
The shoulders of his own unloveliness.
Long-suffering Charles, having cooked and served the meal,
Now brought out little tumblers finely etched
He filled with amber liquor and then passed.
"Say," said the same young man, "in Paris, France,
They do it this way" — bounding to his feet
And touching a lit match to our host's full glass.
A blue flame, gentle, beautiful, came, went
Above the surface. In a hush that fell
We heard the vessel crack. The contents drained
As who should step down from a crystal coach.
Steward of spirits, Charles's glistening hand
All at once gloved itself in eeriness.

The moment passed. He made two quick sweeps and
Was flesh again. "It couldn't matter less,"
He said, but with a shocked, unconscious glance
Into the mirror. Finding nothing changed,
He filled a fresh glass and sank down among us.

1966

Days of 1964

Houses, an embassy, the hospital,
Our neighborhood sun-cured if trembling still
In pools of the night's rain . . .
Across the street that led to the center of town
A steep hill kept one company part way
Or could be climbed in twenty minutes
For some literally breathtaking views,
Framed by umbrella pines, of city and sea.
Underfoot, cyclamen, autumn crocus grew
Spangled as with fine sweat among the relics
Of good times had by all. If not Olympus,
An out-of-earshot, year-round hillside revel.

I brought home flowers from my climbs.
Kyria Kleo who cleans for us
Put them in water, sighing *Virgin, Virgin.*
Her legs hurt. She wore brown, was fat, past fifty,
And looked like a Palmyra matron
Copied in lard and horsehair. How she loved
You, me, loved us all, the bird, the cat!
I think now she *was* love. She sighed and glistened
All day with it, or pain, or both.
(We did not notably communicate.)
She lived nearby with her pious mother
And wastrel son. She called me her real son.

I paid her generously, I dare say.
Love makes one generous. Look at us. We'd known
Each other so briefly that instead of sleeping
We lay whole nights, open, in the lamplight,
And gazed, or traded stories.

One hour comes back — you gasping in my arms
With love, or laughter, or both,
I having just remembered and told you
What I'd looked up to see on my way downtown at noon:
Poor old Kleo, her aching legs,

Trudging into the pines. I called,
Called three times before she turned.
Above a tight, skyblue sweater, her face
Was painted. Yes. Her face was painted
Clown-white, white of the moon by daylight,
Lidded with pearl, mouth a poinsettia leaf,
Eat me, pay me — the erotic mask
Worn the world over by illusion
To weddings of itself and simple need.

Startled mute, we had stared — was love illusion? —
And gone our ways. Next, I was crossing a square
In which a moveable outdoor market's
Vegetables, chickens, pottery kept materializing
Through a dream-press of hagglers each at heart
Leery lest he be taken, plucked,
The bird, the flower of that November mildness,
Self lost up soft clay paths, or found, foothold,
Where the bud throbs awake
The better to be nipped, self on its knees in mud —
Here I stopped cold, for both our sakes;

And calmer on my way home bought us fruit.

Forgive me if you read this. (And may Kyria Kleo,
Should someone ever put it into Greek
And read it aloud to her, forgive me, too.)
I had gone so long without loving,
I hardly knew what I was thinking.

Where I hid my face, your touch, quick, merciful,
Blindfolded me. A god breathed from my lips.
If that was illusion, I wanted it to last long;
To dwell, for its daily pittance, with us there,
Cleaning and watering, sighing with love or pain.
I hoped it would climb when it needed to the heights
Even of degradation, as I for one
Seemed, those days, to be always climbing
Into a world of wild
Flowers, feasting, tears — or was I falling, legs
Buckling, heights, depths,
Into a pool of each night's rain?
But you were everywhere beside me, masked,
As who was not, in laughter, pain, and love.

1966

Days of 1935

Ladder horned against moonlight,
Window hoisted stealthily —
That's what I'd steel myself at night
To see, or sleep to see.

My parents were out partying,
My nurse was old and deaf and slow.
Way off in the servants' wing
Cackled a radio.

On the Lindbergh baby's small
Cold features lay a spell, a swoon.
It seemed entirely plausible
For my turn to come soon,

For a masked and crouching form
Lithe as tiger, light as moth,
To glide towards me, clap a firm
Hand across my mouth,

Then sheer imagination ride
Off with us in its old jalopy,
Trailing bedclothes like a bride
Timorous but happy.

A hundred tenuous dirt roads
Dew spangles, lead to the web's heart.
That whole pale night my captor reads
His brow's unwrinkling chart.

Dawn. A hovel in the treeless
Trembling middle of nowhere,
Hidden from the world by palace
Walls of dust and glare.

A lady out of *Silver Screen*,
Her careful rosebud chewing gum,
Seems to expect us, lets us in,
Nods her platinum

Spit curls deadpan (I will wait
Days to learn what makes her smile)
At a blue enamel plate
Of cold greens I can smell —

But swallow? Never. The man's face
Rivets me, a lightning bolt.

Lean, sallow, lantern-jawed, he lays
Pistol and cartridge belt

Between us on the oilskin (I
Will relive some things he did
Until I die, until I die)
And clears his throat: "Well, Kid,

You've figured out what's happening.
We don't mean to hurt you none
Unless we have to. Everything
Depends on, number one,

How much you're worth to your old man,
And, number two, no more of this —"
Meaning my toothprints on his hand,
Indenture of a kiss.

With which he fell upon the bed
And splendidly began to snore.
"Please, I'm sleepy too," I said.
She pointed to the floor.

The rag rug, a rainbow threadbare,
Was soft as down. For good or bad
I felt her watching from her chair
As no one ever had.

Their names were Floyd and Jean. I guess
They lived in what my parents meant
By sin: unceremoniousness
Or common discontent.

"Gimme — Wait — Hey, watch that gun —
Why don't these dumb matches work —
See you later — Yeah, have fun —
Wise guy — Floozie — Jerk —"

Or else he bragged of bygone glories,
Stores robbed, cars stolen, dolls betrayed,
Escape from two reformatories.
Said Jean, "Wish you'd of stayed."

To me they hardly spoke, just watched
Or gave directions in dumb show.
I nodded back like one bewitched
By a violent glow.

Each morning Floyd went for a ride
To post another penciled note.
Indignation nationwide
Greeted what he wrote.

Each afternoon, brought papers back.
One tabloid's whole front page was spanned
By the headline bold and black:
FIEND ASKS 200 GRAND.

Photographs too. My mother gloved,
Hatted, bepearled, chin deep in fur.
Dad glowering — was it true he loved
Others beside her?

Eerie, speaking likenesses.
One positively heard her mild
Voice temper some slow burn of his,
"Not before the child."

The child. That population map's
Blanknesses and dots were me!
Mine, those swarming eyes and lips,
Centers of industry

Italics under which would say
(And still do now and then, I fear)
Is This Child Alive Today?
Last Hopes Disappear.

Toy ukelele, terrorstruck
Chord, the strings so taut, so few —
Tingling I hugged my pillow. *Pluck*,
Some deep nerve went. I knew

That life was fiction in disguise.
My teeth said, chattering in Morse,
"Are you a healthy wealthy wise
Red-blooded boy? Of course?

Then face the music. Stay. Outwit
Everyone. Captivity
Is beckoning — make a dash for it!
It will set you free."

Sometimes as if I were not there
He put his lips against her neck.
Her head lolled sideways, just like Claire
Coe in *Tehuantepec*.

Then both would send me looks so heaped
With a lazy, scornful mirth,
This was growing up, I hoped,
The first flushed fruits of earth.

One night I woke to hear the room
Filled with crickets — no, bedsprings.
My eyes dilated in the gloom,
My ears made out things.

Jean: The kid, he's still awake . . .
Floyd: Time he learned . . . Oh baby . . . God . . .
Their prone tango, for my sake,
Grew intense and proud.

And one night — pure *Belshazzar's Feast*
When the slave-girl is found out —
She cowered, face a white blaze ("Beast!")
From his royal clout.

Mornings, though, she came and went,
Buffed her nails and plucked her brows.
What had those dark doings meant?
Less than the fresh bruise

Powdered over on her cheek.
I couldn't take my eyes away.
Let hers meet them! Let her speak!
She put down *Photoplay:*

"Do you know any stories, Kid?
Real stories — but not real, I mean.
Not just dumb things people did.
Wouldja tell one to Jean?"

I stared at her — *she* was the child! —
And a tale came back to me.
Bluebeard. At its end she smiled
Half incredulously.

I spun them out all afternoon.
Wunspontime, I said and said . . .
The smile became a dainty yawn
Rose-white and rose-red.

The little mermaid danced on knives,
The beauty slept in her thorn bower.
Who knows but that our very lives
Depend on such an hour?

The fisherman's hut became Versailles
Because he let the dolphin go . . .
Jean's lids have shut. I'm lonely. I
Am pausing on tiptoe

To marvel at the shimmer breath
Inspires along your radii,
Spider lightly running forth
To kiss the simple fly

Asleep. A chance to slip the net,
Wriggle down the dry stream bed,
Now or never! This child cannot.
An iridescent thread

Binds him to her slumber deep
Within a golden haze made plain
Precisely where his fingertip
Writes on the dusty pane

In spit his name, address, age nine
— Which the newspapers and such
Will shortly point to as a fine
Realistic touch.

Grown up, he thinks how S, T, you —
Second childhood's alphabet
Still unmastered, it is true,
Though letters come — have yet

Touched his heart, occasioned words
Not quickened by design alone,
Responses weekly winging towards
Your distance from his own,

Distance that much more complex
For its haunting ritornel:
Things happen to a child who speaks
To strangers, mark it well!

Thinks how you or V — where does
It end, will anyone have done? —
Taking the wheel (cf. those "Days
Of 1971")

Have driven, till his mother's Grade
A controls took charge, or handsome
Provisions which his father made
Served once again as ransom,

Driven your captive far enough
For the swift needle on the gauge
To stitch with delicate kid stuff
His shoddy middle age.

Here was Floyd. The evening sun
Filled his eyes with funny light.
"Junior, you'll be home real soon."
To Jean, "Tomorrow night."

What was happening? Had my parents
Paid? pulled strings? Or maybe I
Had failed in manners, or appearance?
Must this be goodbye?

I'd hoped I was worth more than crime
Itself, which never paid, could pay.
Worth more than my own father's time
Or mother's negligée

Undone where dim ends barely met,
This being a Depression year . . .
I'd hoped, I guess, that they would let
Floyd and Jean keep me here.

We ate in silence. He would stop
Munching and gaze into the lamp.
She wandered out on the dark stoop.
The night turned chill and damp.

When she came in, she'd caught a bug.
She tossed alone in the iron bed.
Floyd dropped beside me on the rug;
Growled, "Sleep." I disobeyed.

Commenced a wary, mortal heat
Run neck by nose. Small fingers felt,
Sore point of all that wiry meat,
A nipple's tender fault.

Time stopped. His arm somnambulist
Had circled me, warm, salt as blood.
Mine was the future in his fist
To get at if I could,

While his heart beat like a drum
And *Oh baby* faint and hoarse
Echoed from within his dream . . .
The next day Jean was worse

— Or I was. Dawn discovered me
Sweating on my bedroom floor.
Was there no curbing fantasy
When one had a flair?

Came those nights to end the tale.
I shrank to see the money tumble,
All in 20s, from a teal
Blue Studebaker's rumble

Down a slope of starlit brush.
Sensed with anguish the foreseen
Net of G-men, heard the hush
Deepen, then Floyd's voice ("Jean,

Baby, we've been doublecrossed!")
Drowned out by punctual crossfire
That left the pillow hot and creased.
By three o'clock, by four,

They stood in handcuffs where the hunt
Was over among blood-smeared rocks
— Whom I should not again confront
Till from the witness-box

I met their stupid, speechless gaze.
How empty they appeared, how weak
By contrast with my opening phrase
As I began to speak:

"You I adored I now accuse . . . "
Would imagination dare
Follow that sentence like a fuse
Sizzling towards the Chair?

See their bodies raw and swollen
Sagging in a skein of smoke?
The floor was reeling where I'd fallen.
Even my old nurse woke

And took me in her arms. I pressed
My guilty face against the void
Warmed and scented by her breast.
Jean, I whispered, Floyd.

A rainy day. The child is bored.
While Emma bakes he sits, half-grown.
The kitchen dado is of board
Painted like board. Its grain

Shiny buff on cinnamon
Mimics the real, the finer grain.
He watches icing sugar spin
Its thread. He licks in vain

Heavenly flavors from a spoon.
Left in the metallic bowl
Is a twenty-five-watt moon.
Somewhere rings a bell.

Wet walks from the east porch lead
Down levels manicured and rolled
To a small grove where pets are laid
In shallow emerald.

The den lights up. A Sazerac
Helps his father face the *Wall
Street Journal.* Jules the colored (black)
Butler guards the hall.

Tel & Tel executives,
Heads of Cellophane or Tin,
With their animated wives
Are due on the 6:10.

Upstairs in miles of spangled blue
His mother puts her make-up on.
She kisses him sweet dreams, but who —
Floyd and Jean are gone —

Who will he dream of? True to life
He's played them false. A golden haze
Past belief, past disbelief . . .
Well. Those were the days.

1972

Syrinx

Bug, flower, bird on slipware fired and fluted,
The summer day breaks everywhere at once.

Worn is the green of things that have known dawns
Before this, and the darkness before them.

Among the wreckage, bent in Christian weeds,
Illiterate — X my mark — I tremble, still

A thinking reed. Who puts his mouth to me
Draws out the scale of love and dread —

O ramify, sole antidote! Foxglove
Each year, cloud, hornet, fatal growths

Proliferating by metastasis
Rooted their total in the gliding stream.

Some formula not relevant any more
To flower children might express it yet

Like $\sqrt{(\frac{x}{y})^n} = 1$
— Or equals zero, one forgets —

The *y* standing for you, dear friend, at least
Until that hour he reaches for me, then

Leaves me cold, the great god Pain,
Letting me slide back into my scarred case

Whose silvery breath-tarnished tones
No longer rivet bone and star in place

Or keep from shriveling, leather round a stone,
The sunbather's precocious apricot

Or stop the four winds racing overhead
Nought
Waste Eased
Sought

1972

Lost in Translation

for Richard Howard

Diese Tage, die leer dir scheinen
und wertlos für das All,
haben Wurzeln zwischen den Steinen
und trinken dort überall.

A card table in the library stands ready
To receive the puzzle which keeps never coming.
Daylight shines in or lamplight down
Upon the tense oasis of green felt.
Full of unfulfillment, life goes on,

Mirage arisen from time's trickling sands
Or fallen piecemeal into place:
German lesson, picnic, see-saw, walk
With the collie who "did everything but talk" —
Sour windfalls of the orchard back of us.
A summer without parents is the puzzle,
Or should be. But the boy, day after day,
Writes in his Line-a-Day *No puzzle.*

He's in love, at least. His French Mademoiselle,
In real life a widow since Verdun,
Is stout, plain, carrot-haired, devout.
She prays for him, as does a curé in Alsace,
Sews costumes for his marionettes,
Helps him to keep behind the scene
Whose sidelit goosegirl, speaking with his voice,
Plays Guinevere as well as Gunmoll Jean.
Or else at bedtime in his tight embrace
Tells him her own French hopes, her German fears,
Her — but what more is there to tell?
Having known grief and hardship, Mademoiselle
Knows little more. Her languages. Her place.
Noon coffee. Mail. The watch that also waited
Pinned to her heart, poor gold, throws up its hands —
No puzzle! Steaming bitterness
Her sugars draw pops back into his mouth, translated:
"Patience, chéri. Geduld, mein Schatz."
(Thus, reading Valéry the other evening
And seeming to recall a Rilke version of "Palme,"
That sunlit paradigm whereby the tree
Taps a sweet wellspring of authority,
The hour came back. Patience dans l'azur.
Geduld im . . . Himmelblau? Mademoiselle.)

Out of the blue, as promised, of a New York
Puzzle-rental shop the puzzle comes —
A superior one, containing a thousand hand-sawn,
Sandal-scented pieces. Many take
Shapes known already — the craftsman's repertoire
Nice in its limitation — from other puzzles:
Witch on broomstick, ostrich, hourglass,
Even (surely not just in retrospect)
An inchling, innocently branching palm.
These can be put aside, made stories of
While Mademoiselle spreads out the rest face-up,
Herself excited as a child; or questioned
Like incoherent faces in a crowd,
Each with its scrap of highly colored
Evidence the Law must piece together.

Sky-blue ostrich? Likely story.
Mauve of the witch's cloak white, severed fingers
Pluck? Detain her. The plot thickens
As all at once two pieces interlock.

Mademoiselle does borders — (Not so fast.
A London dusk, December last.
Chatter silenced in the library
This grown man reenters, wearing grey.
A medium. All except him have seen
Panel slid back, recess explored,
An object at once unique and common
Displayed, planted in a plain tole
Casket the subject now considers
Through shut eyes, saying in effect:
"Even as voices reach me vaguely
A dry saw-shriek drowns them out,
Some loud machinery — a lumber mill?
Far uphill in the fir forest
Trees tower, tense with shock,
Groaning and cracking as they crash groundward.
But hidden here is a freak fragment
Of a pattern complex in appearance only.
What it seems to show is superficial
Next to that long-term lamination
Of hazard and craft, the karma that has
Made it matter in the first place.
Plywood. Piece of a puzzle." Applause
Acknowledged by an opening of lids
Upon the thing itself. A sudden dread —
But to go back. All this lay years ahead.)

Mademoiselle does borders. Straight-edge pieces
Align themselves with earth or sky
In twos and threes, naive cosmogonists
Whose views clash. Nomad inlanders meanwhile
Begin to cluster where the totem
Of a certain vibrant egg-yolk yellow
Or pelt of what emerging animal
Acts on the straggler like a trumpet call
To form a more sophisticated unit.
By suppertime two ragged wooden clouds
Have formed. In one, a Sheik with beard
And flashing sword hilt (he is all but finished)
Steps forward on a tiger skin. A piece
Snaps shut, and fangs gnash out at us!
In the second cloud — they gaze from cloud to cloud
With marked if undecipherable feeling —

Most of a dark-eyed woman veiled in mauve
Is being helped down from her camel (kneeling)
By a small backward-looking slave or page-boy
(Her son, thinks Mademoiselle mistakenly)
Whose feet have not been found. But lucky finds
In the last minutes before bed
Anchor both factions to the scene's limits
And, by so doing, orient
Them eye to eye across the green abyss.
The yellow promises, oh bliss,
To be in time a sumptuous tent.

Puzzle begun I write in the day's space,
Then, while she bathes, peek at Mademoiselle's
Page to the curé: " . . . cette innocente mère,
Ce pauvre enfant, que deviendront-ils?"
Her azure script is curlicued like pieces
Of the puzzle she will be telling him about.
(Fearful incuriosity of childhood!
"Tu as l'accent allemand" said Dominique.
Indeed. Mademoiselle was only French by marriage.
Child of an English mother, a remote
Descendant of the great explorer Speke,
And Prussian father. No one knew. I heard it
Long afterwards from her nephew, a UN
Interpreter. His matter-of-fact account
Touched old strings. My poor Mademoiselle,
With 1939 about to shake
This world where "each was the enemy, each the friend"
To its foundations, kept, though signed in blood,
Her peace a shameful secret to the end.)
"Schlaf wohl, chéri." Her kiss. Her thumb
Crossing my brow against the dreams to come.

This World that shifts like sand, its unforeseen
Consolidations and elate routine,
Whose Potentate had lacked a retinue?
Lo! it assembles on the shrinking Green.

Gunmetal-skinned or pale, all plumes and scars,
Of Vassalage the noblest avatars —
The very coffee-bearer in his vair
Vest is a swart Highness, next to ours.

Kef easing Boredom, and iced syrups, thirst,
In guessed-at glooms old wives who know the worst
Outsweat that virile fiction of the New:
"Insh'Allah, he will tire — " " — or kill her first!"

(Hardly a proper subject for the Home,
Work of — dear Richard, I shall let *you* comb
Archives and learned journals for his name —
A minor lion attending on Gérôme.)

While, thick as Thebes whose presently complete
Gates close behind them, Houri and Afreet
Both claim the Page. He wonders whom to serve,
And what his duties are, and where his feet,

And if we'll find, as some before us did,
That piece of Distance deep in which lies hid
Your tiny apex sugary with sun,
Eternal Triangle, Great Pyramid!

Then Sky alone is left, a hundred blue
Fragments in revolution, with no clue
To where a Niche will open. Quite a task,
Putting together Heaven, yet we do.

It's done. Here under the table all along
Were those missing feet. It's done.

The dog's tail thumping. Mademoiselle sketching
Costumes for a coming harem drama
To star the goosegirl. All too soon the swift
Dismantling. Lifted by two corners,
The puzzle hung together — and did not.
Irresistibly a populace
Unstitched of its attachments, rattled down.
Power went to pieces as the witch
Slithered easily from Virtue's gown.
The blue held out for time, but crumbled, too.
The city had long fallen, and the tent,
A separating sauce mousseline,
Been swept away. Remained the green
On which the grown-ups gambled. A green dusk.
First lightning bugs. Last glow of west
Green in the false eyes of (coincidence)
Our mangy tiger safe on his bared hearth.

Before the puzzle was boxed and readdressed
To the puzzle shop in the mid-Sixties,
Something tells me that one piece contrived
To stay in the boy's pocket. How do I know?
I know because so many later puzzles
Had missing pieces — Maggie Teyte's high notes
Gone at the war's end, end of the vogue for collies,
A house torn down; and hadn't Mademoiselle

Kept back her pitiful bit of truth as well?
I've spent the last days, furthermore,
Ransacking Athens for that translation of "Palme."
Neither the Goethehaus nor the National Library
Seems able to unearth it. Yet I can't
Just be imagining. I've seen it. Know
How much of the sun-ripe original
Felicity Rilke made himself forego
(Who loved French words — verger, mûr, parfumer)
In order to render its underlying sense.
Know already in that tongue of his
What Pains, what monolithic Truths
Shadow stanza to stanza's symmetrical
Rhyme-rutted pavement. Know that ground plan left
Sublime and barren, where the warm Romance
Stone by stone faded, cooled; the fluted nouns
Made taller, lonelier than life
By leaf-carved capitals in the afterglow.
The owlet umlaut peeps and hoots
Above the open vowel. And after rain
A deep reverberation fills with stars.

Lost, is it, buried? One more missing piece?

But nothing's lost. Or else: all is translation
And every bit of us is lost in it
(Or found — I wander through the ruin of S
Now and then, wondering at the peacefulness)
And in that loss a self-effacing tree,
Color of context, imperceptibly
Rustling with its angel, turns the waste
To shade and fiber, milk and memory.

1976

Grass

The river irises
Draw themselves in.
Enough to have seen
Their day. The arras

Also of evening drawn,
We light up between
Earth and Venus
On the courthouse lawn,

Kept by this cheerful
Inch of green
And ten more years — fifteen? —
From disappearing.

1985

Graffito

Deep in weeds, on a smooth chunk of stone
Fallen from the cornice of the church
(Originally a temple to Fortuna),
Appears this forearm neatly drawn in black,
Wearing, lest we misunderstand,
Like a tattoo the cross-within-a-circle
Of the majority — Christian Democrat.

Arms and the man. This arm ends in a hand
Which grasps a neatly, elegantly drawn
Cock — erect and spurting tiny stars —
And balls. One sports . . . a swastika?
Yes, and its twin, if you please, a hammer-and-sickle!
The tiny stars, seen close, are stars of David.
Now what are we supposed to make of that?

Wink from Lorenzo, pout from Mrs. Pratt.
Hold on, I want to photograph this latest
Fountain of Rome, whose twinkling gist
Gusts my way from an age when isms were largely
Come-ons for the priapic satirist,
And any young guy with a pencil felt
He held the fate of nations in his fist.

1988

Self-Portrait in Tyvek™ Windbreaker

The windbreaker is white with a world map.
DuPont contributed the seeming-frail,
Unrippable stuff first used for Priority Mail.
Weightless as shores reflected in deep water,
The countries are violet, orange, yellow, green;
Names of the principal towns and rivers, black.
A zipper's hiss, and the Atlantic Ocean closes
Over my blood-red T-shirt from the Gap.

I found it in one of those vaguely imbecile
Emporia catering to the collective unconscious
Of our time and place. This one featured crystals,
Cassettes of whalesong and rain-forest whistles,
Barometers, herbal cosmetics, pillows like puffins,
Recycled notebooks, mechanized lucite coffins
For sapphire waves that crest, break, and recede,
As they presumably do in nature still.

Sweat-panted and Reeboked, I wear it to the gym.
My terry-cloth headband is green as laurel.
A yellow plastic Walkman at my hip
Sends shiny yellow tendrils to either ear.
All us street people got our types on tape,
Turn ourselves on with a sly fingertip.
Today I felt like Songs of Yesteryear
Sung by Roberto Murolo. Heard of him?

Well, back before animal species began to become
Extinct, a dictator named Mussolini banned
The street-singers of Naples. One smart kid
Learned their repertoire by heart, and hid.
Emerging after the war with his guitar,
He alone bearing the old songs of the land
Into the nuclear age sang with a charm,
A perfect naturalness that thawed the numb

Survivors and reinspired the Underground.
From love to grief to gaiety his art
Modulates effortlessly, like a young man's heart,
Tonic to dominant — the frets so few
And change so strummed into the life of things
That Nature's lamps burn brighter when he sings
Nannetta's fickleness, or chocolate,
Snow on a flower, the moon, the seasons' round.

I picked his tape in lieu of something grosser
Or loftier, say the Dead or Arvo Pärt,
On the hazy premise that what fills the mind
Shows on the face. My face, as a small pärt
Of nature, hopes this musical sunscreen
Will keep the wilderness within it green,
Yet looks uneasy, drawn. I detect behind
My neighbor's grin the oncoming bulldozer

And cannot stop it. Ecosaints — their karma
To be Earth's latest, maybe terminal, fruits —
Are slow to ripen. Even this dumb jacket
Probably still believes in Human Rights,

Thinks in terms of "nations," urban centers,
Cares less (can Tyvek breathe?) for oxygen
Than for the innocents evicted when
Ford bites the dust and Big Mac buys the farm.

Hah. As if greed and savagery weren't the tongues
We've spoken since the beginning. My point is, those
Prior people, fresh from scarifying
Their young and feasting in triumph on their foes,
Honored the gods of Air and Land and Sea.
We, though . . . Cut to dead forests, filthy beaches,
The can of hairspray, oil-benighted creatures,
A star-scarred x-ray of the North Wind's lungs.

Still, not to paint a picture wholly black,
Some social highlights: Dead white males in malls.
Prayer breakfasts. Pay-phone sex. "Ring up as meat."
Oprah. The GNP. The contour sheet.
The painless death of History. The stick
Figures on Capitol Hill. Their rhetoric,
Gladly — no, rapturously (on Prozac) suffered!
Gay studies. Right to Lifers. The laugh track.

And clothes. Americans, blithe as the last straw,
Shrug off accountability by dressing
Younger than their kids — jeans, ski-pants, sneakers,
A baseball cap, a happy-face T-shirt . . .
Like first-graders we "love" our mother Earth,
Know she's been sick, and mean to care for her
When we grow up. Seeing my windbreaker,
People hail me with nostalgic awe.

"Great jacket!" strangers on streetcorners impart.
The Albanian doorman pats it: "Where you buy?"
Over his ear-splitting drill a hunky guy
Yells, "Hey, you'll always know where you are, right?"
"Ever the fashionable cosmopolite,"
Beams Ray. And "Voilà mon pays" — the carrot-haired
Girl in the bakery, touching with her finger
The little orange France above my heart.

Everyman, c'est moi, the whole world's pal!
The pity is how soon such feelings sour.
As I leave the gym a smiling-as-if-I-should-know-her
Teenager — oh but I *mean*, she's wearing "our"
Windbreaker, and assumes . . . Yet I return her wave
Like an accomplice. For while all humans aren't
Countable as equals, we must behave
As if they were, or the spirit dies (Pascal).

"We"? A few hundred decades of relative
Lucidity glinted-through by minnow schools
Between us and the red genetic muck —
Everyman's underpainting. We look up, shy
Creatures, from our trembling pool of sky.
Caught wet-lipped in light's brushwork, fleet but sure,
Flash on shudder, folk of the first fuck,
Likeness breeds likeness, fights for breath — *I live* —

Where the crush thickens. And by season's end,
The swells of fashion cresting to collapse
In breaker upon breaker on the beach,
Who wants to be caught dead in this cliché
Of mere "involvement"? Time to put under wraps
Its corporate synthetic global pitch;
Not throwing out motley once reveled in,
Just learning to live down the wrinkled friend.

Face it, reproduction of any kind leaves us colder
Though airtight-warmer (greenhouse effect) each year.
Remember the figleaf's lesson. Styles betray
Some guilty knowledge. What to dress ours in —
A seer's blind gaze, an infant's tender skin?
All that's been seen through. The eloquence to come
Will be precisely what we cannot say
Until it parts the lips. But as one grows older

— I should confess before that last coat dries —
The wry recall of thunder does for rage.
Erotic torrents flash on screens instead
Of drenching us. Exclusively in dream,
These nights, does a grandsire rear his saurian head,
And childhood's inexhaustible brain-forest teem
With jewel-bright lives. No way now to restage
Their sacred pageant under our new skies'

Irradiated lucite. What then to wear
When — hush, it's no dream! It's my windbreaker
In black, with starry longitudes, Archer, Goat,
Clothing an earphoned archangel of Space,
Who hasn't read Pascal, and doesn't wave . . .
What far-out twitterings he learns by rote,
What looks they'd wake upon a human face,
Don't ask, Roberto. Sing our final air:

Love, grief etc. **** for good reason.
Now only ******* STOP signs
Meanwhile ***** if you or I've ex-
ceeded our [?] *** ~~more than time~~ was needed

To fit a text airless and * * as Tyvek
With breathing spaces and between the lines
Days brilliantly recurring, as once *we* did,
To keep the blue wave dancing in its prison.

1995

b o d y

Look closely at the letters. Can you see,
entering (stage right), then floating full,
then heading off — so soon —
how like a little kohl-rimmed moon
o plots her course from *b* to *d*

as *y*, unanswered, knocks at the stage door?
Looked at too long, words fail,
phase out. Ask, now that *body* shines
no longer, by what light you learn these lines
and what the *b* and *d* stood for.

1995

Days of 1994

These days in my friend's house
Light seeks me underground. To wake
Below the level of the lawn
— Half-basement cool through the worst heat —
Is strange and sweet.
High up, three window-slots, new slants on dawn:
Through misty greens and gilts
An infant sun totters on stilts of shade
Up toward the high
Mass of interwoven boughs,
While close against the triptych panes
Rock bears witness, Dragonfly
Shivers in place
Above tall Queen Anne's lace —
More figures from *The Book of Thel* by Blake
(Lilly & Worm, Cloudlet & Clod of Clay)
And none but drinks the dewy Manna in.

I shiver next, Light walking on my grave . . .
And sleep, and wake. This time, peer out
From just beneath the mirror of the lake

A gentle mile uphill.
Florets — the mountain laurel — float
Openmouthed, devout,
Set swaying by the wake of the flatboat:

Barcarole whose chords of gloom
Draw forth the youngest, purest, faithfullest.
Cool-crystal-casketed
Hands crossed on breast,
Pre-Raphaelite face radiant — and look,
Not dead, O never dead!
To wake, to wake
Among the flaming dowels of a tomb
Below the world, the thousand things
Here risen to if not above
Before day ends:
The spectacles, the book,
Forgetful lover and forgotten love,
Cobweb hung with trophy wings,
The fading trumpet of a car,
The knowing glance from star to star,
The laughter of old friends.

1995

FRANK O'HARA (1926–1966)

Frank O'Hara was born in Baltimore, Maryland. He served in the Navy in World War II. In 1951 he joined his Harvard friends John Ashbery and Kenneth Koch in Manhattan, and the "New York school" was under way. O'Hara was the charismatic hero, the catalyst, the guy who made it all make sense — the divey downtown bars and midtown galleries, the cocktail parties in tuxedos, the afternoon tabloids with a social conscience. Adored by the painters whom he befriended and promoted with selflessness unusual in the competitive world of the arts, he was himself the closest thing to an action painter in verse, typing poems in a mad clatter of keys while listening to the radio. In his "Personism: A Manifesto," O'Hara describes his view of poetic form: "As for measure and other technical apparatus, that's just common sense: if you're going to buy a pair of pants you want them to be tight enough so everyone will want to go to bed with you." O'Hara wrote for *Art News* and worked his way up from postcard clerk to associate curator at the Museum of Modern Art. His monograph on Jackson Pollock appeared in 1959. His books of poems include *Meditations in an Emergency* (1957), *Lunch Poems* (1964), and the posthumous *Collected Poems* (1971). He died in July 1966, having been hit by a dune buggy on Fire Island. Edwin Denby said O'Hara was "everybody's catalyst." The painter Phillip Guston called him "our Apollinaire."

Autobiographia Literaria

When I was a child
I played by myself in a
corner of the schoolyard
all alone.

I hated dolls and I
hated games, animals were
not friendly and birds
flew away.

If anyone was looking
for me I hid behind a
tree and cried out "I am
an orphan."

And here I am, the
center of all beauty!
writing these poems!
Imagine!

1949

Poem

The eager note on my door said "Call me,
call when you get in!" so I quickly threw
a few tangerines into my overnight bag,
straightened my eyelids and shoulders, and

headed straight for the door. It was autumn
by the time I got around the corner, oh all
unwilling to be either pertinent or bemused, but
the leaves were brighter than grass on the sidewalk!

Funny, I thought, that the lights are on this late
and the hall door open; still up at this hour, a
champion jai-alai player like himself? Oh fie!
for shame! What a host, so zealous! And he was

there in the hall, flat on a sheet of blood that
ran down the stairs. I did appreciate it. There are few
hosts who so thoroughly prepare to greet a guest
only casually invited, and that several months ago.

1950

Memorial Day 1950

Picasso made me tough and quick, and the world;
just as in a minute plane trees are knocked down
outside my window by a crew of creators.
Once he got his axe going everyone was upset
enough to fight for the last ditch and heap
of rubbish.
                    Through all that surgery I thought
I had a lot to say, and named several last things
Gertrude Stein hadn't had time for; but then
the war was over, those things had survived
and even when you're scared art is no dictionary.
Max Ernst told us that.
                                        How many trees and frying pans
I loved and lost! Guernica hollered look out!
but we were all busy hoping our eyes were talking
to Paul Klee. My mother and father asked me and
I told them from my tight blue pants we should
love only the stones, the sea, and heroic figures.
Wasted child! I'll club you on the shins! I
wasn't surprised when the older people entered
my cheap hotel room and broke my guitar and my can
of blue paint.
                    At that time all of us began to think
with our bare hands and even with blood all over
them, we knew vertical from horizontal, we never
smeared anything except to find out how it lived.
Fathers of Dada! You carried shining erector sets
in your rough bony pockets, you were generous
and they were lovely as chewing gum or flowers!
Thank you!
                    And those of us who thought poetry
was crap were throttled by Auden or Rimbaud
when, sent by some compulsive Juno, we tried
to play with collages or sprechstimme in their bed.
Poetry didn't tell me not to play with toys
but alone I could never have figured out that dolls
meant death.
                    Our responsibilities did not begin
in dreams, though they began in bed. Love is first of all
a lesson in utility. I hear the sewage singing
underneath my bright white toilet seat and know
that somewhere sometime it will reach the sea:
gulls and swordfishes will find it richer than a river.
And airplanes are perfect mobiles, independent
of the breeze; crashing in flames they show us how
to be prodigal. O Boris Pasternak, it may be silly
to call to you, so tall in the Urals, but your voice

cleans our world, clearer to us than the hospital:
you sound above the factory's ambitious gargle.
Poetry is as useful as a machine!
                                        Look at my room.
Guitar strings hold up pictures. I don't need
a piano to sing, and naming things is only the intention
to make things. A locomotive is more melodious
than a cello. I dress in oil cloth and read music
by Guillaume Apollinaire's clay candelabra. Now
my father is dead and has found out you must look things
in the belly, not in the eye. If only he had listened
to the men who made us, hollering like stuck pigs!

1950

The Critic

I cannot possibly think of you
other than you are: the assassin

of my orchards. You lurk there
in the shadows, meting out

conversation like Eve's first
confusion between penises and

snakes. Oh be droll, be jolly
and be temperate! Do not

frighten me more than you
have to! I must live forever.

1951

Blocks

I

Yippee! she is shooting in the harbor! he is jumping
up to the maelstrom! she is leaning over the giant's
cart of tears which like a lava cone let fall to fly
from the cross-eyed tantrum-tousled ninth grader's
splayed fist is freezing on the cement! he is throwing
up his arms in heavenly desperation, spacious Y of his
tumultuous love-nerves flailing like a poinsettia in
its own nailish storm against the glass door of the

cumulus which is withholding her from these divine
pastures she has filled with the flesh of men as stones!
O fatal eagerness!

II

O boy, their childhood was like so many oatmeal cookies.
I need you, you need me, yum, yum. Anon it became
suddenly

III

like someone always losing something and never knowing what.
Always so. They were so fond of eating bread and butter and
sugar, they were slobs, the mice used to lick the floorboards
after they went to bed, rolling their light tails against
the rattling marbles of granulation. Vivo! the dextrose
those children consumed, lavished, smoked, in their knobby
candy bars. Such pimples! such hardons! such moody loves.
And thus they grew like giggling fir trees.

1952

To the Harbormaster

I wanted to be sure to reach you;
though my ship was on the way it got caught
in some moorings. I am always tying up
and then deciding to depart. In storms and
at sunset, with the metallic coils of the tide
around my fathomless arms, I am unable
to understand the forms of my vanity
or I am hard alee with my Polish rudder
in my hand and the sun sinking. To
you I offer my hull and the tattered cordage
of my will. The terrible channels where
the wind drives me against the brown lips
of the reeds are not all behind me. Yet
I trust the sanity of my vessel; and
if it sinks, it may well be in answer
to the reasoning of the eternal voices,
the waves which have kept me from reaching you.

1954

My Heart

I'm not going to cry all the time
nor shall I laugh all the time,
I don't prefer one "strain" to another.
I'd have the immediacy of a bad movie,
not just a sleeper, but also the big,
overproduced first-run kind. I want to be
at least as alive as the vulgar. And if
some aficionado of my mess says "That's
not like Frank!", all to the good! I
don't wear brown and grey suits all the time,
do I? No. I wear workshirts to the opera,
often. I want my feet to be bare,
I want my face to be shaven, and my heart —
you can't plan on the heart, but
the better part of it, my poetry, is open.

1955

A Step Away From Them

It's my lunch hour, so I go
for a walk among the hum-colored
cabs. First, down the sidewalk
where laborers feed their dirty
glistening torsos sandwiches
and Coca-Cola, with yellow helmets
on. They protect them from falling
bricks, I guess. Then onto the
avenue where skirts are flipping
above heels and blow up over
grates. The sun is hot, but the
cabs stir up the air. I look
at bargains in wristwatches. There
are cats playing in sawdust.
On
to Times Square, where the sign
blows smoke over my head, and higher
the waterfall pours lightly. A
Negro stands in a doorway with a
toothpick, languorously agitating
A blonde chorus girl clicks: he
smiles and rubs his chin. Everything
suddenly honks: it is 12:40 of
a Thursday.

Neon in daylight is a
great pleasure, as Edwin Denby would

write, as are light bulbs in daylight.
I stop for a cheeseburger at JULIET'S
CORNER. Giulietta Masina, wife of
Federico Fellini, é bell' attrice.
And chocolate malted. A lady in
foxes on such a day puts her poodle
in a cab.
There are several Puerto
Ricans on the avenue today, which
makes it beautiful and warm. First
Bunny died, then John Latouche,
then Jackson Pollock. But is the
earth as full as life was full, of them?
And one has eaten and one walks,
past the magazines with nudes
and the posters for BULLFIGHT and
the Manhatten Storage Warehouse,
which they'll soon tear down. I
used to think they had the Armory
Show there.
A glass of papaya juice
and back to work. My heart is in my
pocket, it is Poems by Pierre Reverdy.

1956

Why I Am Not a Painter

I am not a painter, I am a poet.
Why? I think I would rather be
a painter, but I am not. Well,

for instance, Mike Goldberg
is starting a painting. I drop in.
"Sit down and have a drink" he
says. I drink; we drink. I look
up. "You have SARDINES in it."
"Yes, it needed something there."
"Oh." I go and the days go by
and I drop in again. The painting
is going on, and I go, and the days
go by. I drop in. The painting is
finished. "Where's SARDINES?"
All that's left is just
letters, "It was too much," Mike says.

But me? One day I am thinking of
a color: orange. I write a line
about orange. Pretty soon it is a
whole page of words, not lines.
Then another page. There should be
so much more, not of orange, of
words, of how terrible orange is
and life. Days go by. It is even in
prose, I am a real poet. My poem
is finished and I haven't mentioned
orange yet. It's twelve poems, I call
it ORANGES. And one day in a gallery
I see Mike's painting, called SARDINES.

1956

To the Film Industry in Crisis

Not you, lean quarterlies and swarthy periodicals
with your studious incursions toward the pomposity of ants,
nor you, experimental theatre in which Emotive Fruition
is wedding Poetic Insight perpetually, nor you,
promenading Grand Opera, obvious as an ear (though you
are close to my heart), but you, Motion Picture Industry,
it's you I love!

In times of crisis, we must all decide again and again whom we love.
And give credit where it's due: not to my starched nurse, who taught me
how to be bad and not bad rather than good (and has lately availed
herself of this information), not to the Catholic Church
which is at best an oversolemn introduction to cosmic entertainment,
not to the American Legion, which hates everybody, but to you,
glorious Silver Screen, tragic Technicolor, amorous Cinemascope,
stretching Vistavision and startling Stereophonic Sound, with all
your heavenly dimensions and reverberations and iconoclasms! To
Richard Barthelmess as the "tol'able" boy barefoot and in pants,
Jeanette MacDonald of the flaming hair and lips and long, long neck,
Sue Carroll as she sits for eternity on the damaged fender of a car
and smiles, Ginger Rogers with her pageboy bob like a sausage
on her shuffling shoulders, peach-melba-voiced Fred Astaire of the feet,
Eric von Stroheim, the seducer of mountain-climbers' gasping spouses,
the Tarzans, each and every one of you (I cannot bring myself to prefer
Johnny Weissmuller to Lex Barker, I cannot!), Mae West in a furry sled,
her bordello radiance and bland remarks, Rudolph Valentino of the moon,
its crushing passions, and moonlike, too, the gentle Norma Shearer,

Miriam Hopkins dropping her champagne glass off Joel McCrea's yacht
and crying into the dappled sea, Clark Gable rescuing Gene Tierney
from Russia and Allan Jones rescuing Kitty Carlisle from Harpo Marx,
Cornel Wilde coughing blood on the piano keys while Merle Oberon berates,
Marilyn Monroe in her little spike heels reeling through Niagara Falls,
Joseph Cotten puzzling and Orson Welles puzzled and Dolores del Rio
eating orchids for lunch and breaking mirrors, Gloria Swanson reclining,
and Jean Harlow reclining and wiggling, and Alice Faye reclining
and wiggling and singing, Myrna Loy being calm and wise, William Powell
in his stunning urbanity, Elizabeth Taylor blossoming, yes, to you

and to all you others, the great, the near-great, the featured, the extras
who pass quickly and return in dreams saying your one or two lines,
my love!
Long may you illumine space with your marvellous appearances, delays
and enunciations, and may the money of the world glitteringly cover you
as you rest after a long day under the kleig lights with your faces
in packs for our edification, the way the clouds come often at night
but the heavens operate on the star system. It is a divine precedent
you perpetuate! Roll on, reels of celluloid, as the great earth rolls on!

1957

A True Account of Talking to the Sun at Fire Island

The Sun woke me this morning loud
and clear, saying "Hey! I've been
trying to wake you up for fifteen
minutes. Don't be so rude, you are
only the second poet I've ever chosen
to speak to personally

so why
aren't you more attentive? If I could
burn you through the window I would
to wake you up. I can't hang around
here all day."

"Sorry, Sun, I stayed
up late last night talking to Hal."

"When I woke up Mayakovsky he was
a lot more prompt" the Sun said
petulantly. "Most people are up
already waiting to see if I'm going
to put in an appearance."

I tried
to apologize "I missed you yesterday."
"That's better" he said. "I didn't
know you'd come out." "You may be
wondering why I've come so close?"
"Yes" I said beginning to feel hot
wondering if maybe he wasn't burning me
anyway.
"Frankly I wanted to tell you
I like your poetry. I see a lot
on my rounds and you're okay. You may
not be the greatest thing on earth, but
you're different. Now, I've heard some
say you're crazy, they being excessively
calm themselves to my mind, and other
crazy poets think that you're a boring
reactionary. Not me.
Just keep on
like I do and pay no attention. You'll
find that people always will complain
about the atmosphere, either too hot
or too cold too bright or too dark, days
too short or too long.
If you don't appear
at all one day they think you're lazy
or dead. Just keep right on, I like it.

And don't worry about your lineage
poetic or natural. The Sun shines on
the jungle, you know, on the tundra
the sea, the ghetto. Wherever you were
I knew it and saw you moving. I was waiting
for you to get to work.

And now that you
are making your own days, so to speak,
even if no one reads you but me
you won't be depressed. Not
everyone can look up, even at me. It
hurts their eyes."
"Oh Sun, I'm so grateful to you!"

"Thanks and remember I'm watching. It's
easier for me to speak to you out
here. I don't have to slide down
between buildings to get your ear.
I know you love Manhattan, but
you ought to look up more often.

And
always embrace things, people earth
sky stars, as I do, freely and with
the appropriate sense of space. That
is your inclination, known in the heavens
and you should follow it to hell, if
necessary, which I doubt.

Maybe we'll
speak again in Africa, of which I too
am specially fond. Go back to sleep now
Frank, and I may leave a tiny poem
in that brain of yours as my farewell."

"Sun, don't go!" I was awake
at last. "No, go I must, they're calling
me."

"Who are they?"

Rising he said "Some
day you'll know. They're calling to you
too." Darkly he rose, and then I slept.

1958

The Day Lady Died

It is 12:20 in New York a Friday
three days after Bastille day, yes
it is 1959 and I go get a shoeshine
because I will get off the 4:19 in Easthampton
at 7:15 and then go straight to dinner
and I don't know the people who will feed me

I walk up the muggy street beginning to sun
and have a hamburger and a malted and buy
an ugly NEW WORLD WRITING to see what the poets
in Ghana are doing these days

I go on to the bank
and Miss Stillwagon (first name Linda I once heard)
doesn't even look up my balance for once in her life
and in the GOLDEN GRIFFIN I get a little Verlaine
for Patsy with drawings by Bonnard although I do
think of Hesiod, trans. Richmond Lattimore or
Brendan Behan's new play or *Le Balcon* or *Les Nègres*
of Genet, but I don't, I stick with Verlaine
after practically going to sleep with quandariness

and for Mike I just stroll into the PARK LANE
Liquor Store and ask for a bottle of Strega and

then I go back where I came from to 6th Avenue
and the tobacconist in the Ziegfeld Theatre and
casually ask for a carton of Gauloises and a carton
of Picayunes, and a NEW YORK POST with her face on it

and I am sweating a lot by now and thinking of
leaning on the john door in the 5 SPOT
while she whispered a song along the keyboard
to Mal Waldron and everyone and I stopped breathing

1959

Personal Poem

Now when I walk around at lunchtime
I have only two charms in my pocket
an old Roman coin Mike Kanemitsu gave me
and a bolt-head that broke off a packing case
when I was in Madrid the others never
brought me too much luck though they did
help keep me in New York against coercion
but now I'm happy for a time and interested

I walk through the luminous humidity
passing the House of Seagram with its wet
and its loungers and the construction to
the left that closed the sidewalk if
I ever get to be a construction worker
I'd like to have a silver hat please
and get to Moriarty's where I wait for
LeRoi and hear who wants to be a mover and
shaker the last five years my batting average
is .016 that's that, and LeRoi comes in
and tells me Miles Davis was clubbed 12
times last night outside BIRDLAND by a cop
a lady asks us for a nickel for a terrible
disease but we don't give her one we
don't like terrible diseases, then

we go eat some fish and some ale it's
cool but crowded we don't like Lionel Trilling
we decide, we like Don Allen we don't like
Henry James so much we like Herman Melville
we don't want to be in the poets' walk in
San Francisco even we just want to be rich
and walk on girders in our silver hats
I wonder if one person out of the 8,000,000 is

thinking of me as I shake hands with LeRoi
and buy a strap for my wristwatch and go
back to work happy at the thought possibly so

1959

Poem

Light clarity avocado salad in the morning
after all the terrible things I do how amazing it is
to find forgiveness and love, not even forgiveness
since what is done is done and forgiveness isn't love
and love is love nothing can ever go wrong
though things can get irritating boring and dispensable
(in the imagination) but not really for love
though a block away you feel distant the mere presence
changes everything like a chemical dropped on a paper
and all thoughts disappear in a strange quiet excitement
I am sure of nothing but this, intensified by breathing

1959

Poem

Lana Turner has collapsed!
I was trotting along and suddenly
it started raining and snowing
and you said it was hailing
but hailing hits you on the head
hard so it was really snowing and
raining and I was in such a hurry
to meet you but the traffic
was acting exactly like the sky
and suddenly I see a headline
LANA TURNER HAS COLLAPSED!
there is no snow in Hollywood
there is no rain in California
I have been to lots of parties
and acted perfectly disgraceful
but I never actually collapsed
oh Lana Turner we love you get up

1962

W. D. SNODGRASS (b. 1926)

W. D. Snodgrass was born in Wilkinsburg, Pennsylvania. In Donald Hall's opinion, no one "so combines the sonnet and the scream." Lowell credited the Snodgrass of *Heart's Needle* (1959) as part of the impetus behind Lowell's conversion to the "confessional" creed of revelations about the self, candor about misery, self-accusation, and the divulging of intimate details. In *The Fuhrer Bunker* (1977) Snodgrass fashions monologues out of intractable materials: the lives of Hitler, Eva Braun, Goebbels, and other Nazi bigwigs at the end of the Third Reich.

April Inventory

The green catalpa tree has turned
All white; the cherry blooms once more.
In one whole year I haven't learned
A blessed thing they pay you for.
The blossoms snow down in my hair;
The trees and I will soon be bare.

The trees have more than I to spare.
The sleek, expensive girls I teach,
Younger and pinker every year,
Bloom gradually out of reach.
The pear tree lets its petals drop
Like dandruff on a tabletop.

The girls have grown so young by now
I have to nudge myself to stare.
This year they smile and mind me how
My teeth are falling with my hair.
In thirty years I may not get
Younger, shrewder, or out of debt.

The tenth time, just a year ago,
I made myself a little list
Of all the things I'd ought to know,
Then told my parents, analyst,
And everyone who's trusted me
I'd be substantial, presently.

I haven't read one book about
A book or memorized one plot.
Or found a mind I did not doubt.
I learned one date. And then forgot.
And one by one the solid scholars
Get the degrees, the jobs, the dollars.

And smile above their starchy collars.
I taught my classes Whitehead's notions;

One lovely girl, a song of Mahler's.
Lacking a source-book or promotions,
I showed one child the colors of
A luna moth and how to love.

I taught myself to name my name,
To bark back, loosen love and crying;
To ease my woman so she came,
To ease an old man who was dying.
I have not learned how often I
Can win, can love, but choose to die.

I have not learned there is a lie
Love shall be blonder, slimmer, younger;
That my equivocating eye
Loves only by my body's hunger;
That I have forces, true to feel,
Or that the lovely world is real.

While scholars speak authority
And wear their ulcers on their sleeves,
My eyes in spectacles shall see
These trees procure and spend their leaves.
There is a value underneath
The gold and silver in my teeth.

Though trees turn bare and girls turn wives,
We shall afford our costly seasons;
There is a gentleness survives
That will outspeak and has its reasons.
There is a loveliness exists,
Preserves us, not for specialists.

1959

Mementos, 1

Sorting out letters and piles of my old
  Canceled checks, old clippings, and yellow note cards
That meant something once, I happened to find
  Your picture. *That* picture. I stopped there cold,
Like a man raking piles of dead leaves in his yard
      Who has turned up a severed hand.

Still, that first second, I was glad: you stand
  Just as you stood — shy, delicate, slender,
In that long gown of green lace netting and daisies
  That you wore to our first dance. The sight of you stunned

Us all. Well, our needs were different, then,
And our ideals came easy.

Then through the war and those two long years
Overseas, the Japanese dead in their shacks
Among dishes, dolls, and lost shoes; I carried
This glimpse of you, there, to choke down my fear,
Prove it had been, that it might come back.
That was before we got married.

— Before we drained out one another's force
With lies, self-denial, unspoken regret
And the sick eyes that blame; before the divorce
And the treachery. Say it: before we met. Still,
I put back your picture. Someday, in due course
I will find that it's still there.

1967

DAVID WAGONER (b. 1926)

David Wagoner was born in Massillon, Ohio, and grew up in Indiana. After graduating from Pennsylvania State University, he worked as a railway man and reporter before he joined Theodore Roethke on the University of Washington faculty in 1954. He founded *Poetry Northwest* in 1966 and edited the magazine for its entire thirty-six year run. Of the Pacific Northwest, Wagoner has said, "It has for me the central shock of untouched nature. I came from a place where nature was ruined, and here the natural world was still in a pristine state." X. J. Kennedy has written, "Wagoner is so readable a poet, that coming to him after, say, an evening with Pound's later *Cantos*, one practically has a twinge of Puritan guilt, and feels shamelessly entertained — refreshed instead of exhausted."

The Words

Wind, bird, and tree,
Water, grass, and light:
In half of what I write
Roughly or smoothly
Year by impatient year,
The same six words recur.

I have as many floors
As meadows or rivers,
As much still air as wind
And as many cats in mind

As nests in the branches
To put an end to these.

Instead, I take what is:
The light beats on the stones,
And wind over water shines
Like long grass through the trees,
As I set loose, like birds
In a landscape, the old words.

1964

Dead Letter From Out of Town

> When I feel a Northwest town may trigger a poem, before I start writing I assume one or more of the following — . . . David Wagoner has seen the town, assessed it realistically, and decided it is a good place to steer clear of.
>
> — Richard Hugo, *The Triggering Town*

Dick, you were right. I steered clear of that town.
The river that runs through it is as stagnant
As a drainage ditch, the weather an amalgam
Of mildewed paper, slush, dead steam, and phlegm.
The only tavern's built out of used firebrick
And looks like a walk-in safe. The sweet young thing
On the barstool nursing a cooler may have something
But it's in her purse and loaded. The jukebox is broken.
The nearest emergency ward is a trapdoor
In the john — one-way to Ashland. The dork who looks good
For an afternoon of heartbreaking bullshit
Has a badge in his wallet and specializes in busting
Down-on-their-luck nomads who laugh too much.
The card room doubles as the jail: no pens,
No paper, no TV. All games are called
On account of darkness. It's No Smoking forever.
And the girls you might have made, who might have danced
Your way all night and made you feel light-footed?
One lies half-buried in a vacant lot,
Another's caught on a snag in the reservoir,
And the prettiest one, the one voted most likely
To get out of town in time to be somebody,
Is sprouting flowerless plants in a crawl space.
Don't go, old friend. It pulls the trigger once.

2002

Curtains

Grandpa took me along to the hospital
To help him hang new curtains in room after room
Where sick people in bed were going to be
Much better before long. He had to measure

How high and wide the windows were with a tape.
I got to climb a ladder and hold one end
And tell him the right numbers and sometimes
I was the one who wrote them down on a pad.

Some of the people wanted to know my name
And would ask how old I was and say *Oh my!*
Or *Imagine that!* or *Aren't you proud of him?*
To Grandpa, who said nothing but numbers

Because we still had so many rooms to go.
He was tall and gray and bent. His eyes, between eyelids
And eyelashes through his horn-rimmed spectacles
From under his dark eyebrows, measured me.

He was in dry goods. His Ideal Company
Was three floors high with little cars on wires
That ran through floors and ceilings from registers
Toward Grandpa behind glass. I tried to smile

At all the sick people, even the ones who said
They didn't want new curtains or anything else
But peace and quiet. And one man didn't want Grandpa
Covering his windows. He wanted to go on

Seeing God's Outdoors. And he didn't want me
Touching his magazines and looking at him.
Grandpa said he was going to put up curtains
Like it or not because it was his job

And the man should keep a civil tongue in his head
And use it to mind his manners with God indoors
And I should act my age and wait outside
In the corridor where somebody passed by

Under a sheet, who wasn't going to get better.
He was lying on a narrow table with wheels
Behind a blue-and-white nurse who smiled my way
And asked if I'd like to come along for a ride.

2003

Lew Welch (1926–1971)

A handsome, hard-drinking member of the San Francisco Beats, Lew Welch, a native of Phoenix, Arizona, was the model for the character "Dave Wain" in Jack Kerouac's *Big Sur.* In May 1971, Welch walked off with a rifle, leaving a despairing note behind, and was never seen or heard from again.

The Basic Con

Those who can't find anything to live for,
always invent something to die for.

Then they want the rest of us to
die for it, too.

1973

Whenever I Make a New Poem

Whenever I make a new poem,
the old ones sound like gibberish.
How can they ever make sense in a book?

Let them say:

"He seems to have lived in the mountains.
He traveled now and then.
When he appeared in cities,
he was almost always drunk.

"Most of his poems are lost.
Many of those we have were found in
letters to his friends.

"He had a very large number of friends."

1973

John Ashbery (b. 1927)

John Ashbery was born in Rochester, New York. *Some Trees,* his first book, was selected by W. H. Auden for the Yale Younger Poets Prize of 1956. Though a Frank O'Hara manuscript had competed for the distinction, O'Hara was the first to praise Ashbery's book in print, calling it "the most beautiful first book to appear in America since [Wallace Stevens's] *Harmonium.*" Ashbery lived in Paris for ten years. He has earned his living as an art critic: for the *International Herald Tribune* in Paris and, after his return to the United States, for *Art News*, and subsequently for *New York* and *Newsweek* magazines. The epitome of an avant-garde writer, Ashbery faced incomprehension and risked critical dismissal early on, and his conception of the poem still seems revolutionary in some ways, but he gained general acceptance with the triumphant publication of *Self-Portrait in a Convex Mirror* (1975), winner of every book prize in sight. *Other Traditions* (Harvard University Press, 2000) consists of the Norton lectures he gave at Harvard University on such "minor" poets as John Wheelwright, David Schubert, and Laura Riding, to name the three whose work is in this book. ("As I look back on the writers I have learned from, it seems that the majority . . . are what the world calls minor ones.") Assessing the situation of the experimental artist, Ashbery concluded a lecture he gave at Yale University in 1968 by quoting the composer Busoni on the issue of discipleship: "One follows a great example most faithfully if one does not follow it, for it was through turning away from its predecessor that the example became great."

The Instruction Manual

As I sit looking out of a window of the building
I wish I did not have to write the instruction manual on the uses of a
new metal
I look down into the street and see people, each walking with an inner
peace
And envy them — they are so far away from me!
Not one of them has to worry about getting out this manual on schedule.
And, as my way is, I begin to dream, resting my elbows on the desk and
leaning out of the window a little,
Of dim Guadalajara! City of rose-colored flowers!
City I wanted most to see, and most did not see, in Mexico!
But I fancy I see, under the press of having to write the instruction
manual,
Your public square, city, with its elaborate little bandstand!
The band is playing *Scheherazade* by Rimsky-Korsakov.
Around stand the flower girls, handing out rose- and lemon-colored
flowers
Each attractive in her rose-and-blue striped dress (Oh! such shades of
rose and blue),
And nearby is the little white booth where women in green serve you
green and yellow fruit.
The couples are parading; everyone is in a holiday mood.
First, leading the parade, is a dapper fellow
Clothed in deep blue. On his head sits a white hat
And he wears a mustache, which has been trimmed for the occasion.
His dear one, his wife, is young and pretty; her shawl is rose, pink, and
white.
Her slippers are patent leather, in the American fashion,
And she carries a fan, for she is modest, and does not want the crowd to
see her face too often.

But everybody is so busy with his wife or loved one
I doubt they would notice the mustachioed man's wife.
Here come the boys! They are skipping and throwing little things on the sidewalk
Which is made of gray tile. One of them, a little older, has a toothpick in his teeth.
He is silenter than the rest, and affects not to notice the pretty young girls in white.
But his friends notice them, and shout their jeers at the laughing girls.
Yet soon all this will cease, with the deepening of their years,
And love bring each to the parade grounds for another reason.
But I have lost sight of the young fellow with the toothpick.
Wait — there he is — on the other side of the bandstand,
Secluded from his friends, in earnest talk with a young girl
Of fourteen or fifteen. I try to hear what they are saying
But it seems they are just mumbling something — shy words of love, probably.
She is slightly taller than he, and looks quietly down into his sincere eyes.
She is wearing white. The breeze ruffles her long fine black hair against her olive cheek.
Obviously she is in love. The boy, the young boy with the toothpick, he is in love too;
His eyes show it. Turning from this couple,
I see there is an intermission in the concert.
The paraders are resting and sipping drinks through straws
(The drinks are dispensed from a large glass crock by a lady in dark blue),
And the musicians mingle among them, in their creamy white uniforms, and talk
About the weather, perhaps, or how their kids are doing at school.

Let us take this opportunity to tiptoe into one of the side streets.
Here you may see one of those white houses with green trim
That are so popular here. Look — I told you!
It is cool and dim inside, but the patio is sunny.
An old woman in gray sits there, fanning herself with a palm leaf fan.
She welcomes us to her patio, and offers us a cooling drink.
"My son is in Mexico City," she says. "He would welcome you too
If he were here. But his job is with a bank there.
Look, here is a photograph of him."
And a dark-skinned lad with pearly teeth grins out at us from the worn leather frame.
We thank her for her hospitality, for it is getting late
And we must catch a view of the city, before we leave, from a good high place.
That church tower will do — the faded pink one, there against the fierce blue of the sky. Slowly we enter.
The caretaker, an old man dressed in brown and gray, asks us how long we have been in the city, and how we like it here.

His daughter is scrubbing the steps — she nods to us as we pass into the tower.
Soon we have reached the top, and the whole network of the city extends before us.
There is the rich quarter, with its houses of pink and white, and its crumbling, leafy terraces.
There is the poorer quarter, its homes a deep blue.
There is the market, where men are selling hats and swatting flies.
And there is the public library, painted several shades of pale green and beige.
Look! There is the square we just came from, with the promenaders.
There are fewer of them, now that the heat of the day has increased,
But the young boy and girl still lurk in the shadows of the bandstand.
And there is the home of the little old lady —
She is still sitting in the patio, fanning herself.
How limited, but how complete withal, has been our experience of Guadalajara!
We have seen young love, married love, and the love of an aged mother for her son.
We have heard the music, tasted the drinks, and looked at colored houses.
What more is there to do, except stay? And that we cannot do.
And as a last breeze freshens the top of the weathered old tower, I turn my gaze
Back to the instruction manual which has made me dream of Guadalajara.

1956

How Much Longer Will I Be Able to Inhabit the Divine Sepulcher . . .

How much longer will I be able to inhabit the divine sepulcher
Of life, my great love? Do dolphins plunge bottomward
To find the light? Or is it rock
That is searched? Unrelentingly? Huh. And if some day

Men with orange shovels come to break open the rock
Which encases me, what about the light that comes in then?
What about the smell of the light?
What about the moss?

In pilgrim times he wounded me
Since then I only lie
My bed of light is a furnace choking me
With hell (and sometimes I hear salt water dripping).

I mean it — because I'm one of the few
To have held my breath under the house. I'll trade

One red sucker for two blue ones. I'm
Named Tom. The

Light bounces off mossy rocks down to me
In this glen (the neat villa! which
When he'd had he would not had he of
And jests under the smarting of privet

Which on hot spring nights perfumes the empty rooms
With the smell of sperm flushing down toilets
On hot summer afternoons within sight of the sea.
If you knew why then professor) reads

To his friends: Drink to me only with
And the reader is carried away
By a great shadow under the sea.
Behind the steering wheel

The boy took out his own forehead.
His girlfriend's head was a green bag
Or narcissus stems. "OK you win
But meet me anyway at Cohen's Drug Store

In 22 minutes." What a marvel is ancient man!
Under the tulip roots he has figured out a way to be a religious animal
And would be a mathematician. But where in unsuitable heaven
Can he get the heat that will make him grow?

For he needs something or will forever remain a dwarf,
Though a perfect one, and possessing a normal-sized brain
But he has got to be released by giants from things.
And as the plant grows older it realizes it will never be a tree,

Will probably always be haunted by a bee
And cultivates stupid impressions
So as not to become part of the dirt. The dirt
Is mounting like a sea. And we say goodbye

Shaking hands in front of the crashing of the waves
That give our words lonesomeness, and make these flabby hands seem
ours —
Hands that are always writing things
On mirrors for people to see later —

Do you want them to water
Plant, tear listlessly among the exchangeable ivy —
Carrying food to mouth, touching genitals —
But no doubt you have understood

It all now and I am a fool. It remains
For me to get better, and to understand you so
Like a chair-sized man. Boots
Were heard on the floor above. In the garden the sunlight was still
purple

But what buzzed in it had changed slightly
But not forever . . . but casting its shadow
On sticks, and looking around for an opening in the air, was quite as
if it had never refused to exist differently. Guys
In the yard handled the belt he had made

Stars
Painted the garage roof crimson and black
He is not a man
Who can read these signs . . . his bones were stays . . .

And even refused to live
In a world and refunded the hiss
Of all that exists terribly near us
Like you, my love, and light.

For what is obedience but the air around us
To the house? For which the federal men came
In a minute after the sidewalk
Had taken you home? ("Latin . . . blossom . . . ")

After which you led me to water
And bade me drink, which I did, owing to your kindness.
You would not let me out for two days and three nights,
Bringing me books bound in wild thyme and scented wild grasses

As if reading had any interest for me, you . . .
Now you are laughing.
Darkness interrupts my story.
Turn on the light.

Meanwhile what am I going to do?
I am growing up again, in school, the crisis will be very soon.
And you twist the darkness in your fingers, you
Who are slightly older . . .

Who are you, anyway?
And it is the color of sand,
The darkness, as it sifts through your hand
Because what does anything mean,

The ivy and the sand? That boat
Pulled up on the shore? Am I wonder,

Strategically, and in the light
Of the long sepulcher that hid death and hides me?

1962

Decoy

We hold these truths to be self-evident:
That ostracism, both political and moral, has
Its place in the twentieth-century scheme of things;
That urban chaos is the problem we have been seeing into and seeing into,
For the factory, deadpanned by its very existence into a
Descending code of values, has moved right across the road from total financial upheaval
And caught regression head-on. The descending scale does not imply
A corresponding deterioration of moral values, punctuated
By acts of corporate vandalism every five years,
Like a bunch of violets pinned to a dress, that knows and ignores its own standing.
There is every reason to rejoice with those self-styled prophets of commercial disaster, those harbingers of gloom,
Over the imminent lateness of the denouement that, advancing slowly, never arrives,
At the same time keeping the door open to a tongue-and-cheek attitude on the part of the perpetrators,
The men who sit down to their vast desks on Monday to begin planning the week's notations, jotting memoranda that take
Invisible form in the air, like flocks of sparrows
Above the city pavements, turning and wheeling aimlessly
But on the average directed by discernible motives.

To sum up: We are fond of plotting itineraries
And our pyramiding memories, alert as dandelion fuzz, dart from one pretext to the next
Seeking in occasions new sources of memories, for memory is profit
Until the day it spreads out all its accumulation, delta-like, on the plain
For that day no good can come of remembering, and the anomalies cancel each other out.
But until then foreshortened memories will keep us going, alive, one to the other.

There was never any excuse for this and perhaps there need be none,
For kicking out into the morning, on the wide bed,
Waking far apart on the bed, the two of them:
Husband and wife
Man and wife

1970

Soonest Mended

Barely tolerated, living on the margin
In our technological society, we were always having to be rescued
On the brink of destruction, like heroines in *Orlando Furioso*
Before it was time to start all over again.
There would be thunder in the bushes, a rustling of coils,
And Angelica, in the Ingres painting, was considering
The colorful but small monster near her toe, as though wondering
whether forgetting
The whole thing might not, in the end, be the only solution.
And then there always came a time when
Happy Hooligan in his rusted green automobile
Came plowing down the course, just to make sure everything was O.K.,
Only by that time we were in another chapter and confused
About how to receive this latest piece of information.
Was it information? Weren't we rather acting this out
For someone else's benefit, thoughts in a mind
With room enough and to spare for our little problems (so they began to
seem),
Our daily quandary about food and the rent and bills to be paid?
To reduce all this to a small variant,
To step free at last, minuscule on the gigantic plateau —
This was our ambition: to be small and clear and free.
Alas, the summer's energy wanes quickly,
A moment and it is gone. And no longer
May we make the necessary arrangements, simple as they are.
Our star was brighter perhaps when it had water in it.
Now there is no question even of that, but only
Of holding on to the hard earth so as not to get thrown off,
With an occasional dream, a vision: a robin flies across
The upper corner of the window, you brush your hair away
And cannot quite see, or a wound will flash
Against the sweet faces of the others, something like:
This is what you wanted to hear, so why
Did you think of listening to something else? We are all talkers
It is true, but underneath the talk lies
The moving and not wanting to be moved, the loose
Meaning, untidy and simple like a threshing floor.

These then were some hazards of the course,
Yet though we knew the course *was* hazards and nothing else
It was still a shock when, almost a quarter of a century later,
The clarity of the rules dawned on you for the first time.
They were the players, and we who had struggled at the game
Were merely spectators, though subject to its vicissitudes
And moving with it out of the tearful stadium, borne on shoulders, at last.
Night after night this message returns, repeated
In the flickering bulbs of the sky, raised past us, taken away from us,

Yet ours over and over until the end that is past truth,
The being of our sentences, in the climate that fostered them,
Not ours to own, like a book, but to be with, and sometimes
To be without, alone and desperate.
But the fantasy makes it ours, a kind of fence-sitting
Raised to the level of an esthetic ideal. These were moments, years,
Solid with reality, faces, namable events, kisses, heroic acts,
But like the friendly beginning of a geometrical progression
Not too reassuring, as though meaning could be cast aside some day
When it had been outgrown. Better, you said, to stay cowering
Like this in the early lessons, since the promise of learning
Is a delusion, and I agreed, adding that
Tomorrow would alter the sense of what had already been learned,
That the learning process is extended in this way, so that from this
 standpoint
None of us ever graduates from college,
For time is an emulsion, and probably thinking not to grow up
Is the brightest kind of maturity for us, right now at any rate.
And you see, both of us were right, though nothing
Has somehow come to nothing; the avatars
Of our conforming to the rules and living
Around the home have made — well, in a sense, "good citizens" of us,
Brushing the teeth and all that, and learning to accept
The charity of the hard moments as they are doled out,
For this is action, this not being sure, this careless
Preparing, sowing the seeds crooked in the furrow,
Making ready to forget, and always coming back
To the mooring of starting out, that day so long ago.

1970

Self-Portrait in a Convex Mirror

As Parmigianino did it, the right hand
Bigger than the head, thrust at the viewer
And swerving easily away, as though to protect
What it advertises. A few leaded panes, old beams,
Fur, pleated muslin, a coral ring run together
In a movement supporting the face, which swims
Toward and away like the hand
Except that it is in repose. It is what is
Sequestered. Vasari says, "Francesco one day set himself
To take his own portrait, looking at himself for that purpose
In a convex mirror, such as is used by barbers . . .
He accordingly caused a ball of wood to be made
By a turner, and having divided it in half and
Brought it to the size of the mirror, he set himself
With great art to copy all that he saw in the glass,"

Chiefly his reflection, of which the portrait
Is the reflection once removed.
The glass chose to reflect only what he saw
Which was enough for his purpose: his image
Glazed, embalmed, projected at a 180-degree angle.
The time of day or the density of the light
Adhering to the face keeps it
Lively and intact in a recurring wave
Of arrival. The soul establishes itself.
But how far can it swim out through the eyes
And still return safely to its nest? The surface
Of the mirror being convex, the distance increases
Significantly; that is, enough to make the point
That the soul is a captive, treated humanely, kept
In suspension, unable to advance much farther
Than your look as it intercepts the picture.
Pope Clement and his court were "stupefied"
By it, according to Vasari, and promised a commission
That never materialized. The soul has to stay where it is,
Even though restless, hearing raindrops at the pane,
The sighing of autumn leaves thrashed by the wind,
Longing to be free, outside, but it must stay
Posing in this place. It must move
As little as possible. This is what the portrait says.
But there is in that gaze a combination
Of tenderness, amusement and regret, so powerful
In its restraint that one cannot look for long.
The secret is too plain. The pity of it smarts,
Makes hot tears spurt: that the soul is not a soul,
Has no secret, is small, and it fits
Its hollow perfectly: its room, our moment of attention.
That is the tune but there are no words.
The words are only speculation
(From the Latin *speculum*, mirror):
They seek and cannot find the meaning of the music.
We see only postures of the dream,
Riders of the motion that swings the face
Into view under evening skies, with no
False disarray as proof of authenticity.
But it is life englobed.
One would like to stick one's hand
Out of the globe, but its dimension,
What carries it, will not allow it.
No doubt it is this, not the reflex
To hide something, which makes the hand loom large
As it retreats slightly. There is no way
To build it flat like a section of wall:
It must join the segment of a circle,
Roving back to the body of which it seems

So unlikely a part, to fence in and shore up the face
On which the effort of this condition reads
Like a pinpoint of a smile, a spark
Or star one is not sure of having seen
As darkness resumes. A perverse light whose
Imperative of subtlety dooms in advance its
Conceit to light up: unimportant but meant.
Francesco, your hand is big enough
To wreck the sphere, and too big,
One would think, to weave delicate meshes
That only argue its further detention.
(Big, but not coarse, merely on another scale,
Like a dozing whale on the sea bottom
In relation to the tiny, self-important ship
On the surface.) But your eyes proclaim
That everything is surface. The surface is what's there
And nothing can exist except what's there.
There are no recesses in the room, only alcoves,
And the window doesn't matter much, or that
Sliver of window or mirror on the right, even
As a gauge of the weather, which in French is
Le temps, the word for time, and which
Follows a course wherein changes are merely
Features of the whole. The whole is stable within
Instability, a globe like ours, resting
On a pedestal of vacuum, a ping-pong ball
Secure on its jet of water.
And just as there are no words for the surface, that is,
No words to say what it really is, that it is not
Superficial but a visible core, then there is
No way out of the problem of pathos vs. experience.
You will stay on, restive, serene in
Your gesture which is neither embrace nor warning
But which holds something of both in pure
Affirmation that doesn't affirm anything.

The balloon pops, the attention
Turns dully away. Clouds
In the puddle stir up into sawtoothed fragments.
I think of the friends
Who came to see me, of what yesterday
Was like. A peculiar slant
Of memory that intrudes on the dreaming model
In the silence of the studio as he considers
Lifting the pencil to the self-portrait.
How many people came and stayed a certain time,
Uttered light or dark speech that became part of you
Like light behind windblown fog and sand,
Filtered and influenced by it, until no part

Remains that is surely you. Those voices in the dusk
Have told you all and still the tale goes on
In the form of memories deposited in irregular
Clumps of crystals. Whose curved hand controls,
Francesco, the turning seasons and the thoughts
That peel off and fly away at breathless speeds
Like the last stubborn leaves ripped
From wet branches? I see in this only the chaos
Of your round mirror which organizes everything
Around the polestar of your eyes which are empty,
Know nothing, dream but reveal nothing.
I feel the carousel starting slowly
And going faster and faster: desk, papers, books,
Photographs of friends, the window and the trees
Merging in one neutral band that surrounds
Me on all sides, everywhere I look.
And I cannot explain the action of leveling,
Why it should all boil down to one
Uniform substance, a magma of interiors.
My guide in these matters is your self,
Firm, oblique, accepting everything with the same
Wraith of a smile, and as time speeds up so that it is soon
Much later, I can know only the straight way out,
The distance between us. Long ago
The strewn evidence meant something,
The small accidents and pleasures
Of the day as it moved gracelessly on,
A housewife doing chores. Impossible now
To restore those properties in the silver blur that is
The record of what you accomplished by sitting down
"With great art to copy all that you saw in the glass"
So as to perfect and rule out the extraneous
Forever. In the circle of your intentions certain spars
Remain that perpetuate the enchantment of self with self:
Eyebeams, muslin, coral. It doesn't matter
Because these are things as they are today
Before one's shadow ever grew
Out of the field into thoughts of tomorrow.

Tomorrow is easy, but today is uncharted,
Desolate, reluctant as any landscape
To yield what are laws of perspective
After all only to the painter's deep
Mistrust, a weak instrument though
Necessary. Of course some things
Are possible, it knows, but it doesn't know
Which ones. Some day we will try
To do as many things as are possible
And perhaps we shall succeed at a handful

Of them, but this will not have anything
To do with what is promised today, our
Landscape sweeping out from us to disappear
On the horizon. Today enough of a cover burnishes
To keep the supposition of promises together
In one piece of surface, letting one ramble
Back home from them so that these
Even stronger possibilities can remain
Whole without being tested. Actually
The skin of the bubble-chamber's as tough as
Reptile eggs; everything gets "programmed" there
In due course: more keeps getting included
Without adding to the sum, and just as one
Gets accustomed to a noise that
Kept one awake but now no longer does,
So the room contains this flow like an hourglass
Without varying in climate or quality
(Except perhaps to brighten bleakly and almost
Invisibly, in a focus of sharpening toward death — more
Of this later). What should be the vacuum of a dream
Becomes continually replete as the source of dreams
Is being tapped so that this one dream
May wax, flourish like a cabbage rose,
Defying sumptuary laws, leaving us
To awake and try to begin living in what
Has now become a slum. Sydney Freedberg in his
Parmigianino says of it: "Realism in this portrait
No longer produces an objective truth, but a *bizarria*. . . .
However its distortion does not create
A feeling of disharmony. . . . The forms retain
A strong measure of ideal beauty," because
Fed by our dreams, so inconsequential until one day
We notice the hole they left. Now their importance
If not their meaning is plain. They were to nourish
A dream which includes them all, as they are
Finally reversed in the accumulating mirror.
They seemed strange because we couldn't actually see them.
And we realize this only at a point where they lapse
Like a wave breaking on a rock, giving up
Its shape in a gesture which expresses that shape.
The forms retain a strong measure of ideal beauty
As they forage in secret on our idea of distortion.
Why be unhappy with this arrangement, since
Dreams prolong us as they are absorbed?
Something like living occurs, a movement
Out of the dream into its codification.

As I start to forget it
It presents its stereotype again

But it is an unfamiliar stereotype, the face
Riding at anchor, issued from hazards, soon
To accost others, "rather angel than man" (Vasari).
Perhaps an angel looks like everything
We have forgotten, I mean forgotten
Things that don't seem familiar when
We meet them again, lost beyond telling
Which were ours once. This would be the point
Of invading the privacy of this man who
"Dabbled in alchemy, but whose wish
Here was not to examine the subtleties of art
In a detached, scientific spirit: he wished through them
To impart the sense of novelty and amazement to the spectator"
(Freedberg). Later portraits such as the Uffizi
"Gentleman," the Borghese "Young Prelate" and
The Naples "Antea" issue from Mannerist
Tensions, but here, as Freedberg points out,
The surprise, the tension are in the concept
Rather than its realization.
The consonance of the High Renaissance
Is present, though distorted by the mirror.
What is novel is the extreme care in rendering
The velleities of the rounded reflecting surface
(It is the first mirror portrait),
So that you could be fooled for a moment
Before you realize the reflection
Isn't yours. You feel then like one of those
Hoffmann characters who have been deprived
Of a reflection, except that the whole of me
Is seen to be supplanted by the strict
Otherness of the painter in his
Other room. We have surprised him
At work, but no, he has surprised us
As he works. The picture is almost finished,
The surprise almost over, as when one looks out,
Startled by a snowfall which even now is
Ending in specks and sparkles of snow.
It happened while you were inside, asleep,
And there is no reason why you should have
Been awake for it, except that the day
Is ending and it will be hard for you
To get to sleep tonight, at least until late.

The shadow of the city injects its own
Urgency: Rome where Francesco
Was at work during the Sack: his inventions
Amazed the soldiers who burst in on him;
They decided to spare his life, but he left soon after;
Vienna where the painting is today, where

I saw it with Pierre in the summer of 1959; New York
Where I am now, which is a logarithm
Of other cities. Our landscape
Is alive with filiations, shuttlings;
Business is carried on by look, gesture,
Hearsay. It is another life to the city,
The backing of the looking glass of the
Unidentified but precisely sketched studio. It wants
To siphon off the life of the studio, deflate
Its mapped space to enactments, island it.
That operation has been temporarily stalled
But something new is on the way, a new preciosity
In the wind. Can you stand it,
Francesco? Are you strong enough for it?
This wind brings what it knows not, is
Self-propelled, blind, has no notion
Of itself. It is inertia that once
Acknowledged saps all activity, secret or public:
Whispers of the word that can't be understood
But can be felt, a chill, a blight
Moving outward along the capes and peninsulas
Of your nervures and so to the archipelagoes
And to the bathed, aired secrecy of the open sea.
This is its negative side. Its positive side is
Making you notice life and the stresses
That only seemed to go away, but now,
As this new mode questions, are seen to be
Hastening out of style. If they are to become classics
They must decide which side they are on.
Their reticence has undermined
The urban scenery, made its ambiguities
Look willful and tired, the games of an old man.
What we need now is this unlikely
Challenger pounding on the gates of an amazed
Castle. Your argument, Francesco,
Had begun to grow stale as no answer
Or answers were forthcoming. If it dissolves now
Into dust, that only means its time had come
Some time ago, but look now, and listen:
It may be that another life is stocked there
In recesses no one knew of; that it,
Not we, are the change; that we are in fact it
If we could get back to it, relive some of the way
It looked, turn our faces to the globe as it sets
And still be coming out all right:
Nerves normal, breath normal. Since it is a metaphor
Made to include us, we are a part of it and
Can live in it as in fact we have done,
Only leaving our minds bare for questioning

We now see will not take place at random
But in an orderly way that means to menace
Nobody — the normal way things are done,
Like the concentric growing up of days
Around a life: correctly, if you think about it.

A breeze like the turning of a page
Brings back your face: the moment
Takes such a big bite out of the haze
Of pleasant intuition it comes after.
The locking into place is "death itself,"
As Berg said of a phrase in Mahler's Ninth;
Or, to quote Imogen in *Cymbeline*, "There cannot
Be a pinch in death more sharp than this," for,
Though only exercise or tactic, it carries
The momentum of a conviction that had been building.
Mere forgetfulness cannot remove it
Nor wishing bring it back, as long as it remains
The white precipitate of its dream
In the climate of sighs flung across our world,
A cloth over a birdcage. But it is certain that
What is beautiful seems so only in relation to a specific
Life, experienced or not, channeled into some form
Steeped in the nostalgia of a collective past.
The light sinks today with an enthusiasm
I have known elsewhere, and known why
It seemed meaningful, that others felt this way
Years ago. I go on consulting
This mirror that is no longer mine
For as much brisk vacancy as is to be
My portion this time. And the vase is always full
Because there is only just so much room
And it accommodates everything. The sample
One sees is not to be taken as
Merely that, but as everything as it
May be imagined outside time — not as a gesture
But as all, in the refined, assimilable state.
But what is this universe the porch of
As it veers in and out, back and forth,
Refusing to surround us and still the only
Thing we can see? Love once
Tipped the scales but now is shadowed, invisible,
Though mysteriously present, around somewhere.
But we know it cannot be sandwiched
Between two adjacent moments, that its windings
Lead nowhere except to further tributaries
And that these empty themselves into a vague
Sense of something that can never be known
Even though it seems likely that each of us

Knows what it is and is capable of
Communicating it to the other. But the look
Some wear as a sign makes one want to
Push forward ignoring the apparent
Naïveté of the attempt, not caring
That no one is listening, since the light
Has been lit once and for all in their eyes
And is present, unimpaired, a permanent anomaly,
Awake and silent. On the surface of it
There seems no special reason why that light
Should be focused by love, or why
The city falling with its beautiful suburbs
Into space always less clear, less defined,
Should read as the support of its progress,
The easel upon which the drama unfolded
To its own satisfaction and to the end
Of our dreaming, as we had never imagined
It would end, in worn daylight with the painted
Promise showing through as a gage, a bond.
This nondescript, never-to-be defined daytime is
The secret of where it takes place
And we can no longer return to the various
Conflicting statements gathered, lapses of memory
Of the principal witnesses. All we know
Is that we are a little early, that
Today has that special, lapidary
Todayness that the sunlight reproduces
Faithfully in casting twig-shadows on blithe
Sidewalks. No previous day would have been like this.
I used to think they were all alike,
That the present always looked the same to everybody
But this confusion drains away as one
Is always cresting into one's present.
Yet the "poetic," straw-colored space
Of the long corridor that leads back to the painting,
Its darkening opposite — is this
Some figment of "art," not to be imagined
As real, let alone special? Hasn't it too its lair
In the present we are always escaping from
And falling back into, as the waterwheel of days
Pursues its uneventful, even serene course?
I think it is trying to say it is today
And we must get out of it even as the public
Is pushing through the museum now so as to
Be out by closing time. You can't live there.
The gray glaze of the past attacks all know-how:
Secrets of wash and finish that took a lifetime
To learn and are reduced to the status of
Black-and-white illustrations in a book where colorplates

Are rare. That is, all time
Reduces to no special time. No one
Alludes to the change; to do so might
Involve calling attention to oneself
Which would augment the dread of not getting out
Before having seen the whole collection
(Except for the sculptures in the basement:
They are where they belong).
Our time gets to be veiled, compromised
By the portrait's will to endure. It hints at
Our own, which we were hoping to keep hidden.
We don't need paintings or
Doggerel written by mature poets when
The explosion is so precise, so fine.
Is there any point even in acknowledging
The existence of all that? Does it
Exist? Certainly the leisure to
Indulge stately pastimes doesn't,
Any more. Today has no margins, the event arrives
Flush with its edges, is of the same substance,
Indistinguishable. "Play" is something else;
It exists, in a society specifically
Organized as a demonstration of itself.
There is no other way, and those assholes
Who would confuse everything with their mirror games
Which seem to multiply stakes and possibilities, or
At least confuse issues by means of an investing
Aura that would corrode the architecture
Of the whole in a haze of suppressed mockery,
Are beside the point. They are out of the game,
Which doesn't exist until they are out of it.
It seems like a very hostile universe
But as the principle of each individual thing is
Hostile to, exists at the expense of all the others
As philosophers have often pointed out, at least
This thing, the mute, undivided present,
Has the justification of logic, which
In this instance isn't a bad thing
Or wouldn't be, if the way of telling
Didn't somehow intrude, twisting the end result
Into a caricature of itself. This always
Happens, as in the game where
A whispered phrase passed around the room
Ends up as something completely different.
It is the principle that makes works of art so unlike
What the artist intended. Often he finds
He has omitted the thing he started out to say
In the first place. Seduced by flowers,
Explicit pleasures, he blames himself (though

Secretly satisfied with the result), imagining
He had a say in the matter and exercised
An option of which he was hardly conscious,
Unaware that necessity circumvents such resolutions
So as to create something new
For itself, that there is no other way,
That the history of creation proceeds according to
Stringent laws, and that things
Do get done in this way, but never the things
We set out to accomplish and wanted so desperately
To see come into being. Parmigianino
Must have realized this as he worked at his
Life-obstructing task. One is forced to read
The perfectly plausible accomplishment of a purpose
Into the smooth, perhaps even bland (but so
Enigmatic) finish. Is there anything
To be serious about beyond this otherness
That gets included in the most ordinary
Forms of daily activity, changing everything
Slightly and profoundly, and tearing the matter
Of creation, any creation, not just artistic creation
Out of our hands, to install it on some monstrous, near
Peak, too close to ignore, too far
For one to intervene? This otherness, this
"Not-being-us" is all there is to look at
In the mirror, though no one can say
How it came to be this way. A ship
Flying unknown colors has entered the harbor.
You are allowing extraneous matters
To break up your day, cloud the focus
Of the crystal ball. Its scene drifts away
Like vapor scattered on the wind. The fertile
Thought-associations that until now came
So easily, appear no more, or rarely. Their
Colorings are less intense, washed out
By autumn rains and winds, spoiled, muddied,
Given back to you because they are worthless.
Yet we are such creatures of habit that their
Implications are still around *en permanence*, confusing
Issues. To be serious only about sex
Is perhaps one way, but the sands are hissing
As they approach the beginning of the big slide
Into what happened. This past
Is now here: the painter's
Reflected face, in which we linger, receiving
Dreams and inspirations on an unassigned
Frequency, but the hues have turned metallic,
The curves and edges are not so rich. Each person
Has one big theory to explain the universe

But it doesn't tell the whole story
And in the end it is what is outside him
That matters, to him and especially to us
Who have been given no help whatever
In decoding our own man-size quotient and must rely
On second-hand knowledge. Yet I know
That no one else's taste is going to be
Any help, and might as well be ignored.
Once it seemed so perfect — gloss on the fine
Freckled skin, lips moistened as though about to part
Releasing speech, and the familiar look
Of clothes and furniture that one forgets.
This could have been our paradise: exotic
Refuge within an exhausted world, but that wasn't
In the cards, because it couldn't have been
The point. Aping naturalness may be the first step
Toward achieving an inner calm
But it is the first step only, and often
Remains a frozen gesture of welcome etched
On the air materializing behind it,
A convention. And we have really
No time for these, except to use them
For kindling. The sooner they are burnt up
The better for the roles we have to play.
Therefore I beseech you, withdraw that hand,
Offer it no longer as shield or greeting,
The shield of a greeting, Francesco:
There is room for one bullet in the chamber:
Our looking through the wrong end
Of the telescope as you fall back at a speed
Faster than that of light to flatten ultimately
Among the features of the room, an invitation
Never mailed, the "it was all a dream"
Syndrome, though the "all" tells tersely
Enough how it wasn't. Its existence
Was real, though troubled, and the ache
Of this waking dream can never drown out
The diagram still sketched on the wind,
Chosen, meant for me and materialized
In the disguising radiance of my room.
We have seen the city; it is the gibbous
Mirrored eye of an insect. All things happen
On its balcony and are resumed within,
But the action is the cold, syrupy flow
Of a pageant. One feels too confined,
Sifting the April sunlight for clues,
In the mere stillness of the ease of its
Parameter. The hand holds no chalk
And each part of the whole falls off
And cannot know it knew, except

Here and there, in cold pockets
Of remembrance, whispers out of time.

1975

The One Thing That Can Save America

Is anything central?
Orchards flung out on the land,
Urban forests, rustic plantations, knee-high hills?
Are place names central?
Elm Grove, Adcock Corner, Story Book Farm?
As they concur with a rush at eye level
Beating themselves into eyes which have had enough
Thank you, no more thank you.
And they come on like scenery mingled with darkness
The damp plains, overgrown suburbs,
Places of known civic pride, of civil obscurity.

These are connected to my version of America
But the juice is elsewhere.
This morning as I walked out of your room
After breakfast crosshatched with
Backward and forward glances, backward into light,
Forward into unfamiliar light,
Was it our doing, and was it
The material, the lumber of life, or of lives
We were measuring, counting?
A mood soon to be forgotten
In crossed girders of light, cool downtown shadow
In this morning that has seized us again?

I know that I braid too much my own
Snapped-off perceptions of things as they come to me.
They are private and always will be.
Where then are the private turns of event
Destined to boom later like golden chimes
Released over a city from a highest tower?
The quirky things that happen to me, and I tell you,
And you instantly know what I mean?
What remote orchard reached by winding roads
Hides them? Where are these roots?

It is the lumps and trials
That tell us whether we shall be known
And whether our fate can be exemplary, like a star.
All the rest is waiting
For a letter that never arrives,
Day after day, the exasperation

Until finally you have ripped it open not knowing what it is,
The two envelope halves lying on a plate.
The message was wise, and seemingly
Dictated a long time ago.
Its truth is timeless, but its time has still
Not arrived, telling of danger, and the mostly limited
Steps that can be taken against danger
Now and in the future, in cool yards,
In quiet small houses in the country,
Our country, in fenced areas, in cool shady streets.

1975

Wet Casements

When Eduard Raban, coming along the passage,
walked into the open doorway, he saw that it was
raining. It was not raining much.
— Kafka, *Wedding Preparations in the Country*

The concept is interesting: to see, as though reflected
In streaming windowpanes, the look of others through
Their own eyes. A digest of their correct impressions of
Their self-analytical attitudes overlaid by your
Ghostly transparent face. You in falbalas
Of some distant but not too distant era, the cosmetics,
The shoes perfectly pointed, drifting (how long you
Have been drifting; how long I have too for that matter)
Like a bottle-imp toward a surface which can never be approached,
Never pierced through into the timeless energy of a present
Which would have its own opinions on these matters,
Are an epistemological snapshot of the processes
That first mentioned your name at some crowded cocktail
Party long ago, and someone (not the person addressed)
Overheard it and carried that name around in his wallet
For years as the wallet crumbled and bills slid in
And out of it. I want that information very much today,

Can't have it, and this makes me angry.
I shall use my anger to build a bridge like that
Of Avignon, on which people may dance for the feeling
Of dancing on a bridge. I shall at last see my complete face
Reflected not in the water but in the worn stone floor of my bridge.

I shall keep to myself.
I shall not repeat others' comments about me.

1977

At North Farm

Somewhere someone is traveling furiously toward you,
At incredible speed, traveling day and night,
Through blizzards and desert heat, across torrents, through narrow passes.
But will he know where to find you,
Recognize you when he sees you,
Give you the thing he has for you?

Hardly anything grows here,
Yet the granaries are bursting with meal,
The sacks of meal piled to the rafters.
The streams run with sweetness, fattening fish;
Birds darken the sky. Is it enough
That the dish of milk is set out at night,
That we think of him sometimes,
Sometimes and always, with mixed feelings?

1984

One Coat of Paint

We will all have to just hang on for awhile,
It seems, now. This could mean "early retirement"
For some, if only for an afternoon of pottering around
Buying shoelaces and the like. Or it could mean a spell
In some enchanter's cave, after several centuries of which
You wake up curiously refreshed, eager to get back
To the crossword puzzle, only no one knows your name
Or who you are, really, or cares much either. To seduce
A fact into becoming an object, a pleasing one, with some
Kind of esthetic quality, which would also add to the store
Of knowledge and even extend through several strata
Of history, like a pin through a cracked wrist-bone,
Connecting these in such a dynamic way that one would be forced
To acknowledge a new kind of superiority without which the world
Could no longer conduct its business, even simple stuff like
bringing
Water home from wells, coals to hearths, would of course be
An optimal form of it but in any case the thing's got to
Come into being, something has to happen, or all
We'll have left is disagreements, *désagréments*, to name a few.
O don't you see how necessary it is to be around,
To be ferried from here to that near, smiling shore
And back again into the arms of those that love us,
Not many, but of such infinite, superior sweetness
That their lie is for us and it becomes stained, encrusted,
Finally gilded in some exasperating way that turns it
To a truth plus something, delicate and dismal as a star,

Cautious as a drop of milk, so that they let us
Get away with it, some do at any rate?

1987

How to Continue

Oh there once was a woman
and she kept a shop
selling trinkets to tourists
not far from a dock
who came to see what life could be
far back on the island.

And it was always a party there
always different but very nice
New friends to give you advice
or fall in love with you which is nice
and each grew so perfectly from the other
it was a marvel of poetry
and irony

And in this unsafe quarter
much was scary and dirty
but no one seemed to mind
very much
the parties went on from house to house
There were friends and lovers galore
all around the store
There was moonshine in winter
and starshine in summer
and everybody was happy to have discovered
what they discovered

And then one day the ship sailed away
There were no more dreamers just sleepers
in heavy attitudes on the dock
moving as if they knew how
among the trinkets and the souvenirs
the random shops of modern furniture
and a gale came and said
it is time to take all of you away
from the tops of the trees to the little houses
on little paths so startled

And when it became time to go
they none of them would leave without the other

for they said we are all one here
and if one of us goes the other will not go
and the wind whispered it to the stars
the people all got up to go
and looked back on love

1992

My Philosophy of Life

Just when I thought there wasn't room enough
for another thought in my head, I had this great idea —
call it a philosophy of life, if you will. Briefly,
it involved living the way philosophers live,
according to a set of principles. OK, but which ones?

That was the hardest part, I admit, but I had a
kind of dark foreknowledge of what it would be like.
Everything, from eating watermelon or going to the bathroom
or just standing on a subway platform, lost in thought
for a few minutes, or worrying about rain forests,
would be affected, or more precisely, inflected
by my new attitude. I wouldn't be preachy,
or worry about children and old people, except
in the general way prescribed by our clockwork universe.
Instead I'd sort of let things be what they are
while injecting them with the serum of the new moral climate
I thought I'd stumbled into, as a stranger
accidentally presses against a panel and a bookcase slides back,
revealing a winding staircase with greenish light
somewhere down below, and he automatically steps inside
and the bookcase slides shut, as is customary on such occasions.
At once a fragrance overwhelms him — not saffron, not lavender,
but something in between. He thinks of cushions, like the one
his uncle's Boston bull terrier used to lie on watching him
quizzically, pointed ear-tips folded over. And then the great rush
is on. Not a single idea emerges from it. It's enough
to disgust you with thought. But then you remember something
  William James
wrote in some book of his you never read — it was fine, it had the
  fineness,
the powder of life dusted over it, by chance, of course, yet
  still looking
for evidence of fingerprints. Someone had handled it
even before he formulated it, though the thought was his and
  his alone.

It's fine, in summer, to visit the seashore.
There are lots of little trips to be made.
A grove of fledgling aspens welcomes the traveler. Nearby
are the public toilets where weary pilgrims have carved
their names and addresses, and perhaps messages as well,
messages to the world, as they sat
and thought about what they'd do after using the toilet
and washing their hands at the sink, prior to stepping out
into the open again. Had they been coaxed in by principles,
and were their words philosophy, of however crude a sort?
I confess I can move no farther along this train of thought —
something's blocking it. Something I'm
not big enough to see over. Or maybe I'm frankly scared.
What was the matter with how I acted before?
But maybe I can come up with a compromise — I'll let
things be what they are, sort of. In the autumn I'll put up jellies
and preserves, against the winter cold and futility,
and that will be a human thing, and intelligent as well.
I won't be embarrassed by my friends' dumb remarks,
or even my own, though admittedly that's the hardest part,
as when you are in a crowded theater and something you say
riles the spectator in front of you, who doesn't even like the idea
of two people near him talking together. Well he's
got to be flushed out so the hunters can have a crack at him —
this thing works both ways, you know. You can't always
be worrying about others and keeping track of yourself
at the same time. That would be abusive, and about as much fun
as attending the wedding of two people you don't know.
Still, there's a lot of fun to be had in the gaps between ideas.
That's what they're made for! Now I want you to go out there
and enjoy yourself, and yes, enjoy your philosophy of life, too.
They don't come along every day. Look out! There's a big one . . .

1995

A Poem of Unrest

Men duly understand the river of life,
misconstruing it, as it widens and its cities grow
dark and denser, always farther away.

And of course that remote denseness suits
us, as lambs and clover might have
if things had been built to order differently.

But since I don't understand myself, only segments
of myself that misunderstand each other, there's no
reason for you to want to, no way you could

even if we both wanted it. Do those towers even exist?
We must look at it that way, along those lines
so the thought can erect itself, like plywood battlements.

1995

This Room

The room I entered was a dream of this room.
Surely all those feet on the sofa were mine.
The oval portrait
of a dog was me at an early age.
Something shimmers, something is hushed up.

We had macaroni for lunch every day
except Sunday, when a small quail was induced
to be served to us. Why do I tell you these things?
You are not even here.

2000

The History of My Life

Once upon a time there were two brothers.
Then there was only one: myself.

I grew up fast, before learning to drive,
even. There was I: a stinking adult.

I thought of developing interests
someone might take an interest in. No soap.

I became very weepy for what had seemed
like the pleasant early years. As I aged

increasingly, I also grew more charitable
with regard to my thoughts and ideas,

thinking them at least as good as the next man's.
Then a great devouring cloud

came and loitered on the horizon, drinking
it up, for what seemed like months or years.

2000

GALWAY KINNELL (b. 1927)

Galway Kinnell was born in Providence, Rhode Island. A U.S. Navy veteran, he was educated at Princeton, where he and W. S. Merwin became friends. Kinnell was living in France in the 1960s when he got wind of the civil rights movement in the United States. He returned and worked on registering black voters in Louisiana. "I have no interest in any poem in which the poet does not bring everything he knows," he has said. He told an interviewer in 2001: "I try to see past the usual clichés about things. 'Pig' is a pejorative word, but if you get to know them, get a feeling for them, you see that they have an extraordinary beauty. When creatures don't have an extraordinary beauty, it's because the person in contact with them is not seeing it. I feel more and more in love with other creatures as I get older."

Saint Francis and the Sow

The bud
stands for all things,
even for those things that don't flower,
for everything flowers, from within, of self-blessing;
though sometimes it is necessary
to reteach a thing its loveliness,
to put a hand on its brow
of the flower
and retell it in words and in touch
it is lovely
until it flowers again from within, of self-blessing;
as Saint Francis
put his hand on the creased forehead
of the sow, and told her in words and in touch
blessings of earth on the sow, and the sow
began remembering all down her thick length,
from the earthen snout all the way
through the fodder and slops to the spiritual curl of the tail,
from the hard spininess spiked out from the spine
down through the great broken heart
to the sheer blue milken dreaminess spurting and shuddering
from the fourteen teats into the fourteen mouths sucking and
   blowing beneath them:
the long, perfect loveliness of sow.

1980

The Man Splitting Wood in the Daybreak

The man splitting wood in the daybreak
looks strong, as though if one weakened
one could turn to him and he would help.
Gus Newland was strong. When he split wood

he struck hard, flashing the bright steel
through air of daybreak so fast rock maple
leapt apart — as they think marriages will
in countries about to institute divorce —
and even willow, which though stacked
to dry a full year, on separating
actually weeps — totem wood, therefore,
to the married-until-death — sniffled asunder.
But Gus is dead. We could turn to our fathers,
but they protect us only through the harsh
grace of the numerals cut into their headstones.
Or to our mothers, whose love, so devastated,
can't, even in spring, break through the hard earth.
Our spouses weaken at the same rate we do.
We have to hold our children up to lean on them.
Everyone who could help goes or hasn't arrived.
What about the man splitting wood in the daybreak,
who looked strong? That was years ago.
I myself was that man splitting wood in the daybreak.

1985

Hitchhiker

After a moment, the driver, a salesman
for Travelers Insurance heading for
Topeka, said, "What was that?"
I, in my Navy uniform, still useful
for hitchhiking though the war was over,
said, "I think you hit somebody."
I knew he had. The round face, opening
in surprise as the man bounced off the fender,
had given me a look as he swept past.
"Why didn't you say something?" The salesman
stepped hard on the brakes. "I thought you saw,"
I said. I didn't know why. It came to me
I could have sat next to this man all the way
to Topeka without saying a word about it.
He opened the car door and looked back.
I did the same. At the roadside,
in the glow of a streetlight, was a body.
A man was bending over it. For an instant
it was myself, in a time to come,
bending over the body of my father.
The man stood and shouted at us, "Forget it!
He gets hit all the time!" Oh.
A bum. We were happy to forget it.
The rest of the way, into dawn in Kansas,
when the salesman dropped me off, we did not speak,

except, as I got out, I said, "Thanks,"
and he said, "Don't mention it."

1994

Why Regret?

Didn't you like the way the ants help
the peony globes open by eating off the glue?
Weren't you cheered to see the ironworkers
sitting on an I-beam dangling from a cable,
in a row, like starlings, eating lunch, maybe
baloney on white with fluorescent mustard?
Wasn't it a revelation to waggle from the estuary
all the way up the river, the pirle,
the kill, the run, the brook, the beck,
the sike gone dry, to the shock of a spring?
Didn't you almost shiver, hearing the book lice
clicking their sexual syncopation inside the old
Webster's *New International* — perhaps having just
eaten out of it *izle*, *xyster* and *thalassacon?*
What did you imagine lay in store anyway
at the end of a world whose sub-substance is
ooze, gleet, birdlime, slime, mucus, muck?
Don't worry about becoming emaciated — think of the wren
and how little flesh is needed to make a song.
Didn't it seem somehow familiar when the nymph
split open and the mayfly struggled free
and flew and perched and then its own back split open
and the imago, the true adult, somersaulted
out backwards and took flight
toward the swarm, mouth-parts vestigial,
alimentary canal unfit to digest food,
a day or hour left to find the desired one?
Or when Casanova threw the linguine in squid ink
out the window, telling his startled companion,
"The perfected lover does not eat."
As a child didn't you find it calming to think
of the pinworms as some kind of tiny batons
giving cadence to the squeezes and releases
around the downward march of debris?
Didn't you once glimpse what seemed your
own inner blazonry in the monarchs, wobbling
and gliding, in desire, in the middle air?
Weren't you reassured at the thought that these flimsy,
hinged beings might navigate their way to Mexico
by the flair of the dead bodies of ancestors
who fell in the same migration a year ago?
Isn't it worth missing whatever joy

you might have dreamed, to wake in the night and find
you and your beloved are holding hands in your sleep?

1999

W. S. MERWIN (b. 1927)

W. S. Merwin was born in New York City, and grew up in Union City, New Jersey, and in Scranton, Pennsylvania. He graduated from Princeton, and from 1949 to 1951 he worked as a tutor in France, Portugal, and Majorca, later earning his living by translating works from French, Spanish, Latin, and Portuguese. Merwin has also lived in England and in Mexico. He has translated *Sir Gawain and the Green Knight*, Dante's *Purgatorio*, *The Poem of the Cid*, and *The Song of Roland*. *A Mask for Janus*, his first book of poems, was chosen by W. H. Auden as the 1952 volume in the Yale Series of Younger Poets. *The Miner's Pale Children* (1970) is a seminal volume of prose poems. The absence of punctuation in much of his verse reflects his belief that "punctuation is predominantly a mark of allegiance to the protocols of prose and of the printed word." Omitting punctuation "maintains a living line to the spoken word and its intonations and motions." When Louise Glück selected "The Stranger" for *The Best American Poetry 1993*, Merwin wrote that he had found a prose summary of the legend told in that poem "and tried to tell it as the Guarani would tell it." The Guarani are rainforest Indians from the central part of South America, where Paraguay, Brazil, and Bolivia meet. "They are to South America what the Hopi are to the American Southwest: the museum, compendium, and storehouse for the spiritual life of that region."

Departure's Girl Friend

Loneliness leapt in the mirrors, but all week
I kept them covered like cages. Then I thought
Of a better thing.

And though it was late night in the city
There I was on my way
To my boat, feeling good to be going, hugging
This big wreath with the words like real
Silver: *Bon Voyage.*

                    The night
Was mine but everyone's, like a birthday.
Its fur touched my face in passing. I was going
Down to my boat, my boat,
To see it off, and glad at the thought.
Some leaves of the wreath were holding my hands
And the rest waved good-bye as I walked, as though
They were still alive.

And all went well till I came to the wharf, and no one,

I say no one, but I mean
There was this young man, maybe
Out of the merchant marine,
In some uniform, and I knew who he was; just the same
When he said to me where do you think you're going,
I was happy to tell him.

But he said to me, it isn't your boat,
You don't have one. I said, it's mine, I can prove it:
Look at this wreath I'm carrying to it,
Bon Voyage. He said, this the stone wharf, lady,
You don't own anything here.
                                        And as I
Was turning away, the injustice of it
Lit up the buildings, and there I was
In the other and hated city
Where I was born, where nothing is moored, where
The lights crawl over the stone like flies, spelling now,
Now, and the same fate chances roll
Their many eyes; and I step once more
Through a hoop of tears and walk on, holding this
Buoy of flowers in front of my beauty,
Wishing myself the good voyage.

1963

Dusk in Winter

The sun sets in the cold without friends
Without reproaches after all it has done for us
It goes down believing in nothing
When it has gone I hear the stream running after it
It has brought its flute it is a long way

1967

For the Anniversary of My Death

Every year without knowing it I have passed the day
When the last fires will wave to me
And the silence will set out
Tireless traveller
Like the beam of a lightless star

Then I will no longer
Find myself in life as in a strange garment
Surprised at the earth

And the love of one woman
And the shamelessness of men
As today writing after three days of rain
Hearing the wren sing and the falling cease
And bowing not knowing to what

1967

A Thing of Beauty

Sometimes where you get it they wrap it up in a clock and you take it home with you and since you want to see it it takes you the rest of your life to unwrap it trying harder and harder to be quick which only makes the bells ring more often.

1970

Yesterday

My friend says I was not a good son
you understand
I say yes I understand

he says I did not go
to see my parents very often you know
and I say yes I know

even when I was living in the same city he says
maybe I would go there once
a month or maybe even less
I say oh yes

he says the last time I went to see my father
I say the last time I saw my father

he says the last time I saw my father
he was asking me about my life
how I was making out and he
went into the next room
to get something to give me

oh I say
feeling again the cold
of my father's hand the last time

he says and my father turned
in the doorway and saw me
look at my wristwatch and he
said you know I would like you to stay
and talk with me

oh yes I say

but if you are busy he said
I don't want you to feel that you
have to
just because I'm here

I say nothing

he says my father
said maybe
you have important work you are doing
or maybe you should be seeing
somebody I don't want to keep you

I look out the window
my friend is older than I am
he says and I told my father it was so
and I got up and left him then
you know

though there was nowhere I had to go
and nothing I had to do

1983

The Stranger

After a Guarani legend recorded by Ernesto Morales

One day in the forest there was somebody
who had never been there before
it was somebody like the monkeys but taller
and without a tail and without so much hair
standing up and walking on only two feet
and as he went he heard a voice calling Save me

as the stranger looked he could see a snake
a very big snake with a circle of fire
that was dancing all around it
and the snake was trying to get out
but every way it turned the fire was there

so the stranger bent the trunk of a young tree
and climbed out over the fire until he
could hold a branch down to the snake
and the snake wrapped himself around the branch
and the stranger pulled the snake up out of the fire

and as soon as the snake saw that he was free
he twined himself around the stranger
and started to crush the life out of him
but the stranger shouted No No
I am the one who has just saved your life
and you pay me back by trying to kill me

but the snake said I am keeping the law
it is the law that whoever does good
receives evil in return
and he drew his coils tight around the stranger
but the stranger kept on saying No No
I do not believe that is the law

so the snake said I will show you
I will show you three times and you will see
and he kept his coils tight around the stranger's neck
and all around his arms and body
but he let go of the stranger's legs
Now walk he said to the stranger Keep going

so they started out that way and they came
to a river and the river said to them
I do good to everyone and look what they
do to me I save them from dying of thirst
and all they do is stir up the mud
and fill my water with dead things

the snake said One

the stranger said Let us go on and they did
and they came to a carandá-i palm
there were wounds running with sap on its trunk
and the palm tree was moaning I do good
to everyone and look what they do to me
I give them my fruit and my shade and they cut me
and drink from my body until I die

the snake said Two

the stranger said Let us go on and they did
and came to a place where they heard whimpering

and saw a dog with his paw in a basket
and the dog said I did a good thing
and this is what came of it
I found a jaguar who had been hurt
and I took care of him and he got better

and as soon as he had his strength again
he sprang at me wanting to eat me up
I managed to get away but he tore my paw
I hid in a cave until he was gone
and here in this basket I have
a calabash full of milk for my wound
but now I have pushed it too far down to reach

will you help me he said to the snake
and the snake liked milk better than anything
so he slid off the stranger and into the basket
and when he was inside the dog snapped it shut
and swung it against a tree with all his might
again and again until the snake was dead

and after the snake was dead in there
the dog said to the stranger Friend
I have saved your life
and the stranger took the dog home with him
and treated him the way the stranger would treat a dog

1993

One of the Lives

If I had not met the red-haired boy whose father
   had broken a leg parachuting into Provence
to join the resistance in the final stage of the war
   and so had been killed there as the Germans were moving north
out of Italy and if the friend who was with him
   as he was dying had not had an elder brother
who also died young quite differently in peacetime
   leaving two children one of them with bad health
who had been kept out of school for a whole year by an illness
   and if I had written anything else at the top
of the examination form where it said college
   of your choice or if the questions that day had been
put differently and if a young woman in Kittanning
   had not taught my father to drive at the age of twenty
so that he got the job with the pastor of the big church
   in Pittsburgh where my mother was working and if
my mother had not lost both parents when she was a child
   so that she had to go to her grandmother's in Pittsburgh

I would not have found myself on an iron cot
  with my head by the fireplace of a stone farmhouse
that had stood empty since some time before I was born
  I would not have travelled so far to lie shivering
with fever though I was wrapped in everything in the house
  nor have watched the unctuous doctor hold up his needle
at the window in the rain light of October
  I would not have seen through the cracked pane the darkening
valley and the river sliding past the amber mountains
  nor have wakened hearing plums fall in the small hour
thinking I knew where I was as I heard them fall

1995

Waves in August

There is a war in the distance
with the distance growing smaller
the field glasses lying at hand
are for keeping it far away

I thought I was getting better
about that returning childish
wish to be living somewhere else
that I know was impossible
and now I find myself wishing
to be here to be alive here
it is impossible enough
to still be the wish of a child

in youth I hid a boat under
the bushes beside the water
knowing I would want it later
and come back and would find it there
someone else took it and left me
instead the sound of the water
with its whisper of vertigo

terror reassurance an old
old sadness it would seem we knew
enough always about parting
but we have to go on learning
as long as there is anything

1999

James Wright (1927–1980)

James Wright was born in Martins Ferry, Ohio. He served in the army in Japan during the U.S. occupation following World War II. He attended Kenyon College on the GI Bill, studying with John Crowe Ransom, and did graduate work at the University of Washington under the direction of Theodore Roethke. W. H. Auden chose Wright's first book, *The Green Wall*, for the Yale Younger Poets series in 1957. Wright translated works by Pablo Neruda, Cesar Vallejo, and Georg Trakl. He died of throat cancer in New York City in 1980.

Lying in a Hammock at William Duffy's Farm in Pine Island, Minnesota

Over my head, I see the bronze butterfly,
Asleep on the black trunk,
Blowing like a leaf in green shadow.
Down the ravine behind the empty house,
The cowbells follow one another
Into the distances of the afternoon.
To my right,
In a field of sunlight between two pines,
The droppings of last year's horses
Blaze up into golden stones.
I lean back, as the evening darkens and comes on.
A chicken hawk floats over, looking for home.
I have wasted my life.

1963

Autumn Begins in Martins Ferry, Ohio

In the Shreve High football stadium,
I think of Polacks nursing long beers at Tiltonsville,
And gray faces of Negroes in the blast furnace at Benwood,
And the ruptured night watchman of Wheeling Steel,
Dreaming of heroes.

All the proud fathers are ashamed to go home.
Their women cluck like starved pullets,
Dying for love.

Therefore,
Their sons grow suicidally beautiful
At the beginning of October,
And gallop terribly against each other's bodies.

1963

A Blessing

Just off the highway to Rochester, Minnesota,
Twilight bounds softly forth on the grass.
And the eyes of those two Indian ponies
Darken with kindness.
They have come gladly out of the willows
To welcome my friend and me.
We step over the barbed wire into the pasture
Where they have been grazing all day, alone.
They ripple tensely, they can hardly contain their happiness
That we have come.
They bow shyly as wet swans. They love each other.
There is no loneliness like theirs.
At home once more,
They begin munching the young tufts of spring in the darkness.
I would like to hold the slenderer one in my arms,
For she has walked over to me
And nuzzled my left hand.
She is black and white,
Her mane falls wild on her forehead,
And the light breeze moves me to caress her long ear
That is delicate as the skin over a girl's wrist.
Suddenly I realize
That if I stepped out of my body I would break
Into blossom.

1963

In Response to a Rumor that the Oldest Whorehouse in Wheeling, West Virginia, Has Been Condemned

I will grieve alone,
As I strolled alone, years ago, down along
The Ohio shore.
I hid in the hobo jungle weeds
Upstream from the sewer main,
Pondering, gazing.

I saw, down river,
At Twenty-third and Water Streets
By the vinegar works,
The doors open in early evening.
Swinging their purses, the women
Poured down the long street to the river
And into the river.

I do not know how it was
They could drown every evening.

What time near dawn did they climb up the other shore,
Drying their wings?

For the river at Wheeling, West Virginia,
Has only two shores:
The one in hell, the other
In Bridgeport, Ohio.

And nobody would commit suicide, only
To find beyond death
Bridgeport, Ohio.

1968

Youth

Strange bird,
His song remains secret.
He worked too hard to read books.
He never heard how Sherwood Anderson
Got out of it, and fled to Chicago, furious to free himself
From his hatred of factories.
My father toiled fifty years
At Hazel-Atlas Glass,
Caught among girders that smash the kneecaps
Of dumb honyaks.
Did he shudder with hatred in the cold shadow of grease?
Maybe. But my brother and I do know
He came home as quiet as the evening.

He will be getting dark, soon,
And loom through new snow.
I know his ghost will drift home
To the Ohio River, and sit down, alone,
Whittling a root.
He will say nothing.
The waters flow past, older, younger
Than he is, or I am.

1968

Hook

I was only a young man
In those days. On that evening
The cold was so God damned

Bitter there was nothing.
Nothing. I was in trouble
With a woman, and there was nothing
There but me and dead snow.

I stood on the street corner
In Minneapolis, lashed
This way and that.
Wind rose from some pit,
Hunting me.
Another bus to Saint Paul
Would arrive in three hours,
If I was lucky.

Then the young Sioux
Loomed beside me, his scars
Were just my age.

Ain't got no bus here
A long time, he said.
You got enough money
To get home on?

What did they do
To your hand? I answered.
He raised up his hook into the terrible starlight
And slashed the wind.

Oh, that? he said.
I had a bad time with a woman. Here,
You take this.

Did you ever feel a man hold
Sixty-five cents
In a hook,
And place it
Gently
In your freezing hand?

I took it.
It wasn't the money I needed.
But I took it.

1977

DONALD HALL (b. 1928)

Donald Hall was born in New Haven, Connecticut. He attended Phillips Exeter, Harvard, and Oxford. A friend of George Plimpton, founding editor of the *Paris Review*, he was the magazine's first poetry editor (1953–1962), choosing the poems appearing in its pages and conducting interviews with such eminences as Ezra Pound and T. S. Eliot. Hall taught at the University of Michigan, where his students included Tom Clark, Lawrence Joseph, Jane Kenyon, and Bob Perelman. After leaving his tenured post to become a full-time freelance writer living on his family farm in New Hampshire, he founded the *Poets on Poetry* series for the University of Michigan Press and served as its general editor until 1994. He has written criticism, fiction, and sports journalism; edited anthologies of contemporary poetry (including *The Best American Poetry 1989);* debunked shibboleths (that the "death of poetry" has occurred) and inveighed against the "McPoem," which is "the product of the workshops of Hamburger University." Hall's own poems exhibit great versatility in form and rhetoric.

T. R.

Granted that what we summon is absurd:
Moustaches and the stick, the New York fake
In cowboy costume grinning for the sake
Of cameras that always just occurred;
Granted that his Rough Riders fought a third-
Rate army badly run, and had to make
Headlines to fatten Hearst; that one can take
Trust-busting not precisely at its word;

Robinson, who was drunken and unread,
Received a letter with a White House frank.
To court the Muse, T. R. might well have killed her,
And had her stuffed, yet here this mountebank
Chose to belaurel Robinson instead
Of famous men like Richard Watson Gilder.

1958

The Impossible Marriage

The bride disappears. After twenty minutes of searching
we discover her in the cellar, vanishing against a pillar
in her white gown and her skin's original pallor.
When we guide her back to the altar, we find the groom
in his slouch hat, open shirt, and untended beard
withdrawn to the belltower with the healthy young sexton
from whose comradeship we detach him with difficulty.
Oh, never in all the cathedrals and academies
of compulsory Democracy and free-thinking Calvinism

will these poets marry! — O pale, passionate
anchoret of Amherst! O reticent kosmos of Brooklyn!

1983

Prophecy

I will strike down wooden houses; I will burn aluminum
clapboard skin; I will strike down garages
where crimson Toyotas sleep side by side; I will explode
palaces of gold, silver, and alabaster: — the summer
great house and its folly together. Where shopping malls
spread plywood and plaster out, and roadhouses
serve steak and potatoskins beside Alaska King Crab;
where triangular flags proclaim tribes of identical campers;
where airplanes nose to tail exhale kerosene,
weeds and ashes will drowse in continual twilight.

I reject the old house and the new car; I reject
Tory and Whig together, I reject the argument
that modesty of ambition is sensible because the bigger
they are the harder they fall; I reject Waterford;
I reject the five-and-dime; I reject Romulus and Remus;
I reject Martha's Vineyard and the slamdunk contest;
I reject leaded panes; I reject the appointment made
at the tennis net or on the seventeenth green; I reject
the Professional Bowling Tour; I reject matchboxes;
I reject purple bathrooms with purple soap in them.

Men who lie awake worrying about taxes, vomiting
at dawn, whose hands shake as they administer Valium, —
skin will peel from the meat of their thighs.
Armies that march all day with elephants past pyramids
and roll pulling missiles past Generals weary of saluting
and past President-Emperors splendid in cloth-of-gold, —
soft rumps of armies will dissipate in rain. Where square
miles of corn waver in Minnesota, where tobacco ripens
in Carolina and apples in New Hampshire, where wheat
turns Kansas green, where pulpmills stink in Oregon,

dust will blow in the darkness and cactus die
before it flowers. Where skiers wait for chairlifts,
wearing money, low raspberries will part rib-bones.
Where the drive-in church raises a chromium cross,
dandelions and milkweed will straggle through blacktop.
I will strike from the ocean with waves afire;
I will strike from the hill with rainclouds of lava;
I will strike from darkened air

with melanoma in the shape of decorative hexagonals.
I will strike down embezzlers and eaters of snails.

I reject Japanese smoked oysters, potted chrysanthemums
allowed to die, Tupperware parties, Ronald McDonald,
Karposi's sarcoma, the Taj Mahal, holsteins wearing
electronic necklaces, the Algonquin, Tunisian aqueducts,
Phi Beta Kappa keys, the Hyatt Embarcadero, carpenters
jogging on the median, and betrayal that engorges
the corrupt heart longing for criminal surrender:
I reject shadows in the corner of the atrium
where Phyllis or Phoebe speaks with Billy or Marc
who says that afternoons are best although not reliable.

Your children will wander looting the shopping malls
for forty years, suffering for your idleness,
until the last dwarf body rots in a parking lot.
I will strike down lobbies and restaurants in motels
carpeted with shaggy petrochemicals
from Maine to Hilton Head, from the Skagit to Tucson.
I will strike down hanggliders, wiry adventurous boys;
their thighbones will snap, their brains
slide from their skulls. I will strike down
families cooking wildboar in New Mexico backyards.

Then landscape will clutter with incapable machinery,
acres of vacant airplanes and schoolbuses, ploughs
with seedlings sprouting and turning brown through colters.
Unlettered dwarves will burrow for warmth and shelter
in the caves of dynamos and Plymouths, dying
of old age at seventeen. Tribes wandering
in the wilderness of their ignorant desolation,
who suffer from your idleness, will burn your illuminated
missals to warm their rickety bodies.
Terrorists assemble plutonium because you are idle

and industrious. The whip-poor-will shrivels and the pickerel
chokes under the government of self-love. Vacancy burns
air so that you strangle without oxygen like rats
in a biologist's bell jar. The living god sharpens
the scythe of my prophecy to strike down red poppies
and blue cornflowers. When priests and policemen
strike my body's match, Jehovah will flame out;
Jehovah will suck air from the vents of bombshelters.
Therefore let the Buick swell until it explodes;
therefore let anorexia starve and bulimia engorge.

When Elzira leaves the house wearing her tennis dress
and drives her black Porsche to meet Abraham,

quarrels, returns to husband and children, and sobs
alseep, drunk, unable to choose among them, —
lawns and carpets will turn into tar together
with lovers, husbands, and children.
Fat will boil in the sacs of children's clear skin.
I will strike down the nations, astronauts and judges;
I will strike down Babylon, I will strike acrobats,
I will strike algae and the white birches.

Because Professors of Law teach ethics in dumbshow,
let the Colonel become President; because Chief Executive
Officers and Commissars collect down for pillows,
let the injustice of cities burn city and suburb;
let the countryside burn; let the pineforests of Maine
explode like a kitchenmatch and the Book of Kells turn
ash in a microsecond; let oxen and athletes
flash into grease: — I return to Appalachian rocks;
I shall eat bread; I shall prophesy through millennia
of Jehovah's day until the sky reddens over cities:

Then houses will burn, even houses of alabaster,
the sky will disappear like a scroll rolled up
and hidden in a cave from the industries of idleness.
Mountains will erupt and vanish, becoming deserts,
and the sea wash over the sea's lost islands
and the earth split open like a corpse's gassy
stomach and the sun turn as black as a widow's skirt
and the full moon grow red with blood swollen inside it
and stars fall from the sky like wind-blown apples, —
while Babylon's managers burn in the rage of the Lamb.

1988

When the Young Husband

When the young husband picked up his friend's pretty wife
in the taxi one block from her townhouse for their
first lunch together, in a hotel dining room
with a room key in his pocket,

midtown traffic gridlocked and was abruptly still.
For one moment before klaxons started honking,
a prophetic voice spoke in his mind's ear despite
his pulse's erotic thudding:

"The misery you undertake this afternoon
will accompany you to the ends of your lives.
She knew what she did when she agreed to this lunch,
although she will not admit it;

and you've constructed your playlet a thousand times:
cocktails, an omelet, wine; the revelation
of a room key; the elevator rising as
        the penis elevates; the skin

flushed, the door fumbled at, the handbag dropped; the first
kiss with open mouths, nakedness, swoon, thrust-and-catch;
endorphins followed by endearments; a brief nap;
                another fit; restoration

of clothes, arrangements for another encounter,
the taxi back, and the furtive kiss of goodbye.
Then, by turn: tears, treachery, anger, betrayal;
                marriages and houses destroyed;

small children abandoned and inconsolable,
their foursquare estates disestablished forever;
the unreadable advocates; the wretchedness
                of passion outworn; anguished nights

sleepless in a bare room; whiskey, meth, cocaine; new
love, essayed in loneliness with miserable
strangers, that comforts nothing but skin; hours with sons
                and daughters studious always

to maintain distrust; the daily desire to die
and the daily agony of the requirement
to survive, until only the quarrel endures."
                Prophecy stopped; traffic started.

1993

Her Garden

        I let her garden go.
            let it go, let it go
    How can I watch the hummingbird
            Hover to sip
            With its beak's tip
The purple bee balm — whirring as we heard
            It years ago?

        The weeds rise rank and thick
            let it go, let it go
    Where annuals grew and burdock grows,
            Where standing she
            At once could see
The peony, the lily, and the rose
            Rise over brick

She'd laid in patterns. Moss
let it go, let it go
Turns the bricks green, softening them
By the gray rocks
Where hollyhocks
That lofted while she lived, stem by tall stem,
Dwindle in loss.

2001

PHILIP LEVINE (b. 1928)

Philip Levine worked in automobile factories in his native Detroit, Michigan, after graduating from college. "I was resentful of the factory work I had to do," he told an interviewer, "partly because I saw it as something that was either going to delay my arrival into the kingdom of poetry or deny my entry. Little did I know it would become my subject matter." The "default landscape" of many of Levine's poems is the blighted streets of working-class Detroit.

Baby Villon

He tells me in Bangkok he's robbed
Because he's white; in London because he's black;
In Barcelona, Jew; in Paris, Arab:
Everywhere & at all times, & he fights back.

He holds up seven thick little fingers
To show me he's rated seventh in the world,
And there's no passion in his voice, no anger
In the flat brown eyes flecked with blood.

He asks me to tell all I can remember
Of my father, his uncle; he talks of the war
In North Africa and what came after,
The loss of his father, the loss of his brother,

The windows of the bakery smashed and the fresh bread
Dusted with glass, the warm smell of rye
So strong he ate till his mouth filled with blood.
"Here they live, here they live and not die,"

And he points down at his black head ridged
With black kinks of hair. He touches my hair,
Tells me I should never disparage
The stiff bristles that guard the head of the fighter.

Sadly his fingers wander over my face,
And he says how fair I am, how smooth.
We stand to end this first and last visit.
Stiff, 116 pounds, five feet two,

No bigger than a girl, he holds my shoulders,
Kisses my lips, his eyes still open,
My imaginary brother, my cousin,
Myself made otherwise by all his pain.

1968

They Feed They Lion

Out of burlap sacks, out of bearing butter,
Out of black bean and wet slate bread,
Out of the acids of rage, the candor of tar,
Out of creosote, gasoline, drive shafts, wooden dollies,
They Lion grow.
                        Out of the gray hills
Of industrial barns, out of rain, out of bus ride,
West Virginia to Kiss My Ass, out of buried aunties,
Mothers hardening like pounded stumps, out of stumps,
Out of the bones' need to sharpen and the muscles' to stretch,
They lion grow.
                        Earth is eating trees, fence posts,
Gutted cars, earth is calling in her little ones,
"Come home, Come home!" From pig balls,
From the ferocity of pig driven to holiness,
From the furred ear and the full jowl come
The repose of the hung belly, from the purpose
They Lion grow.
                        From the sweet glues of the trotters
Come the sweet kinks of the fist, from the full flower
Of the hams the thorax of caves,
From "Bow Down" come "Rise Up,"
Come they Lion from the reeds of shovels,
The grained arm that pulls the hands,
They Lion grow.
                        From my five arms and all my hands,
From all my white sins forgiven, they feed,
From my car passing under the stars,
They Lion, from my children inherit,
From the oak turned to a wall, they Lion,
From they sack and they belly opened
And all that was hidden burning on the oil-stained earth
They feed they Lion and he comes.

1972

You Can Have It

My brother comes home from work
and climbs the stairs to our room.
I can hear the bed groan and his shoes drop
one by one. You can have it, he says.

The moonlight streams in the window
and his unshaven face is whitened
like the face of the moon. He will sleep
long after noon and waken to find me gone.

Thirty years will pass before I remember
that moment when suddenly I knew each man
has one brother who dies when he sleeps
and sleeps when he rises to face this life,

and that together they are only one man
sharing a heart that always labors, hands
yellowed and cracked, a mouth that gasps
for breath and asks, Am I gonna make it?

All night at the ice plant he had fed
the chute its silvery blocks, and then I
stacked cases of orange soda for the children
of Kentucky, one gray boxcar at a time

with always two more waiting. We were twenty
for such a short time and always in
the wrong clothes, crusted with dirt
and sweat. I think now we were never twenty.

In 1948 in the city of Detroit, founded
by de la Mothe Cadillac for the distant purposes
of Henry Ford, no one wakened or died,
no one walked the streets or stoked a furnace,

for there was no such year, and now
that year has fallen off all the old newspapers,
calendars, doctors' appointments, bonds,
wedding certificates, drivers licenses.

The city slept. The snow turned to ice.
The ice to standing pools or rivers
racing in the gutters. Then bright grass rose
between the thousands of cracked squares,

and that grass died. I give you back 1948.
I give you all the years from then to the

coming one. Give me back the moon
with its frail light falling across a face.

Give me back my young brother, hard
and furious, with wide shoulders and a curse
for God and burning eyes that look upon
all creation and say, You can have it.

1979

The Return

All afternoon my father drove the country roads
between Detroit and Lansing. What he was looking for
I never learned, no doubt because he never knew himself,
though he would grab any unfamiliar side road
and follow where it led past fields of tall sweet corn
in August or in winter those of frozen sheaves.
Often he'd leave the Terraplane beside the highway
to enter the stunned silence of mid-September,
his eyes cast down for a sign, the only music
his own breath or the wind tracking slowly through
the stalks or riding above the barren ground. Later
he'd come home, his dress shoes coated with dust or mud,
his long black overcoat stained or tattered
at the hem, sit wordless in his favorite chair,
his necktie loosened, and stare at nothing. At first
my brothers and I tried conversation, questions
only he could answer: Why had he gone to war?
Where did he learn Arabic? Where was his father?
I remember none of this. I read it all later,
years later as an old man, a grandfather myself,
in a journal he left my mother with little drawings
of ruined barns and telephone poles, receding
toward a future he never lived, aphorisms
from Montaigne, Juvenal, Voltaire, and perhaps a few
of his own: "He who looks for answers finds questions."
Three times he wrote, "I was meant to be someone else,"
and went on to describe the perfumes of the damp fields.
"It all starts with seeds," and a pencil drawing
of young apple trees he saw somewhere or else dreamed.
I inherited the book when I was almost seventy,
and with it the need to return to who we were.
In the Detroit airport I rented a Taurus;
the woman at the counter was bored or crazy:
Did I want company? she asked; she knew every road
from here to Chicago. She had a slight accent,
Dutch or German, long black hair, and one frozen eye.
I considered but decided to go alone,

determined to find what he had never found.
Slowly the autumn morning warmed; flocks of starlings
rose above the vacant fields and blotted out the sun.
I drove on until I found the grove of apple trees
heavy with fruit, and left the car, the motor running,
beside a sagging fence, and entered his life
on my own for maybe the first time. A crow welcomed
me home, the sun rode above, austere and silent,
the early afternoon was cloudless, perfect.
When the crow dragged itself off to another world,
the shade deepened slowly in pools that darkened around
the trees; for a moment everything in sight stopped.
The wind hummed in my good ear, not words exactly,
not nonsense either, nor what I spoke to myself,
just the language creation once wakened to.
I took off my hat, a mistake in the presence
of my father's God, wiped my brow with what I had,
the back of my hand, and marveled at what was here:
nothing at all except the stubbornness of things.

1999

ANNE SEXTON (1928–1974)

Anne Sexton was born Anne Gray Harvey in Newton, Massachusetts. When she was twenty-eight, she had a psychotic breakdown and attempted suicide. "One night I saw I. A. Richards on educational television reading a sonnet and explaining its form. I thought to myself, 'I could do that, maybe; I could try.' So I sat down and wrote a sonnet. The next day I wrote another one, and so forth. My doctor encouraged me to write more. 'Don't kill yourself,' he said. 'Your poems might mean something to someone else someday.'" Like Sylvia Plath, Sexton studied with Robert Lowell and participated in the "confessional" impulse established by him and W. D. Snodgrass; Lowell characterized Sexton as "Edna Millay after Snodgrass." Sexton told her *Paris Review* interviewer that "Sylvia [Plath] and I would talk at length about our first suicide, in detail and depth" at the Ritz where they and fellow poet George Starbuck would go for martinis following Lowell's class at Boston University. Sexton was found dead inside an idling car parked in a garage on 4 October 1974.

All My Pretty Ones

All my pretty ones?
Did you say all? O hell-kite! All?
What! all my pretty chickens and their dam
At one fell swoop? . . .
I cannot but remember such things were,
That were most precious to me.
— *Macbeth*

Father, this year's jinx rides us apart
where you followed our mother to her cold slumber,
a second shock boiling its stone to your heart,
leaving me here to shuffle and disencumber
you from the residence you could not afford:
a gold key, your half of a woollen mill,
twenty suits from Dunne's, an English Ford,
the love and legal verbiage of another will,
boxes of pictures of people I do not know.
I touch their cardboard faces. They must go.

But the eyes, as thick as wood in this album,
hold me. I stop here, where a small boy
waits in a ruffled dress for someone to come . . .
for this soldier who holds his bugle like a toy
or for this velvet lady who cannot smile.
Is this your father's father, this commodore
in a mailman suit? My father, time meanwhile
has made it unimportant who you are looking for.
I'll never know what these faces are all about.
I lock them into their book and throw them out.

This is the yellow scrapbook that you began
the year I was born; as crackling now and wrinkly
as tobacco leaves: clippings where Hoover outran
the Democrats wiggling his dry finger at me
and Prohibition; news where the *Hindenburg* went
down and recent years where you went flush
on war. This year, solvent but sick, you meant
to marry that pretty widow in a one-month rush.
But before you had that second chance, I cried
on your fat shoulder. Three days later you died.

These are the snapshots of marriage, stopped in places.
Side by side at the rail toward Nassau now;
here, with the winner's cup at the speedboat races,
here, in tails at the Cotillion, you take a bow,
here, by our kennel of dogs with their pink eyes,
running like show-bred pigs in their chain-link pen;
here, at the horseshow where my sister wins a prize;
and here, standing like a duke among groups of men.
Now I fold you down, my drunkard, my navigator,
my first lost keeper, to love or look at later.

I hold a five-year diary that my mother kept
for three years, telling all she does not say
of your alcoholic tendency. You overslept,
she writes. My God, father, each Christmas Day
with your blood, will I drink down your glass

of wine? The diary of your hurly-burly years
goes to my shelf to wait for my age to pass.
Only in this hoarded span will love persevere.
Whether you are pretty or not, I outlive you,
bend down my strange face to yours and forgive you.

1962

Wanting to Die

Since you ask, most days I cannot remember.
I walk in my clothing, unmarked by that voyage.
Then the almost unnameable lust returns.

Even then I have nothing against life.
I know well the grass blades you mention,
the furniture you have placed under the sun.

But suicides have a special language.
Like carpenters they want to know *which tools.*
They never ask *why build.*

Twice I have so simply declared myself,
have possessed the enemy, eaten the enemy,
have taken on his craft, his magic.

In this way, heavy and thoughtful,
warmer than oil or water,
I have rested, drooling at the mouth-hole.

I did not think of my body at needle point.
Even the cornea and the leftover urine were gone.
Suicides have already betrayed the body.

Still-born, they don't always die,
but dazzled, they can't forget a drug so sweet
that even children would look on and smile.

To thrust all that life under your tongue! —
that, all by itself, becomes a passion.
Death's a sad bone; bruised, you'd say,

and yet she waits for me, year after year,
to so delicately undo an old wound,
to empty my breath from its bad prison.

Balanced there, suicides sometimes meet,
raging at the fruit, a pumped-up moon,
leaving the bread they mistook for a kiss,

leaving the page of the book carelessly open,
something unsaid, the phone off the hook
and the love, whatever it was, an infection.

1964

The Fury of Cocks

There they are
drooping over the breakfast plates,
angel-like,
folding in their sad wing,
animal sad,
and only the night before
there they were
playing the banjo.
Once more the day's light comes
with its immense sun,
its mother trucks,
its engines of amputation.
Whereas last night
the cock knew its way home,
as stiff as a hammer,
battering in with all
its awful power.
That theater.
Today it is tender,
a small bird,
as soft as a baby's hand.
She is the house.
He is the steeple.
When they fuck they are God.
When they break away they are God.
When they snore they are God.
In the morning they butter the toast.
They don't say much.
They are still God.
All the cocks of the world are God,
blooming, blooming, blooming
into the sweet blood of woman.

1974

JOHN HOLLANDER (b. 1929)

John Hollander was born in New York City the day the stock market crashed in October 1929. He was educated at Columbia and at the Harvard Society of Fellows. W. H. Auden chose

Hollander's first book, *A Crackling of Thorns* (1958), for the Yale Younger Poets series. Hollander has distinguished himself as a scholar and critic (*The Figure of Echo*), editor (the *Oxford Anthology of English Literature*), and influential Yale professor. The long poem *Reflections on Espionage* (1976) spins out the conceit that the poet and such colleagues as James Merrill are spies with covers and code names. *Rhyme's Reason*, the best of manuals, in which each form is described or defined by an example, some of them produced for the occasion, was published in 1981. *Powers of Thirteen* (1983) shows Hollander at the height of his powers of invention: a variant on the standard sonnet sequence, it consists of 169 poems (or thirteen squared), each consisting of thirteen lines, each line consisting of thirteen syllables.

The Lady's-Maid's Song

When Adam found his rib was gone
   He cursed and sighed and cried and swore
And looked with cold resentment on
   The creature God had used it for.
All love's delights were quickly spent
   And soon his sorrows multiplied:
He learned to blame his discontent
   On something stolen from his side.

And so in every age we find
   Each Jack, destroying every Joan,
Divides and conquers womankind
   In vengeance for his missing bone.
By day he spins out quaint conceits
   With gossip, flattery, and song,
But then at night, between the sheets,
   He wrongs the girl to right the wrong.

Though shoulder, bosom, lip, and knee
   Are praised in every kind of art,
Here is love's true anatomy:
   His rib is gone; he'll have her heart.
So women bear the debt alone
   And live eternally distressed,
For though we throw the dog his bone
   He wants it back with interest.

1958

Swan and Shadow

The last shape

Dusk
Above the
water hang the
loud
flies
Here
O so
gray
then
What A pale signal will appear
When Soon before its shadow fades
Where Here in this pool of opened eye
In us No Upon us As at the very edges
of where we take shape in the dark air
this object bares its image awakening
ripples of recognition that will
brush darkness up into light
even after this bird this hour both drift by atop the perfect sad instant now
already passing out of sight
toward yet-untroubled reflection
this image bears its object darkening
into memorial shades Scattered bits of
light No of water Or something across
water Breaking up No Being regathered
soon Yet by then a swan will what
gone Yes out of mind into what
vast
pale
hush
of a
place
past
sudden dark as
if a swan
sang

1968

The Bird

from the Yiddish of Moishe Leib Halpern

Well, this bird comes, and under his wing is a crutch,
And he asks why I keep my door on the latch;
So I tell him that right outside the gate
Many robbers watch and wait
To get at the hidden bit of cheese,
Under my ass, behind my knees.

Then through the keyhole and the crack in the jamb
The bird bawls out he's my brother Sam,

And tells me I'll never begin to believe
How sorely he was made to grieve
On shipboard, where he had to ride
Out on deck, he says, from the other side.

So I get a whiff of what's in the air,
And leave the bird just standing there.
Meanwhile — because one never knows,
I mean — I'm keeping on my toes,
Further pushing my bit of cheese
Under my ass and toward my knees.

The bird bends his wing to shade his eyes
— Just like my brother Sam — and cries,
Through the keyhole, that *his* luck should shine
Maybe so blindingly as mine,
Because, he says, he's seen my bit
Of cheese, and he'll crack my skull for it.

It's not so nice here anymore.
So I wiggle slowly towards the door,
Holding my chair and that bit of cheese
Under my ass, behind my knees,
Quietly. But then as if I care,
I ask him whether it's cold out there.

They are frozen totally,
Both his poor ears, he answers me,
Declaring with a frightful moan
That, while he lay asleep alone
He ate up his leg — the one he's lost.
If I let him in, I can hear the rest.

When I hear the words "ate up," you can bet
That I'm terrified; I almost forget
To guard my bit of hidden cheese
Under my ass there, behind my knees.
But I reach below and, yes, it's still here,
So I haven't the slightest thing to fear.

Then I move that we should try a bout
Of waiting, to see which first gives out,
His patience, there, behind the door,
Or mine, in my own house. And more
And more I feel it's funny, what
A lot of patience I have got.

And that's the way it's stayed, although
That was some seven years ago.

I still call out "Hi, there!" through the door.
He screams back " 'Lo there" as before.
"Let me out" I plead, "don't be a louse"
And he answers, "Let me in the house."

But I know what he wants. So I bide
My time and let him wait outside.
He enquires about the bit of cheese
Under my ass, behind my knees;
Scared, I reach down, but, yes, it's still here,
I haven't the slightest thing to fear.

1971

Adam's Task

> And Adam gave names to all cattle, and
> to the fowl of the air, and to every
> beast of the field . . . Gen. 2:20

Thou, paw-paw-paw; thou, glurd; thou, spotted
  Glurd; thou, whitestap, lurching through
The high-grown brush; thou, pliant-footed,
  Implex; thou, awagabu.

Every burrower, each flier
  Came for the name he had to give:
Gay, first work, ever to be prior,
  Not yet sunk to primitive.

Thou, verdle; thou, McFleery's pomma;
  Thou; thou; thou — three types of grawl;
Thou, flisket; thou, kabasch; thou, comma-
  Eared mashawk; thou, all; thou, all.

Were, in a fire of becoming,
  Laboring to be burned away,
Then work, half-measuring, half-humming,
  Would be as serious as play.

Thou, pambler; thou, rivarn; thou, greater
  Wherret, and thou, lesser one;
Thou, sproal; thou, zant; thou, lily-eater.
  Naming's over. Day is done.

1971

from *Powers of Thirteen*

162

At thirteen already single-minded Abraham
Smashed up all the idols in his father's house that were
Likenesses of nothing, and turned his inner eye toward
The Lord of Nonrepresentation, whose sole image
Lies encoded somewhere in our own. So at thirteen,
Boys with minds aswim are called up out of their Third World
To sing the old law aloud from an opened scroll, to
Stand up and be counted, and yet more: to count themselves
Fortunate and wise in not coming of age at twelve
Or ten or twenty (months, toes and fingers keeping those
Accounts) but at a time whose number, even more odd,
Signifies its own solitariness and whose square
(One sixty-nine years old?) breeds doubt ("I should live so long!")

163

*J*ust the right number of letters — half the alphabet;
*O*r the number of rows on this monument we both
*H*ave to share in the building of. We start out each course
*N*ow, of dressed stone, with something of me, ending where you
*H*andle the last block and leave something of you within
*O*r outside it. So we work and move toward a countdown,
*L*oving what we have done, what we have left to do. A
*L*ong day's working makes us look up where we started from
*A*nd slowly to read down to the end, down to a base,
*N*ot out, to some distant border, the terminal bland
*D*estructions at their ends that lines of time undergo,
*E*ndings as of blocks of text, unlit by the late sun
*R*eally underlie our lives when all is said and done.

164

Is it the plenitude of seasons, then, the number
Of weeks each one must have for its full hand of cards, that
Gives us a sense of its completeness? The seasons sit
Around the annular table each holding a pure
Run: Winter wields only the spades, Summer brandishes
Hot, black clubs, Spring showers hearts about and Autumn shows
A fall of diamonds in our climate of extremes.
Our parents in Eden, deathless, parentless, were dealt
The perfect year's full hand of intermingled weeks when
Continual spring and fall scattered variations
Of face and number in among the months, whose first names
Were merely decorative. Now seasons play for keeps:
Death deals, and cheats with the false promise of final trumps.

1983

An Old-Fashioned Song

"Nous n'irons plus au bois"

No more walks in the wood:
The trees have all been cut
Down, and where once they stood
Not even a wagon rut
Appears along the path
Low brush is taking over

No more walks in the wood;
This is the aftermath
Of afternoons in the clover
Fields where we once made love
Then wandered home together
Where the trees arched above,
Where we made our own weather
When branches were the sky.
Now they are gone for good,
And you, for ill, and I
Am only a passer-by.

We and the trees and the way
Back from the fields of play
Lasted as long as we could.
No more walks in the wood.

1990

RICHARD HOWARD (b. 1929)

Richard Howard was born in Cleveland, Ohio. Educated at Columbia University, he has said that at the age of five he learned French from a Viennese aunt during a five-day car ride from Cleveland to Miami. He has gone on to translate more than 150 books from the French, including works by de Gaulle, Barthes, Camus, Baudelaire, and Stendhal. Until recently he was poetry editor of two literary periodicals (the *Paris Review* and *Western Humanities Review*) and has used these positions as well as his teaching appointment at Columbia to encourage young talent. In *Alone with America* (1969) he wrote long essays about the major figures of his own poetic generation as no one has done for the poets since. Figuratively a child of Auden (as are Anthony Hecht, John Hollander, and James Merrill), Howard has adopted the Robert Browning model of the dramatic monologue to his own devices. "The Job Interview" was written for a Festschrift in honor of André Breton's memory but was rejected as insufficiently laudatory of "surrealism's pope."

209 Canal

Not hell but a street, not
Death but a fruit-stand, not
Devils just hungry devils
Simply standing around the stoops, the stoops.

We find our way, wind up
The night, wound uppermost,
In four suits, a funny pack
From which to pick ourselves a card, any card:

Clubs for beating up, spades
For hard labor, diamonds
For buying up rough diamonds,
And hearts, face-up, face-down, for facing hearts.

Dummies in a rum game
We count the tricks that count
Waiting hours for the dim bar
Like a mouth to open wider After Hours.

1971

Like Most Revelations

after Morris Louis

It is the movement that incites the form,
discovered as a downward rapture — yes,
it is the movement that delights the form,
sustained by its own velocity. And yet

it is the movement that delays the form
while darkness slows and encumbers; in fact
it is the movement that betrays the form,
baffled in such toils of ease, until

it is the movement that deceives the form,
beguiling our attention — we supposed
it is the movement that achieves the form.
Were we mistaken? What does it matter if

it is the movement that negates the form?
Even though we give (give up) ourselves
to this mortal process of continuing,
it is the movement that creates the form.

1994

The Job Interview

with André Breton, 1957

The question, Monsieur Gracq advised, had best
be asked, and answered, in the Old Lion's den:
would I, duly scrutinized, be allowed
    to translate *Nadja?*

Factors in my favor: I did speak French
— the one parlance necessarily shared —
and my links to certain Proscribed Figures
    were, to him, unknown.

Bravely enough, therefore, I proceeded
through the Place Blanche and up the Rue Fontaine,
though in my heart (or in some other place)
    I knew the danger:

Breton's legendary loathing of queers . . .
Ever since Jacques Vaché had overdosed
on opium in a Nantes hotel, naked
    with another man,

Surrealism's pope had unchurched men
of my kind, condemned our "perverted race"
to a paltry outer darkness, claiming
    he could sense, could *smell*

an intolerable presence . . . Fee fo fum.
Climbing his stairs, I wondered if I give
off the emanations of turpitude:
    would he detect me

by the scent of my "disgusting practice"?
Was I entitled to conceal from him
— indeed *could* I conceal the taint which made
    whatever talent

I might have merely an interference,
an imposture? A scuffle of slippers,
and the author of *Nadja* let me in
    past the museum

of surreal objects, himself another
museum of sorts, who had shown epigones
how to read, how to live, and how to love.
    Some epigones.

Others had failed, — rejections, suicides;
Of which no hint discolored our encounter,
affable to a fault. Perhaps the three
    decades since Nadja

had revealed to the world her Accidents
of Sublimity had blunted Breton's
erotic stipulations; and I was so
    pusillanimous

as to keep my *tendencies* to myself,
where they fluttered helplessly enough:
of course I knew in my heart that the one
    surrealist act

— O coward heart! would be to challenge this
champion of liberation, this foe of all
society's constraints, but I could do
    nothing of the kind,

nor need I have. O reason not the need:
I left the Master of the Same New Things
with every warrant of his trust in me
    as his translator

(*Traditorre — tradutore!* in fact,
if not in French), and forty years have passed
since that traduced encounter. Where are we?
    Nadja in English is still

in print, and lots of people still hate queers.
I allay that heart of mine with the words
Breton wrote to the first of his three wives
    (Simone, a Jew like me):

criticism will be love, or will not be.

1999

Among the Missing

Know me? I am the ghost of Gansevoort Pier.
        Out of the Trucks, beside the garbage scow
        where rotten pilings form a sort of prow.
I loom, your practiced shadow, waiting here

for celebrants who cease to come my way,
        though mine were limbs as versatile as theirs

and eyes as vagrant. Odd that no one cares
to ogle me now where I, as ever, lay

myself out, all my assets and then some,
weather permitting. Is my voice so faint?
Can't you hear me over the river's complaint?
Too dark to see me? Have you all become

ghosts? What earthly good is that? I want
incarnate lovers hungry for my parts,
longing hands and long-sincere lonely hearts!
It is your living bodies I must haunt,

and while the Hudson hauls its burdens past,
having no hosts to welcome or repel
disclosures of the kind I do so well,
I with the other ghosts am laid at last.

1999

At 65

The tragedy, Colette said, is that one
does *not* age. Everyone else does, of course
(as Marcel was so shocked to discover),
and upon one's mask odd disfigurements
are imposed; but that garrulous presence
we sometimes call the self, sometimes deny

it exists at all despite its carping
monologue, is the same as when we stole
the pears, spied on mother in the bath, ran
away from home. What has altered is what
Kant called Categories: the shape of *time*
changes altogether! Days, weeks, months,

and especially years are reassigned.
Famous for her timing, a Broadway wit
told me her "method": asked to do something,
anything, she would acquiesce *next year* —
"I'll commit suicide, provided it's
next year." But after sixty-five, next year

is now. Hours? there are none, only a few
reckless postponements before *it is time* . . .
When was it you "last" saw Jimmy — last spring?
last winter? That scribbled arbiter
your calendar reveals — betrays — the date:
over a year ago. Come again? No

time like the present, endlessly deferred.
Which makes a difference: once upon a time
there was only time (. . . *as the day is long)*
between the wanting self and what it wants.
Wanting still, you have no dimension where
fulfillment or frustration can occur.

Of course you have, but you must cease waiting
upon it: simply turn around and look
back. Like Orpheus, like Mrs. Lot, you
will be petrified — astonished — to learn
memory is endless, life very long,
and you — you are immortal after all.

1999

ADRIENNE RICH (b. 1929)

Adrienne Rich was born in Baltimore, Maryland. In 1951, the year she graduated from Radcliffe College, W. H. Auden chose her book *A Change of World* for the Yale Younger Poets series. In the 1960s, Rich's poetry underwent a signal change; she outgrew her interest in traditional poetic structures and grew increasingly committed to radical feminism and to a poetry of community. Of the role of the poet in the modern world she has written: "We may feel bitterly how little our poems can do in the face of seemingly out-of-control technological power and seemingly limitless corporate greed, yet it has always been true that poetry can break isolation, show us to ourselves when we are outlawed or made invisible, remind us of beauty where no beauty seems possible, remind us of kinship where all is represented as separation. . . . Maturity in poetry, as in ordinary life, surely means taking our places in history, in accountability, in a web of responsibilities met or failed, of received and changing forms, arguments with community or tradition, a long dialogue between art and justice."

Aunt Jennifer's Tigers

Aunt Jennifer's tigers prance across a screen,
Bright topaz denizens of a world of green.
They do not fear the men beneath the tree;
They pace in sleek chivalric certainty.

Aunt Jennifer's fingers fluttering through her wool
Find even the ivory needle hard to pull.
The massive weight of Uncle's wedding band
Sits heavily upon Aunt Jennifer's hand.

When Aunt is dead, her terrified hands will lie
Still ringed with ordeals she was mastered by.

The tigers in the panel that she made
Will go on prancing, proud and unafraid.

1951

The Middle-Aged

Their faces, safe as an interior
Of Holland tiles and Oriental carpet,
Where the fruit-bowl, always filled, stood in a light
Of placid afternoon — their voices' measure,
Their figures moving in the Sunday garden
To lay the tea outdoors or trim the borders,
Afflicted, haunted us. For to be young
Was always to live in other peoples' houses
Whose peace, if we sought it, had been made by others,
Was ours at second-hand and not for long.
The custom of the house, not ours, the sun
Fading the silver-blue Fortuny curtains,
The reminiscence of a Christmas party
Of fourteen years ago — all memory,
Signs of possession and of being possessed,
We tasted, tense with envy. They were so kind,
Would have given us anything; the bowl of fruit
Was filled for us, there was a room upstairs
We must call ours: but twenty years of living
They could not give. Nor did they ever speak
Of the coarse stain on that polished balustrade,
The crack in the study window, or the letters
Locked in a drawer and the key destroyed.
All to be understood by us, returning
Late, in our own time — how that peace was made,
Upon what terms, with how much left unsaid.

1955

Living in Sin

She had thought the studio would keep itself;
no dust upon the furniture of love.
Half heresy, to wish the taps less vocal,
the panes relieved of grime. A plate of pears,
a piano with a Persian shawl, a cat
stalking the picturesque amusing mouse
had risen at his urging.
Not that at five each separate stair would writhe
under the milkman's tramp; that morning light
so coldly would delineate the scraps
of last night's cheese and three sepulchral bottles;

that on the kitchen shelf among the saucers
a pair of beetle-eyes would fix her own —
envoy from some village in the moldings . . .
Meanwhile, he, with a yawn,
sounded a dozen notes upon the keyboard,
declared it out of tune, shrugged at the mirror,
rubbed at his beard, went out for cigarettes;
while she, jeered by the minor demons,
pulled back the sheets and made the bed and found
a towel to dust the table-top,
and let the coffee-pot boil over on the stove.
By evening she was back in love again,
though not so wholly but throughout the night
she woke sometimes to feel the daylight coming
like a relentless milkman up the stairs.

1955

A Marriage in the Sixties

As solid-seeming as antiquity,
you frown above
the *New York Sunday Times*
where Castro, like a walk-on out of *Carmen*,
mutters into a bearded henchman's ear.

They say the second's getting shorter —
I knew it in my bones —
and pieces of the universe are missing.
I feel the gears of this late afternoon
slip, cog by cog, even as I read.
"I'm old," we both complain,
half-laughing, oftener now.

Time serves you well. That face —
part Roman emperor, part Raimu —
nothing this side of Absence can undo.
Bliss, revulsion, your rare angers can
only carry through what's well begun.

When
I read your letters long ago
in that half-defunct
hotel in Magdalen Street
every word primed my nerves.
A geographical misery
composed of oceans, fogbound planes
and misdelivered cablegrams
lay round me, a Nova Zembla

only your live breath could unfreeze.
Today we stalk
in the raging desert of our thought
whose single drop of mercy is
each knows the other there.
Two strangers, thrust for life upon a rock,
may have at last the perfect hour of talk
that language aches for; still —
two minds, two messages.

Your brows knit into flourishes. Some piece
of mere time has you tangled there.
Some mote of history has flown into your eye.
Will nothing ever be the same,
even our quarrels take a different key,
our dreams exhume new metaphors?
The world breathes underneath our bed.
Don't look. We're at each other's mercy too.

Dear fellow-particle, electric dust
I'm blown with — ancestor
to what euphoric cluster —
see how particularity dissolves
in all that hints of chaos. Let one finger
hover toward you from There
and see this furious grain
suspend its dance to hang
beside you like your twin.

1961

Ghost of a Chance

You see a man
trying to think.

You want to say
to everything:
Keep off! Give him room!
But you only watch,
terrified
the old consolations
will get him at last
like a fish
half-dead from flopping
and almost crawling
across the shingle,
almost breathing
the raw, agonizing

air
till a wave
pulls it back blind into the triumphant
sea.

1962

A Valediction Forbidding Mourning

My swirling wants. Your frozen lips.
The grammar turned and attacked me.
Themes, written under duress.
Emptiness of the notations.

They gave me a drug that slowed the healing of wounds.

I want you to see this before I leave:
the experience of repetition as death
the failure of criticism to locate the pain
the poster in the bus that said:
my bleeding is under control.

A red plant in a cemetery of plastic wreaths.

A last attempt: the language is a dialect called metaphor.
These images go unglossed: hair, glacier, flashlight.
When I think of a landscape I am thinking of a time.
When I talk of taking a trip I mean forever.
I could say: those mountains have a meaning
but further than that I could not say.

To do something very common, in my own way.

1970

Translations

You show me the poems of some woman
my age, or younger
translated from your language

Certain words occur: *enemy, oven, sorrow*
enough to let me know
she's a woman of my time

obsessed

with Love, our subject:
we've trained it like ivy to our walls
baked it like bread in our ovens
worn it like lead on our ankles
watched it through binoculars as if
it were a helicopter
bringing food to our famine
or the satellite
of a hostile power

I begin to see that woman
doing things: stirring rice
ironing a skirt
typing a manuscript till dawn

trying to make a call
from a phonebooth

The phone rings unanswered
in a man's bedroom
she hears him telling someone else
Never mind. She'll get tired —
hears him telling her story to her sister

who becomes her enemy
and will in her own time
light her own way to sorrow

ignorant of the fact this way of grief
is shared, unnecessary
and political

1972

Diving into the Wreck

First having read the book of myths,
and loaded the camera,
and checked the edge of the knife-blade,
I put on
the body-armor of black rubber
the absurd flippers
the grave and awkward mask.
I am having to do this
not like Cousteau with his
assiduous team
aboard the sun-flooded schooner
but here alone.

There is a ladder.
The ladder is always there
hanging innocently
close to the side of the schooner.
We know what it is for,
we who have used it.
Otherwise
it's a piece of maritime floss
some sundry equipment.

I go down.
Rung after rung and still
the oxygen immerses me
the blue light
the clear atoms
of our human air.
I go down.
My flippers cripple me,
I crawl like an insect down the ladder
and there is no one
to tell me when the ocean
will begin.

First the air is blue and then
it is bluer and then green and then
black I am blacking out and yet
my mask is powerful
it pumps my blood with power
the sea is another story
the sea is not a question of power
I have to learn alone
to turn my body without force
in the deep element.

And now: it is easy to forget
what I came for
among so many who have always
lived here
swaying their crenellated fans
between the reefs
and besides
you breathe differently down here.

I came to explore the wreck.
The words are purposes.
The words are maps.
I came to see the damage that was done
and the treasures that prevail.
I stroke the beam of my lamp

slowly along the flank
of something more permanent
than fish or weed

the thing I came for:
the wreck and not the story of the wreck
the thing itself and not the myth
the drowned face always staring
toward the sun
the evidence of damage
worn by salt and sway into this threadbare beauty
the ribs of the disaster
curving their assertion
among the tentative haunters.

This is the place.
And I am here, the mermaid whose dark hair
streams black, the merman in his armored body
We circle silently
about the wreck
we dive into the hold.
I am she: I am he

whose drowned face sleeps with open eyes
whose breasts still bear the stress
whose silver, copper, vermeil cargo lies
obscurely inside barrels
half-wedged and left to rot
we are the half-destroyed instruments
that once held to a course
the water-eaten log
the fouled compass

We are, I am, you are
by cowardice or courage
the one who find our way
back to this scene
carrying a knife, a camera
a book of myths
in which
our names do not appear.

1973

One Life

A woman walking in a walker on the cliffs
recalls great bodily joys, much pain.
Nothing in her is apt to say

My heart aches, though she read those words
in a battered college text, this morning
as the sun rose. It is all too
mixed, the heart too mixed with laughter
raucousing the grief, her life
too mixed, she shakes her heavy
silvered hair at all the fixed
declarations of baggage. I should be dead and I'm alive
don't ask me how; I don't eat like I should
and still I like how the drop of vodka
hits the tongue. I was a worker and a mother,
that means a worker and a worker
but for one you don't pay union dues
or get a pension; for the other
the men ran the union, we ran the home.
It was terrible and good, we had more than half a life,
I had four lives at least, one out of marriage
when I kicked up all the dust I could
before I knew what I was doing.
One life with the girls on the line during the war,
yes, painting our legs and jitterbugging together
one life with a husband, not the worst,
one with your children, none of it just what you'd thought.
None of it what it could have been, if we'd known.
We took what we could.
But even this is a life, I'm reading a lot of books
I never read, my daughter brought home from school,
plays where you can almost hear them talking,
Romantic poets, Isaac Babel. A lot of lives
worse and better than what I knew. I'm walking again.
My heart doesn't ache; sometimes though it rages.

1989

Living Memory

Open the book of tales you knew by heart,
begin driving the old roads again,
repeating the old sentences, which have changed
minutely from the wordings you remembered.
A full moon on the first of May
drags silver film on the Winooski River.
The villages are shut
for the night, the woods are open
and soon you arrive at a crossroads
where late, late in time you recognize
part of yourself is buried.   Call it Danville,
village of water-witches.

From here on instinct is uncompromised and clear:
the tales come crowding like the Kalevala
longing to burst from the tongue. Under the trees
of the backroad you rumor the dark
with houses, sheds, the long barn
moored like a barge on the hillside.
Chapter and verse.   A mailbox.   A dooryard.
A drink of springwater from the kitchen tap.
An old bed, old wallpaper.   Falling asleep like a child
in the heart of the story.

Reopen the book.   A light mist soaks the page,
blunt naked buds tip the wild lilac scribbled
at the margin of the road, no one knows when.
Broken stones of drywall mark the onset
of familiar paragraphs slanting up and away
each with its own version, nothing ever
has looked the same from anywhere.

We came like others to a country of farmers —
Puritans, Catholics, Scotch Irish, Québecois:
bought a failed Yankee's empty house and barn
from a prospering Yankee,
Jews following Yankee footprints,
prey to many myths but most of all
that Nature makes us free.   That the land can save us.
Pioneer, indigenous; we were neither.

You whose stories these farms secrete,
you whose absence these fields publish,
all you whose lifelong travail
took as given this place and weather
who did what you could with the means you had —
it was pick and shovel work
done with a pair of horses, a stone boat
a strong back, and an iron bar: clearing pasture —
Your memories crouched, foreshortened in our text.
Pages torn.   New words crowding the old.

I knew a woman whose clavicle was smashed
inside a white clapboard house with an apple tree
and a row of tulips by the door.   I had a friend
with six children and a tumor like a seventh
who drove me to my driver's test and in exchange
wanted to see Goddard College, in Plainfield.   She'd heard
women without diplomas could study there.
I knew a woman who walked
straight across cut stubble in her bare feet away,
women who said, *He's a good man, never*
laid a hand to me as living proof.

A man they said fought death
to keep fire for his wife for one more winter, leave
a woodpile to outlast him.

I was left the legacy of a pile of stovewood
split by a man in the mute chains of rage.
The land he loved as landscape
could not unchain him.   There are many,
Gentile and Jew, it has not saved.   Many hearts have burst
over these rocks, in the shacks
on the failure sides of these hills.   Many guns
turned on brains already splitting
in silence.   Where are those versions?
Written-across like nineteenth-century letters
or secrets penned in vinegar, invisible
till the page is held over flame.

I was left the legacy of three sons
— as if in an old legend of three brothers
where one changes into a rufous hawk
one into a snowy owl
one into a whistling swan
and each flies to the mother's side
as she travels, bringing something she has lost,
and she sees their eyes are the eyes of her children
and speaks their names and they become her sons.
But there is no one legend and one legend only.

This month the land still leafless, out from snow
opens in all directions, the transparent woods
with sugar-house, pond, cellar-hole unscreened.
Winter and summer cover the closed roads
but for a few weeks they lie exposed,
the old nervous-system of the land.   It's the time
when history speaks in a row of crazy fence-poles
a blackened chimney, houseless, a spring
soon to be choked in second growth
a stack of rusting buckets, a rotting sledge.

It's the time when your own living
laid open between seasons
ponders clues like the *One Way* sign defaced
to *Bone Way*, the stones
of a graveyard in Vermont, a Jewish cemetery
in Birmingham, Alabama.
How you have needed these places,
as a tall gaunt woman used to need to sit
at the knees of bronze-hooded *Grief*
by Clover Adams' grave.

But you will end somewhere else, a sift of ashes
awkwardly flung by hands you have held and loved
or, nothing so individual, bones reduced
with, among, other bones, anonymous,
or wherever the Jewish dead
have to be sought in the wild grass overwhelming
the cracked stones.   Hebrew spelled in wilderness.

All we can read is life.   Death is invisible.
A yahrzeit candle belongs
to life.   The sugar skulls
eaten on graves for the Day of the Dead
belong to life.   To the living.   The Kaddish is to the living,
the Day of the Dead, for the living.   Only the living
invent these plumes, tombs, mounds, funeral ships,
living hands turn the mirrors to the walls,
tear the boughs of yew to lay on the casket,
rip the clothes of mourning.   Only the living
decide death's color: is it white or black?
The granite bulkhead
incised with names, the quilt of names, were made
by the living, for the living.
        I have watched
films from a Pathé camera, a picnic
in sepia, I have seen my mother
tossing an acorn into the air;
my grandfather, alone in the heart of his family;
my father, young, dark, theatrical;
myself, a six-month child.
Watching the dead we see them living
their moments, they were at play, nobody thought
they would be watched so.
        When Selma threw
her husband's ashes into the Hudson
and they blew back on her and on us, her friends,
it was life.   Our blood raced in that gritty wind.

Such details get bunched, packed, stored
in these cellar-holes of memory
so little is needed
to call on the power, though you can't name its name:
It has its ways of coming back:
a truck going into gear on the crown of the road
the white-throat sparrow's notes
the moon in her fullness standing
right over the concrete steps the way
she stood the night they landed there.
                                        From here
nothing has changed, and everything.

The scratched and treasured photograph Richard showed me
taken in '29, the year I was born:
it's the same road I saw
strewn with the Perseids one August night,
looking older, steeper than now
and rougher, yet I knew it.   Time's
power, the only just power — would you
give it away?

1988

1948: Jews

A mother's letter, torn open
in a college mailroom:
. . . *Some of them will be*
the most brilliant, fascinating
you'll ever meet
but don't get taken up by any clique
trying to claim you

— *Marry out, like your father*
she didn't write   She wrote for   wrote
against   him

It was a burden for anyone
to be fascinating, brilliant
after the six million
Never mind just coming home
and trying to get some sleep
like an ordinary person

1990

HARRY MATHEWS (b. 1930)

A New Yorker by birth, Harry Mathews has lived primarily in France since graduating from Harvard in 1952. An uncompromisingly experimental novelist and poet, he is the sole American member of the OuLiPo (Ouvroir de Litterature Potentielle, or Workshop for Potential Literature), a Paris-based association of mathematicians and writers committed to the development of constrictive new forms and methods of composition. With John Ashbery, Kenneth Koch, and James Schuyler — three mainstays of the "New York school" — Mathews founded the avant-garde literary magazine *Locus Solus* in 1960. In "Histoire" (French for both "story" and "history"), the characters "Seth" and "Tina" merge into a unified sestina; the disintegration of meaning in the six end words parallels the fulfillment of the verse form, and the completion of the poem coincides with the consummation of the characters' love affair.

Histoire

Tina and Seth met in the midst of an overcrowded militarism.
"Like a drink?" he asked her. "They make great Alexanders over at the Marxism-Leninism."
She agreed. They shared cocktails. They behaved cautiously, as in a period of pre-fascism.
Afterwards he suggested dinner at a restaurant renowned for its Maoism.
"O.K.," she said, but first she had to phone a friend about her ailing Afghan, whose name was Racism.
Then she followed Seth across town past twilit alleys of sexism.

The waiter brought menus and announced the day's specials. He treated them with condescending sexism,
So they had another drink. Tina started her meal with a dish of militarism,
While Seth, who was hungrier, had a half portion of stuffed baked racism.
Their main dishes were roast duck for Seth, and for Tina broiled Marxism-Leninism.
Tina had pecan pie à la for dessert, Seth a compote of stewed Maoism.
They lingered. Seth proposed a liqueur. They rejected sambuca and agreed on fascism.

During the meal, Seth took the initiative. He inquired into Tina's fascism,
About which she was reserved, not out of reticence but because Seth's sexism
Had aroused in her a desire she felt she should hide — as though her Maoism
Would willy-nilly betray her feelings for him. She was right. Even her deliberate militarism
Couldn't keep Seth from realizing that his attraction was reciprocated. His own Marxism-Leninism
Became manifest, in a compulsive way that piled the Ossa of confusion on the Peleion of racism.

Next, what? Food finished, drinks drunk, bills paid — what racism
Might not swamp their yearning in an even greater confusion of fascism?
But women are wiser than words. Tina rested her hand on his thigh and, a-twinkle with Marxism-Leninism,
Asked him, "My place?" Clarity at once abounded under the flood-lights of sexism,
They rose from the table, strode out, and he with the impetuousness of young militarism
Hailed a cab to transport them to her lair, heaven-haven of Maoism.

In the taxi he soon kissed her. She let him unbutton her Maoism
And stroke her resilient skin, which was quivering with shudders of racism.
When beneath her jeans he sensed the superior Lycra of her militarism,
His longing almost strangled him. Her little tongue was as potent as fascism
In its elusive certainty. He felt like then and there tearing off her sexism
But he reminded himself: "Pleasure lies in patience, not in the greedy violence of Marxism-Leninism."

Once home, she took over. She created a hungering aura of Marxism-Leninism
As she slowly undressed him where he sat on her overstuffed art-deco Maoism,
Making him keep still, so that she could indulge in caresses, in sexism,
In the pursuit of knowing him. He groaned under the exactness of her racism
— Fingertip sliding up his nape, nails incising his soles, teeth nibbling his fascism.
At last she guided him to bed, and they lay down on a patchwork of Old American militarism.

Biting his lips, he plunged his militarism into the popular context of her Marxism-Leninism,
Easing one thumb into her fascism, with his free hand coddling the tip of her Maoism,
Until, gasping with appreciative racism, both together sink into the revealed glory of sexism.

1982

GARY SNYDER (b. 1930)

Gary Snyder was born in San Francisco, raised on a farm outside Seattle, and educated at Reed College in Oregon. As a young man, he worked as a fire watcher in the mountains of Washington State and as a seaman on a Pacific tanker. Impressed by tales of Snyder's hikes and mountain climbing, Jack Kerouac used Snyder as the model for the Beat poet Japhy Ryder in his 1958 novel *The Dharma Bums.* From 1956 to 1964, Snyder studied Buddhism at the Rinzai Zen temple of Shokoku-ji in Japan. Snyder defines "riprap" as "a cobble of stone laid on steep slick rock to make a trail for horses in the mountains," and he has called poetry "a riprap on the slick road of metaphysics." Of the influence of Buddhism on his writing, Snyder observes, "In poetry and in meditation you must be shameless, have no secrets from yourself, be constantly alert, make no judgment of wise and foolish, high or low class, and give everything its full due." The "things to do" poem seems to have been a simultaneous invention of Snyder and James Schuyler, each working without the knowledge of the other.

Piute Creek

One granite ridge
A tree, would be enough
Or even a rock, a small creek,
A bark shred in a pool.
Hill beyond hill, folded and twisted
Tough trees crammed
In thin stone fractures
A huge moon on it all, is too much.
The mind wanders. A million
Summers, night air still and the rocks
Warm. Sky over endless mountains.
All the junk that goes with being human
Drops away, hard rock wavers
Even the heavy present seems to fail
This bubble of a heart.
Words and books
Like a small creek off a high ledge
Gone in the dry air.
A clear, attentive mind
Has no meaning but that
Which sees is truly seen.
No one loves rock, yet we are here.
Night chills. A flick
In the moonlight
Slips into Juniper shadow:
Back there unseen
Cold proud eyes
Of Cougar or Coyote
Watch me rise and go.

1959

Riprap

Lay down these words
Before your mind like rocks.
            placed solid, by hands
In choice of place, set
Before the body of the mind
            in space and time:

Solidity of bark, leaf, or wall
            riprap of things:
Gobble of milky way.
            straying planets,
These poems, people,
            lost ponies with
Dragging saddles —
            and rocky sure-foot trails.
The worlds like an endless
            four-dimensional
Game of *Go*.
            ants and pebbles
In the thin loam, each rock a word
            a creek-washed stone
Granite: ingrained
            with torment of fire and weight
Crystal and sediment linked hot
            all change, in thoughts,
As well as things.

1959

Mid-August at Sourdough Mountain Lookout

Down valley a smoke haze
Three days heat, after five days rain
Pitch glows on the fir-cones
Across rocks and meadows
Swarms of new flies.

I cannot remember things I once read
A few friends, but they are in cities.
Drinking cold snow-water from a tin cup
Looking down for miles
Through high still air.

1959

Above Pate Valley

We finished clearing the last
Section of trail by noon,
High on the ridge-side
Two thousand feet above the creek
Reached the pass, went on
Beyond the white pine groves,
Granite shoulders, to a small

Green meadow watered by the snow,
Edged with Aspen — sun
Straight high and blazing
But the air was cool.
Ate a cold fried trout in the
Trembling shadows. I spied
A glitter, and found a flake
Black volcanic glass — obsidian —
By a flower. Hands and knees
Pushing the Bear grass, thousands
Of arrowhead leavings over a
Hundred yards. Not one good
Head, just razor flakes
On a hill snowed all but summer.
A land of fat summer deer,
They came to camp. On their
Own trails. I followed my own
Trail here. Picked up the cold-drill,
Pick, singlejack and sack
Of dynamite.
Ten thousand years.

1959

Things to Do Around San Francisco

Catch eels in the rocks below the Palace of the Legion of Honor.
Four in the morning — congee at Sam Wo.
Walk up and down Market, upstairs playing pool,
Turn on at Aquatic park — seagulls steal bait sardine
Going clear out to Oh's to buy bulghur.
Howard Street Goodwill
Not paying traffic tickets; stopping the phone.
Merry-go-round at the beach, the walk up to the cliff house,
sea lions and tourists — the old washed-out road that goes
on —
Play chess at Mechanics'
Dress up and go looking for work
Seek out the Wu-t'ung trees in the park arboretum.
Suck in the sea air and hold it — miles of white walls —
sunset shoots back from somebody's window high in the
Piedmont hills
Get drunk all the time. Go someplace and score.
Walk in and walk out of the Asp
Hike up Tam
Keep quitting and starting at Berkeley
Watch the pike in the Steinhart Aquarium: he doesn't move.
Sleeping with strangers
Keeping up on the news

Chanting sutras after sitting
Practicing yr frailing on guitar
Get dropped off in the fog in the night
Fall in love twenty times
Get divorced
Keep moving — move out to the Sunset
Get lost — or
Get found

1966

The Snow on Saddle Mountain

The only thing that can be relied on
is the snow on Kurakake Mountain.
fields and woods
thawing, freezing, and thawing,
totally untrustworthy.
it's true, a great fuzzy windstorm
like yeast up there today, still
the only faint source of hope
is the snow on Kurakake mountain.

1968

What You Should Know to Be a Poet

all you can about animals as persons.
the names of trees and flowers and weeds.
names of stars, and the movements of the planets
                        and the moon.

your own six senses, with a watchful and elegant mind.

at least one kind of traditional magic:
divination, astrology, the *book of changes*, the tarot;

dreams.
the illusory demons and illusory shining gods;

kiss the ass of the devil and eat shit;
fuck his horny barbed cock,
fuck the hag,
and all the celestial angels
                        and maidens perfum'd and golden —

& then love the human: wives   husbands   and friends.

children's games, comic books, bubble-gum,
the weirdness of television and advertising.

work, long dry hours of dull work swallowed and accepted
and livd with and finally lovd.   exhaustion,
                              hunger, rest.

the wild freedom of the dance, *extasy*
silent solitary illumination, *enstasy*

real danger.   gambles.   and the edge of death.

1970

SYLVIA PLATH (1932–1963)

Sylvia Plath was born in Boston. Her father, who taught German at Boston University and published a study of bees, died in 1940 when Plath was eight years old. She attended Smith College, won a fellowship to Cambridge University in England, and married the English poet Ted Hughes in 1956. She separated from her husband in October 1962 and committed suicide on 11 February 1963. The posthumous publication of *Ariel* (1965) cemented her reputation and made her simultaneously a feminist heroine, an icon, a martyr in the eyes of her fans, and a major poet. Her marriage to Hughes has been endlessly discussed and analyzed. Robert Lowell's description of *Ariel* sounds like a summary statement of confessional poetry: "Everything in these poems [*Ariel*] is personal, confessional, felt, but the manner of feeling is controlled hallucination, the autobiography of a fever."

The Hanging Man

By the roots of my hair some god got hold of me.
I sizzled in his blue volts like a desert prophet.

The nights snapped out of sight like a lizard's eyelid:
A world of bald white days in a shadeless socket.

A vulturous boredom pinned me in this tree.
If he were I, he would do what I did.

1960

Mirror

I am silver and exact. I have no preconceptions.
Whatever I see I swallow immediately
Just as it is, unmisted by love or dislike.
I am not cruel, only truthful —
The eye of a little god, four-cornered.
Most of the time I meditate on the opposite wall.
It is pink, with speckles. I have looked at it so long
I think it is a part of my heart. But it flickers.
Faces and darkness separate us over and over.

Now I am a lake. A woman bends over me,
Searching my reaches for what she really is.
Then she turns to those liars, the candles or the moon.
I see her back, and reflect it faithfully.
She rewards me with tears and an agitation of hands.
I am important to her. She comes and goes.
Each morning it is her face that replaces the darkness.
In me she has drowned a young girl, and in me an old woman
Rises toward her day after day, like a terrible fish.

1961

The Applicant

First, are you our sort of a person?
Do you wear
A glass eye, false teeth or a crutch,
A brace or a hook,
Rubber breasts or a rubber crotch,

Stitches to show something's missing? No, no? Then
How can we give you a thing?
Stop crying.
Open your hand.
Empty? Empty. Here is a hand

To fill it and willing
To bring teacups and roll away headaches
And do whatever you tell it.
Will you marry it?
It is guaranteed

To thumb shut your eyes at the end
And dissolve of sorrow.
We make new stock from the salt.
I notice you are stark naked.

How about this suit —

Black and stiff, but not a bad fit.
Will you marry it?
It is waterproof, shatterproof, proof
Against fire and bombs through the roof.
Believe me, they'll bury you in it.

Now your head, excuse me, is empty.
I have the ticket for that.
Come here, sweetie, out of the closet.
Well, what do you think of *that?*
Naked as paper to start

But in twenty-five years she'll be silver,
In fifty, gold.
A living doll, everywhere you look.
It can sew, it can cook,
It can talk, talk, talk.

It works, there is nothing wrong with it.
You have a hole, it's a poultice.
You have an eye, it's an image.
My boy, it's your last resort.
Will you marry it, marry it, marry it.

1962

Lady Lazarus

I have done it again.
One year in every ten
I manage it —

A sort of walking miracle, my skin
Bright as a Nazi lampshade,
My right foot

A paperweight,
My face a featureless, fine
Jew linen.

Peel off the napkin
O my enemy.
Do I terrify? —

The nose, the eye pits, the full set of teeth?
The sour breath
Will vanish in a day.

Soon, soon the flesh
The grave cave ate will be
At home on me

And I a smiling woman.
I am only thirty.
And like the cat I have nine times to die.

This is Number Three.
What a trash
To annihilate each decade.

What a million filaments.
The peanut-crunching crowd
Shoves in to see

Them unwrap me hand and foot —
The big strip tease.
Gentleman, ladies,

these are my hands,
My knees.
I may be skin and bone,

Nevertheless, I am the same, identical woman.
The first time it happened I was ten.
It was an accident.

The second time I meant
To last it out and not come back at all.
I rocked shut

As a seashell.
They had to call and call
And pick the worms off me like sticky pearls.

Dying
Is an art, like everything else.
I do it exceptionally well.

I do it so it feels like hell.
I do it so it feels real.
I guess you could say I've a call.

It's easy enough to do it in a cell.
It's easy enough to do it and stay put.
It's the theatrical

Comeback in broad day
To the same place, the same face, the same brute
Amused shout:

"A miracle!"
That knocks me out.
There is a charge

For the eyeing of my scars, there is a charge
For the hearing of my heart —
It really goes.

And there is a charge, a very large charge,
For a word or a touch
Or a bit of blood

Or a piece of my hair or my clothes.
So, so, Herr Doktor.
So, Herr Enemy.

I am your opus,
I am your valuable,
The pure gold baby

That melts to a shriek.
I turn and burn.
Do not think I underestimate your great concern.

Ash, ash —
You poke and stir.
Flesh, bone, there is nothing there —

A cake of soap,
A wedding ring,
A gold filling.

Herr God, Herr Lucifer,
Beware
Beware.

Out of the ash
I rise with my red hair
And I eat men like air.

1962

Elm

for Ruth Fainlight

I know the bottom, she says. I know it with my great tap root:
It is what you fear.
I do not fear it: I have been there.

Is it the sea you hear in me,
Its dissatisfactions?
Or the voice of nothing, that was your madness?

Love is a shadow.
How you lie and cry after it.
Listen: these are its hooves: it has gone off, like a horse.

All night I shall gallop thus, impetuously,
Till your head is a stone, your pillow a little turf,
Echoing, echoing.

Or shall I bring you the sound of poisons?
This is rain now, this big hush.
And this is the fruit of it: tin-white, like arsenic.

I have suffered the atrocity of sunsets.
Scorched to the root
My red filaments burn and stand, a hand of wires.

Now I break up in pieces that fly about like clubs.
A wind of such violence
Will tolerate no bystanding: I must shriek.

The moon, also, is merciless: she would drag me
Cruelly, being barren.
Her radiance scathes me. Or perhaps I have caught her.

I let her go. I let her go
Diminished and flat, as after radical surgery.
How your bad dreams possess and endow me.

I am inhabited by a cry.
Nightly it flaps out
Looking, with its hooks, for something to love.

I am terrified by this dark thing
That sleeps in me;
All day I feel its soft, feathery turnings, its malignity.

Clouds pass and disperse.
Are those the faces of love, those pale irretrievables?
Is it for such I agitate my heart?

I am incapable of more knowledge.
What is this, this face
So murderous in its strangle of branches? —

Its snaky acids kiss.
It petrifies the will. These are the isolate, slow faults
That kill, that kill, that kill.

1962

Daddy

You do not do, you do not do
Any more, black shoe
In which I have lived like a foot
For thirty years, poor and white,
Barely daring to breathe or Achoo.

Daddy, I have had to kill you.
You died before I had time —
Marble-heavy, a bag full of God,
Ghastly statue with one grey toe
Big as a Frisco seal

And a head in the freakish Atlantic
Where it pours bean green over blue
In the waters off beautiful Nauset.
I used to pray to recover you.
Ach, du.

In the German tongue, in the Polish town
Scraped flat by the roller
Of wars, wars, wars.
But the name of the town is common.
My Polack friend

Says there are a dozen or two.
So I never could tell where you
Put your foot, your root,
I never could talk to you.
The tongue stuck in my jaw.

It stuck in a barb wire snare.
Ich, ich, ich, ich,

I could hardly speak.
I thought every German was you.
And the language obscene

An engine, an engine
Chuffing me off like a Jew.
A Jew to Dachau, Auschwitz, Belsen.
I began to talk like a Jew.
I think I may well be a Jew.

The snows of the Tyrol, the clear beer of Vienna
Are not very pure or true.
With my gypsy ancestress and my weird luck
And my Taroc pack and my Taroc pack
I may be a bit of a Jew.

I have always been scared of *you*,
With your Luftwaffe, your gobbledygoo.
And your neat moustache
And your Aryan eye, bright blue.
Panzer-man, panzer-man, O You —

Not God but a swastika
So black no sky could squeak through.
Every woman adores a Fascist,
The boot in the face, the brute
Brute heart of a brute like you.

You stand at the blackboard, daddy,
In the picture I have of you,
A cleft in your chin instead of your foot
But no less a devil for that, no not
Any less the black man who

Bit my pretty red heart in two.
I was ten when they buried you.
At twenty I tried to die
And get back, back, back to you.
I thought even the bones would do.

But they pulled me out of the sack,
And they stuck me together with glue.
And then I knew what to do.
I made a model of you,
A man in black with a Meinkampf look

And a love of the rack and the screw.
And I said I do, I do.
So daddy, I'm finally through.

The black telephone's off at the root,
The voices just can't worm through.

If I've killed one man, I've killed two —
The vampire who said he was you
And drank my blood for a year,
Seven years, if you want to know.
Daddy, you can lie back now.

There's a stake in your fat black heart
And the villagers never liked you.
They are danci[illegible]nping on you.
They always *kn*[illegible]ou.
Daddy, daddy, [illegible], I'm through.

1962

Words

Axes
After whose stroke the wood rings,
And the echoes!
Echoes traveling
Off from the center like horses.

The sap
Wells like tears, like the
Water striving
To re-establish its mirror
Over the rock

That drops and turns,
A white skull,
Eaten by weedy greens.
Years later I
Encounter them on the road —

Words dry and riderless,
The indefatigable hoof-taps.
While
From the bottom of the pool, fixed stars
Govern a life.

1963

Fever 103°

Pure? What does it mean?
The tongues of hell
Are dull, dull as the triple

Tongues of dull, fat Cerberus
Who wheezes at the gate. Incapable
Of licking clean

The aguey tendon, the sin, the sin.
The tinder cries.
The indelible smell

Of a snuffed candle!
Love, love, the low smokes roll
From me like Isadora's scarves, I'm in a fright

One scarf will catch and anchor in the wheel.
Such yellow sullen smokes
Make their own element. They will not rise,

But trundle round the globe
Choking the aged and the meek,
The weak

Hothouse baby in its crib,
The ghastly orchid
Hanging its hanging garden in the air,

Devilish leopard!
Radiation turned it white
And killed it in an hour.

Greasing the bodies of adulterers
Like Hiroshima ash and eating in.
The sin. The sin.

Darling, all night
I have been flickering, off, on, off, on.
The sheets grow heavy as a lecher's kiss.

Three days. Three nights.
Lemon water, chicken
Water, water make me retch.

I am too pure for you or anyone.
Your body
Hurts me as the world hurts God. I am a lantern —

My head a moon
Of Japanese paper, my gold beaten skin
Infinitely delicate and infinitely expensive.

Does not my heat astound you. And my light.
All by myself I am a huge camellia
Glowing and coming and going, flush on flush.

I think I am going up,
I think I may rise —
The beads of hot metal fly, and I, love, I

Am a pure acetylene
Virgin
Attended by roses,

By kisses, by cherubim,
by whatever these pink things mean.
Not you, nor him

Not him, nor him
(My selves dissolving, old whore petticoats) —
To Paradise.

1963

The Arrival of the Bee Box

I ordered this, this clean wood box
Square as a chair and almost too heavy to lift.
I would say it was the coffin of a midget
Or a square baby
Were there not such a din in it.

The box is locked, it is dangerous.
I have to live with it overnight
And I can't keep away from it.
There are no windows, so I can't see what is in there.
There is only a little grid, no exit.

I put my eye to the grid.
It is dark, dark,
With the swarmy feeling of African hands
Minute and shrunk for export,
Black on black, angrily clambering.

How can I let them out?
It is the noise that appalls me most of all,
The unintelligible syllables.
It is like a Roman mob,
Small, taken one by one, but my god, together!

I lay my ear to furious Latin.
I am not a Caesar.
I have simply ordered a box of maniacs.
They can be sent back.
They can die, I need feed them nothing, I am the owner.

I wonder how hungry they are.
I wonder if they would forget me
If I just undid the locks and stood back and turned into a tree.
There is the laburnum, its blond colonnades,
And the petticoats of the cherry.

They might ignore me immediately
In my moon suit and funeral veil.
I am no source of honey
So why should they turn on me?
Tomorrow I will be sweet God, I will set them free.

The box is only temporary.

1963

Edge

The woman is perfected.
Her dead

Body wears the smile of accomplishment,
The illusion of a Greek necessity

Flows in the scrolls of her toga,
Her bare

Feet seem to be saying:
We have come so far, it is over.

Each dead child coiled, a white serpent,
One at each little

Pitcher of milk, now empty.
She has folded

Them back into her body as petals
Of a rose close when the garden

Stiffens and odors bleed
From the sweet, deep throats of the night flower.

The moon has nothing to be sad about,
Staring from her hood of bone.

She is used to this sort of thing.
Her blacks crackle and drag.

1963

Poppies in October

Even the sun-clouds this morning cannot manage such skirts.
Nor the woman in the ambulance
Whose red heart blooms through her coat so astoundingly —

A gift, a love gift
Utterly unasked for
By a sky

Palely and flamily
Igniting its carbon monoxides, by eyes
Dulled to a halt under bowlers.

O my God, what am I
That these late mouths should cry open
In a forest of frost, in a dawn of cornflowers.

1962

TED BERRIGAN (1934–1983)

Ted Berrigan was born in Providence, Rhode Island. After military service in Korea, he enrolled at the University of Tulsa. While there he met Ron Padgett, then still in high school, and the two formed a lifelong friendship that flowered in New York City. To Berrigan, who never held a regular job or had a bank account, poetry was something you did twenty-four hours day. A mainstay of the second generation of the "New York school," Berrigan worked variations on Frank O'Hara's "I do this I do that" poem and James Schuyler's "Things to Do" format. His best book is *The Sonnets* (1964), an exhilarating sequence in which he uses the techniques of the collage and the cutup, repeats lines in shifting contexts, and incorporates lines from a translation of Arthur Rimbaud's "Le bateau ivre" ("The Drunken Boat").

from *The Sonnets*

XV

In Joe Brainard's collage its white arrow
He is not in it, the hungry dead doctor.
Of Marilyn Monroe, her white teeth white-
I am truly horribly upset because Marilyn
and ate King Korn popcorn," he wrote in his
of glass in Joe Brainard's collage
Doctor, but they say "I LOVE YOU"
and the sonnet is not dead.
takes the eyes away from the gray words,
Diary. The black heart beside the fifteen pieces
Monroe died, so I went to a matinee B-movie
washed by Joe's throbbing hands. "Today
What is in it is sixteen ripped pictures
does not point to William Carlos Williams.

XXXVI

after Frank O'Hara

It's 8:54 a.m. in Brooklyn it's the 28th of July and
it's probably 8:54 in Manhattan but I'm
in Brooklyn I'm eating English muffins and drinking
pepsi and I'm thinking of how Brooklyn is New
York city too how odd I usually think of it as
something all its own like Bellows Falls like Little
Chute like Uijongbu
                                        I never thought on the Williams-
burg bridge I'd come so much to Brooklyn
just to see lawyers and cops who don't even carry
guns taking my wife away and bringing her back
                                                                                    No
and I never thought Dick would be back at Gude's
beard shaved off long hair cut and Carol reading
his books when we were playing cribbage and
watching the sun come up over the Navy Yard
across the river
                              I think I was thinking when I was
ahead I'd be somewhere like Perry Street erudite
dazzling slim and badly loved
contemplating my new book of poems
to be printed in simple type on old brown paper
feminine marvelous and tough

LXX

after Arthur Rimbaud

Sweeter than sour apples flesh to boys
The brine of brackish water pierced my hulk
Cleansing me of rot-gut wine and puke
Sweeping away my anchor in its swell
And since then I've been bathing in the poem
Of the star-steeped milky flowing mystic sea
Devouring great sweeps of azure green and
Watching flotsam, dead men, float by me
Where, dyeing all the blue, the maddened flames
And stately rhythms of the sun, stronger
Than alcohol, more great than song,
Fermented the bright red bitterness of love
I've seen skies split with light, and night,
And surfs, currents, waterspouts; I know
What evening means, and doves, and I have seen
What other men sometimes have thought they've seen

1964

Living with Chris

for Christina Gallup

It's not exciting to have a bar of soap
in your right breast pocket
it's not boring either
it's just what's happening in America, in 1965

If there is no Peace in the world
it's because there is no Peace
in the minds of men. You'd be surprised, however
at how much difference
a really good cup of coffee & a few pills can make
in your day

I would like to get hold of
the owner's manual
for a 1965 model "DREAM"
(Catalogue number CA-77)

I am far from the unluckiest woman in the world

I am far from a woman

An elephant is tramping in my heart

Alka-Seltzer   Palmolive   Pepsodent   Fab
Chemical New York

There is nothing worse than elephant love

Still, there is some Peace in the world. It is
night. You are asleep. So I must be at peace

The barometer at 29.58 and wandering

But who are you?

For god's sake, is there anyone out there listening?

If so, Peace.

1965

My Autobiography

For love of Megan I danced all night,
fell down, and broke my leg in two places.
I didn't want to go to the doctor.
Felt like a goddam fool, that's why.
But Megan got on the phone, called
my mother. Told her, Dick's broken
his leg, & he won't go to the doctor!
Put him on the phone, said my mother.
Dickie, she said, you get yourself
up to the doctor right this minute!
Awwww, Ma, I said. All right, Ma.
Now I've got a cast on my leg from
hip to toe, and I lie in bed all day
and think. God, how I love that girl!

1988

JOSEPH CERAVOLO (1934–1988)

Born in the Astoria section of Queens, New York, Joseph Ceravolo began writing poetry while serving in the U.S. Army in Germany in 1957. He wrote his first poems while on all-night guard duty in a stockade tower. A civil engineer by trade, he studied poetry with Kenneth Koch at the New School in New York City in 1959. "Drunken Winter" owes its effect to "the *things* in it," Koch maintains. "Even the words *like like* seem thinglike." Ceravolo lived quietly with his wife and three children in Bloomfield, New Jersey, and was 54 when he died of an inoperable tumor on 4 September 1988.

The Wind Is Blowing West

I

I am trying to decide to go swimming,
But the sea looks so calm.
All the other boys have gone in.
I can't decide what to do.

I've been waiting in my tent
Expecting to go in.
Have you forgotten to come down?
Can I escape going in?
I was just coming

I was just going in
But lost my pail

II

A boisterous tide is coming up;
I was just looking at it.
The pail is near me
again. My shoulders have sand on them.

Round the edge of the tide
Is the shore. The shore
Is filled with waves.
They are tin waves.

Boisterous tide coming up.
The tide is getting less.

III

Daytime is not a brain,
Living is not a cricket's song.
Why does light diffuse
As earth turns away from the sun?

I want to give my food
To a stranger. I want
to be taken.
What kind of a face do

I have while leaving?
I'm thinking of my friend.

IV

I am trying to go swimming
But the sea looks so calm
All boys are gone
I can't decide what to do

I've been waiting to go
Have you come down?
Can I escape

I am just coming
Just going in

1967

Drunken Winter

Oak oak! like like
it then
cold some wild paddle
so sky then;
flea you say
"geese geese" the boy
June of winter
of again
Oak sky

1967

Happiness in the Trees

O height dispersed and head
in sometimes joining
these sleeps. O primitive touch
between fingers and dawn
on the back

You are no more
simple than a cedar tree
whose children change
the interesting earth
and promise to shake her
before the wind blows
away from you
in the velocity of rest

1967

Rain

Rain is not surrounded by sleep like a drum
that pours song for song
all the body's soft weakness.
That's why I'm afraid.

So I don't feel sorry,
o chatter of birds' wings in
the clouds.

1967

Dusk

Before the dusk grows deeper
Now comes a little moth dressed in
rose pink, wings bordered with yellow. Now
a tiger moth, now another and another another

1967

Fill and Illumined

God created his image.
I love him like the door.
Speak to me now.
Without god there is no god.
Forget everything!
Lie down and be circumscribed
              and circumcised.
Yet there is no pain.
Yet there is no joy.

1967

MARK STRAND (b. 1934)

Mark Strand was born to American parents in Prince Edward Island, Canada. His father was an executive with Pepsi-Cola and the family traveled widely. Strand went to Antioch College and then to Yale, where he studied painting with Josef Albers; he has continued to make prints, etchings, and collages, and to write about art and photography. He has edited several anthologies, including *The Best American Poetry 1991*. "A book of Strand's is like a long night train with a single passenger riding in it," Charles Simic observes. "He is bent over with a small flashlight reading from the book of his life. From time to time, he raises his head, straining to glimpse something of the landscape rushing by beyond the dark window, only to catch sight of his ghostly reflection in the glass. He whispers to himself, hoping that he is being overheard."

Keeping Things Whole

In a field
I am the absence
of field.
This is
always the case.
Wherever I am
I am what is missing.

When I walk
I part the air
and always
the air moves in
to fill the spaces
where my body's been.

We all have reasons
for moving.
I move
to keep things whole.

1964

Reading in Place

Imagine a poem that starts with a couple
Looking into a valley, seeing their house, the lawn
Out back with its wooden chairs, its shady patches of green,
Its wooden fence, and beyond the fence the rippled silver sheen
Of the local pond, its far side a tangle of sumac, crimson
In the fading light. Now imagine somebody reading the poem
And thinking, "I never guessed it would be like this,"
Then slipping it into the back of a book while the oblivious
Couple, feeling nothing is lost, not even the white
Streak of a flicker's tail that catches their eye, nor the slight
Toss of leaves in the wind, shift their gaze to the wooded dome
Of a nearby hill where the violet spread of dusk begins,
But the reader, out for a stroll in the autumn night, with all
The imprisoned sounds of nature dying around him, forgets
Not only the poem, but where he is, and thinks instead

Of a bleak Venetian mirror that hangs in a hall
By a curving stair, and how the stars in the sky's black glass
Sink down and the sea heaves them ashore like foam.
So much is adrift in the ever-opening rooms of elsewhere,
He cannot remember whose house it was, or when he was there.
Now imagine he sits years later under a lamp
And pulls a book from the shelf; the poem drops
To his lap. The couple are crossing a field
On their way home, still feeling that nothing is lost,
That they will continue to live harm-free, sealed
In the twilight's amber weather. But how will the reader know,
Especially now that he puts the poem, without looking,
Back in the book, the book where a poet stares at the sky
And says to a blank page, "Where, where in Heaven am I?"

1990

Orpheus Alone

It was an adventure much could be made of: a walk
On the shores of the darkest known river,
Among the hooded, shoving crowds, by steaming rocks
And rows of ruined huts half buried in the muck;
Then to the great court with its marble yard
Whose emptiness gave him the creeps, and to sit there
In the sunken silence of the place and speak
Of what he had lost, what he still possessed of his loss,
And, then, pulling out all the stops, describing her eyes,
Her forehead, where the golden light of evening spread,
The curve of her neck, the slope of her shoulders, everything
Down to her thighs and calves, letting the words come,
As if lifted from sleep, to drift upstream,
Against the water's will, where all the condemned
And pointless labor, stunned by his voice's cadence,
Would come to a halt, and even the crazed, dishevelled
Furies, for the first time, would weep, and the soot-filled
Air would clear just enough for her, the lost bride,
To step through the image of herself and be seen in the light.
As everyone knows, this was the first great poem,
Which was followed by days of sitting around
In the houses of friends, with his head back, his eyes
Closed, trying to will her return, but finding
Only himself, again and again, trapped
In the chill of his loss, and, finally,
Without a word, taking off to wander the hills
Outside of town, where he stayed until he had shaken
The image of love and put in its place the world
As he wished it would be, urging its shape and measure

Into speech of such newness that the world was swayed,
And trees suddenly appeared in the bare place
Where he spoke and lifted their limbs and swept
The tender grass with the gowns of their shade,
And stones, weightless for once, came and set themselves there,
And small animals lay in the miraculous fields of grain
And aisles of corn, and slept. The voice of light
Had come forth from the body of fire, and each thing
Rose from its depths and shone as it never had.
And that was the second great poem,
Which no one recalls anymore. The third and greatest
Came into the world as the world; out of the unsayable,
Invisible source of all longing to be, it came
As things come that will perish, to be seen or heard
A while, like the coating of frost or the movement
Of wind, and then no more; it came in the middle of sleep
Like a door to the infinite, and, circled by flame,
Came again at the moment of waking, and sometimes,
Remote and small, it came as a vision with trees
By a weaving stream, brushing the bank
With their violet shade, with somebody's limbs
Scattered among the matted, mildewed leaves nearby,
With his severed head rolling under the waves,
Breaking the shifting columns of light into a swirl
Of slivers and flecks; it came in a language
Untouched by pity, in lines lavish and dark,
Where death is reborn and sent into the world as a gift,
So the future, with no voice of its own, or hope
Of ever becoming more than it will be, might mourn.

1990

The Idea

for Nolan Miller

For us, too, there was a wish to possess
Something beyond the world we knew, beyond ourselves,
Beyond our power to imagine, something nevertheless
In which we might see ourselves; and this desire
Came always in passing, in waning light, and in such cold
That ice on the valley's lakes cracked and rolled,
And blowing snow covered what earth we saw,
And scenes from the past, when they surfaced again,
Looked not as they had, but ghostly and white
Among false curves and hidden erasures;
And never once did we feel we were close
Until the night wind said, "Why do this,

Especially now? Go back to the place you belong;"
And there appeared, with its windows glowing, small,
In the distance, in the frozen reaches, a cabin;
And we stood before it, amazed at its being there,
And would have gone forward and opened the door,
And stepped into the glow and warmed ourselves there,
But that it was ours by not being ours,
And should remain empty. That was the idea.

1990

The Philosopher's Conquest

for Harry Ford

This melancholy moment will remain,
So, too, the oracle beyond the gate,
And always the tower, the boat, the distant train.

Somewhere to the south a Duke is slain,
A war is won. Here, it is too late.
This melancholy moment will remain.

Here, an autumn evening without rain,
Two artichokes abandoned on a crate,
And always the tower, the boat, the distant train.

Is this another scene of childhood pain?
Why do the clockhands say 1:28?
This melancholy moment will remain.

The green and yellow light of love's domain
Falls upon the joylessness of fate,
And always the tower, the boat, the distant train.

The things our vision wills us to contain,
The life of objects, their unbearable weight.
This melancholy moment will remain,
And always the tower, the boat, the distant train.

1998

2002

I am not thinking of Death, but Death is thinking of me.
He leans back in his chair, rubs his hands, strokes
His beard and says, "I'm thinking of Strand, I'm thinking

That one of these days I'll be out back, swinging my scythe
Or holding my hourglass up to the moon, and Strand will appear
In a jacket and tie, and together under the boulevards'
Leafless trees we'll stroll into the city of souls. And when
We get to the Great Piazza with its marble mansions, the crowd
That had been waiting there will welcome us with delirious cries,
And their tears, turned hard and cold as glass from having been
Held back so long, will fall, and clatter on the stones below.
O let it be soon. Let it be soon."

2002

2032

It is evening in the town of X,
where Death, who used to love me, sits
in a limo with a blanket spread across his thighs,
waiting for his driver to appear. His hair
is white, his eyes have gotten small, his cheeks
have lost their lustre. He has not swung his scythe
in years, or touched his hourglass. He is waiting
to be driven to the Blue Hotel, the ultimate resort,
where an endless silence fills the lilac-scented air,
and marble fish swim motionless in marble seas,
and where . . . Where is his driver? Ah, there she is,
coming down the garden steps, in heels, velvet evening gown,
and golden boa, blowing kisses to the trees.

2003

JAY WRIGHT (b. 1935)

Jay Wright was born in Albuquerque, New Mexico. "A young man, hearing me read some of my poems, said that I seemed to be trying to weave together a lot of different things," Wright has said. "My answer was that they are already woven, and I'm just trying to uncover the weave." In some of his poems Wright adopts the persona of Benjamin Banneker, the self-taught son of two freed slaves, who was called the first African-American inventor and was appointed by President Thomas Jefferson to the planning committee developing the nation's capital. Wright lives in Bradford, Vermont.

The Homecoming Singer

The plane tilts in to Nashville,
coming over the green lights
like a toy train skipping past

the signals on a track.
The city is livid with lights,
as if the weight of all the people
shooting down her arteries
had inflamed them.
It's Friday night,
and people are home for the homecomings.
As I come into the terminal,
a young black man, in a vested gray suit,
paces in the florid Tennessee air,
breaks into a run like a halfback
in open field, going past the delirious faces,
past the poster of Molly Bee,
in her shiny chaps, her hips tilted forward
where the guns would be, her legs set,
as if she would run, as if she were
a cheerleader who doffs her guns
on Saturday afternoon and careens
down the sidelines after some broken field runner,
who carries it in, for now,
for all the state of Tennessee
with its nut-smelling trees,
its stolid little stone walls
set out under thick blankets of leaves,
its crisp lights dangling on the porches
of homes that top the graveled driveways,
where people who cannot yodel or yell
putter in the grave October afternoons,
waiting for Saturday night and the lights
that spatter on Molly Bee's silver chaps.
I don't want to think of them,
or even of the broken field runner in the terminal,
still looking for his girl, his pocket
full of dates and parties, as I come
into this Friday night of homecomings
and hobble over the highway in a taxi
that has its radio tuned to country music.
I come up to the campus,
with a large wreath jutting up
under the elegant dormitories,
where one girl sits looking down at the shrieking cars,
as the lights go out, one by one, around her
and the laughter drifts off, rising, rising,
as if it would take flight away
from the livid arteries of Nashville.
Now, in sleep, I leave my brass-headed bed,
and see her enter with tall singers,
they in African shirts, she in a robe.

She sits among them, as a golden lance
catches her, suddenly chubby, with soft lips
and unhurried eyes, quite still in the movement
around her, waiting, as the other voices fade,
as the movement stops, and starts to sing,
her voice moving up from its tart entrance
until it swings as freely
as an ecstatic dancer's foot,
rises and plays among the windows
as it would with angels and falls,
almost visible, to return to her,
and leave her shaking with the tears
I'm ashamed to release, and leave her
twisting there on that stool with my shame
for the livid arteries, the flat Saturdays,
the inhuman homecomings of Nashville.
I kneel before her. She strokes my hair,
as softly as she would a cat's head,
and goes on singing, her voice shifting
and bringing up the Carolina calls,
the waterboy, the railroad cutter, the jailed,
the condemned, all that had been forgotten
on this night of homecomings, all
that had been misplaced in those livid arteries.
She finishes, and leaves,
her shy head tilted and wrinkled,
in the green-tinged lights of the still campus.
I close my eyes and listen,
as she goes out to sing this city home.

1971

The Cradle Logic of Autumn

En mi país el otoño nace de una flor seca, de algunos pájaros …
o del vaho penetrante de ciertos ríos de la llanura.
—Molinari, "Oda a una larga tristeza"

Each instant comes with a price, the blue-edged bill
on the draft of a bird almost incarnadine,
the shanked ochre of an inn that sits as still
as the beavertail cactus it guards (the fine
rose of that flower gone as bronze as sand),
the river's chalky white insistence as it
moves past the gray afternoon toward sunset.
Autumn feels the chill of a late summer lit
only by goldenrod and a misplaced strand
of blackberries; deplores all such sleight-of-hand;
turns sullen, selfish, envious, full of regret.

Someone more adept would mute its voice. The spill
of its truncated experience would shine
less bravely and, out of the dust and dunghill
of this existence (call it hope, in decline),
as here the blue light of autumn falls, command
what is left of exhilaration and fit
this season's unfolding to the alphabet
of turn and counterturn, all that implicit
arc of a heart searching for a place to stand.
Yet even that diminished voice can withstand
the currying of its spirit. Here lies — not yet.

If, and only if, the leafless rose he sees,
or thinks he sees, flowered a moment ago,
this endangered heart flows with the river that flees
the plain, and listens with eye raised to the slow
revelation of cloud, hoping to approve
himself, or to admonish the rose for slight
transgressions of the past, this the ecstatic
ethos, a logic that seems set to reprove
his facility with unsettling delight.
Autumn might be only desire, a Twelfth-night
gone awry, a gift almost too emphatic.

Logic in a faithful light somehow appeases
the rose, and stirs the hummingbird's vibrato.
By moving, I can stand where the light eases
me into the river's feathered arms, and, so,
with the heat of my devotion, again prove
devotion, if not this moment, pure, finite.
Autumn cradles me with idiomatic
certainty, leaves me nothing to disapprove.
I now acknowledge this red moon, to requite
the heart alone given power to recite
its faith, what a cradled life finds emblematic.

1995

Russell Edson (b. 1935)

Russell Edson was born in Stamford, Connecticut, and continues to live in the nutmeg state. A specialist in prose poems, Edson could have been summing up his practice in the poem "Antimatter": "On the other side of a mirror there's an inverse world, where the insane go sane, where bones climb out of the earth and recede to the first slime of love." On the subject of the prose poem he has remarked that "time flows through prose, and around poetry. Poetry is the sense of the permanent, of time held. Prose is the sense of normal time, time flowing. . . . And it is the two edges of contradictory time touching, fusing in unlikely combinations, that creates the central metaphor of the prose poem."

The Fall

There was a man who found two leaves and came indoors holding them out saying to his parents that he was a tree.

To which they said then go into the yard and do not grow in the living-room as your roots may ruin the carpet.

He said I was fooling I am not a tree and he dropped his leaves.

But his parents said look it is fall.

1969

Antimatter

On the other side of a mirror there's an inverse world, where the insane go sane, where bones climb out of the earth and recede to the first slime of love.

And in the evening the sun is just rising.

Lovers cry because they are a day younger, and soon childhood robs them of their pleasure.

In such a world there is much sadness which, of course, is joy . . .

1973

The Neighborhood Dog

A neighborhood dog is climbing up the side of a house.

I don't like to see that, I don't like to see a dog like that, says someone passing in the neighborhood.

The dog seems to be making for that 2nd story window. Maybe he wants to get his paws on the sill; he may want to hang there and rest; his tongue throbbing from his open mouth.

Yet, in the room attached to that window (the one just mentioned) a woman is looking at a cedar box; this is of course where she keeps her hatchet: in that same box, the one in the room, the one she is looking at.

That person passing in the neighborhood says, that dog is making for that 2nd story window . . . This is a nice neighborhood, that dog is wrong.

If the dog gets his paws on the sill of the window, which is attached to the same room where the woman is opening her hatchet box, she may chop at his paws with that same hatchet. She might want to chop at something; it is after all, getting close to chopping time . . .

Something is dreadful, I feel a sense of dread, says that same person passing in the neighborhood, it's that dog that's not right, not that way . . .

In the room attached to the window that the dog has been making for, the woman is beginning to see two white paws on the sill of that same window, which is attached to the same room where that same woman is beginning to see two white paws on the sill of that same window, which looks out over the neighborhood.

She says, it's wrong . . . Something . . . The windowsill . . . Something . . . The windowsill

She wants the hatchet. She thinks she's going to need it now.

The person passing in the neighborhood says, something may happen … That dog . . . I feel a sense of dread . . .

The woman goes to the hatchet in its box. She wants it. But it's gone bad. It's soft and nasty. It smells dead. She wants to get it out of its box (that same cedar box where she keeps it). But it bends and runs through her fingers . . .

Now the dog is coming down, crouched low to the wall, backwards, leaving a wet streak with its tongue down the side of the house.

And that same person passing in the neighborhood says, that dog is wrong . . . I don't like to see a dog get like that . . .

1976

The Rule and Its Exception

The big toe located on each of the two feet of man (*Homo sapiens*, "man, the wise") has as its main functions the growing of a toenail and the production of pain when stepped on …

Death is the exception to this rule.

Goodbye, my friends . . .

2001

MARY OLIVER (b. 1935)

Mary Oliver was born in the Cleveland suburb of Maple Heights. She attended Ohio State and Vassar, and assisted Edna St. Vincent Millay's sister Norma with Millay's papers. "I see something and look at it and look at it," she has said. "I see myself going closer and closer just to see it better, as though to see its meaning out of its physical form. And then, I take something emblematic from it and then it transcends the actual."

Some Questions You Might Ask

Is the soul solid, like iron?
Or is it tender and breakable, like
the wings of a moth in the beak of the owl?
Who has it, and who doesn't?
I keep looking around me.
The face of the moose is as sad
as the face of Jesus.
The swan opens her white wings slowly.
In the fall, the black bear carries leaves into the darkness.
One question leads to another.
Does it have a shape? Like an iceberg?
Like the eye of a hummingbird?
Does it have one lung, like the snake and the scallop?
Why should I have it, and not the anteater
who loves her children?
Why should I have it, and not the camel?
Come to think of it, what about the maple trees?
What about the blue iris?
What about all the little stones, sitting alone in the moonlight?
What about roses, and lemons, and their shining leaves?
What about the grass?

1990

Rain

1

All afternoon it rained, then
such power came down from the clouds
on a yellow thread,
as authoritative as God is supposed to be.
When it hit the tree, her body
opened forever.

2 The Swamp

Last night, in the rain, some of the men climbed over
   the barbed-wire fence of the detention center.
In the darkness they wondered if they could do it, and knew
   they had to try to do it.
In the darkness they climbed the wire, handful after handful
   of barbed wire.
Even in the darkness most of them were caught and sent back
   to the camp inside.
But a few are still climbing the barbed wire, or wading through
   the blue swamp on the other side.

What does barbed wire feel like when you grip it, as though
   it were a loaf of bread, or a pair of shoes?
What does barbed wire feel like when you grip it, as though
   it were a plate and a fork, or a handful of flowers?
What does barbed wire feel like when you grip it, as though
   it were the handle of a door, working papers, a clean sheet
   you want to draw over your body?

3

Or this one: on a rainy day, my uncle
lying in the flower bed,
cold and broken,
dragged from the idling car
with its plug of rags, and its gleaming
length of hose. My father
shouted,
then the ambulance came,
then we all looked at death,
then the ambulance took him away.
From the porch of the house
I turned back once again
looking for my father, who had lingered,
who was still standing in the flowers,
who was that motionless muddy man,
who was that tiny figure in the rain.

4 Early Morning, My Birthday

The snails on the pink sleds of their bodies are moving
   among the morning glories.
The spider is asleep among the red thumbs
   of the raspberries.
What shall I do, what shall I do?

The rain is slow.
The little birds are alive in it.
Even the beetles.
The green leaves lap it up.
What shall I do, what shall I do?

The wasp sits on the porch of her paper castle.
The blue heron floats out of the clouds.
The fish leap, all rainbow and mouth, from the dark water.

This morning the water lilies are no less lovely, I think,
  than the lilies of Monet.
And I do not want anymore to be useful, to be docile, to lead
children out of the fields into the text
of civility, to teach them that they are (they are not) better
  than the grass.

5 At the Edge of the Ocean

I have heard this music before,
saith the body.

6 The Garden

The kale's
puckered sleeve,
the pepper's
hollow bell,
the lacquered onion.

Beets, borage, tomatoes.
Green beans.

I came in and I put everything
on the counter: chives, parsley, dill,
the squash like a pale moon,
peas in their silky shoes, the dazzling
rain-drenched corn.

7 The Forest

At night
under the trees
the black snake
jellies forward
rubbing
roughly

the stems of the bloodroot,
the yellow leaves,
little boulders of bark,
to take off
the old life.
I don't know
if he knows
what is happening.
I don't know
if he knows
it will work.
In the distance
the moon and the stars
give a little light.
In the distance
the owl cries out.

In the distance
the owl cries out.
The snake knows
these are the owl's woods,
these are the woods of death,
these are the woods of hardship
where you crawl and crawl,
where you live in the husks of trees,
where you lie on the wild twigs
and they cannot bear your weight,
where life has no purpose
and is neither civil nor intelligent.

Where life has no purpose,
and is neither civil nor intelligent,
it begins
to rain,
it begins
to smell like the bodies
of flowers.
At the back of the neck
the old skin splits.
The snake shivers
but does not hesitate.
He inches forward.
He begins to bleed through
like satin.

1992

CHARLES WRIGHT (b. 1935)

Charles Wright was born in the small town of Pickwick Dam, Tennessee, and grew up near Knoxville. He majored in history at Davidson College in North Carolina and did not discover his poetic vocation until he went to Verona, Italy, as a member of a U.S. Army counterintelligence unit in 1958. Since 1983 he has taught at the University of Virginia. The critic Ted Genoways characterizes Wright's work as a synthesis of Tu Fu, Gerard Manley Hopkins, and Ezra Pound. Wright himself has said, "All my poetry seems to be an ongoing argument with myself about the unlikelihood of salvation." Wright's "Self-Portrait" might profitably be compared to John Ashbery's "Self-Portrait in a Convex Mirror," Donald Justice's "Self-Portrait as Still Life," and James Merrill's "Self-Portrait in Tyvek™ Windbreaker" in this volume.

Snow

If we, as we are, are dust, and dust, as it will, rises,
Then we will rise, and recongregate
In the wind, in the cloud, and be their issue,

Things in a fall in a world of fall, and slip
Through the spiked branches and snapped joints of the evergreens,
White ants, white ants and the little ribs.

1977

Reunion

Already one day has detached itself from all the rest up ahead.
It has my photograph in its soft pocket.
It wants to carry my breath into the past in its bag of wind.

I write poems to untie myself, to do penance and disappear
Through the upper right-hand corner of things, to say grace.

1977

Self-Portrait

Charles on the Trevisan, night bridge
To the crystal, infinite alphabet of his past.
Charles on the San Trovaso, earmarked,
Holding the pages of a thrown-away book, dinghy the color of honey
Under the pine boughs, the water east-flowing.

The wind will edit him soon enough,
And squander his broken chords
                                        in tiny striations above the air,
No slatch in the undertow.
The sunlight will bear him out,
Giving him breathing room, and a place to lie.

And why not? The reindeer still file through the bronchial trees,
Holding their heads high.
The mosses still turn, the broomstraws flash on and off.
Inside, in the crosslight, and St. Jerome
And his creatures . . . St. Augustine, striking the words out.

1981

The Other Side of the River

Easter again, and a small rain falls
On the mockingbird and the housefly,
                                        on the Chevrolet
In its purple joy
And the TV antennas huddled across the hillside —

Easter again, and the palm trees hunch
Deeper beneath their burden,
                                        the dark puddles take in
Whatever is given them,
And nothing rises more than halfway out of itself —

Easter with all its little mouths open into the rain.

* * *

There is no metaphor for the spring's disgrace,
No matter how much the rose leaves look like bronze dove
   hearts,
No matter how much the plum trees preen in the wind.

For weeks I've thought about the Savannah River,
For no reason,
            and the winter fields around Garnett, South Carolina
My brother and I used to hunt
At Christmas,
            Princess and Buddy working the millet stands
And the vine-lipped face of the pine woods
In their languorous zig-zags,

The quail, when they flushed, bursting like shrapnel points
Between the trees and the leggy shrubs
                                        into the undergrowth,
Everything else in motion as though under water,
My brother and I, the guns, their reports tolling from far away
Through the aqueous, limb-filtered light,
December sun like a single tropical fish
Uninterested anyway,
                            suspended and holding still
In the coral stems of the pearl-dusked and distant trees . . .

There is no metaphor for any of this,
Or the meta-weather of April,
The vinca blossoms like deep bruises among the green.

* * *

It's linkage I'm talking about,
                        and harmonies and structures
And all the various things that lock our wrists to the past.

Something infinite behind everything appears,
                                        and then disappears.

It's all a matter of how
                            you narrow the surfaces.
It's all a matter of how you fit in the sky.

* * *

Often, at night, when the stars seem as close as they do now,
    and as full,
And the trees balloon and subside in the way they do
                                        when the wind is right,
As they do now after the rain,
                                the sea way off with its false sheen,
And the sky that slick black of wet rubber,
I'm 15 again, and back on Mt. Anne in North Carolina
Repairing the fire tower,
Nobody else around but the horse I packed in with,
                                    and five days to finish the job.
Those nights were the longest nights I ever remember,
The lake and pavilion 3,000 feet below
                                    as though modeled in tinfoil,
And even more distant than that,
The last fire out, the after-reflection of Lake Llewellyn
Aluminum glare in the sponged dark,
Lightning bugs everywhere,

the plump stars
Dangling and falling near on their black strings.

These nights are like that,
The silvery alphabet of the sea
increasingly difficult to transcribe,
And larger each year, everything farther away, and less clear,
Than I want it to be,
not enough time to do the job,
And faint thunks in the earth,
As though somewhere nearby a horse was nervously pawing
the ground.

* * *

I want to sit by the bank of the river,
in the shade of the evergreen tree,
And look in the face of whatever,
the whatever that's waiting for me.

* * *

There comes a point when everything starts to dust away
More quickly than it appears,
when what we have to comfort the dark
Is just that dust, and just its going away.

Twenty-five years ago I used to sit on this jut of rocks
As the sun went down like an offering through the glaze
And backfires of Monterey Bay,
And anything I could think of was mine because it was there
in front of me, numinously everywhere,
Appearing and piling up . . .

So to have come to this,
remembering what I did do, and what I
didn't do,
The gulls whimpering over the boathouse,
the monarch butterflies
Cruising the flower beds,
And all the soft hairs of spring thrusting up through the wind,
And the sun, as it always does,
dropping into its slot without a click,
Is a short life of trouble.

1984

In Praise of Han Shan

Cold Mountain and Cold Mountain became the same thing in the mind,
The first last seen
          slipping into a crevice in the second.
Only the poems remained,
               scrawled on the rocks and trees,
Nothing's undoing among the self-stung unfolding of things.

2004

FREDERICK SEIDEL (b. 1936)

The reclusive Frederick Seidel was born in St. Louis, Missouri, and now lives in New York City. From 23 March 2000 to 13 December 2001, he published on commission a series of poems in the *Wall Street Journal*, fifteen in all, each with the name of the month as its title. (A dozen appear in his book *Area Code 212*.) A motorcycle enthusiast, Seidel has written on the subject for the same newspaper: "Motorcycles are blasts of form with a purpose, flowing on two wheels, smoothed to go fast, and as a result look very fine standing still."

Racine

When civilization was European,
I knew every beautiful woman
In the Grand Hôtel et de Milan,
Which the Milanese called "The Millin,"
Where Verdi died, two blocks from La Scala,
And lived in every one of them
Twenty-some years ago while a motorcycle was being made
For me by the MV Agusta
Racing Department in Cascina Costa,
The best mechanics in the world
Moonlighting for me after racing hours.
One of the "Millin" women raced cars, a raving beauty.
She owned two Morandis, had met Montale.
She recited verses from the Koran
Over champagne in the salon and was only eighteen
And was too good to be true.
She smilingly recited Leopardi in Hebrew.
The most elegant thing in life is an Italian Jew.
The most astonishing thing in life to be is an Italian Jew.
It helps if you can be from Milan, too.
She knew every *tirade* in Racine
And was only eighteen.
They thought she was making a scene
When she started declaiming Racine.
Thunderbolts in the bar.

With the burning smell of Auschwitz in my ear.
With the gas hissing from the ceiling.
Racine raved on racing tires at the limit of adhesion.
With the gas hissing from the showers.
I remember the glamorous etching on the postcard
The hotel continued to reprint from the original 1942 plate.
The fantasy hotel and street
Had the haughty perfect ease of haute couture,
Chanel in stone. A tiny tailored doorman
Stood as in an architectural drawing in front of the façade and streamlined
Cars passed by.
The cars looked as if they had their headlights on in the rain.
In the suave, grave
Milanese sunshine.

1998

Love Song

I shaved my legs a second time,
Lagoon approaching the sublime,
To cast a moonlight spell on you.
TriBeCa was Tahiti, too.

I know I never was on time.
I was downloading the sublime
To cast a moonlight spell on you.
TriBeCa was Tahiti, too.

The melanoma on my skin
Resumes what's wrong with me within.
My outside is my active twin.
Disease I'm repetitious in.

The sun gives life but it destroys.
It burns the skin of girls and boys.
I cover up to block the day.
I also do so when it's gray.

The sunlight doesn't go away.
It causes cancer while they play.
Pre-cancerous will turn out bad.
I had an ice pick for a dad.

A womanizing father, he's
The first life-threatening disease.
His narcissistic daughter tried
To be his daughter but he died.

The richest man in Delaware
Died steeplechasing, debonair.
One company of ours made napalm.
That womanizing ice pick's gray calm

Died steeplechasing in a chair,
The jockey underneath the mare.
She posted and she posted and
Quite suddenly he tried to stand

And had a heart attack and died,
The ice pick jockey's final ride.
The heart attack had not been planned.
He saw my eyes and tried to stand.

My satin skin becomes the coffin
The taxidermist got it off in.
He stuffed me, made me lifelike. Fatten
My corpse in satin in Manhattan!

My body was flash-frozen. God,
I am a person who is odd.
I am the ocean and the air.
I'm acting out. I cut my hair.

You like the way I do things, neat
Combined with craziness and heat.
My ninety-eight point six degrees,
Warehousing decades of deep freeze,

Can burst out curls and then refreeze
And have to go to bed but please
Don't cure me. Sickness is my me.
My terror was you'd set me free.

My shrink admired you. He could see.
Sex got me buzzing like a bee
With Parkinson's! Catastrophe
Had slaughtered flowers on the tree.

My paranoia was revived.
I love it downtown and survived.
I loved downtown till the attack.
Love Heimlich'd me and brought me back.

You brought me life, glued pollen on
My sunblock. Happy days are gone
Again. My credit cards drip honey.
The tabloids dubbed me *Maid of Money*.

Front-page divorce is such a bore.
I loathed the drama they adore.
You didn't love me for my money.
You made the stormy days seem sunny.

2004

C. K. Williams (b. 1936)

Born in Newark, New Jersey, C. K. Williams spends half of each year in Paris, the other half teaching at Princeton. He favors long lines bursting with modifiers. Williams's poems have the force "of the best journalism — human interest stories, editorials, news flashes from around the world and across the street, all of it rendered in a level tone that one is surprised to find so surprising," Tom Disch has written.

Love: Beginnings

They're at that stage where so much desire streams between them, so much frank need and want,
so much absorption in the other and the self and the self-admiring entity and unity they make —
her mouth so full, breast so lifted, head thrown back *so* far in her laughter at his laughter,
he so solid, planted, oaky, firm, so resonantly factual in the headiness of being craved so,
she almost wreathed upon him as they intertwine again, touch again, cheek, lip, shoulder, brow,
every glance moving toward the sexual, every glance away soaring back in flame into the sexual —
that just to watch them is to feel again that hitching in the groin, that filling of the heart,
the old, sore heart, the battered, foundered, faithful heart, snorting again, stamping in its stall.

1987

The Lover

When she stopped by, just passing, on her way back from picking up the kids at school,
taking them to dance, just happened by the business her husband owned and her lover worked in,

their glances, hers and the lover's, that is, not the husband's, seemed so
  decorous, so distant,
barely, just barely touching their fiery wings, their clanging she thought
  so well muffled,
that later, in the filthy women's bathroom, in the stall, she was horrified to
  hear two typists
coming from the office laughing, about them, all of them, their boss, her
  husband, "the blind pig,"
one said, and laughed, "and her, the horny bitch," the other said, and they
  both laughed again,
"and *him*, did you see *him*, that sanctimonious, lying bastard — I thought
  he was going to *blush*."

1987

Money

How did money get into the soul; how did base dollars and cents ascend
  from the slime
to burrow their way into the crannies of consciousness, even it feels like
  into the flesh?

Wants with no object, needs with no end, like bacteria bringing their
  fever and freezing,
viruses gnawing at neurons, infecting even the sanctuaries of altruism
  and self-worth.

We asked soul to be huge, encompassing, sensitive, knowing, all-
  knowing, but not this,
not money roaring in with battalions of pluses and minus, setting up
  camps of profit and loss,

not joy become calculation, life counting itself, compounding itself like
  a pocket of pebbles:
sorrow, it feels like; a weeping, unhealable wound, an affront at all costs
  to be avenged.

Greed, taint and corruption, this sickness, this buy and this miserable
  sell;
soul against soul, talons of caustic tungsten: *what has been done to us,
  what have we done?*

1997

CHARLES SIMIC (b. 1938)

Charles Simic was born in Belgrade, Yugoslavia. In *A Fly in the Soup*, his absorbing memoir, Simic tells of growing up in war-torn Yugoslavia: "My family, like so many others, got to see the world for free, thanks to Hitler's wars and Stalin's takeover of East Europe." Simic and his little friends played soldiers as the war went on: "A boy a little older than I had disappeared. It turned out that he had slipped out to watch the bombs fall. When the men brought him back, his mother started slapping him hard and yelling she's going to kill him if he ever does that again. I was more frightened of her slaps than of the sound of the bombs." When the Americans arrived in Belgrade, they took the Simic family to the barracks and gave them chewing gum, chocolate, bacon, and eggs. In 1954 young Charlie, his brother, and his mother joined his father in Manhattan. The brothers watched a Dodgers-Giants game on television, ate burgers and fries, and ended up in a jazz club (the Metropole): "I was all absorbed in the music. This was definitely better than any radio. It was heaven." He has also written, "Awe is my religion, and mystery is its church." When Mark Strand selected "Country Fair" for *The Best American Poetry 1991*, Simic wrote that he had witnessed the scene "in the mid-1970s at the nearby fair in Deerfield, New Hampshire. What a life, I thought at the time. It's not enough to have six legs, they want you to do tricks, too. Then it occurred to me. That's what a poet is: a six-legged dog."

My Shoes

Shoes, secret face of my inner life:
Two gaping toothless mouths,
Two partly decomposed animal skins
Smelling of mice-nests.

My brother and sister who died at birth
Continuing their existence in you,
Guiding my life
Toward their incomprehensible innocence.

What use are books to me
When in you it is possible to read
The Gospel of my life on earth
And still beyond, of things to come?

I want to proclaim the religion
I have devised for your perfect humility
And the strange church I am building
With you as the altar.

Ascetic and maternal, you endure:
Kin to oxen, to Saints, to condemned men,
With your mute patience, forming
The only true likeness of myself.

1967

Watermelons

Green Buddhas
On the fruit stand.
We eat the smile
And spit out the teeth.

1974

My Beloved

after D. Khrams

In the fine print of her face
Her eyes are two loopholes.
No, let me start again.
Her eyes are flies in milk,
Her eyes are baby Draculas.

To hell with her eyes.
Let me tell you about her mouth.
Her mouth's the red cottage
Where the wolf ate Grandma.

Ah, forget about her mouth,
Let me talk about her breasts.
I get a peek at them now and then
And even that's more than enough
To make me lose my head,
So I better tell you about her legs.

When she crosses them on the sofa
It's like the jailer unwrapping a parcel
And in that parcel is a Christmas cake
And in that cake a sweet little file
That gasps her name as it files my chains.

1981

December

It snows
and still the derelicts
go
carrying sandwich boards —

    one proclaiming
the end of the world
    the other
the rates of a local barbershop.

1986

St. Thomas Aquinas

I left parts of myself everywhere
The way absent-minded people leave
Gloves and umbrellas
Whose colors are sad from dispensing so much bad luck.

I was on a park bench asleep.
It was like the Art of Ancient Egypt.
I didn't wish to bestir myself.
I made my long shadow take the evening train.

"We give death to a child when we give it a doll,"
Said the woman who had read Djuna Barnes.
We whispered all night. She had traveled to darkest Africa.
She had many stories to tell about the jungle.

I was already in New York looking for work.
It was raining as in the days of Noah.
I stood in many doorways of that great city.
Once I asked a man in a tuxedo for a cigarette.
He gave me a frightened look and stepped out into the rain.

Since "man naturally desires happiness,"
According to St. Thomas Aquinas,
Who gave irrefutable proof of God's existence and purpose,
I loaded trucks in the Garment Center.
Me and a black man stole a woman's red dress.
It was of silk; it shimmered.

Upon a gloomy night with all our loving ardors on fire,
We carried it down the long empty avenue,
Each holding one sleeve.
The heat was intolerable causing many terrifying human faces
To come out of hiding.

In the Public Library Reading Room
There was a single ceiling fan barely turning.

I had the travels of Herman Melville to serve me as a pillow.
I was on a ghost ship with its sails fully raised.
I could see no land anywhere.
The sea and its monsters could not cool me.

I followed a saintly-looking nurse into a doctor's office.
We edged past people with eyes and ears bandaged.
"I am a medieval philosopher in exile,"
I explained to my landlady that night.
And, truly, I no longer looked like myself.
I wore glasses with a nasty spider crack over one eye.

I stayed in the movies all day long.
A woman on the screen walked through a bombed city
Again and again. She wore army boots.
Her legs were long and bare. It was cold wherever she was.
She had her back turned to me, but I was in love with her.
I expected to find wartime Europe at the exit.

It wasn't even snowing! Everyone I met
Wore a part of my destiny like a carnival mask.
"I'm Bartleby the Scrivener," I told the Italian waiter.
"Me, too," he replied.
And I could see nothing but overflowing ashtrays
The human-faced flies were busy examining.

1990

The Devils

You were a "victim of semiromantic anarchism
In its most irrational form."
I was "ill at ease in an ambiguous world

Deserted by Providence." We drank gin
And made love in the afternoon. The neighbors'
TV's were tuned to soap operas.

The unhappy couples spoke little.
There were interminable pauses.
Soft organ music. Someone coughing.

"It's like Strindberg's *Dream Play*," you said.
"What is?" I asked and got no reply.
I was watching a spider on the ceiling.

It was the kind St. Veronica ate in her martyrdom.
"That woman subsisted on spiders only,"
I told the janitor when he came to fix the faucet.

He wore dirty overalls and a derby hat.
Once he had been an inmate of a notorious
state institution.
"I'm no longer Jesus," he informed us happily.

He believed only in devils now.
"This building is full of them," he confided.
One could see their horns and tails

If one caught them in their baths.
"He's got Dark Ages on his brain," you said.
"Who does?" I asked and got no reply.

The spider had the beginnings of a web
Over our heads. The world was quiet
Except when one of us took a sip of gin.

1990

The Scarecrow

God's refuted but the devil's not.

This year's tomatoes are something to see.
Bite into them, Martha,
As you would into a ripe apple.
After each bite add a little salt.

If the juices run down your chin
Onto your bare breasts,
Bend over the kitchen sink.

From there you can see your husband
Come to a dead stop in the empty field
Before one of his bleakest thoughts,
Spreading his arms like a scarecrow.

1990

Country Fair

for Hayden Carruth

If you didn't see the six-legged dog,
It doesn't matter.

We did and he mostly lay in the corner.
As for the extra legs,

One got used to them quickly
And thought of other things.
Like, what a cold, dark night
To be out at the fair.

Then the keeper threw a stick
And the dog went after it
On four legs, the other two flapping behind,
Which made one girl shriek with laughter.

She was drunk and so was the man
Who kept kissing her neck.
The dog got the stick and looked back at us.
And that was the whole show.

1992

Evening Chess

The Black Queen raised high
In my father's angry hand.

1992

Cameo Appearance

I had a small, nonspeaking part
In a bloody epic. I was one of the
Bombed and fleeing humanity.
In the distance our great leader
Crowed like a rooster from a balcony,
Or was it a great actor
Impersonating our great leader?

That's me there, I said to the kiddies.
I'm squeezed between the man
With two bandaged hands raised
And the old woman with her mouth open
As if she were showing us a tooth

That hurts badly. The hundred times
I rewound the tape, not once
Could they catch sight of me
In that huge gray crowd,
That was like any other gray crowd.

Trot off to bed, I said finally.
I know I was there. One take
Is all they had time for.
We ran, and the planes grazed our hair,
And then they were no more
As we stood dazed in the burning city,
But, of course, they didn't film that.

1996

FRANK BIDART (b. 1939)

Frank Bidart was born in Bakersfield, California. He came east to study at Harvard and formed close friendships with Robert Lowell (whose collected poems Bidart has edited) and Elizabeth Bishop. Bidart is drawn to extreme states of mind; he has spoken through such characters as the anorexic Ellen West and the flamboyant Russian dancer Vaslav Nijinsky, and has adopted a highly idiosyncratic system of punctuation, with frequent use of emphatic devices (italics, uppercase letters) and with lines distributed around the page. "His art, like the story of the Garden, creates narratives designed to account for what would otherwise be inexplicable suffering" (Louise Glück). Bidart has explained that the "you" addressed in "Curse" are those who brought down the World Trade Center towers. His most spirited and best efforts are his long poems, impossible to excerpt. After completing one of these, he said, "I've just been through hell."

Another Life

Peut-être n'es-tu pas suffisamment mort.
C'est ici la limite de notre domaine. Devant
toi coule un fleuve.
—Valéry

" — In a dream I never *exactly* dreamed,
but that is, somehow, the quintessence
of what I *might* have dreamed,
Kennedy is in Paris

again; it's '61; once again
some new national life seems possible,
though desperately, I try to remain unduped,
even cynical . . .
He's standing in an open car,

brilliantly lit, bright orange
next to a grey de Gaulle, and they stand
not far from me, slowly moving up the Champs-Elysées . . .

Bareheaded in the rain, he gives a short
choppy wave, smiling like a sun god.

— I stand and
look, suddenly at peace; once again mindlessly
moved,
          as they bear up the fields of Elysium

the possibility of Atlantic peace,

reconciliation between all that power, energy,
optimism, —
                    and an older wisdom, without
illusions, without force, the austere source
of nihilism, corrupted only by its dream of Glory . . .

But no — ; as I
watch, the style is

                         not quite right — ;

                         Kennedy is *too* orange . . .

And de Gaulle, white, dead
white, ghost white, not even grey . . .

                                        As my heart
began to grieve for my own awkwardness and
ignorance, which would never be
soothed by the informing energies
                                        of whatever
wisdom saves, —

                         I saw a young man, almost
my twin, who had written
                                   'MONSTER'
in awkward lettering with a crayon across
the front of his sweat shirt.
                                   He was gnawing on his arm,

in rage and anger gouging up
pieces of flesh — ; but as I moved to stop him, somehow
help him,
          suddenly he looked up,

and began, as I had, to look at Kennedy and de Gaulle:

and then abruptly, almost as if I were seeing him
through a camera lens, his figure

split in two, —
                    or doubled, —

and all the fury
                    drained from his stunned, exhausted face . . .

But only for a moment. Soon his eyes turned down
to the word on his chest. The two figures
again became one,

and with fresh energy he attacked the mutilated arm . . .

— Fascinated, I watched as this
pattern, this cycle,
                    repeated several times.

Then he reached out and touched me.

— Repelled,
                I pulled back . . . But he became
frantic, demanding that I become
the body he split into:
                              'It's harder
to manage *each* time! Please,
give me your energy; — *help me!*'

                              — I said it was impossible,
there was *no part* of us the same:
we were just watching a parade together:
(and then, as he reached for my face)
                                        leave me *alone!*

He smirked, and said
I was never alone.

                    I told him to go to hell.

He said that this was hell.

                              — I said it was impossible,
there was *no part* of us the same:
we were just watching a parade together:
                                        when I saw

Grief, avenging Care, pale
Disease, Insanity, Age, and Fear,
                              — all the raging desolations

which I had come to learn were my patrimony;
the true progeny of my parents' marriage;
the gifts hidden within the mirror;

— standing guard at the gate of this place,
triumphant,
                    striking poses
                                        eloquent of the disasters they embodied . . .

— I took several steps to the right, and saw
Kennedy was paper-thin,
                                        as was de Gaulle;
mere cardboard figures
whose possible real existence
lay buried beneath a million tumbling newspaper photographs . . .

— I turned, and turned, but now all that was left
was an enormous
                              fresco; — on each side, the unreadable
                                                                  fresco of my life . . . "

1973

The Yoke

don't worry   *I know you're dead*
but tonight

turn your face again
toward me

when I hear your voice there is now
no direction in which to turn

I sleep and wake and sleep and wake and sleep and wake and

but tonight
turn your face again

toward me

see   *upon my shoulders is the yoke*
that is not a yoke

don't worry   I know you're dead
but tonight

turn your face again

1997

For the Twentieth Century

Bound, hungry to pluck again from the thousand
technologies of ecstasy

boundlessness, the world that at a drop of water
rises without boundaries,

I push the PLAY button: —

. . . *Callas, Laurel & Hardy, Szigeti*

you are alive again, —

the slow movement of K.218
once again no longer

bland, merely pretty, nearly
banal, as it is

in all but Szigeti's hands

* * *

Therefore you and I and Mozart
must thank the Twentieth Century, for

it made you pattern, form
whose infinite

repeatability within matter
defies matter —

Malibran. Henry Irving. The young
Joachim. They are lost, a mountain of

newspaper clippings, become words
not their own words. The art of the performer.

1999

Curse

May breath for a dead moment cease as jerking your

head upward you hear as if in slow motion floor

collapse evenly upon floor as one hundred and ten

floors descend upon you.

May what you have made descend upon you.
May the listening ears of your victims their eyes their

breath

enter you, and eat like acid
the bubble of rectitude that allowed you breath.

May their breath now, in eternity, be your breath.

* * *

Now, as you wished, you cannot for us
not be. May this be your single profit.

Of your rectitude at last disenthralled, you
seek the dead. Each time you enter them

they spit you out. The dead find you are not food.
Out of the great secret of morals, *the imagination to enter*
the skin of another, what I have made is a curse.

2002

CARL DENNIS (b. 1939)

Carl Dennis has written of a poem of his ("Sarit Narai") that it "implies a protest against the brute fact that we live in time, that the present is always sliding away from us into a past no future will ever be able to restore" — but the poem also "suggests some power to resist time by enlarging the present, and so it allies itself with traditional notions of the difference between poetry and history: namely, the greater place poetry gives to individual human agency." In Dennis's view, all poetry participates in a common impulse, the refusal "to let time have the last word."

History

I too could give my heart to history.
I too could turn to it for illumination,
For a definition of who we are, what it means to live here
Breathing this atmosphere at the end of the century.
I too could agree we aren't pilgrims
Resting for the night at a roadside hermitage,
Uncertain about the local language and customs,
But more like the bushes and trees around us,
Sprung from this soil, nurtured by the annual rainfall
And the slant of the sun in our temperate latitudes.

If only history didn't side with survivors,
The puny ones who in times of famine
Can live on nothing, or the big and greedy.
If only it didn't conclude that the rebels who take the fort
Must carry the flag of the future in their knapsacks
While the rebels who fail have confused their babble
With the voice of the people, which announces by instinct
The one and only path to posterity.

The people are far away in the provinces
With their feet on the coffee table
Leafing through magazines on barbecuing and sailing.
They're dressing to go to an uncle's funeral,
To a daughter's rehearsal dinner. They're listening,
As they drive to work, to the radio.
Caesar's ad on law and order seems thoughtful.
Brutus's makes some useful points about tyranny.
But is either candidate likely to keep his promises?

When ice floes smashed the barges on the Delaware
And Washington drowned with all his men, it was clear
To the world the revolt he led against excise taxes
And import duties was an overreaction.
When the South routed the North at Gettysburg
It was clear the scheme of merchants to impose their values
On cotton planters was doomed from the start
Along with Lincoln's mystical notion of union,
Which sadly confused the time-bound world we live in
With a world where credos don't wear out.

2001

World History

Better to wonder if ten thousand angels
Could waltz on the head of a pin
And not feel crowded than to wonder if now's the time
For the armies of the Austro-Hungarian Empire
To teach the Serbs a lesson they'll never forget
For shooting Archduke Franz Ferdinand in Sarajevo.

Better to go door to door in Düsseldorf or Marseilles
And leave the taxpayers scratching their heads
At your vague report of a kingdom within
Than argue it's time for Germany to display
A natural love for its Austrian kin, or time
For France to make good on its pledge to Russia,
Or time for England to honor its word to France
Or give up thinking itself a gentleman.

To wonder, after a month without one convert,
If other people exist, if they share the world
That you inhabit, if you've merely dreamed them
To keep from feeling lonely — that's enough
To make the silence that falls when your words give out
A valley of shadows you fear to pass through.
But it can't compare to the silence of bristling nations
Standing toe to toe in a field, each army certain
It couldn't be anywhere else, given the need
Of great nations to be ready for great encounters.

And if it's hard to believe that spirit
Is anything more than a word when defined
As something separate from what is mortal,
It's easy to recognize the spirit of the recruit
Not convinced his honor has been offended
Who decides it's time to step from the line
And catch a train back to his cottage
Deep in the boondocks, where his wife and daughter
Are waiting to serve him supper and hear the news.

2003

TOM DISCH (b. 1940)

Tom Disch was born in Iowa, grew up in Minnesota, moved to New York City after graduating from high school in 1958, and became a full-time writer after dropping out of New York University. Versatile and prolific, Disch has long enjoyed a commanding international reputation for his science fiction novels, such as *Camp Concentration* (1968), and he has written theater criticism, book reviews, plays, and an "interactive" computer novel. The virtues of Disch's prose — wit, invention, boyish wonder, and intellectual sophistication — are to be found in his verse as well.

A Concise History of Music

When the wells of song were sweet
In the childhood of the world
And tambourines jingled and bagpipes skirled
And drums would beat with the beat
Of the heart, there was no art that hands and feet
Didn't perfectly understand.
And wasn't life grand?
O, life was grand.

But the wells of song grew foul,
And no one who heard them knew why

The hautboy would scream like a jet in the sky
      And viols would seem to howl
And the harpstring's sound was the cry of an owl.
   No, no one understood
      How songs so lovely could
      Cease to be good.

1978

The Crumbling Infrastructure

A limb snaps, the hive is smashed, and the survivors
Buzz off to colonize another neck of the woods.
No nest is sacrosanct. Abandoned churches may serve
A while as discothèques. Steel towns may hope
To be retooled to meet the needs of foreign banks
Anxious to reinvest evaporating capital
Beyond the reach of ruin. But generally decay's
The aftermath of desuetude. Rome,
What's left of it, falls to the Hun, and all
Its noble plumbing is undone. The fountains
Of Versailles run dry, and the Bourbons are remembered
As a lower-class alternative to Scotch.
In all these matters money rules, but not as the sun,
Benign, inscrutable, and far away, but as a river would,
Collating the waters of a hundred townships,
Tolerant of dams, a source of wonder and a force
Even the Federal Reserve cannot coerce.
Basements flood, canoeists (i.e., small investors)
Drown, and nothing can be done about the mosquitoes,
But on the whole one does well to dwell in the valley.
Money, like water, yields an interest hard to deny.
Every dawn brings new quotations in the pages
Of *The Times*; every sunset gilds the thought of death
As though it were the mummy of a king.
Then is every man an Emerson,
Aghast at the everlasting, wild with surmise,
His daily paper dewy with the news
Of history's long, slow slouch toward
That Götterdämmerung dearest to pulp
Illustrators: Liberty's torch thrust up,
Excalibur-like, from the sands of a new Sahara
Or the waves of a new flood, her bronze flame
All that remains of Babylon. A pretty sight —
But meanwhile Liberty's toes are dry, bridges
And tunnels still traversible, and someone had better
Be paid to patch these goddamn potholes, that's all

I'm trying to say, because if they're not,
Someone's going to break an axle, and it could be one of us.

1990

Fanny Howe (b. 1940)

Fanny Howe was born in Buffalo, New York, the daughter of Irish-born playwright and actress Mary Manning and Harvard law professor Mark DeWolfe Howe. She took classes at Stanford University but dropped out and drifted to New York City and then Boston, where she met and married Carl Senna, a half-black, half-Chicano writer and activist, with whom she had three children. A devout Catholic, she is committed to a radical ideal in her writing and in her politics. She has taught at the University of California, San Diego, and at the New School in New York City, and has published novels and essays as well as poems and prose poems.

Veteran

I don't believe in ashes; some of the others do.
I don't believe in better or best; some of the others do.
I don't believe in a thousand flowers or the first robin
of the year or statues made of dust. Some of the others do

I don't believe in seeking sheet music
by Boston Common on a snowy day, don't believe
in the lighting of malls seasonably
When I'm sleeping I don't believe in time
as we own it, though some of the others might

Sad lace on green. Veterans stamping the leafy snow
I don't believe in holidays
long-lasting and artificial. Some of the others do
I don't believe in starlings of crenelated wings
I don't believe in berries, red & orange, hanging on
threadlike twigs. Some of the others do

I don't believe in the light on the river
moving with it or the green bulbs hanging on the elms
Outdoors, indoors, I don't believe in a gridlock of ripples
or the deep walls people live inside

Some of the others believe in food & drink & perfume
I don't. And I don't believe in shut-in time
for those who committed a crime
of passion. Like a sweetheart
of the iceberg or wings lost at sea

the wind is what I believe in,
the One that moves around each form

1992

Goodbye, Post Office Square

Where wrought iron spears
punctuate the common and rain
turns to snow a minute
I learned six poems
equal the dirt in the road
twenty more make a cobweb
thirty five muddy bodies equal a wall
one and a half jobs don't make a living
great novels are stainglass
their pain is their color

Never welcome on the hill
I looked like a fool with my daily thanks
but the wine was my joke, it was really water
Two stones equal two kisses up there
a leather jacket equals a terrier

In the next world I discovered
a hovel where a naked I writes with a nail
There you're as small as zero, the hole in the wall
the mouse goes in
with a whorl of cheese
for the littlest glass-cutter to eat
To paint one rose equals a life in that place
and on the thorny path outside
one cathedral is equal to the sky

1992

9-11-01

The first person is an existentialist

Like trash in the groin of the sand dunes
Like a brown cardboard home beside a dam

Like seeing like things the same
Between Death Valley and the desert of Pavan

An earthquake a turret with arms and legs
The second person is the beloved

Like winners taking the hit
Like looking down on Utah as if

It was Saudi Arabia or Pakistan
Like war-planes out of Miramar

Like a split cult a jolt of coke New York
Like Mexico in its deep beige couplets

Like this, like that . . . like call us all It,
Thou It. "Sky to Spirit! Call us all It!"

The third person is a materialist.

2001

ROBERT PINSKY (b. 1940)

Robert Pinsky was born in Long Branch, New Jersey. He was educated at Rutgers and studied with Yvor Winters at Stanford. He has written, in addition to poetry, several books of criticism and an acclaimed translation of Dante's *Inferno.* As U.S. poet laureate, he started the Favorite Poem Project, a video and audio archive featuring Americans from all walks of life reading their favorite poems. The third stanza of Pinsky's "Ode to Meaning" is in the form of an abecedarius, recapitulating the alphabet. The impetus for "Samurai Song" came from hearing a welder in Salina, Kansas, read a fourteenth-century Japanese poem based on the formula "When I . . . then I . . ."

Shirt

The back, the yoke, the yardage. Lapped seams,
The nearly invisible stitches along the collar
Turned in a sweatshop by Koreans or Malaysians

Gossiping over tea and noodles on their break
Or talking money or politics while one fitted
This armpiece with its overseam to the band

Of cuff I button at my wrist. The presser, the cutter,
The wringer, the mangle. The needle, the union,
The treadle, the bobbin. The code. The infamous blaze

At the Triangle Factory in nineteen-eleven.
One hundred and forty-six died in the flames
On the ninth floor, no hydrants, no fire escapes —

The witness in a building across the street
Who watched how a young man helped a girl to step
Up to the windowsill, then held her out

Away from the masonry wall and let her drop.
And then another. As if he were helping them up
To enter a streetcar, and not eternity.

A third before he dropped her put her arms
Around his neck and kissed him. Then he held
Her into space, and dropped her. Almost at once

He stepped to the sill himself, his jacket flared
And fluttered up from his shirt as he came down,
Air filling up the legs of his gray trousers —

Like Hart Crane's Bedlamite, "shrill shirt ballooning."
Wonderful how the pattern matches perfectly
Across the placket and over the twin bar-tacked

Corners of both pockets, like a strict rhyme
Or a major chord. Prints, plaids, checks,
Houndstooth, Tattersall, Madras. The clan tartans

Invented by mill-owners inspired by the hoax of Ossian,
To control their savage Scottish workers, tamed
By a fabricated heraldry: MacGregor,

Bailey, MacMartin. The kilt, devised for workers
To wear among the dusty clattering looms.
Weavers, carders, spinners. The loader,

The docker, the navvy. The planter, the picker, the sorter
Sweating at her machine in a litter of cotton
As slaves in calico headrags sweated in fields:

George Herbert, your descendant is a Black
Lady in South Carolina, her name is Irma
And she inspected my shirt. Its color and fit

And feel and its clean smell have satisfied
Both her and me. We have culled its cost and quality
Down to the buttons of simulated bone,

The buttonholes, the sizing, the facing, the characters
Printed in black on neckband and tail. The shape,
The label, the labor, the color, the shade. The shirt.

1990

From the Childhood of Jesus

One Saturday morning he went to the river to play.
He modeled twelve sparrows out of the river clay

And scooped a clear pond, with a dam of twigs and mud.
Around the pond he set the birds he had made,

Evenly as the hours. Jesus was five. He smiled,
As a child would who had made a little world

Of clear still water and clay beside a river.
But a certain Jew came by, a friend of his father,

And he scolded the child and ran at once to Joseph,
Saying, "Come see how your child has profaned the Sabbath,

Making images at the river on the Day of Rest."
So Joseph came to the place and took his wrist

And told him, "Child, you have offended the Word."
Then Jesus freed the hand that Joseph held

And clapped his hands and shouted to the birds
To go away. They raised their beaks at his words

And breathed and stirred their feathers and flew away.
The people were frightened. Meanwhile, another boy,

The son of Annas the scribe, had idly taken
A branch of driftwood and leaning against it had broken

The dam and muddied the little pond and scattered
The twigs and stones. Then Jesus was angry and shouted,

"Unrighteous, impious, ignorant, what did the water
Do to harm you? Now you are going to wither

The way a tree does, you shall bear no fruit
And no leaves, you shall wither down to the root."

At once, the boy was all withered. His parents moaned,
The Jews gasped, Jesus began to leave, then turned

And prophesied, his child's face wet with tears:
"Twelve times twelve times twelve thousands of years

Before these heavens and this earth were made,
The Creator set a jewel in the throne of God

With Hell on the left and Heaven to the right,
The Sanctuary in front, and behind, an endless night

Endlessly fleeing a Torah written in flame.
And on that jewel in the throne, God wrote my name."

Then Jesus left and went into Joseph's house.
The family of the withered one also left the place,

Carrying him home. The Sabbath was nearly over.
By dusk, the Jews were all gone from the river.

Small creatures came from the undergrowth to drink
And foraged in the shadows along the bank.

Alone in his cot in Joseph's house, the Son
Of Man was crying himself to sleep. The moon

Rose higher, the Jews put out their lights and slept,
And all was calm and as it had been, except

In the agitated household of the scribe Annas,
And high in the dark, where unknown even to Jesus

The twelve new sparrows flew aimlessly through the night,
Not blinking or resting, as if never to alight.

1990

Round

What was the need like driving rain
That struck the house and pelted the garden
So poorly planned? What was the creature
That needed to hide from the stunning torrent
Among the piers of the stone foundation
Under the house

That groaned in the wind? The seedlings floated
And spun in furrows that turned to runnels
Of muddy water while the hidden watched
Apart from the ones that lived inside.
The house was pounded and stung by the wind
That flailed the siding

And pried at the roof. Though the beams looked sound
The rooms all shook. Who were the ones
Shaken inside and the one that hid
Among the stones all through the storm
While the whole failed garden melted to ruin?
What was the need?

1996

Ode to Meaning

Dire one and desired one,
Savior, sentencer —

In an old allegory you would carry
A chained alphabet of tokens:

Ankh Badge Cross.
Dragon,
Engraved figure guarding a hallowed intaglio,
Jasper kinema of legendary Mind,
Naked omphalos pierced
By quills of rhyme or sense, torah-like: unborn
Vein of will, xenophile
Yearning out of Zero.

Untrusting I court you. Wavering
I seek your face, I read
That Crusoe's knife
Reeked of you, that to defile you
The soldier makes the rabbi spit on the torah.
"I'll drown my book" says Shakespeare.

Drowned walker, revenant.
After my mother fell on her head, she became
More than ever your sworn enemy. She spoke
Sometimes like a poet or critic of forty years later.
Or she spoke of the world as Thersites spoke of the heroes,
"I think they have swallowed one another. I
Would laugh at that miracle."

You also in the laughter, warrior angel:
Your helmet the zodiac, rocket-plumed
Your spear the beggar's finger pointing to the mouth
Your heel planted on the serpent Formulation
Your face a vapor, the wreath of cigarette smoke crowning
Bogart as he winces through it.

You not in the words, not even
Between the words, but a torsion,
A cleavage, a stirring.
Stirring even in the arctic ice,
Even at the dark ocean floor, even
In the cellular flesh of a stone.

You stirring even in the arctic ice,
Gas. Gossamer. My poker friends
Question your presence
In a poem by me, passing the magazine
One to another.

Not the stone and not the words, you
Like a veil over Arthur's headstone,
The passage from Proverbs he chose
While he was too ill to teach
And still well enough to read, *I was*
Beside the master craftsman
Delighting him day after day, ever
At play in his presence — you

A soothing veil of distraction playing over
Dying Arthur playing in the hospital,
Thumbing the Bible, fuzzy from medication,
Ever courting your presence,
And you the prognosis.
You in the cough.

Gesturer, when is your spur, your cloud?
You in the airport rituals of greeting and parting.
Indicter, who is your claimant?
Bell at the gate. Spiderweb iron bridge.
Cloak, video, aroma, rue, what is your
Elected silence, where was your seed?

What is Imagination
But your lost child born to give birth to you?

Dire one. Desired one.
Savior, sentencer —

Absence,
Or presence ever at play:
Let those scorn you who never
Starved in your dearth. If I
Dare to disparage
Your harp of shadows I taste
Wormwood and motor oil, I pour
Ashes on my head. You are the wound. You
Be the medicine.

2000

Samurai Song

When I had no roof I made
Audacity my roof. When I had
No supper my eyes dined.

When I had no eyes I listened.
When I had no ears I thought.
When I had no thought I waited.

When I had no father I made
Care my father. When I had no
Mother I embraced order.

When I had no friend I made
Quiet my friend. When I had no
Enemy I opposed my body.

When I had no temple I made
My voice my temple. I have
No priest, my tongue is my choir.

When I have no means fortune
Is my means. When I have
Nothing, death will be my fortune.

Need is my tactic, detachment
Is my strategy. When I had
No lover I courted my sleep.

2000

XYZ

The cross the fork the zigzag — a few straight lines
For pain, quandary and evasion, the last of signs.

2005

TOM CLARK (b. 1941)

Tom Clark grew up in Chicago and was educated at the University of Michigan and Cambridge University. For ten years starting in 1963, he served as poetry editor of the *Paris Review*. A prolific poet, prose writer, and journalist, he has written critical biographies of Robert Creeley, Edward Dorn, Jack Kerouac, and Charles Olson. His "Dover Beach" is one of a number of poems based on Matthew Arnold's poem of that title and should be read alongside it. (Two other noteworthy instances are Anthony Hecht's "The Dover Bitch" in this volume and the title poem of John Brehm's *Sea of Faith*.)

Dover Beach

The sea is calm to-night,
The tide is full, the moon lies fair
Upon the Straits; — on the French
Toast, the light
Syrup gleams but a moment,
And is gone
Down the hatch; for it is the light of France.
The cliffs of England stand
Made all of cardboard; a hand
Claps by itself. It gives itself a standing ovation.

Sophocles long ago
Heard it on the Aegean, and it brought
Into his mind
A state of crashing ignorance.

1978

Elegy

It's a pity we have to suffer
The bluejay said to me with a wink
If any part of the body be cut off
No part of the soul perishes but
Is sucked into that soul that remains
In that which remains of the body
These aren't tears anyway just eye gunk
And you've always taught me to be brave
As the last kindly rays of February
Sun warm bare ruined plum tree choirs
And light them up with a gaggle of buds
From which a few white blossoms are just
Starting to pop open as traffic hums
And in this moment there is nothing lost

1997

Prophet

So then he wandered out into the street and began to testify
Something about life being a long journey of the soul
An endless voyaging turning into a voyaging with an end
One knows how but one does not know when
No one yet knows when as the traffic bore down on him

As the traffic bore down on him my mind drifted in the wilderness
Or was it that my mind having been adrift all along
I've just grown to regard the wilderness as my resting or laughing place
He cried but those were not yet his last words
As the traffic parted around him as around one charmed

2004

BILLY COLLINS (b. 1941)

Billy Collins was born in New York City. After toiling in obscurity for years, teaching at Lehman College in the Bronx and publishing his books with respected university presses, Collins achieved extraordinary popularity in his late fifties — to the point that a legal battle broke out between the University of Pittsburgh Press and Random House for the right to publish his poetry. On the first anniversary of 11 September 2001, he read a poem he had written for the occasion to a special joint session of Congress. His poems are characterized by warmth of personality, a conversational style, wit, humor, and a knack for taking the reader on a journey from a familiar place to an uncanny conclusion. Collins has cited Coleridge's "conversation" poems (such as "Frost at Midnight" and "This Lime-Tree Bower My Prison") as a precedent. A number of Collins's poems concern poetry ("Introduction to Poetry," "Workshop") and virtually define a poetics by casual implication. For "Litany" he appropriated the first two lines of a love poem encountered in a magazine. Introducing the poem at a public reading, he remarked that the profligate use of analogies — which he lampoons in "Litany" — suggests that, in the mind of some poets, the correct answer to Freud's "insulting" question "What do women want?" is "Similes."

Introduction to Poetry

I ask them to take a poem
and hold it up to the light
like a color slide

or press an ear against its hive.

I say drop a mouse into a poem
and watch him probe his way out,

or walk inside the poem's room
and feel the walls for a light switch.

I want them to waterski
across the surface of a poem
waving at the author's name on the shore.

But all they want to do
is tie the poem to a chair with a rope
and torture a confession out of it.

They begin beating it with a hose
to find out what it really means.

1988

Another Reason Why I Don't Keep a Gun in the House

The neighbors' dog will not stop barking.
He is barking the same high, rhythmic bark
that he barks every time they leave the house.
They must switch him on on their way out.

The neighbors' dog will not stop barking.
I close all the windows in the house
and put on a Beethoven symphony full blast
but I can still hear him muffled under the music,
barking, barking, barking,

and now I can see him sitting in the orchestra,
his head raised confidently as if Beethoven
had included a part for barking dog.

When the record finally ends he is still barking,
sitting there in the oboe section barking,
his eyes fixed on the conductor who is
entreating him with his baton

while the other musicians listen in respectful
silence to the famous barking dog solo,
that endless coda that first established
Beethoven as an innovative genius.

1988

Workshop

I might as well begin by saying how much I like the title.
It gets me right away because I'm in a workshop now

so immediately the poem has my attention
like the ancient mariner grabbing me by the sleeve.

And I like the first few stanzas,
the way they establish this mode of self-pointing
that runs through the whole poem
and tells us the words are food thrown down
on the ground for other words to eat.
I can almost taste the tail of the snake
in its own mouth,
if you know what I mean.

But what I'm not sure about is the voice
which sounds in places very casual, very blue jeans,
but other times seems very standoffish,
professorial in the worst sense of the word,
like the poem is blowing pipe smoke in my face.
But maybe that's just what it wants to do.

What I did find engaging were the middle stanzas,
especially the fourth one.
I like the image of clouds flying like lozenges,
which gives me a very clear picture.
And I really like how this drawbridge operator
just appears out of the blue
with his feet up on the iron railing
and his fishing pole jigging — I like jigging —
a hook in the slow industrial canal below.
I love slow industrial canal below. All those *I*'s.

Maybe it's just me,
but the next stanza is where I start to have a problem.
I mean how can the evening bump into the stars?
And what's an obbligato of snow?
Also, I roam the decaffeinated streets.
At that point I'm lost. I need help.

The other thing that throws me off,
and maybe this is just me,
is the way the scene keeps shifting around.
First, we're in what seems like an aerodrome
and the speaker is inspecting a row of dirigibles,
which makes me think this could be a dream.
Then he takes us into his garden,
the part with the dahlias and the coiling hose,
though that's nice, the coiling hose,
and then I'm not sure where we're supposed to be.
The rain and the mint green light,
that makes it feel outdoors, but what about this wallpaper?

Or is it a kind of indoor cemetery?
There's something about death going on here.

In fact, I start to wonder if what we have now
is really two poems, or three, or four,
or possibly none.

But then there's that last stanza, my favorite.
This is where the poem wins me back,
especially the lines that are spoken in the voice of the mouse.
I mean we've seen these images in cartoons before,
but I still love the details he uses
when he's describing where he lives.
The tiny arch of an entrance in the white baseboard,
his bed made out of a rolled-back sardine can,
the spool of thread for a table.
I start thinking about how hard the mouse had to work
night after night collecting all those things
while the people in the house were fast asleep,
and that gives me a very strong feeling,
a very powerful sense of something.
But I don't know if anyone else was feeling that.
Maybe that's just me.
Maybe that's just the way I read it.

1995

Lines Composed Over Three Thousand Miles From Tintern Abbey

I was here before, a long time ago,
and now I am here again
is an observation that occurs in poetry
as frequently as rain occurs in life.

The fellow may be gazing
over an English landscape,
hillsides dotted with sheep,
a row of tall trees topping the downs,

or he could be moping through the shadows
of a dark Bavarian forest,
a wedge of cheese and a volume of fairy tales
tucked into his rucksack.

But the feeling is always the same.
It was better the first time.

This time is not nearly as good.
I'm not feeling as chipper as I did back then.

Something is always missing —
swans, a glint on the surface of a lake,
some minor but essential touch.
Or the quality of things has diminished.

The sky was a deeper, more dimensional blue,
clouds were more cathedral-like,
and water rushed over rock
with greater effervescence.

From our chairs we have watched
the poor author in his waistcoat
as he recalls the dizzying icebergs of childhood
and mills around in a field of weeds.

We have heard the poets long-dead
declaim their dying
from a promontory, a riverbank,
next to a haycock, within a copse.

We have listened to their dismay,
the kind that issues from poems
the way water issues forth from hoses,
the way the match always gives its little speech on fire.

And when we put down the book at last,
lean back, close our eyes,
stinging with print,
and slip in the bookmark of sleep,

we will be schooled enough to know
that when we wake up
a little before dinner
things will not be nearly as good as they once were.

Something will be missing
from this long, coffin-shaped room,
the walls and windows now
only two different shades of gray

the glossy gardenia drooping
in its chipped terra-cotta pot.
Shoes, socks, ashtray, the shroud of curtains,
the browning core of an apple.

Nothing will be as it was
a few hours ago, back in the glorious past
before our naps, back in that Golden Age
that drew to a close sometime shortly after lunch.

1998

Shoveling Snow with Buddha

In the usual iconography of the temple or the local Wok
you would never see him doing such a thing,
tossing the dry snow over the mountain
of his bare, round shoulder,
his hair tied in a knot,
a model of concentration.

Sitting is more his speed, if that is the word
for what he does, or does not do.

Even the season is wrong for him.
In all his manifestations, is it not warm and slightly humid?
Is this not implied by his serene expression,
that smile so wide it wraps itself around the waist of the
universe?

But here we are, working our way down the driveway,
one shovelful at a time.
We toss the light powder into the clear air.
We feel the cold mist on our faces.
And with every heave we disappear
and become lost to each other
in these sudden clouds of our own making,
these fountain-bursts of snow.

This is so much better than a sermon in church,
I say out loud, but Buddha keeps on shoveling.
This is the true religion, the religion of snow,
and sunlight and winter geese barking in the sky,
I say, but he is too busy to hear me.

He has thrown himself into shoveling snow
as if it were the purpose of existence,
as if the sign of a perfect life were a clear driveway
you could back the car down easily
and drive off into the vanities of the world
with a broken heater fan and a song on the radio.

All morning long we work side by side,
me with my commentary

and he inside the generous pocket of his silence,
until the hour is nearly noon
and the snow is piled high all around us;
then, I hear him speak.

After this, he asks,
can we go inside and play cards?

Certainly, I reply, and I will heat some milk
and bring cups of hot chocolate to the table
while you shuffle the deck,
and our boots stand dripping by the door.

Aaah, says the Buddha, lifting his eyes
and leaning for a moment on his shovel
before he drives the thin blade again
deep into the glittering white snow.

1998

Dharma

The way the dog trots out the front door
every morning
without a hat or an umbrella,
without any money
or the keys to her dog house
never fails to fill the saucer of my heart
with milky admiration.

Who provides a finer example
of a life without encumbrance?
Thoreau in his curtainless hut
with a single plate, a single spoon?
Gandhi with his staff and his holy diapers?

Off she goes into the material world
with nothing but her brown coat
and her modest blue collar,
following only her wet nose,
the twin portals of her steady breathing,
followed only by the plume of her tail.

If only she did not shove the cat aside
every morning
and eat all his food
what a model of self-containment she would be,
what a paragon of earthly detachment.
If only she were not so eager

for a rub behind the ears,
so acrobatic in her welcomes,
if only I were not her god.

1999

Man Listening to Disc

This is not bad —
ambling along 44th Street
with Sonny Rollins for company,
his music flowing through the soft calipers
of these earphones,

as if he were right beside me
on this clear day in March,
the pavement sparkling with sunlight,
pigeons fluttering off the curb,
nodding over a profusion of bread crumbs.

In fact, I would say
my delight at being suffused
with phrases from his saxophone —
some like honey, some like vinegar —
is surpassed only by my gratitude

to Tommy Potter for taking the time
to join us on this breezy afternoon
with his most unwieldy bass
and to the esteemed Arthur Taylor
who is somehow managing to navigate

this crowd with his cumbersome drums.
And I bow deeply to Thelonious Monk
for figuring out a way
to motorize — or whatever — his huge piano
so he could be with us today.

The music is loud yet so confidential
I cannot help feeling even more
like the center of the universe
than usual as I walk along to a rapid
little version of "The Way You Look Tonight,"

and all I can say to my fellow pedestrians,
to the woman in the white sweater,
the man in the tan raincoat and the heavy glasses,
who mistake themselves for the center of the universe —

all I can say is watch your step

because the five of us, instruments and all,
are about to angle over
to the south side of the street
and then, in our own tightly knit way,
turn the corner at Sixth Avenue.

And if any of you are curious
about where this aggregation,
this whole battery-powered crew,
is headed, let us just say
that the real center of the universe,

the only true point of view,
is full of the hope that he,
the hub of the cosmos
with his hair blown sideways,
will eventually make it all the way downtown.

2000

No Time

In a rush this weekday morning,
I tap the horn as I speed past the cemetery
where my parents are buried
side by side under a smooth slab of granite.

Then, all day long, I think of him rising up
to give me that look
of knowing disapproval
while my mother calmly tells him to lie back down.

2002

Litany

> You are the bread and the knife,
> The crystal goblet and the wine . . .
> —Jacques Crickillon

You are the bread and the knife,
the crystal goblet and the wine.
You are the dew on the morning grass
and the burning wheel of the sun.
You are the white apron of the baker

and the marsh birds suddenly in flight.

However, you are not the wind in the orchard,
the plums on the counter,
or the house of cards.
And you are certainly not the pine-scented air.
There is just no way you are the pine-scented air.

It is possible that you are the fish under the bridge,
maybe even the pigeon on the general's head,
but you are not even close
to being the field of cornflowers at dusk.

And a quick look in the mirror will show
that you are neither the boots in the corner
nor the boat asleep in its boathouse.

It might interest you to know,
speaking of the plentiful imagery of the world,
that I am the sound of rain on the roof.
I also happen to be the shooting star,
the evening paper blowing down an alley,
and the basket of chestnuts on the kitchen table.

I am also the moon in the trees
and the blind woman's tea cup.
But don't worry, I am not the bread and the knife.
You are still the bread and the knife.
You will always be the bread and the knife,
not to mention the crystal goblet and — somehow —
the wine.

2003

Bob Dylan (b. 1941)

The songwriter and singer Bob Dylan was born Robert Zimmerman in Duluth, Minnesota, and spent much of his boyhood in Hibbing, near the Canadian border. He named himself after the Welsh poet Dylan Thomas. The lyrics in three of his record albums from the mid-1960s — *Bringing It All Back Home*, *Highway 61 Revisited*, and *Blonde on Blonde* — particularly reward close analysis of the sort given to demanding examples of modern poetry. Read on the page, independent of musical accompaniment or vocal delivery, "Desolation Row" may be his finest lyric. The critic Christopher Ricks, who had previously written books about Milton, Keats, Tennyson, T. S. Eliot, and Samuel Beckett, devoted a lengthy volume to *Dylan's Visions of Sin* in 2004. Ricks analyzes a stanza in "Desolation Row" — the one in which Ezra Pound and T. S. Eliot are "fighting in the captain's tower" — in relation to Eliot's "Love Song of J. Alfred Prufrock." Archibald MacLeish once complimented Dylan on the same lines. "Pound and Eliot were too scholastic, weren't they?" MacLeish said. "I knew them both. Hard men. We have to go through them. But I know what you mean when you say they are fighting in a captain's tower." Recalling MacLeish's words, Dylan made no comment other than to allow that he liked Eliot, who was "worth reading," but disapproved of Pound's anti-American propaganda from Italy in World War II and never did read him.

Desolation Row

They're selling postcards of the hanging
They're painting the passports brown
The beauty parlor is filled with sailors
The circus is in town
Here comes the blind commissioner
They've got him in a trance
One hand is tied to the tight-rope walker
The other is in his pants
And the riot squad they're restless
They need somewhere to go
As Lady and I look out tonight
From Desolation Row

Cinderella, she seems so easy
"It takes one to know one," she smiles
And puts her hands in her back pockets
Bette Davis style
And in comes Romeo, he's moaning
"You Belong to Me I Believe"
And someone says, "You're in the wrong place, my friend
You better leave"
And the only sound that's left
After the ambulances go
Is Cinderella sweeping up
On Desolation Row

Now the moon is almost hidden
The stars are beginning to hide
The fortunetelling lady
Has even taken all her things inside
All except for Cain and Abel
And the hunchback of Notre Dame
Everybody is making love
Or else expecting rain
And the Good Samaritan, he's dressing
He's getting ready for the show
He's going to the carnival tonight

On Desolation Row

Now Ophelia, she's 'neath the window
For her I feel so afraid
On her twenty-second birthday
She already is an old maid
To her, death is quite romantic
She wears an iron vest
Her profession's her religion
Her sin is her lifelessness
And though her eyes are fixed upon
Noah's great rainbow
She spends her time peeking
Into Desolation Row

Einstein, disguised as Robin Hood
With his memories in a trunk
Passed this way an hour ago
With his friend, a jealous monk
He looked so immaculately frightful
As he bummed a cigarette
Then he went off sniffing drainpipes
And reciting the alphabet
Now you would not think to look at him
But he was famous long ago
For playing the electric violin
On Desolation Row

Dr. Filth, he keeps his world
Inside of a leather cup
But all his sexless patients
They're trying to blow it up
Now his nurse, some local loser
She's in charge of the cyanide hole
And she also keeps the cards that read
"Have Mercy on His Soul"
They all play on penny whistles
You can hear them blow
If you lean your head out far enough
From Desolation Row

Across the street they've nailed the curtains
They're getting ready for the feast
The Phantom of the Opera
A perfect image of a priest
They're spoonfeeding Casanova
To get him to feel more assured
Then they'll kill him with self-confidence
After poisoning him with words

And the Phantom's shouting to skinny girls
"Get Outa Here If You Don't Know
Casanova is just being punished for going
To Desolation Row"

Now at midnight all the agents
And the superhuman crew
Come out and round up everyone
That knows more than they do
Then they bring them to the factory
Where the heart-attack machine
Is strapped across their shoulders
And then the kerosene
Is brought down from the castles
By insurance men who go
Check to see that nobody is escaping
To Desolation Row

Praise be to Nero's Neptune
The Titanic sails at dawn
And everybody's shouting
"Which Side Are You On?"
And Ezra Pound and T. S. Eliot
Fighting in the captain's tower
While calypso singers laugh at them
And fishermen hold flowers
Between the windows of the sea
Where lovely mermaids flow
And nobody has to think too much
About Desolation Row

Yes, I received your letter yesterday
(About the time the door knob broke)
When you asked how I was doing
Was that some kind of joke?
All these people that you mention
Yes, I know them, they're quite lame
I had to rearrange their faces
And give them all another name
Right now I can't read too good
Don't send me no more letters no
Not unless you mail them
From Desolation Row

1965

Robert Hass (b. 1941)

Robert Hass was born in San Francisco. He grew up in Marin County and attended St. Mary's College of California and Stanford University. *Field Guide*, his first book, was selected by Stanley Kunitz as the winner of the Yale Younger Poets competition for 1973. For many years Hass collaborated with Czeslaw Milosz on the translations of Milosz's poems from the Polish. Hass has also edited a volume of Tomas Transtromer's selected poems and translated most of the contents of *The Essential Haiku: Versions of Basho, Buson, and Issa*. For two years starting in 1995 he served as the nation's poet laureate. He was the guest editor of *The Best American Poetry 2001*. "I started out imagining myself as a novelist or essayist," he has said, "but then Gary Snyder and Allen Ginsberg came along; and poetry, imbued with the whole lifestyle of the Beats, was much more exciting."

On the Coast Near Sausalito

1
I won't say much for the sea
except that it was, almost,
the color of sour milk.
The sun in that clear
unmenacing sky was low,
angled off the grey fissure of the cliffs,
hills dark green with manzanita.

Low tide: slimed rocks
mottled brown and thick with kelp
like the huge backs of ancient tortoises
merged with the grey stone
of the breakwater, sliding off
to antediluvian depths.
The old story: here filthy life begins.

2
Fish-
ing, as Melville said,
"to purge the spleen,"
to put to task my clumsy hands
my hands that bruise by
not touching
pluck the legs from a prawn,
peel the shell off,
and curl the body twice about a hook.

3
The cabezone is not highly regarded
by fishermen, except Italians
who have the grace

to fry the pale, almost bluish flesh
in olive oil with a sprig
of fresh rosemary.

The cabezone, an ugly atavistic fish,
as old as the coastal shelf
it feeds upon
has fins of duck's-web thickness,
resembles a prehistoric toad,
and is delicately sweet.

Catching one, the fierce quiver of surprise
and the line's tension
are a recognition.

4
But it's strange to kill
for the sudden feel of life.
The danger is
to moralize
that strangeness.
Holding the spiny monster in my hands
his bulging purple eyes
were eyes and the sun was
almost tangent to the planet
on our uneasy coast.
Creature and creature,
we stared down centuries.

1973

Meditation at Lagunitas

All the new thinking is about loss.
In this it resembles all the old thinking.
The idea, for example, that each particular erases
the luminous clarity of a general idea. That the clown-
faced woodpecker probing the dead sculpted trunk
of that black birch is, by his presence,
some tragic falling off from a first world
of undivided light. Or the other notion that,
because there is in this world no one thing
to which the bramble of *blackberry* corresponds,
a word is elegy to what it signifies.
We talked about it late last night and in the voice
of my friend, there was a thin wire of grief, a tone
almost querulous. After a while I understood that,
talking this way, everything dissolves: *justice*,

pine, *hair*, *woman*, *you* and *I*. There was a woman
I made love to and I remembered how, holding
her small shoulders in my hands sometimes,
I felt a violent wonder at her presence
like a thirst for salt, for my childhood river
with its island willows, silly music from the pleasure boat,
muddy places where we caught the little orange-silver fish
called *pumpkinseed*. It hardly had to do with her.
Longing, we say, because desire is full
of endless distances. I must have been the same to her.
But I remember so much, the way her hands dismantled bread,
the thing her father said that hurt her, what
she dreamed. There are moments when the body is as numinous
as words, days that are the good flesh continuing.
Such tenderness, those afternoons and evenings,
saying *blackberry*, *blackberry*, *blackberry*.

1979

Against Botticelli

I

In the life we lead together every paradise is lost.
Nothing could be easier: summer gathers new leaves
to casual darkness. So few things we need to know.
And the old wisdoms shudder in us and grow slack.
Like renunciation. Like the melancholy beauty
of giving it all up. Like walking steadfast
in the rhythms, winter light and summer dark.
And the time for cutting furrows and the dance.
Mad seed. Death waits it out. It waits us out,
the sleek incandescent saints, earthly and prayerful.
In our modesty. In our shamefast and steady attention
to the ceremony, its preparation, the formal hovering
of pleasure which falls like the rain we pray not to get
and are glad for and drown in. Or spray of that sea,
irised: otters in the tide lash, in the kelp-drench,
mammal warmth and the inhuman element. Ah, that is the secret.
That she is an otter, that Botticelli saw her so.
That we are not otters and are not in the painting
by Botticelli. We are not even in the painting by Bosch
where the people are standing around looking at the frame
of the Botticelli painting and when Love arrives, they throw up.
Or the Goya painting of the sad ones, angular and shriven,
who watch the Bosch and feel very compassionate
but hurt each other often and inefficiently. We are not in any
painting.
If we do it at all, we will be like the old Russians.

We'll walk down through scrub oak to the sea
and where the seals lie preening on the beach
we will look at each other steadily
and butcher them and skin them.

II

The myth they chose was the constant lovers.
The theme was richness over time.
It is a difficult story and the wise never choose it
because it requires a long performance
and because there is nothing, by definition, between the acts.
It is different in kind from a man and the pale woman
he fucks in the ass underneath the stars
because it is summer and they are full of longing
and sick of birth. They burn coolly
like phosphorus, and the thing need be done
only once. Like the sacking of Troy
it survives in imagination,
in the longing brought perfectly to closing,
the woman's white hands opening, opening,
and the man churning inside her, thrashing there.
And light travels as if all the stars they were under
exploded centuries ago and they are resting now, glowing.
The woman thinks what she is feeling is like the dark
and utterly complete. The man is past sadness,
though his eyes are wet. He is learning about gratitude,
how final it is, as if the grace in Botticelli's *Primavera*,
the one with sad eyes who represents pleasure,
had a canvas to herself, entirely to herself.

1979

A Story About the Body

The young composer, working that summer at an artist's colony, had watched her for a week. She was Japanese, a painter, almost sixty, and he thought he was in love with her. He loved her work, and her work was like the way she moved her body, used her hands, looked at him directly when she made amused and considered answers to his questions. One night, walking back from a concert, they came to her door and she turned to him and said, "I think you would like to have me. I would like that too, but I must tell you that I have had a double mastectomy," and when he didn't understand, "I've lost both my breasts." The radiance that he had carried around in his belly and chest cavity — like music — withered very quickly, and he made himself look at her when he said, "I'm sorry. I don't think I could." He walked back to his own cabin through the pines, and in the morning he found a small blue bowl on the porch outside his door. It looked to be full of rose petals, but he found when he picked it up that the rose petals were on top; the rest of the bowl — she must have swept them from the corners of her studio — was full of dead bees.

1989

Forty Something

She says to him, musing, "If you ever leave me,
and marry a younger woman and have another baby,
I'll put a knife in your heart." They are in bed,
so she climbs onto his chest, and looks directly
down into his eyes. "You understand? Your heart."

1996

Misery and Splendor

Summoned by conscious recollection, she
would be smiling, they might be in a kitchen talking,
before or after dinner. But they are in this other room,
the window has many small panes, and they are on a couch
embracing. He holds her as tightly
as he can, she buries herself in his body.
Morning, maybe it is evening, light
is flowing through the room. Outside,
the day is slowly succeeded by night,
succeeded by day. The process wobbles wildly
and accelerates: weeks, months, years. The light in the room
does not change, so it is plain what is happening.
They are trying to become one creature,
and something will not have it. They are tender
with each other, afraid
their brief, sharp cries will reconcile them to the moment
when they fall away again. So they rub against each other,
their mouths dry, then wet, then dry.
They feel themselves at the center of a powerful
and baffled will. They feel
they are an almost animal,
washed up on the shore of a world —
or huddled against the gate of a garden —
to which they can't admit they can never be admitted.

1996

Lyn Hejinian (b. 1941)

Lyn Hejinian was born in the San Francisco Bay area and was educated at Radcliffe. *My Life* is a kind of indirect and abstract autobiography. The initial version, written in 1978 when Hejinian was thirty-seven, consisted of thirty-seven sections containing thirty-seven sentences each. The revised version of 1987 has eight additional sections containing forty-five sentences each and adds eight sentences to each of the original sections. *The Fatalist* is based on the letters and email messages Hejinian wrote in 2001 and 2002: "By massively deleting and obsessively lineating (and without adding anything or moving anything around), I sculpted the poems out of the raw epistolary material." She was the guest editor of *The Best American Poetry 2004*.

from *My Life*

What is the meaning hung from that depend

A dog bark, the engine of a truck, an airplane hidden by the trees and rooftops. My mother's childhood seemed a kind of holy melodrama. She ate her pudding in a pattern, carving a rim around the circumference of the pudding, working her way inward toward the center, scooping with the spoon, to see how far she could separate the pudding from the edge of the bowl before the center collapsed, spreading the pudding out again, lower, back to the edge of the bowl. You could tell that it was improvisational because at that point they closed their eyes. A pause, a rose, something on paper. Solitude was the essential companion. The branches of the redwood trees hung in a fog whose moisture they absorbed. Lasting, "what might be," its present a future, like the life of a child. The greatest solitudes are quickly strewn with rubbish. All night the radio covered the fall of a child in the valley down an abandoned well-fitting, a clammy narrow pipe 56 feet deep, in which he was wedged, recorded, and died. Stanza there. The synchronous, which I have characterized as spatial, is accurate to reality but it has been debased. Daisy's plenty pebbles in the gravel drive. It is a tartan not a plaid. There was some disparity between my grandfather's reserve, the result of shyness and disdain, and his sense that a man's natural importance was characterized by bulk, by the great depth of his footprint in the sand — in other words, a successful man was no lightweight. A flock of guard geese are pecking in a cold rain, become formal behind the obvious flower's bloom. The room, in fact, was used as a closet as well, for as one sat at the telephone table, one faced a row of my grandparents' overcoats, raincoats, and hats, which were hung from a line of heavy, polished wooden hooks. The fog burned off and I went for a walk alone, then was lost between the grapevines, unable to return, until they set a mast, a pole, into the ground and hung a colored flag that I could see from anywhere around. A glass snail was set among real camellias in a glass bowl upon the table. Pure duration, a compound plenum in which nothing is repeated. Photographed in a blue pinafore. The way Dorothy Wordsworth often, I think, went out to "get" a sight. But language is restless. They say there has been too much roughhousing. The heat waves wobbled over the highway — on either side were flat brown fields tilted slightly toward the horizon — and in the distance ahead of the car small blue ponds lay in our path, evaporating suddenly, as if in a single piece, at the instant prior to our splashing in. I saw a line of rocks topped by a foghorn protecting the little harbor from the tide. Fruit peels and the heels of bread were left to get moldy. But then we'd need, what, a bird, to eat the fleas from the rug. When what happens is not intentional, one can't ascribe meaning to it, and unless what happens is necessary, one can't expect it to occur again. Because children will spill food, one needs a dog. Rubber books for bathtubs. Coast laps. One had merely to turn around in order to see it. Elbows off the table. The portrait, a photograph, had been made so that my grandmother was looking just over the head of the observer, into a little distance, not so far as to be a space into which she might seem to be staring, but at some definite object, some noun, just behind one. Waffle man everywhere. She had come upon a set of expressions ("peachy" being one of them and "nuts to you" another) which exactly suited her, and so, though the expressions went out of everyone else's vocabulary, even years later, when everyone else was saying "far out" or "that's nowhere," she continued to have a "perfectly peachy time" on her vacations. This was Melody Ranch, daring and resourceful. As for we who "love to be astonished," we might go to the zoo and see the famous hippo named "Bubbles." The sidesaddle was impossible, and yet I've seen it used successfully, even stunningly, the woman's full skirts spread like a wing as the horse jumped a hurdle and they galloped on. Lasting, ferries, later, trolleys from Berkeley to the Bridge. This is one of those things which continues, and hence seems important, and so ever what one says over and over again. Soggy sky, which then dries out, lifting slightly turning white — and then banks toward the West. If I see fishing boats that's the first thing I think. Insane, in common parlance.

1987

from *The Fatalist*

I arrived with biographical context
and that sometimes inhibits freely flowing conversation, as I said
unprofessionally when you came to see me
but after all it was the very first discussion we've had,
no matter the intelligence, duration, or precision
that you were interested in and — well, I don't remember
your exact words, but the gist of it (if I understood
correctly) was that he and she are very clearly specific in every case
but they aren't necessarily the same from one case
to another, I don't know why — perhaps because I associate
slouching with lurking. The reference to Thanksgiving evokes
the U.S. — the shift to "I," the decision, the question.
Race, identity, repetition — that's America. Identity
as a socio-sexual problem and hence as a problem
of affinities, allegiances, and accommodation, a problem
fixated on norms but also on love — that's America.

Though the plots of the stories can be quickly told, they cannot be called
thin. This is how an American life if it were a purely domestic affair
would proceed: the American would have a loving heart, limited
imagination (and hence no pressing ambitions), and a capacity for offering
a portrait of herself that is affectionate but also wry
and even slightly self-mocking though Americans are very rarely given
to this because mockery is provided by others and it comes
to the same conclusion, namely that people
who are fundamentally different from each other are attracted to each other
but despite all the "talking and listening" they undertake no understanding
between them is possible so we had that to celebrate, too. We left
the house and the gift certificate somewhere in the 20 feet between
the ticket booth and the gate. The first to approach
was a silent man with olives. O, for the olive pits. How fat
he had been as an adolescent!

2003

MARILYN HACKER (b. 1942)

Marilyn Hacker was born in the Bronx and was educated at the Bronx High School of Science and New York University. She favors traditional forms and structures for subject matter that is social and political. "Form can be a medium of homage and challenge between poets," she has written. She celebrates the "pleasures of good-natured bardic competition," in which the poet tries to outdo a predecessor. "Evelyn Ashford will never race Jesse Owens, nor will I trade epigrams with James Wright; but she can pace herself against his time, and I can match his metrics." She spends half of each year in France and has translated French poetry.

Nights of 1964–66: The Old Reliable

The laughing soldiers fought to their defeat
—James Fenton, "In a Notebook"

White decorators interested in art,
Black file clerks with theatrical ambitions,
kids making pharmaceutical revisions
in journals Comp. instructors urged they start,
the part-Cherokee teenage genius (maybe)
the secretary who hung out with fairies,
the copywriter wanting to know, where is
my husband? the soprano with the baby,
all drank draft beer or lethal sweet Manhattans
or improvised concoctions with tequila

in summer, when, from Third Street, we could feel a
night breeze waft in whose fragrance were Latin.
The place was run by Polish refugees:
squat Margie, gaunt Speedy (whose sobriquet
transliterated what?) He'd brought his play
from Łódź. After a while, we guessed Margie's
illiteracy was why *he* cashed checks
and *she* perched near the threshold to ban pros,
the underage, the fugitive, and those
arrayed impertinently to their sex.
The bar was talk and cruising; in the back
room, we danced: Martha and the Vandellas,
Smokey and the Miracles, while sellers
and buyers changed crisp tens for smoke and smack.
Some came in after work, some after supper,
plumage replenished to meet who knew who.
Behind the bar, Margie dished up beef stew.
On weeknights, you could always find an upper
to speed you to your desk, and drink till four.
Loosened by booze, we drifted, on the ripples
of Motown, home in new couples, or triples
were back at dusk, with ID's, at the door.
Bill was my roommate, Russell drank with me,
although they were a dozen years my seniors.
I walked off with the eighteen-year-old genius
— an Older Woman, barely twenty-three.
Link was new as Rimbaud, and better looking,
North Beach bar *paideon* of doomed Jack Spicer,
like Russell, our two-meter artificer,
a Corvo whose *ecclesia* was cooking.
Bill and Russell were painters. Bill had been
a monk in Kyoto. Stoned, we sketched together,
till he discovered poppers and black leather
and Zen consented to new discipline.
We shared my Sixth Street flat with a morose
cat, an arch cat, and pot-plants we pruned daily.
His boyfriend had left him for an Israeli
dancer; my husband was on Mykonos.
Russell loved Harold who was Black and bad
and lavished on him dinners "meant for men"
like Escoffier and Brillat-Savarin.
Staunch blond Dora made rice. When she had
tucked in the twins, six flights of tenement
stairs they'd descend, elevenish, and stroll
down Third Street, desultory night patrol
gone mauve and green under the virulent
streetlights, to the bar, where Bill and I
(if we'd not come to dinner), Link, and Lew,
and Betty had already had a few.

One sweat-soaked night in pitiless July,
wedged on booth-benches of cracked Naugahyde,
we planned a literary magazine
where North Beach met the Lower East Side scene.
We could have called it *When Worlds Collide*.
Dora was gone, "In case the children wake up."
Link lightly had decamped with someone else
(the German engineer? Or was he Bill's?).
Russell's stooped *vale* brushed my absent makeup.
Armed children spared us home, our good-night hugs
laisser-passer. We railed against the war.
Soon, some of us bussed South with SNCC and CORE.
Soon, some of us got busted dealing drugs.
The file clerks took exams and forged ahead.
The decorators' kitchens blazed persimmon.
The secretary started kissing women,
and so did I, and my three friends are dead.

1990

LINDA GREGG (b. 1942)

Linda Gregg was born in Suffern, New York. She lived for many years in Greece. When Robert Hass selected "The Singers Change, the Music Goes On" for *The Best American Poetry 2001*, Gregg wrote that the poem seeks to "make a whole out of a contradiction. The permanence in myths, shards, temples and song, but also the permanence that was lived in the body and place. Love and revelations. Lasting, because of its heartbreaking momentariness."

Marriage and Midsummer's Night

It has been a long time now
since I stood in our dark room looking
across the court at my husband in her apartment.
Watched them make love.
She was perhaps more beautiful
from where I stood than to him.
I can say it now: She was like a vase
lit the way milky glass is lighted.
He looked more beautiful there
than I remember him the times
he entered my bed with the light behind.
It has been three years since I sat
at the open window, my legs over the edge
and the knife close like a discarded idea.
Looked up at the Danish night,

that pale, pale sky where the birds that fly
at dawn flew on those days all night long,
black with the light behind. They were caught
by their instincts, unable to end their flight.

1985

A Dark Thing Inside the Day

So many want to be lifted by song and dancing,
and this morning it is easy to understand.
I write in the sound of chirping birds hidden
in the almond trees, the almonds still green
and thriving in the foliage. Up the street,
a man is hammering to make a new house as doves
continue their cooing forever. Bees humming
and high above that a brilliant clear sky.
The roses are blooming and I smell the sweetness.
Everything desirable is here already in abundance.
And the sea. The dark thing is hardly visible
in the leaves, under the sheen. We sleep easily.
So I bring no sad stories to warn the heart.
All the flowers are adult this year. The good
world gives and the white doves praise all of it.

1991

The Singers Change, the Music Goes On

No one really dies in the myths.
No world is lost in the stories.
In being wondered at. We grow up
and grow old in our land of grass
and blood moons, birth and goneness.
A place of absolutes. Of returning.
We live our myth in the recurrence,
pretending we will return another day.
Like the morning coming every morning.
The truth is we come back as a choir.
Otherwise Eurydice would be forever
in the dark. Our singing brings her
back. Our dying keeps her alive.

2001

ANN LAUTERBACH (b. 1942)

Ann Lauterbach was born and raised in Manhattan. In 1967 she embarked on a three-week trip to Europe and extended it into a seven-year stay in London, where she worked at the Institute of Contemporary Arts. She returned to New York City in 1973 and worked in art galleries. She has taught at the City University of New York and is now a professor at Bard College. Her poems are highly abstract and yet intimate; "Hum" was written in the wake of the terrorist attacks of 11 September 2001.

Santa Fe Sky

A spare radiance blooms, blooms again, expires.
This is the radical mark
Of an insatiable wish.
Things look like other things, as was said.
Those that are unleashed
Come upon the hot earth
Toward the toward, violently
Unproven. Thrall is a curse,
A woven rival place indissolubly conditioned.
This you may have seen and endured
As it came nearer, threading its term.
But to act would be the vanishing we know:
Ocean in its wholeness, river in its time,
Lake holding the persistent, domestic sky,
Each an episode in the will to be parted.
But to be that, to be weather
In the distance, fallen, dreamed of; also imagined.

1991

Invocation

to Beruadette Mayer

Speak, Mistress Quaker, a parable waits from which
blessings issue, conditionally, as in a hunt, a possible hearing
wherein the manifest flirts, beguiling, almost at home.
Speak on, Troubled Specter, as in a calm
carefree silence whose message embraces its
quick. Seed that, so
the trail is viable, literal, glad
as in love's timing: tick-tock luck.
A siege of incipient cures! A brevity so enhanced
the Pilgrim finds her way along the path of red berries
through the wild into the dilated Spot where following ends and begins
and ends again. *You were in a tale*, a choice you had not made,
whose dim constellation gathers dew on the sleeve of hours,

the iteration of just cause, saving one against the others, as in a court.
Be kind, Mistress of Woes, Hooligan of Ages. Be a Treaty we sign.
Chafe against brittle nudity, swallow the excellent potion,
remain among thieves.
Remain among thieves, steal Advent from avarice, dark from idiot sight.

1997

Hum

The days are beautiful.
The days are beautiful.

I know what days are.
The other is weather.

I know what weather is.
The days are beautiful.

Things are incidental.
Someone is weeping.

I weep for the incidental.
The days are beautiful.

Where is tomorrow?
Everyone will weep.

Tomorrow was yesterday.
The days are beautiful.

Tomorrow was yesterday.
Today is weather.

The sound of the weather
Is everyone weeping.

Everyone is incidental.
Everyone weeps.

The tears of today
Will put out tomorrow.

The rain is ashes.
The days are beautiful.

The rain falls down.
The sound is falling.

The sky is a cloud.
The towers are raining.

The towers are rain.
The days are beautiful.

The sky is dust.
The weather is yesterday.

The weather is yesterday.
The sound is weeping.

What is this dust?
The weather is nothing.

The days are beautiful.
The towers are yesterday.

The towers are incidental.
What are these ashes?

Here is the hat
That does not travel

Here is the robe
That smells of the night

Here are the words
Retired to their books

Here are the stones
Loosed from their settings

Here is the bridge
Over the water

Here is the place
Where the sun came up

Here is a season
Dry in the fireplace.

Here are the ashes.
The days are beautiful.

2005

WILLIAM MATTHEWS (1942–1997)

William Matthews was born in Cincinnati. He once observed that most published poems fall into one of four thematic categories: "1. I went out into the woods today and it made me feel, you know, sort of religious. 2. We're not getting any younger. 3. It sure is cold and lonely (a) without you, honey, or (b) with you, honey. 4. Sadness seems but the other side of the coin of happiness, and vice versa, and in any case the coin is too soon spent and on we know not what." In his own poems Matthews eulogized jazz, poetry, Freud, Nabokov, good food, and wine. Like many American poets he taught in English departments and creative writing programs. In a late poem, "Job Interview," he recalls landing a job because he luckily spoke "fluent fog."

Bud Powell, Paris, 1959

I'd never seen pain so bland.
Smack, though I didn't call it smack
in 1959, had eaten his technique.
His white-water right hand clattered
missing runs nobody else would think
to try, nor think to be outsmarted
by. Nobody played as well
as Powell, and neither did he,
stalled on his bench between sets,
stolid and vague, my hero,
his mocha skin souring gray.
Two bucks for a Scotch in this dump,
I thought, and I bought me
another. I was young and pain
rose to my ceiling, like warmth,
like a story that makes us come true
in the present. Each day's
melodrama in Powell's cells
bored and lulled him. Pain loves pain
and calls it company, and it is.

1979

Mingus at The Showplace

I was miserable, of course, for I was seventeen,
and so I swung into action and wrote a poem,

and it was miserable, for that was how I thought
poetry worked: you digested experience and shat

literature. It was 1960 at The Showplace, long since
defunct, on West 4th St., and I sat at the bar,

casting beer money from a thin reel of ones,
the kid in the city, big ears like a puppy.

And I knew Mingus was a genius. I knew two
other things, but as it happened they were wrong.

So I made him look at the poem.
"There's a lot of that going around," he said,

and Sweet Baby Jesus he was right. He glowered
at me but he didn't look as if he thought

bad poems were dangerous, the way some poets do.
If they were baseball executives they'd plot

to destroy sandlots everywhere so that the game
could be saved from children. Of course later

that night he fired his pianist in mid-number
and flurried him from the stand.

"We've suffered a diminuendo in personnel,"
he explained, and the band played on.

1995

Inspiration

Rumpled, torpid, bored, too tasteful to rhyme
"lethargy" with "laundry," or too lazy,
I'll not spend my afternoon at the desk
cunningly weaving subjunctives and lithe
skeins of barbed colloquial wire. Today

I loathe poetry. I hate the clotted,
dicty poems of the great modernists,
disdainful of their truant audience,
and I hate also proletarian
poetry, with its dutiful rancors

and sing-along certainties. I hate
poetry readings and the dreaded verb
"to share." Let me share this knife with your throat,
suggested Mack. Today I'm a gnarl, a knot,
a burl. I'm furled in on myself and won't

be opened. I'm the bad mood if you try
to cheer me out of I'll smack you. Impasse

is where I come to escape from. It takes
a deep belief in one's own ignorance;
it takes, I tell you, desperate measures.

1998

Vermin

"What do you want to be when you grow up?"
What child cries out, "An exterminator!"?
One diligent student in Mrs. Taylor's
class will get an ant farm for Christmas, but
he'll not see industry; he'll see dither.
"The ant sets an example for us all,"
wrote Max Beerbohm, a master of dawdle,
"but it is not a good one." These children
don't hope to outlast the doldrums of school
only to heft great weights and work in squads
and die for their queen. Well, neither did we.
And we knew what we didn't want to be:
the ones we looked down on, the lambs of God,
blander than snow and slow to be cruel.

1997

SHARON OLDS (b. 1942)

Sharon Olds was born in San Francisco. She grew up in California in a "hellfire Episcopalian religion." After receiving her doctorate at Columbia in 1972, she vowed, for the sake of her poems, to renounce all she had learned in graduate school. Olds has long taught at New York University and organized writing workshops for the disabled at Goldwater Hospital. She writes about sexual desire in explicit terms, which has won her a very large following but has also led to charges that her poems are, in Helen Vendler's term, "pornographic." Unfazed by the criticism, Olds has said, "I have tried writing poems. I have tried not writing poems. And I find not writing poems to be much harder than writing them."

Satan Says

I am locked in a little cedar box
with a picture of shepherds pasted onto
the central panel between carvings.
The box stands on curved legs.
It has a gold, heart-shaped lock
and no key. I am trying to write my

way out of the closed box
redolent of cedar. Satan
comes to me in the locked box
and says, *I'll get you out. Say*
My father is a shit. I say
my father is a shit and Satan
laughs and says, *It's opening.*
Say your mother is a pimp.
My mother is a pimp. Something
opens and breaks when I say that.
My spine uncurls in the cedar box
like the pink back of the ballerina pin
with a ruby eye, resting beside me on
satin in the cedar box.
Say shit, say death, say fuck the father,
Satan says, down my ear.
The pain of the locked past buzzes
in the child's box on her bureau, under
the terrible round pond eye
etched around with roses, where
self-loathing gazed at sorrow.
Shit. Death. Fuck the father.
Something opens. Satan says
Don't you feel a lot better?
Light seems to break on the delicate
edelweiss pin, carved in two
colors of wood. I love him too,
you know, I say to Satan dark
in the locked box. I love them but
I'm trying to say what happened to us
in the lost past. *Of course*, he says
and smiles, *of course. Now say: torture.*
I see, through blackness soaked in cedar,
the edge of a large hinge open.
Say: the father's cock, the mother's
cunt, says Satan, *I'll get you out.*
The angle of the hinge widens
until I see the outlines of
the time before I was, when they were
locked in the bed. When I say
the magic words, Cock, Cunt,
Satan softly says, *Come out.*
But the air around the opening
is heavy and thick as hot smoke.
Come in, he says, and I feel his voice
breathing from the opening.
The exit is through Satan's mouth.
Come in my mouth, he says, *you're there*
already, and the huge hinge

begins to close. Oh no, I loved
them, too, I brace
my body tight
in the cedar house.
Satan sucks himself out the keyhole.
I'm left locked in the box, he seals
the heart-shaped lock with the wax of his tongue.
It's your coffin now, Satan says.
I hardly hear;
I am warming my cold
hands at the dancer's
ruby eye —
the fire, the suddenly discovered knowledge of love.

1980

The One Girl at the Boys Party

When I take my girl to the swimming party
I set her down among the boys. They tower and
bristle, she stands there smooth and sleek,
her math scores unfolding in the air around her.
They will strip to their suits, her body hard and
indivisible as a prime number,
they'll plunge into the deep end, she'll subtract
her height from ten feet, divide it into
hundreds of gallons of water, the numbers
bouncing in her mind like molecules of chlorine
in the bright-blue pool. When they climb out,
her ponytail will hang its pencil lead
down her back, her narrow silk suit
with hamburgers and french fries printed on it
will glisten in the brilliant air, and they will
see her sweet face, solemn and
sealed, a factor of one, and she will
see their eyes, two each,
their legs, two each, and the curves of their sexes,
one each, and in her head she'll be doing her
wild multiplying, as the drops
sparkle and fall to the power of a thousand from her body.

1983

The Pope's Penis

It hangs deep in his robes, a delicate
clapper at the center of a bell.

It moves when he moves, a ghostly fish in a
halo of silver seaweed, the hair
swaying in the dark and the heat — and at night
while his eyes sleep, it stands up
in praise of God.

1987

Topography

After we flew across the country we
got in bed, laid our bodies
delicately together, like maps laid
face to face, East to West, my
San Francisco against your New York, your
Fire Island against my Sonoma, my
New Orleans deep in your Texas, your Idaho
bright on my Great Lakes, my Kansas
burning against your Kansas your Kansas
burning against my Kansas, your Eastern
Standard Time pressing into my
Pacific Time, my Mountain Time
beating against your Central Time, your
sun rising swiftly from the right my
sun rising swiftly from the left your
moon rising slowly from the left my
moon rising slowly from the right until
all four bodies of the sky
burn above us, sealing us together,
all our cities twin cities,
all our states united, one
nation, indivisible, with liberty and justice for all.

1987

The Race

When I got to the airport I rushed up to the desk,
bought a ticket, ten minutes later
they told me the flight was cancelled, the doctors
had said my father would not live through the night
and the flight was cancelled. A young man
with a dark blond moustache told me
another airline had a non-stop
leaving in seven minutes. See that

elevator over there, well go
down to the first floor, make a right, you'll
see a yellow bus, get off at the
second Pan Am terminal, I
ran, I who have no sense of direction
raced exactly where he'd told me, a fish
slipping upstream deftly against
the flow of the river. I jumped off that bus with those
bags I had thrown everything into
in five minutes, and ran, the bags
wagged me from side to side as if
to prove I was under the claims of the material,
I ran up to a man with a white flower on his breast,
I who always go to the end of the line, I said
Help me. He looked at my ticket, he said
Make a left and then a right, go up the moving stairs and then
run. I lumbered up the moving stairs,
at the top I saw the corridor,
and then I took a deep breath, I said
Goodbye to my body, goodbye to comfort,
I used my legs and heart as if I would
gladly use them up for this,
to touch him again in this life. I ran, and the
bags banged against me, wheeled and coursed
in skewed orbits, I have seen pictures of
women running, their belongings tied
in scarves grasped in their fists, I blessed my
long legs he gave me, my strong
heart I abandoned to its own purpose,
I ran to Gate 17 and they were
just lifting the thick white
lozenge of the door to fit it into
the socket of the plane. Like the one who is not
too rich, I turned sideways and
slipped through the needle's eye, and then
I walked down the aisle toward my father. The jet
was full, and people's hair was shining, they were
smiling, the interior of the plane was filled with a
mist of gold endorphin light,
I wept as people weep when they enter heaven,
in massive relief. We lifted up
gently from one tip of the continent
and did not stop until we set down lightly on the
other edge, I walked into his room
and watched his chest rise slowly
and sink again, all night
I watched him breathe.

1992

RON PADGETT (b. 1942)

Ron Padgett was born in Tulsa, Oklahoma, the son of Wayne Padgett, bootlegger for Tulsa's Dixie Mafia, who became "on a local level, a legendary public figure, somewhat like Pretty Boy Floyd and John Wesley Hardin," as his son would later recollect. As an undergraduate at Columbia, Padgett came under the influence of Kenneth Koch, and like his mentor he worked toward improving the teaching of writing in schools; from 1980 until 2000, he was director of publications for Teachers and Writers Collaborative. Padgett collaborated frequently with the artist Joe Brainard and the poet Ted Berrigan, and has written memoirs of both. He tells his father's story in *Oklahoma Tough: My Father, King of the Tulsa Bootleggers* (2003).

Reading Reverdy

The wind that went through the head left it plural.

* * *

The half-erased words on the wall of bread.

* * *

Someone is grinding the color of ears.
She looks like and at her.

* * *

A child draws a man and the earth
Is covered with snow.

* * *

He comes down out of the night
When the hills fall.

* * *

The line part of you goes out to infinity.

* * *

I get up on top of an inhuman voice.

1969

Poetic License

This license certifies
That Ron Padgett may tell whatever lies

His heart desires
Until it expires

1976

Voice

I have always laughed
when someone spoke of a young writer
"finding his voice." I took it
literally: had he lost his voice?
Had he thrown it and had it
not returned? Or perhaps they
were referring to his newspaper
the *Village Voice?* He's trying
to find his *Voice*.
  What isn't
funny is that so many young writers
seem to have found this notion
credible: they set off in search
of their voice, as if it were
a single thing, a treasure
difficult to find but worth
the effort. I never thought
such a thing existed. Until
recently. Now I know it does.
I hope I never find mine. I
wish to remain a phony the rest of my life.

1976

LOUISE GLÜCK (b. 1943)

Louise Glück was born in New York City. She skipped college and at age eighteen enrolled in a poetry workshop with Leonie Adams at Columbia. She also studied with Stanley Kunitz. She has taught at Williams College, was the guest editor of *The Best American Poetry 1993*, and was named the nation's poet laureate in 2003. "My compositional process," Glück told an interviewer in 1999, "almost always begins in a kind of despondency, or hopelessness, or desolation, usually born of a conviction that I will never write again." Glück wrote "Vespers" as one of eight poems in the summer of 1990, as part of "an argument with the divine." The following summer she wrote the rest of her Pulitzer-winning book, *The Wild Iris*, "with a kind of wild ease for which my life affords no precedent."

Gratitude

Do not think I am not grateful for your small

kindness to me.
I like small kindnesses.
In fact I actually prefer them to the more
substantial kindness, that is always eying you,
like a large animal on a rug,
until your whole life reduces
to nothing but waking up morning after morning
cramped, and the bright sun shining on its tusks.

1975

The Drowned Children

You see, they have no judgment.
So it is natural that they should drown,
first the ice taking them in
and then, all winter, their wool scarves
floating behind them as they sink
until at last they are quiet.
And the pond lifts them in its manifold dark arms.

But death must come to them differently,
so close to the beginning.
As though they had always been
blind and weightless. Therefore
the rest is dreamed, the lamp,
the good white cloth that covered the table,
their bodies.

And yet they hear the names they used
like lures slipping over the pond:
What are you waiting for
come home, come home, lost
in the waters, blue and permanent.

1980

The Mirror

Watching you in the mirror I wonder
what it is like to be so beautiful
and why you do not love
but cut yourself, shaving
like a blind man. I think you let me stare
so you can turn against yourself
with greater violence,
needing to show me how you scrape the flesh away
scornfully and without hesitation

until I see you correctly,
as a man bleeding, not
the reflection I desire.

1980

Mock Orange

It is not the moon, I tell you.
It is these flowers
lighting the yard.

I hate them.
I hate them as I hate sex,
the man's mouth
sealing my mouth, the man's
paralyzing body —

and the cry that always escapes,
the low, humiliating
premise of union —

In my mind tonight
I hear the question and pursuing answer
fused in one sound
that mounts and mounts and then
is split into the old selves,
the tired antagonisms. Do you see?
We were made fools of.
And the scent of mock orange
drifts through the window.

How can I rest?
How can I be content
when there is still
that odor in the world?

1985

The Triumph of Achilles

In the story of Patroclus
no one survives, not even Achilles
who was nearly a god.
Patroclus resembled him; they wore
the same armor.

Always in these friendships
one serves the other, one is less than the other:

the hierarchy
is always apparent, though the legends
cannot be trusted —
their source is the survivor,
the one who has been abandoned.

What were the Greek ships on fire
compared to this loss?

In his tent, Achilles
grieved with his whole being
and the gods saw

he was a man already dead, a victim
of the part that loved,
the part that was mortal.

1985

Celestial Music

I have a friend who still believes in heaven.
Not a stupid person, yet with all she knows, she literally talks to god,
she thinks someone listens in heaven.
On earth, she's unusually competent.
Brave, too, able to face unpleasantness.

We found a caterpillar dying in the dirt, greedy ants crawling over it.
I'm always moved by weakness, by disaster, always eager to oppose vitality.
But timid, also, quick to shut my eyes.
Whereas my friend was able to watch, to let events play out
according to nature. For my sake, she intervened,
brushing a few ants off the torn thing, and set it down across the road.

My friend says I shut my eyes to god, that nothing else explains
my aversion to reality. She says I'm like the child who buries her head in the pillow
so as not to see, the child who tells herself
that light causes sadness —
My friend is like the mother. Patient, urging me
to wake up an adult like herself, a courageous person —

In my dreams, my friend reproaches me. We're walking
on the same road, except it's winter now;

she's telling me that when you love the world you hear celestial music:
look up, she says. When I look up, nothing.
Only clouds, snow, a white business in the trees
like brides leaping to a great height —
Then I'm afraid for her; I see her
caught in a net deliberately cast over the earth —

In reality, we sit by the side of the road, watching the sun set;
from time to time, the silence pierced by a birdcall.
It's this moment we're both trying to explain, the fact
that we're at ease with death, with solitude.
My friend draws a circle in the dirt; inside, the caterpillar
doesn't move.
She's always trying to make something whole, something
beautiful, an image
capable of life apart from her.
We're very quiet. It's peaceful sitting here, not speaking, the
composition
fixed, the road turning suddenly dark, the air
going cool, here and there the rocks shining and glittering —
it's this stillness that we both love.
The love of form is a love of endings.

1990

Vespers

In your extended absence, you permit me
use of earth, anticipating
some return on investment. I must report
failure in my assignment, principally
regarding the tomato plants.
I think I should not be encouraged to grow
tomatoes. Or, if I am, you should withhold
the heavy rains, the cold nights that come
so often here, while other regions get
twelve weeks of summer. All this
belongs to you: on the other hand,
I planted the seeds, I watched the first shoots
like wings tearing the soil, and it was my heart
broken by the blight, the black spot so quickly
multiplying in the rows. I doubt
you have a heart, in our understanding of
that term. You who do not discriminate
between the dead and the living, who are, in consequence,
immune to foreshadowing, you may not know
how much terror we bear, the spotted leaf,
the red leaves of the maple falling

even in August, in early darkness: I am responsible
for these vines.

1992

The Red Poppy

The great thing
is not having
a mind. Feelings:
oh, I have those; they
govern me. I have
a lord in heaven
called the sun, and open
for him, showing him
the fire of my own heart, fire
like his presence.
What could such glory be
if not a heart? Oh my brothers and sisters,
were you like me once, long ago,
before you were human? Did you
permit yourselves
to open once, who would never
open again? Because in truth
I am speaking now
the way you do. I speak
because I am shattered.

1992

Siren

I became a criminal when I fell in love.
Before that I was a waitress.

I didn't want to go to Chicago with you.
I wanted to marry you, I wanted
your wife to suffer.

I wanted her life to be like a play
in which all the parts are sad parts.

Does a good person
think this way? I deserve

credit for my courage —

I sat in the dark on your front porch.
Everything was clear to me:

If your wife wouldn't let you go
that proved she didn't love you.
If she loved you
wouldn't she want you to be happy?

I think now
if I felt less I would be
a better person. I was
a good waitress.
I could carry eight drinks.

I used to tell you my dreams.
Last night I saw a woman sitting in a dark bus —
in the dream, she's weeping, the bus she's on
is moving away. With one hand
she's waving; the other strokes
an egg carton full of babies.

The dream doesn't rescue the maiden.

1996

Circe's Power

I never turned anyone into a pig.
Some people are pigs; I make them
look like pigs.

I'm sick of your world
that lets the outside disguise the inside.

Your men weren't bad men;
undisciplined life
did that to them. As pigs,

under the care of
me and my ladies, they
sweetened right up.

Then I reversed the spell,
showing you my goodness
as well as my power. I saw

we could be happy here,
as men and women are
when their needs are simple. In the same breath,

I foresaw your departure,
your men with my help braving
the crying and pounding sea. You think

a few tears upset me? My friend,
every sorceress is
a pragmatist at heart; nobody
sees essence who can't
face limitation. If I wanted only to hold you

I could hold you prisoner.

1996

MICHAEL PALMER (b. 1943)

A leading practitioner of avant-garde poetics, Michael Palmer is often grouped together with the Language poets, though his work reflects not only that movement's concern with language and its limitations as a medium but also an engagement with Objectivism on the one hand and French surrealism on the other. He traces the origin of "I Do Not" to two sentences he encountered in the translator's preface to a French edition of Gertrude Stein: "Je ne sais pas l'anglais [I do not know English]" and "Je ne sais pas l'anglais mais j'ai traduit lettre par lettre et virgule par virgule [I do not know English but I have translated letter by letter and comma by comma]." He has lived in San Francisco since 1969.

Fifth Prose

Because I'm writing about the snow not the sentence
Because there is a card — a visitor's card — and on that card
    there are words of ours arranged in a row

and on those words we have written house, we have written
    leave this house, we
have written be this house, the spiral of a house, channels
    through this house

and we have written The Provinces and The Reversal and
    something called the Human Poems
though we live in a valley on the Hill of Ghosts

Still for many days the rain will continue to fall
A voice will say Father I am burning

Father I've removed a stone from a wall, erased a picture from
    that wall,
a picture of ships — cloud ships — pressing toward the sea

words only
taken limb by limb apart

Because we are not alive not alone
but ordinary extracts from the tablets

Hassan the Arab and his wife
who did vaulting and balancing

Coleman and Burgess, and Adele Newsome
pitched among the spectators one night

Lizzie Keys
and Fred who fell from the trapeze

into the sawdust
and wasn't hurt at all

and Jacob Hall the rope-dancer
Little Sandy and Sam Sault

Because there is a literal shore, a letter that's blood-red
Because in this dialect the eyes are crossed or quartz

seeing swimmer and seeing rock
statue then shadow

and here in the lake
first a razor then a fact

1988

"A man undergoes pain sitting at a piano"

A man undergoes pain sitting at a piano
knowing thousands will die while he is playing

He has two thoughts about this
If he should stop they would be free of pain

If he could get the notes right he would be free of pain
In the second case the first thought would be erased

causing pain

It is this instance of playing

he would say to himself
my eyes have grown hollow like yours

my head is enlarged
though empty of thought

Such thoughts destroy music
and this at least is good

1988

I Do Not

"Je ne sais pas l'anglais."
— Georges Hugnet

I do not know English.

I do not know English, and therefore I can have nothing to say about this latest war, flowering through a nightscope in the evening sky.

I do not know English and therefore, when hungry, can do no more than point repeatedly to my mouth.

Yet such a gesture might be taken to mean any number of things.

I do not know English and therefore cannot seek the requisite permissions, as outlined in the recent protocol.

Such as: May I utter a term of endearment; may I now proceed to put my arm or arms around you and apply gentle pressure; may I now kiss you directly on the lips; now on the left tendon of the neck; now on the nipple of each breast? And so on.

Would not in any case be able to decipher her response.

I do not know English. Therefore I have no way of communicating that I prefer this painting of nothing to that one of something.

No way to speak of my past or hopes for the future, of my glasses mysteriously shattered in Rotterdam, the statue of Eros and Psyche in the Summer Garden, the sudden, shrill cries in the streets of São Paulo, a watch abruptly stopping in Paris.

No way to tell the joke about the rabbi and the parrot, the bartender and the duck, the Pope and the porte-cochère.

You will understand why you have received no letters from me and
why yours have gone unread.

Those, that is, where you write so precisely of the confluence of
the visible universe with the invisible, and of the lens of dark
matter.

No way to differentiate the hall of mirrors from the meadow of
mullein, the beetlebung from the pinkletink, the kettlehole
from the ventifact.

Nor can I utter the words science, seance, silence, language and
languish.

Nor can I tell of the arboreal shadows elongated and shifting along
the wall as the sun's angle approaches maximum hibernal
declination.

Cannot tell of the almond-eyed face that peered from the well, the
ship of stone whose sail was a tongue.

And I cannot report that this rose has twenty-four petals, one slightly
cankered.

Cannot tell how I dismantled it myself at this desk.

Cannot ask the name of this rose.

I cannot repeat the words of the Recording Angel or those of the
Angel of Erasure.

Can speak neither of things abounding nor of things disappearing.
Still the games continue. A muscular man waves a stick at a ball. A
woman in white, arms outstretched, carves a true circle in space.
A village turns to dust in the chalk hills.

Because I do not know English I have been variously called Mr.
Twisted, The One Undone, The Nonrespondent, The Truly
Lost Boy, and Laughed-At-By-Horses.

The war is declared ended, almost before it has begun.

They have named it The Ultimate Combat between Nearness and
Distance.

I do not know English.

2000

James Tate (b. 1943)

James Tate was born in Kansas City, Missouri. When the future poet was less than a year old, his father, a fighter pilot, was lost on a combat mission, a subject treated in the title poem of Tate's first volume, *The Lost Pilot*, which was chosen for the Yale Younger Poets series when its author was twenty-three years old. "To write a poem out of nothing at all is Tate's genius," Charles Simic has written. "For him, the poem is something one did not know was there until it was written down. Image evokes image, as rhyme evokes rhyme in formal prosody, until there is a poem. The poet is like a fortune-teller with a mirror and a dictionary." While he is sometimes described as a surrealist, the more salient truth is that Tate's poetry in one mode is as homespun American as the movies of Preston Sturges, while in another mode he calls to mind the equally American imagination of Edgar Allan Poe. Some of Tate's poems are mirthful, hilarious when read aloud, though Tate has commented that "poetry-reading audiences invariably giggle at the most tragic passages."

The Lost Pilot

for my father, 1922–1944

Your face did not rot
like the others — the co-pilot,
for example, I saw him

yesterday. His face is corn-
mush: his wife and daughter,
the poor ignorant people, stare

as if he will compose soon.
He was more wronged than Job.
But your face did not rot

like the others — it grew dark,
and hard like ebony;
the features progressed in their

distinction. If I could cajole
you to come back for an evening,
down from your compulsive

orbiting, I would touch you,
read your face as Dallas,
your hoodlum gunner, now,

with the blistered eyes, reads
his braille editions. I would
touch your face as a disinterested

scholar touches an original page.
However frightening, I would
discover you, and I would not

turn you in; I would not make
you face your wife, or Dallas,
or the co-pilot, Jim. You

could return to your crazy
orbiting, and I would not try
to fully understand what

it means to you. All I know
is this: when I see you,
as I have seen you at least

once every year of my life,
spin across the wilds of the sky
like a tiny, African god,

I feel dead. I feel as if I were
the residue of a stranger's life,
that I should pursue you.

My head cocked toward the sky,
I cannot get off the ground,
and, you, passing over again,

fast, perfect, and unwilling
to tell me that you are doing
well, or that it was mistake

that placed you in that world,
and me in this; or that misfortune
placed these worlds in us.

1967

Failed Tribute to the Stonemason of Tor House, Robinson Jeffers

We traveled down to see your house,
Tor House, Hawk Tower, in Carmel,
California. It was not quite what
I thought it would be: I wanted it
to be on a hill, with a view of the ocean
unobstructed by other dwellings.
Fifty years ago I know you had

a clean walk to the sea, hopping
from boulder to boulder, the various
seafowl rightly impressed with
your lean, stern face. But today

with our cameras cocked we had to
sneak and crawl through trimmed lawns
to even verify the identity of
your strange carbuncular creation,
now rented to trillionaire non-
literary folk from Pasadena.
Edged in on all sides by trilevel
pasteboard phantasms, it took
a pair of good glasses to barely see
some newlyweds feed popcorn
to an albatross. Man *is*

a puny thing, divorced,
whether he knows it or not, and
pays his monthly alimony,
his child-support. Year after year
you strolled down to this exceptionally
violent shore and chose your boulder;
the arms grew as the house grew
as the mind grew to exist outside
of time, beyond the dalliance
of your fellows. Today I hate
Carmel: I seek libation in the Tiki

Bar: naked native ladies are painted
in iridescent orange on velvet cloth:
the whole town loves art.
And I donate this Singapore Sling
to the memory of it, and join
the stream of idlers simmering outside.
Much as hawks circled your head
when you cut stone all afternoon,
kids with funny hats on motorscooters
keep circling the block.
Jeffers, . . .

1970

Teaching the Ape to Write Poems

They didn't have much trouble
teaching the ape to write poems:
first they strapped him into the chair,

then tied the pencil around his hand
(the paper had already been nailed down).
Then Dr. Bluespire leaned over his shoulder
and whispered into his ear:
"You look like a god sitting there.
Why don't you try writing something?"

1972

Distance from Loved Ones

After her husband died, Zita decided to get the face-lift she had always wanted. Half way through the operation her blood pressure started to drop, and they had to stop. When Zita tried to fasten her seat belt for her sad drive home, she threw out her shoulder. Back at the hospital the doctor examined her and found cancer was rampant throughout her shoulder and arm and elsewhere. Radiation followed. And, now, Zita just sits there in her beauty parlor, bald, crying and crying.

My mother tells me all this on the phone, and I say: Mother, who is Zita?

And my mother says, I am Zita. All my life I have been Zita, bald and crying. And you, my son, who should have known me best, thought I was nothing but your mother.

But, Mother, I say, I am dying. . . .

1990

I Am a Finn

I Am a Finn

I am standing in the post office, about
to mail a package back to Minnesota, to my family.
I am a Finn. My name is Kasteheimi (Dewdrop).

Mikael Agricola (1510–1557) created the Finnish language.
He knew Luther and translated the New Testament.
When I stop by the Classé Café for a cheeseburger

no one suspects that I am a Finn.
I gaze at the dimestore reproductions of Lautrec
on the greasy walls, at the punk lovers afraid

to show their quivery emotions, secure
in the knowledge that my grandparents really did
emigrate from Finland in 1910 — why

is everybody leaving Finland, hundreds of
thousands to Michigan and Minnesota, and now Australia?
Eighty-six percent of Finnish men have blue

or gray eyes. Today is Charlie Chaplin's
one hundredth birthday, though he is not
Finnish or alive: "Thy blossom, in the bud

laid low." The commonest fur-bearing animals
are the red squirrel, musk-rat, pine-marten
and fox. There are about 35,000 elk.

But I should be studying for my exam.
I wonder if Dean will celebrate with me tonight,
assuming I pass. Finnish literature

really came alive in the 1860s.
Here, in Cambridge, Massachusetts,
no one cares that I am a Finn.

They've never even heard of Frans Eemil Sillanpää,
winner of the 1939 Nobel Prize in Literature.
As a Finn, this infuriates me.

I Am Still a Finn

I failed my exam, which is difficult
for me to understand because I am a Finn.
We are a bright, if slightly depressed, people.

Pertti Palmroth is the strongest name
in Finnish footwear design; his shoes and boots
are exported to seventeen countries.

Dean bought champagne to celebrate
my failure. He says I was just nervous.
Between 1908 and 1950, 33 volumes

of *The Ancient Poetry of the Finnish People*
were issued, the largest work of its kind
ever published in any language.

So why should I be nervous? Aren't I
a Finn, descendant of Johan Ludvig Runeberg
(1804–1877), Finnish national poet?

I know he wrote in Swedish, and this
depresses me still. Harvard Square
is never "empty." There is no chance

that I will ever be able to state honestly
that "Harvard Square is empty tonight."
A man from Nigeria will be opening

his umbrella, and a girl from Wyoming
will be closing hers. A Zulu warrior
is running to catch a bus and an over-

painted harlot from Buenos Aires will
be fainting on schedule. And I, a Finn,
will long for the dwarf birches of the north

I have never seen. For 73 days the sun
never sinks below the horizon. O
darkness, mine! I shall always be a Finn.

1990

How the Pope Is Chosen

Any poodle under ten inches high is a toy.
Almost always a toy is an imitation
of something grown-ups use.
Popes with unclipped hair are called *corded popes*.
If a Pope's hair is allowed to grow unchecked,
it becomes extremely long and twists
into long strands that look like ropes.
When it is shorter it is tightly curled.
Popes are very intelligent.
There are three different sizes.
The largest are called standard Popes.
The medium-sized ones are called miniature Popes.
I could go on like this, I could say:
"He is a squarely built Pope, neat,
well-proportioned, with an alert stance
and an expression of bright curiosity,"
but I won't. After a poodle dies
all the cardinals flock to the nearest 7-Eleven.
They drink Slurpies until one of them throws up
and then he's the new Pope.
He is then fully armed and rides through the wilderness alone,
day and night in all kinds of weather.
The new Pope chooses the name he will use as Pope,
like "Wild Bill" or "Buffalo Bill."

He wears red shoes with a cross embroidered on the front.
Most Popes are called "Babe" because
growing up to become a Pope is a lot of fun.
All the time their bodies are becoming bigger and stranger,
but sometimes things happen to make them unhappy:
They have to go to the bathroom by themselves,
and they spend almost all of their time sleeping.
Parents seem to be incapable of helping their little popes grow up.
Fathers tell them over and over again not to lean out of windows,
but the sky is full of them.
It looks as if they are just taking it easy,
but they are learning something else.
What, we don't know, because we are not like them.
We can't even dress like them.
We are like red bugs or mites compared to them.
We think we are having a good time cutting cartoons out of the
paper,
but really we are eating crumbs out of their hands.
We are tiny germs that cannot be seen under microscopes.
When a Pope is ready to come into the world,
we try to sing a song, but the words do not fit the music too well.
Some of the full-bodied popes are a million times bigger than us.
They open their mouths at regular intervals.
They are continually grinding up pieces of the cross
and spitting them out. Black flies cling to their lips.
Once they are elected they are given a bowl of cream
and a puppy clip. Eyebrows are a protection
when the Pope must plunge through dense underbrush

in search of a sheep.

1994

Inspiration

The two men sat roasting in their blue suits
on the edge of a mustard field.
Lucien Cardin, a local painter,
had suggested a portrait.
President and Vice President of the bank branch,
maybe it would hang in the lobby
inspiring confidence. It might even
cast a little grace and dignity
on the citizens of their hamlet.
They were serious men with sober thoughts
about an unstable world.
The elder, Gilbert, smoked his pipe
and gazed through his wire-rims beyond the painter.

The sky was eggshell blue,
and Lucien knew what he was doing
when he begged their pardon
and went to fetch the two straw hats.
They were farmers' hats, for working in the sun.
Gilbert and Tom agreed to wear them
to staunch their perspiration,
but they knew too the incongruity
their appearance now suggested.
And, as for the lobby of their bank,
solidarity with the farmers, their customers.
The world might go to war — Louis flattened
Schmeling the night before — but a portrait
was painted that day in a field of mustard
outside of Alexandria, Ontario;
of two men, even-tempered and levelheaded,
and of what they did next there is no record.

1994

Dream On

Some people go their whole lives
without ever writing a single poem.
Extraordinary people who don't hesitate
to cut somebody's heart or skull open.
They go to baseball games with the greatest of ease
and play a few rounds of golf as if it were nothing.
These same people stroll into a church
as if that were a natural part of life.
Investing money is second nature to them.
They contribute to political campaigns
that have absolutely no poetry in them
and promise none for the future.
They sit around the dinner table at night
and pretend as though nothing is missing.
Their children get caught shoplifting at the mall
and no one admits that it is poetry they are missing.
The family dog howls all night,
lonely and starving for more poetry in his life.
Why is it so difficult for them to see
that, without poetry, their lives are effluvial.
Sure, they have their banquets, their celebrations,
croquet, fox hunts, their seashores and sunsets,
their cocktails on the balcony, dog races,
and all that kissing and hugging, and don't
forget the good deeds, the charity work,
nursing the baby squirrels all through the night,

filling the birdfeeders all winter,
helping the stranger change her tire.
Still, there's that disagreeable exhalation
from decaying matter, subtle but ever present.
They walk around erect like champions.
They are smooth-spoken, urbane and witty.
When alone, rare occasion, they stare
into the mirror for hours, bewildered.
There was something they meant to say, but didn't:
"And if we put the statue of the rhinoceros
next to the tweezers, and walk around the room three times,
learn to yodel, shave our heads, call
our ancestors back from the dead —"
poetrywise it's still a bust, bankrupt.
You haven't scribbled a syllable of it.
You're a nowhere man misfiring
the very essence of your life, flustering
nothing from nothing and back again.
The hereafter may not last all that long.
Radiant childhood sweetheart,
secret code of everlasting joy and sorrow,
fanciful pen strokes beneath the eyelids:
all day, all night meditation, knot of hope,
kernel of desire, pure ordinariness of life,
seeking, through poetry, a benediction
or a bed to lie down on, to connect, reveal,
explore, to imbue meaning on the day's extravagant labor.
And yet it's cruel to expect too much.
It's a rare species of bird
that refuses to be categorized.
Its song is barely audible.
It is like a dragonfly in a dream —
here, then there, then here again,
low-flying amber-wing darting upward
and then out of sight.
And the dream has a pain in its heart
the wonders of which are manifold,
or so the story is told.

1997

The Promotion

I was a dog in my former life, a very good dog, and, thus, I was promoted to a human being. I liked being a dog. I worked for a poor farmer guarding and herding his sheep. Wolves and coyotes tried to get past me almost every night, and not

once did I lose a sheep. The farmer rewarded me
with good food, food from his table. He may have
been poor, but he ate well. And his children
played with me, when they weren't in school or
working in the field. I had all the love any dog
could hope for. When I got old, they got a new
dog, and I trained him in the tricks of the trade.
He quickly learned, and the farmer brought me into
the house to live with them. I brought the farmer
his slippers in the morning, as he was getting
old, too. I was dying slowly, a little bit at a
time. The farmer knew this and would bring the
new dog in to visit me from time to time. The
new dog would entertain me with his flips and
flops and nuzzles. And then one morning I just
didn't get up. They gave me a fine burial down
by the stream under a shade tree. That was the
end of my being a dog. Sometimes I miss it so
I sit by the window and cry. I live in a highrise
that looks out at a bunch of other high-rises.
At my job I work in a cubicle and barely speak
to anyone all day. This is my reward for being
a good dog. The human wolves don't even see me.
They fear me not.

2002

Bounden Duty

I got a call from the White House, from the
president himself, asking me if I'd do him a personal
favor. I like the president, so I said, "Sure, Mr.
President, anything you like." He said, "Just act
like nothing's going on. Act normal. That would
mean the world to me. Can you do that, Leon?" "Why,
sure, Mr. President, you've got it. Normal, that's
how I'm going to act. I won't let on, even if I'm
tortured," I said, immediately regretting that "tortured"
bit. He thanked me several times and hung up. I was
dying to tell someone that the president himself called
me, but I knew I couldn't. The sudden pressure to
act normal was killing me. And what was going on
anyway. I didn't know anything was going on. I
saw the president on TV yesterday. He was shaking
hands with a farmer. What if it wasn't really a
farmer? I needed to buy some milk, but suddenly
I was afraid to go out. I checked what I had on.
I looked "normal" to me, but maybe I looked more

like I was trying to be normal. That's pretty
suspicious. I opened the door and looked around.
What was going on? There was a car parked in front
of my car that I had never seen before, a car that
was trying to look normal, but I wasn't fooled.
If you need milk, you have to get milk, otherwise
people will think something's going on. I got into
my car and sped down the road. I could feel those
little radar guns popping behind every tree and bush,
but, apparently, they were under orders not to stop
me. I ran into Kirsten in the store. "Hey, what's
going on, Leon?" she said. She had a very nice smile.
I hated to lie to her. "Nothing's going on. Just
getting milk for my cat," I said. "I didn't know
you had a cat," she said. "I meant to say coffee.
You're right, I don't have a cat. Sometimes I
refer to my coffee as my cat. It's just a private
joke. Sorry," I said. "Are you all right?" she
asked. "Nothing's going on, Kirsten. I promise
you. Everything is normal. The president shook
hands with a farmer, a real farmer. Is that such
a big deal?" I said. "I saw that," she said, "and
that man was definitely not a farmer." "Yeah, I
know," I said, feeling better.

2004

DOUGLAS CRASE (b. 1944)

Douglas Crase was born in Battle Creek, Michigan. He has published only one book of poems, *The Revisionist* (1981), but on its strength rests a formidable underground reputation. Crase has edited a volume of Emerson's essays, compiled a book of quotations from American writers, and written a lyrical account of the fifty-year friendship of two avant-garde botanists (*Both*, 2004). He is the "Doug" in James Schuyler's poem "Dining Out with Doug and Frank."

The Continent as the Letter M

Think of it starting out this way: in profile
Two almost immediate peaks, but widely opposite,
The basin humming with weather in between
And approaching speech as summary ineffectual
As the oceans beside its feet, their murmuring
Montauk, at Monterey. Think of the central
Organizing mound of it, around which
An alphabet of fir mounts up to fall away

Just at the timberline, the solid crown of it
When seen from cabin windows, imposing crash sites
Seen from stricken planes. Ponderous,
The name of our country is ponderous and brown,
Laborious as a growing mastodon, its own huge shoulders
The only thing it's hanging on. Columbia,
Paumanok, say it, the Alamo — we build
Outward from this middle interior sound
So far until, unsupported,
Our imaginations begin to let us down.
To the soft soil of that consonant we return,
Made Massey-Ferguson fertile and turning over
A train of little *m*'s behind the plow. America:
So many centuries thicken its animal sound,
This mammoth that holds us between its knees,
Maumee, Menominee, Michilimackinac,
Deep, past Appalachian deep
The inarticulate lives in its hold on me.

1981

There Is No Real Peace in the World

The fact of life is it's no life-or-death matter,
Which is supposed to make it easier to choose. People die,
For sure, and that's a personal apocalypse for them
And a revision of heaven and earth for those "left
To follow after" (as your great-grandfather's obituary would say)
So that a few are always being rearranged on maps
Redrawn by family accident or folly, like separate Europes
After their awful wars. War isn't the easiest metaphor
To go by though, nor, here's the point, is it reliable
Since all the individual hells added up remain exactly
Individual, and whether they blaze like Berlin or not
Are kept in those unassailable bunkers, Born and Died,
Passed in and out of this world, the whole world minus one,
Which never felt the flames nor ever knew. No,
No sooner has one perished than the rest survive,
Which ought to be proof that yes-or-no options aren't final
As they seem to be, except for the problem that the survivor
In our time includes memories out of all proportion to
The experience ahead of him and is intent on living up to them,
On Germany where there's only Idaho. It's inescapable
How history has targeted the tiniest, safest life
With the knowledge that chance and power, unmitigated,
Are always impending out of the godless distance toward it
The way there is always a comet impending toward the earth

And it's only a question now of how close and when,
A recombinant message which has breached the world
And altered the code so thoroughly that issues graceful once
As travel or turning the calendar beget features of flight,
Contortion and alarm instead. If it's in the inheritance
It's in the life, and why should it be disregarded
Because the evidence, the rock-hard impact,
Is still to occur? By then it would be too late
For the genius of worry is to duck the Gotterdammerungs
That might establish its validity, to live close enough
To the border to get away and know where to do it
(Minnesota, Montana, never Niagara Falls), to have
Plenty of birth certificates on hand, a respectable lawyer
And a self-sufficient farm tucked into an unknown corner
Of that same Idaho. But the truth is, as I said, to date
It's only Idaho, a kind of demilitarized zone at most
Where life is interchangeable with the regrets expressed
When it is over, nothing to touch off the silos for.
There's grain in the hopper and wives sweet with biphenyls
Under the skin, or else fatigue — who knows for sure ? The cows
Are freshening off schedule again. There is nothing to fear.

1981

Astropastoral

As much as the image of you, I have seen
You again, live, as in live indecision you brighten
The limbs of an earth that so earnestly turns
To reflect you, the sky's brightest body
And last best beacon for those who are everywhere
Coded in spirals and want to unbend,
Who bear in the dark turned toward you
This message they have to deliver even to live,
To linger in real rime before you, to meet or to
Blow you away — and yes I have seen you receive them
But you are not there. Though I've tried to ignore you,
Go solo, light out beyond you,
I have seen you on every horizon, how you are stored
And encouraged and brought to the brim
Until the round bounds of one planet could not hold you in
But were ready to set near space ringing
As if from the ranking capacitor outside the sun.
I have seen you discharged, and then how you swell
Toward heaven and how you return, transmitting the fun
Of the firmament, all of it yours. And these things
Have happened, only you are not there.
At night in the opposite high-rise I'd see how you glow,

And in the adjacent one too, the same would-be blue,
And I've looked on the glow in the waters
Around the reactor, that also blue, how
Whatever would match your expression you
Wouldn't be there. I have seen the impressions you leave
At the margin of error in exit polls, monitored polls
That you never entered — I can tell what I see:
Saw you vote with your feet and hit the ground running,
Kiss the ground, rescued, and (this wasn't a drill)
Saw you fall to your knees on the ground
By the body of your friend on the ground
And though these fall beside you like gantries, it is
You who are rising above them and you are not there.
Like a rocket in winter, I have been there to see you
Logged in as a guest among stars — only you,
Though you're lovely to look at, expensive to own,
And though in demand without letup, you are not there.

2000

PAUL VIOLI (b. 1944)

Paul Violi, who grew up in Greenlawn, Long Island, joined the Peace Corps after graduating from Boston University and traveled through Europe, Africa, and Asia. "Index" demonstrates his flair for comic invention and his penchant for unusual forms. He had been reading an autobiography and noticed that "the author's egotism even seeped into the end papers, especially the index which by condensing his life seemed to magnify his faults." In the poem, the page numbers work "like dates," conveying a sense of chronology. Violi has also written poems in the form of *TV Guide* listings and the acknowledgments page of a poetry collection.

Index

Hudney, Sutej IX, X, XI, 7, 9, 25, 58, 60, 61, 64
    Plates 5, 10, 15
    Childhood 70, 71
    Education 78, 79, 80
    Early relationship with family 84
    Enters academy, honors 84
    Arrest and bewilderment 85
    Formation of spatial theories 90
    "Romance of Ardoy, The" 92
    Second arrest 93
    Early voyages, life in the Pyrenees 95
    Marriage 95
    Abandons landscape painting 96
    Third arrest 97

Weakness of character, inconstancy 101
First signs of illness, advocation
of celibacy 106, 107
Advocates abolishment of celibacy 110
Expulsion from Mazar 110
Collaborations with Fernando Gee 111
Composes lines beginning: "Death, wouldst that I had
died/While thou wert still a mystery." 117
Consequences of fame, violent rows,
professional disputes 118, 119
Disavows all his work 120
Bigamy, scandals, illness, admittance of
being "easily crazed, like snow." 128
Theories of perspective published 129
Birth of children 129
Analysis of important works:
Wine glass with fingerprints
Nude on a blue sofa
The drunken fox trappers
Man wiping tongue with large towel
Hay bales stacked in a field
Self portrait
Self portrait with cat
Self portrait with frozen mop
Self portrait with belching duck 135
Correspondence with Cecco Angolieri 136
Dispute over attribution of lines: "I have as large
supply of evils/as January has not flowerings." 137
Builds first greenhouse 139
Falling-out with Angolieri 139
Flees famine 144
Paints *Starved cat eating snow* 145
Arrested for selling sacks of wind
to gullible peasants 146
Imprisonment and bewilderment 147
Disavows all his work 158
Invents the collar stay 159
Convalescence with third wife 162
Complains of "a dense and baleful wind
blowing the words I write off the page." 165
Meets with Madam T. 170
Departures, mortal premonitions, "I think
I'm about to snow." 176
Disavows all his work 181
Arrest and pardon 182
Last days 183
Last words 184, 185, 186, 187, 188, 189, 190

1981

Appeal to the Grammarians

We, the naturally hopeful,
Need a simple sign
For the myriad ways we're capsized.
We who love precise language
Need a finer way to convey
Disappointment and perplexity.
For speechlessness and all its inflections,
For up-ended expectations,
For every time we're ambushed
By trivial or stupefying irony,
For pure incredulity, we need
The inverted exclamation point.
For the dropped smile, the limp handshake,
For whoever has just unwrapped a dumb gift
Or taken the first sip of a flat beer,
Or felt love or pond ice
Give way underfoot, we deserve it.
We need it for the air pocket, the scratch shot,
The child whose ball doesn't bounce back,
The flat tire at journey's outset,
The odyssey that ends up in Weehawken.
But mainly because I need it — here and now
As I sit outside the Caffè Reggio
Staring at my espresso and cannoli
After this middle-aged couple
Came strolling by and he suddenly
Veered and sneezed all over my table
And she said to him, "See, *that's* why
I don't like to eat outside."

2004

JOHN KOETHE (b. 1945)

John Koethe was born in San Diego. He began writing poetry in his sophomore year at Princeton, the same time that he decided to major in philosophy. The author of a book on Wittgenstein, he has long taught philosophy at the University of Wisconsin, Milwaukee. "I still think of philosophy and poetry as separate activities, though I don't mind using language and ideas from philosophy in poetry (though I don't mind using practically anything in poetry), and so in that sense I don't mind being called a philosophical poet, though I don't think of myself as one," Koethe says. The reader may compare Koethe's "Sorrento Valley" to villanelles in this anthology by Robinson, Auden, Bishop, Justice, and Strand.

Morning in America

It gradually became a different country
After the reversal, dominated by a distant,
Universal voice whose favorite word was *never*;
Changing its air of quiet progress into one of
Rapidly collapsing possibilities, and making me,
Even here at home, a stranger. I felt its tones
Engaging me without expression, leaving me alone
And waiting in the vacuum of its public half-life,
Quietly confessing my emotions, taking in its cold
Midwinter atmosphere of violence and muted rage. I
Wanted to appropriate that anger, to convey it, not
In a declamatory mode, but in some vague and private
Language holding out, against the clear, inexorable
Disintegration of a nation, the claims of a renewed
Internal life, in these bleak months of the new year.
That was my way of ruling out everything discordant,
Everything dead, cruel, or soulless — by assiduously
Imagining the pages of some legendary volume marked
Forever; but without ever getting any closer. As I
Got older it began to seem more and more hopeless,
More and more detached — until it only spoke to me
Impersonally, like someone gradually retreating,
Not so much from his life as from its settings,
From the country he inhabits; as the darkness
Deepens in the weeks after the solstice.

1997

Sorrento Valley

On a hillside somewhere in Sorrento Valley,
My aunts and uncles sat in canvas chairs
In the blazing sun, facing a small ash tree.

There was no wind. In the distance I could see
Some modern buildings, hovering in the air
Above the wooded hillsides of Sorrento Valley.

I followed the progress of a large bumblebee
As the minister stood, offering a prayer,
Next to the young white California ash tree.

Somewhere a singer went right on repeating
When I Grow Too Old to Dream. Yet to dream where,
I wondered — on a hillside in Sorrento Valley,

Half-way between the mountains and the sea?
To be invisible at last, and released from care,
Beneath a stone next to a white tree?

— As though each of us were alone, and free,
And the common ground we ultimately shared
Were on a hillside somewhere in Sorrento Valley,
In the shade of a small ash tree.

1997

Moore's Paradox

I don't like poems about philosophy,
But then, what is it? Someone
Sees the world dissolving in a well,
Another sees the moving image of eternity
In a shard of time, in what we call a moment.
Are they philosophers? I guess so,
But does it matter? G. E. Moore
Maintained we dream up theories
Incompatible with things we really know, a
Paradox which hardly seems peculiar to our breed.
Poets are worse, or alternately, better
At inhabiting the obviously untrue and
Hoisting flags of speculation in defiance of the real —
In a way that's the point, isn't it?
Whatever holds, whatever occupies the mind
And lingers, and takes flight?

Then from deep within the house
I heard the sound of something I'd forgotten;
Raindrops on the window and the thrashing
Noise the wind makes as it pulses through the trees.
It brought me back to what I meant to say
As time ran out, a mind inside an eggshell boat,
The elements arrayed against it:
Reason as a song, a specious
Music played between the movements of two dreams,
Both dark. I hear the rain.
The silence in the study is complete.
The sentence holds me in its song
Each time I utter it or mentally conceive it,
Calling from a primitive domain
Where time is like a moment
And the clocks stand silent in the chambers,
And it's raining, and I don't believe it.

2002

BERNADETTE MAYER (b. 1945)

Bernadette Mayer was born in Brooklyn. In the 1970s she began teaching her influential *Experiments in Poetry* workshop at the Poetry Project of St. Mark's Church in New York City's East Village. She has compiled a list of her favorite experiments, which include the following: eliminate all adjectives from a work in progress; omit words beginning with "s" from a Shakespeare sonnet; "rewrite someone else's writing"; "write a letter that will never be sent to a person who does or does not exist," and repeat the exercise every day for a month; write a novel in the form of ten paragraphs; "write a work that intersperses love with landlords"; "write a poem or series of poems that will change the world."

Sonnet

Love is a babe as you know and when you
Put your startling hand on my cunt or arm or head
Or better both your hands to hold in them my own
I'm awed and we laugh with questions, artless
Of me to speak so ungenerally of thee & thy name
I have no situation and love is the same, you live at home
Come be here my baby and I'll take you elsewhere where
You ain't already been, my richer friend, and there
At the bottom of my sale or theft of myself will you
Bring specific flowers I will not know the names of
As you already have and already will and already do
As you already are with your succinctest cock
All torn and sore like a female masochist that the rhyme
Of the jewel you pay attention to becomes your baby born

1989

Sonnet

You jerk you didn't call me up
I haven't seen you in so long
You probably have a fucking tan
& besides that instead of making love tonight
You're drinking your parents to the airport
I'm through with you bourgeois boys
All you ever do is go back to ancestral comforts
Only money can get — even Catullus was rich but

Nowadays you guys settle for a couch
By a soporific color cable t.v. set
Instead of any arc of love, no wonder
The G.I. Joe team blows it every other time

Wake up! It's the middle of the night
You can either make love or die at the hands of
the Cobra Commander

* * *

To make love, turn to Page 32.
To die, turn to Page 110.

1989

Holding the Thought of Love

And to render harmless a bomb or the like
Of such a pouring in different directions of love
Love scattered not concentrated love talked about,
So let's not talk of love the diffuseness of which
Round our heads (that oriole's song) like on the platforms
Of the subways and at their stations is today defused
As if by the scattering of light rays in a photograph
Of the softened reflection of a truck in a bakery window

You know I both understand what we found out and I don't
Hiking alone is too complex like a slap in the face
Of any joyous appointment even for the making of money

Abandoned to too large a crack in the unideal sphere of lack of summer
When it's winter, of wisdom in the astronomical arts, we as A & B
Separated then conjoin to see the sights of Avenue C

1989

Sonnet

So long honey, don't ever come around again, I'm sick of you
& of your friends, you take up all my time & I don't write
Poems cause I spend all my time wanting to fuck you & then
You put the apple onto the grilled cheese, I tie you up

Save me from your respective beauties, keep them home
Thanks for all the rock & roll music, if such a
Thing can be said. Who are those guys? The B-52's?
That's what Ethie told me. Can I believe her?

You wanna get married? You tie me up with
Garter belts & less than Heidegger & Kierkegaard the fact
That as we know the poem is not the thought so a slap

Might notice that Uranus suspected a comet? Let me know

He kicks her fallen hat & they are not grownup
Any more than a vase of flowers is, painted, so what?

1989

J. D. McClatchy (b. 1945)

J. D. McClatchy was born in Bryn Mawr, Pennsylvania. He is the editor of the *Yale Review* and has edited contemporary poetry anthologies, written opera libretti and poetry criticism, and taught at Princeton and Yale. He has brought out new editions of poems by Jean Garrigue and Edna St. Vincent Millay. In his own poems, McClatchy sets store by wit, wordplay, and formal dexterity, traits he shares with such mentors as James Merrill and John Hollander. "Pibroch" is a musical term referring to variations on a traditional dirge or martial theme for highland bagpipes in Scotland.

The Landing

Through the blinds, it must have been the searchlight I saw
That silvered the woodwork. Step by step, its shadow was

Measuring out tonight. The climb itself has become a cloud
That thickens with the effort. I'd look up if I could.

Three lines erased in the address book. The thumbed pages
Of those last weeks through which the halflit end still gapes,

Unwritten. And what I miss goes without saying. Has
The explanation even there been brief as a flame and its ash?

I speak to the air that takes these things finally as its own.
Tell me who that is beyond the stairwell's next turning now.

1990

What They Left Behind

The room with double beds, side by side.
One was the bed of roses, still made up,
The other the bed of nails, all undone.
In the nightstand clamshell, two Marlboro butts.

On the shag, a condom with a tear in its tip
Neither of them noticed — or would even suspect
For two years more. A ballpoint embossed
By a client's firm: Malpractice Suits.

A wad of gum balled in a page of proverbs
Torn from the complimentary Bible.
His lipstick. Her aftershave.

A dream they found the next day they'd shared:
All the dogs on the island were dying
And the birds had flown up into the lonely air.

1998

Pibroch

But now that I am used to pain,
Its knuckles in my mouth the same
Today as yesterday, the cause
As clear-obscure as who's to blame,

A fascination with the flaws
Sets in — the plundered heart, the pause
Between those earnest, oversold
Liberties that took like laws.

What should have been I never told,
Afraid of outbursts you'd withhold.
Why are desires something to share?
I'm shivering, though it isn't cold.

Beneath your window, I stand and stare.
The planets turn. The trees are bare.
I'll toss a pebble at the pane,
But softly, knowing you are not there.

2002

ALICE NOTLEY (b. 1945)

Alice Notley was born in Bisbee, Arizona, and grew up in Needles, California. She was married to the poet Ted Berrigan ("the single greatest influence on my being a poet") from 1972 until his death in 1983. She married the British poet Douglas Oliver in 1988 and moved to Paris with him four years later. Notley has proclaimed her kinship with other second-generation "New York school" poets Bernadette Mayer and Anne Waldman. "I was obsessed with the fact that there was no sound in American poetry that presaged mine; that there was no poetry that corresponded to my experience," she has written. In the voices of Waldman and Mayer she says she "heard a way a young woman might sound."

"A woman came into"

"A woman came into" "a car I rode" "about thirty-seven" "maybe
forty" "Face" "a harsh response to" "what she did" "had to do"
"face rigid" "but she was beautiful" "Was," "we could see,"
"one of the ones who" "strip for coins" "on the subway —"

"They simply" "very quickly" ("illegally") "remove all their
clothes" "Stand, for a moment" "Turning to face" "each end"
"of the car" "Then dress quickly," "pass quickly" "the cup."
"But she — this one —" "face of hating to so much that" "as she

took off her blouse," "her face" "began to change" "Grew
feathers, a small beak" "& by the time she was naked," "she wore the
head" "of an eagle" "a crowned eagle" "a raptor" "herself —"
"And as she stood" "& faced the car" "her body" "was changing"

"was becoming entirely" "that bird" "those wings," "she shrank to
become the bird" "but grew wings that" "were wider" "than she had been
tall" "Instantly," "instantly, a man caught her" "A cop came"
"As if ready" "as if they knew" "Her wings were clipped,"

"talons cut" "as if as quickly" "as possible" "She was released
then, to the car" "to the subway" "Perched" "on the bar the
straps hang from"

1992

April Not an Inventory But a Blizzard

I met Ted at two parties at the same house
at the first he insulted me because, he said later,
he was mad at girls that night; at the second we danced
an elaborate fox-trot with dipping — he had once taken one lesson
at an Arthur Murray's. First I went into an empty
room and waited for him to follow me. I liked the way
his poems looked on the page open but delicately arranged.

I like him because he's funny he talks more like
me than like books or words: he likes my knowledge and
accepts its sources. I know that there are Channel swimmers
and that they keep warm with grease because of
an Esther Williams movie. We differ as to what kind
of grease it is I suggest bacon he says it's bear

really in the movie it was dark brown like grease from a car
Who's ever greased a car? Not him I find he prefers to white out
all the speech balloons in a Tarzan comic
and print in new words for the characters. Do you want
to do some? he says — No — We go to a movie where Raquel Welch
and Jim Brown are Mexican revolutionaries I make him
laugh he says something about a turning point in the plot
Do you mean, I say, when she said We shood have keeled him long ago?
Finally a man knows that I'm being funny

He's eleven years older than me and takes pills
I take some a few months later and write
I think it's eighty-three poems I forget about Plath and James Wright
he warns me about pills in a slantwise way See this
nose? he says, It's the ruins of civilization
I notice some broken capillaries who cares

I wonder who I am now myself though I haven't
anticipated me entirely I have such an appetite
to write not to live I'm certainly living quite fully
We're good together he says because we can be like
little boy and little girl I give him much later a
girl's cheap Dutch brooch Delft blue and white
a girl and a boy holding hands and windmills
But now it's summer in Iowa City he leaves for
Europe gives me the key to his library stored
in a room at The Writers Workshop
I write mildly yet oh there's a phrase "the Gilbert curve"
how a street turns that sensation to make it permanent
a daily transition as the curve opens and is walked on
of the kinds of experience still in between the ones
talked about in literature and even in Ted's library
which finally makes poetry possible for me but I've
not read a voice like my own like my own voice will be

1997

KAY RYAN (b. 1945)

Kay Ryan was born Kay Pedersen in San Jose, California, the daughter of an oil driller. She received her bachelor's and master's degrees in English literature at UCLA. On not obtaining her Ph.D., she commented: "I couldn't bear the idea of being a doctor of something I couldn't fix." Her poems are characteristically brief, rich in internal rhyme, centering on a perception nourished by the author's skeptical intelligence. They result, Ryan says, from "self-imposed emergencies." Her "Failure" might be compared to Katha Pollitt's poem of the same title.

A Bad Time for the Sublime

The sublime is now
a less popular topic
than if El Greco was myopic.
Yes El Greco may very well
have been, which may very
well have made his men
so thin and his women so
distressed. If pressed,
the oculists confess that
the shape taken by the
aqueous humor makes
or breaks us, and have
devised anti-vision devices
that restore noses to their
right lengths and places.
Witness how a speckled plain
condenses to a field
or farmyard, the ecstasy
or pain of space
erased by moving the lens
back or forward.
We now discover there were
many thin kings and
many chubby martyrs,
many ordinary trees
and water always very
similar to our water.

1985

Poetry Is a Kind of Money

Poetry is a kind of money
whose value depends on reserves.
It's not the paper it's written on
or its self-announced denomination,
but the bullion, sweated from the earth
and hidden, which preserves its worth.
Nobody knows how this works,
and how can it? Why does something
stacked in some secret bank or cabinet,
some miser's trove, far back, lambent,
and gloated over by its golem, make us
so solemnly convinced of the transaction

when Mandelstam says *love,* even
in translation?

1989

Blandeur

If it please God,
let less happen.
Even out Earth's
rondure, flatten
Eiger, blanden
the Grand Canyon.
Make valleys
slightly higher,
widen fissures
to arable land,
remand your
terrible glaciers
and silence
their calving,
halving or doubling
all geographical features
toward the mean.
Unlean against our hearts.
Withdraw your grandeur
from these parts.

2000

Failure

Like slime
inside a
stagnant tank

its green
deepening
from lime
to emerald

a dank
but less
ephemeral
efflorescence

than success
is in general.

2000

Home to Roost

The chickens
are circling and
blotting out the
day. The sun is
bright, but the
chickens are in
the way. Yes,
the sky is dark
with chickens,
dense with them.
They turn and
then they turn
again. These
are the chickens
you let loose
one at a time
and small —
various breeds.
Now they have
come home
to roost—all
the same kind
at the same speed.

2004

Terence Winch (b. 1945)

Born in the Bronx, Terence Winch made a living writing and performing traditional Irish music until 1985, when he took a job as an editor at the Smithsonian Institution. Like "Crime Club" by Weldon Kees, Winch's "Mysteries" derives its subject matter from the genre of detective fiction. The simian solution of "The Murders in the Rue Morgue," which launched the genre, may seem "pretty ridiculous" but perhaps sublime as well when it is recalled that the story antedated Darwin's theory of evolution. The solution, or conclusion, of Winch's poem is a concise illustration of the spirit of postmodernism.

Mysteries

All last night I kept speaking in this
archaic language, because I had been reading
Poe and thinking about him. I read "The Murders
in the Rue Morgue" which is supposedly the first
detective story. Who dun it? I wondered.
It turns out an orangutan was the murderer.
It looks to me like the detective story got off
to a pretty ridiculous start. I used to visit
Poe's house in the Bronx. I used to think,
God, Poe must have been a midget. Everything
was so small. Poe died in Baltimore and I can see why.
In Baltimore, all the people are very big and sincere.
During dinner last night, I told Doug and Susan
about "Murders in the Rue Morgue." I said I hadn't
finished it yet, but it looked like the murderer
was going to turn out to be an orangutan, unless
the plot took a surprising new twist. Then Doug
suggested that he and I collaborate
on a series of detective stories in which
the murderer is *always* an orangutan.

1994

PATTI SMITH (b. 1946)

Born in Chicago, Patti Smith, the well-known singer and performance artist, gave an electrifying reading at St. Mark's Church in New York City's East Village in 1971. Her first album, *Horses* (1975), blurs the line between lyrics and poetry. The album opens with "Gloria," a cover of the Van Morrison song that is also an elaboration of Smith's poem "Oath" ("Jesus died for somebody's sins / but not mine"). Allen Ginsberg praised her "Rimbaud kind of Buddhist thing."

dream of rimbaud

I am a widow. could be charleville could be anywhere.
move behind the plow. the fields. young arthur lurks
about the farmhouse (roche?) the pump the artesian
well. throws green glass alias crystal broken.
gets me in the eye.

I am upstairs. in the bedroom bandaging my wound. he
enters. leans against the four-poster. his ruddy cheeks.
contemptuous air big hands. I find him sexy as hell.
how did this happen he asks casually. too casually.

I lift the bandage. reveal my eye a bloodied mess;
a dream of Poe. he gasps.

I deliver it hard and fast. someone did it. you did it.
he falls prostrate. he weeps he clasps my knees. I grab
his hair. it all but burns my fingers. thick fox fire.
soft yellow hair. yet that unmistakable red tinge.
rubedo. red dazzle. hair of the One.

Oh jesus I desire him. filthy son of a bitch. he licks
my hand. I sober. leave quickly your mother waits. he
rises, he's leaving. but not without the glance, from
those cold blue eyes, that shatters. he who hesitates
is mine. we're on the bed. I have a knife to his smooth
throat. I let it drop. we embrace. I devour his scalp.
lice fat as baby thumbs. lice the skulls caviar.

Oh arthur arthur. we are in Abyssinia Aden. making love
smoking cigarettes. we kiss. but its much more. azure.
blue pool. oil slick lake. sensations telescope, animate.
crystalline gulf. balls of colored glass exploding.
seam of berber tent splitting. openings, open as a cave,
open wider. total surrender.

1973

RAE ARMANTROUT (b. 1947)

A native of Vallejo, California, Rae Armantrout has lived for many years in San Diego. According to the poet Ron Silliman, she writes "poems that at first glance appear contained and perhaps even simple, but which upon the slightest examination rapidly provoke a sort of vertigo effect as element after element begins to spin wildly toward more radical … possibilities." "Traveling through the Yard" is a response to William Stafford's "Traveling through the Night" and should be read alongside it.

Traveling Through The Yard

for William Stafford

It was lying near my back porch
in the gaudy light of morning —
a dove corpse, oddly featherless,
alive with flies.
I stopped,
dustpan in hand, and heard

them purr over their feast.
To leave that there would make some stink!
So thinking hard for all of us,
I scooped it up, heaved it
across the marriage counselor's fence.

2001

Articulation

I

With whom
do you leave yourself
during reveries?

The one making coffee
or doing the driving —

that is the real
person in your life.
Now that one is gone

or has tagged along with you
like a small child
behind Mother.

"No!" you explain
in the crowded aisle.

"Without articulation
there's *no* sense of place."

II

When I dreamed about flying,
it was as a skill
I needed to regain.

I'd make practice runs
and float high
over the page. Pleasure

was a confirmation.
I remembered the way
and I was right!

Still,
one should be patient

with the present
as if with a child.

To follow its prattle —
glitter on water —

indulgently
is only polite.

2001

Aaron Fogel (b. 1947)

Aaron Fogel was born in New York City and was educated at Columbia and Cambridge universities. A professor at Boston University, he has written strikingly original literary criticism on such subjects as hoaxes, "double alliteration" as an exercise or method of composition, and the secret importance of the abbreviated word "trans." in Frank O'Hara's poem "The Day Lady Died."

The Printer's Error

Fellow compositors
and pressworkers!

I, Chief Printer
Frank Steinman,
having worked fifty-seven
years at my trade,
and served for five years
as president
of the Holliston
Printers' Council,
being of sound mind
though near death,
leave this testimonial
concerning the nature
of printers' errors.

First: I hold that
all books and all
printed matter have
errors, obvious or no,
and that these are
their most significant moments,
not to be tampered with
by the vanity and folly

of ignorant, academic
textual editors.
Second: I hold that there are
three types of errors, in ascending
order of importance:
One: chance errors
of the printer's trembling hand
not to be corrected incautiously
by foolish scholars
and other such rabble
because trembling is part
of divine creation itself.
Two: silent, cool sabotage
by the printer,
the manual laborer
whose protests
have at times taken this
historical form,
covert interferences
not to be corrected
censoriously by the hand
of the second and far
more ignorant saboteur,
the textual editor.
Three: errors
from the touch of God,
divine and often
obscure corrections
of whole books by
nearly unnoticed changes
of single letters
sometimes meaningful but
about which the less said
by preemptive commentary
the better.
Third: I hold that all three
sorts of error,
errors by chance,
errors by workers' protest,
and errors by
God's work,
are in practice the
same and indistinguishable.

Therefore I,
Frank Steinman,
typographer
for thirty-seven years,
and cooperative Master

of the Holliston Guild
eight years,
being of sound mind and body
though near death
urge the abolition
of all editorial work
whatsoever
and manumission
from all textual editing
to leave what was
as it was, and
as it became,
except insofar as editing
is itself an error, and

therefore also divine.

1995

JANE KENYON (1947–1995)

Born in Ann Arbor, Jane Kenyon met her husband, the poet Donald Hall, at the University of Michigan. They married in 1972 and moved in 1975 to Hall's family farm in Eagle Pond Farm, New Hampshire. She found solace in poetry but suffered, she once remarked, from "disabling, soul-crushing depression, the kind that puts your face in the dust." She contracted leukemia in 1994 and died on 22 April 1995.

Let Evening Come

Let the light of late afternoon
shine through chinks in the barn, moving
up the bales as the sun moves down.

Let the cricket take up chafing
as a woman takes up her needles
and her yarn. Let evening come.

Let dew collect on the hoe abandoned
in long grass. Let the stars appear
and the moon disclose her silver horn.

Let the fox go back to its sandy den.
Let the wind die down. Let the shed
go black inside. Let evening come.

To the bottle in the ditch, to the scoop
in the oats, to air in the lung
let evening come.

Let it come, as it will, and don't
be afraid. God does not leave us
comfortless, so let evening come.

1990

Otherwise

I got out of bed
on two strong legs.
It might have been
otherwise. I ate
cereal, sweet
milk, ripe, flawless
peach. It might
have been otherwise.
I took the dog uphill
to the birch wood.
All morning I did
the work I love.

At noon I lay down
with my mate. It might
have been otherwise.
We ate dinner together
at a table with silver
candlesticks. It might
have been otherwise.
I slept in a bed
in a room with paintings
on the walls, and
planned another day
just like this day.
But one day, I know,
it will be otherwise.

1993

Man Eating

The man at the table across from mine
is eating yogurt. His eyes, following
the progress of the spoon, cross briefly

each time it nears his face. Time,

and the world with all its principalities,
might come to an end as prophesied
by the Apostle John, but what about
this man, so completely present

to the little carton with its cool,
sweet food, which has caused no animal
to suffer, and which he is eating
with a pearl-white plastic spoon.

1994

YUSEF KOMUNYAKAA (b. 1947)

Yusef Komunyakaa was born in Bogalusa, Louisiana. He received the Bronze Star for his military service in Vietnam. "Facing It" was written in 1984: "I had meditated on the Vietnam Veterans Memorial as if the century's blues songs had been solidified into something monumental and concrete," Komunyakaa commented. "Our wailing, our ranting, our singing of spirituals and kaddish and rock anthems, it was all captured and refined into a shaped destiny," which "became a shrine overnight: a blackness that plays with light — a reflected motion in the stone that balances a dance between the grass and sky." With Sascha Feinstein, Komunyakaa has edited several anthologies devoted to "jazz poetry." He was the guest editor of *The Best American Poetry 2003*.

Tu Do Street

Music divides the evening.
I close my eyes & can see
men drawing lines in the dust.
America pushes through the membrane
of mist & smoke, & I'm a small boy
again in Bogalusa. *White Only*
signs & Hank Snow. But tonight
I walk into a place where bar girls
fade like tropical birds. When
I order a beer, the mama-san
behind the counter acts as if she
can't understand, while her eyes
skirt each white face, as Hank Williams
calls from the psychedelic jukebox.
We have played Judas where
only machine-gun fire brings us
together. Down the street

black GIs hold to their turf also.
An off-limits sign pulls me
deeper into alleys, as I look
for a softness behind these voices
wounded by their beauty & war.
Back in the bush at Dak To
& Khe Sanh, we fought
the brothers of these women
we now run to hold in our arms.
There's more than a nation
inside us, as black & white
soldiers touch the same lovers
minutes apart, tasting
each other's breath,
without knowing these rooms
run into each other like tunnels
leading to the underworld.

1988

We Never Know

He danced with tall grass
for a moment, like he was swaying
with a woman. Our gun barrels
glowed white-hot.
When I got to him,
a blue halo
of flies had already claimed him.
I pulled the crumbled photograph
from his fingers.
There's no other way
to say this: I fell in love.
The morning cleared again,
except for a distant mortar
& somewhere choppers taking off.
I slid the wallet into his pocket
& turned him over, so he wouldn't be
kissing the ground.

1988

Thanks

Thanks for the tree
between me & a sniper's bullet.
I don't know what made the grass

sway seconds before the Viet Cong
raised his soundless rifle.
Some voice always followed,
telling me which foot
to put down first.
Thanks for deflecting the ricochet
against that anarchy of dusk.
I was back in San Francisco
wrapped up in a woman's wild colors,
causing some dark bird's love call
to be shattered by daylight
when my hands reached up
& pulled a branch away
from my face. Thanks
for the vague white flower
that pointed to the gleaming metal
reflecting how it is to be broken
like mist over the grass,
as we played some deadly
game for blind gods.
What made me spot the monarch
writhing on a single thread
tied to a farmer's gate,
holding the day together
like an unfingered guitar string,
is beyond me. Maybe the hills
grew weary & leaned a little in the heat.
Again, thanks for the dud
hand grenade tossed at my feet
outside Chu Lai. I'm still
falling through its silence.
I don't know why the intrepid
sun touched the bayonet,
but I know that something
stood among those lost trees
& moved only when I moved.

1988

Facing It

My black face fades,
hiding inside the black granite.
I said I wouldn't,
dammit: No tears.
I'm stone. I'm flesh.
My clouded reflection eyes me
like a bird of prey, the profile of night

slanted against morning. I turn
this way — the stone lets me go.
I turn that way — I'm inside
the Vietnam Veterans Memorial
again, depending on the light
to make a difference.
I go down the 58,022 names,
half-expecting to find
my own in letters like smoke.
I touch the name Andrew Johnson;
I see the booby trap's white flash.
Names shimmer on a woman's blouse
but when she walks away
the names stay on the wall.
Brushstrokes flash, a red bird's
wings cutting across my stare.
The sky. A plane in the sky.
A white vet's image floats
closer to me, then his pale eyes
look through mine. I'm a window.
He's lost his right arm
inside the stone. In the black mirror
a woman's trying to erase names:
No, she's brushing a boy's hair.

1988

No-Good Blues

I

I try to hide in Proust,
Mallarme, & Camus,
but the no-good blues
come looking for me. Yeah,
come sliding in like good love
on a tongue of grease & sham,
built up from the ground.
I used to think a super-8 gearbox
did the job, that a five-hundred-dollar suit
would keep me out of Robert Johnson's
shoes. I rhyme Baudelaire
with Apollinaire, hurting
to get beyond crossroads & goofer
dust, outrunning a twelve-bar
pulsebeat. But I pick up
a hitchhiker outside Jackson.
Tasseled boots & skin-tight
jeans. You know the rest.

II

I spend winter days
with Monet, seduced
by his light. But the no-good
blues come looking for me.
It takes at least a year
to erase a scar
on a man's heart. I come home nights
drunk, the couple next door
to keep me company, their voices
undulating through my bedroom wall.
One evening I turn a corner
& step inside Bearden's *Uptown*
Sunday Night Session. Faces
Armstrong blew from his horn
still hanging around the Royal Gardens — all
in a few strokes, & she suddenly leans out of
a candy-apple green door & says,
"Are you from Tougaloo?"

III

At The Napoleon House
Beethoven's *Fifth* draws shadows
from the walls, & the no-good blues
come looking for me. She's here,
her left hand on my knee.
I notice a big sign
across the street that says
The Slave Exchange.
She scoots her chair closer.
I can't see betrayal
& arsenic in Napoleon's hair —
they wanted their dying emperor
under the Crescent City's
Double Scorpio. But nothing
can subdue these African voices
between the building's false floors,
this secret song from the soil
left hidden under my skin.

IV

Working swing shift at McGraw-
Edison, I shoot screws
into cooler cabinets as if I were born
to do it. But the no-good blues come
looking for me. She's from Veracruz,
& never wears dead colors of the factory,
still in Frida Kahlo's world of monkeys.
She's a bird in the caged air.

The machines are bolted down
to the concrete floor,
everything moves with the same big
rhythm Mingus could get out of
a group. Humming the syncopation
of punch presses & conveyer belts,
work grows into our dance
when the foreman
hits the speed-up button
for a one-dollar bonus.

V

My hands are white
with chalk at The Emporium
in Colorado Springs, but the no-good
blues come looking for me. I miscue
when I look up & see sunlight
slanting through her dress
at the back door. That shot
costs me fifty bucks.
I let the stick glide along the V
of two fingers, knowing men who
wager their first born to conquer
snowy roller coasters & myths.
I look up, just when
the faith drains out of
my right hand. It isn't
a loose rack. But more like —
well, I know I'm in trouble
when she sinks her first ball.

VI

I'm cornered at Birdland
like a two-headed man hexing
himself. But the no-good blues
come looking for me. A prayer
holds me in place,
balancing this sequinned
constellation. I've hopped boxcars
& thirteen state lines to where
she stands like Ma Rainey.
Gold tooth & satin. Rotgut
& God Almighty. Moonlight
wrestling a Texas-jack.
A meteor of desire burns
my last plea to ash. Blues
don't care how many tribulations
you lay at my feet, I'll go

with you if you promise
to bring me home to Mercy.

1998

Troubling the Water

As if that night
  on Fire Island
    never happened — the dune

buggy that cut
  like a scythe of moonlight
    across the sand — I see

Frank O'Hara
  with Mapplethorpe's
    book of photographs.

He whistles "Lover
  Man" beneath his breath,
    nudging that fearful

40th year into the background,
  behind those white waves
    of sand. A quick

lunch at Moriarty's
  with someone called LeRoi,
    one of the sixty best friends

in the city. He's hurting
  to weigh Melville's concept
    of evil against Henry

James. That woman begging
  a nickel has multiplied
    a hundredfold since

he last walked past the House
  of Seagram. They speak
    of Miles Davis

clubbed twelve times
  outside Birdland by a cop,
  & Frank flips through pages

of Mapplethorpe as if searching

for something to illustrate
  the cop's real fear.

A dog for the exotic —
  is this what he meant?
    The word Nubian

takes me to monuments
  in Upper Egypt, not
    the "kiss of birds

at the end of the penis"
  singing in the heart
    of America. Julie Harris

merges with images of Bob Love
  till *East of Eden* is
    a compendium of light

& dark. Is this O'Hara's
  Negritude? The phallic temple
    throbs like someone

breathing on calla lilies
  to open them: Leda's
    room of startled mouths.

2004

Susan Mitchell (b. 1947)

Susan Mitchell grew up in New York City and was educated at Wellesley College. Of "Havana Birth," she has written that "though the specific event the poem dramatizes is the Cuban revolution, I imagine the speaker as someone who, on entering adolescence, detaches herself from the narrow interests of her own socioeconomic group to identify with the larger interests of humanity. So the poem found its own definition of birth, not only as freeing oneself from the mother, but more important, as the struggle to enter the world."

Havana Birth

Off Havana the ocean is green this morning
of my birth. The conchers clean their knives on leather
straps and watch the sky while three couples
who have been dancing on the deck of a ship

in the harbor, the old harbor of the fifties, kiss
each other's cheeks and call it a night.

On a green velour sofa five dresses wait
to be fitted. The seamstress kneeling at Mother's feet
has no idea I am about to be born. Mother
pats her stomach which is flat
as the lace mats on the dressmaker's table. She thinks
I'm playing in my room. But as usual, she's wrong.

I'm about to be born in a park in Havana. Oh,
this is important, everything in the dressmaker's house
is furred like a cat. And Havana leans right up
against the windows. In the park, the air
is chocolate, the sweet breath of a man
smoking an expensive cigar. The grass

is drinkable, dazzling, white. In a moment
I'll get up from a bench, lured
by a flock of pigeons, lazily sipping the same syrupy
music through a straw.
Mother is so ignorant, she thinks
I'm rolled like a ball of yarn under the bed. What

does she know of how I got trapped in my life?
She thinks it's all behind her, the bloody
sheets, the mirror in the ceiling
where I opened such a sudden furious blue, her eyes
bruised shut like mine. The pigeon's eyes
are orange, unblinking, a doll's. Mother always said

I wanted to touch everything because
I was a child. But I was younger than that.
I was so young I thought whatever I
wanted, the world wanted too. Workers
in the fields wanted the glint of sun on their machetes.
Sugarcane came naturally sweet, you

had only to lick the earth where it grew.
The music I heard each night outside
my window lived in the mouth of a bird. I was so young
I thought it was easy as walking
into the ocean which always had room
for my body. So when I held out my hands

I expected the pigeon to float between them
like a blossom, dusting my fingers with the manna
of its wings. But the world is wily, and doesn't want
to be held for long, which is why

as my hands reached out, workers lay down
their machetes and left the fields, which is why

a prostitute in a little *calle* of Havana dreamed
the world was a peach and flicked
open a knife. And Mother, startled, shook
out a dress with big pigeons splashed like dirt
across the front, as if she had fallen
chasing after me in the rain. But what could I do?

I was about to be born, I was about to have
my hair combed into the new music
everyone was singing. The dressmaker sang it, her mouth
filled with pins. The butcher sang it and wiped
blood on his apron. Mother sang and thought her body
was leaving her body. And when I tried

I was so young the music beat right
through me, which is how the pigeon got away.
The song the world sings day after day
isn't made of feathers, and the song a bird pours
itself into is tough as a branch
growing with the singer and the singer's delight.

1990

MOLLY PEACOCK (b. 1947)

Molly Peacock was born in Buffalo, New York. Her books of poetry include *Cornucopia: New and Selected Poems* (2002) and several prose works including *How to Read a Poem and Start a Poetry Circle* (1999) and a memoir, *Paradise, Piece by Piece* (1998). In her tenure as president of the Poetry Society of America from 1989 to 1994, the organization initiated its successful "Poetry in Motion" campaign to put poems on placards in New York City subway cars and buses. "One of the pleasures of being a poet at the end of the twentieth century," she notes, "is writing about a subject that has existed in its richness since the beginning of the species but has until now been little found in literature: female sexuality."

The Lull

The possum lay on the tracks fully dead.
I'm the kind of person who stops to look.
It was big and white with flies on its head,
a thick healthy hairless tail, and strong, hooked
nails on its racoon-like feet. It was a full-
grown possum. It was sturdy and adult.
Only its head was smashed. In the lull

that it took to look, you took the time to insult
the corpse, the flies, the world, the fact that we were
traipsing in our dress shoes down the railroad tracks.
"That's disgusting." You said that. Dreams, brains, fur
and guts: what we are. That's my bargain, the Pax
Peacock, with the world. Look hard, life's soft. Life's cache
is flesh, flesh, and flesh.

1984

Next Afternoon

The phlox is having fun, the purple phlox
is having fun, peonies are having fun,
the car is bouncing down the road, a box
of pansies overturns, the fox kit is having fun
catching bugs in the hay in the field
beyond the irises' purple yield
beyond the stream as the muffler warbles
when the car bounces down the bridge. And I
had fun, too. And so did you. Sex is a sort
of racing whitish purple at 3 A.M. Why
does love run so far to be near? No retort.
You're not here. The day's fun is a soft but clear
violet violence of were and we're.

1984

Buffalo

Many times I wait there for my father,
in parking lots of bars or in the bars
themselves, drinking a cherry Coke, Father
joking with a bartender who ignores
him, except to take the orders. I think
of the horrible discipline of bartenders,
and how they must feel to serve, how some shrink
from any conversation to endure
the serving, serving, serving of disease.
I think I would be one of these, eternally
hunched around myself, turning to appease
monosyllabically in the dimness. To flee
enforced darkness in the afternoon
wasn't possible, where was I to go?
Home was too far to walk to, my balloon,
wrinkling in the front seat in the cold, too
awful to go out and play with. Many

times I wait there for Daddy, stupefied
with helpless rage. *Looks old for her age*, any
one of the bartenders said. Outside, the wide
endlessly horizontal vista raged
with sun and snow: it was Buffalo, gleaming
below Great Lakes. Behind bar blinds we were caged,
some motes of sunlight cathedrally beaming.

1989

Bob Perelman (b. 1947)

Bob Perelman was born in Youngstown, Ohio. He is frequently identified as a Language poet. He wrote "Chronic Meanings" on hearing the news that a friend had contracted AIDS. About the method of the poem, each line or sentence ending after five words, Perelman commented that the poem was an attempt "to see what happened to meaning as it was interrupted" in the way that death interrupts a life. "I wanted to feel what real life, conventional articulation felt like when it was halted in the middle."

Chronic Meanings

for Lee Hickman

The single fact is matter.
Five words can say only.
Black sky at night, reasonably.
I am, the irrational residue.

Blown up chain link fence.
Next morning stronger than ever.
Midnight the pain is almost.
The train seems practically expressive.

A story familiar as a.
Society has broken into bands.
The nineteenth century was sure.
Characters in the withering capital.

The heroic figure straddled the.
The clouds enveloped the tallest.
Tens of thousands of drops.
The monster struggled with Milton.

On our wedding night I.
The sorrow burned deeper than.

Grimly I pursued what violence.
A trap, a catch, a.

Fans stand up, yelling their.
Lights go off in houses.
A fictional look, not quite.
To be able to talk.

The coffee sounds intriguing but.
She put her cards on.
What had been comfortable subjectivity.
The lesson we can each.

Not enough time to thoroughly.
Structure announces structure and takes.
He caught his breath in.
The vista disclosed no immediate.

Alone with a pun in.
The clock face and the.
Rock of ages, a modern.
I think I had better.

Now this particular mall seemed.
The bag of groceries had.
Whether a biographical junkheap or.
In no sense do I.

These fields make me feel.
Mount Rushmore in a sonnet.
Some in the party tried.
So it's not as if.

That always happened until one.
She spread her arms and.
The sky if anything grew.
Which left a lot of.

No one could help it.
I ran farther than I.
That wasn't a good one.
Now put down your pencils.

They won't pull that over.
Standing up to the Empire.
Stop it, screaming in a.
The smell of pine needles.

Economics is not my strong.
Until one of us reads.
I took a breath, then.
The singular heroic vision, unilaterally.

Voices imitate the very words.
Bed was one place where.
A personal life, a toaster.
Memorized experience can't be completely.

The impossibility of the simplest.
So shut the fucking thing.
Now I've gone and put.
But that makes the world.

The point I am trying.
Like a cartoon worm on.
A physical mouth without speech.
If taken to an extreme.

The phone is for someone.
The next second it seemed.
But did that really mean.
Yet Los Angeles is full.

Naturally enough I turn to.
Some things are reversible, some.
You don't have that choice.
I'm going to Jo's for.

Now I've heard everything, he.
One time when I used.
The amount of dissatisfaction involved.
The weather isn't all it's.

You'd think people would have.
Or that they would invent.
At least if the emotional.
The presence of an illusion.

Symbiosis of home and prison.
Then, having become superfluous, time.
One has to give to.
Taste: the first and last.

I remember the look in.
It was the first time.
Some gorgeous swelling feeling that.
Success which owes its fortune.

Come what may it can't.
There are a number of.
But there is only one.
That's why I want to.

1993

DAVID SHAPIRO (b. 1947)

David Shapiro was born in Newark, New Jersey. A child prodigy as a violinist, he wrote "Canticle" at the age of fourteen, "Giants" at fifteen, and "For the Princess Hello" as a Columbia undergraduate. His first book of poems, *January*, appeared in 1965 and was followed by *Poems from Deal* four years later. He has subsequently published many poetry collections as well as monographs on such artists as Piet Mondrian, Jasper Johns, and Jim Dine. He has written that "paint was invented to represent the flesh. And poetry, to represent desire."

Canticle

I

I was on a white coast once.
My father was with me on his head.
I said:
Father, father, I can't fall down.
I was born for the sun and the moon.

I looked at the clouds
and all the clouds were mounting.
My friends made a blue ring.
O we hung down with the birds.

II

I loved the snow
when the summer ran away.
Once I said:

Cricket, cricket, aren't you afraid
that you're really too loud ?
He said:

David,
I don't think so.

III

Monstrous night!

I want light now! now!
I want those great stars again!
I want to know
why I keep asking my father
what he's doing on that shore.
What is he doing, anyway ?
Why isn't he over here?

I saw the Red Bird too.
But where's its Wing?

I want to tell my father what I saw:
That Bird is full of fear.

1965

Giants

Giants are much too beautiful.
They live in a house called bigger dimensions
They never suffer from delusions of grandeur
and I have met many giants and this is always true
A giant will always pity you

Still, giants sleep with their eyes on their business
which mainly now is the killing of tourists
the flow is getting smaller since the end of the summer
the fall of leaves keeps many customers away
still, I could never say goodbye
to all my friends among the giants
and they have frightened all my enemies away.

The giants know that I'll be strong some day
for I have planned one insuperable attack
against this habit of closing my eyes when I sleep.
because I want to hold on to light as long as I can
and because I want to kiss the small of your back.

1965

For the Princess Hello

Bridges that, a little because of absence,
Have like circuses changed their sites,
And the wood rots due to circumstance,
And, I believe, because of their engagement

To light, and something like light,
Whose voltage will run dry,
These bridges come like all bridges
To change and be re-painted.

Stone cries when it spans a void,
Wood thinks about the last century,
Both hate each other by custom
And can't contain their mountainous
Duality, like a turkey with two feathers
Pushed by the wind, turning
Into feathers of nothing without sweat:
A turkey's definition of change.

The old bridges faint under caresses,
Discovering the constant in a circle
Around forty-seven plane figures
Which they invented in foreign ports;
The liar and his lie
Win over a racially mixed city!
And these bridges come like all bridges
To change and be re-painted.

It's sweet to follow the trace of a bridge
And get angry without knowing why
Which one of the architects will succeed
In vaulting, character, and facing.
All the days of nine committees
Have been concerned with city bridges!
Now you will see the proof
That each has been re-painted.

Both stone and wooden bridges promise
Elevated above us, to separate
The hardened student from the breaths
Of a young girl, mouth open:
Each conserves the advantage
Of forces despite everything you say
In each of your false languages:
In its turn will be re-painted.

1969

Father Knows Best

It is the old show, but the young son can fly.
He sees pink and blue and red umbrellas in the air.
They teach him how to fly.

Of course the family does not see and has resentments.

One day at a snow party he tries to prove he can fly.
But he only leaps a bit and loses the jumping contest.
Then Father realizes son must enclose but a few electrons
of air in his fist
Then son flies high above the family garage and trees,
branch by branch.

There are no umbrellas, there are only frosty parachutes,
Little angels who instruct him how to fly.
He must not struggle too much with his hands,
Which having practised the violin now dog-paddle in air.

High above the invigorated gulf the air walks down its
own road.
And sister jumps up in a dual column of wind.
Inside, Mother serves breakfast; the bluejay gulps at
the feeding-station.
The family now knows he can fly, but still father knows best.

1973

To My Son

King Oedipus has one eye too many, perhaps. — Hölderlin

I love you so much
I am going to let you kill me.
Pathos your thin arms your
neck your hair rich
without perfume
and your eyes bright as a brooch
You say you will kill me tomorrow
and I believe you
but for now you must sleep
in my arms like a cheat at cards
Five years we have lived together
counting like the Chinese
I fear every narrow road
on which we will eventually meet
But do not banish me so fast, my son
Your clubfoot that I have pierced
is more beautiful, to me, than your mother's breast.

1994

JAMES CUMMINS (b. 1948)

James Cummins was born in Columbus, Ohio. In 1986 he published *The Whole Truth*, a book of sestinas devoted to the cast of characters in the Perry Mason mystery novels and television shows. Richard Howard characterized the book as "a relentless, sometimes goofy, and always graphic sequence wherein the dread concepts of plot and character [are] goaded through the most unyielding formal baffles that occidental poetry has yet devised." The reader might compare the sestina that follows with examples of the form in this anthology by Ezra Pound, Elizabeth Bishop, Anthony Hecht, and Harry Mathews.

Fling

He wanted to tell her the weekend idea was "neat,"
But he kept hearing himself repeat the word "funny."
She named the names of trees, flowers: *sycamore*, *tulip*.
He asked her who did she think she was, Gary Snyder?
Above the car, then over the hotel, the spring moon
Was full, orange. "This isn't just another fling,"

She said suddenly. "Don't dare think it's some fling."
The Jack Daniel's arrived, hers on the rocks, his neat.
"I didn't think that at all." Behind her, the moon
Looked away. She fretted. "I just — I feel funny."
Amazingly, it occurred to him something Gary Snyder
Once said was appropriate. He repeated it. "Tulips,"

She smiled back. "Let's take a walk through the tulips."
Later, they didn't make love. She was shy. Some fling,
He brooded. Did she really think he *liked* Gary Snyder —
That he, too, thought he had it all summed up in a neat
Little package? Funny, he groaned. Worse than funny.
I get it all right for once: drinks, room, even the moon

Cooperates. How often can you count on a spring moon
Slipping through the sycamores, picking out the tulips
In the night air? She should feel romantic, not "funny!"
Lying next to her, he felt so restless, eager to fling
His body atop hers — seeking, yet in control, his need
Ascetic, sensual, yet poised — a suburban Gary Snyder . . .

In the dark, she teased: "Thinking about Gary Snyder?"
Then: "I'm not so shy now." He thought about the moon,
And a Grace Paley character who "liked his pussy neat."
Then she was touching him, needing him, her two lips
Soft flowers, emissaries of her body, softly ruffling
Against him, moving him, so powerfully it wasn't funny . . .

Afterward, they were awkward, shy, trying to be funny.
They couldn't get any more mileage out of Gary Snyder.
"Some fling," he said, and she flung back, "Some fling!"
But mostly they were quiet. Outside, the big yellow moon
Yawned. He made a mental note to send her some tulips.
She stared out the window, thinking about the word "neat."

* * *

He thought of how she'd fling her hair. And the moon . . .
It was *finito*. Next week he got a book by Gary Snyder
In the mail. That was funny. He sent her the tulips.

1997

RACHEL HADAS (b. 1948)

Rachel Hadas was born in New York City, the daughter of Columbia University classics professor Moses Hadas. She majored in classics at Radcliffe and spent four years living in Greece. She lives in Manhattan's Upper West Side, the setting for the two poems included here. In an interview she has likened the self to "a park through which one meanders, always getting home for supper."

The Red Hat

It started before Christmas. Now our son
Officially walks to school alone.
Semi-alone, it's accurate to say:
I or his father track him on the way.
He walks up on the east side of West End,
we on the west side. Glances can extend
(and do) across the street; not eye contact.
Already ties are feeling and not fact.
Straus Park is where these parallel paths part;
he goes alone from there. The watcher's heart
stretches, elastic in its love and fear,
toward him as we see him disappear,
striding briskly. Where two weeks ago,
holding a hand, he'd dawdle, dreamy, slow,
he now is hustled forward by the pull
of something far more powerful than school.

The mornings we turn back to are no more
than forty minutes longer than before,
but they feel vastly different — flimsy, strange,
wavering in the eddies of this change,

empty, unanchored, perilously light
since the red hat vanished from our sight.

1995

Riverside Park

I've always loved the autumn. Trees bleed amber,
the sun moves south to sink into the river.
For several of these seasons you were here —
if not precisely this noon, bench, or air,
still in New York, October, and inside
my heart. Our timing's trick
was elegantly simple: although sick,
you had not yet died.

How could I resist the chance to share
(shyly at first; more freely the last year)
fusses, ideas, encounters, daily weather?
So for a space we took life in together
reciprocally, since what came your way
you passed along to me.
Experience doubled and then halved kept giving
itself to both as long as both were living.

I pause to watch the afternoon's red ray
advance another notch. Across the way
a mother tends her toddler, and a pair
of strolling lovers vanish in the glare
flung from the river by the westering sun.
I can hardly claim to be alone.
Nevertheless, of all whom autumn's new
russet brocades are draping, none is you.

1995

LAWRENCE JOSEPH (b. 1948)

Lawrence Joseph was born in Detroit, the grandson of Lebanese and Syrian Catholic immigrants. His family operated a grocery store in a Detroit neighborhood that was torched in the race riots of the summer of 1967. Joseph studied literature at the University of Michigan and at Cambridge University in England, then attended law school in Ann Arbor. In 1981 he moved to New York City and worked on securities fraud, bankruptcy, and products liability litigation for the law firm of Shearman and Sterling. He wrote his prose book *Lawyerland* (1997) about his experiences as a practicing attorney in New York City. Joseph's poetry is committed to what he calls the "poetry of reality."

Some Sort of Chronicler I Am

Some sort of chronicler I am, mixing
emotional perceptions and digressions,

choler, melancholy, a sanguine view.
Through a transparent eye, the need, sometimes,

to see everything simultaneously
— strange need to confront everyone

with equal respect. Although the citizen
across the aisle on the Number Three

subway doesn't appreciate my respect.
Look at his eyes — both of them popping

from injections of essence of poppy;
listen to his voice bordering on a shrill.

His declaration: he's a victim of acquired
immune deficiency syndrome. His addiction

he acquired during the Indo-Chinese war.
Specified "underclass" by the Department of Labor

— he's underclass, all right: no class
if you're perpetually diseased and poor.

Named "blessed" by one of our Parnassians
known to make the egotistical sublime

— blessed, indeed; he's definitely blessed.
His wounds open, here, on the surface:

you might say he's shrieking his stigmata.
I know — you'd prefer I change the subject

(I know how to change the subject).
Battery Park's atmosphere changes

mists in which two children play and scratch
like a couple of kittens until the green

layers of light cover them completely,
a sense of anguished fulfillment arising

without me, beauty needled into awareness
without me, beauty always present in

what happened that instant her silhouette
moved across the wall, magnified sounds

her blouse made scraped against her skin
— workers, boarded storefronts, limousines

with tinted windows, windows with iron bars,
lace-patterned legs, someone without legs,

merged within the metathetical imagination
we're all part of, no matter how personal

we think we are. Has anyone considered
during the depression of 1921

Carlos Williams felt a physician's pain,
vowed to maintain the most compressed

expression of perceptions and ardors
— intrinsic, undulant, physical movement —

revealed in the speech he heard around him
(dynamization of emotions into imagined

form as a reality in itself).
Wallace Stevens — remember his work

covered high-risk losses — knowingly chose
during the bank closings of early '33

to suspend his grief between social planes
he'd transpose into thoughts, figures, colors

— you don't think he saw the woman beneath
golden clouds tortured by destitution,

fear too naked for her own shadow's shape?
In 1944, an Alsatian who composed

poems in French and in German, exiled
for fear of death in a state-created camp —

his eye structure, by law, defined as "Jewish" —
sensed the gist. Diagnosed with leukemia,

Yvan Goll gave the name Lackawanna
Manahatta to our metropolis — Manahatta

locked in Judgment's pregnant days, he sang,
Lackawanna of pregnant nights and sulphurous

pheasant mortality riddled with light
lying dormant in a shock of blond hair

half made of telephones, half made of tears.
The heavy changes of the light — I know.

Faint sliver of new moon and distant Mars
glow through to Lackawanna Manahatta.

Above a street in the lower Nineties
several leaves from an old ginkgo tree

twist through blackish red on golden air
outside a fashionable bistro where a man

with medals worn across a tailor-cut suit
chides a becoming woman half his age.

"From now on, my dear," he says with authority,
"from now on it's every man for himself."

1993

HEATHER MCHUGH (b. 1948)

Heather McHugh was born in San Diego, California. McHugh, who sometimes elevates word-play into a species of philosophical meditation, has affinities with the "metaphysical" poets of the seventeenth century. "According to a bon mot of La Rochefoucauld (a shrewd late seventeenth-century figure himself), the true use of speech is to conceal our thoughts," McHugh has written. "One might equally say, since Vesalius, that the true use of the flesh is to conceal our nakedness. A poem's content no less than its form can be a cover: *what* it means may reveal less than *how* it is seen *through*."

Form

We were wrong to think
form a frame, a still

shot of the late
beloved, or the pot thrown
around water. We wanted
to hold what we had.

But the clay contains
the breaking, and the man
is dead — the scrapbook
has him — and the form of life
is a motion. So from all this
sadness, the bed being touched,

the mirror being filled,
we learn what carrying on
is for. We move, we are moved.
It runs in the family.
For the life of us
we cannot stand to stay.

1981

I Knew I'd Sing

A few sashay, a few finagle.
Some make whoopee, some
make good. But most make
diddly-squat. I tell you this

is what I love about
America — the words it puts
in my mouth, the mouth where once
my mother rubbed

a word away with soap. The word
was *cunt*. She stuck that bar
of family-size in there
until there was no hole to speak of,

so she hoped. But still
I'm full of it — the cunt,
the prick, short u, short i,
the words that stood

for her and him. I loved the thing
they must have done, the love they must
have made, to make
an example of me. After my lunch of Ivory I said

vagina for a day or two, but knew
from that day forth which word
struck home like sex itself. I knew
when I was big I'd sing

a song in praise of cunt — I'd want
to keep my word, the one with teeth in it.
Forevermore (and even after I was raised) I swore

nothing — but nothing — would be beneath me.

1987

ID

Did I? Is it?
Hit below the belt, the ego

doesn't know the difference,
KO, OK, ego can't
identify its problem, can't
identify itself. O cogito,

it says, O sum.
And then, in its cape,

freed from the pay phone, who
says "I have come," and in the name

of whom? Somebody's
living in here, deep inside, but still

the elevator's stuck, the clock
is slow, the news is yellow

in the hallway stack. The ego's
middle name is mud. There's trouble in 4A and now

there's trouble in 2B; the plumbing
leaks, a hole is in the head, and tell me

how did all this happen?
Is the super dead?

1988

What He Thought

for Fabbio Doplicher

We were supposed to do a job in Italy
and, full of our feeling for
ourselves (our sense of being
Poets from America) we went
from Rome to Fano, met
the mayor, mulled
a couple matters over (what's
cheap date, they asked us; what's
flat drink). Among Italian literati

we could recognize our counterparts:
the academic, the apologist,
the arrogant, the amorous,
the brazen and the glib — and there was one

administrator (the conservative), in suit
of regulation gray, who like a good tour guide
with measured pace and uninflected tone narrated
sights and histories the hired van hauled us past.
Of all, he was most politic and least poetic,
so it seemed. Our last few days in Rome
(when all but three of the New World Bards had flown)
I found a book of poems this
unprepossessing one had written: it was there
in the *pensione* room (a room he'd recommended)
where it must have been abandoned by
the German visitor (was there a bus of *them*?)
to whom he had inscribed and dated it a month before.
I couldn't read Italian, either, so I put the book
back into the wardrobe's dark. We last Americans

were due to leave tomorrow. For our parting evening then
our host chose something in a family restaurant, and there
we sat and chatted, sat and chewed,
till, sensible it was our last
big chance to be poetic, make
our mark, one of us asked
"What's poetry?
Is it the fruits and vegetables and
marketplace of Campo dei Fiori, or
the statue there?" Because I was

the glib one, I identified the answer
instantly, I didn't have to think — "The truth
is both, it's both," I blurted out. But that

was easy. That was easiest to say. What followed
taught me something about difficulty,
for our underestimated host spoke out,
all of a sudden, with a rising passion, and he said:

The statue represents Giordano Bruno,
brought to be burned in the public square
because of his offense against
authority, which is to say
the Church. His crime was his belief
the universe does not revolve around
the human being: God is no
fixed point or central government, but rather is
poured in waves through all things. All things
move. "If God is not the soul itself, He is
the soul of the soul of the world." Such was
his heresy. The day they brought him
forth to die, they feared he might
incite the crowd (the man was famous
for his eloquence). And so his captors
placed upon his face
an iron mask, in which

he could not speak. That's
how they burned him. That is how
he died: without a word, in front
of everyone.
                    And poetry —
                                        (we'd all
put down our forks by now, to listen to
the man in gray; he went on
softly) —
                    poetry is what

he thought, but did not say.

1994

LYNN EMANUEL (b. 1949)

Lynn Emanuel was born in Mt. Kisco, New York, and was educated at Bennington College, the City College of New York (where she studied with Adrienne Rich), and the University of Iowa. She has written a sequence of "film noir" poems and explained that one attraction of crime movies is that their recurrent conventions seem to function like the returning end words in a sestina: plot elements that act like formal devices. To communicate the essence of noir, one can do worse than quote Emanuel's "At the Ritz," which specifies that the indispensable ingredients of noir include blondes, sarcasm, "babeness," and money.

Of Your Father's Indiscretions and the Train to California

One summer he stole the jade buttons
Sewn like peas down Aunt Ora's dress
And you, who loved that trail of noise and darkness
Hauling itself across the horizon,
Moths spiraling in the big lamps,
Loved the oily couplings and the women's round hats
Haunting all the windows
And the way he held you on his knee like a ventriloquist
Discussing the lush push of grass against the tree's roots
Or a certain crookedness in the trunk.
Now everything is clearer.
Now when the train pulls away from the station
And the landscape begins to come around, distant and yet
  familiar,
That odd crease of yellow light
Or the woods' vague sweep framed in the window forever
Remind you of the year you were locked up at the Hotel
  Fiesta.
While father went out with fast black minks.
And how wonderful it was
When he was narrow as a hat pin in this tux
And to have come all that way on his good looks.
How wonderful to have discovered lust
And know that one day you would be on its agenda
Like the woman who drank and walked naked through
  the house
In her black hat, the one you used to watch
Through a stammer in the drapes.
In that small town of cold hotels, you were the girl
  in the dress,
Red as a house burning down.

1984

Blonde Bombshell

Love is boring and passé, all the old baggage,
the bloody bric-a-brac, the bad, the gothic,
retrograde, obscurantist hum and drum of it
needs to be swept away. So, night after night,
we sit in the dark of the Roxy beside grandmothers
with their shanks tied up in the tourniquets
of rolled stockings and open ourselves, like earth

to rain, to the blue fire of the movie screen
where love surrenders suddenly to gangsters
and their cuties. There in the narrow,
mote-filled finger of light, is a blonde
so blond, so blinding, she is a blizzard, a huge
spook, and lights up like the sun the audience
in its galoshes. She bulges like a deuce coupe.
When we see her we say good-bye to Kansas.
She is everything spare, cool, and clean,
like a gas station on a dark night or the cold
dependable light of rage coming in on schedule like a bus.

1988

At The Ritz

How and where they met is cause for speculation.
All up and down the avenue, blondes — lacquered
in intelligence, sarcasm, babeness, and money —
gossiped into the ears of investment bankers
so impeccably groomed you could see them
checking their Windsor knots in the chrome
toes of their wing tip shoes.

He was so handsome that when he walked in
the room just rearranged its axis from south
to north, the scene came to a halt and hovered
as though the weight of him had tilted the planet
and everything was beginning a slow slide off.
Martinis tremble in their fragile glasses.
Against her mink a gardenia erupts in a Vesuvius

of white. These two haven't met. Until they do,
her job will be to pout beside her wealthy father who,
weighted with an enormous white mustache
(what brilliance: in this scene, hair is money),
is lying in the sedate and lacquered gleam of the coffin.
Above his stern but kindly visage some pricey
lilies droop. He's dead; she sulks.

But this is all a long way off. Now we're
at the Ritz where, as we've seen, the joint's atremble,
the tablecloths on the table so white, so limp,
they look like they have fainted. When he walks in,
she says, there is no here here, let's go down the street
to Izzy's. The street's grown quiet. Not even the moon
can move. Its grainy bulk, stolid and sinister at once,

won't budge. Behind them — the pale, small stares of the hotel
lobby, a taxi hauls a smudge of exhaust into place,
and a town staggers to its feet as he follows her like a prisoner
into the sentence of this story.

1999

KATHA POLLITT (b. 1949)

Katha Pollitt was born in New York City and educated at Radcliffe College, where she studied with Elizabeth Bishop, and at Columbia University. A noted feminist author, she is an associate editor of the *Nation*, to which she contributes a regular column, "Subject to Debate." A gathering of her columns was published as *Reasonable Creatures* in 1994. In her poem "Mind-Body Problem," the metaphor equating the relations between mind and body to "Tony Curtis / and Sidney Poitier fleeing handcuffed together" is a reference to Stanley Kramer's 1958 movie *The Defiant Ones*, in which a white and a black convict are shackled together as they flee from the police in the segregationist South.

Failure

You'd never set foot in this part of town before,
so how could the landlady wink as if she recognized you?
Still, it's uncanny, the way when you open the door
to your room the scratched formica bureau and table
give off a gleam of welcome, the foldaway bed
sags happily into itself like an old friend,
and look, the previous tenant has considerately
left you his whole library: *Ferns of the World*
and *How to Avoid Probate*. Even the water stain
spreading on the ceiling has your profile.

Well, never mind. Unpack your suitcase, put
boric acid out for the roaches. Here
too there are plenty of tears for things, probably, but
don't think about that just now. Outside your window
ailanthus trees, bringing you an important message
about the nutritive properties of garbage,
wave their arms for attention, third-world raiders,
scrawny, tough, your future if you're lucky.

1982

Mind-Body Problem

When I think of my youth I feel sorry not for myself
but for my body. It was so direct
and simple, so rational in its desires,
wanting to be touched the way an otter
loves water, the way a giraffe
wants to amble the edge of the forest, nuzzling
the tender leaves at the tops of the trees. It seems
unfair, somehow, that my body had to suffer
because I, by which I mean my mind, was saddled
with certain unfortunate high-minded romantic notions
that made me tyrannize and patronize it
like a cruel medieval baron, or an ambitious
English-professor husband ashamed of his wife —
her love of sad movies, her budget casseroles
and regional vowels. Perhaps
my body would have liked to make some of our dates,
to come home at four in the morning and answer my scowl
with "None of your business!" Perhaps
it would have liked more presents: silks, mascaras.
If we had had a more democratic arrangement
we might even have come, despite our different backgrounds,
to a grudging respect for each other, like Tony Curtis
and Sidney Poitier fleeing handcuffed together
instead of the current curious shift of power
in which I find I am being reluctantly
dragged along by my body as though by some
swift and powerful dog. How eagerly
it plunges ahead, not stopping for anything,
as though it knows exactly where we are going.

2000

CHARLES BERNSTEIN (b. 1950)

The Harvard-educated Charles Bernstein was born in New York City. A leading figure of the Language poets, he is a prolific theorist and poet and has a comic flair that suggests affinities with the "New York school." In *My Way: Speeches and Poems* (1999), from which the following selection is taken, Bernstein has a poker-faced essay arguing that a poem needs to have water in it if it is to stand any chance of being published in the *New Yorker.*

Solidarity Is the Name We Give to What We Cannot Hold

I am a nude formalist poet, a sprung
syntax poet, a multitrack poet, a
wondering poet, a social expressionist
poet, a Baroque poet, a constructivist poet,
an ideolectical poet. I am a New York poet in
California, a San Francisco poet on
the Lower East Side, an Objectivist poet
in Royaumont, a surrealist poet in Jersey,
a Dada poet in Harvard Square,
a zaum poet in Brooklyn, a merz poet
in Iowa, a cubo-futurist poet in Central Park.
I am a Buffalo poet in Providence, a London
poet in Cambridge, a Kootenay School
of Writing poet in Montreal, a local poet
in Honolulu.
I am a leftist poet in my armchair
and an existential poet on the street;
an insider poet among my friends,
an outsider poet in midtown.
I am a serial poet, a paratactic poet, a
disjunctive poet, a discombobulating poet,
a montage poet, a collage poet, a hypertextual
poet, a nonlinear poet, an abstract poet,
a nonrepresentational poet, a process poet,
a polydiscourse poet, a conceptual poet.
I am a vernacular poet, a talk poet, a dialect
poet, a heteroglossic poet, a slang poet, a
demotic poet, a punning poet, a comic poet.
I am an iambic poet I am,
a dactylic poet, a tetrameter poet,
an anapestic poet.
I am a capitalist poet in Leningrad
and a socialist poet in St. Petersburg;
a bourgeois poet at Zabar's, a union poet
in Albany; an elitist poet on TV,
a political poet on the radio.
I am a fraudulent poet, an incomprehensible poet, a degenerate
poet, an incompetent poet, an indecorous poet, a crude poet,
an incoherent poet, a flat-footed poet, a disruptive poet, a
fragmenting poet, a contradictory poet, a self-imploding poet,
a conspiratorial poet, an ungainly poet, an anti-dogmatic poet,
an infantile poet, a theoretical poet, an awkward poet, a sissy
poet, an egghead poet, a perverse poet, a clumsy poet,
a cacophonous poet, a vulgar poet, a warped
poet, a silly poet, a queer poet, an
erratic poet, an erroneous poet, an anarchic poet,

a cerebral poet, an unruly poet,
an emotional poet, a (no) nonsense poet. I am a language
poet wherever people try to limit the modes of
expression or nonexpression. I am an experimental poet
to those who value craft over interrogation, an
avant-garde poet to those who see the future
in the present. I am a Jewish poet hiding in the shadow
of my great-grandfather and great-grandmother.
I am a difficult poet in Kent, a visual poet in
Cleveland, a sound poet in Cincinnati.
I am a modernist poet to postmodernists and a postmodern poet
to modernists. I am a book artist in Minneapolis
and a language artist in Del Mar.
I am a lyric poet in Spokane, an analytic
poet in South Bend, a narrative poet
in Yellow Knife, a realist
poet in Berkeley.
I am an antiabsorptive poet in the morning,
an absorptive poet in the afternoon,
and a sleepy poet at night.
I am a parent poet, a white poet, a man poet, an urban poet, an
angered poet, a sad poet,
an elegiac poet, a raucous poet, a frivolous poet, a detached
poet, a roller-coaster poet, a
volcanic poet, a dark poet, a skeptical poet, an eccentric poet, a
misguided poet, a reflective
poet, a dialectical poet, a polyphonic poet, a hybrid poet, a
wandering poet, an odd poet, a
lost poet, a disobedient poet, a bald poet, a virtual poet.
& I am none of these things,
nothing but the blank wall of my aversions
writ large in disappearing ink —

1999

ANNE CARSON (b. 1950)

Anne Carson was born in Toronto, Canada, the daughter of a banker. She studied Greek and Latin, wrote a doctoral dissertation on Sappho at the University of Toronto, and became a professor of classics at McGill University; she has also taught at the University of Michigan and at Berkeley. Her *Autobiography of Red*, a novel in verse, turns the myth of Geryon and Herakles, monster and slayer, into the story of a boy's struggle with homosexuality during high school. Asked about her preference for "old and battered" things, Carson told her *Paris Review* interviewer that "in surfaces, perfection is less interesting. For instance, a page with a poem on it is less attractive than a page with a poem on it and some tea stains. Because the tea stains add a bit of history." A practicing Catholic, she describes herself as "baffled" rather than "devout," and says, "If God were knowable, why would we believe in him?"

from *The Truth about God*

My Religion

My religion makes no sense
and does not help me
therefore I pursue it.

When we see
how simple it would have been
we will thrash ourselves.

I had a vision
of all the people in the world
who are searching for God

massed in a room
on one side
of a partition

that looks
from the other side
(God's side)

transparent
but we are blind.
Our gestures are blind.

Our blind gestures continue
for some time until finally
from somewhere

on the other side of the partition there we are
looking back at them.
It is far too late.

We see how brokenly
how warily
how ill

our blind gestures
parodied
what God really wanted

(some simple thing).
The thought of it
(this simple thing)

is like a creature
let loose in a room
and battering

to get out.
It batters my soul
with its rifle butt.

By God

Sometimes by night I don't know why
I awake thinking of prepositions.
Perhaps they are clues.

"Since by Man came Death."
I am puzzled to hear that Man is the agent of Death.
Perhaps it means

Man was standing at the curb
and Death came by.
Once I had a dog

would go with anyone.
Perhaps listening for
little by little the first union.

God's Woman

Are you angry at nature? said God to His woman.
Yes I am angry at nature I do not want nature stuck
up between my legs on your pink baton

or ladled out like geography whenever
your buckle needs a lick.
What do you mean *Creation*?

God circled her.
Fire. Time. Fire.
Choose, said God.

God's Mother

She doesn't get to say much in the official biography —
I believe they are out of wine, etc.,
practical things —

watching with one eye as he goes about the world
calling himself The Son Of Man.
Naturalists tell us

that the hatching crow is fed by the male
but when it flies, by the mother:

Love	Fly	Man
Loves	Flies	Mans
Loved	Flew	Manned
Loving	Flying	Manning
Loved	Flown	Woman.

It is what grammarians call a difference of tense and aspect.

God's Justice

In the beginning there were days set aside for various tasks.
On the day He was to create justice
God got involved in making a dragonfly

and lost track of time.
It was about two inches long
with turquoise dots all down its back like Lauren Bacall.

God watched it bend its tiny wire elbows
as it set about cleaning the transparent case of its head.
The eye globes mounted on the case

rotated this way and that
as it polished every angle.
Inside the case

which was glassy black like the windows of a downtown bank
God could see the machinery humming
and He watched the hum

travel all the way down turquoise dots to the end of the tail
and breathe off as light.
Its black wings vibrated in and out.

God's Christ Theory

God had no emotions but wished temporarily
to move in man's mind
as if He did: Christ.

Not passion but compassion.
Com — means "with."
What kind of withness would that be?

Translate it.
I have a friend named Jesus
from Mexico.

His father and grandfather are called Jesus too.
They account me a fool with my questions about salvation.
They say they are saving to move to Los Angeles.

God's List of Liquids

It was a November night of wind.
Leaves tore past the window.
God had the book of life open at PLEASURE

and was holding the pages down with one hand
because of the wind from the door.
For I made their flesh as a sieve

wrote God at the top of the page
and then listed in order:
Alcohol
Blood
Gratitude
Memory
Semen
Song
Tears
Time.

God's Work

Moonlight in the kitchen is a sign of God.
The kind of sadness that is a black suction pipe extracting you
from your own navel and which the Buddhists call

"no mindcover" is a sign of God.
The blind alleys that run alongside human conversation
like lashes are a sign of God.

God's own calmness is a sign of God.
The surprisingly cold smell of potatoes or money.
Solid pieces of silence.

From these diverse signs you can see
how much work remains to do.
Put away your sadness, it is a mantle of work.

1995

CAROLYN FORCHÉ (b. 1950)

Carolyn Forché was born in Detroit. Stanley Kunitz chose her first book, *Gathering the Tribes*, for the Yale Younger Poets series in 1976. Committed to a politically engaged poetics, Forché spent the following year in El Salvador working with the human rights activist Archbishop Oscar Humberto Romero. Her second book, *The Country Between Us* (1982), grew out of her experiences there, and sparked controversy for the overtly political nature of some of its poems. Forché has edited the anthology *Against Forgetting: Twentieth-Century Poetry of Witness* (1993), which she describes as "a symphony of utterance, a living memorial to those who had died and those who survived the horrors of the 20th century."

The Colonel

What you have heard is true. I was in his house. His wife carried a tray of coffee and sugar. His daughter filed her nails, his son went out for the night. There were daily papers, pet dogs, a pistol on the cushion beside him. The moon swung bare on its black cord over the house. On the television was a cop show. It was in English. Broken bottles were embedded in the walls around the house to scoop the kneecaps from a man's legs or cut his hands to lace. On the windows there were gratings like those in liquor stores. We had dinner, rack of lamb, good wine, a gold bell was on the table for calling the maid. The maid brought green mangoes, salt, a type of bread. I was asked how I enjoyed the country. There was a brief commercial in Spanish. His wife took everything away. There was some talk of how difficult it had become to govern. The parrot said hello on the terrace. The colonel told it to shut up, and pushed himself from the table. My friend said to me with his eyes: say nothing. The colonel returned with a sack used to bring groceries home. He spilled many human ears on the table. They were like dried peach halves. There is no other way to say this. He took one of them in his hands, shook it in our faces, dropped it into a water glass. It came alive there. I am tired of fooling around he said. As for the rights of anyone, tell your people they can go fuck themselves. He swept the ears to the floor with his arm and held the last of his wine in the air. Something for your poetry, no? he said. Some of the ears on the floor caught this scrap of his voice. Some of the ears on the floor were pressed to the ground.

1978

DANA GIOIA (b. 1950)

Born in Los Angeles to working-class parents, Dana Gioia graduated from an all-boys Catholic high school, then attended Stanford, studied comparative literature at Harvard, and returned to Stanford for business school. For fifteen years he worked for General Foods, handling the Kool-Aid and Jell-O accounts. He quit business to devote himself full-time to writing and moved with his family to Santa Rosa, California, in 1992. His essay "Can Poetry Matter?" generated considerable comment and controversy when it appeared in the *Atlantic* in 1991. He has written on the New Formalism and is considered one of the leaders of that movement. He became the chairman of the National Endowment for the Arts in February 2003.

The Archbishop

for a famous critic

O do not disturb the Archbishop,
Asleep in his ivory chair.
You must send all the workers away,
Though the church is in need of repair.

His Reverence is tired from preaching
To the halt, and the lame, and the blind.
Their spiritual needs are unsubtle,
Their notions of God unrefined.

The Lord washed the feet of His servants.
"The first shall be last," He advised.
The Archbishop's edition of Matthew
Has that troublesome passage revised.

The Archbishop declines to wear glasses,
So his sense of the world grows dim.
He thinks that the crowds at Masses
Have gathered in honor of him.

In the crypt of the limestone cathedral
A friar recopies St. Mark,
A nun serves stew to a novice,
A choirboy sobs in the dark.

While high in the chancery office
His Reverence studies the glass,
Wondering which of his vestments
Would look best at Palm Sunday Mass.

The saints in their weather-stained niches
Weep as the Vespers are read,

And the beggars sleep on the church steps,
And the orphans retire unfed.

On Easter the Lord is arisen
While the Archbishop breakfasts in bed,
And the humble shall find resurrection,
And the dead shall lie down with the dead.

2001

Summer Storm

We stood on the rented patio
While the party went on inside.
You knew the groom from college.
I was a friend of the bride.

We hugged the brownstone wall behind us
To keep our dress clothes dry
And watched the sudden summer storm
Floodlit against the sky.

The rain was like a waterfall
Of brilliant beaded light,
Cool and silent as the stars
The storm hid from the night.

To my surprise, you took my arm —
A gesture you didn't explain —
And we spoke in whispers, as if we two
Might imitate the rain.

Then suddenly the storm receded
As swiftly as it came.
The doors behind us opened up.
The hostess called your name.

I watched you merge into the group,
Aloof and yet polite.
We didn't speak another word
Except to say good-night.

Why does that evening's memory
Return with this night's storm —
A party twenty years ago,
Its disappointments warm?

There are so many *might-have-beens*,
What-ifs that won't stay buried,

Other cities, other jobs,
Strangers we might have married.

And memory insists on pining
For places it never went,
As if life would be happier
Just by being different.

2001

JORIE GRAHAM (b. 1950)

Born in New York City, Jorie Graham spent her childhood in Rome and studied at the Sorbonne in Paris before she was expelled for participating in the student uprising of 1968. She had also worked on sets of Antonioni films in Rome, an experience that led her to film studies at New York University. Describing Graham's practice of substituting blanks for words at strategic moments (exemplified here in "Orpheus and Eurydice"), Helen Vendler has explained that when Graham "comes to a concept not yet conceivable she leaves a gap in the middle of a sentence." Her poem "Fission" takes place in a movie theater on 22 November 1963, with Stanley Kubrick's *Lolita* on the screen. Graham taught at the Iowa Writers' Workshop for many years and was the guest editor of *The Best American Poetry 1990*. She succeeded Seamus Heaney as the Boylston Professor of Rhetoric at Harvard University.

Orpheus and Eurydice

Up ahead, I know, he felt it stirring in himself already, the glance,
the darting thing in the pile of rocks,

already in him, there, shiny in the rubble, hissing Did you want to remain
completely unharmed? —

the point-of-view darting in him, shiny head in the ash-heap,

hissing Once upon a time, and then Turn now darling give me that look,

that perfect shot, give me that place where I'm erased....

The thing, he must have wondered, could it be put to rest, there, in the
glance,
could it lie back down into the dustiness, giving its outline up?

When we turn to them — limbs, fields, expanses of dust called meadow and
avenue —
will they be freed then to slip back in?

Because you see he could not be married to it anymore, this field with
minutes in it
called woman, its presence in him the thing called

future — could not be married to it anymore, expanse tugging his mind out
into it,
tugging the wanting-to-finish out.

What he dreamed of was this road (as he walked on it), this dustiness,
but without their steps on it, their prints, without
song —

What she dreamed, as she watched him turning with the bend in the road
(can you
understand this?) — what she dreamed

was of disappearing into the seen

not of disappearing, lord, into the real —

And yes she could feel it in him already, up ahead, that wanting-to-turn-and-cast-the-outline-over-her

by his glance,

sealing the edges down,

saying I know you from somewhere darling, don't I,
saying You're the kind of woman who etcetera —

(Now the cypress are swaying) (Now the lake in the distance)
(Now the view-from-above, the aerial attack of *do you
remember?*) —

now the glance reaching her shoreline wanting only to be recalled,
now the glance reaching her shoreline wanting only to be taken in,

(somewhere the castle above the river)

(somewhere you holding this piece of paper)

(what will you do next?) (— feel it beginning?)

now she's raising her eyes, as if pulled from above,

now she's looking back into it, into the poison the beginning,

giving herself to it, looking back into the eyes,

feeling the dry soft grass beneath her feet for the first time now the mind

looking into that which sets the ________ in motion and seeing in there

a doorway open nothing on either side
(a slight wind now around them, three notes from up the hill)

through which morning creeps and the first true notes —

For they were deep in the earth and what is possible swiftly took hold.

1987

Fission

The real electric lights light upon the full-sized
screen
on which the greater-than-life-size girl appears,
almost nude on the lawn — sprinklers on —
voice-over her mother calling her name out — loud —
camera angle giving her lowered lids their full
expanse — a desert — as they rise

out of the shabby annihilation,
out of the possibility of never-having-been-seen,
and rise,
till the glance is let loose into the auditorium,
and the man who has just stopped in his tracks
looks down
for the first

time. Tick tock. It's the birth of the mercantile
dream (he looks down). It's the birth of
the dream called
new world (looks down). She lies there. A corridor of light
filled with dust
flows down from the booth to the screen.
Everyone in here wants to be taken off

somebody's list, wants to be placed on
somebody else's list.
Tick. It is 1963. The idea of history is being
outmaneuvered.
So that as the houselights come on — midscene —
not quite killing the picture which keeps flowing beneath,

a man comes running down the aisle
asking for our attention —

Ladies and Gentlemen.
I watch the houselights lap against the other light — the tunnel
of image-making dots licking the white sheet awake —
a man, a girl, her desperate mother — daisies growing in the
corner —

I watch the light from our real place
suck the arm of screen-building light into itself
until the gesture of the magic forearm frays,
and the story up there grays, pales — them almost lepers now,
saints, such
white on their flesh in
patches — her thighs like receipts slapped down on a
slim silver tray,

her eyes as she lowers the heart-shaped shades,
as the glance glides over what used to be the open,
the free,
as the glance moves, pianissimo, over the glint of day,
over the sprinkler, the mother's voice shrieking like a grappling
hook,
the grass blades aflame with being-seen, here on the out-

skirts. . . . You can almost hear the click at the heart of
the silence
where the turnstile shuts and he's *in* — our hero —
the moment spoked,
our gaze on her fifteen-foot eyes,
the man hoarse now as he waves his arms,
as he screams to the booth to cut it, cut the sound,
and the sound is cut,
and her sun-barred shoulders are left to turn

soundless as they accompany
her neck, her face, the
looking-up.
Now the theater's skylight is opened and noon slides in.
I watch as it overpowers the electric lights,
whiting the story out one layer further

till it's just a smoldering of whites
where she sits up, and her stretch of flesh
is just a roiling up of graynesses,
vague stutterings of
light with motion in them, bits of moving zeros

in the infinite virtuality of light,
some *likeness* in it but not particulate,

a grave of possible shapes called *likeness* — see it? — something
scrawling up there that could be skin or daylight or even

the expressway now that he's gotten her to leave with him —
(it happened rather fast) (do you recall) —

the man up front screaming the President's been shot, waving
his hat, slamming one hand flat
over the open
to somehow get
our attention,

in Dallas, behind him the scorcher — whites, grays,
laying themselves across his face —
him like a beggar in front of us, holding his hat —
I don't recall what I did,
I don't recall what the right thing to do would be,
I wanted someone to love. . . .

There is a way she lay down on that lawn
to begin with,
in the heart of the sprinklers,
before the mother's call,
before the man's shadow laid itself down,

there is a way to not yet be wanted,

there is a way to lie there at twenty-four frames
per second — no faster —
not at the speed of plot,
not at the speed of desire —
the road out — expressway — hotels — motels —
no telling what we'll have to see next,
no telling what all we'll have to want next
(right past the stunned rows of houses),
no telling what on earth we'll have to marry marry marry. . . .

Where the three lights merged:
where the image licked my small body from the front, the story
playing
all over my face my
forwardness,
where the electric lights took up the back and sides,
the unwavering houselights,
seasonless,

where the long thin arm of day came in from the top
to touch my head,
reaching down along my staring face —
where they flared up around my body unable to

merge into each other
over my likeness,
slamming down one side of me, unquenchable — here static

there flaming —
sifting grays into other grays —
mixing the split second into the long haul —
flanking me — undressing something there where my
body is
though not my body —
where they play on the field of my willingness,

where they kiss and brood, filtering each other to no avail,
all over my solo
appearance,
bits smoldering under the shadows I make —
and aimlessly — what we call *free* — there

the immobilism sets in,
the being-in-place more alive than the being,
my father sobbing beside me, the man on the stage
screaming, the woman behind us starting to
pray,
the immobilism, the being-in-place more alive than

the being,
the squad car now faintly visible on the screen
starting the chase up,
all over my countenance,
the velvet armrest at my fingers, the dollar bill

in my hand,
choice the thing that wrecks the sensuous here the glorious
here —

that wrecks the beauty,
choice the move that rips the wrappings of light, the
ever-tighter wrappings

of the layers of the
real: what is, what also is, what might be that is,
what could have been that is, what
might have been that is, what I say that is,

what the words say that is,
    what you imagine the words say that is — Don't move, don't

wreck the shroud, don't move —

1991

EDWARD HIRSCH (b. 1950)

Edward Hirsch was born in Chicago. He attended Grinnell College in Iowa, did graduate work at the University of Pennsylvania, and taught at the University of Houston. He has written, in addition to six books of poetry, three volumes of prose, including *How to Read a Poem: And Fall in Love with Poetry* (1999). When Charles Simic selected "Man on a Fire Escape" for *The Best American Poetry 1992*, Hirsch wrote that part of his intention was to "imagine and dwell upon an extended apocalyptic moment, the world being destroyed, and then to see that moment transfigured and withdrawn, the twilight seeping into evening, the world continuing on as before."

Man on a Fire Escape

He couldn't remember what propelled him
out of the bedroom window onto the fire escape
of his fifth-floor walkup on the river,

so that he could see, as if for the first time,
sunset settling down on the dazed cityscape
and tugboats pulling barges up the river.

There were barred windows glaring at him
from the other side of the street
while the sun deepened into a smoky flare

that scalded the clouds gold-vermillion.
It was just an ordinary autumn twilight —
the kind he had witnessed often before —

but then the day brightened almost unnaturally
into a rusting, burnished, purplish-red haze
and everything burst into flame;

the factories pouring smoke into the sky,
the trees and shrubs, the shadows,
of pedestrians scorched and rushing home. . . .

There were storefronts going blind and cars
burning on the parkway and steel girders
collapsing into the polluted waves.

Even the latticed fretwork of stairs
where he was standing, even the first stars
climbing out of their sunlit graves

were branded and lifted up, consumed by fire.
It was like watching the start of Armageddon,
like seeing his mother dipped in flame. . . .

And then he closed his eyes and it was over.
Just like that. When he opened them again
the world had reassembled beyond harm.

So where had he crossed to? Nowhere.
And what had he seen? Nothing. No foghorns
called out to each other, as if in a dream,

and no moon rose over the dark river
like a warning — icy, long forgotten —
while he turned back to an empty room.

1994

Days of 1968

She walked through Grant Park during the red days of summer.
One morning she woke up and smelled tear gas in her hair.

She liked Big Brother and the Holding Company, Bob Dylan,
Sly & the Family Stone, The Mothers of Invention.

When Jimi Hendrix played *Purple Haze* in a jam session
she had a vision of the Trail of Tears and the Cherokee Nation.

She dropped acid assiduously for more than a year.
She sang, "I want to take you higher and higher,"

and dreamt of cleansing the doors of perception.
After she joined the Sky Church I never saw her again . . .

Days of 1968, sometimes your shutters open
and I glimpse a star gleaming in the constellations.

I can almost reach up and snag her by the hand.
I can go to her if I don't look back at the ground.

1998

RODNEY JONES (b. 1950)

Rodney Jones was born in Hartselle, Alabama. He studied at the University of Alabama and the University of North Carolina at Greensboro. His poems address a range of subjects: the southern drawl, the last days of William Carlos Williams, the theories of Jacques Derrida. He writes about manhood and masculinity with particular candor and eloquence.

My Manhood

My head battered against the culvert wall, nose
letting down a dark sprig of un-Christian blood,
finally I just sat down in the ditch and gave up,
my oaths softened, all my victories compromised.
I knew the ball I had carried through cheers
would turn black and rot, what hearts I had won
would just as easily be lost. I raised my arms
and still the knee came up blunt against one ear.
The world shrieked at temple and rang in gut.
In my breath, which would not come, kings swallowed
their tongues, and in my right eye, which
would not open, Mussolini dangled from a hook.
If I could have, I would have taken it all back:
the heavy masculine god, the invincible ghost,
but I brought it on, raised it, and provoked it,
so I drank its puddle water and ate its dirt.
Finally, in the name of reason, I had to ask
the boot that kicked me to walk back to the job,
and I had to watch the bored face smugly turn
among those above me who had been my friends.
Surely defeat, like victory, is larger than man,
its legend stretched out long, imperfect as doubt.
My own ruined, at the most, two minutes,
and then work resumed, hammer and crowbar,
the boss coming, and four more forms had to
be ripped from the wall before quitting time.
What more was there to lose? The secret,
the bitter lie of triumph? The inviolable
face hidden beneath my face? I worked quietly
through the reruns where I won, and others
where I died, humiliated, slow, and small —
a wren wrapped in tissue paper, a salted slug.

This year I was never farther from all that.
This year was the breezy cafés along the Seine,
the doors of Ghiberti, the jewels of Van Eyck.
Very gently, south of Venice, the track unrolls
golden hills, tunnels, medieval villages
in the Apennines. My wife slept beside me,

a glad odor of peace, of watered leaves,
but I felt the power that blasted the gneiss
and heard the one who had laid the crossties
whisper, "On your knees, like it, now kiss it,"
and not the artisan of palaces and cathedrals
but the soldier filled me, the Hun included me,
helpless before his wrath, as he drove south,
indomitable, priapic beast who would claim
all beauty with his fists, not to love art,
but to hold it holy in his rough ideal of
dominion, in his dream of a perfect polygamy.

1989

Small Lower-Middle-Class White Southern Male

Missing consonant, silent vowel in everyone,
pale cipher omitted from the misery census,
eclipsed by lynchings before you were born,
it cannot even be said now that you exist

except as a spittoon exists in an antique store
or a tedious example fogs a lucid speech.
Your words precede you like cumulus
above melodrama's favorite caricatures.

In novels, you're misfit and Hogganbeck;
in recent cinema, inbreeding bigotry
or evolving to mindless greed: a rancher
of rainforests, an alchemist of genocide.

You're dirt that dulls the guitar's twang,
blood-soaked bible, and burning cross.
You cotton to the execution of retards,
revile the blues, and secretly assume

Lindbergh's underground America that sided
with the Germans in World War II.
Other types demand more probity;
you may be Bubbaed with impunity

This makes some feel prematurely good.
They hear your voice and see Jim Crow.
But the brothers wait. Any brother knows
that there are no honorary negroes.

2002

JOHN YAU (b. 1950)

John Yau was born in Lynn, Massachusetts, shortly after his parents left Shanghai. He graduated from Bard College and studied with John Ashbery at Brooklyn College. A professional art critic, he has written books on Andy Warhol and Jasper Johns. He has also collaborated on multimedia projects with such artists as Archie Rand. "I let the music take over the poem sometimes," he has said, explaining that when he writes he does not want to know what is coming next.

January 18, 1979

So often artists have painted a woman
washing, or combing her hair.
And nearby is a mirror.
And there you were, crouched in the tub.
It was cold in the apartment.
It is always cold in winter.
But you were brushing out your hair
and singing to yourself.
And, for a moment, I think I saw
what those artists saw —
someone half in love with herself
and half in love with the world.

1983

Domestic Bliss

If I am as cute as a button
why have you spent the past hour
hunting for the one that rolled down your sleeve

onto the aluminum siding bus
carrying rows of disillusioned tourists
toward the chimney heart of our once famous city

Didn't you say that you didn't like that coat
that the buttons were too big for someone
possessing your delicate bone structure

Why isn't there more meat on this chicken
It's as if the damned thing began starving itself
once it knew what the future had in store for it

Is this what they mean by "organic"
I agree. We don't need to go on
fighting like this. We could learn

another way to fight, one that wouldn't
expend so many baccalaureates of bituminous energy
Perhaps a nap from which we would wake up

refreshed as fish dropped back into a forest pond
Okay, platinum mousetrap of a higher celestial order
one of us would whisper to the other

you get on your side of the rubber volcano
and I'll get on mine. But before you do
would you mind mending my hind paws

I need to get that sand back into my open veins

2002

Copyrights

Conrad Aiken, I, XIX, and XXXIII from "Preludes" from *Selected Poems*. Copyright 1931, © 1959 by Conrad Aiken. Reprinted with the permission of Brandt & Hochman Literary Agents, Inc.

A. R. Ammons, "So I Said I Am Ezra," "Corsons Inlet," "Cascadilla Falls," "The City Limits," "Triphammer Bridge," "Still," and "Mansion" from *Collected Poems 1951–1971*. Copyright © 1955, 1963, 1972 by A. R. Ammons. "Mountain Talk" and "Reflective" from *The Selected Poems, Expanded Edition*. Copyright © 1987, 1977, 1975, 1974, 1972, 1971, 1970, 1966, 1965, 1964, 1955 by A. R. Ammons. "Ballad" from *Diversifications*. Copyright © 1975 by A. R. Ammons. "Easter Morning" from *A Coast of Trees*. Copyright © 1981 by A. R. Ammons. "Anxiety's Prosody" from *Brink Road*. Copyright © 1996 by A. R. Ammons. "Their Sex Life" from *The Really Short Poems of A. R. Ammons*. Copyright © 1990 by A. R. Ammons. "In View of the Fact" from *Bosh and Flapdoodle*. Copyright © 2005 by John R. Ammons. All reprinted with the permission of W. W. Norton & Company, Inc.

Rae Armantrout, "Traveling through the Yard" and "Articulation" from *Veil: New and Selected Poems*. Copyright © 2001 by Rae Armantrout. Reprinted with the permission of Wesleyan University Press.

John Ashbery, "This Room" and "The History of My Life" from *Your Name Here*. Copyright © 2000 by John Ashbery. "My Philosophy of Life" and "A Poem of Unrest" from *Can You Hear, Bird*. Copyright © 1995 by John Ashbery. All reprinted with the permission of Farrar, Straus & Giroux, LLC. "The Instruction Manual" from *Some Trees*. Copyright © 1956 by John Ashbery. "One Coat of Paint" from *April Galleons*. Copyright © 1987 by John Ashbery. "'How Much Longer Will I Be Able to Inhabit the Divine Sepulcher . . .'" and "Decoy" from *The Mooring of Starting Out: The First Five Books of Poetry* (New York: The Ecco Press, 1997). Copyright © 1997 by John Ashbery. "At North Farm" from *A Wave* (New York: Viking, 1984). Copyright © 1984 by John Ashbery. "Wet Casements" from *Houseboat Days*. Copyright © 1987, 1979 by John Ashbery. All reprinted with the permission of Georges Borchardt, Inc. for the author. "The One Thing That Can Save America" and "Self-Portrait in a Convex Mirror" from *Self-Portrait in a Convex Mirror*. Copyright © 1976 by John Ashbery. Both reprinted with the permission of Viking, a division of Penguin Group (USA) Inc. from *Self-Portrait in a Convex Mirror*. Copyright © 1976 by John Ashbery. "How to Continue" from *Hotel Lautremont*. Copyright © 1992 by John Ashbery. Reprinted with the permission of Alfred A. Knopf, a division of Random House, Inc.

W. H. Auden, "XXVI" ["It's no use raising a shout."] from *The English Auden: Poems, Essays and Dramatic Writings 1927–1939*. Copyright © 1977 by Edward Mendelson, William Meredith, and Monroe K. Spears, Executors of the Estate of W. H. Auden. Reprinted with the permission of Curtis Brown, Ltd. "As I Walked Out One Evening," "Musée des Beaux Arts," "In Memory of William Butler Yeats," "September 1, 1939," "Law, say the gardeners, is the sun (Law Like Love)," "In Memory of Sigmund Freud," "A Healthy Spot," "Under Which Lyre," "In Praise of Limestone," "The Shield of Achilles," "The More Loving One," "VII: Domesday Song" from "Ten Songs," and "If I Could Tell You Now" from *Collected Poems*. Copyright 1940 and renewed © 1968 by W. H. Auden. Copyright 1945, 1951, 1952, © 1957 by W. H. Auden. Copyright © 1976 by Edward Mendelson, William Meredith and Monroe K. Spears, Executors of the Estate of W. H. Auden. Reprinted with the permission of Random House, Inc.

Stephen Vincent Benét, "American Names" from *Selected Works of Stephen Vincent Benét* (New York: Holt, Rinehart and Winston, 1955). Copyright 1927 by Stephen Vincent Benét, renewed © 1955 by Rosemary Carr Benét. Reprinted with the permission of Brandt & Hochman Literary Agents, Inc.

Charles Bernstein, "Solidarity Is the Name We Give to What We Cannot Hold" from *My Way: Speeches and Poems* (Chicago: The University of Chicago Press, 1999). Originally published in *Political Diction* (1996). Reprinted with the permission of the author.

Ted Berrigan, XV ["In Joe Brainard's collage its white arrow"], LXX ["After Arthur Rimbaud"], and XXVI ["It's 8:45 am in Brooklyn, it's the 258th of July . . . "] from *The Sonnets*, edited by Alice Notley. Copyright © 2000 by Alice Notley, Literary Executrix of the Estate of Ted Berrigan. Reprinted with the permission of Viking Penguin, a division of Penguin Group (USA), Inc. "Living with Chris" and "My Autobiography" from *Collected Poems by Ted Berrigan*, edited by Alice Notley. Copyright © 2005 by. Reprinted with the permission of University of California Press and Alice Notley, Executor of the Estate of Ted Berrigan.

John Berryman, "Winter Landscape," "The Traveler," and "Henry's Understanding" from *Collected Poems*. Copyright © 1989 by Kate Donahue Berryman. Dream Songs 13, 14, 23 ["The Lay of Ike"], 29, 61, 147, and 235 from *The Dream Songs*. Copyright © 1969, 1991 by John Berryman. All reprinted with the permission of Farrar, Straus & Giroux, LLC.

Frank Bidart, "Another Life" from *In the Western Night: Collected Poems 1965–1990*. Copyright © 1990 by Frank Bidart. "The Yoke" from *Desire*. Copyright © 1997 by Frank Bidart. "For the Twentieth Century" and "The Curse" from *Star Dust*. Copyright © 2005 by Frank Bidart. All reprinted with the permission of Farrar, Straus & Giroux, LLC.

Elizabeth Bishop, "A Miracle for Breakfast" "Seascape," "Rain Towards Morning," "The Shampoo," "Exchanging Hats," "Questions of Travel," "Sestina (September rain falls on the house)," "In the Waiting Room," "Roosters," "Questions of Travel," "Over 2000 Illustrations and a Complete Concordance," "At the Fishhouses," "Crusoe in England," "One Art," and "Five Flights Up" from *The Complete Poems: 1927–1979*. Copyright © 1979, 1983 by Alice Helen Methfessel. Reprinted with the permission of Farrar, Straus & Giroux, LLC.

Robert Bly, "Johnson's Cabinet Watched by Ants" and "After the Industrial Revolution, All Things Happen at Once" from *The Light Around the Body*. Copyright © 1967 and renewed 1995 by Robert Bly. Reprinted with the permission of HarperCollins Publishers. "The Resemblance

Between Your Life and a Dog" from *Morning Poems*. Copyright © 1997 by Robert Bly. "The Night Abraham Called to the Stars" from *The Night Abraham Called to the Stars*. Copyright © 2002 by Robert Bly. All reprinted with the permission of HarperCollins Publishers. "After Long Busyness" from *Silence in the Snowy Fields* (Middletown, Conn.: Wesleyan University Press, 1962). Copyright © 1962 by Robert Bly. "My Father at 85" from *Common Ground: A Gathering of Poets from the 1986 Marshall Festival*, edited by Mark Vinz and Thom Tammaro (Moorehead, Minn.: Dacotah Territory Press, 1988). Both reprinted with the permission of the author.

Louise Bogan, "Last Hill in a Vista," "Winter Swan," "Juan's Song," "Men Loved Wholly Beyond Wisdom," and "Evening in the Sanitarium" from *The Blue Estuaries: Poems 1923–1968*. Copyright © 1968 by Louise Bogan and renewed 1996 by Ruth Limmer. Reprinted with the permission of Farrar, Straus & Giroux, LLC.

William Bronk, "I Thought it was Harry" and "The Ignorant Lust After Knowledge" (William Bronk Papers, Rare Book and Manuscript Library, Columbia University). Reprinted with the permission of The Trustees of Columbia University in the City of New York.

Gwendolyn Brooks, "A Song in the Front Yard," "The Mother," "Negro Hero," "still do I keep my look, my identity," and "We Real Cool." Reprinted with the permission of Brooks Permissions.

Sterling Brown, "Bitter Fruit of the Tree," "Harlem Happiness," "Master and Man," "Southern Cop," and "Legend" from *The Collected Poems of Sterling A. Brown*, edited by Michael S. Harper. Copyright 1932 by Harcourt, Brace & Co., copyright renewed © 1960 by Sterling A. Brown. Copyright © 1980 by Sterling A. Brown. Reprinted with the permission of HarperCollins Publishers.

Charles Bukowski, "my old man" from *Love is a Dog from Hell: Poems 1974–1977*. Copyright © 1977 by Charles Bukowski. "comments upon my last book of poesy:" from *What Matters Most is How Well You Walk Through the Fire*. Copyright © 1999 by Linda Lee Bukowski. "me against the world" from *Betting on the Muse: Poems and Stories*. Copyright © 1996 by Linda Lee Bukowski. "freaky time" from *The Last Night of the Earth Poems*. Copyright © 1992 by Charles Bukowski. "so you want to be a writer" from *Sifting Through the Madness for The Word, The Line, The Way*. Copyright © 2003 by Linda Lee Bukowski. All reprinted with the permission of HarperCollins Publishers.

Anne Carson, "My Religion," "By God," "God's Woman," "God's Mother," "God's Justice," "God's Christ Theory," "God's List of Liquids," and "God's Work" from *Glass, Irony, and God*. Copyright © 1995 by Anne Carson. Reprinted with the permission of New Directions Publishing Corporation.

Joseph Ceravolo, "Dusk," "The Wind is Blowing West," "Fill and Illumined," "Drunken Winter," and "Happiness in the Trees" from *The Green Lake Is Awake: Selected Poems of Joseph Ceravolo*. Copyright © 1994 by the Estate of Joseph Ceravolo. Reprinted with the permission of Coffee House Press, Minneapolis, Minnesota. "Rain" from *Wildflowers Out of Gas*. Copyright © 1967 by Joseph Ceravolo. Reprinted with the permission of Rosemary Ceravolo.

Amy Clampitt, "Marine Surface, Low Overcast," "The Sun Underfoot Among the Sundews," and "Palm Sunday" from *The Kingfisher*. Copyright © 1983 by Amy Clampitt. Reprinted with the permission of Alfred A. Knopf, a division of Random House, Inc.

Edwin Denby, "Summer," "The Silence at Night," "On the Home Front — 1943," and "Alex Katz paints his north window" from *The Collected Poems of Edwin Denby* (New York: Full Court Press, 1975). Reprinted with the permission of Yvonne Jacquette Burckhardt.

Carl Dennis, "History" from *Practical Gods*. Copyright © 2001 by Carl Dennis. Reprinted with the permission of Viking Penguin, a division of Penguin Group (USA) Inc. "World History" from *New and Selected Poems*. Copyright © 2004 by Carl Dennis. Reprinted with the permission of Penguin, a division of Penguin Group (USA) Inc.

Thomas Disch, "A Concise History of Music" from *Yes, Let's: New and Selected Poems* (Baltimore: The Johns Hopkins University Press, 1989). Copyright © 1989 by Thomas M. Disch. "The Crumbling Infrastructure" from *Southwest Review* (1990). Copyright © 1990 by Thomas Disch. Both reprinted with the permission of the author.

Robert Duncan, "My Mother Would Be a Falconress" and "The Torso" from *Bending the Bow*. Copyright © 1968 by Robert Duncan. "Often I am Permitted to Return to a Meadow," "The Temple of the Animals," and "Poetry, a Natural Thing" from *The Opening of the Field*. Copyright © 1960 by Robert Duncan. All reprinted with the permission of New Directions Publishing Corporation.

Bob Dylan, "Desolation Row." Copyright © 1965 by Warner Bros. Inc. Copyright renewed 1993 by Special Rider Music. All rights reserved. International copyright secured. Reprinted with permission.

Russell Edson, "The Fall," "Antimatter," and "The Neighborhood Dog" from *The Tunnel: Selected Poems*. Copyright © 1994. Reprinted with the permission of Oberlin College Press. "The Rule and Its Exception" from *The Tormented Mirror*. Copyright © 2001 by Russell Edson. Reprinted with the permission of the University of Pittsburgh Press.

T. S. Eliot, "The Hollow Men" and "The Journey of the Magi" from *Collected Poems 1909–1962*. Copyright 1936 by Harcourt, Inc., copyright © 1964, 1963 by T. S. Eliot. "Little Gidding" from *T. S. Eliot: The Complete Poems and Plays 1909–1950*. Copyright 1922, 1925, 1927 1941 by T. S. Eliot. Reprinted with the permission of Harcourt, Inc.

Lynn Emanuel, "Of Your Father's Indiscretions and the Train to California" and "Blonde Bombshell" from *The Dig and Hotel Fiesta*. Copyright © 1984, 1992, 1995 by Lynn Emanuel. Reprinted with the permission of the poet and University of Illinois Press. "At the Ritz" from *Then, Suddenly*. Copyright © 1999 by Lynn Emanuel. Reprinted with the permission of the University of Pittsburgh Press.

Kenneth Fearing, "Green Light," "Dirge," and "X Minus X" from *Complete Poems*. Copyright 1929 and renewed © 1957 by Kenneth Fearing. Copyright 1934 by Kenneth Fearing, renewed © 1962 by The Estate of Kenneth Fearing. Reprinted with the permission of Russell & Volkening, Inc., as agents for the author.

Aaron Fogel, "The Printer's Error" from *The Printer's Error*. Copyright © 2001 by Aaron Fogel. Reprinted with the permission of Miami University Press.

Carolyn Forché, "The Colonel" from *The Country Between Us*. Originally appeared in *Women's International Resource Exchange*. Copyright © 1981 by Carolyn Forché. Reprinted with the permission of HarperCollins Publishers.

Robert Frost, "Fire and Ice," "Dust of Snow," "Nothing Gold Can Stay," "For Once, Then, Something," "Stopping By Woods on a Snowy Evening," "To Earthward," "Spring Pools," "Two Tramps in Mud Time," "Desert Places," "Neither Out Far Nor In Deep," "Design," "Provide, Provide," "Come In," "The Most of It," "Never Again Would Birds' Song Be the Same," "Acquainted with the Night," "The Gift Outright," and "Directive" from *The Poetry of Robert Frost*, edited by Edward Connery Lathem. Copyright 1951 by Robert Frost. Copyright 1923, © 1969 by Henry Holt and Co., Inc. Reprinted with the permission of Henry Holt and Company, LLC.

Jean Garrigue, "Dialog" from *Antaeus* (1971). Copyright © 1971 by Jean Garrigue. Reprinted with the permission of the Estate of Jean Garrigue. "Movie Actors Scribbling Letters Very Fast in Crucial Scenes," "Grenoble Café," "Song in Sligo" and "Bad Times Song" from *Selected Poems*. Copyright © 1992 by the Estate of Jean Garrigue. Reprinted with the permission of the University of Illinois Press.

Allen Ginsberg, "A Supermarket in California," "Kaddish (I)," "Kaddish (III–V)," "America," and "To Aunt Rose" from *Selected Poems 1947–1995*. Copyright © 2001 by Allen Ginsberg. "City Midnight Junk Strains" from *Collected Poems: 1947–1980*. Copyright © 1984 by Allen Ginsberg. All reprinted with the permission of HarperCollins Publishers.

Dana Gioia, "The Archbishop" and "The Summer Storm" from *Interrogation at Noon*. Copyright © 2001 by Dana Gioia. Reprinted with the permission of Graywolf Press, Saint Paul, Minnesota.

Louise Glück, "Mock Orange," "The Triumph of Achilles," "Gratitude," "The Mirror" and "The Drowned Children" from *The First Four Books of Poems*. Copyright © 1995 by Louise Glück. "Celestial Music" from *Ararat*. Copyright © 1990 by Louise Glück. "Siren" and "Circe's Power" from *Meadowlands*. Copyright © 1996 by Louise Glück. Louise Glück, "The Red Poppy" and "Vespers" ["In your extended absence, you permit me"] from *The Wild Iris*. Copyright © 1992 by Louise Glück. All reprinted with the permission of HarperCollins Publishers.

Paul Goodman, "The Lordly Hudson," "I Planned to Have a Border of Lavender," and "A Chess Game" from *Collected Poems*. Copyright © 1973 by Paul Goodman. Reprinted with the permission of Sally Goodman.

Jorie Graham, "Orpheus and Eurydice" from *The Dream of the Unified Field: Selected Poems, 1974–1994*. Copyright © 1995 by Jorie Graham. "Fission" from *Region of Unlikeness*. Copyright © 1991 by Jorie Graham. Both reprinted with the permission of HarperCollins Publishers.

Linda Gregg, "Marriage and a Midsummer's Night" from *Too Bright to See & Alma*. Copyright © 1985, 2002 by Linda Gregg. "A Dark Thing Inside the Day" from *The Sacraments of Desire*. Copyright © 1991 by Linda Gregg. "The Singers Change, the Music Goes On" from *The Middle Distance*. Copyright © 2006 by Linda Gregg. All reprinted with the permission of Graywolf Press, Saint Paul, Minnesota.

Angela Grimke, "Fragment." Reprinted with the permission of the Moorland-Springarn Research Center, Howard University.

Barbara Guest, "Parachutes, My Love, Could Carry Us Higher," "On the Verge of the Path," and "Words" from *Collected Poems*. Copyright © 1995 by Barbara Guest. Reprinted with the permission of the author and Wesleyan University Press.

Marilyn Hacker, "Nights of 1965–66: The Old Reliable" from *Going Back to the River*. Copyright © 1990 by Marilyn Hacker. Reprinted with the permission of Frances Collin Literary Agent.

Rachel Hadas, "The Red Hat" and "Riverside Park" from *Halfway Down the Hall: New and Selected Poems*. Copyright © 1998 by Rachel Hadas. Reprinted with the permission of Wesleyan University Press.

Donald Hall, "T.R." and "The Impossible Marriage," "Prophecy," "When the Young Husband," and "Her Garden" from *Old and New Poems*. Copyright © 1990 by Donald Hall. Reprinted with the permission of Houghton Mifflin Company. All rights reserved.

Robert Hass, "Against Botticelli" and "Meditation at Lagunitas" from *Praise*. Copyright © 1979 by Robert Hass. "A Story about the Body" and "Misery and Splendor" from *Human Wishes*. Copyright © 1989 by Robert Hass. "Forty Something" from *Sun Under Wood*. Copyright © 1989 by Robert Hass. All reprinted with the permission of HarperCollins Publishers. "On the Coast Near Saulsalito" from *Field Guide*. Copyright © 1973 by Robert Hass. Reprinted with permission of Yale University Press. All rights reserved.

Robert Hayden, "Those Winter Sundays," "Middle Passage," and "Homage to the Empress of the Blues" from *The Collected Poems of Robert Hayden*, edited by Frederick Glaysher. Copyright © 1962, 1966 by Robert Hayden. Copyright © 1985 by Emma Hayden. Reprinted with the permission of Liveright Publishing Corporation.

H. D. (Hilda Doolittle), "The Moon In Your Hands" from *Selected Poems*. Copyright © 1957 by Norman Holmes Pearson. Reprinted with permission. "The Helmsman," "Helen," and "Epitaph" from *Collected Poems, 1912–1944*. Copyright © 1982 by The Estate of Hilda Doolittle. Reprinted with the permission of New Directions Publishing Corporation.

Anthony Hecht, "The Dover Bitch," "Third Avenue in Sunlight," and "A Hill" from *Collected Earlier Poems*. Copyright © 1990 by Anthony Hecht. "The Book of Yolek" from *The Transparent Man*. Copyright © 1990 by Anthony E. Hecht. "To Fortuna Parvulorum" from *Flight Among the Tombs*. Copyright © 1995, 1996 by Anthony E. Hecht. Wood engravings copyright © 1995 by Leonard Baskin. All reprinted with the permission of Alfred A. Knopf, a division of Random House, Inc.

Lyn Hejinian, excerpt from *My Life* (Los Angeles: Sun & Moon, 1987), pp. 16–18. Copyright © 1980, 1987 by Lyn Hejinian. Reprinted with the permission of the publisher. Excerpt ["I arrived with biographical context"] from *The Fatalist*. Copyright © 2003 by Lyn Hejinian. Reprinted with the permission of Omnidawn Publishing.

Ruth Herschberger, "The Virgin" and "Page Torn from a Notebook" from *A Way of Happening* (New York: Pellegrini & Cudahy, 1948). "The Huron" from *Nature and Love Poems* (New York: Eakins Press, 1969). All reprinted with the permission of the author.

Edward Hirsch, "Days of 1968," from *On Love*. Copyright © 1998 by Edward Hirsch. "Man on the Fire Escape" from *Earthly Measures*. Copyright © 1994 by Edward Hirsch. Both reprinted with the permission of Alfred A. Knopf, a division of Random House, Inc.

John Hollander, "The Lady's-Maid's Song" from *Selected Poetry*. Copyright © 1993 by John Hollander. "The Bird" from *Selected Poetry*. Copyright © 1993 by John Hollander. 162, 163, and 164 from "Powers of Thirteen"; and "Adam's Task" from *Selected Poetry*. Copyright © 1993 by John Hollander. "An Old-Fashioned Song" from *Tesserae and Other Poems*. Copyright © 1993 by John Hollander. All reprinted with the permission of Alfred A. Knopf, a division of Random House, Inc. "Swan and Shadow" from *Types of Shape*. Copyright © 1968 by John Hollander. Reprinted with the permission of Yale University Press.

Richard Howard, "Like Most Revelations," "Job Interview," "Among the Missing," and "At 65" from *Inner Voices: Selected Poems, 1963–2003*. Copyright © 2004 by Richard Howard. Reprinted with the permission of Farrar, Straus & Giroux, LLC. "209 Canal" from *Quantities/Damages: Early Poems*. Copyright © 1971, 1984 by Richard Howard. Reprinted with the permission of Wesleyan University Press.

Fanny Howe, "Veteran," "Goodbye, Post Office Square," and "9-11-01" from *Selected Poems*. Copyright © 2000 by the Regents of the University of California. Reprinted with the permission of University of California Press.

Langston Hughes, "Dream Boogie," "Passing," "Nightmare Boogie," "Neighbor," "Chord," "Fact," "Hope," "Dream Boogie: Variation," "Harlem," "Good Morning," "Same in Blues," "Comment on Curb," "Juke Box Love Song," "The Weary Blues," "Dream Variations" and "Luck" from *The Collected Poems of Langston Hughes*. Copyright © 1994 by The Estate of Langston Hughes. Reprinted with the permission of Alfred A. Knopf, a division of Random House, Inc.

Richard Hugo, "Montesano Unvisited" and "Degrees of Gray in Philipsburg" from *Making Certain It Goes On: The Collected Poems of Richard Hugo*. Copyright © 1984 by Richard Hugo. Reprinted with the permission of W. W. Norton & Company, Inc.

Jacobsen, Josephine, "The Blue Eyed Exterminator" and "The Birthday Party" from *In the Crevice of Time: New and Selected Poems*. Copyright © 1995 by Josephine Jacobsen. Printed with permission of The Johns Hopkins University Press. "The Monosyllable" from *The Chinese Insomniacs*. Copyright © 1981 by Josephine Jacobsen. Printed with permission of The University of Pennsylvania Press.

Randall Jarrell, "The Death of the Ball Turret Gunner," "A Sick Child," "The Woman at the Washington Zoo," "The Lost Children," and "The Player Piano" from *The Complete Poems*. Copyright © 1969, renewed 1997 by Mary von S. Jarrell. Reprinted with the permission of Farrar, Straus & Giroux, LLC.

Robinson Jeffers, "To the Stone-Cutters," "Shine, Perishing Republic," "Hurt Hawks" and "Rock and Hawk" from *The Selected Poetry of Robinson Jeffers*. Copyright 1935 and © 1963 by Donnan Jeffers and Garth Jeffers. Reprinted with the permission of Random House, Inc. "Ave Caesar" and "Fire on the Hills" from *The Collected Poetry of Robinson Jeffers, Vol. II, 1928–1938*, Tim Hunt, editor. Copyright 1938 and renewed © 1966 by Donnan and Garth Jeffers, the Jeffers Literary Properties. All rights reserved. Reprinted with the permission of Stanford University Press, www.sup.org. "Credo" from *The Collected Poetry of Robinson Jeffers, Volume I, 1920–1928*, edited by Tim Hunt. Copyright © by Jeffers Literary Properties. Reprinted with the permission of Stanford University Press, www.sup.org.

Rodney Jones, "My Manhood" and "Small Lower-Middle-Class White Southern Male" from *Transparent Gestures*. Copyright © 1989 by Rodney Jones. Reprinted with the permission of Houghton Mifflin Company. All rights reserved.

Lawrence Joseph, "Some Sort of Chronicler I Am" from *Codes, Precepts, Biases, Taboos*. Copyright © 2005 by Lawrence Joseph. Reprinted with the permission of Farrar, Straus & Giroux, LLC.

Donald Justice, "Self-Portrait as Still Life," "On the Death of Friends in Childhood," "But That Is Another Story," "Men at Forty," "The Tourist from Syracuse," "Villanelle at Sundown" and "In the Attic" from *Collected Poems*. Copyright © 2004 by Donald Justice. Reprinted with the permission of Alfred A. Knopf, a division of Random House, Inc.

Weldon Kees, "For My Daughter," "Crime Club," "Robinson," "River Song," "Round," "Aspects of Robinson," and "1926" from *The Collected Poems of Weldon Kees*, edited by Donald Justice. Copyright © 1975 by the University of Nebraska Press. Reprinted with the permission of the publishers.

Jane Kenyon, "Let Evening Come," "Otherwise," and "Man Eating" from *Collected Poems*. Copyright © 2005 by The Estate of Jane Kenyon. Reprinted with the permission of Graywolf Press, Saint Paul, Minnesota.

Galway Kinnell, "Why Regret?" from *The New Yorker* (1999). Reprinted with the permission of the author. "Hitchhiker" from *Imperfect Thirst*. Copyright © 1994 by Galway Kinnell. "Saint Francis and the Sow" and "The Man Splitting Wood in the Daybreak" from *Three Books*. Copyright © 2002 by Galway Kinnell. Reprinted with the permission of Houghton Mifflin Company. All rights reserved.

Lincoln Kirstein, "Rank" from *Rhymes of a PFC* (New York: New Directions Publishing Corporation, 1964). Copyright © 1964 by Lincoln Kirstein. Reprinted with the permission of the Estate of Lincoln Kirstein.

Carolyn Kizer, "The Erotic Philosophers" and "Bitch" from *Cool, Calm, and Collected: Poems 1960–2000*. Copyright © 2001 by Carolyn Kizer. Reprinted with the permission of Copper Canyon Press, P.O. Box 271, Port Townsend, WA 98368-0271.

Kenneth Koch, "You Were Wearing," "Permanently," "The Railway Stationery," "Variations on a Theme by William Carlos Williams," "The Circus" (1962), "The Circus" (1975), "One Train May Hide Another," "To World War II," and "Proverb." All reprinted with the permission of the Kenneth Koch Literary Estate.

John Koethe, "Sorrento Valley" and "Moore's Paradox" from *North Point North: New and Selected Poems*. Copyright © 2002 by John Koethe. "Morning in America" from *Falling Water*. Copyright © 1997 by John Koethe. All reprinted with the permission of HarperCollins Publishers.

Yusef Komunyakaa, "Tu Do Street," "We Never Know," and "Thanks" from *Dien Cai Dau*. Copyright © 1988 by Yusef Komunyakaa. "No-Good Blues" from *Thieves of Paradise*. Copyright © 1998 by Yusef Komunyakaa, "Facing It" from *Pleasure Dome: New and Collected Poems*. Copyright © 2001 by Yusef Komunyakaa. All reprinted with the permission of Wesleyan

J. D. McClatchy, "The Landing" from *The Rest of the Way*. Copyright © 1990 by J. D. McClatchy. "What They Left Behind" from *Ten Commandments*. Copyright © 1998 by J. D. McClatchy. "Pibroch" from *Hazmat*. Copyright © 2002 by J. D. McClatchey. All reprinted with the permission of Alfred A. Knopf, a division of Random House, Inc.

Heather McHugh, "Form," "I Knew I'd Sing," "ID," and "What He Thought" from *Hinge & Sign: Poems, 1968–1993*. Copyright © 1994 by Heather McHugh. Reprinted with the permission of Wesleyan University Press.

James Merrill, "A Dedication," "Charles on Fire," "Days of 1964," "Days of 1935," "Syrinx," "Grass," "Self-Portrait in Tyvek™ Windbreaker," "b o d y," "Days of 1994," and "Lost in Translation" from *Collected Poems*. Copyright © 2001 by the literary Estate of James Merrill at Washington University. "Graffito" from *The Inner Room*. Copyright © 1988 by James Merrill. All reprinted with the permission of Alfred A. Knopf, a division of Random House, Inc.

W. S. Merwin, "The Stranger," "Departure's Girl-Friend," "Dusk in Winter," "Yesterday," and "For the Anniversary of My Death" from *Migration: New & Selected Poems* (Port Townsend, WA: Copper Canyon Press, 2005). Copyright © 2005 by W. S. Merwin. "A Thing of Beauty." Copyright © 1970 by W. S. Merwin. All reprinted with the permission of The Wylie Agency, Inc. "One of the Lives" from *The Vixen*. Copyright © 1995 by W. S. Merwin. "Waves in August" from *The River Sound*. Copyright © 1999 by W. S. Merwin. Both reprinted with the permission of Alfred A. Knopf, a division of Random House, Inc.

Josephine Miles, "Center," "Government Injunction Restraining Harlem Cosmetics Co.," "December 7, 1941," "Ride," "Reason," "The Doctor Who Sits at the Bedside of a Rat," "As difference blends into identity," and "Conception" from *Collected Poems*. Copyright © 1983 by Josephine Miles. Reprinted with the permission of the University of Illinois Press.

Edna St. Vincent Millay, Sonnet ["Pity me not because the light of day"], Sonnet ["What lips my lips have kissed, and where, and why"], Sonnet ["Love is not all: it is not meat nor drink"], and "Rendevous" ["Not for these lovely blooms . . . "] from *Collected Poems*. Copyright 1931, © 1958 by Edna St. Vincent Millay and Norma Millay Ellis. Reprinted with the permission of Elizabeth Barnett, Literary Executor.

Susan Mitchell, "Havana Birth" from *Rapture*. Copyright © 1992 by Susan Mitchell. Reprinted with the permission of HarperCollins Publishers, Inc.

Marianne Moore, "To a Steamroller," "To a Snail" "Poetry," "Poetry Abridged," "An Octopus," "The Student," "No Swan So Fine," "The Past Is Present," "The Fish," "Silence," "Critics and Connoisseurs," "Marriage," and "What Are Years?" from *Collected Poems of Marianne Moore*. Copyright 1935 by Marianne Moore, renewed © 1963 by Marianne Moore and T. S. Eliot. Reprinted with the permission of Scribner, an imprint of Simon & Schuster, Inc. "The Steeple-Jack" from *Collected Poems of Marianne Moore*. Copyright 1935 by Marianne Moore, renewed © 1963 by Marianne Moore and T. S. Eliot. Reprinted with the permission of Viking Penguin, a division of Penguin Group (USA) Inc.

Howard Moss, "King Midas" and "The Long Island Night" from *New Selected Poems* (New York: Atheneum, 1985). Copyright © 1985 by Howard Moss. "The Summer Thunder" and "Making a Bed" from *Rules of Sleep* (New York: Atheneum, 1984). Copyright © 1984 by Howard Moss. All reprinted with the permission of The Estate of Howard Moss.

Joan Murray, "Lullaby," "You Talk of Art," and "Men and Women Have Meaning Only as Men and Women" from *Poems 1917–1942*. Copyright 1947, © 1975 by Yale University Press. Reprinted with the permission of Yale University Press.

Ogden Nash, "Long Time No See, 'Bye Now'" from *The New Yorker* (1949) and "Just How Low Can a Highbrow Go When a Highbrow Lowers His Brow" from *The New Yorker* (1958). Copyright 1949, © 1958 by Ogden Nash. Reprinted with the permission of Curtis Brown, Ltd.

Howard Nemerov, "Brainstorm," "Style," and "Because You Asked About the Line Between Prose and Poetry" from *The Collected Poems of Howard Nemerov*. Copyright © 1977 by Howard Nemerov. Reprinted with the permission of Margaret Nemerov.

Lorine Niedecker, "If I Were a Bird," "Poet's Work," "Who Was Mary Shelley?" "My Life By Water," "Lake Superior," "I married," and "Wilderness" from *Collected Works*. Reprinted with the permission of University of California Press.

Alice Notley, "A woman came into" from *The Descent of Alette*. Copyright © 1992 by Alice Notley. "April Not an Inventory but a Blizzard" from *Mysteries of Small Houses*. Copyright © 1998 by Alice Notley. Both reprinted with the permission of Viking Penguin, a division of Penguin Group (USA) Inc.

Frank O'Hara, "The Day Lady Died," "A Step Away from Them," "Personal Poem," and "Poem" ["Lana Turner has collapsed"] from *Lunch Poems*. Copyright © 1964 by Frank O'Hara. Reprinted with the permission of City Lights Books. "To the Harbormaster," "Poem: 'The eager note on my door . . .'" and "To the Film Industry in Crisis" from *Meditations in an Emergency*. Copyright © 1957 by Frank O'Hara. Reprinted with the permission of Grove/Atlantic, Inc. "Autobiographia Literaria," "Memorial Day 1950," "The Critic," "Blocks," "My Heart," "A True Account of Talking to the Sun on Fire Island," and "Poem (Light clarity avocado salad in the morning)," and "Why I am Not a Painter" from *Collected Poems*. Copyright © 1971 by Maureen Granville-Smith, Executrix of the Estate of Frank O'Hara. All reprinted with the permission of Alfred A. Knopf, a division of Random House, Inc.

Sharon Olds, "The One Girl at the Boys Party" from *The Dead and the Living*. Copyright © 1987 by Sharon Olds. "The Pope's Penis" and "Topography" from *The Gold Cell*. Copyright © 1987 by Sharon Olds. "The Race" from *The Father*. Copyright © 1992 by Sharon Olds. All reprinted with the permission of Alfred A. Knopf, a division of Random House, Inc. "Satan Says" from *Satan Says*. Copyright © 1980 by Sharon Olds. Reprinted with the permission of University of Pittsburgh Press.

Mary Oliver, "Some Questions You Might Ask" and "Rain" from *New and Selected Poems, Volume One*. Copyright © 1992 by Mary Oliver. Reprinted with the permission of Beacon Press, Boston.

Charles Olson, "The Kingfishers" from *The Collected Poems of Charles Olson*. Copyright © 1987 by the Regents of the University of California. Reprinted with the permission of University of California Press.

George Oppen, "Chartres," "The Undertaking in New Jersey," "Boy's Room," "The Gesture," "Psalm," and "The Building of the Skyscraper" from *Collected Poems*. Copyright © 1962, 1965, 1975 by George Oppen. Reprinted with the permission of New Directions Publishing Corporation.

Ron Padgett, "Reading Reverdy" from *Great Balls of Fire*. Copyright © 1969, 1990 by Ron Padgett. Reprinted with the permission of Coffee House Press, Minneapolis, Minnesota. "Poetic License" from *Toujours l'Amour*. Copyright © 1976 by Ron Padgett. "Voice" from *New & Selected Poems*. Copyright © 1995 by Ron Padgett. Both reprinted with the permission of the author.

Michael Palmer, "Fifth Prose" and "A man undergoes pain sitting at a piano" from *The Lion Bridge: Selected Poems 1972–1995*. Copyright © 1998 by Michael Palmer. "I do not" from *The Promises of Glass*. Copyright © 1999 by Michael Palmer. All reprinted with the permission of New Directions Publishing Corporation.

Dorothy Parker, "Resume," "Unfortunate Coincidence," "Observation," and "News Item" from *The Portable Dorothy Parker*, edited by Brendan Gill. Copyright 1926, 1928, renewed 1954, © 1956 by Dorothy Parker. Reprinted with the permission of Viking Penguin, a division of Penguin Group (USA) Inc.

Molly Peacock, "The Lull," "Next Afternoon," and "Buffalo" from *New and Selected Poems*. Copyright © 2002 by Molly Peacock. Reprinted with the permission of W. W. Norton & Company, Inc.

Bob Perelman, "Chronic Meanings" from *Ten to One*. Copyright © 1999 by Bob Perelman. Reprinted with the permission of Wesleyan University Press.

Robert Pinsky, "Round" from *The Figured Wheel: New and Collected Poems 1966–1996*. Copyright © 1996 by Robert Pinsky. "Ode to Meaning," and "Samurai Song" from *Jersey Rain*. Copyright © 2000 by Robert Pinsky. All reprinted with the permission of Farrar, Straus & Giroux, LLC. "Shirt" from *The Want Bone*. Copyright © 1990 by Robert Pinsky. "From the Childhood of Jesus" from *The Want Bone*. Copyright © 1990 by Robert Pinsky. Both reprinted with the permission of HarperCollins Publishers. "XYZ." Reprinted with the permission of Robert Pinsky.

Sylvia Plath, "The Hanging Man," "Mirror," "The Applicant," "Lady Lazarus," "Elm," "Daddy," "Words," "Fever 103°," "The Arrival of the Bee Box," "Edge," and "Poppies in October" from *Collected Poems*. Copyright © 1960, 1965, 1971, 1981 by the Estate of Sylvia Plath. Editorial matter copyright © 1981 by Ted Hughes. Reprinted with the permission of HarperCollins Publishers.

Katha Pollitt, "The Mind-Body Problem" from *The Atlantic Monthly*. Reprinted with the permission of the author. "Failure" from *Antarctic Traveller*. Copyright © 1982 by Katha Pollitt. Reprinted with the permission of Alfred A. Knopf, a division of Random House, Inc.

Anne Porter, "For My Son Johnny" from *Living Things: Collected Poems*. Copyright © 1994 Anne Porter. Reprinted with the permission of Zoland Books, an imprint of Steerforth Press of Hanover, New Hampshire.

Ezra Pound, Canto XLV and excerpt from Canto LXXXI, and Canto XIII from *The Cantos of Ezra Pound*. Copyright 1934, 1937, 1940, 1948, © 1956, 1959, 1962, 1963, 1966, 1968 by Ezra Pound. Reprinted with the permission of New Directions Publishing Corporation.

H. Phelps Putnam, "Bill Gets Burned," "Sonnet to Some Sexual Organs," and "Ship of State and Grandpa" from *The Collected Poems of H. Phelps Putnam*. Copyright © 1970. Reprinted with the permission of Farrar, Straus & Giroux, LLC.

John Crowe Ransom, "Bells for John Whiteside's Daughter," "Captain Carpenter," "Piazza Piece," "Vision by Sweetwater," and "Agitato ma non troppo" from *Selected Poems, Revised and Enlarged Edition*. Copyright © 1964 by John Crowe Ransom. Reprinted with the permission of Alfred A. Knopf, a division of Random House, Inc.

Kenneth Rexroth, "Delia Rexroth," "Vitamins and Roughage," "The Signature of all Things," and "Empty Mirror" from *Collected Shorter Poems*. Copyright 1944, 1949, 1952 by Kenneth Rexroth. Reprinted with the permission of New Directions Publishing.

Charles Reznikoff, "Beggar Woman," IV from "Testimony" ["Outside the night was cold . . . "], "The Bridge," "Te Deum," "The Old Man," "Similes," and "Epitaph" from *The Poems of Charles Reznikoff, 1918–1975*, edited by Seamus Cooney. Copyright © 2005 by the Estate of Charles Reznikoff. Reprinted with the permission of Black Sparrow Books, an imprint of David R. Godine Publisher, Inc.

Adrienne Rich, "Aunt Jennifer's Tigers," "Living in Sin," and "A Valediction Forbidding Mourning" from *The Fact of a Doorframe: Selected Poems 1950–2001*. Copyright © 1971 by W. W. Norton & Company, Inc. Copyright © 2002, 1955, 1951 by Adrienne Rich. "Translations" from *Diving into the Wreck: Poems 1971–1972*. Copyright © 1973 by Adrienne Rich. "The Middle-Aged," "A Marriage in the 'Sixties," and "Ghost of a Chance" from *Collected Early Poems*. Copyright © 1993, 1967, 1963, 1955 by Adrienne Rich. "1948: Jews" from *An Atlas of the Difficult World: Poems 1988–1991*. Copyright © 1991 by Adrienne Rich. "Diving into the Wreck" from *The Fact of A Doorframe: Poems Selected and New 1950–1984*. Copyright © 1984 by Adrienne Rich. "One Life" and "Living Memory" from *Time's Power: Poems 1985–1988*. Copyright © 1989 by Adrienne Rich. All reprinted with the permission of the author and W. W. Norton & Company, Inc.

Laura Riding, "Postponement of Self," "Opening of Eyes," "The Unthronged Oracle," "The World and I," and "Because of Clothes" from *The Poems of Laura Riding*. Copyright © 1991 by the Board of Literary Management of the late Laura (Riding) Jackson. Reprinted with the permission of Persea Books, Inc., In conformity with the late author's wish, her Board of Literary Management asks us to record that, in 1941, Laura (Riding) Jackson renounced, on grounds of linguistic principle, the writing of poetry: she had come to hold that "poetry obstructs general attainment to something better in our linguistic way-of-life than we have."

Edwin Arlington Robinson, "The House on the Hill," "An Old Story," and "The Sheaves" from *Collected Poems* (New York: Macmillan, 1937). Reprinted with the permission of Scribner, an imprint of Simon & Schuster Adult Publishing Group.

Theodore Roethke, "The Minimal," "My Papa's Waltz," "Root Cellar," "Dolor," "The Lost Son," "The Waking," "The Waking," "I Knew a Woman," and "In a Dark Time" from *The Collected Poems of Theodore Roethke*. Copyright 1942 by Hearst Magazines, Inc. Copyright 1943 by Modern Poetry Association, Inc. Copyright 1947, 1953, 1954 © 1960 by Theodore Roethke. Reprinted with the permission of Doubleday, a division of Random House, Inc.

Muriel Rukeyser, "Waiting for Icarus" and "Myth" from *The Collected Poems of Muriel Rukeyser* (Pittsburgh: University of Pittsburgh Press, 2005). Copyright © 1973 by Muriel Rukeyser. Reprinted with the permission of International Creative Management, Inc.

Kay Ryan, "A Bad Time for the Sublime" from *Strangely Marked Meats*. Copyright © 1985 by Kay Ryan. Reprinted with the permission of Copper Beech Press. "Blandeur" and "Failure" from

Say Uncle. Copyright © 2000 by Kay Ryan. Reprinted with the permission of Grove/Atlantic, Inc. "Poetry Is a Kind of Money." Copyright © 1989 by Kay Ryan. Reprinted with the permission of the author. "Home to Roost" from *The Niagara River* (New York: Grove/Atlantic, 2005). Originally in *Poetry* (May 2003). Reprinted with the permission of the author.

David Schubert, "Kind Valentine," "Peter and Mother," and "Midston House" from *Works and Days*. Copyright © 1983 by David Schubert. Published by the Quarter Review of Literature, Poetry Book Publications. Reprinted with permission.

James Schuyler, "Things To Do," "Korean Mums," "Dec. 28, 1974," "Dining Out with Doug and Frank," "Haze," and "A White City" from *Collected Poems*. Copyright © 1993 by the Estate of James Schuyler. Reprinted with the permission of Farrar, Straus & Giroux, LLC.

Delmore Schwartz, "Far Rockaway," "All clowns are masked," and "Pleasure" from *Selected Poems: Summer Knowledge*. Copyright © 1959 by Delmore Schwartz. Reprinted with the permission of New Directions Publishing Corporation.

Frederick Seidel, "Love Song" from *Fence* 6, no.1 (Spring/Summer 2003). Copyright © 2003 by Frederick Seidel. Reprinted with the permission of the author. "Racine" from *Going Fast*. Copyright © 1998 by Frederick Seidel. Reprinted with the permission of Farrar, Straus & Giroux, LLC.

Anne Sexton, "All My Pretty Ones," "Waiting to Die," and "The Fury of Cocks" from *The Complete Poems of Anne Sexton*. Copyright © 1981 by Linda Gray Sexton and Loring Conant, Jr. Reprinted with the permission of Houghton Mifflin Company. All rights reserved.

David Shapiro, "For the Princess Hello" from *Poems from Deal* (New York: E. P. Dutton, 1969). Copyright © 1969 by David Shapiro. Reprinted with the permission of the author. "Father Knows Best" from *The Page-Turner*. Copyright © 1972, 1973 by David Shapiro. Reprinted with the permission of Liveright Publishing Corporation. "To My Son" from *After a Lost Original*. Copyright © 1994 by David Shapiro. Reprinted with the permission of The Overlook Press. "Canticle" and "Giants" from *January* (New York: Holt, Rinehart, 1965). Copyright © 1965 by David Shapiro. Reprinted with the permission of the author.

Karl Shapiro, "Buick" and "Troop Train" from *Collected Poems 1940–1978*. Copyright © 1978 by the Estate of Karl Shapiro. "The Funeral of Poetry" from *The Bourgeois Poet*. Copyright © 1964 by the Estate of Karl Shapiro. All reprinted with the permission of Wieser & Elwell, Inc.

Charles Simic, "December" from *Unending Blues*. Copyright © 1986, 1985, 1984, 1983 by Charles Simic. Reprinted with the permission of Harcourt, inc. "Country Fair" and "Evening Chess" from *Hotel Insomnia*. Copyright © 1992 by Charles Simic. "Cameo Appearance" from *Walking the Black Cat*. Copyright © 1996 by Charles Simic. "The Scarecrow," "St. Thomas Aquinas," and "The Devils" from *The Book of Gods and Devils*. Copyright © 1990 by Charles Simic. All reprinted with the permission of Harcourt, Inc. "My Shoes," "Watermelons" and "My Beloved" from *Selected Early Poems*. Copyright © 1999 by Charles Simic. Reprinted with the permission of George Braziller, Inc.

Louis Simpson, "The Silent Generation," "To the Western World," and "My Father in the Night Commanding No" from *The Owner of the House: New Collected Poems 1940–2001*. Copyright © 2003 by Louis Simpson. Reprinted with the permission of BOA Editions, Ltd., www.boaeditions.org.

Patti Smith, "dream of rimbaud" from *Early Work: 1970–1979*. Copyright © 1994 by Patti Smith. Reprinted with the permission of W. W. Norton & Company, Inc.

W. D. Snodgrass, "Mementos I" and "April Inventory" from *Selected Poems, 1957–1987*. Copyright © 1987 by W. D. Snodgrass. Reprinted with the permission of the author.

Gary Snyder, "Piute Creek" and "Riprap" from *Riprap and Cold Mountain Poems*. Copyright © 2003 by Gary Snyder. "Mid-August at Sourdough Mountain Lookout" and "Above Pate Valley" from *Riprap and Cold Mountain Poems*. Copyright © 2003 by Gary Snyder. All reprinted with the permission of Shoemaker & Hoard. "The Snow on Saddle Mountain" from *The Back Country*. Copyright © 1968 by Gary Snyder. "What You Should Know to Be a Poet" from *Regarding Wave*. Copyright © 1970 by Gary Snyder. All reprinted with the permission of New Directions Publishing Corporation. "Things to Do Around San Francisco" from *Mountains and Rivers Without End*. Copyright © 1996 by Gary Snyder. Reprinted with the permission of Counterpoint Press, a member of Perseus Books, LLC.

Jack Spicer, "A Red Wheelbarrow," "Improvisations on a Sentence by Poe," "A Book of Music," "Thing Language," and "The Sporting Life" from *The Collected Books of Jack Spicer*. Copyright © 1975 by Jack Spicer. Reprinted with the permission of The Estate of Jack Spicer.

William Stafford, "Traveling Through the Dark," "Ask Me," and "An Archival Print" from *The Way It Is: New and Selected Poems*. Copyright © 1962, 1977, 1991, 1998 by the Estate of William Stafford. Reprinted with the permission of Graywolf Press, Saint Paul, Minnesota.

Gertrude Stein, "If I Told Him: A Completed Portrait of Picasso" from *Writings: 1903–1932* (New York: The Library of America, 1998). "Guillaume Apollinaire" and "Cezanne" from *Portraits and Prayers*. Copyright 1934 by Gertrude Stein. "Key to Closet," "Fish," "Had a Horse," "In Question," "Much Later," "Emily," "There," "In English," "Not Surprising," "A Wish," and "Fifty" from *A Book Concluding with As a Wife Has a Cow a Love Story*. All reprinted with the permission of the Estate of Gertrude Stein through its Literary Executor, Mr. Stanford Gann, Jr. of Levin and Gann, P. A.

Wallace Stevens, "Not Ideas about the Thing but the Thing Itself," "A High Toned Old Christian Woman," "Bantams in Pine Wood," "Peter Quince at the Clavier," "The Sense of the Sleight-of-Hand Man," "A Clear Day and No Memories," "Reality is an Activity of the Most August Imagination," "The Man on the Dump," "Of Modern Poetry," and "Of Mere Being," "Tea at the Palaz of Hoon," "Disillusionment of Ten O'Clock," "The Idea of Order at Key West," "The Snow Man," "The Man Whose Pharynx Was Bad," "The Death of a Soldier," and "The Poems of Our Climate," "Autumn Refrain," "The American Sublime," "Study of Two Pears," "The Motive for Metaphor," "The House was Quiet and the World was Calm," "The Plain Sense of Things," and "The Planet on the Table" from *The Collected Poems of Wallace Stevens*. Copyright 1954 by Wallace Stevens and renewed 1964 by Holly Stevens. All reprinted with the permission of Alfred A. Knopf, a division of Random House, inc.

Ruth Stone, "Train Ride" from *In the Next Galaxy*. Copyright © 2002 by Ruth Stone. Reprinted with the permission of Copper Canyon Press, P. O. Box 271, Port Townsend, WA 98368-0271. "Resonance" and "For My Dead Red-Haired Mother" from *Simplicity*. Copyright © 1995 by Ruth Stone. Reprinted with the permission of Paris Press, Inc., www.parispress.org. "Winter" and "The Latest Hotel Guest Walks over Particles that Revolve in Seven Other Dimensions Controlling Latticed Space" from *Second-Hand Coat: Poems New and Selected* (Cambridge: Yellow Moon Press, 1991). Reprinted with the permission of the author.

Mark Strand, "Keeping Things Whole" from *Reasons for Moving; Darker; The Sargentville Notebook*. Copyright © 1973 by Mark Strand. "Reading in Place," "Orpheus Alone," and "The Idea" from *The Continuous Life*. Copyright © 1990 by Mark Strand. "The Philosopher's Conquest" from *Blizzard of One*. Copyright © 1998 by Mark Strand. All reprinted with the permission of Alfred A. Knopf, a division of Random House, Inc. "2002" from *The New Yorker* (December 19, 2002). Copyright © 2002 by Mark Strand. "2032" from *The New Yorker* (November 10, 2003). Copyright © 2003 by Mark Strand. Both reprinted with the permission of the author.

May Swenson, "Four-Word Lines" from *Half Sun, Half Sleep* (New York: Charles Scribner's Sons, 1967). Copyright © 1967 by May Swenson. "Riding the A" from *To Mix with Time* (New York: Charles Scribner's Sons, 1963). Copyright © 1963 by Mary Swenson. Both reprinted with the permission of The Literary Estate of May Swenson. "Question," "The Wave and the Dune," "Waterbird," and "Staring at the Sea on the Day of the Death of Another" from *Nature: Poems Old and New*. Copyright © 1994 by May Swenson. Reprinted with the permission of Houghton Mifflin Company. All rights reserved.

Allen Tate, "The Ivory Tower," "Ode to the Confederate Dead," "The Wolves," and "The Mediterranean" from *The Collected Poems 1919–1976*. Copyright © 1977 by Allen Tate. Reprinted with the permission of Farrar, Straus & Giroux, LLC.

James Tate, "The Lost Pilot," "Failed Tribute to the Stonemason of Tor House, Robinson Jeffers," and "Teaching the Ape to Write Poems" from *Selected Poems*. Copyright © 1991 by James Tate. "Distance from Loved Ones" and "I Am a Finn / I Am Still a Finn" from *Distance from Loved Ones*. Copyright © 1990 by James Tate. Reprinted with the permission of Wesleyan University Press. All reprinted with the permission of Wesleyan University Press. "How the Pope is Chosen" and "Inspiration" from *Worshipful Company of Fletchers*. Copyright © 1994 by James Tate. "Dream On" from *The Shroud of the Gnome*. Copyright © 1997 by James Tate. "The Promotion" and "Bounden Duty" from *Return to the City of White Donkeys*. Copyright © 2004 by James Tate. Reprinted with the permission of HarperCollins Publishers.

Melvin B. Tolson, "Sootie Joe" from *Gallery of Harlem Portraits* (Columbia: University of Missouri Press, 1979). "Mu" from *Harlem Gallery Harlem Gallery: Book I, The Curator* (New York: Twayne, 1965). Both reprinted with the permission of Melvin B. Tolson, Jr.

Jean Toomer, "November Cotton Flower," "Reapers," "Georgia Dusk," "Beehive," and "The Gods Are Here" from *Cane*. Copyright 1923 by Boni & Liveright, renewed 1951 by Jean Toomer. Reprinted with the permission of Liveright Publishing Corporation. "The Gods Are Here" from *The Collected Poems of Jean Toomer* (Chapel Hill: The University of North Carolina Press, 1988). Reprinted with the permission of the Yale Literary Property Committee.

Mark Van Doren, "My Brother Lives Too Far Away" and "Orbit" from *Good Morning*. Copyright © 1973 by The Estate of Mark Van Doren, Reprinted with the permission of Farrar, Straus & Giroux, LLC.

Mona van Duyn, "Open Letter from a Constant Reader," "Relationships," and "Causes" from *If It Be Not I: Collected Poems*. Copyright © 1994 by Mona van Duyn. Reprinted with the permission of Alfred A. Knopf, a division of Random House, Inc.

Paul Violi, "Appeal to the Grammarians" from *BAP* (2004). Copyright © 2002 by Paul Violi. "Index" from *Splurge* (New York: Sun Publishing, 1982). Copyright © 1982 by Paul Violi. Both reprinted with the permission of the author.

David Wagoner, "The Words" from *Traveling Light: Collected and New Poems*. Copyright © 1999 by David Wagoner. "Dead Letter from Out of Town" from *House of Song*. Copyright © 1999 by David Wagoner. "Curtains" from *Good Morning and Good Night*. Copyright © 2005 by David Wagoner. All reprinted with the permission of the poet and the University of Illinois Press.

Robert Penn Warren, "Watershed" and "The Whole Question" from *The Collected Poems of Robert Penn Warren*. Copyright © 1998 by the Estate of Robert Penn Warren. "Brotherhood in Pain" from *The Collected Poems of Robert Penn Warren*. Copyright © 1998 by the Estate of Robert Penn Warren. All reprinted with the permission of William Morris Agency.

Lew Welch, "Whenever I make a new poem" and "The Basic Con" from *Ring of Bone: Collected Poems 1950–1971*. Copyright © 1979 by Lew Welch. Reprinted with the permission of Grey Fox Press.

John Wheelwright, "There Is No Opera Like Lohengrin" from *The New Yorker* (1939). Copyright 1939. Reprinted permission. "Why Must You Know?" "Would You Think?" "Train Ride," and "A Poem by David McCord" from *Collected Poems of John Wheelwright*. Copyright © 1971 by Louise Wheelwright Damon. Reprinted with the permission of New Directions Publishing Corporation.

Richard Wilbur, "The Beautiful Changes" from *The Beautiful Changes and Other Poems*. Copyright © 1947 and renewed 1975 by Richard Wilbur. "Boy at the Window," "Love Calls Us to the Things of This World," "Mind," and "A Baroque Wall Fountain in the Villa Sciara" from *Things of This World*. Copyright © 1956 and renewed 1984 by Richard Wilbur. "Advice to a Prophet" and "Shame" from *Advice to a Prophet and Other Poems*. Copyright © 1961 and renewed 1989 by Richard Wilbur. "Man Running" and "Lying" from *Collected Poems 1943–2004*. Copyright © 2004 by Richard Wilbur. "A Shallot" from *The Mind-Reader*. Copyright © 1975 by Richard Wilbur. All reprinted with the permission of Harcourt, Inc.

C. K. Williams, "Love: Beginnings" and "The Lover" from *Flesh and Blood*. Copyright © 1987 by C. K. Williams. "Money" from *The Vigil*. Copyright © 1997 by C. K. Williams. All reprinted with the permission of Farrar, Straus & Giroux, LLC.

William Carlos Williams, "A Coronal," "Fine Work with Pitch and Copper," "Great Mullen," "Nantucket," "Poem ("As the cat . . . "), "Proletarian Portrait," "Spring and All, Section XIV: Of death / the barber," Spring and All, Section XXV: Somebody dies every four minutes," "The Locust Tree in Flower" (second version), "This is Just to Say," "To a Poor Old Woman," "The Young Housewife," "Rain," "By the Road to the Contagious Hospital," VII: "The rose is obsolete," XVIII: "To Elsie," XXII: "The Red Wheelbarrow," and "These" from *Collected Poems: 1909–1939, Volume I*. Copyright 1938 by New Directions Publishing Corporation. "Landscape with the Fall of Icarus" from *Collected Poems: 1939-1962, Volume II*. Copyright 1953 by New

Directions Publishing Corporation. "The Hunters in the Snow" from *The Selected Poems of William Carlos Williams*. Copyright © 1962 by William Carlos Williams. All reprinted with the permission of New Directions Publishing Corporation.

Terence Winch, "Mysteries" from *The Great Indoors*. Copyright © 1994 by Terence Winch. Reprinted with permission of the author and Story Line Press (www.storylinepress.com).

Yvor Winters, "Before Disaster," "A Summer Commentary," "Much in Little," and "At the San Francisco Airport" from *The Selected Poems of Yvor Winters*, edited by R. L. Barth. Copyright © 1999 by Yvor Winters. Reprinted with the permission of Swallow Press/Ohio University Press, Athens, Ohio.

Charles Wright, "The Other Side of the River" from *The World of Ten Thousand Things: Poems 1980–1990*. Copyright © 1990 by Charles Wright. "In Praise of Han Shan" from *Buffalo Yoga*. Copyright © 2004 by Charles Wright. All reprinted with the permission of Farrar, Straus & Giroux, LLC.

James Wright, "Lying in a Hammock at William Duffy's Farm in Pine Island, Minnesota" and "A Blessing" from *Collected Poems*. Copyright © 1971 by James Wright. "Autumn Begins in Martins Ferry, Ohio" from *The Branch Will Not Break*. Copyright © 1963 by James Wright. "In Response to a Rumor That the Oldest Whorehouse in Wheeling, West Virginia, Has Been Condemned" and "Youth" from *Shall We Gather at the River*. Copyright © 1968 by James Wright. All reprinted with the permission of Wesleyan University Press. "Hook" from *Above the River: The Complete Poems*. Copyright © 1990 by Anne Wright. Reprinted with the permission of Farrar, Straus & Giroux, LLC.

Jay Wright, "The Homecoming Singer" and "The Cradle Logic of Autumn" from *Transfigurations: Collected Poems*. Copyright © 2000 by Jay Wright. Reprinted with the permission of the author.

John Yau, "January 18, 1979" from *Corpse and Mirror*. Copyright © 1983 by John Yau. Reprinted with the permission of Henry Holt and Company, LLC. "Domestic Bliss" from *Borrowed Love Poems*. Copyright © 2002 by John Yau. Reprinted with the permission of Penguin, a division of Penguin Group (USA), Inc.

Louis Zukofsky, "To my wash-stand" and "No it was no dream of coming death" from *Complete Short Poetry*. Copyright © 1991 by Louis Zukofsky. Reprinted with the permission of The Johns Hopkins University Press. "A" B 11 from *A*. Copyright © 1978 by Celia and Louis Zukofsky. Reprinted with the permission of the University of California Press.

Index

Authors *Titles* First Lines

G

H

I

N

O

P

Q

R

S

T

U